THE CROWELL EDUCATION SERIES

JAMES C. STONE, *University of California, Berkeley*
General Editor in Education

READINGS IN READING

Practice · Theory · Research

EDITED BY

Delwyn G. Schubert

Professor of Education
California State College, Los Angeles

IN CONSULTATION WITH

Theodore L. Torgerson

Professor Emeritus of Education
University of Wisconsin

THOMAS Y. CROWELL COMPANY
New York · Established 1834

Library of Congress Catalog Card Number: 68–24594

Manufactured in the United States of America

In memory of Trixie-Ann Gehrung Schubert

Preface

The materials found in this book were carefully chosen to give the reader insight into the *historical* development trends, theory, research, and current practices in reading instruction. The vast number of articles and research studies of the last decade reflect profound changes in the philosophy and teaching of reading. To fully appreciate these changes, the editor feels it is of paramount importance to focus attention, not only on the present, but on the writings and research of the pioneers of the reading field. *The writings of such authorities as Gray, Huey, Judd, Mann, Thorndike, et al., must not be overlooked. Their contribution to the teaching of reading today is tremendous and their influence on current practice pronounced.*

Readings in Reading is organized in conformity to the chapter content of most basic textbooks in reading. In terms of time, the reader will find selections covering almost one and one-half centuries. They date from the Horace Mann reports of the 1800's (he wrote about the teaching of reading in a fascinating up-to-date manner) to the present decade. The specific date of publication of each selection appears directly alongside the author's name.

Articles have been chosen from books, monographs, pamphlets, yearbooks, conference proceedings, and educational periodicals. Selections vary in length, although the majority of the articles are short in order to present as great a variety as possible.

A study* by the editor has shown that the average teacher's library in the reading area is woefully inadequate. Teachers do not have the variety of authoritative reference books on the subject that we might expect. This volume will provide busy teachers with valuable references in a convenient and usable form.

Although *Readings in Reading* has been evolved with the classroom teacher, remedial teacher, and reading specialist in mind, it also will provide a valuable source book for students who are preparing to become the teachers of tomorrow. And since all references and biblio-

* Delwyn G., Schubert, "Do Teachers Read About Reading?" *California Journal of Educational Research,* XI (March, 1960), 94–96.

graphical listings associated with the articles are intact, the student has at his fingertips additional sources to pursue should he desire more information.

The editor wishes to acknowledge his indebtedness to the many authors and publishers who gave permission to have writings reproduced in this volume.

D. G. S.

Contents

I. Reading—Yesterday and Today 1

1. Reading for Effective Personal Living
DAVID H. RUSSELL 3
2. Reading Ability and High School Drop-Outs
RUTH C. PENTY 11
3. Reading Achievement of School Children—Then and Now
VERA V. MILLER and WENDELL C. LANTON 15
4. Influences Shaping American Reading Instruction
NILA BANTON SMITH 24
5. Who Shall Teach Reading?
EMMETT ALBERT BETTS 36

II. Psychology and Nature of the Reading Process 45

6. Reading as Reasoning: A Study of Mistakes in Paragraph Reading
EDWARD L. THORNDIKE 47
7. The Work of the Eye in Reading
EDMUND B. HUEY 57
8. The Nature of Recognition
HARRY G. WHEAT 62
9. The Inner Speech of Reading and the Mental and Physical Characteristics of Speech
EDMUND B. HUEY 69
10. An Experimental Study of Eye–Voice Span
GUY T. BUSWELL 73
11. How Children and Adults Perceive Words in Reading
MILES A. TINKER 75

III. Learning to Read 89

12. When Should Children Begin to Read?
MABEL VOGEL MORPHETT and CARLETON WASHBURNE 90

13. The Necessary Mental Age for Beginning Reading
ARTHUR I. GATES 98
14. Reading Readiness
LUCILLE M. HARRISON 100
15. Laying the Foundations in Reading
WILLIAM G. CARR 102
16. Preschool and Kindergarten Experience
DONALD D. DURRELL and ALICE K. NICHOLSON 122
17. Laying the Foundation for Word Perception
WILLIAM S. GRAY 133
18. Classroom Help for Children with Beginning Reading Problems
A. STERL ARTLEY 136

IV. Developmental Reading—Basic Skills 141

19. How to Cope with Deficiencies in Basic Reading Skills That Block Progress in Learning Activities
GERALD A. YOAKAM 142
20. A Basic Word List from Basal Readers
DAVID R. STONE and VILDA BARTSCHI 148
21. Methods of Teaching Vocabulary
LUELLA COLE 158
22. How and When Word Attack Skills Should Be Taught
A. STERL ARTLEY 162
23. Some Misconceptions Concerning Phonics
GERTRUDE HILDRETH 169
24. Results of Teaching a System of Phonics
ARTHUR I. GATES 173
25. The Utility of Phonic Generalizations in the Primary Grades
THEODORE CLYMER 179

V. Developmental Reading—Comprehension and Rate 189

26. Measuring Reading Comprehension
WALTER B. BARBE 191
27. Reading in Subject Matter Fields
NILA BANTON SMITH 195
28. The Prerequisite: Knowing How to Read Critically
DAVID H. RUSSELL 200

29. Speed Reading: Its Value and Place in a School Program
A. STERL ARTLEY 203
30. Machines and Reading: A Review of Research
ROBERT KARLIN 208
31. Oral and Silent Reading
LUELLA COLE 214
32. Rate of Comprehension—Needed Research
EMERALD DECHANT 218

VI. Individual Differences 223

33. Individual Differences in Reading Achievement
IRVING H. ANDERSON and WALTER F. DEARBORN 225
34. Individualizing Reading Instruction—A Backward Look
RUSSELL G. STAUFFER 231
35. Procedures Used in Directing Individualized Reading Instruction
GUY L. BOND 241
36. Needs of Slow-Learning Pupils
PAUL WITTY 249
37. Reading Instruction for Children of Superior Ability
GERTRUDE WHIPPLE 256
38. Reading Help for the Disadvantaged
NEA Newsletter 264
39. Culturally Disadvantaged Children Can Be Helped
LESSIE CARLTON and ROBERT H. MOORE 268
40. Criteria for Grouping for Reading Instruction
THEODORE CLYMER 272

VII. Methods and Materials 281

41. Second Report to the Massachusetts Board of Education
HORACE MANN 283
42. An Appraisal of the Non-Oral Method of Teaching Reading
GUY T. BUSWELL 287
43. Reading: The Approaches We Use
ARTHUR V. OLSON 295
44. How Are Basal Readers Used?
RALPH C. STAIGER 302

45. Whose Brand of Reading Methods Is the "Best Buy"?
DELWYN G. SCHUBERT 307
46. An Evaluation of Techniques for Teaching Word Recognition
ROBERT E. MILLS 309
47. Locating, Introducing and Using Easy-to-Read, High-Interest Reading Matter
JEANNE S. CHALL 316

VIII. Diagnosis and Correction of Reading Problems 323

48. Identifying Readers Who Need Corrective Instruction
MARY C. AUSTIN 325
49. Know the Cause Before Applying the Cure
DELWYN G. SCHUBERT 333
50. A Critical Evaluation of Visual Diagnostic Materials
ALFRED A. ROSENBLOOM, JR. 336
51. Understanding and Handling Reading–Personality Problems
DELWYN G. SCHUBERT 343
52. Psychiatric Insights into Reading Problems
MANDEL SHERMAN 347
53. Specific Principles Essential to Classroom Diagnosis
WILLIAM D. SHELDON 351
54. General Principles of Diagnosis of Reading Disabilities
MARION MONROE 359
55. Clinical Procedures in Diagnosing Seriously Retarded Readers
HELEN M. ROBINSON 363
56. Remedial Cases in Reading: Their Diagnosis and Treatment
WILLIAM S. GRAY 370
57. Basic Principles of Remedial Instruction
GUY L. BOND and MILES A. TINKER 372

IX. Evaluating the Reading Program 399

58. The Essential Aspects of Evaluation
RALPH W. TYLER 401
59. Evaluating the Effectiveness of Teaching Reading
MILDRED C. LETTON 407

60. Determining Reading Achievement
WILLIAM G. CARR 416
61. What Constitutes an Adequate Testing Program
THEODORE L. TORGERSON 423
62. Values and Limitations of Standardized Reading Tests
ARTHUR E. TRAXLER 427

X. Research in Reading 435

63. Needed Improvement in Research Design in Reading
DONALD L. CLELAND 436
64. Reactions to Research on Reading
RUTH STRANG 444
65. Some Thoughts on the Current State of Research in Reading
ALTON L. RAYGOR 451
66. The Hawthorne Effect and Reading Research
DESMOND L. COOK 452
67. The Real Frontier in Reading Research
THEODORE CLYMER 460
68. The Future of Research in Reading
ARTHUR I. GATES 467

XI. Issues and Trends in Reading 481

69. Faculty Opinion on Significant Issues
MARY C. AUSTIN 484
70. Reading in the Kindergarten
MARY C. AUSTIN 494
71. Neuro-Psychological Factors as Causes of Reading Disabilities
CARL H. DELACATO 499
72. Color: A New Dimension in Teaching Reading
SISTER M. RAPHAEL 503
73. The Value of ITA: "We're Enthusiastic"
JOHN DOWNING and IVAN ROSE 506
74. The Value of ITA: "It's Too Soon to Know Definitely"
WARREN G. CUTTS 508
75. The Controversial History of Phonics
DOLORES DURKIN 511
76. Individualized Reading—An Evaluation
HARRY W. SARTAIN 517

77. Linguistics and the Teaching of Reading
RUTH G. STRICKLAND 524
78. Speed Reading
EVELYN N. WOOD 528
79. Speed Reading
EUGENE EHRLICH 530
80. Vision and Rapid Reading
HOWARD N. WALTON 533
81. Reading Problems, Research and Changes
MARY C. AUSTIN 543
82. What We Should Be Doing Soon
ARTHUR I. GATES 549

I. Reading–Yesterday and Today

Skills have an important place in everyday life. But one skill dwarfs all others in its importance. That skill is reading. Reading and living are almost synonymous in our society. Without the ability to read, the doors to accomplishment are tightly closed. All fields of endeavor demand reading skill. Through reading we enlarge our vicarious experiences and we live many lives; through reading we can enter the minds of men both past and present. Because of its permeating importance, reading proves to be one of the most important keys to an enlightened citizenship. There is little doubt: reading is the supreme skill.

In spite of its obvious value, many students ask the question, "Why read?" The frequency with which this query is being met may lead one to believe, according to Russell (1), that we are in the twilight of the printed page. To meet the competition offered by other activities and media, teachers must help students experience reading as a process that provides useful solutions to personal problems. Russell feels that we should "teach reading for competencies, but even more for its effects on personal living."

How is reading related to learning and success in school? It is not surprising to learn that the incidence of school dropouts is considerably greater among disabled readers. As a matter of fact, Penty (2) reveals that 90 percent of those who leave high school prematurely have reading problems. And when these students do leave school, they soon discover that it is difficult and usually impossible to acquire or maintain competence on any job because of their impaired reading skill.

Society must assume the responsibility of educating the young. It has no choice. If the society is primitive, the home, of course, is obligated to do the major part of the job. But in a democratic society such as ours, public and private schools shoulder the responsibility. Naturally, during times of stress and rapid change, schools are strongly criticized for incompetence as reflected in pupil performance. Because of its fundamental importance, the teaching of reading bears the brunt of such criticism. Critics invariably assert that children of today do not read as well as those in former years. They advocate a return to the "good old days when everyone could read."

How well do today's students read? A number of then-and-now studies have been conducted to provide information relevant to reading achievement of children in the past with those currently enrolled in school. In this connection the reader will be especially interested in the study by Miller and Lanton (3), "Reading Achievement of School Children—Then and Now." This study, along with many others that have been made during the past decade, lends little support to the contention that a return to the "good old days" is warranted.

What forces have exerted an influence on reading problems as we know them? Smith (4) helps us answer this question as she traces the historical developments and influences that have been fundamentally responsible for changes in the teaching of reading, the most significant of which was the scientific movement in education accompanied by the development of standardized tests.

Smith tells us that educators who feel that no future era in reading could be as productive as the years since 1900 are probably wrong. Those of us who are involved in one or more aspects of reading instruction have "thrilling new worlds to conquer." With this in mind Smith concludes by saying, ". . . may progress in reading instruction march forward with ever-accelerating vigor and fertility, and may all of us join productively in the procession."

A timely selection by Betts (5) closes this chapter. He poses the question "Who Shall Teach Reading?" and concludes that only through better teacher preparation today are we readying ourselves for more effective reading instruction tomorrow.

1. Reading for Effective Personal Living

DAVID H. RUSSELL (1958)

One of my colleagues at the University of California, George R. Stewart, has written an article entitled "The Twilight of the Printed Book." This scarehead title would not be remarkable except for the fact that Mr. Stewart is a professor of English and is himself the author of quite a few books. Despite our coming to this meeting two or three thousand strong, are we in a period of the twilight of the book—and the newspaper and magazine? Are teachers a little like the old-time railroad men who refused to take the automobile seriously?

The question about the place of reading in modern life may be put another way. Some time ago a teacher in Los Angeles County said to me, "Dr. Russell, how would you answer this question? A big seventh-grade boy, who can't read very well, came up to me and said, 'Why should I read better? I can get all the information I want, and all the entertainment I want from radio and television. Why read?' " I repeat the question to you seriously. In 1958, why read? As the fourteen-year-old in the Russell family says, "It's a good question, Pop; let's face it."

It is not my purpose to compare the advantages and disadvantages of reading versus the mass media. We all know that good television has an immediacy, an impact, which not all books can match. We know that both books and TV can deal in trivia. We know that in books, however, there is a storehouse of ideas unmatched by all the movies, radio, and TV of all times. We know that in reading a child can go at his own pace, can repeat, can think over what he is reading undisturbed by the "hard sell" of the commercial. Because he can go at his own pace, and occasionally dream over a book, it may mean more in his inner life.

But despite such beliefs in the superiority of reading, it is still true that many of our children are like the seventh-grade boy. They want to

---

SOURCE: *Proceedings of the International Reading Association,* III (1958), 12–17. Reprinted with the permission of the International Reading Association.

see more clearly that reading has values for them personally. Accordingly, today I am going to stress some of the personal values in reading for effective living. My hypothesis is that children and adults will become constant readers, develop permanent interests and habits of reading only if they have a fairly high level of skill and only if reading meets some of their deepest needs. In these days of competition with television, with travel, with other mass media, and with Disneyland, I want to suggest that the teaching of reading for superior skills is not enough. High-level reading abilities are important, and several sections of this convention program are devoted to them, but the day has gone by when we can defend the place of reading in schools only on the basis of developing effective reading skills. In the years ahead, reading can keep its present place in the school curriculum only if it helps the individual on some of his important personal problems. We can give reading the same time and energy only as it deals with some of the child's basic concerns or the adolescent's deepest needs. If we are to avoid a twilight of reading, increasingly our concern must be with the effects of reading on the lives of boys and girls.

Today, then, I want to emphasize a new concept of reading—reading not as a process of eye movements or word-recognition skills but reading as the product, as uses and results in the lives of people. I am asking what happens to a girl who reads in her school reader a story about children in Norway or Indonesia? What happens to a boy who has been enthralled by *Treasure Island?* Does he, in the superb ending of Stevenson's own words "start upright in bed with the sharp voice of Captain Flint still ringing in (his) ears: 'Pieces of eight! Pieces of eight!' "? Today, I am saying to you all with Bourne, "Youth does not get ideas—ideas get him." Perhaps I am saying too with Walt Whitman, "All music is what awakes from you when you are reminded by the instruments."

How did this change in viewpoint, this new concept of reading appear? How have we come to look upon reading as an idea-getting and idea-producing process? Historically, reading instruction started in this country as an effort at mere literacy. In Colonial days people learned their alphabets, and were able to plod through a few books for their factual content. The first school readers used the alphabet method, then Webster and McGuffey had word lists, and were read and re-read by the child many times. The emphasis shifted from literal interpretation of words to meaning of paragraphs and passages, but rote memory was the usual requirement. As late as 1920 a widely used silent reading test, the *Burgess Silent Reading,* measured only speed and accuracy—the latter in terms of recall of facts.

I'm afraid that this tradition persists in schools today. Some teachers in second grade are more likely to ask the question "What was the color of Mary's dress?" rather than the question "Is Mary the kind of a girl you would like to have as a friend?" Even at the seventh-grade level, after a group reads an adventure story some teachers are likely to ask a question like, "What is a flash flood?" rather than a question like, "How did Peter show courage in the emergency of the flash flood?"

During the 1920's and 30's, however, we became more conscious of the many purposes for which we may read—the main idea, the sequence of events, following directions, and the more creative activities of enjoying humor and imagery, judging character, reacting to values. Gradually, then, our concept shifted from one of reading for regurgitative facts to one of reading for a variety of comprehensions or interpretations, all of which involved thinking by the reader. Even more recently, we have become concerned with the effects of reading, with the use the reader makes of the material in his own activities.

There are many ways of studying reading as understanding, interpretation, and use but, today, I have only time to suggest that the whole process has two sides. These may be called (1) the cognitive or knowing aspects of reading, and (2) the responsive or appreciative aspects of reading. These may be labeled reading as thinking and reading as creating, if you wish. It is my thesis that, if reading is to endure in the lives of boys and girls, we must emphasize both these aspects of it in our teaching.

In regard to thinking may I make three short suggestions:

(1) *Reading can be a source of thinking materials.* If we regard reading as a thinking process we immediately think of the reservoir of ideas in printed materials. Reading can provide the raw materials of thinking—the facts, the images, the concepts, the stimuli to memory that we all need as part of our materials of thinking. The fourth-reader story gives facts about a prairie blizzard or a social-studies text hints at concepts like *justice* and *cooperation.*

Such raw materials are useful only if the child can locate them. Accordingly, beginning in the primary grades the teacher develops skills in discovering facts—how to use the table of contents and later the index, the dictionary, the graph, the card file, and typographical aids in books. Skills in locating will give the child accessibility to more facts, concepts, and images as materials for his thinking. "The world is so full of a number of things." I'm not sure we can all be happy as kings, unless we know how to find and select them. There are so many new ideas bursting on us that, like Alice and the Red Queen, we all have to run very fast just to keep in the same place. In all this complexity of a world bursting with facts and meanings, the teacher helps the child use reading as a check on old ideas and a discovery of new ones.

(2) *Reading can be an aid in selecting and evaluating ideas.* TV quiz shows suggest that facts by themselves are interesting, but you and I know they become even more valuable as they are selected, weighed, and organized into larger ideas. We teach children to read for the main idea (what is a title for the story?), the sequence of ideas (what happened next?), or for the arguments pro and con. Children today need help in the selection of ideas—all we need to do is to look at our corner newsstand for proof of this necessity. Teachers can use their wider experience in helping children distinguish between the relevant and irrelevant, the important and the trivial. In your reading group you ask children to judge the adequacy of an action or idea. You ask, "Did Bill do the right thing when he went into the dangerous cave?" or "Which of these words describe the city of London?"

The evaluating of ideas comes pretty close to what we call critical thinking. I should like to suggest that reading is one of the few activities that can encourage the child to be critical, to set standards. Aimed at entertainment, television and radio can't or won't do it. Somewhere around twelve or thirteen years, without much help, children can become conscious of the clichés of the soap opera or the Western. As they have a chance at good books the process may be speeded up. Critical thinking is a matter of having standards—reading can give these standards of judgment better than most other activities.

(3) *Reading can develop into concept formation and problem-solving.* Whether we teach a third-grade, tenth-grade, or college class we are under pressure to get things done. We want students to get the story read, the report written, the book closed. As I said above, that's why we occasionally ask questions like "What is the color of Mary's dress?" or "What is a flash flood?" instead of *how* and *why* questions. But every so often a bit of magic descends upon our classroom. For a few moments, the voices in the playground outside the window are gone, the trucks on the nearby road are still, and the other groups are reasonably quiet and busy. Then for a few moments teacher and a group of children may stop and think over what they have been reading. In the pause that comes when a story has been savored, the teacher says, "What kind of a girl do you think Bess was?" "What would you have done if you had been in that town?" "What touch of greatness does Lincoln show in this episode?" "What is the author trying to say about truth or courage or loyalty or all the other lovely words?" Here, then, are the times when the children begin to grasp important concepts, ideas which help form a "lacework of coherence" in our culture. Here, too, are the opportunities

for solving problems. Sometimes these may be little ones like, "Did Jack do the right thing when he went to visit the mayor in the story?" Sometimes they may be important problems of what we adults call ethics and values. I know there are dangers in forcing a point of view, in discussing problems stated in a teacher's manual but not in children's minds, but I still maintain that the reading program is one of our best opportunities for asking important questions and attacking vital problems. Television, the movies, and spectator sports won't usually attack problems for us. The reading and literature program is one of our main outposts in the battle for men's minds.

In the cognitive aspects, then, reading can be a source of ideas, can give practice in selecting and evaluating ideas, and can develop into concept formation and problem-solving. In addition to these three facets of reading as thinking, the whole process has a second component of interpretation and use—that of the appreciative response in reading. This is what we may call creative thinking growing out of reading. In this process the reader adds something of himself to the words—he reads between the lines; he goes beyond the superficial facts, explicitly stated, to do some relational thinking which produces fresh outcomes. This may be evaluation of an idea or identification with a character in a story. For example, the child may come across the statement, "Mexicans are lazy," and use his past experience to be critical of this statement. Or in terms of identification, in the best things he reads a child will find himself or part of himself. To encourage this feeling the primary teacher asks, "What person in the story is most like you?" Or the junior-high-school teacher says, "Which of these people would you want for a friend?"

In this reaction there will be knowing of factual aspects but there will also be more personal involvement. This may be hard to get with a pseudo-sophisticated eighth-grader and some so-called "classic" literature on the prescribed list. However, with the wide resources of today, a skilled teacher can match boy and book; somewhere there are stories, poems, articles which mean a lot in the inner life of each boy and girl in your class. Chief Justice Holmes has said that "A word is the skin of an idea." Similarly, a story of family life or death or courage can be a skin for an idea with clear and direct meaning in the personal life of a child. I don't know what pieces of literature affect you this way. To this day I cannot read Benét's poem "Nancy Hanks" without getting a lump in my throat. All of you know this poem of the drab setting and a mother's love, "How's my Abe? Did he get on?"

Of course, we as teachers know that not all readers will react in this personal way. Sometimes the material is just too hard for them to read;

sometimes the theme seems trivial; sometimes the child or youth will reject the main idea in a story. Perhaps a child in a broken home simply cannot face a story of happy home life, or an adolescent with his own problems of growing up builds defenses against a story about shyness or one about first love. I have recently tried to put together over fifty research studies on the impact of reading on individuals. One of my conclusions is that the effects of materials are not always predictable. You, as a teacher of reading or literature, are confronted with apparently erratic responses or individual and shallow stereotypes. Recently one of my students had his high-school class in California read J. D. Salinger's *Catcher in the Rye.* Here are some of the things the high-school people wrote about Holden Caulfield, the central character. They said such individual things as "Holden is a bum," "He's a crazy mixed-up kid," "He's a sensitive boy," "He's almost like myself," "Holden should have minded his parents," and "I can understand how he felt about school." As teachers, then, we must understand that the same story, whether at third grade or eleventh grade, produces different effects in different people. Let's avoid trying for the same responses from all children.

If the situation is so individual in the person's reactions to stories, what can we as teachers do about it? There are several things: (1) We can provide a wide range of reading materials so that somewhere each child finds something with ideas in it which are important for him. In the primary grades, of course, this underlines the significance of the teacher reading something to his class every day—a delightful habit which should continue all through school. Often the reading may be followed by short discussion of characters or values in the story. (2) We can provide times for free reading regularly scheduled in the week's program, provided there are library facilities to undergird such activities. (3) We can snatch a few minutes from a busy day to talk with a child individually about what he has read. These interviews may be supplemented with an individual folder on reading interests, needs, list of things read, and reactions to some of them. (4) We can arrange for small groups with similar interests and motivations to come together informally. The group may form for one period or for three weeks to share likes and dislikes, to react to ideas, to attempt creative activities growing out of the reading.

None of these suggestions is new and many of you here are attempting them in an effort to enhance appreciative and creative activities growing out of reading. But I do want to add what I hope is a new concept for some of you. It grows out of a letter that Howard Pease, author of some twenty adventure books for adolescents, wrote to a fifteen-year-old friend about three levels of reading. I am trying to suggest that you, as the most experienced person in the classroom, can help boys and girls see that some materials are to be read only superficially—parts of the daily newspaper, all of the comics, and fiction in women's magazines probably fall in this category. But some stories, poems, and books may be read at a deeper level—there is a second or even a third layer of meaning to be found in them. Let me illustrate by materials all of you know:

(a) *Tom Sawyer*—on the surface, a story of a boy's adventures; at a second level, an account of life on the Mississippi a hundred years ago; on the third level, a more universal theme—the tug between respectability and the raffish life which we all experience, with respectability exemplified by Aunt Polly and the ne'er-do-well by Huck Finn and his father.

(b) Hans C. Andersen's *The Red Shoes*—a story and a movie but also a symbol: the shoes that danced themselves to death are a symbol of vanity, or the frivolous life.

(c) *Little Women*—superficially, a story of family life in America; at a deeper level, some of the problems of growing up; at a still deeper level, the greater truth of the importance of individual differences.

These are my personal reactions and, as I said, yours are probably different. But, since modern writers do not tack on an explanation, as did Aesop in his fables, we must help children learn how to hunt, how to dig. Pease writes to the fifteen-year-old, "You might begin your search by studying a popular song such as 'Bali Hai,' from *South Pacific*, which says that most people live on a lonely island lost in the middle of a foggy sea, and that most people really long for another island—Bali Hai! Don't take this literally, Pat. This is figurative language. You might say in your own words that the song's idea, or theme, is 'Greener pastures over the fence,' or 'Beyond the horizon is a lovelier place to live.' In this idea you'll find that which we call a universal truth.

"Take one of my simplest books, my fifth, *Secret Cargo*. On the surface, this is an action and mystery story about a locked chest hidden in the hold of a ship. But there is also a hidden cargo that my hero, Larry, knows nothing about until the end of his adventures. When the lid of the modern chest is raised, there is nothing of value inside. Then why is the book titled *Secret Cargo?* Because its theme, a belief I still hold to, is this: In all of us, in our unplumbed depths, there are certain hidden qualities, abilities, talents—call them what you will—which few of us ever discover and bring to light and put to use. So seldom do any of us ever reach the limits even of our own short range!

"This, for what it is worth, is the theme I attempted to dramatize in this story. The secret cargo is in Larry himself. The brass-bound chest, hidden in the ship, is a symbol. What do I mean by that? Well, a lion is a symbol of courage. The object used as a symbol represents something else, a quality, an idea of greater magnitude, something you cannot see or put your hands on. To use a symbol is one way of trying to give more depth, more meaning to a story. *Now, Pat, stand on the first level, but hold yourself ready to dive.* On the surface this book is the story of a locked chest hidden on a ship at sea. *Now dive to the second level!* The story is about the secret cargo that Larry discovers within himself, certain abilities he did not know he had until his adventures showed them to him. *Now plunge down to the third level and touch bottom.* The story is fundamentally about hidden cargoes to be found in ALL OF US."

So it is with other stories. We as teachers need to help young people to discover for themselves some of the hidden values in what they read. Not all children are going to read Faulkner or even Hemingway in their post-school years but all can be helped in discriminating between the superficial and the profound. All can be encouraged to develop the habit of dipping below the surface for the symbol or even the universal truth. I have never yet been able to find a universal truth in a Hollywood musical or in a typical TV Western, but they may exist. And may I say in passing that the typical basic reader contains ideas at least at the second depth. It may be maligned for repetitious vocabulary or middle-class standards but its stories often contain important meanings to be suggested to a group. A simple preprimer story of a trip to an airport and a return home can tell a lot about a family's feelings for its home. A fourth-reader story of a boy exploring a cave can raise important questions of foolhardiness versus courage. That is, the story can present these questions if you as the teacher will find a theme, look for symbols, pick out the human values involved, and encourage children to think on these things.

Over the past years many of us have begun to feel about reading as the song in *My Fair Lady*, "I've grown accustomed to his face." We have grown accustomed to the face of reading such as the ability to call words or answer factual questions. But the activity goes deeper.

Reading is a thinking process and an active, appreciative response. Youth will read, in competition with other activities, only if reading fulfills some of their basic needs for information, for enjoyment, for escape, or for answers to deep-laid problems. Only as reading provides useful solutions to personal problems, or has favorable effects on personality itself will it be given a place in an enduring pattern of activities. Let us teach reading for competencies, but even more for its effects on personal living.

2. Reading Ability and High School Drop-Outs

RUTH C. PENTY (1956)

There has been a growing feeling in the United States that the secondary school has not been meeting the needs of the youth which it should be serving and that, therefore, large numbers of those youth are each year leaving school before graduation. Numerous studies have been made to determine the characteristics of these school leavers and why they are dropping out of school before the conclusion of their secondary school education. All of the research done on school leaving points to the multiplicity of reasons for its occurrence and also to the interrelatedness of these reasons.

A few researchers have recognized low reading achievement as one of the factors which may play a role in the school leaving of high school students; however, the factual data related to reading ability as a factor in school drop-out are extremely limited in the literature on holding power. The prevalence of low reading achievement among high school students, especially among those students who are school leavers, and the small amount of research done on the relation of reading achievement to drop-out pointed to the need for further investigation of this relationship and prompted this study.

More than three times as many poor readers as good readers dropped out of school before graduation; the peak of the school leaving among the drop-outs was during the tenth grade.

There was no significant difference between the reading scores at the tenth grade level of the poor readers who dropped out of school before graduation and of the poor readers who remained in school until graduation.

The interview data emphasized that difficulty in reading played a very important role in the school leaving of boys and girls, especially when certain other problems and pressures were also present.

SOURCE: Ruth C. Penty, *Reading Ability and High School Drop-Outs* (New York: Teachers College Press, 1956), pp. 72–77.

It was evident from the data that the poor readers who remained in school also had difficulty in reading. However, the better emotional and social adjustment of the graduates, probably the result of home security, interest, and economic status superior to that of the boys and girls who dropped out of school, and also of more fortunate school experiences, permitted them to be less burdened by a multiplicity of problems among which the reading problem was one. Among the poor readers who graduated were some who felt that people expected them to graduate: they had always expected to graduate from high school; their parents encouraged them; their teachers and counselors helped them; they had "made up their minds" to graduate and had set this as their goal. A few thought a high school education would help them get a better job. Last, but not least, they were getting some real satisfactions from school: they enjoyed the school dances, athletics, and other extraclass activities, were interested in doing well in one or more subjects, and "liked the kids" in their school. These seemed to be some of the reasons why pupils of low reading ability persisted in school until they graduated. To prevent a high percentage of drop-out, these conditions should be more widely created.

A study of the disparity between reading ages and mental ages of the poor readers who dropped out of school and of the poor readers who remained in school but who experienced difficulty in reading, revealed that a very large percentage of the young people in both groups had potential for growth in reading ability. With proper help, these students could have shown marked improvement in reading ability, which would have resulted in better scholastic achievement and personality adjustment.

The data showed difference in educational potentialities between good and poor readers. However, it must be borne in mind that even though reading achievement and intelligence as measured by group tests are closely related, it is difficult to predict the amount of improvement that persons with limited intelligence can make in reading ability.

The evaluation test data, though inadequate, suggested that more rapid growth in reading ability would be possible for the boys and girls who received special reading help than for the boys and girls who received only incidental help in reading. There was also less school leaving among boys and girls who received special help in reading.

Implications for Education

The ability to read well is very important to boys and girls of high school age. They feel inferior and ashamed and want to leave school when they are unable to read with understanding the books which are the basic part of the school curriculum. When they are handicapped by poor reading ability, they try harder to get information necessary to their school success from films and discussions; however, they do not find these avenues of learning sufficient to meet their needs. Neither are they satisfied to be passed from grade to grade on the basis of class attendance, if their reading handicap is recognized, as this embarrasses them and makes them feel that they are "not getting any place." They wish to achieve as well as the other boys and girls in their classes.

Both students and educators have frequently failed to give the underlying reasons for dropping out of school or of poor school adjustment. They have not recognized *trouble with reading*, from which many other difficulties stem. The students would say: "I didn't know how to study," "I cannot get anything out of school," "I had difficulty with school work," "I was discouraged over my grades," "I found school work hard," and "I felt inferior." When students were given opportunity, in the interviews, to describe the kinds of trouble they had had with school subjects and in classroom situations, these statements were usually found to mean: *I had trouble with reading*. Corresponding reasons which are frequently given by educators for early school leaving and which in large part can be attributed to poor reading ability have been poor study habits, lack of application, no interest in academic work, discouragement over grades, work not adapted to ability, lack of school success, and poor foundation.

In this study, the problems and conditions found most regularly associated with early school leaving were these: (1) frequent academic failure, (2) reading difficulty, (3) lack of school friends, (4) nonparticipation in school activities, (5) feeling of inferiority, (6) financial problems, (7) lack of home security and encouragement, and (8) family history of early school drop-out.

In the interviews held with drop-outs, the emotional factors seemed to have great importance. This suggests that much attention should be given to working with parents in an attempt to change home conditions; but the whole burden cannot be placed upon the home. It is apparent that the conditions in the emotional lives of boys and girls which free them to learn and which block them from learning are not peculiar to the home. Educators cannot escape responsibility by isolating those factors which point to the failure of the home to provide a climate in which boys and girls can develop into emotionally stable young people, free of pressures which keep them from optimum growth at school.

Some of the boys and girls who seemed to be making a good adjustment in school were able to remain in school despite their reading handicap; however, they felt inadequate in the school situation because they could not read well. Moreover, a very large percentage of the boys and girls who dropped out of school did so because they had various problems in connection with school. If they had met with school success, there would have been more likelihood of their remaining in school.

Among the provisions which the secondary school has recognized as important in reducing school drop-out are these: (1) adequate guidance service, to help prevent problems from occurring and to diagnose and relieve those which have developed; (2) expanded extracurricular programs; (3) efforts to help young people increase their feeling of belonging and satisfaction in their human relations; and (4) placement in part-time work opportunities to assist with finances. Less recognition has been given to the development of reading programs on the secondary level from the standpoint of school leaving.

It is understandable that the secondary school teacher may question whether the teaching of reading is his responsibility and not alone that of the elementary school teacher. However, when boys and girls have need for any useful skills for which they have potential for growth, it is the responsibility of the good teacher to assist them to obtain those skills to the extent that he is able. In this study, it was shown that (1) 70 percent of the 276 boys and girls who dropped out of school could have been helped to develop their reading ability until they were reading at or above the sixth grade reading level, which would have given them better opportunity for school satisfaction; (2) among the boys and girls who remained in school, 84 percent could have been helped to read at or above the sixth grade level, and this growth in reading ability would have insured them greater scholastic success and happier school experience. There is no reason to believe that this situation is an atypical one; rather, it seems certain that similar numbers of boys and girls who are poor readers need help in developing their reading skills in high schools throughout the country.

It is also the responsibility of the teacher to give attention to the child who has probably fulfilled his reading potential and who may not be able to learn to read much beyond the fourth or fifth grade level if he is to remain in school. His greatest need is to receive help in planning tasks through which he can experience success. He will need help in locating books and materials which he can read with understanding and to have socially and emotionally satisfying experiences arranged for him.

Several other findings of this study emphasize the need for giving help to boys and girls in the improvement of reading skills throughout the secondary schools if they are to remain in school in greater numbers until graduation. The past practice in most school systems, of terminating special help in reading at the close of the sixth grade, is not meeting the needs of students who are expected to read increasingly difficult and varied materials without receiving help in the techniques of reading those materials. The prevalence of drop-out in the tenth grade points to the need for special help in reading between the sixth and the tenth grades. It is also undoubtedly desirable to continue giving reading help throughout the high school grades.

3. Reading Achievement of School Children – Then and Now

VERA V. MILLER and
WENDELL C. LANTON (1956)

Are the children of today learning to read as well as those of twenty years ago? Are the teacher techniques in use today as successful as those of the past? Is too much time being devoted to music, arts and crafts, dramatics, and unit work to the detriment of the "Three R's"?

These are questions being raised by parents and educators in increasing numbers. Research studies conducted in an attempt to answer these questions have been inconclusive in many cases.

Since few large-scale "past-present" comparative studies have been conducted in strategic geographic places throughout the country, each local school system must provide its own data if a nationwide "past-present" evaluation is to be made.

This need for carefully planned and scientifically controlled "then and now" researches at local school levels has led investigators to conduct studies in order to provide objective data on the "then and now" reading abilities of elementary-school children. Representative of such studies are those that have been conducted in St. Louis and Springfield, Missouri (1) (3); Grand Rapids and Dearborn, Michigan (2) (4);

SOURCE: *Elementary English*, XXXIII (February, 1956), 91–97. Reprinted with the permission of the National Council of Teachers of English and Vera V. Miller and Wendell C. Lanton.

and Lincoln, Nebraska (9), in the United States; and St. Catharines, Ontario (8), in Canada.

The Evanston "Then and Now" Studies

In order to provide data on the relative achievement of present-day elementary-school children in Evanston, Illinois, with that of children in the past, three "then and now" studies have been conducted in the Evanston public elementary schools. This paper summarizes the findings of the reading comparisons made in a pilot study of the achievement of fourth-grade pupils in 1932 and 1952 (7); that of the achievement of third- and fifth-grade pupils in 1934 and 1953 (5); and finally, that of the achievement of eighth-grade pupils in 1933 and 1954 (6).

The basic plan of the studies was the administration of the same standardized tests to children today as those taken by children enrolled in the same grades and schools twenty years ago. This plan was feasible because the community was comparatively stable, good records had been maintained, and the tests had always been given by the Research and Testing Department which excluded the variable of teacher-administered tests. Then, too, the present-day groups of pupils and those of the past were similar in most respects.

Community Described

For years, Evanston schools have had a good reputation for high standards of attainment and, according to a recent opinion survey (10), adults in Evanston are generally favorable to their school program. Thus, these studies were conducted in the absence of any community charges that the schools were neglecting the fundamentals.

Several other community conditions provided a favorable setting for these studies. The area has not experienced expanded school boundaries. The population has remained relatively stable during the last twenty-five years. The area contains a cross section of people of different races and of varied social and economic status—a cross section that typifies the above-average large suburban university city.

Tests Used

The 1929 edition of the *New Stanford Achievement Test* was used for the fourth-grade pilot study; two levels of the 1933 edition of the *Metropolitan Achievement Tests* were selected for the third- and fifth-grade study; and the 1933 edition of the *New Stanford Achievement Test* was chosen for the eighth-grade study.

children, because these forms may not be rigorously parallel. Differences in mental abilities measured in this way may be assignable in part to differences in the two forms. The use of exactly the same editions and forms of the achievement tests in these studies, on the other hand, had the possible disadvantage of being less appropriate for children today since the achievement tests used in these studies contain items based upon textbooks and courses of study used in the 1920's and were standardized more than a quarter-century ago.

Differences in Reading Achievement

Table 4 shows the reading grade-equivalent means by grade, sex, and subtest as measured by the 1933 edition of the *Metropolitan Achievement Test*, Form A, Primary II Battery, for Grade III-B. This test was administered during the last week in September and the first week in

TABLE 4. Differences Between the Grade-equivalent Means of Reading Achievement of Evanston Third and Fifth Grade Pupils

Sex and Grade	*Test*	*Grade-equivalent Means* 1934	1953	*Difference Between Means* a]
Third Grade:				
Girls:	Reading Completion	3.56	3.75	†.19*
	Paragraph Meaning	3.51	3.86	†.35*
	Vocabulary	3.18	3.73	†.55*
Boys:	Reading Completion	3.26	3.53	†.27*
	Paragraph Meaning	3.26	3.44	†.18*
	Vocabulary	3.05	3.32	†.27*
Girls and Boys:	Reading Completion	3.42	3.64	†.22*
	Paragraph Meaning	3.39	3.65	†.26*
	Vocabulary	3.14	3.52	†.38*
Fifth Grade:				
Girls:	Reading Comprehension	5.83	6.15	†.32*
	Vocabulary	6.10	6.39	†.29*
Boys:	Reading Comprehension	5.64	5.81	†.17
	Vocabulary	5.92	6.19	†.27*
Girls and Boys:	Reading Comprehension	5.73	5.97	†.24*
	Vocabulary	6.01	6.29	†.28*

a] † indicates data favorable to present-day group.
* indicates chances are at least 95 (or better) in 100 of a true difference. Differences not marked (*) are negligible from a statistical standpoint.

Although these tests were out of print, exact copies of the original tests were obtained by an offset printing made possible with the permission of the World Book Company.

Conditions surrounding the administration of the tests in the present duplicated those of the past as nearly as possible. The Director of the Research and Testing Department who had supervised the administration in the past supervised it again in the present. The children in each school were tested on or near the day of the month that the tests were given in the past. Two trained and experienced test administrators gave the tests, the manual of directions was followed strictly, and the tests were scored in a central place by experienced persons.

In both years and grades, children who had not attended Evanston schools for one full year were excluded from the study. The children in the third- and fifth-grade study were enrolled in eight different schools of former District 75 (schools in North Evanston) and those included in the eighth-grade study attended a junior high school which draws students from the same eight schools.

Fourth-Grade Pilot Study, 1932–1952

Three schools typifying average, superior, and below-average economic groups in Evanston were chosen for the study. The fourth-grade classes in these schools were given the 1929 edition of the *New Stanford Achievement Test*, Form V, and the *Kuhlmann-Anderson Intelligence Test* (fourth edition in 1932 and sixth edition in 1952). Since the numbers in a class and the range in chronological age differed considerably from the 1932 groups, it was decided to match individuals in the two groups as closely as possible in chronolgical age and intelligence and to use only these subjects in the study. This reduced the number to 58 pupils in each group or 116 cases in all.

From a study of Table 1, it appears that the 1952 class did not suffer from the comparison. The 1952 groups earned scores 6 months higher

TABLE 1. Median Scores in Reading Comprehension, Vocabulary, Intelligence Quotients, and Range of Scores in Fourth Grade, October, 1932 and 1952

	Median 1932	*Median 1952*	*Difference*	*Range 1932*	*Range 1952*
Reading Comp.	4.6	5.2	+.6	2.5–7.8	2.6–8.8
Vocabulary	4.6	5.4	+.8	2.6–8.4	2.3–7.8
I.Q.	104	109	+.5	89–126	89–123

in reading comprehension and 8 months higher in vocabulary than did their predecessors of twenty years ago.

While the results were encouraging, it was felt that more complete studies should be made at other grade levels.

Third-Grade Pupils Studied

This paper combines the information from the eight schools, although the full study gives complete details for each one. Table 2 shows that the number of girls was about the same as the number of boys in each of the years, 1934 and 1953. Also, girls for girls and boys for boys, the mean chronological ages and the mean intelligence quotients were essentially the same in the two years.

TABLE 2. Number, Mean Chronological Age, and Mean Intelligence Quotient of Grade III-B and Grade V-B Children, 1934 and 1953

Item	*Girls*		*Boys*	
	1934	*1953*	*1934*	*1953*
Third Grade:				
Number	153	166	151	162
Mean C.A. (months)	100.86	100.21	100.83	100.03
Mean I.Q.	106.53	106.87	105.35	103.64
Fifth Grade:				
Number	142	187	154	175
Mean C.A. (months)	125.89	125.24	125.69	127.42
Mean I.Q.	108.70	106.38	107.01	101.85

The mean intelligence quotients were derived from the fourth edition of the *Kuhlmann-Anderson Intelligence Tests* in 1934 and from the fifth edition in 1953.

Grade V-B Children Studied

Table 2 also shows a reasonable balance between boys and girls in Grade V-B in 1934 and again in 1953. The difference in size between the 1934 and 1953 groups, however, was not of special concern to the study. As in Grade III-B, the mean chronological ages of Grade V-B girls were about the same in the two years, and the similarity was also true of the Grade V-B boys. The mean intelligence quotients of Grade V-B

boys showed the only significant differences in any of the group cc parisons.† This difference was in favor of the 1934 boys.

The full study included information on the variation within groups which does not appear in Table 2. All 1934 groups showe wider variation in both chronological ages and intelligence quotie than the 1953 groups. The writers believe that this suggests changes t have transpired in promotional practices since 1934, when slower c dren were more readily retained in grades and more double promoti were awarded to bright children than at the present time.

TABLE 3. Comparison of the Mean Intelligence Quotients, Menta Ages, and Chronological Ages of Grade VIII-B Pupils in 1933 and 1954

Item	*Girls*		*Boys*		*Girls and Boy*	
	1933	*1954*	*1933*	*1954*	*1933*	*195*
Number	102	143	126	158	228	301
Mean I.Q.	108.77	113.86*	105.62	109.84	107.03	111.[illegible]
Mean M.A. (in months)	174.19	181.33*	171.78	175.53	172.85	178.[illegible]
Mean C.A. (in years)	13–5	13–3	13–8*	13–3	13–7*	13–[illegible]
Mean C.A. (in months)	161.42	159.43	163.85*	159.34	162.76*	159.[illegible]

* Indicates chances are at least 95 (or better) in 100 of a true difference. Differen not marked (*) are negligible from a statistical standpoint.

Grade VIII-B Children Studied

Table 3 shows the mean intelligence quotients, mental ages, a chronological ages of Grade VIII-B pupils in 1933 and 1954. The pup in 1954 were younger than those in 1933, and the 1954 group also earn higher intelligence quotients as measured by the fourth edition of t *Kuhlmann-Anderson Intelligence Tests* in 1933 and by the sixth editi in 1954. The limitations of two forms of any tests must be recogniz before generalizations can be made about the mental abilities of t

† Significant difference is used in its technical statistical sense. It is determined reducing differences to standard units. The full study interpreted significant diff ences at four levels of confidence. This summary combines the information on r ability of the differences and uses the term "significant" as an indication of odds at least 95 (or better) in 100 that an obtained difference in means was true and r due to chance.

October in 1934 and 1953. Table 4 also shows the reading achievement of Grade V-B children who were given the 1933 edition of the *Metropolitan Achievement Test,* Form A, Intermediate Battery, during the last week in October and the first week in November in 1934 and 1953.

These grades were selected because the third grade represents the primary level when most children have had at least two years of instruction in the so-called Three R's, and the fifth grade represents the intermediate level after two more years of instruction in the Three R's have been given and a broader curriculum has been introduced.

Reading Achievement of Grade III-B Children

The grade-equivalent mean of Grade III-B girls was about two months higher in reading completion, about four months higher in paragraph meaning, and about six months higher in vocabulary. Grade III-B boys in 1953 earned a grade-equivalent mean score of approximately three months higher in reading completion, about two months higher in paragraph meaning, and about three months higher in vocabulary.

When the girls' and boys' scores were combined, Grade III-B pupils in 1953 earned grade-equivalent scores that were two months higher in reading completion, about three months higher in paragraph meaning, and about four months higher in vocabulary.

Reading Achievement of Grade V-B Children

Grade V-B girls in 1953 earned a grade-equivalent score that was three months higher in reading comprehension and about three months higher in vocabulary. Grade V-B boys in 1953 earned grade-equivalent scores that were about two months higher in reading comprehension and about three months higher in vocabulary. The combined scores of girls and boys in 1953 were two months higher in reading comprehension and about three months higher in vocabulary.

Total Difference Favored the 1953 Group

In addition to determining the differences by total class groups, the full study showed differences between the means for each of the eight Evanston schools by the categories of grade, sex, and subtest. When all these differences for Grade III-B were considered, 96 reading comparisons were made between the pupils in 1934 and 1953. Eighty-seven percent of the differences favored the 1953 groups.

When the grade, sex, and subtest comparisons were combined for Grade V-B comparisons, 83 percent favored the 1953 group in reading comprehension and 92 percent favored the 1953 group in vocabulary.

Eighth-Grade Reading Comparisons

Table 5 shows Grade VIII-B reading comparisons measured by the 1932 edition of the *New Stanford Achievement Test,* Form V. This test was administered to Grade VIII-B pupils during the last week in September and the first week in October in 1933 and in 1954.

TABLE 5. Differences Between the Grade-equivalent Means of Reading Achievement of Evanston Grade VIII-B Pupils in 1933 and 1954

Sex and Grade	*Test*	*Grade-equivalent Means*		*Difference Between Means a]*
		1933	*1954*	
Eighth Grade:				
Girls:	Reading Comprehension	9.3	9.8	†.5
	Vocabulary	9.0	9.5	†.5
Boys:	Reading Comprehension	8.9	9.5	†.6*
	Vocabulary	9.0	9.5	†.5
Girls and Boys:	Reading Comprehension	9.2	9.7	†.5*
	Vocabulary	9.0	9.5	†.5*

a] † indicates data favorable to present-day group.
* indicates chances are at least 95 (or better) in 100 of a true difference. Differences not marked (*) are negligible from a statistical standpoint.

The table shows that Grade VIII-B girls earned a grade-equivalent score which was five months higher in reading comprehension and vocabulary. Grade VIII-B boys in 1954 earned a grade-equivalent score which was six months higher in reading comprehension and five months higher in vocabulary. The combined grade-equivalent scores for Grade VIII-B girls and boys in 1954 were five months higher in reading comprehension and vocabulary.

Concluding Statement

This report summarizes the findings of three studies of the "then and now" reading achievement of 1,828 children in the 1930's and 1950's.

It was found that present-day pupils attending Evanston schools at the primary, intermediate, and junior-high-school levels read with more comprehension and understand the meaning of words better than did children who were enrolled in the same grades and schools more than two decades ago.

Bibliography

1. Boss, Mable E. "Reading, Then and Now," *School and Society,* LI (January 13, 1940), 62–64.
2. Gray, William S. "Comparative Study of Achievement in Reading, 1916 and 1949." Grand Rapids School Survey, Grand Rapids, Michigan. Grand Rapids: Board of Education, 1949. Chapter 11, pp. 273–79.
3. Illini Survey Associates, College of Education, University of Illinois. *A Look at Springfield Schools.* Champaign, Illinois: Stipes Publishing Co., 1948. Chapter 8, "Results of Formal Tests on Fundamental Skills," pp. 97–127.
4. Jackson, Joseph. *A Quarter Century of Three R's.* Dearborn, Michigan: Board of Education, 1953.
5. Lanton, Wendell C. "Comparison of the Reading, Arithmetic, and Spelling Achievement of Third and Fifth Grade Pupils in 1953 and in 1934." Unpublished doctoral dissertation, Northwestern University, Evanston, Illinois, 1954. 251 pp. *Summary: The "Past-Present" Achievement of Evanston School Children.* Washington, D.C.: NEA Research Division, National Education Association of the United States (September, 1954). 23 pp. (offset).
6. Lanton, Wendell C., Miller, Vera V., and Clark, Edward L. *Comparison of the Reading, Spelling, and Arithmetic Achievement of Eighth Grade Children, 1933–1954.* Research Bulletin No. 4. Evanston, Illinois: Community Consolidated Schools, District 65, Cook County (May 16, 1955), 46 pp.
7. Miller, Vera V. "Comparative Study of the Achievement of Fourth-Grade Children in 1932 and 1952." Evanston, Illinois: Research Department, Community Consolidated Schools, District 65, Cook County, 1952.
8. Partlow, Hugh R. "A Comparison of St. Catharine's Public School Standards in Arithmetic and Reading, 1933–38 and 1952–54." Unpublished doctoral dissertation, University of Toronto, 1955.
9. Worcester, D. A., and Kline, Ann. *Reading Achievement in Lincoln, Nebraska Schools—1921 and 1947.* Lincoln: University of Nebraska Teachers College, 1947.
10. Steffen, Dale S. "A School Opinion Survey of Adults in the Evanston Public Elementary Schools, District Number 65, County of Cook, State of Illinois." Unpublished doctoral dissertation, Northwestern University, 1954.

4. Influences Shaping American Reading Instruction

NILA BANTON SMITH (1965)

The story of American reading instruction from 1607 to 1965 is a fascinating one to pursue. Evolutionary progress in teaching this skill has been marked with a series of turning points. For a period of time methods and materials are quite similar. Then rather suddenly, both of these aspects of reading instruction change in design and in intent. What influences are responsible for bringing about these changes? What causes are sufficiently strong to wrest established procedures from the classroom and to initiate new ones?

More often than not these changes are brought about by the occurrence of a deep stress situation in American life. When an event occurs that threatens the national welfare and happiness of any people, reading instruction changes. Reading seems to be so intricately interwoven with the woof and warp of life that it becomes a part of the living fabric of the American people during crucial epochs in our history.

I shall attempt to sketch the influences that have been basically responsible for change and to indicate ways in which these influences have affected reading instruction.

The Period of Religious Emphasis (1607–1776)

The pioneers of America were, in general, deeply religious. Many of these early settlers came from among those people and from those lands which had embraced some form of the Protestant faith, and their purpose in coming to America was to enjoy a religious freedom not possible in their own country. It was their religious convictions which caused these pioneers to face the dangers attendant upon the establishment of colonies in the wilderness of a new country, and it was these same religious convictions which caused them so courageously to endure the hardships with which they were confronted in the early years. Since the religious motive was the all-controlling force in their lives, it is quite

---

SOURCE: IRA Invitational Address, 1965. Reprinted with the permission of Nila B. Smith and the International Reading Association.

natural that we should find it permeating and directing the instruction in their schools.

As a consequence, this concern was reflected in their teaching of reading both in the content of their readers and in their method. The materials for teaching reading consisted almost wholly of religious selections which it was deeemed necessary for children to memorize in their "green and tender years." Oral reading played an important role in the lives of these people. There was a great dearth of reading materials during the colonial period. The Bible, generally speaking, was the only book the home libraries contained, and many families did not even have a Bible. Furthermore, illiteracy was highly prevalent at this time; so it was customary for the uneducated members of the family or the community to gather in little groups in the evenings and on Sabbaths to listen to the oral reading of the Scriptures by one who had mastered the art of reading, and many memorized long passages of scripture. Oral reading and memorization had strong functions to perform in the social and religious lives of these people. Consequently, reading was taught by oral and memorization methods and the content was entirely religious in nature. Thus reading instruction was shaped by the deep out-of-school concerns of early American settlers.

The Period of Patriotic Emphasis (1776–1840)

By the latter part of the eighteenth century the vividness of the early strife for religious freedom had been dimmed in the birth of new generations, who had learned of the ardent efforts and bitter struggles of their forebears only through hearsay, and whose own hearts and minds were completely occupied with the struggle for political freedom and the business of developing a young nation, strong, unified, and harmonious.

Reader content and method now departed from the religious objective and concerned itself with inculcation of loyalty for the new nation. Readers now contained selections which had to do with the traditions, occupations, and resources of America and with orations and poems written by American authors. Methods now came to lay great stress upon unification of the diversity of dialects; hence phonics was introduced by Noah Webster in his "Blue-Back" Speller to purify different brands of English in America. Memorizing was now replaced with *eloquent* oral reading which might move its listeners to exalted heights of patriotism. So again we see how reading instruction was drastically changed by an out-of-school influence, emanating from a profound national concern.

Emphasis on Promoting Intelligent Citizenship (1840–1880)

We noted in the preceding period that the birth of our nation was followed by an emotional outburst of patriotism. As we neared the second half of the new century the effort to inculcate this intense type of patriotism began to subside and was replaced with a less emotional but still deeply felt national aim—that of preparing the great masses to discharge their duties of citizenship. Leaders now came to realize that the success of the new democracy depended not so much upon arousing patriotic sentiment as upon developing the intelligence of the people, whose ballots were to choose the leaders and determine its policies.

The aim of promoting good citizenry was two-fold: to provide information in all fields of learning, and to develop high morals.

The subject matter of readers now became broader. We find the intensive patriotic type of materials all but disappearing. There were some moralistic selections designed to develop noble and righteous citizens. With the new emphasis, however, upon reading as a means of obtaining information, we find the upper-grade readers filled with a wide range of informative selections in science, history, art, philosophy, economics and politics.

Our leaders in education eager to cooperate in the effort to provide a more effective education for the masses began to visit some of the experimental schools in Europe and came back with the ideas of organizing classrooms by grades and of teaching reading by the word method; hence McGuffey's readers, the first graded series to be published, and Webb's readers titled "The New Word Method" appeared. Methods and materials changed again, abruptly and rather completely.

Emphasis upon Reading as a Cultural Asset (1880–1910)

Sometime in the early 1880's a new movement began to shape itself in the field of reading instruction. At this time in history we have reached a status of tranquillity and security. With the success of the American democracy assured, with threats of major wars no longer impending, with a population comfortable in a prosperous economy, a new trend emerged which affected the nature of reading instruction. The nation now had the leisure and peace of mind to turn to cultural pursuits in music, art, and literature. This concern for cultural development resulted in an emphasis upon the use of reading as a medium for awakening a permanent interest in literary material which would be a cultural asset to the individual in adult life.

Simultaneously with this settled state of affairs the Herbartian principles exerted a strong influence on reading instruction in America. Johann Herbart, who strongly advocated the teaching of literature, was responsible for a wave of educational enthusiasm known as the Herbartian movement in Europe and America. American educators went to Europe to study Herbart's theories, they returned and wrote books on these theories, and zeal for Herbart's ideas ran so high that the Herbartian Society was organized in 1892, and was very active for several years. It later became our present National Society for the Study of Education. Reading instruction was affected by the enthusiastic acceptance of Herbart's ideas.

Readers now became vehicles for acquainting children with folk tales in the primary grades and with the classics in the upper grades. Expressive oral reading for appreciation was the method adopted because it best served the purpose of these times.

The favorite procedure for introducing first-grade children to reading was to have them memorize, dramatize, and then finally read a folk story. "The Little Red Hen" was a story from literature which was especially appropriate for such treatment and this selection was used as the first story in practically all beginning readers. But finally "The Little Red Hen" was demised, and emphasis upon reading as a cultural asset passed away with her.

Initial Period of Emphasis upon Scientific Investigations in Reading (1910–1925)

The dramatic period beginning within the year of 1910 ushered in the first truly great breakthrough in American reading instruction. While there was no strong nationalistic aim for education or for reading at this time, a new development suddenly shaped up which had startling effects in changing reading methods and materials.

This era in the history of reading was marked by the birth of the scientific movement in education. In 1909 Thorndike made the initial presentation of his handwriting scale before a meeting of the American Association for the Advancement of Science, and in 1910 it was published. Generally speaking, the publication of the Thorndike scale has been recognized as the beginning of the contemporary movement for measuring educational products scientifically. In the immediately ensuing years scales and tests appeared rapidly: Courtis arithmetic tests, Hilligas' Composition Scale, Buckingham Spelling Scale, and then a reading test—The Gray Standardized Oral Reading Paragraphs. This test was published in 1915. Other reading tests, mostly silent reading tests, followed shortly.

With the advent of these instruments of measurement it was possible for the first time to obtain scientific information about the effectiveness of reading methods and materials and of administrative arrangements for teaching reading in the classroom. As a result, more innovations in reading instruction issued forth during this period than in all of the centuries of the past.

The initial period of emphasis upon scientific investigation in reading as described in this era extended from 1910 up to but not including 1925. This was, indeed, an eventful moment in the history of reading.

Up to the date of 1910 only 24 researches in reading had been reported in the English language and all of these had been of the laboratory type. From 1910 to 1924, a total of 436 accounts of reading studies had been published by investigators in the United States. This phenomenal spurt in scientific investigation in reading was due to the development of the basic tools of research—standardized tests. As would be expected, the majority of the first studies was concerned with tests and testing. As the period proceeded broader interests were reflected in the problems chosen for investigation. The great majority of these studies now had their settings in public schools, but some laboratory research continued.

The first doctoral dissertations in reading which came to my attention were conducted at the University of Chicago in 1917. Among these studies was a dissertation titled *Studies of Elementary-School Reading through Standardized Tests* by William S. Gray, who was our first great reading authority. Between 1917 and 1924 thirteen additional doctoral dissertations on reading were reported and among these there was a study bearing the title *The Psychology of Reading and Spelling: With Special Reference to Disability*. And who was the young student who did this dissertation? None other than Arthur I. Gates, another "giant" in the field of reading. These two pioneers began their studies early in this initial period of scientific investigation and continued them throughout the years.

Now to note the effects of this influence: for one thing, research conducted during this period was largely responsible for causing the most drastic change in method that had ever taken place—the change-over from oral to silent reading. From the beginning of reading instruction, oral reading had maintained its supreme and undisputed claim over classroom methods. In marked contrast to this traditional practice, we find a period of years, let us say approximately between 1918 and 1925, marked with an exaggerated and, in some cases, almost exclusive emphasis upon silent reading procedures. Research had revealed that individuals could read silently with better understanding of meaning and with more speed. Thus two new techniques were ushered into the teaching of reading: those of silent reading and of speed.

The content of readers changed accordingly. Reading literary selections for appreciation was not consistent with procedures of detailed checking of comprehension or the development of speed, so readers now came to devote their pages to factual materials.

The use of standardized reading tests also ushered in an entire constellation of other new concepts and practices. Through their use it was found that wide individual differences in reading ability existed. As a result we first heard about "individual progression" in reading as developed by Washburne in Winnetka and Dalton in New York. Tests also revealed that large numbers of children were having difficulty in learning to read, and so the specialized branch of reading instruction known as remedial reading now became established in the public schools. And along with the remedial reading movement concerns began to take root in regard to reading specialization in teacher preparation.

It was a great day when the movement in scientific education began to operate in the field of reading. Even though investigators only scratched the surface during this initial period of research this was a momentous epoch in the history of reading, for it truly marked our first great breakthrough in improvement of reading instruction.

The First Period of Intensive Research and Wide Application (1925–1935)

While research got under way during the preceding period, during the next ten years it became intensive, extensive and widely applied. The years between 1925 and 1935 were remarkable in productivity of reading research. From July 1, 1924, to June 30, 1935, a total of 654 published studies were reported, dealing with problems related to an extraordinarily wide variety of topics. This wide and extensive research, together with its application, was the influence largely responsible for the innovations effected at this time.

One effect of this research was a broadening of the reading program in scope. In the new instruction, objectives were not strongly directed toward the development of any one or two skills or end points, but rather toward the development of several different abilities needed in the various purposes for which reading was used in well-rounded living. No one type of instruction was given an exaggerated emphasis overshadowing all others, as had been true in preceding periods.

Without a doubt the various investigations in regard to the reading interests, purposes, and habits of both children and adults were more influential than any other single factor in bringing about this emphasis upon a broader reading program. This decade was unusually fruitful in producing investigations of this type.

In addition to broadening reader content, skill programs, and methods, other notable developments were made—particularly, the initiation of the readiness concept for beginning reading and major advances in devising techniques for diagnosing reading deficiency.

The growing recognition of the complexity of the reading process and the multitude of problems associated with the teaching of reading carried in its wake increasing interest in supervision and in reading courses for teachers. The first supervisors of reading were appointed during this period, and colleges and universities began providing reading courses of varied types.

Period of International Conflict (1935–1950)

Once more an out-of-school stress situation began shaping reading instruction, even as it did in the Period of Religious Emphasis, even as it did in Revolutionary days. An event resulting from progress in science overshadowed all other indications of progress during the period of 1935 to 1950. The "birthday of the atomic age" is officially set as December 2, 1942, when Dr. Enrico Fermi turned on the first successful nuclear energy machine in Chicago. The first atomic bomb destroyed Hiroshima on August 6, 1945. The atomic age and reading immediately become interactive.

But we didn't realize this at the time. We were too close to this earth-shaking event to sense its import for reading instruction. The full impact did not become apparent until the period to be discussed in the next epoch. However, because of its grave significance in the future I am mentioning the initial release of nuclear energy at this point.

While the explosion of the atomic bomb had a delayed reaction on reading, international problems and World War II had some immediate effects, and I shall briefly review the events which brought about these changes.

During the years elapsing since World War I, the United States and other nations had lived through a period of peace. In the early 1930's, however, increasing dissatisfaction was heard concerning treaties and pacts, and in 1933 Hitler began to reveal his aggressive tendencies and continued to do so in the immediate years ahead. So the beginning years of the period covering 1935 to 1950 were marked with international strife and stress. This unrest continued and eventuated in the beginning of World War II in 1939. The United States soon became involved indirectly, but it did not declare war until after the Japanese attack on Pearl Harbor, December 7, 1941. Several trying war-torn years followed.

While the war ended in 1945, many problems still plagued the United States in the way of labor disputes; shortages in food, clothing and shelter; and Russian aggressiveness in building up communist governments in other countries and in extending its communistic party activities in our own country.

It is apparent then, that the entire period of 1935 to 1950 was marked with national and international unrest eventuating in another war.

With this brief consideration of national and international conflict in mind, I shall sketch its effects on reading instruction.

Probably the most obvious effect was a reduction in output of research and instructional materials. Research suffered a severe setback. While accounts of published research had previously numbered over one hundred per year, during the war year 1943–1944 only 54 appeared. Recovery in numbers was not achieved all through the 1940 decade. The number of doctoral dissertations completed was also drastically reduced.

The number of new series of basal readers published during this period decreased sharply. Sixteen basal series were listed as new in the preceding period. During this period, four series were published before the war, and two more got under way only in publishing their primary programs during the last two years of the period.

Another effect of world-wide tension was that it caused a few forethinkers to state a fresh viewpoint in regard to the contribution which reading might make to the American democracy. For half a century we had been concentrating in succession on literary appreciation, silent reading, and a broader program of skills with no mention of nationalism. During this new period the aim of living effectually in our democracy began to crop up. Social effects and uses of reading became a matter of concern. These indications of changing viewpoints concerning purposes of reading instruction were few in number, but even so they probably were the most significant effects of the new national tensions.

The content of basal reading series did not change drastically. The general acceptance of the readiness concept now caused authors for the first time to provide readiness books for the children and readiness instructions to the teacher. Preprimers were increased from one to two, three and four.

Advances in method included provisions for utilizing interrelationships of reading with the other language arts, addition of the use of context clues and structural analysis, and extensions in comprehension and work-study skills.

Interest in reading disability increased rapidly. The multiple-causation theory was developed, informal diagnosis was used for the first time, mechanical aids to reading appeared, and there was a beginning trend toward the development of clinics in public school systems.

Finally, a development in reading supervision should be mentioned. A number of school systems at this time had appointed a special person for supervisory service in reading, and the term "reading consultant" made its initial appearance in educational literature.

Expanding Knowledge and Technological Revolution (1950–1965)

In this long journey of reading instruction from 1607 to 1965 we have finally arrived at the epoch in which all of us are now living. Never since Revolutionary days has our national situation been so tense. Never since then have our democratic ideals been threatened. Once more, Americans are living in a critical period of national stress, perhaps the most critical one of our existence. What influences are causing strain in these troubled times? How are these influences affecting reading instruction?

Two of the influences which are fundamental in our current civilization and which are basically influential in shaping reading instruction are: expanding knowledge and technological revolution. Underscoring both of these and adding motive and impetus to them is deep concern for the survival of democracy. During this period United States citizens have become increasingly aware of the need for vigorous effort in maintaining our leadership as a nation and in preserving the way of life which we as a people cherish.

These combined influences have plunged us into the most serious problems in the history of mankind, and unexpectedly these problems are flinging out many new challenges to those engaged in the teaching of reading. In fact, because of these problems reading has suddenly leapt into a new magnitude.

The key solution and the one most frequently proposed for solving the problems that are currently plaguing humanity is *education* and *reading is basic to education.* Education cannot proceed without reading, hence there is a compelling new objective to increase literacy. This new objective is lifting the horizon of reading far above its established bounds, and revealing vast new frontiers—frontiers of creativity, of responsibility, of obligation and of privilege. The door to an exciting new epoch in the history of reading would seem to be not only ajar, but swinging wide open.

Now let us sketch broadly the more direct effects which these influences are having on the actual teaching of reading.

First, the accumulation of knowledge. We are living in the midst of an explosion of knowledge—social, scientific, ideological, economic, and political. This vast expansion of knowledge is changing continuously and will undoubtedly continue to change at ever-accelerating rates. We realize now that what a child is learning in school today or what an adult learned in school yesterday may be of little or no use to him tomorrow, metaphorically speaking. Therefore, if children in school and adults in present-day life are to keep in step with our ever-changing age they must be able to read well and with discriminating understanding in all fields of endeavor. So it is that these expanding and changing accumulations of knowledge are placing heavy new responsibilities on those who teach reading in all subjects and at all levels.

The technological revolution is also affecting reading instruction. Technology is rapidly replacing manpower with machines. Education will be necessary in holding the jobs of the future. Furthermore, the entire population will be consumers of products of this ever-advancing technology and as such they must read to make decisions as to whether or not to buy some of these technological products, how to use those that they do buy, how to live effectually with those not within their control. This situation in technological developments opens up an entirely new frontier in the field of reading.

Now to discuss the nationalistic concern. All through the late 1940's differences between the Western Powers and Russia continued to divide the world, and Russia's intention to expand communism was plainly evident in the fact that she had taken over seven small countries.

In 1950, shortly after communists had attacked the Republic of Korea, President Truman declared a national emergency as a means of strengthening the United States against communism. This meant enlarging our armed forces and producing large quantities of weapons. The feeling for nationalism now became strong, and its effect was immediately felt in education.

The concern for preservation of our democracy caused changes to be made in materials that children had to read in school, particularly in the fields of social studies and science, in trade books, and in weekly magazines taken for children in many school systems. Teaching reading in the content fields became more important. Interest in the whole subject of improving reading as a national asset picked up quickly.

It was not until 1957, however, that extraordinary concern about the teaching of reading began to manifest itself. This was undoubtedly due to an event of grave international significance—the release of the first Russian satellite, Sputnik. Up to this time the United States had possessed the most deadly weapon of warfare, and it had already sent a rocket 250 miles into space. These achievements assured its supremacy as a nation able to defend itself against aggression. But now the Russians were developing atom bombs, and, furthermore, on October 4, 1957, they startled the world by sending Sputnik 560 miles into space, where it began its orbit around the earth. The supremacy of the United States was now challenged by the technological achievements of another nation which avowedly was determined to establish world communism.

Education in all of its branches felt this challenge. As William Carr said in the January *N.E.A. Journal*, "The first Sputnik was followed by a thundering public demand for education." As a part of this general demand reading instruction now became a subject charged with unprecedented activity.

Educators and laymen alike awakened to the sharp realization that we must put forth more vigorous effort if we were to preserve and improve the American way of life. In all aspects of national endeavor pressures were felt to produce more and more and to do it faster and faster. In reading, pressure to produce higher competency in a shorter time immediately became apparent. This trend reflected the larger motive and tempo which is now controlling increased production in all other aspects of American life. Investigators, authors, and publishers have been working feverishly in seeking new methods and in preparing new materials which they hope will produce faster and better results in learning to read. All this following the advent of Sputnik.

The culminating influence of this period and the one which more than any other gave a fresh and hitherto unrecognized status to competency in reading was governmental concern for and support of education for the masses. Former President John F. Kennedy took an unusual interest in education and asked Congress to approve larger amounts to promote education than had previously been requested by other Presidents. In 1964 President Lyndon B. Johnson announced his intention to make war on joblessness, and on poverty, and to provide "Civil Rights" for all citizens. The basic medium advocated for furthering all three of these objectives was education, and, as previously stated, reading is commonly recognized as the foundation upon which education is built.

The strong new interest in teaching youth and adults who are not in attendance at school extends reading instruction far beyond its established bounds. First, in our history, we provided reading instruction to children in primary grades. It was then extended through the elementary school, then to high-school students, on to college students and in a limited way to adults outside of college. Now it suddenly has become mandatory that we teach millions of adults and millions of youths *out of school* to read better in order that they may hold jobs and lead productive lives.

Thus it is that the government's plans for improving the social and economic lives of our people involve education as a basic first step. The present administration fully recognizes the need for this basic step and is providing for it. In his message to Congress delivered on January 13, 1965, President Johnson proposed an expanded aid-to-education program and asked for new spending authority for the unprecedented sum of $1.3

billion for the coming fiscal year to finance the legislation he had proposed, and he received the amount that he requested.

So it is that the President of the United States and Congress in the interest of our national freedom and welfare, are advocating policies which require education for solution of our current problems, and are providing financial aid to implement their recommendations. Withal, it is gratifying to note that recognition is given to reading as the stepping stone to educational progress.

Never in the history of our country has reading been the subject of such high interest. Never have opportunities to learn to read been extended to so many individuals at all age levels, in school and out. Truly reading instruction has grown to entirely new dimensions in the enlarged and important role that it has to play in achieving national goals.

As a result of these stimulating influences authors of basal reading series are enlarging their programs with multiple texts and rapidly initiating methods reflecting the most recent research and trends. Many new approaches to beginning reading are being published. New reading materials are being prepared for teaching youth and adults who are illiterate or functionally illiterate. Interest in reading disability is expanding and increasingly making use of contributions from other disciplines. The demand for well-trained reading specialists is greater than the supply. Several states are now setting up special reading requirements in preservice and postservice preparation, and several require certification for reading specialists. Research, the common denominator in *all* aspects of reading, is now at an unprecedented high both in quantity and quality. And so this story of American reading instruction has a happy ending.

Change in the present century has been most exciting. In looking back in retrospect we might wonder whether ever another sixty-five years could be so productive as those which have elapsed since 1900. In consideration of the newly developed tools of investigation, evidence of our deep-seated motives to learn, the multitude of studies conducted, we might reason that practically all facets of reading instruction have been explored and thus another era could never be so great as this.

If we do reason to this conclusion, we probably are wrong. We pioneered during this period in unexplored territory. Metaphorically speaking, we chopped down and cleared away the large virgin trees, but perhaps some of the humble shrubs or creeping vines or fragile mosses may hold even more significance for us than the strikingly obvious, first-sight timbers. These more obscure constituents won't yield their significance with the use of heavy saws and axes. We shall need fresh, piercing insights in choosing which of these to select for dislodgment, and then we shall need unique, delicate tools to pry them loose from their tangled environment and to test the potency of their effect; and withal, great ingenuity will be required in shaping reading methods and materials in the image of our findings.

So to you who are involved in any aspect of reading instruction please be assured that there still are thrilling new worlds to conquer. With this expectation in mind, may progress in reading instruction march forward with ever-accelerating vigor and fertility, and may all of us join productively in the procession.

5. Who Shall Teach Reading?

EMMETT ALBERT BETTS (1962)

From available evidence, reading is being taught as well or as poorly as it was one or more generations ago. But the *status quo* is not unchallenged. Citizens are giving their support to the appointment of reading consultants and special reading teachers, to the establishment of reading clinics, to the upgrading of teacher education institutions, and to in-service teacher-education programs.

Equally important, educators are challenging rather than defending the *status quo*. A specialist in reading has been appointed by the U.S. Department of Health, Education and Welfare. Some state departments of education have made similar appointments for the purpose of improving reading instruction from kindergarten through college. Counties, cities, and other large units are delegating this responsibility to a staff member, who often has a core of reading specialists.

These appointees are under the spotlight of public and professional opinion. If they fail to produce facts regarding the improvement of reading instruction under their leadership, the void will continue to be filled by charlatans who offer one-shot palliatives but no cures. Their responsibilities are serious, indeed.

SOURCE: *The Reading Teacher*, XV (May, 1962), 409–414. Reprinted with the permission of Emmett Albert Betts and the International Reading Association.

Excellence: Abstraction to Fact

For many decades, liberal appropriations have been made to improve agriculture. Achievement could be measured in terms of increased bushels of grain to an acre or increased weight of livestock over shorter feeding periods—in units readily understood by most citizens.

International attention is now focused on education—especially on the pursuit of excellence. In this situation, however, the tangibles and intangibles embrace values, attitudes, skills, concepts and thinking abilities. Techniques and instruments for measuring these learnings are neither as precise nor as explicit as the bushels, pounds, and other measures used in agriculture.

Much of the progress in agriculture has been made by inventions of labor-saving machinery. But in most classrooms today, the conscientious teacher is burdened with the hand grading of pupil's work and tests and with many other clerical duties—as in Ichabod Crane's day. The conveniences of mechanical and electronic devices which could offer many plus values are yet to be realized.

Progress in agriculture also has been achieved by selective breeding, improved nutrition, and controlled environments to produce desirable characteristics, such as rust-free wheat. But in education, there is a commitment to teach all the children of all the people. There is, however, a growing awareness of the impact of the community on pupil achievement in the classroom—as evidenced by increasing concern with the community setting of the school. Then, too, there is a concerted effort to individualize instruction and make early identification of the pupil who is learning-disability-prone.

In short, educators, psychologists, and others concerned with the improvement of education, especially with reading instruction, are being challenged to make meaningful that high-level abstraction: Excellence. But excellence, as a goal of education, has different meanings for children with different potentialities and from different cultures.

At this crucial time, the importance of being obvious needs cautious emphasis!

Trends: The Place to Begin

With a clear mandate from their citizens, state departments of education are taking definite steps to improve reading instruction. Rather than doing mountain climbing over molehills, they are taking a close look at the preparation of teachers and clinicians—at the adequacy of professional courses and the levels of competence of graduates. This first step is aimed at a sensible program for the certification of teachers.

This assessment of the source of teacher supply and the quality of teacher preparation is long overdue. But it is no indictment of the intelligence or the earnestness of classroom teachers!

In general, these are the trends:

1. *Liberal Arts.* Two or more years of study before admission to a school of education.

2. *Admission Tests.* Standardized tests for admission (a) to a school of education, (b) to graduate work, (c) to the teaching profession.

3. *Methods Courses.* One or more courses on the teaching of reading for certification in both elementary and secondary education. (This requirement is being considered also for teachers in junior colleges.)

4. *Cognate Disciplines.* Courses in (a) phonetics (as a basis for teaching phonics), (b) semantics, structural linguistics, and psychology of thinking (as a basis for teaching pupils how to think), and (c) human development (as a basis for understanding the development of interests, motivation, etc.).

5. *Special Reading Teachers.* Additional demonstration-laboratory courses on the psychology and pedagogy of reading at elementary, secondary, and college levels.

6. *Reading "Consultants."* Special courses for staff members who demonstrate for and consult with classroom teachers—with emphasis on previous experience as a successful classroom teacher.

7. *Clinicians.* Experience in a reading clinic plus laboratory courses dealing with the causes and remedies of extreme reading disabilities (language disturbances).

Members of many professions are required by law (1) to attend accredited professional schools, (2) to serve an internship and (3) to pass "state boards." Specialists must take additional courses and internships. These requirements give society some measure of insurance that adequate service will be rendered.

Slowly, surely, and somewhat belatedly, this insurance is being extended to cover teaching and closely related services (e.g., school psychology). But merit pay, special certification, and the accrediting of schools of education are complex problems to be studied carefully. The great number of teachers required to staff schools is a staggering problem, especially since there are so few from whom to choose. But the professional competence of the teacher and the specialist is the keystone of improved reading instruction; ways to evaluate competence are being developed because they are so urgently needed.

Classroom Teachers

Recently, Sterling McMurrin, U.S. Commissioner of Education, stated:

> The identification and education of teachers for our schools is now a matter of major concern for the Nation. It is a national tragedy that the generality of our teachers are not fully qualified to assume the burden of responsibility that we must place upon them in the future. Many are lacking the native talent demanded by the art of teaching. Others in large numbers are inadequately prepared by general education or education in their teaching specialties. The responsibility for this rests partially upon our society as a whole, for it has failed to raise the teaching profession to that level of stature and esteem that would make it attractive to highly talented people in numbers adequate to fully satisfy the demand for qualified teaching personnel, and our public leaders have not insisted that our colleges and universities devote their best efforts to the education of teachers.*

The above statement would be as disastrous as attacking motherhood if Dr. McMurrin had said "all teachers"—but he didn't.

A course on how to teach reading has not always been a requirement for the certification of elementary-school teachers. Probably one of the first courses for secondary-school teachers was offered in 1936. But how many of today's English or English-social studies teachers have had one course on the teaching of reading?

Since classroom teachers are "general practitioners" rather than specialists in reading, there are sensible considerations regarding the number of courses required for certification. Today, however, state departments are increasingly concerned with the content of courses as well as with their number. Decisive action is being taken to spell out what a teacher needs to know: (1) identifying and providing for individual differences, (2) understanding the development of interests and the essentials of motivation, (3) teaching phonic skills in their perceptual settings and (4) inventorying and developing concepts and thinking abilities.

To Have and Have Not

Another concern is that of prerequisites or co-requisites for a course on reading methods. When a graduate (or undergraduate) student has a basic knowledge of speech sounds (phonetics), he is ready to study

* (Comments on "The Present Condition of American Education," page 7, *Hearings Before the Subcommittee of the Committee on Appropriations, House of Representatives:* Washington, D.C., U.S. Government Printing Office, May 8, 1961)

the teaching of phonic skills and the interpretation of pronunciation symbols in the dictionary. When the student has a basic knowledge of structural linguistics, semantics, and the psychology of thinking, he is prepared to study the development of concepts and thinking abilities. Otherwise, he is as lost as a pupil forced into long division without having mastered multiplication.

A surfeit of courses on reading methods—one piled on top of another—may produce the same disappointing results as studying the teaching of mathematics without a foundation in mathematics. There is much ado about nothing and a profusion of confusion.

When the requisites for taking a course on teaching reading are blueprinted and given reality, one basic laboratory-demonstration course may be adequate for classroom teachers. The requisites also apply to the teaching of listening, science, history, and other areas of the curriculum. To have a course in reading methods may mean to have professional competence to teach reading—when there is depth to the preparation!

There is equal concern regarding how a course is taught. Does the course consist of lectures and reading textbooks—better known as the art of communicating very little profoundly? Or does the instructor demonstrate how to estimate reading "levels" and needs, to direct reading-study activities, etc.—often bringing the class into the demonstration? Does the instructor provide supervised laboratory practice for his students?

Special Reading Teachers

Since 1930 there has been a sharp increase in the appointment of special reading teachers in elementary and secondary schools and in colleges. But the demand for reading teachers far exceeds the supply, a situation that is likely to exist for some time.

In 1962, for example, one state department reported on the professional preparation of special reading teachers. Only fifty percent of these "specialists" had as much as one course on the foundations of reading instruction. About half of them had studied corrective and/or remedial reading. From these and other data in the report it appears that special reading teachers "get that way" by appointment rather than meeting specific requirements.

The basic problem, then, is how to improve reading instruction by establishing reasonable certification requirements and at the same time upgrade the professional preparation of present appointees.

Special reading teachers are being licensed to teach both developmental and corrective reading. In elementary schools, the cross-grade grouping plan—introduced in 1931—is often used. This plan, while reducing the range of abilities, does not eliminate the need for group or individualized reading. It tends to put most of the low achievers from grades four to six, for example, in the same group. In this low group are pupils with hearing impairments, visual problems, neurological and emotional handicaps, and a wide range of intelligence.

In junior and senior high schools (and in colleges), the sectioning of students for reading instruction is often more easily achieved. But at these school levels there is still a tendency to overemphasize the needs of the poor student by neglecting the basic reading needs of others, especially superior students. And, too often, reading practices are based on the erroneous assumption that all pupils can be "brought up to grade level."

Out on a Limb

In some communities, special reading teachers are called "remedial teachers"—regardless of their levels of professional competence. The announcement of these appointments has raised the hopes of some parents, without justification. This hope proved to be another illusion and the special reading teacher's halo slipped lower to become a noose.

Some large school systems have appointed hundreds of "remedial" teachers as a first step toward upgrading the reading instruction, and thereby have created a dangerous situation. None too soon, thinking leaders raise the question, "If we need so many people to remedy our reading ills, what is the cause?" The answer puts the board of education out on a dead limb. This awkward position is a tragedy.

On Solid Ground

This situation, too, is being corrected. More attention is being given to the prevention rather than the correction of reading and related learning difficulties. In-service programs are being developed as leadership programs, beginning with administrators and supervisors. These leaders, in turn, work with classroom teachers. The old plan of preparing enlightened teachers and leaving the leadership uninformed is going "by the board." Instead, administrators are taking seriously their instructional leadership function, showing more concern about (1) plans for differentiating instruction (i.e., releasing the brakes on learning), (2) methods of teaching reading, and (3) materials for an effective reading-study program.

Reading Clinics

Regardless of the prattlings of some journalists who view reading instruction with jaundiced eyes, there is no *one* cause of reading difficulties. Of course, many pupils are in difficulty because of mismanagement in the classroom. These are the mild, or corrective, reading problems of which there are too many. But their number is being reduced as reading instruction is improved through increased professional competence of teachers.

But there is a significant number of students with reading problems which cannot be put at the doorstep of the classroom teacher, the general practitioner in education. After all, a general practitioner in medicine is not prepared or licensed to be a neurosurgeon or a psychiatrist, nor is the classroom teacher prepared or licensed to deal with learning disabilities which are symptoms of a basic handicap—an emotional disturbance or a neurological problem, complicated by hearing impairments, visual inefficiency, etc.

For this reason, reading clinics are being licensed as clinics rather than as schools. Special certification is being required for reading "clinicians." Often, the reading clinic is a psychological clinic in a medical setting. But the need for reading clinicians who know how to deal with these students is urgent.

Schizoids and other types of emotionally disturbed students require special help. So do those pupils with neurological handicaps. In some instances, the student's basic problem contributes to deficits in perception. These students need more than phonics. In other instances the student's basic problem contributes to disabilities in concept formation. These students, too, need special help.

In the 1960's, too many of these students are assigned to courses on how to study or to speed-reading courses. Obviously, either type of course is contra-indicated for these students. For these reasons, attention is being given in some states to the certification or licensing of reading clinicians who work in one area of clinical psychology: learning disabilities.

Conclusion

Who shall teach reading? This question is not easy to answer. But, right or wrong, answers are being obtained.

First, the professional preparation of the classroom teacher is coming under the spotlight of public opinion. This preparation is the starting point in the improvement of reading instruction, because the teacher is in the front line of action. However, the bottleneck, literally and figuratively, is at the top. Hence, leadership programs involving administrators and supervisors are pointing the way to improved conditions for teaching.

Second, special reading teachers are of concern to those responsible for their certification. Certainly they need more preparation than the general practitioner in a self-contained classroom.

Third, the whole concept of "a specialist in reading" is being revised. Do these people "get that way" by appointment or by professional preparation? Are they to serve as "consultants" to *classroom* teachers or as "reading clinicians"?

Both the public and the teaching profession are challenging the *status quo* by taking vigorous action. There is now good reason to expect more research to improve on the *status quo* and to expect a speed-up in the translation of research into practice.

The improvement of the reading situation can be and is being accelerated. This is the beginning of a new era.

II. Psychology and Nature of the Reading Process

What is reading? The question isn't simple. Ask a dozen reading specialists for their definition and chances are no two will agree. There seem to be almost as many definitions of reading as there are reading specialists.

Although we may never agree on an exact definition of reading, few would disagree with the statement that reading is more than a mechanical process of calling words; or, as someone has facetiously stated it, "barking at the print." Reading is a meaningful process that depends on cortical activity. And the first man to prove it was the great psychologist and father of the scientific method, Edward L. Thorndike. Thorndike's momentous study (6), "Reading as Reasoning," was published in 1917. The idea that the reading process is as involved and as complex as thinking itself was so fundamental and so far-reaching in its implications that its effects on reading instruction remain with us today.

Little has been added to our knowledge regarding the mechanical aspects of the reading process since the pioneer work of Javal in 1879 and that of Erdman and Dodge, who in 1898 evolved means of photographing eye movements during reading. As a result, it is not surprising to find that Huey (7), in his treatment of eye movements done in 1908, is amazingly up to date. Comparable passages are found in current reading texts.

The discovery that poor readers make more fixations and regressions per line than good readers led to the erroneous conclusion that inefficient eye movements caused poor reading. Today's authorities recognize that inefficient eye movement patterns are symptoms rather than causes of reading disability. As reading skill improves, eye movement patterns immediately mirror the improvement.

Wheat (8) delved into the nature of visual perception during the 1920's. He pointed out, among other things, that a reader rarely perceives words letter by letter but recognizes them as wholes. In discussing "The Nature of Word Perception" Wheat also stressed mind set and cue reduction as factors inextricably related to visual perception.

Another aspect of the reading process treated by Huey (9) dealt with the relationship of inner speech to silent reading. Before perusing Huey's material, it might be interesting for the reader to ask, "Do I hear my voice as I read silently? Am I a visual reader or do I function on the auditory level?"

In order to illustrate the difference between the reading habits of a beginner and a mature reader, Buswell (10) studied eye-voice span in oral reading at various grade levels. He learned that the beginner looks at each word as he pronounces it. The mature reader, on the other hand, allows his eyes to lead his voice. Pioneer studies such as this helped give us our first basic understandings of how reading skills develop.

A recent article by Tinker (11) closes this chapter. Tinker provides us with an understanding of how children and adults perceive words. He stresses the importance of sight vocabulary mastery and word analysis skill. In discussing the perceptual processes employed by the beginner and the mature reader, he pinpoints the contributions of current writers as well as those made by early researchers.

Insight into the word perception process carries with it strong instructional implications. What are these implications? How would they affect teaching methodology at the primary and adult levels?

6. Reading as Reasoning: A Study of Mistakes in Paragraph Reading

EDWARD L. THORNDIKE (1917)

It seems to be a common opinion that reading (understanding the meaning of printed words) is a rather simple compounding of habits. Each word or phrase is supposed, if known to the reader, to call up its sound and meaning and the series of word or phrase meanings is supposed to be, or be easily transmuted into, the total thought. It is perhaps more exact to say that little attention has been paid to the dynamics whereby a series of words whose meanings are known singly produces knowledge of the meaning of a sentence or paragraph.

It will be the aim of this article to show that reading is a very elaborate procedure, involving a weighing of each of many elements in a sentence, their organization in the proper relations one to another, the selection of certain of their connotations and the rejection of others, and the cooperation of many forces to determine final response. In fact, we shall find that the act of answering simple questions about a simple paragraph like the one shown below includes all the features characteristic of typical reasonings.

J

Read this and then write the answers to 1, 2, 3, 4, 5, 6, and 7. Read it again as often as you need to.

In Franklin, attendance upon school is required of every child between the ages of seven and fourteen on every day when school is in session unless the child is so ill as to be unable to go to school, or some person in his house is ill with a contagious disease, or the roads are impassable.

1. What is the general topic of the paragraph?

____

2. On what day would a ten-year-old girl not be expected to attend school?

____

SOURCE: *The Journal of Educational Psychology,* VIII (June, 1917), 323–332. Reprinted by permission of the publisher.

3. Between what years is attendance upon school compulsory in Franklin?

____

4. How many causes are stated which make absence excusable?

____

5. What kind of illness may permit a boy to stay away from school, even though he is not sick himself?

____

6. What condition in a pupil would justify his non-attendance?

____

7. At what age may a boy leave school to go to work in Franklin?

____

Consider first the following responses which were found among those made to Questions 1, 2, 5 and 6 above by two hundred pupils in Grade 6. (All are quoted exactly save that capitals are used at the beginning here regardless of whether the pupils used them.)

		Percents	*Number per thousand*
J	1. Unanswered	18	180
	Franklin	4½	45
	In Franklin	1	10
	Franklin attendance	1	10
	Franklin School	1½	15
	Franklin attending school	1	10
	Days of Franklin	½	5
	School days of Franklin	½	5
	Doings at Franklin	1	10
	Pupils in Franklin	½	5
	Franklin attends to his school	½	5
	It is about a boy going to Franklin	½	5
	It was a great inventor	½	5
	Because its a great invention	½	5
	The attendance of the children	½	5
	The attendance in Franklin	½	5
	School	7½	75
	To tell about school	½	5
	About school	4	40
	What the school did when the boy was ill	½	5
	What the child should take	½	5
	If the child is ill	2	20
	How old a child should be	½	5

"Scarlet fever, chicken pox, measles or diphtheria," through "Scarlet fever," "headache," "Serious," "Hay fever," "Pimple," to "Contagious or roads impassable," and "All kinds of disease." Thus *Paragraph* in J 1 when over-potent produces responses ranging from "A group of sentences making sense" through "A group of sentences," and "A few sentences," to "The sentence," "Subject and predicate," "Begin with a capital," "A letter," and "Commas and periods."

In particular, the relational words, such as pronouns, conjunctions and prepositions, have meanings of many degrees of exactitude. They also vary in different individuals in the amount of force they exert. A pupil may know exactly what *though* means, but he may treat a sentence containing it much as he would treat the same sentence with *and* or *or* or *if* in place of the *though*.

The importance of the correct weighting of each element is less appreciated. It is very great, a very large percentage of the mistakes made being due to the over-potency of certain elements or the under-potency of others.

Consider first the over-potency of elements in the questions. The first question about paragraph J was, "What is the general topic of the paragraph?" A large group of answers show over-potency of *paragraph*. Such are those quoted above to show variation in the understanding of the word. We also find an over-potency of *top* (in topic) combined with that of paragraph, resulting in such responses as: "Leave a half-inch space," "An inch and a half," "An inch and a half capital letter," "The topic of paragraph is one inch in."

The second question was: "On what day would a ten-year-old girl not be expected to attend school?" We find under-potency of *not* resulting in answers like "When school is in session" or "Five days a week." We find under-potency of *day* resulting in responses like "She is allowed to go to school when 6 years," "Age 11," and "Fourteen years."

We find over-potency of *day* shown by "Monday," "Wednesday," and "Friday"; of *ten-year-old girl* in "The ten-year-old girl will be 5 a."

Ten-year-old is over-potent in an interesting way, namely, in the very large number of responses of "On her birthday." Over-potency of *Attend school* seems to be one part of the causation of "To attendance with Franklin," "Ever morning at half past 8," "She should," and "Because he did learn."

Consider next over-potency and under-potency of the words or phrases in the paragraph. The following list of responses shows that each of ten words taken from the paragraph is over-potent so as to appear clearly influential in the response to each of the first three questions (and in seven of the cases to the fourth question as well). These occur within

		Percents	*Number per thousand*
	If the child is sick or contagious disease	½	5
	Illness	1	10
	On diseases	½	5
	Very ill	3	30
	An excuse	2	20
	The roads are impassable	1	10
	Even rods are impossible	½	5
	A few sentences	½	5
	Made of complete sentences	½	5
	A sentence that made sense	½	5
	A group of sentences making sense	½	5
	A group of sentences	3	30
	Subject and predicate	½	5
	Subject	½	5
	The sentence	½	5
	A letter	½	5
	Capital	5½	55
	A capital letter	½	5
	To begin with a capital	2	20
	The first word	½	5
	A general topic	½	5
	Good topic	½	5
	Leave half an inch space	2½	25
	The heading	½	5
	Period	½	5
	An inch and a half	½	5
	An inch and a half capital letter	½	5
	The topic is civics	½	5
	The answer	½	5
J 2.	Unanswered	6	60
	Unless the child is so ill as to be unable to go to school	41	410
	Unless the child is unable to go to school	½	5
	Unless she is ill or the roads are impassable	1	10
	Roads are impassable	1	10
	When his baby or brother have some kind of disease	1	10
	When a parent is ill	½	5
	If her father or mother died	½	5
	On her birthday	6½	65
	On her fourteenth birthday	½	5
	On every day	4	40
	On any day	½	5

	Percents	Number per thousand
Expected every day	1½	15
On Monday and for 5 days a week	½	5
On Monday	1	10
On Friday	1	10
When school is in session	1	10
The beginning of the term	½	5
Fourteen year	½	5
Age 11	½	5
She is allowed to go to school when 6 years	½	5
A very bad throat	½	5
When better	½	5
J 5. Unanswered	2	20
If mother is ill	5½	55
Headache, ill	½	5
A sore neck	½	5
Headache, toothache or earache	½	5
When a baby is sick	½	5
Playing sickness	½	5
Serious	½	5
When the roads cannot be used	½	5
Contagious disease, roads impassable	1½	15
He cannot pass the ball	½	5
A note	½	5
J 6. Unanswered	15	150
Ill with a contagious disease	5	50
Seven years old	½	5
By bringing a note	6	60
When going with his mother to his cousin	½	5
Is to go his mother	½	5
When he is well and strong	½	5
To have a certificate from a doctor that the disease is all over	½	5
Somebody else must have a bad disease	½	5
Torn shoes	½	5
Neat attendance	½	5
When he acts as if he is innocent	½	5
Being good	½	5
By being early	½	5
Get up early	½	5
Come to school	1½	15
Be at school every day	½	5
If he lost his lessons	½	5
Illness lateness or truancy	½	5

	Percents	Number per thousand
A bad boy	½	5
By not going to school	½	5
None	½	5
Not sick no condition and mother not ill	½	5
Not very good	½	5
When you come you get your attendance marked	½	5
Of being absent	½	5
His attendance was fair	½	5
Truant	1	10
If someone at his house has a contagious disease	6½	65
When roads	½	5
If he was excused	½	5
Not smart	½	5
If his father or mother died	½	5
By not staying home or playing hookey	½	5

In general, in this and all similar tests of reading, the responses do not fall into a few clearly defined groups—correct, unanswered, error No. 1, error No. 2, and so on. On the contrary, they show a variety that threatens to baffle any explanation. We can, however, progress toward an explanation, by using the following facts and principles:

In correct reading (1) each word produces a correct meaning, (2) each such element of meaning is given a correct weight in comparison with the others, and (3) the resulting ideas are examined and validated to make sure that they satisfy the mental set or adjustment or purpose for whose sake the reading was done. Reading may be wrong or inadequate (1) because of wrong connections with the words singly, (2) because of over-potency or under-potency of elements, or (3) because of failure to treat the ideas produced by the reading as provisional, and so to inspect and welcome or reject them as they appear.

Everybody, of course, understands that (1) plays a part, but it is not so clearly understood that a word may produce all degrees of erroneous meaning for a given context, from a slight inadequacy to an extreme perversion.

Thus *Franklin* in the paragraph quoted (J) varies from its exact meaning as a local unit through degrees of vagueness to meaning a man's name (as in "Franklin attends to his school" as a response to question 1), or to meaning a particular personage (as in "It was a great inventor" as a response to question 1). Thus *Contagious* in paragraph J permit responses to question 5 (What kind of illness may permit a boy to sta away from school, even though he is not sick himself?) ranging fro

five hundred responses made by children within grades 5 to 8. Cases of under-potency would be still easier to collect.

The questions, I may remind the reader, were as follows:

1. What is the general topic of the paragraph?
2. On what day would a ten-year-old girl not be expected to attend school?
3. Between what years is attendance upon school compulsory in Franklin?
4. How many causes are stated which make absence excusable?

(The numbers refer to the question to which the words were the response.)

Franklin	1. Franklin. 1. Franklin and the diseases. 1. Franklin topic.
	2. Franklin.
	3. Because it is a small city. 3. Franklin was in school 141 years.
attendance	1. Attendance.
	2. To attendance with Franklin.
	3. In Franklin attendance upon school is required. Attending school 130 days.
school	1. School. 1. They must know their lessons.
	2. In the beginning of school.
	3. School in session. 3. In the years of school.
seven	1. Seven and fourteen. 1. How old a child should be.
	2. He should attend school at 7 years. 2. Between seven and fourteen.
	3. Seven years.
	4. Under seven.
fourteen	1. Every child between seven and fourteen. In Franklin how old they are.
	2. Fourteenth of every day. 2. Fourteen years.
	3. Fourteen years. 3. Fourteen.
	4. 7 to 14.
every	1. Every child.
	2. Expected every day. 2. On every day.
	3. Every year. 3. Every child between fourteen or thirteen.
	4. Every day.
ill	1. Illness. 1. Very ill. 1. If the child is ill.
	2. Ill. 2. A very bad throat.
	3. He cannot go to school unless ill.
	4. When child is ill. 4. Must be sick.
contagious	1. Contagious disease.
	2. If she is sick or has a contagious disease.
	3. Contagious disease.
	4. Contagious disease.
disease	1. Fever. 1. About disease.
	2. Often sick.

	3. Unless ill or contagious disease.	3. Disease.
	4. A terrible disease going out.	4. Because when a boy has disease.
impassable	1. The roads are impassable.	1. Snow.
	2. When roads are impassable.	
	3. Seven to fourteen years or the roads are impassable.	
	4. Or the roads are impassable.	

To make a long story short, inspection of the mistakes shows that the potency of any word or word group in a question may be far above or far below its proper amount in relation to the rest of the question. The same holds for any word or word group in the paragraph. Understanding a paragraph implies keeping these respective weights in proper proportion from the start or varying their proportions until they together evoke a response which satisfies the purpose of the reading.

Understanding a paragraph is like solving a problem in mathematics. It consists of selecting the right elements of the situation and putting them together in the right relations, and also with the right amount of weight or influence or force for each. The mind is assailed as it were by every word in the paragraph. It must select, repress, soften, emphasize, correlate and organize, all under the influence of the right mental set or purpose or demand.

Consider the complexity of the task in even a very simple case such as answering question 6 on paragraph D, in the case of children of grades 6, 7, and 8 who well understand the question itself.

John had two brothers who were both tall. Their names were Will and Fred. John's sister, who was short, was named Mary. John liked Fred better than either of the others. All of these children except Will had red hair. He had brown hair.

6. Who had red hair?

The mind has to suppress a strong tendency for *Will had red hair* to act irrespective of the *except* which precedes it. It has to suppress a tendency for *all these children . . . had red hair* to act irrespective of the *except Will*. It has to suppress weaker tendencies for *John, Fred, Mary, John and Fred, Mary and Fred, Mary and Will, Mary Fred and Will,* and every other combination that could be a "*Who*," to act irrespective of the satisfying of the requirement "had red hair according to the paragraph." It has to suppress tendencies for John and Will or brown and red to exchange places in memory, for irrelevant ideas like *nobody* or *brothers* or *children* to arise. That it has to suppress them is shown by the failures to do so which occur. The *Will had red hair* in fact causes one-fifth of children in grades 6, 7, and 8 to answers wrongly,* and about two-fifths of children in grades 3, 4, and 5. Insufficient potency of *except Will** makes about one child in twenty in grades 6, 7, and 8 answer wrongly with "all the children," "all," or "Will Fred Mary and John."

Reading may be wrong or inadequate because of failure to treat the responses made as provisional and to inspect, welcome, and reject them as they appear. Many of the very pupils who gave wrong responses to the questions would respond correctly if confronted with them in the following form:

Is this foolish or is it not?

The day when a girl should *not* go to school is the day when school is in session.

The day when a girl should not go to school is the beginning of the term.

The day etc. . . . is Monday.

The day is fourteen years.

The day is age eleven.

The day is a very bad throat.

Impassable roads are a kind of illness.

He cannot pass the ball is a kind of illness.

They do not, however, of their own accord test their responses by thinking out their subtler or more remote implications. Even very gross violations against common sense are occasionally passed, such as letting Mary give Tom a blue dog, or giving "Thought the man fat out" as an answer to I 1. Usually, however, the irrelevance or inconsistency concerns something in the question or the paragraph and the failure to heed it is closely akin to the under-potency of certain elements.

I.

Nearly fifteen thousand of the city's workers joined in the parade on September seventh, and passed before the hundred thousand cheering spectators. There were workers of both sexes in the parade, though the men far out-numbered the women.

1. What is said about the number of persons who marched in the parade?

It thus appears that reading an explanatory or argumentative paragraph in his textbooks on geography or history or civics and (though to a less degree) reading a narrative or description involves the same sort of organization and analytic action of ideas as occur in thinking of sup-

* Some of these errors are due to essential ignorance of "except," though that should not be common in pupils of grades 6 or higher.

posedly higher sorts. This view is supported by the high correlations between such reading and verbal completion tests, Binet-Simon tests, analogies tests and the like. These correlations, when corrected for attenuation, are probably, for children of the same age, as high as + .80.

It appears likely, therefore, that many children fail in certain features of these subjects not because they have understood and remembered the facts and principles but have been unable to organize and use them; or because they have understood them but have been unable to remember them; but because they never understood them.

It appears likely also that a pupil may read fluently and feel that the series of words are arousing appropriate thoughts without really understanding the paragraph. Many of the children who made notable mistakes would probably have said that they understood the paragraph and, upon reading the questions on it, would have said that they understood them. In such cases the reader finds satisfying solutions of those problems which he does raise and so feels mentally adequate; but he raises only a few of the problems which should be raised and makes only a few of the judgments which he should make. Thus one may read paragraph I with something like the following actual judgments:

Fifteen thousand did something—there was a parade—September seventh was the day—there were two hundred thousand something—there was cheering—workers were in the parade—both sexes in the parade—the men outnumbered the women.

Contrast these with the following which may be in the mind of the expert reader:

Nearly fifteen thousand—not quite, but nearly—of the city's workers—people who worked for a living—joined in the parade—a big parade of nearly 15,000—on September seventh—the parade was in the fall—they passed before two thousand hundred cheering spectators—two hundred thousand saw the parade—they cheered it—they were workers of both sexes—there were men workers and women workers in the parade—the men far outnumbered the women. Many more men than women were in the parade.

In educational theory, then, we should not consider the reading of a textbook or reference as a mechanical, passive, undiscriminating task, on a totally different level from the task of evaluating or using what is read. While the work of judging and applying doubtless demands a more elaborate and inventive organization and control of mental connections, the demands of mere reading are also for the active selection which is typical of thought. It is not a small or unworthy task to learn "what the book says."

In school practice it appears likely that exercises in silent reading to find the answers to given questions, or to give a summary of the matter read, or to list the questions which it answers, should in large measure replace oral reading. The vice of the poor reader is to say the words to himself without actively making judgments concerning what they reveal. Reading aloud or listening to one reading aloud may leave this vice unaltered or even encouraged. Perhaps it is in their outside reading of stories and in their study of geography, history, and the like that many school children really learn to read.

7. The Work of the Eye in Reading

EDMUND B. HUEY (1908)

If we sit directly before one who is reading and watch his eyes closely; or, more conveniently, perhaps, if we have him hold a hand mirror flat on the adjoining page as he reads, while we look over his shoulder, we will notice that his eyes move pretty regularly from side to side along the printed lines. We may count these sweeps from left to right, as a page is read, and at the end will find that they correspond to the number of lines on the page. The reader may insist that he reads several lines or even a paragraph with one sweep of the eye. He has perhaps grasped the thought of the lines or paragraph in one unitary act; and being quite unconscious of the movements of his eyes, he may very naturally suppose that he has taken but one "look" at the lines. However, I have been able without fail to count the lines of the page from the movement of the reader's eyes, whenever the whole page was actually read, not skimmed; and in using apparatus which recorded every movement, the eyes have been found in every case to move from side to side, line by line, without missing any line.

SOURCE: Edmund B. Huey, *Psychology and Pedagogy of Reading* (New York: The Macmillan Company, 1908), pp. 15–24.

As you watch the reading, you notice, too, that the eyes do not move continuously from left to right along the line, but proceed by a succession of quick, short movements to the end, then return in one quick, usually unbroken movement to the left. You find all this very evident. And yet most of those who have studied the eye have curiously failed to note that the movement was discontinuous; and up to about 1879, when Professor Javal called attention to it, I find no mention of the fact in the literature. Indeed, I have not myself seen mention of these reading movements until 1898, except in the writings of Professor Javal and some other French authors who took up his discovery, and in a paper published in 1895 by Professor Alexander Brown, of Edinburgh. It is a curious instance of the failure of scientists to make first-hand observations except along certain lines that have become habitual.

You will find that there are at least two pauses for every line, and almost always more than that for lines of this length—from three to five pauses, usually, and even more when the reading proceeds very slowly. The movements are so very quick that you may wonder as you try to follow them whether the reader has time to see anything during the movement, and you may forecast, as Professor Javal did, what later experiments have seemed to prove, that there is practically no reading, or rather no direct seeing of the words and letters, except during the pauses.

You will find it impossible to determine just what word is being looked at, or fixated, as we say, at any moment; and the reader himself cannot give a much more accurate account of this than can the onlooker, although he often supposes that he can.

An attempt to count the pauses for each line will give rise to some curious difficulties, in case you "lay it on your conscience" to get the number right. If the movements occurred at regular time intervals, so many per second, you might get on very well with them; but it has been found that they vary greatly in extent, and that some of the pauses are very much longer than others. This irregularity prevents the rhythmic grouping which helps so much in counting, and forces one to make a particular counting reaction, say to tap with a pencil or to inwardly say "one, two," etc., for each movement. One may do this for a reader who is not very speedy, but I doubt if it is possible, even with special training, to make accurate counts, by this method, of the movements of the eyes of persons who read rather fast. Besides the difficulty of the counting itself, there is always the possibility of losing movements that occur while your own eye is in motion, as you are practically blind to what occurs while you are changing your own fixation—just as in boxing, one may be startled by a blow that started while his eye was moving, attracted by a feint. And we know the rule, as Professor Dodge observes, that the fencer should look his opponent *in the eye,* trusting to indirect vision for information about his movements.

Professor Javal, of the University of Paris, seems, as has been said, to have been the first to note the actual character of the eye's movements in reading. He concluded that there was a pause about every ten letters, and thought that this was about the amount that could be seen clearly at one fixation. He found that after reading he had after-images of straight gray lines corresponding to the parallel lines of print, and concluded that the eye's fixation point did not leave the line as it moved forward in reading. Finding that the upper half of the line was most important for reading, as can be seen at once by dividing a line in halves horizontally and comparing the legibility of the upper and lower halves, he concluded, from this and other observations, that the fixation point moves along between the middle and top of the small letters. He also stated that the movement was such as to prevent the seeing of what was read except during the reading pauses.

While not all of Professor Javal's observations are conclusive, he deserves more than does any one else the credit for making the initial discoveries in this field, and for initiating a considerable number of later studies. His own further work was prevented by his losing his sight, although, upon calling to see him a few years ago, I found him busily engaged in experimenting upon the reading of the blind.

M. Lamare, working with Professor Javal, found it simpler to count a series of sounds produced, in a microphone, by the eye movements. The eyelid is displaced a little at each movement of the eye, and this gave the necessary stimulus in an electric circuit. Some information about the movements was thus obtained, although the author is careful to acknowledge the inadequacy of even this method of counting, and guards himself against making more than general conclusions. M. Landolt, continuing the study at the University of Paris, and observing the movements directly, concluded that on an average 1.55 words were read per reading pause, at the ordinary reading distance. Reading of a foreign language required more pauses, as did also the reading of detached words, numbers, and lists of proper names. He found that the small movements were very fatiguing, and that, since the angular excursion increases as the reading matter is brought nearer to the eye, this may account for the tendency of children to bring their books too near the eye. Relief is thus obtained from the fatigue incident to small-angled movements, but the work of the muscles of accommodation and convergence is correspondingly increased, with the resulting tendency to myopia. Doubling the distance of the page from the eye increased the number of movements in the ratio of nine to seven, the number of eye movements seeming to depend upon the number of words per line rather than upon the visual angle subtended. Landolt's method obliged him, as he states, to have his readers read slowly, and more movements are made by the slow readers.

Dr. Ahrens, at the University of Rostock, Germany, attached a light ivory cup to the cornea of a reader's eye; and fastening a bristle pointer to the cup, he attempted to get from this a tracing of the eye's movements written on a smoked surface. He was unsuccessful, but he had given a valuable suggestion.

Dr. Lough, at Harvard University, and Professor Delabarre, at Brown University, at a considerably later time, attached a plaster of Paris cup to the cornea and obtained some records of the movements of the eye, but apparently obtained no record of the movements in reading.

Erdmann and Dodge, in an extended investigation of reading made at the University of Halle, Germany, and published in 1898, studied the movements of the eye in reading, using the mirror method of direct observation referred to on a previous page. They found that the number of pauses did not vary greatly from line to line, for the same reader and with easy familiar reading matter. There were fewer pauses with familiar matter. In reading lines from a familiar philosophical treatise, printed in English, with line 83 millimeters in length, Dodge, an American, averaged from three to five pauses per line, according to the familiarity of the passages read. Erdmann, a German, averaged from five to seven pauses per line, under the same conditions, in reading a familiar German scientific work, with lines 122 millimeters in length. In the initial readings, Dodge averaged five pauses per line and Erdmann seven. The variations above and below these latter averages were small and infrequent. More pauses were made in reading a foreign language. Proofreading required about three times as many pauses as regular reading, in the case of Erdmann. In writing there seemed to be a pause for about every two letters, but they could not be sure that they noted all of the movements here.

By watching a reader's eye through a telescope arranged to permit measurement of horizontal distances observed, they found that the first pause was almost always within the line, and that the last was still farther from the end of the line. The more familiar a text, the greater was the indentation at the left, and more especially still at the right. They consider that the greater indentation at the right is because the previous context makes it easier to fill out the end of the line apperceptively, and also because the last section of the line is seen longer in indirect vision than is the first section, the reader getting no data from the beginning of the line until he arrives at it.

These authors made some observations which seemed to indicate that the fixations of the eye in reading were almost exclusively upon words, upon the middle of the word usually. However, the experiments were not conclusive, and did not permit of the marking of the actual places fixated.

Erdmann and Dodge did not measure the speed of the eye's movements in reading. Lamansky had measured the speed of the eye's movements in general, by counting the number of after-images produced during a given movement of a pencil of light flashed into the eye at regular intervals through the perforations in a rotating disk. Dodge repeated these experiments, and then carried over the results obtained for the speed of eye movements as they occur in moving voluntarily from one fixation point to another, to the movements that occur in reading. The results, as published in 1898, did not agree with those of Lamansky, and indicated that the time required for an eye movement in reading was about .015 second. These experimenters had no means of measuring the duration of the reading pauses, but seem to have supposed them to be of tolerably uniform length for a given reading. The pauses have later, however, been shown to vary greatly in length.

Professor Dodge has succeeded in photographing upon a moving plate a beam of light reflected from the eye at different angles during its movement from one fixation point to another, thus permitting a computation of the rate of movement. The tests that he made of the movement in reading showed that the forward movements varied from two to seven degrees, and that the time occupied by these was, on an average for three readers, nearly .023 second. The return movement through twelve to fourteen degrees required a little less than .041 second. As the lines subtended an angle of sixteen degrees, the eye evidently passed over but three-fourths to seven-eighths of each line.

In experimenting upon the psychology of reading, in 1897-1898, it seemed to me impossible, from my own observations and from those of all earlier experimenters who had tried direct observations of the reader's eye, to get trustworthy account, by direct observation, of the speed, nature, and even number of the eye's movements in reading of the length and variation of the reading pauses, etc. Nor could the reader himself give even so good an account. For him the succession of movements and pauses is practically nonexistent, except when the eyes are very tired or in some way abnormal. In certain cases of abnormal vision, it is true, some valuable observations may be made by the reader. For example, a patient who had no use of the left halves of his retinæ and thus could not see any letters that lay to the right of the point fixated, was quite conscious of the jerky forward movement of his eyes as section after section of new matter came into view. Again, some readers become quite conscious of the presence of the muscæ volitantes, or flitting spots that appear more or less in the vision of most people; and these give some notion of the jerky character of the movements.

Most of us, however, find ourselves getting over the page rather smoothly and continuously, apparently seeing distinctly a considerable portion of it at once, and without interruptions of any kind. Words, letters, and letter-groups flash into greater distinctness from moment to moment, and there is some thought of a mental traversing of the lines. If we watch closely, we are apt to find some sort of inner utterance of what is being read, and we have a notion of the meaning of it all, although we cannot very well describe this consciousness of meaning. Thus reading appears to the casual introspection of the reader. We find, however, that underneath this apparent simplicity, there is an astounding complexity of processes. These have been built up slowly, and by an immense amount of practice, until they have organized and settled into the smoothly running machinery of our present-day reading. The psychologist's analysis discloses a condition which impresses one, to use Francis Galton's figure, as "when the basement of our house happens to be under thorough sanitary repairs, and we realize for the first time the complex system of drains and gas and water pipes, flues, bell-wires, and so forth, upon which our comfort depends, but which are usually hidden out of sight, and with whose existence, so long as they acted well, we had never troubled ourselves."

8. The Nature of Recognition

HARRY G. WHEAT (1923)

I. The Process

The former conception emphasized the importance of letters. It was formerly believed, as it is quite commonly believed today, that recognition in reading proceeds letter by letter. The eyes, one might be told, move across the line of print in a continuous, steady movement, noting

SOURCE: Harry G. Wheat, *The Teaching of Reading* (Boston: Ginn and Company, 1923), pp. 64–71. Reprinted with the permission of the publishers, Ginn and Company; copyright 1923.

each letter separately, but doing it so rapidly that the letters fuse themselves into words in our minds without our being at all conscious of the process. A word is determined by its constituent letters; therefore it is necessary for the eye to take in and the mind to relate each letter as it appears in the word, before recognition of the word is complete. Words are spelled letter by letter; they are written letter by letter; naturally, the argument might run, they are recognized and read letter by letter. The argument is very plausible. There is not a doubt that behind some such an argument the old alphabet method of teaching children to read defended itself for so long a time in educational practice.

"From simple to complex" was the dominant principle. The alphabet method of teaching children to read was logically the first and only method of earlier pedagogical practice. A later chapter, "The Development of Modern Methods in Reading," will treat of it in some detail. For our present purpose it is enough to examine briefly the underlying principle of the method. The writings of Pestalozzi provide for us the most evident clue to an understanding of the reason why the alphabet method continued for so long a time to be the only one devised by the minds of teachers of children.

Pestalozzi, fired by the "Emile" of the visionary Rousseau, decided, as he said, "to psychologize teaching" and to arrange the order of topics in each subject and present them in the way by which pupils can learn them best. In order to carry out his designs he adopted and followed to the letter that principle of method which had always been dominant in the teaching of reading. All teaching was to "proceed from the simple to the complex." The manner in which such an apparently harmless principle led Pestalozzi astray in the teaching of reading, as well as in the teaching of other subjects, is illustrated in the following quotations from his writings:

> I once more began crying my A B C's from morning to night. . . . I was indefatigable in putting syllables together and arranging them in a graduated series. I did the same for numbers; I filled whole notebooks with them; I sought by every means to simplify the elements of reading and arithmetic, and by grouping them psychologically [to] enable the child to pass easily and surely from the first step to the second, from the second to the third, and so on. The pupils no longer drew letters on their slates, but lines, curves, angles, and squares.
>
> In every branch of popular knowledge or talent, I set to work to organize a graduated series of exercises, the starting point of which was within everybody's comprehension, and the unbroken action of which, always exercising the child's powers without exhausting them, resulted in a continuous, easy, and attractive progress.

The spelling book must contain the entire range of sounds of which the language consists, and portions of it should be repeated daily in every family. . . . No one imagines to what a degree the attention of infants is aroused by the repetition of such simple sounds as *ba, ba, ba, da, da, da, ma, ma, ma, la, la, la.*[1]

Thus we see that to Pestalozzi and to the pedagogues of a former day "from simple to complex" meant to start with the letter and proceed to the syllable, word, phrase, and sentence. To them the letter and the syllable were the simple elements; the word, the phrase, and the sentence the complex.

The present conception emphasizes the importance of words and phrases. Students of education are coming to believe that the old and still somewhat common idea of recognition is entirely wrong. The careful reader of the preceding chapter cannot but be convinced that recognition in reading can and does proceed in a way that is more rapid and comprehensive than letter by letter. The present conception of recognition is that it proceeds not letter by letter but in word-wholes, in phrase-wholes, and sometimes even in sentence-wholes. In support of this conception let us review, first, the records of eye movement in reading which were presented in the preceding chapter; second, the findings of certain experimenters who have carried on investigations in the subject of recognition.

Records of eye movement. The records of eye movement which were presented in the preceding chapter reveal facts of recognition which stand out in most striking contradiction to the former letter-by-letter conception of the process. Let us turn back to a typical record, Fig. 1, for example. Here we find an adult silent reader taking into consciousness from one to four words at a single peep at the line. Since there is no perception in eye movement from pause to pause, as it was pointed out in a preceding discussion, we are obliged to conclude that the whole of perception, or recognition, takes place during the time consumed in the reading pauses. A mathematical division of a given line into as many parts as there are pauses in the line is conclusive that the reader's span of recognition is of an extent sufficient to cover the space of several letters. In line 2, for example, we note that the span of recognition is able to compass words and groups of words which are made up of six to thirteen letters. In lines 2 to 6, inclusive, forty-six words are read in twenty-two fixation pauses. That is to say, recognition is proceeding at the average rate of slightly more than two words at a time. It is not difficult for us to draw a conclusion from such a record.

[1] S. C. Parker, General Methods of Teaching in Elementary Schools, pp. 144–145. Ginn and Company, Boston, 1919.

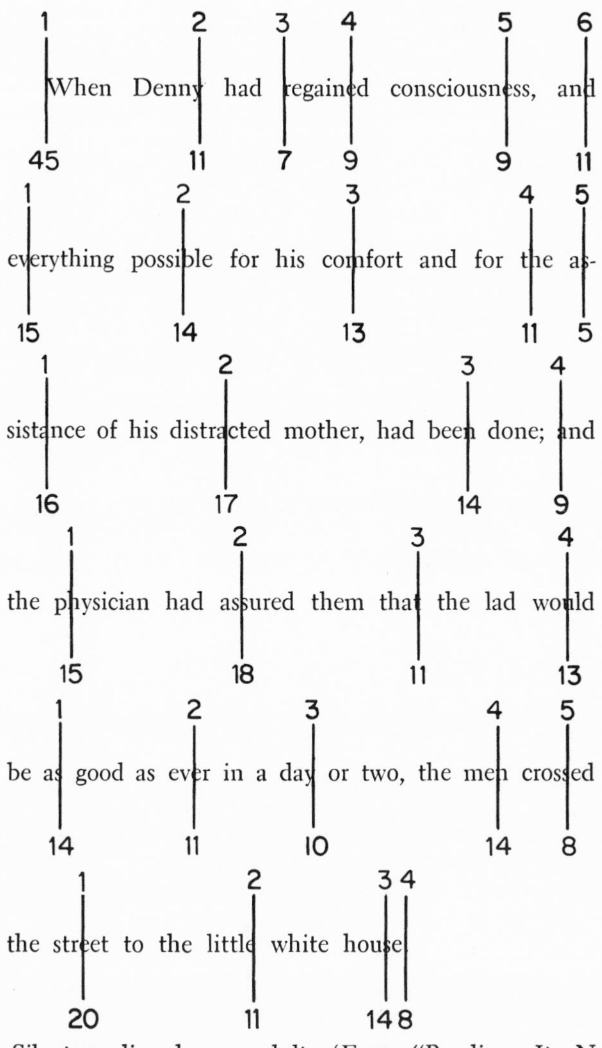

Figure 1. Silent reading by an adult. (From "Reading: Its Nature and Development," by C. H. Judd.)

In like manner the records of the eye movements of children, shown in Figs. 4–7, point to very definite conclusions. The important facts of the four records are summarized in Table I. The most significant data are to be found in the fifth, sixth, and seventh columns of the table. An examination of these data leads one to the conclusion that the former letter-by-letter conception of recognition is very erroneous. The development of the span of recognition, which is indicated in the increase in the average number of letters and words recognized per reading pause,

TABLE I. The Development of the Recognition Span—the Average Number of Words and Letters Recognized per Pause—from Grades III to VII

Figure	*Grade of Reader*	*Number of Letters in Line*	*Number of Words in Line*	*Number of Pauses per Line*	*Number of Letters per Pause*	*Number of Words per Pause*
4	3rd	35	10	7	5	1.4
5	4th	35	8	6	5.8	1.3
6	6th	39	9	5	7.8	1.8
7	7th	40	9	4	10	2.2

is brought to our attention in a very striking way. We are led to the additional conclusion that as the child reader approaches maturity he be-becomes capable of recognizing in larger and larger units.

Records of short exposure of words. The process of recognition may be studied by the so-called short-exposure method. The method, in brief, is as follows: The subject is caused to fixate a given point in a rectangular blank space. Within this blank space, by means of a specially designed apparatus, letters, words, phrases, etc. are momentarily exposed. The subject endeavors to recognize as much as he can at each exposure. Part of the findings of two experimenters, Erdmann and Dodge, is summarized by Huey in the following paragraph:

> Erdmann and Dodge argue strongly for the theory of perception in word-wholes, on the basis of numerous and varied experiments. . . . They base their argument mainly upon the following facts: First, words are recognized when lying too far from the fixation point to permit recognition of their component letters. Second, words are recognized when formed of letters so small that the letters could not be singly identified. Third, in about half the cases tried, words were recognized at distances at which the letters, when singly exposed, could not be recognized. Fourth, in the latter experiment the words were more readily recognized when they were long, or of optically characteristic form. Fifth, when twenty-six selected words were learned thoroughly in a fixed order, as the alphabet is known, and then exposed beyond the distances at which the letters could be recognized, the words could be distinguished and recognized in almost every instance. Sixth, words of four letters are named somewhat more quickly than single letters, and words of eight, twelve, and sixteen letters need comparatively little more time, the longest words needing only about one fifth more time than the shortest.[1]

Erdmann and Dodge point out that it is not the constituent parts of any given form that make it recognizable, but it is the familiar total arrangement.

[1] From Huey's "Psychology and Pedagogy of Reading," pp. 73–74. Used by permission of The Macmillan Company, publisher.

The facts which are now before us are quite conclusive that recognition in reading proceeds in word-wholes and phrase-wholes. They appear so conclusive even as to contradict one of the important facts of vision, which was discussed in the preceding chapter, that the limit of *distinct* vision is so small as to include no more than three or four letters. The careful reader of the preceding chapter no doubt has already encountered in his own mind the problem of bringing this fact of vision into agreement with the facts of recognition which have been discussed. The apparent disagreement between these two seemingly contradictory sets of facts introduces us now to one of the most important discussions of the present chapter; namely, that the mind supplies what the eye fails to behold.

II. Characteristics

The eye notes the general outline; the mind supplies the details. As the eye in reading moves from fixation pause to fixation pause, the successive impressions which leave their records on the retina to be reported by the optic nerve to the visual centers of the brain are very defective as photographs. About three letters in the center of each retinal image stand out with any degree of clearness; the rest on either side of the center are less and less distinct as the distance to the limits of the recognition span becomes greater. If we put together the facts of eye movement, as revealed in the records of duration and number per line of the reading pauses, with the facts of vision, we shall become aware that only very indistinct retinal pictures of the words in a line are needed by the mature reader in order to set going the process of recognition. The eye is able to behold only the *outstanding characteristics*, the *striking forms*, the *dominant features*, of letters, words, and phrases. We shall see that these are all that the mind requires of the eye; indeed, all the raw material of sensation that the mind *needs* in order to perform its proper function as an agent of recognition. Whatever of detail is necessary in order to complete the very inadequate retinal photographs the mind is able to supply, and does.

Examples. It we glance at a familiar landscape, we are able to recognize it immediately. The one glance seems sufficient to produce a mental picture of the landscape in all its detail—the general contour of the land, the position of every tree and shrub, paths and roadways, rocks and grassy knolls. A closer examination of the landscape will reveal a number of details which we were quite sure we had seen at first glance. Yet if we are questioned regarding the landscape immediately after the first glance, we can be absolutely sure of having seen only a few of its details. Regarding many of the more familiar details, we are not able to tell exactly whether we have just seen them or are having them pictured for us in our "mind's eye." Indeed, a second glance will often reveal a number of details which we were quite sure we had seen at the first glance, greatly altered and some entirely disappeared.

Again, the mind does not require any great amount of sensory experience in order to enable us to recognize a friend. A mere glimpse of him in passing, the sound of his footsteps, an insignificant mannerism—any of these is sufficient sensory material to enable us to recognize him and to be just as sure of our judgment as we should be had we met him face to face and had we scrutinized his appearance in greatest detail. Some one thing about his general appearance, some especial peculiarity or mannerism, is sufficient to set going the process of recognition. In like manner we may see a building in the distance and recognize it as being a house because of one distinguishing feature—smoke rising from a particular corner, for example. This is sufficient sensory material to result in recognition. It is not necessary for us to be able to see a single window or door.

The reading of the blind as an illustration. The reading of the blind is a frequently quoted illustration of the general character of recognition. In the Braille system of printing the letters of the alphabet are represented by tangible points and dots raised above the page. A practiced reader of these raised-letter pages goes ahead with the fingers of his right hand to examine the total form, or general outline, of the word. The fingers of the left hand follow, moving successively over the letters in order to sense the details of each word. However, only a part of the letters are examined, while the fingers move over the others without touching the points. Thus only a part of the letters are read; the rest are conjectured. Thus the blind need to sense only a part of the details of a word in order to recognize it.

A *mistake in reading as an illustration.* Professor Parker reports the following incident from his own personal experience to illustrate the influence of a person's frame of mind in determining his response to a situation:

I was riding in a train and happened to look over the shoulder of the man in front of me at the newspaper he was reading. I could just see the top of the paper and read there the following large headline, extending clear across the page:

GOOD HATS A QUARTER

Inasmuch as I always take advantage of end-of-the-season reduction sales of men's furnishings, this statement interested me (although good hats for a quarter seemed impossible) and I decided to look into the matter further when I got a chance. Soon the man left his seat to go into the smoking car.

I picked up the paper and, turning to the desired page, found that instead of reading

GOOD HATS A QUARTER

the headline read

GOD HATES A QUITTER

It was Monday morning and the paper in question contained reports of Sunday sermons printed with large-type headlines running clear across the page. If I had been in the religious frame of mind, instead of the bargain-hunting frame of mind, I might have read the headline correctly at the first glance.

9. The Inner Speech of Reading and the Mental and Physical Characteristics of Speech

EDMUND B. HUEY (1908)

The fact of inner speech forming a part of silent reading has not been disputed, so far as I am aware, by any one who has experimentally investigated the process of reading. Its presence has been established, for most readers, when adequate tests have been made. Its characteristics and functions have been variously described by many writers on general psychology and philosophy and on the psychology of language.

Purely visual reading is quite possible, theoretically; and Secor, in a study made at Cornell University, found that some readers could read visually while whistling or doing other motor tasks that would hinder inner speech. We might perhaps all have learned a sort of visual reading, and might yet require ourselves to read so in a measure. But although there is an occasional reader in whom the inner speech is not very noticeable, and although it is a foreshortened and incomplete speech in most of us, yet it is perfectly certain that the inner hearing or pronouncing, or both, of what is read, is a constituent part of the reading

SOURCE: Edmund B. Huey, *Psychology and Pedagogy of Reading* (New York: The Macmillan Company, 1908), pp. 117–123.

of by far the most of people, as they ordinarily and actually read. The evidence is cumulative from many sources, and cannot all be given here, but there is no doubt as to the fact. We shall here consider some of the experiments which throw light upon the presence and character of this inner speech.

In the writer's own experiments in which single unrelated words were exposed for four seconds each, the reader to state just what was suggested as he saw each, the words were usually "mentally pronounced" immediately after or accompanying the recognition of their visual form. When other words or phrases were suggested, as often occurred, these were almost always mentally pronounced. The conjunctive and relational words, definitive adjectives, etc., aroused few associations other than verbal ones, the latter usually being phrases of which the words customarily form a part. The inner pronunciation of these words and of the suggested phrases constituted much the most prominent part of the reader's consciousness of them. When sense matter was exposed similarly, giving the reader four seconds for each consecutive word or phrase, the words and phrases were almost always mentally pronounced, and usually with a strong feeling that they belonged with a preceding pronunciation or were to be followed by another, or both.

In another series of experiments, the readers read equivalent pages from an interesting novel, by various methods assigned them. Sometimes the instructions were to read "the way you like to read"; sometimes they were to "say it all to themselves"; again they "read aloud"; then they thought of "how it would sound" as they read; and sometimes they were directed to use lip-movement. Sometimes the readings were at the ordinary and most comfortable speed, and again they would be as fast as possible. The time required for the reading of each page was carefully taken and will be referred to in discussing the rate of reading. In many cases these experiments brought the readers to an awareness of their inner speech in reading when this had gone unnoticed before. When asked to say the words over to themselves, they found that really this was what they had been doing all along in their ordinary reading, and was the one thing that they could not escape doing when they tried. In such cases, the time required for reading a page in the assigned way would be nearly the same as when the page was read "the way you like to read." In the same way the reader's habit of hearing the sound of what he read, or of using lip-movement, etc., was often revealed. Of nearly thirty adults who were thus tested, the large majority found inner speech in some form to be a part of their ordinary reading. Purely visual reading was not established for any of the readers, although the test did not show that it was not present for a few. Motorizing with lips closed at the "comfortable" speed gave nearly the same average rate as when the reading was by the reader's "own method," 5.29 words per second for the former and 5.35 for the latter, for twenty readers tested. Of twenty post-graduate students who were tested, but two or three used lip-movement when reading "as they liked." Many of the others who "motorized" said that the pronunciation was "up in the head," and it usually seemed to be without any very noticeable movements of the articulatory apparatus.

For the readers tested in these experiments it seemed that the inner speech was a combination of auditory and motor elements, with one or the other predominating according to the reader's habitual mode of imaging. Sometimes when the inner speech was very prominent it was difficult for the reader to say whether it was auditory or motor, although it seemed to him to be of but one kind. The fact is that what we say is always heard as well, and there comes to be an indissoluble union of the auditory and motor elements. Our hearing, too, has an active aspect which may go so far as to include an inner saying, or imitation, of what is heard. And so the auditory and motor types of readers are really apt to be audito-motor types, with one or the other aspect leading in many cases.

That the speech of silent reading is simpler than in reading aloud is indicated by the fact that it was faster for each of the readers tested, both when the reading was at normal speed and when it was as fast as possible. Reading aloud was 66 percent slower than reading silently, at the normal rate, and 56 percent slower at the maximal rate, on an average for twenty readers. In reading aloud, as in talking, generally, the words are practically all pronounced as the breath is expired, and there are pauses at the inspirations. The inner speech of reading, on the other hand, goes on during inspiration as well, and thus time is saved. Then, as Professor Dodge shows in his "Die Motorische Wortvorstellungen," the inner articulations do not call into play the chest and larynx muscles that are used in speaking aloud, and there is a shortening of the pronunciation, a slurring of the words, and indeed the omission of many for some readers. Professor Dodge states that in his own ordinary silent reading almost every word is pronounced, but that in his fastest silent reading only the beginnings of words are pronounced. In his fastest reading of very familiar matter only certain words were pronounced. His speed of reading seems to be determined by the speed with which his motor word-ideas can follow one another. He finds, as I have found, that auditory elements are present in the reading of those who motorize, and that those who auditize are apt to have more or less of the motor present.

Zeitler and Messmer did not investigate the inner speech of reading, but Messmer asserts that "in visual reading the auditory and motor centres work along," and that purely visual reading is normally not to be found.

Quantz found lip-movement, and consequently inner speech, to be universal in the early reading of children. The lip-movement decreases with practice and usually, although not always, disappears in the rapid and more intelligent readers. He found that "lip-movement in silent reading is not an acquired habit, but a reflex action, the physical tendency to which is inherited." "It is a specific manifestation of the general psycho-physical law of dynamogenesis by which every mental state tends to express itself in muscular movement." Reading without lip-movement is "an acquired habit," the natural thing being to use the lips, as almost all of us do in practice when we come to a difficult place requiring close attention.

My own observations indicate that the disappearance of the lip-movement is no indication of the absence of inner speech in reading. In my own case, the lips are seldom moved, but I can never escape the inner pronunciation that forms a part of all my reading.

It would be easy to quote authority almost endlessly for the presence of inner speech in reading and, indeed, in most thinking. The simple fact is that the inner saying or hearing of what is read seems to be the core of ordinary reading, the "thing in itself," so far as there is such a part of such a complex process. It is so in all use of language. The spoken language is the language *par excellence*, as Professor Whitney says in his "Life and Growth of Language," "gesture and writing being its subordinates and auxiliaries." The child comes to his first reader with his habits of spoken language fairly well formed, and these habits grow more deeply set with every year. His meanings inhere in this spoken language and belong but secondarily to the printed symbols; and always, for most readers, we can say with M. Egger that "to read is, in effect, to translate writing into speech." And while this inner speech is but an abbreviated and reduced form of the speech of everyday life, a shadow copy as it were, it nevertheless retains the essential characteristics of the original. . . .

10. An Experimental Study of Eye–Voice Span

GUY T. BUSWELL (1920)

Summary of Analysis of Eye-Voice Span

The relations of the eye-voice span to other factors of reading as described in this chapter may be summarized as follows:

1. There is a positive correlation between a wide eye-voice span and mature reading. The average span for good readers is greater than that of poor readers in every school grade.

2. The development of the eye-voice span through the school period does not show a consistent increase from grade to grade, but is very irregular. The average span for the high school is greater than that of the elementary school. The average span of the adult subjects is greater than that of those from high school. But some good readers from the elementary school have a span greater than most of the high school subjects.

3. The width of the eye-voice span shows little correlation with position in the line, except that the span at the end of a line is slightly narrower. A high correlation is shown between eye-voice span and position in the sentence. The average width of the span at the beginning of a sentence is greater than at the end of the sentence by 46 percent, while the average within the sentence is greater than that at the end by 23 percent. These percentages are for all fifty-four subjects, including both good and poor readers.

4. A comparison of reading rate with eye-voice span shows that rate of reading and width of eye-voice span increase together. There is a high positive correlation between these two factors of reading.

5. A negative correlation exists between the eye-voice span and the number of fixations per line. As the span increases in width the number of fixations per line decreases.

6. Little correlation is evident between eye-voice span and the number of regressive movements per line. However if the regressive move-

---

SOURCE: Guy Buswell, "An Appraisal of the Non-Oral Method of Teaching Reading," Supplementary Educational Monograph No. 61, 1945, pp. 51–57. Reprinted by permission of the University of Chicago Press.

ments are analyzed into their various types, a positive correlation is shown between eye-voice span and that type of regressive movements caused by too long a forward sweep of the eye. As the width of the eye-voice span increases, the percentage of regressive movements caused by this habit of attempting a long forward movement increases. This type of regressive movement must be considered as a characteristic of mature reading.

This study shows that a wide eye-voice span occurs in common with good quality of reading, rapid rate of reading, a small number of fixations per line, and a certain type of regressive movement. All of these qualities may be described as characteristic of a mature reader. It is also evident from the data shown that a narrow eye-voice span occurs with a poor quality of reading, a slow rate, a large number of fixations per line, and a larger percentage of a type of regressive movement which is not characteristic of good reading. These qualities may be considered as characteristic of persons whose reading habits are immature.

The results of the preceding analysis make it very clear that the development of a wide eye-voice span is a significant element in oral reading. As will be shown later, in silent reading a similar meaning-recognition span exists which appears to be closely related, in its development, to the eye-voice span. Since the width of eye-voice span is a factor of mature reading it should receive very definite attention in methods of teaching reading. However, it is difficult to find any allusion to the subject in any of the method texts or manuals. No evidence can be found that elementary teachers in the public schools give any attention to the problem in their teaching, probably because no specific methods are available for dealing with it. Expert teachers of primary reading have worked out a few devices, based upon rapid scanning of phrases and the use of familiar material, which they use in their own classes, but they say that there is nothing available in the literature of reading methods which deals specifically with training for a wider eye-voice span. It is not the function of this investigation to devise methods of teaching, but it is in place to state that here is a significant factor of reading which is in need of specific training methods. The problem is to devise methods which will develop a habit of pushing the eye farther ahead of the voice in order that there may be interpretation of meaning in larger units.

11. How Children and Adults Perceive Words in Reading

MILES A. TINKER (1965)

In beginning reading, children perceive words differently than adult, mature readers. The aim in this discussion is to describe how children, as they begin to learn to read, perceive words and how they progress to the more effective perception employed by mature readers on the adult level. Since word perception by good readers at the adult level is one of the hallmarks of effective reading, this will be considered first. Then the discussion will describe the immature methods ordinarily employed by beginning readers and how the transition to more effective techniques takes place. The implications for reading instruction in the primary grades will then be noted.

In general, perception includes stimulation, preparation for a response, and the response. The graphic symbol is the stimulus in reading and the perception, which involves the meanings and interpretations, is derived from the reader's past experiences. This perceptual response relates meaning to the printed or written symbol. Vernon (20) states that perception and reading of words need to be dealt with apart from perception of other visual objects since they involve processes that are not essential to the latter.

Word identification, recognition and perception need definition. The original inspection of a new word entails identification of its printed or written symbol in terms of its visual appearance and its sound. As the visual form is matched with its sound, the correct pronunciation is achieved either aloud or mentally as inner speech. And the meaning present with identification may be slight or great, depending upon associated experiences and the degree of help available from the verbal context in which the word occurs. If the new word is in the reader's usage vocabulary, even though he has not met it in print before, it will tend to carry considerable meaning. Otherwise the meaning is apt to be

---

SOURCE: IRA Invitational Address, 1965. Reprinted with the permission of Miles A. Tinker and the International Reading Association.

slight. But increased meaning does come with repeatedly meeting the word in various contexts.

Word recognition and identification are interrelated. Tinker and McCullough (18) state that to recognize a word means to identify it as a word previously known. Instant or relatively rapid recognition occurs only for words that are well known through frequent encounters in previous reading. Words that have been met but which are less familiar are recognized less promptly, ordinarily only after a slight delay. Such words require a somewhat more thorough visual inspection and some aid from word recognition clues.

Perception occurs both in identification and in recognition of words. The more meaning present, the more adequate the perception. Because all words are primarily speech units, the word read derives directly from the word as spoken. Some traces of auditory and vocal processes always occur during reading. And word perception involves something beyond apprehension of its visual and auditory form. Awareness of the meaning of word symbol requires some appreciation of the idea or experience it signifies. The perception of words, therefore, depends upon the meanings present in their identification and recognition. Since meanings come from experience, perception is basically associated with experience. It may be emphasized that the person who brings the most extensive experience and verbal facility to his reading gets the most from the printed page.

For the mature, adult reader, word recognition and assimilation are rapid. Furthermore, the imagery, associations, interpretation, and evaluation involved tend to be rich and varied. Thus the adult reader seems to pass directly from visual perception to these meanings and thought processes.

How Adults Perceive Words

Let us now turn to a consideration of word perception by adults who have learned to read well. Keep in mind that facile word perception is essential for effective reading. Without this, the thinking side of reading would be impossible.

Ordinarily, in the investigations designed to discover how words are perceived, a short exposure device called a tachistoscope has been used. The apparatus can be adjusted to give the reader a single glimpse of a word, phrase, or sentence. What occurs in normal reading is similar. In reading, the eyes make several stops, or fixation pauses, along a line of print with very rapid saccadic moves between pauses. The printed material is perceived only during the fixation pauses. These pauses are, on the average, about one-fourth of a second in duration.

Although the area of clearest vision for the eyes covers only about four letter spaces, Ruediger (17) found that letters in eleven point type could be perceived fairly accurately at one inch (12 to 15 letter spaces) from the fixation point. There were no distinct boundaries to this area, as the clearness of form definition fades off gradually. The images of words need not be at maximum clearness in all details to be perceived accurately. In fact, the unclear images of words to the right of the fixation point have important cue values. Hamilton (10), in studying the reading of continuous prose by means of successive short exposures, discovered at each fixation pause a relatively small area of distinct vision along with marginal impressions of words and letters located mainly to the right of the clearly defined fixated area. These marginal impressions, which vary greatly in clearness, provide preparatory partial perception of successive words. Furthermore, they orient the reader for the perception of successive words in the phrase or sentence as well as provide indispensable stimuli for successive fixation pauses of the eyes. In addition, these vague word forms and letter groups seen in peripheral vision furnish premonitions of coming meanings that are then cleared up sufficiently in succeeding fixations to give correct word perception. Thus, in continuous reading, all words need not be seen in foveal vision and with maximum clearness to be perceived.

The perceptual span in reading is the number of items, such as letters, numerals, or words, that can be perceived and reproduced after the reader has had a single brief view of the material. Usually the glimpse of the material is provided by an exposure of 100 milli-seconds or less. Numerous investigations show that the perceptual span for adults is about 3 to 4 letters in unrelated (not word) arrangement. If the letters are grouped in nonsense syllables (pronounceable units that do not make words as "zap," "tuk," or "gokem") the span is about 7 letters. And when unrelated words are exposed briefly, the number of letters is further increased, although the number of words grasped is comparable to the number of letters in an unrelated arrangement, i.e., 3 to 4 words or up to about 19 letters. But when the words exposed are in a sentence, the span is increased by a word or two. These are typical findings. In general, the literature indicates that there is a natural tendency for a mature reader to combine the various elements of a visual impression into larger perceptual units whenever subjective grouping is possible. This occurs in perceiving letters arranged in the form of nonsense syllables or words, and in the perception of words in phrases or sentences.

Thus, in perceiving printed symbols presented briefly as in a short exposure or a fixation pause, adults tend to organize the materials subjectively in accordance with the meaning. Therefore, when the meaning becomes clearer, this organization achieves a greater perceptual span, that is, more letters are grasped in words than in less meaningful material.

What then are the roles played by individual letters, small letter groups, and word forms in perception as adults read? Does the person with considerable skill in reading read by letters or by word units? No simple or unequivocal answer is possible. Later discussion will reveal that both individual letters and total word forms provide cues to perception in reading.

Since an adult may at times read in a sentence words containing 20 to 30 letters, with an average of 8 to 10 in one fixation pause, but can grasp only 3 to 4 unrelated letters per fixation, the indication is that perception in reading must occur by some means other than recognition of letter after letter as once supposed (13). This deeply rooted assumption of earlier days was based largely on the notion that the eyes moved continuously along a line of print as successive letters were recognized. Now that research has demonstrated how the eyes move in reading and that perception occurs only during the fixation pauses, the notion of reading letter by letter has been discarded. It is now clear that, during each fixation, several letters grouped in words stimulate the eyes as a single act of vision, not as one letter after another.

Data published by Cattell (4) in 1885 led to the conclusion that mature readers perceive printed material as units—whole words, sometimes even a phrase or short sentence. Single words were grasped as readily as single letters. He states that educated adults perceive a word as a whole.

Erdmann and Dodge (6) reported results that support the view that perception in reading is by word wholes by means of the characteristic general shape of the word—the word form. And Huey (13) stated that "The arrangement, the total form, is the main thing, whether in the recognition of letters, numbers, words, or objects of whatever sort."

There is not complete unanimity, however, on how words are perceived. Goldscheider and Müller (8) emphasize that certain letters and letter complexes (determining letters) are more influential than others (indifferent letters) in determining the recognition of words, particularly the more familiar words. The determining letters are considered important because they give characteristic form to the word. The authors also pointed out that the familiarity or difficulty of a word determines whether it is read letter by letter, by groups of letters, by syllables, or by word wholes. According to them, the characteristic shape of a word, the word form, is conditioned mainly by the determining letters present. And Messmer (15) adds that total word form is determined principally by the length of the word and by its vertical profile. This is not in conflict with Goldscheider and Müller. Erdmann and Dodge (6), who employed exposures of 100 milli-seconds, criticized the other authors for using very short exposure times, too short for a clearing up of the visual sensation created by the stimulation. With the shorter exposures, prominent features of words would stand out and be remembered to the exclusion of other features of a word.

In their analysis, Woodworth and Schlosberg (21) point out that Erdmann and Dodge's "general word shape" probably meant the external configuration of the printed word, while Cattell's "total word picture" covers also the internal pattern of curves and vertical strokes. For instance, the external outlines of the words "consonants" and "communifs" look alike but the internal patterns are different enough to prevent their being easily confused (p. 101). Also, in Pillsbury's experiment (16) on perception of mutilated words, the readers frequently noted the wrong letter inserted, or the missing letter, although they perceived the word correctly. That is, the reader often sees details which he disregards in reading a word (for example, "fashxon" read "fashion"). "Now if such details are visible when he cannot use them, correct details must also be visible in an unmutilated word and help to make up the complete word picture. Therefore, the visual impression received during a brief exposure must be much more complete and detailed than is implied by the phrase 'general word shape.'" (p. 102)

In tachistoscope experiments, although the subject can report only a few of the letters, he believes he has seen all of them clearly. Thus, while getting a glimpse of a word either during a fixation pause or a very short exposure, the word is not spelled out letter by letter even though all the letters may be seen. Hence, without verbalizing the successive letters, the reader has all the cues he could desire for accurate perception of the word. Apparently this is what Woodworth and Schlosberg mean when they approve the "total word picture" as used for perception in reading. The bare outline of a word, the *total word shape*, may cease to function in the normal reading situation. But the total word picture, the *total word structure*, which includes the details of the internal pattern, may still function as a cue. Although this may appear to be a minor distinction, it has important implications as we shall see.

In examining the errors made in normal reading, Vernon (19) found a tendency to omit letters, especially in long words. Inasmuch as ascending letters were rarely omitted in comparison with descending letters, readers apparently attend to the upper contour or shape of the word more than to the lower. This is in agreement with the finding of Huey (12) that printed material in which the lower half of the words had been eliminated was read much more easily than material in which the upper halves of the words had been deleted. This contrast is illustrated in Fig. 1. Nevertheless, Huey (13) notes that, during the fixation pauses in normal reading, many if not all parts of a word can affect consciousness somewhat and provide clues which help in perception. Thus, while dominating letters may play a prominent role in word perception, the others have an important part, too. This is in harmony with the view of Woodworth and Schlosberg cited above.

According to Vernon (19), the part of a word that is most important for perception depends upon the particular word. It may be the first part, the middle, or the last part. Ordinarily, the root is the most important part of a word and must be apprehended to recognize the word. In many words of Anglo-Saxon or Old English derivation, the root is the first syllable, or the word may have only one syllable. But words of

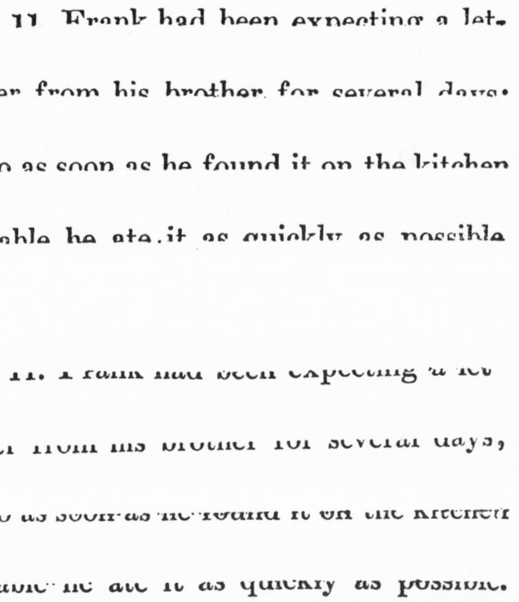

Figure 1. The upper half of a printed line provides more clues to word perception than the lower half. Adapted from D. G. Paterson and M. A. Tinker, *How to Make Type Readable*. New York: Harper and Row, 1940, by permission of the authors.

Latin derivation frequently have the root in the middle with a prefix before and a suffix after it. For example:

Anglo-Saxon: whaling, home
Latin: unsuccessful, subservient

Although the root must be apprehended, other syllables are also important, i.e., in normal reading, perception is achieved by simultaneous view of the entire word.

What then is the relative importance of the total word form, individual letters, determining letters, vowels, and syllables in word perception? In the normal reading situation it is doubtful if many words are perceived correctly when the cue is merely the word shape as determined by the bare outline of the word. Apparently the process of perception begins with the visual appearance of the total word shape and then is completed when enough details, such as initial consonant or consonant blend, a vowel or a syllable, or the final letter are apprehended to achieve recognition of a word that fits the meaning of the verbal context in which it appears.

This process of perception in reading, in which the word form has an important cue value, operates only for sight words, i.e., words which have become thoroughly familiar to the reader through meeting them frequently in his reading. From beginning reading on through life, if he continues to read, a person keeps adding to his bank of sight words. These words are perceived at a glance. The skillful adult reader has accumulated a large store of sight words. Without this word bank, reading would remain a slow, laborious process of analyzing practically every word in a sentence. The more familiar words possess greater cue value in their word form.

To perceive unfamiliar words is a different matter, for they require analysis. And the amount of analysis depends upon the degree of familiarity. Any degree of familiarity less than that which produces a sight word requires some analysis for perception. Then the total word structure, which includes details of the internal pattern of which the reader obtains an adequate simultaneous view of all its parts, operates in word perception. However in the case of new words that are completely unfamiliar because they have not been seen before, an exception occurs. Analysis of such words requires rather complete visual scrutiny of their elements in order to sound out the word mentally or subvocally. After identifying the pronunciation, the reader uses the verbal context in which the word appears plus association with any experience he has had with the sound of the word to achieve meaning and perception. At times the use of a dictionary is needed to discover its meaning. Thus, although word form or shape may be sufficient to yield recognition of familiar words, it fails as an adequate cue when words are unfamiliar.

The meaning of the verbal context in which a new word occurs provides an important aid to accurate perception of the word. To pronounce a word accurately without understanding its meaning does not result in perception. But the context of a sentence or paragraph frequently makes it possible to infer the meaning of a new word. The proficient reader makes fairly constant use of clues in verbal context, not only to recognize a relatively unfamiliar word but also to infer its exact meaning and thus enhance perception of it.

From the above, we appreciate how skillful adult readers perceive words. We now turn to a discussion of how beginners in reading perceive words and how they progress to the adult level.

Children's Approach to Word Perception

According to Vernon (19), in any perceptual situation, the young child tends to respond in terms of those aspects which appeal to his interest and can be comprehended. He seldom notes minute details of form and structure. With a complex stimulus, the child will report objects and activities familiar to him and may invent others which he associates with those actually seen. And if the stimulus object contains relatively little of interest to him, as for example a single word or collection of letters, the child's eyes will rove around looking for something attractive. If nothing is found, he may invent something. Types of perception in young children are apparently subjective in nature, i.e., the objective stimulus is secondary to the role of familiarity and interest. It is not surprising, therefore, that as they start to learn to read children do not adopt proficient techniques for perceiving words.

Children may have difficulty in learning to read until they are able and willing to perceive the small dissimilarities of form that differentiate letters and words from each other. For the average child this apparently occurs soon after he begins to learn to read. But in the kindergarten and early first grade many children adopt ineffective techniques of perceiving words. This seems to result in part from the method of instruction employed. According to Anderson and Dearborn (1), investigators tend to agree that the start in reading is best made with the "word" or "look-and-say" method. Initially a word is learned by viewing it, perhaps with a picture, while it is pronounced. It is assumed that the visual total word structure is associated with the spoken word and the heard sound. Then, when a few words are learned, they can be used in a simple story.

It would seem that the word method also receives strong support from Hildreth (11) who states that there is abundant evidence that young children recognize (i.e., perceive) words as wholes. Her argument is largely concerned with teaching the beginner words by the look-and-say method rather than by teaching the separate letters or sounds first. But if the look-and-say method continues to be used beyond the initial stage, and especially if it is used without supplementation by other techniques for teaching word perception, problems are apt to rise.

The word method was introduced to get away from the tedious and irksome practice, common in the early nineteenth century, of long continued drill on letter names and sounds before allowing children to attempt reading words and sentences. And when the researches of Cattell (4) and Erdmann and Dodge (6) revealed that adults tend to read words as units rather than letter by letter, the word method received further impetus, for it was assumed, apparently wrongly, that children perceive words the same way adults do. For a time, teachers discarded all forms of word analysis. But it was soon evident that the look-and-say or word method by itself was ineffective. Furthermore, most writers now agree that only a few young children perceive and recognize words by total word structure. As stated by Durrell (5), a part of a word often stands out and serves the child as a clue for recall of the whole. This often leads to errors.

Although the alphabet method of learning to read by compounding letters was rightly discarded, the word method, while useful in initial learning, has limitations. If the teaching of reading to children is to be as effective as possible, there must be a more widespread understanding of how children start out in reading and how they can progress most readily to the adult stage.

Cues to Word Perception by Young Children

The word method frequently employed as pupils begin to learn to read assumes that a child will learn each word as a unit by perceiving the word form as a total unified structure. Apparently, however, few children achieve this ability during early reading instruction. For instance, Bowden (3) discovered that pupils in learning to read individual words pay little attention to the total word form or general shape. The characteristic aspects of total word form, derived from distribution of ascending and descending letters as well as an alteration of straight and curved letters, do not help children to perceive words correctly as they do adults. The reading of these children was a rather imperfect kind of word perception in which recognition depended upon noting the presence or absence of certain familiar letters. And Gates and Boeker

(7) also stress the role of individual letters rather than total word form in perception of words by children. Additional evidence presented by Meek (14) led to the conclusion that certain letters or small groups of letters were the chief cues for word perception by beginners. Young children, it seems, recognize words by remembering some small thing or detail that characterizes the word for them. The detail varies from child to child. For instance (7), the word *monkey* was remembered by the *hole* (of o), or the funny chair (of *k*), or the tail middle or the *monkey's tail* (*y*) at the end. And *pig* was recognized by the dot over the *i* and *box* by the *funny cross* at the end. One child remembered *look* because it had two eyes it used to look at you. An extreme case is given by Durrell (5). After a child had successfully read the word *children* on a flash card he could not read it in a book, maintaining that he had never seen it before. He was then shown the flash card again and asked how he knew the word was *children*. The reply was, "By the smudge over the corner."

As put by Anderson and Dearborn (1), young readers do not seem to have much of an eye for word shape or structure. Only an occasional bright and able reader among young pupils appears to make much use of word form. Most children, at least during the early stages of learning to read, search out some small detail of the word, usually a single letter or two, a prefix or suffix, or some other letter group, which then comes to stand for the whole word. That is, some small detail that stands out is selected as the cue for perceiving the word. Furthermore, the letter or letters used for word recognition are not necessarly perceived as such. They are only a specific detail that stands for the word. The obvious result is inaccurate word perception, due to lack of attention to the constituent parts of the word.

Obviously young children just learning to read have not yet developed an habitual tendency to attend to the total structure of words. And it would seem that the very method ordinarily employed to teach the initial sight vocabulary, the word method, permits or even fosters a number of problems, including inaccurate word perception. As a single technique, the word method imposes a strict limitation on the size of the reading vocabulary, avoids word analysis, and encourages word by word reading. Apparently, too frequently the word method continues to receive undue emphasis beyond the time at which an initial sight vocabulary is acquired.

It is probable that most first grade teachers fail to realize that their pupils seize upon some minor detail of a word for perception rather than attending to its total structure. The assumption that the child makes use of the whole word picture in attempting to learn the word is for the most part fallacious.

What is to be done to teach the child to move away from his inadequate method of perceiving words? It is necessary at an early date to de-emphasize the use of the word method as the sole technique of teaching word identification and word recognition. That is, there is need to employ teaching methods that make it possible for the child to discard as soon as he can his inadequate technique of perceiving words. This is possible provided the teacher understands the problem and knows how to teach by a combination of methods. When this is done, most children will move along more promptly in the developmental program to the place where they will perceive words as adults do.

Developing Word Perception

Most experienced teachers prefer to introduce their pupils to reading by use of sentences or very short paragraphs (2). This procedure, however, does not avoid for long the task of learning to perceive accurately the individual words the sentences contain. This is achieved by combining the word method with other techniques. The combined approach is intended to furnish the child with the available techniques and to teach him to be versatile in applying them (18). Basic to the combined or any other program of teaching word perception is emphasis on adequate visual and auditory discrimination. Word perception involves matching the visual symbol with the sound of the spoken word and the meaning represented by the printed symbol. Therefore, there must be correct discrimination of the sounds represented in a word and precise visual discrimination of both total word form and details of its structure.

It is probably true that most teachers have not realized that young children employ limited and rudimentary methods of word recognition to the extent described above. Therefore they may not have realized the urgent need for early introduction of instructional techniques to supplant faulty procedures. Any real progress in learning to read will be blocked until this change from the word method is instituted. This does not mean that the word method for getting reading underway should be abandoned. However, it does appear that methods designed to serve the pupil throughout his school years should be adopted as soon as possible. Actually there is no justification for permitting a child to continue identifying words by some minor detail such as the tail on the word *monkey* or the funny cross at the end of the word *box*.

Although some authors suggest that 50 to 100 words be learned by the word method before other techniques are introduced, it is difficult for most beginners to learn even 50 words this way. Fortunately some teachers are departing from a strictly look-and-say method early in the first grade. A beginning of instruction for use of the simpler phonetic techniques is possible after learning only a few words. As soon as these words have common characteristics, such as the initial consonant in *box, ball, boy,* and *bell,* the child should be encouraged to notice that these words begin with the same sound and the same letter. At the same time, the teacher points out the details of the word form such as the middle vowel and the ending letters. In general, consonants are taught first, then vowels. Progress is from the simple to the complex. A complete program of word perception techniques is given by Gray in *On Their Own in Reading,* revised edition (9).

As already noted, few children attend to word form in beginning reading. The use of word form clues without special training does not ordinarily occur until a child has made considerable progress in learning to read. Eventually, as a word becomes more familiar by frequent encounters, the visual clues from total word structure become more potent. This happens more readily when a word has a distinctive shape or form. The presence of definite word form is shown in the left column and its absence in the right column below:

mother	come
father	common
stopped	some
school	noise
children	across
largely	seven

Casual inspection of several pages in a dictionary or a textbook reveals that a large majority of words have characteristic word forms due to the alternation of long and short letters.

It might be well for the primary teacher to direct the pupils' attention to word form clues. At the same time she will need to point out that some words have like shapes and may be confused, as *horse* and *house.* Visual examination of the details of such words are necessary. It seems desirable, in the developmental program, to place some stress upon teaching pupils to attend to the characteristic shape of words, and to develop the habit of combining word form and context clues with phonetic clues. This will emphasize the need for close visual examination of a word for accurate perception. As soon as a child has caught on to this procedure, little or no further training in use of word form clues for perception will be necessary.

As the program of learning to read develops, the child progresses toward the adult level of word perception. Clues from word form, verbal context, phonics, structural analysis, and syllabication are mastered as the learning continues through the grades. As the clues are taught, the child learns how to choose the most suitable clue or combination of clues to identify, recognize, or perceive words in any specific situation. For instance, suppose the child meets the word *telescope* in the sentence: "One clear night Jim looked through the *telescope* and saw mountains on the moon." He could use one of the following methods to perceive the new word: (a) letter-by-letter sounding and blend the sounds; (b) note the syllables *tel -e- scope* and blend the pronunciation of the syllables; or ((c) use the contextual meaning of the rest of the sentence, note the initial consonant, and infer the identity of the word. Ordinarily the last method, using a combination of clues with phonics (sound of the initial consonant, or more if necessary) will be effective and most rapid. Skilled use of syllabication is nearly as rapid. But the letter-by-letter sounding and blending is laborious, slow, and usually difficult to use.

The progression from the initial ineffectual method of word perception to the skillful level of the adult reader is a long but not impossible journey. The main objective of this discussion has been to alert teachers to the precise nature of the ineffective methods most children employ to perceive words as they begin to learn to read. With this realization, the teacher will be better able to guide the child at an early date into the use of procedures designed to bring about smooth progress toward adult word perception.

References

1. Anderson, I. H., and Dearborn, W. F., *The psychology of teaching reading*. New York: Ronald Press Company, 1952.
2. *Better reading instruction—A survey of research and successful practice.* Research Bulletin of the National Education Association, Washington: Research Division of the National Education Association, 1935, Vol. 13, No. 5, pp. 273–325.
3. Bowden, J. H., "Learning to read," *Elem. Sch. J.*, 1911, 12, pp. 21–33.
4. Cattell, J. M., "Ueber die Zeit der Erkennung und Benennung von Schriftzeichen, Bildern und Farben," *Phil. Stud.*, 1885, 2, pp. 634–650.
5. Durrell, D. D., *Improving reading instruction*. New York: Harcourt, Brace and World, 1956.
6. Erdmann, B., and Dodge, R., *Psychologische Untersuchungen ueber das Lesen auf experimenteller Grundlage*. Halle: Max Niemeyer, 1898.
7. Gates, A. I., and Boeker, E., "A study of initial stages in reading by preschool children," *Teachers College Record*, 1923, 24, pp. 469–488.
8. Goldscheider, A., and Müller, R. F., "Zur Physiologie und Pathologie des Lesen," *Zsch. f. Klin. Med.*, 1893, 23, pp. 131–167.
9. Gray, W. S., *On their own in reading*, rev. ed. Chicago: Scott, Foresman and Company, 1960.
10. Hamilton, F. M., *The perceptual factors in reading*. Archives of Psychology, 1907, 1. No. 9.

11. Hildreth, G., *Teaching reading.* New York: Holt, Rinehart and Winston, 1958.
12. Huey, E. B., "On the Psychology and Physiology of Reading," *Amer. J. Psychol.*, 1900, 11, pp. 283–302; 1901, 12, pp. 292–313.
13. Huey, E. B., *The psychology and pedagogy of reading.* New York: The Macmillan Company, 1908, p. 75.
14. Meek, L. H., A *study of learning and retention in young children.* Teachers College Contr. to Educ., No. 164. New York: Bureau of Publications, Teachers College, Columbia University, 1925.
15. Messer, O., "Zur Psychologie des Lesen bei Kindern und Erwachsennen," *Arch. f. d. ges. Psychol.*, 1903, 2, pp. 190–298.
16. Pillsbury, W. B., "A Study in Apperception," *Amer. J. Psychol.*, 1897, 8, 315–393.
17. Ruediger, W. C., *The field of distinct vision.* Archives of Psychology, 1907, 1, No. 5.
18. Tinker, M. A., and McCullough, C. M., *Teaching elementary reading,* 2nd ed. New York: Appleton-Century-Crofts, 1962.
19. Vernon, M. D., *The experimental study of reading.* Cambridge: Cambridge University Press, 1931.
20. Vernon, M. D., *Visual perception.* Cambridge: Cambridge University Press, 1937.
21. Woodworth, R. S., and Schlosberg, H., *Experimental psychology,* rev. ed. New York: Holt, Rinehart and Winston, 1954.

III. Learning to Read

Although authorities do not agree as to the minimum mental age for beginning reading, the figure six years and six months is most often cited. Because this figure is quoted so widely, one would assume that many students corroborate it. This is not the case. A pioneer study conducted by Morphett and Washburne (12) in 1931 is principally responsible. The reader will want to evaluate the article carefully and decide for himself whether the generalization was justified.

As might be expected, the work of Morphett and Washburne did not go unchallenged. In 1937, Gates (13) wrote about mental age and beginning reading. He contended that determination of an optimum mental age for beginning reading was difficult to arrive at because teachers vary in their ability to meet individual differences; they also differ widely in the methods, procedures, and materials they employ.

A child's reading readiness is dependent on much more than mental maturity. The complex nature of reading readiness and its importance have been recognized by reading specialists for many years. Three decades ago, Harrison (14) wrote penetratingly about the subject. The reader will find the introduction to her book *Reading Readiness* rewarding reading. Of interest, too, is an excerpt from a NEA research bulletin (15) which was published in 1935. It devoted considerable space to "the preparatory period of reading instruction." The reader should find it intensely interesting to compare these early writings with the more recent treatment of reading readiness by Durrell and Nicholson (16) in their article, "Preschool and Kindergarten Experience."

The widely known reading authority, the late William S. Gray, felt that efficient habits of word perception were basic to fluent and thoughtful reading. His short article (17), "Laying the Foundation for Word Perception," contains some wise advice as to how teachers can help promote growth in reading perception for the neophyte reader.

Nipping reading problems in the bud—a prophylactic approach to major reading disability—is the responsibility of the classroom teacher. Artley (18) reminds teachers of the importance of detecting and alleviating beginning reading problems which, if left untreated, develop into serious reading disabilities. How may the teacher detect a reading problem in its incipient stage?

12. When Should Children Begin to Read?

MABEL VOGEL MORPHETT and
CARLETON WASHBURNE (1931)

In tracing back to their origins the reading difficulties of some children and their distaste for the subject, the Department of Educational Counsel in Winnetka found that in several instances the children's mental ages on entering the first grade had been low and that discouragement had resulted from their first attempts to learn to read. This discouragement sometimes resulted in a mental set against reading, which lasted for years and which hampered all their school work. The research department, therefore, with the aid of the primary-grade teachers, set about the task of discovering the period in the mental development of children when, as a rule, there is the best chance of their learning to read readily.

In September 1928, all Winnetka first-grade children, 141 in number, were given the Detroit First-Grade Intelligence Test. The eight first-grade teachers were not told the mental ages of the children and attempted to teach all of them to read. The method, in accordance with the Winnetka technique, was largely individual, so that the slow chil-

SOURCE: *Elementary School Journal*, XXXI (1931), 496–503. Reprinted by permission of the University of Chicago Press.

dren did not retard the fast ones. In February 1929, the reading progress of these children was measured for the purpose of determining the amount of progress made by children at each mental level.

In order that the reading progress might be measured, the first large teaching unit was divided into definite steps, which were measurable by the teachers. Twenty-one steps took the children through the beginning reading materials.[1] Each further step represented the reading of a primer or first reader. Reading progress was measured by the number of these steps which the child had completed by February.

In addition to these progress steps the sight-word score of each child was measured. Each child in Winnetka is required to know at least 139 words at sight before passing from first-grade reading to second-grade reading. These words are those most frequently used in primers and first readers. The children were tested individually with flash cards, and the number of words recognized by each child was recorded as his sight-word score. In some cases the children knew some of the second-grade sight words as well as the 139 first-grade words. In such cases the score was the total number of first- and second-grade words recognized.

The first-grade teachers, all of whom had had several years of experience with the reading materials, agreed that children who seemed ready for reading from the beginning of the year had usually completed at least thirteen progress steps and knew at least thirty-seven sight words by February. Therefore, thirteen progress steps and thirty-seven sight words were accepted as the measure of the minimum degree of satisfactory progress.

The Detroit First-Grade Intelligence Test and the Stanford Revision of the Binet-Simon Scale were used to determine the mental ages of the children. The Detroit tests were given to all first-grade children entering in September. The Stanford-Binet test was given later in the year, and the mental ages were calculated as of September 1928. In this way comparison between the mental ages determined by the Detroit and Stanford-Binet tests was made possible.

Table 1 gives the correlations which were found between the sight-word scores and intelligence and between reading progress and intelligence. Since the data proved to be non-linear, the correlation ratios rather than the correlation coefficients are given. When the relation between reading progress and intelligence was calculated, it was necessary to use the rank method of figuring correlations since the intervals of progress were not necessarily of equal difficulty. The correlations show that there is a fairly high degree of relationship between mental age

[1] Livia Youngquist and Carleton Washburne, Winnetka Primary Reading Materials. Chicago: Rand McNally & Co., 1928.

TABLE 1. Correlations Between Achievement in Reading of 141 First-Grade Children and Their Intelligence as Measured by Detroit Test and Stanford-Binet Test

Factors Correlated	*Detroit Test*	*Stanford-Binet Test*
Sight-word score and mental age	.65	.58
Sight-word score and average of mental and chronological age as of September 1, 1928	.57	.49
Sight-word score and intelligence quotient	.56	.54
Reading progress and mental age	.59	.51
Reading progress and average of mental and chronological age as of September 1, 1928	.55	.49
Reading progress and intelligence quotient	.50	.53

and reading progress. The Detroit test shows more relation to progress than does the Stanford-Binet test. Of the three measures of intelligence—mental age, average of the mental and chronological ages, and intelligence quotient—mental age shows the greatest degree of relationship, although the differences are slight. In the calculations that follow, mental age alone is used as the method of figuring intelligence.

The scores were next divided into groups based on the children's mental ages in September. The percentage of children of each mental age making satisfactory progress (thirteen steps or more) and the percentage making satisfactory sight-word scores (thirty-seven or more) were determined. Tables 2 and 3 show the results.

Table 2 shows that a small percentage of children who began reading with a mental age of less than six years were able to achieve satisfactory reading progress but that for the group having a mental age between six years and six years and six months there was a sharp rise in the percentage making satisfactory progress. This fact is shown graphically in Figure 1. The curves for the Stanford-Binet and the Detroit tests are essentially alike, although final flattening occurs later on the Stanford-Binet curve.

The curve of the results on the Stanford-Binet test seems to indicate that children would gain considerably in speed of learning if they could wait until they had attained a mental age of seven years and six months before beginning to read. However, the curve of the results of the Detroit test shows that the children with mental ages of six years and six months made progress practically as satisfactory as that of the children with higher mental ages. Since the results of the Detroit test show a higher correlation with reading progress than do the results of the Stan-

TABLE 2. Number of Children of Each Mental Age and Percentage Making Satisfactory Reading Progress

MENTAL AGE IN YEARS AND MONTHS*	NUMBER OF CHILDREN†		PERCENTAGE MAKING SATISFACTORY READING PROGRESS‡	
	Detroit Test	*Stanford-Binet Test*	*Detroit Test*	*Stanford-Binet Test*
4–5 to 4–11	1	1	....	....
5–0 to 5–5	12	1	0	....
5–6 to 5–11	12	12	0	8
6–0 to 6–5	17	22	47	41
6–6 to 6–11	23	38	78	68
7–0 to 7–5	29	31	79	68
7–6 to 7–11	16	15	75	87
8–0 to 8–5	7	11	....	82
8–6 to 9–0	8	2	....	....

* Intervals are half sigmas above and below the mean of the entire group as determined by the Detroit test.
† Because the tests were given on different dates, some children who were given the Detroit test were not given the Stanford-Binet test and vice versa.
‡ No percentages were figured for groups of less than ten children.

TABLE 3. Number of Children of Each Mental Age and Percentage Making Satisfactory Sight-Word Scores

MENTAL AGE IN YEARS AND MONTHS	NUMBER OF CHILDREN*		PERCENTAGE MAKING SATISFACTORY SIGHT-WORD SCORES	
	Detroit Test	*Stanford-Binet Test*	*Detroit Test*	*Stanford-Binet Test*
4–5 to 4–11	1	1	....	....
5–0 to 5–5	12	1	0	....
5–6 to 5–11	12	12	0	8
6–0 to 6–5	17	25	71	52
6–6 to 6–11	23	43	87	77
7–0 to 7–5	31	35	84	89
7–6 to 7–11	23	18	83	94
8–0 to 8–5	10	11	90	91
8–6 to 9–0	12	3	100	....

* The numbers of children whose sight-word progress is compared differ from the numbers whose reading progress is compared in Table II because one group of children not taught by the indivdual method was omitted from the reading-progress group.

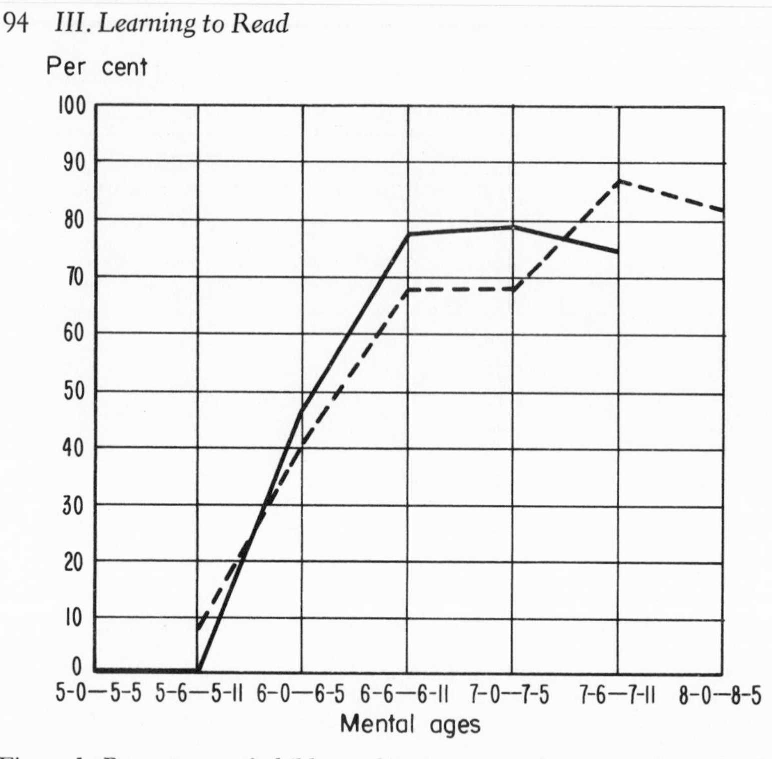

Figure 1. Percentages of children of various mental ages, as determined by the Detroit First-Grade Intelligence Test (solid line) and by the Stanford Revision of the Binet-Simon Scale (broken line), making satisfactory reading progress in school year 1928–29.

ford-Binet test and since the Detroit test is more practicable to administer than the Stanford-Binet test, it seems reasonable to use the Detroit test as a basis for determining children's readiness for reading. The mental level of six years and six months is the breaking point in the curve, that is, the point beyond which there is very little gain in postponing the teaching of reading. This break is evident to some extent on the Stanford-Binet curve and markedly true on the curve of Detroit test scores.

Figure 2 points to the same conclusion—that it pays to postpone beginning reading until a child has attained a mental age of six years and six months. If this practice is followed, 78 percent of the children may be expected to make satisfactory general progress, and 87 percent of the children may be expected to make satisfactory progress in learning sight words.

A similar study was carried on during the school year 1929–30 for the purpose of checking the results of the 1928–29 experiment.

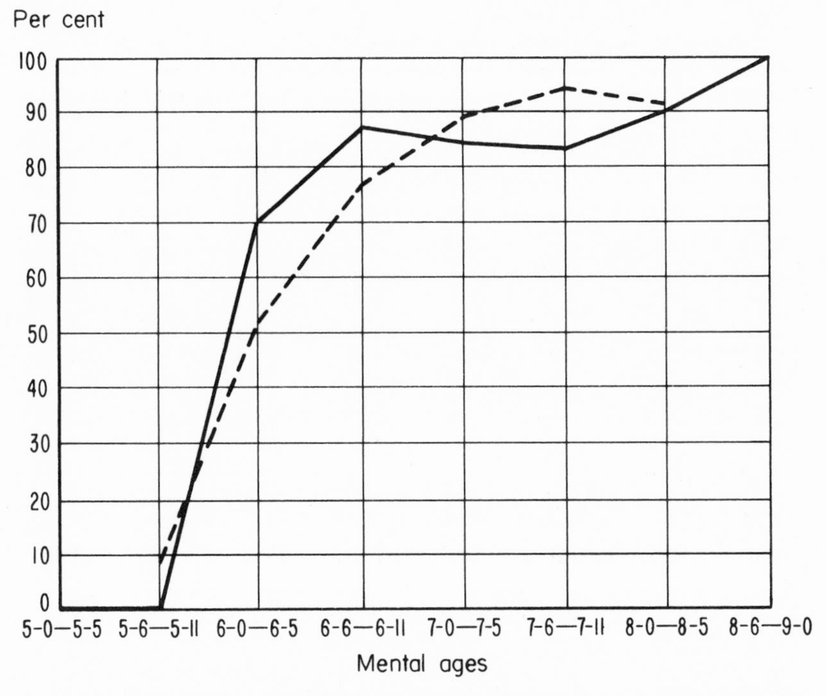

Figure 2. Percentages of children of various mental ages, as determined by the Detroit First-Grade Intelligence Test (solid line) and by the Stanford Revision of the Binet-Simon Scale (broken line), making satisfactory sight-word scores in school year 1928–29.

All children who were mentally six years of age or more were taught reading from the beginning of the year. The previous study made it seem futile to try to teach younger children, but a few with lower mental ages were taught reading for the purpose of the experiment. Mental ages were determined this time by the Detroit First-Grade Intelligence Test and the Pintner-Cunningham Primary Mental Test.

At the end of the year (June, 1930) the children were tested on the sight-word list and the Gray Standardized Oral Reading Check Test. A child was considered to have made satisfactory progress if he knew the entire sight-word list (139 words) and read the Gray test in fifty seconds or less with three errors or less. This standard has been set by Gray for Grade I. Table 4 gives the number of children of each mental age and the percentage of children at each mental level making satisfactory scores in both sight words and oral reading. Figure 3 makes the data of Table 4 graphic. As in Figures 1 and 2, the perentage of children who learned to read satisfactorily is greatest at the mental ages of

TABLE 4. Number of Children of Each Mental Age and Percentage Making Satisfactory Sight-Word Scores and Oral-Reading Scores

MENTAL AGE IN YEARS AND MONTHS*	NUMBER OF CHILDREN		PERCENTAGE MAKING SATISFACTORY PROGRESS	
	Sight-Word Test	*Oral-Reading Test*	*Sight-Word Test*	*Oral-Reading Test*
5–0 to 5–5	1	0	....	....
5–6 to 5–11	10	9	....	....
6–0 to 6–5	25	24	64	58
6–6 to 6–11	23	23	87	83
7–0 to 7–5	23	23	87	91
7–6 to 7–11	12	12	83	92
8–0 to 8–5	5	5	....	....
8–6 to 9–0	1	1	....	....

* Average of scores on Detroit test and Pintner-Cunningham test.

six years and six months and of seven years. The curve for sight-word scores breaks at the mental age of six years and six months, while the curve on the Gray Standardized Oral Reading Check Test breaks at the mental age of seven.

The second year's experiment, therefore, in which a different set of children, different teachers, a different method of determining mental age, and a different method of determining progress were used and in

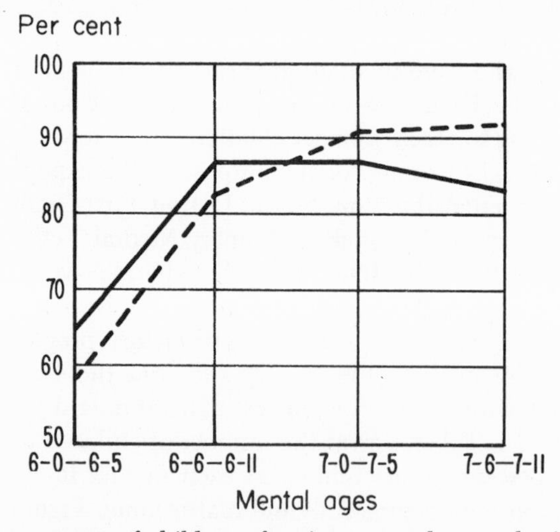

Figure 3. Percentages of children of various mental ages who in school year 1929–30 made satisfactory sight-word scores (solid line) and satisfactory scores on the Gray Standardized Oral Reading Check Test (broken line).

which a whole year's work instead of a half year's was taken as the measure of progress confirms the experiment of the first year.

Summary

1. Correlations between mental age and ability to learn to read, as measured by reading progress and sight-word scores, showed a fairly high degree of relationship. The correlations ranged from .50 to .65.

2. The correlations between mental age and reading progress were somewhat higher when mental age was measured by the Detroit First-Grade Intelligence Test than when mental age was measured by the Stanford Revision of the Binet-Simon Scale.

3. Mental age alone showed a larger degree of correlation with reading progress than did the intelligence quotient or the average of mental and chronological ages.

4. When the Detroit test was used as a basis for determining mental-age groups, the children who had a mental age of six years and six months made far better progress than did the less mature children and practically as satisfactory progress as did the children of a higher mental age.

5. When mental age was measured by the Stanford Revision of the Binet-Simon Scale, the children with a mental age of six years and six months again made very much better progress in reading than did those of less maturity, but they made less satisfactory progress than did those whose mental age was six months greater. The gain in ability up to six years and six months of mental age, however, was much greater than the subsequent gain.

6. A repetition of the experiment in 1929–30 with different teachers, different children, and different tests confirmed the earlier experiment in all its basic conclusions.

7. Consequently, it seems safe to state that, by postponing the teaching of reading until children reach a mental level of six and a half years, teachers can greatly decrease the chances of failure and discouragement and can correspondingly increase their efficiency.

13. The Necessary Mental Age for Beginning Reading

ARTHUR I. GATES (1937)

For some time the problem of determining the optimum or necessary mental age level at which reading can be successfully introduced has been under investigation. Recently, in books written primarily for professional workers, statements have been made which implied that this problem is fairly well solved. Such statements usually imply, more specifically, that success with *typical* first-grade reading programs requires a stipulated mental age, six and a half years being the age usually given.

The fact remains, however, that it has been by no means proved as yet that a mental age of six and one half years is a proper minimum to prescribe for learning to read by *all* types of teaching skill and procedures. Representative data gathered by the writer indicate rather clearly that statements concerning the necessary mental age at which a pupil can be intrusted to learn to read are essentially meaningless. The age for learning to read under one program or teaching method may be entirely different from that required under other circumstances. The crucial mental age will vary with the materials; the type of instruction; the skill of the teacher; the size of the class; the amount of preceding preparatory work; the frequency and the treatment of special difficulties, such as visual defects; and other factors.

Among a number of classes analyzed in this connection, four groups may be cited. In the first, the teaching was done under the supervision of Miss Florence W. Raguse of the State Teachers College at Indiana, Pennsylvania. Not only was the teaching rather closely supervised, the teachers were provided with a larger amount of easy-reading and self-diagnostic material than usual, and with supplementary practice and teach-and-test materials made up for the purpose. With this modern and effective instruction, well adjusted to individual differences, a mental age of 5.0 years appeared to be sufficient. Of the children equaling or exceed-

SOURCE: *The Education Digest,* XI (May, 1937), 42–43. Reprinted with the permission of *The Education Digest.*

ing this mental age only 7 percent fell below a reading grade of 1.95, the corresponding average for American pupils at large.

A second group was taught in a New York City School by teachers judged to be more expert than the average, and who used experimental materials developed by the writer and his colleagues. Here the minimum reading age was about half a year higher. Pupils with a mental age of less than 5.0 years were not so successful as in the class reported by Raguse. But of those who began with a mental age of 5.5 or higher, only 12 percent fell below 1.95.

A third group had good teaching with better-than-average classroom reading material and other equipment, but without the specially prepared types of material employed in the two groups just mentioned. Here a mental age of six was required.

The fourth group was from a metropolitan public school. The teachers were judged to be somewhat below the average in the system, and the reading materials and other equipment were inferior. The classes were taught by mass methods with little individual work. In this group children with a mental age of 6.5 fared none too well, and some with mental ages of 7.0 or higher had difficulty. Of the latter, 36 percent failed to exceed the national norms.

Obviously, therefore, general statements that any given mental age should be achieved by the pupil before he begins to learn to read are misleading. In the four groups mentioned the correlations between mental age and reading grade were .62, .55, .44, and .34, respectively, varying directly—and significantly—with the quality of instruction provided. More specifically, the magnitude of the correlation seems to vary directly with the effectiveness of the provision for individual differences. When the teacher uses a mass method, pointed at pupils with a certain equipment and background, these pupils seem to get on rather well but others encounter difficulty. If each pupil is to be given an opportunity to apply his mentality most effectively, attention must be given to his particular difficulties and limitations as well as to his special aptitudes and interests.

This study shows that the determination of the optimum mental age and other factors in reading readiness is not so simple as some recent pronouncements would imply. Reading is begun by very different methods, materials, and procedures, some of which a pupil can master with reasonable ease at the mental age of five, others of which would give him difficulty at the mental age of seven. It is necessary for each teacher to determine exactly what mental age, what background of previous experience, what special aptitudes, her particular program requires.

Finally, nothing in this report answers the question: At what age is it best to introduce reading? The data indicate that it is *possible* to organize materials and methods to teach children to learn to read at mental age 5.0 or higher, but they do not, in any way, imply that it is *desirable* to do so. Research is needed on this point.

14. Reading Readiness

LUCILLE M. HARRISON (1936)

Reading is and probably always will be the most fundamental skill taught and used in and out of school. The first grade of the elementary school is thought of as the grade in which this skill gets its basic foundation for the later periods of growth and development. It has, in the minds of many educators, no more important function than that of carrying the child well through the major portion of what is called the "Initial Stage" in reading. Each teacher who brings her pupils through this stage in the traditional period of time is usually designated as the successful teacher and she who fails to do so is deemed a failure. As we study the statistics of success and failure among pupils in the first grade, we are appalled by the large percentage who fail. This failure is judged quite consistently by reading achievement alone.

In defense of earnest and conscientious teachers and pupils we have at last come to the point of endeavoring to find the cause of these extensive failures. Psychologists and educators have analyzed the reading process sufficiently so that we now are in possession of facts which indicate clearly its complexity, and we find that to read requires that very specific and accurate verbal responses be made to very specific visual stimuli. Certain well-developed psycho-physical organizations are required for the accurate reception of the specific visual stimuli and for co-ordinating impressions of these stimuli with learned patterns of verbal response. If these organizations for reception and co-ordination are undeveloped or are interfered with in any way, we cannot have reading. If patterns of verbal response are inadequate or are impaired,

---

SOURCE: Lucille M. Harrison, *Reading Readiness* (Boston: Houghton Mifflin Company, 1936), pp. 1–4. Reprinted by permission of the publisher.

reading cannot be adequately carried on. In case such lack of development occurs, or if normal development is interfered with in a functional way by other factors, the desired and necessary reading abilities do not usually result, no matter how skillful the teacher nor what the nature of her teaching methods may be. This means that there is a need of readiness for reading before adequate reading can result.

In studying the maturing process of children as evidenced by their behavior, we find that readiness to do things appears at rather definite periods or within certain age limits and that to force a child to a particular type of activity before he is ready usually causes strain, may result in negativistic attitudes toward it, and accomplishes little so far as the desired activity is concerned. For example, there is a stage at which children walk, preceded by adequate muscular and nervous development to make the process possible. There is another stage at which children talk, with corresponding preparatory periods of babbling, single-word utterances, and the using of very simple types of sentences. We find also that the age limits for beginning these activities are comparatively broad, with individuals coming into the period at widely varying ages. In spite of our knowledge of these facts and our research concerning failures in the first grade, many school systems are still following the dictates of state laws and tradition in introducing the child to the initial stage of reading instruction whether he has evidenced readiness or not. The result is failure for the child who is unprepared, with its corresponding detrimental effects upon the child's whole personality.

The assumption has been that if a child does not read at the time reading is introduced, he is either stupid or lazy or perhaps he cannot see or hear. Experimental evidence based upon studies of non-readers in the first grade has shown us that very intelligent children sometimes fail to read but enjoy the content of reading material very much when others do the reading for them. We also find children who can read words fluently but are not capable of comprehending what is read. We find still others who are too unstable emotionally to carry out the reading process even though they may be very intelligent, are free from physical defects of eye and ear and are able to comprehend ideas read to them and to carry out well-developed processes of thought. Other children may be handicapped by meager experiences, malnutrition, or lack of social adjustment. These children need not be classed as defectives; instead, we must merely consider them as unready for reading in some respect. We must allow for traits of readiness to develop, and we can in the case of many of these traits stimulate their development in a preparatory period for reading instruction.

15. Laying the Foundations in Reading

WILLIAM G. CARR (1935)

Practices in the teaching of reading during the preparatory period and the period of initial instruction are matters of direct and immediate concern to teachers in the kindergarten and in the primary grades. Indirectly, these practices concern other teachers as well, for they determine in large measure the reading achievement which pupils later attain.

The Preparatory Period

SPECIFIC AIMS

The same national committee which defined the general objectives of reading instruction in terms of growth periods also suggested the specific aims appropriate for each period. According to their analysis, the child during the preparatory period should acquire:

1. Wide experience, along the line of his interests; experience which will enable him to understand the stories and activities about which he will read.
2. Reasonable facility in the use of ideas, in conversation, and in doing simple reasoning.
3. Sufficient command of simple English sentences to speak with ease and freedom.
4. A relatively wide speaking vocabulary.
5. Accuracy in enunciation and pronunciation.
6. A genuine desire to read.[1]

SOURCE: *Laying the Foundations in Reading,* NEA Research Bulletin, XIII, 5 (November, 1935), 279–289. Reprinted by permission of the author and publisher.

[1] National Society for the Study of Education. *Report of the National Committee on Reading.* Twenty-fourth Yearbook, Part I. Bloomington, Ill.: Public School Publishing Co., 1925. p. 27.

USE OF A PRE-PRIMER PERIOD

Although the development of reading readiness is one of the major purposes of kindergarten training, first-grade teachers also are interested in the problem, for often they must delay formal instruction for a while and encourage development along the lines indicated above. In many cases children enter the first grade with no kindergarten training. Other pupils have had a certain amount of kindergarten training, but still are not ready to learn to read. Ninety-five percent of the first-grade teachers who responded to the present inquiry into the classroom practices of successful teachers make use of a pre-primer period to assure reading readiness. The length of the period varies with the needs of the pupils; sometimes it lasts only a few days, sometimes several weeks.

ACTIVITIES OF THE PRE-PRIMER PERIOD

A few of the important activities engaged in by teachers and pupils during the pre-primer period are listed below, arranged according to frequency of mention in reports from the 288 successful first-grade teachers who cooperated in this study.

1. Providing various experiences as a basis for stories; e.g., trips and excursions, interesting toys, pets, parties, and activity projects of various types.
2. Making charts about children's own experiences.
3. Games to develop word recognition.
4. Use of action words and sentences.
5. Matching words with pictures and objects.
6. Story telling.
7. Display and discussion of pictures.
8. Dramatization.
9. Use of workbooks and seat work of other types.
10. Making booklets.
11. Learning the names of labeled objects in the room.
12. Learning nursery rhymes.
13. Following printed directions.
14. Reading to children.
15. Drawing and handwork.
16. Singing and rhythm games.
17. Informal conversation and free play.
18. Flash-card exercises.
19. Looking at books in the "reading corner."

This list would have to be extended greatly to include all the activities mentioned in the questionnaire replies. Many related activities, and numerous variations and adaptations, are suggested by these general categories.

WHEN READING INSTRUCTION SHOULD BEGIN

One of the crucial issues in first-grade teaching is the question of when to introduce the children to reading. The teacher must be able not only to cultivate reading readiness through appropriate experiences and activities, but also to determine accurately when the pre-primer period has served its purpose. Numerous suggestions on how to determine reading readiness are available in books and articles on primary reading.[2] In general they correspond to the practices listed in Table 1 based on reports from 288 successful first-grade teachers in reply to the question, "How do you determine when a child is ready to read?" Among the definite symptoms which teachers may watch for are the following:[3]

Attitudes:

- Joy in the use of books.
- Sense of responsibility toward group activities; spirit of cooperation.
- Sense in handling books; respect for other people's books.
- Interest in the environment of home, school, and community.
- Realization of the pleasures and values found in reading.
- Self-reliance; little need of encouragement.
- Persistence in carrying out activities begun.

Knowledge:

- Rich fund of meanings related to child interests.
- Knowledge of several simple stories, some folklore, and many nursery rhymes and poems.
- An adequate vocabulary.

Abilities:

- To express meanings or desires in good oral sentences.
- To listen attentively to rhymes and stories and comprehend them.

[2] See especially: National Society for the Study of Education, *op. cit.*, p. 27. Holmes, Margaret C. "Investigation of Reading Readiness of First Grade Entrants." *Childhood Education* 3: 215–21; January, 1927. International Kindergarten Union (now the Association for Childhood Education). *Points of View on the Problem of Reading Readiness.* Washington, D.C.: the Union, 1929. Clark, Hazel, and Shank, Spencer, "Supervising a Reading Readiness Program." *The Principal and Supervison.* Tenth Yearbook. Washington, D.C.: Department of Elementary School Principals, National Education Association, 1931. Pp. 460–70.

[3] Adapted from: U.S. Department of the Interior, Office of Education. *The Activity Program and the Teaching of Reading.* Bulletin, 1931, No. 2. Washington, D.C.: Government Printing Office, 1931, 95 p. Also, Lee, J. M.; Clark, W. W.; and Lee, Doris M. "Measuring Reading Readiness." *Elementary School Journal* 34: 656–66; May, 1934.

TABLE 1. Methods of Determining Reading Readiness as Reported by 288 Successful First-Grade Teachers

Evidence considered	*Number of times mentioned*
1	2
Interest (pretending to read; looking at pictures; children's inquiries; etc.)	189
Reading readiness test results	54
Mental age	43
Ability in oral expression	42
Sufficient background; adequate range of experiences	35
Ability to match words	17
Chronological age	14
Physical condition (including muscular control)	14
Kindergarten teachers' judgments	8
Ability to concentrate	7
Social adjustment	5

To follow a line of thought.
To retell a story told or read to the group.
To recall experiences.
To repeat brief rhymes or messages correctly.
To supply missing words in familiar rhymes and stories.
To sense emotional coloration in stories heard.
To anticipate what comes next in stories.
To carry on activities that will develop reading interests.
To dramatize simple stories.
To follow oral directions.
To classify pictures or other objects.
To recognize and distinguish forms.
To discriminate between sounds.
To recognize reading situations—signs, labels, names of objects, own name, titles of pictures, etc.
To handle books properly, turning the pages with care.

It is generally agreed that reading instruction should be postponed until the child's mental age is at least six or perhaps six and one-half years. It is important, too, that he be free from defects of vision or hearing. Several good tests of reading readiness are available, some measuring the child's range of information and experiences, others his ability to distinguish differences in word-form, and to follow directions.[4] Intelligence tests for preschool children also, such as the Pintner-Cunningham and others of similar type, are useful in determining children's mental maturity. Smith found that word-matching ability was an excellent criterion of readiness, showing a correlation of .87 with the achievement made by 200 first-grade pupils.[5] Nice emphasizes length of children's sentences as a criterion of maturity.[6] She suggests that 30 to 100 samples of children's sentences be taken, and the average number of words per sentence be used as one indication of maturity.

The Period of Initial Instruction

SPECIFIC AIMS

During the initial period of reading instruction rapid progress should be made in:

1. Associating meanings with written or printed symbols.
2. Developing a thoughtful reading attitude.
3. Interpreting simple passages, thus securing new experiences through reading and enlarging the meanings of familiar words.
4. Acquiring a sight vocabulary.
5. Developing independence in the recognition of simple but unfamiliar words.
6. Establishing correct basic habits, such as speed and accuracy in word recognition, a wide span of recognition, regular progress along the lines, and accurate return sweeps of the eyes from the end of one line to the beginning of the next.[7]

[4] Among the readiness tests available are: *The Betts Ready to Read Tests* obtainable from the Keystone View Co., Meadville, Pa. *The Metropolitan Readiness Test.* World Book Co., Yonkers-on-Hudson, New York. *The Lee-Clark Reading Readiness Test.* Southern California Book Depository, Hollywood, Calif. *The Minneapolis Reading Readiness Scales.* Minneapolis Public Schools, Curriculum Department. *Reading Aptitude Tests* (by Marion Monroe). Houghton Mifflin Company, Boston, Mass. *Reading Readiness Chart,* a diagnostic chart accompanied by definite teaching suggestions: Hahn, Julia H. *First Grade Manual To Accompany the Child Development Readers.* Boston: Houghton Mifflin Company, 1935. p. xx-xxvi.

Two other tests are described in: Berry, Frances M. "The Baltimore Reading Readiness Test." *Childhood Education* 3: 222–23; January, 1927. Deputy, Erby C. *Predicting First-Grade Reading Achievement.* Contributions to Education, No. 426. New York: Teachers College, Columbia University, 1930. 55 p.

[5] Smith, Nila B. "Matching Ability as a Factor in First Grade Reading." *Journal of Educational Psychology* 19: 560–71; November, 1928.

[6] Nice, Margaret M. "Length of Sentences as a Criterion of a Child's Progress in Speech." *Journal of Educational Psychology* 16: 370–79; September, 1925.

[7] National Society for the Study of Education, *op. cit.*, p. 35–36. For another helpful outline of first-grade objectives given in terms of attitudes, skills, habits, and knowledges see: Hahn, Julia L. *First Grade Manual To Accompany the Child Development Readers.* Boston: Houghton Mifflin Company, 1935. p. xl-xliii.

ABILITIES DEVELOPED IN FIRST-GRADE CLASSES

More than 50 percent of the first-grade teachers participating in the present study make a conscious effort to develop the specific abilities listed in Table 2. All except the last ability listed are goals of achievement in more than three-fourths of the classrooms.

TABLE 2. Specific Abilities Used as Definite Objectives by 288 Successful First-Grade Teachers

The ability to: 1	*Percent of teachers* 2
Recognize words in groups; i. e., in phrases or thought units	96.5
Recognize both words and word-groups more quickly	95.1
Follow printed directions	87.8
Recognize words of which the pupil already knows the meaning	86.5
Get the meaning of new words from context	83.7
Find the answer to fact questions	75.3
Observe punctuation marks	52.4

TEACHING EMPHASIS

Phases of reading instruction emphasized by the same group of teachers afford further insight into appropriate first-grade objectives. . . . More than 75 percent of the group emphasize comprehension more than rate, assimilative reading more than cursory reading, and directed reading more than free reading. Prevailing practice among these teachers also favors strongly (1) greater emphasis on meaning than on mechanics, (2) more oral reading than silent reading, and (3) more extensive use of literary materials than factual materials. Sixty-nine percent of the group place equal emphasis on habits and attitudes. Agreement on other pairs is less complete, particularly the last, where 36 percent use basal texts more than other books, 32 percent use them less, and 32 percent make equal use of texts and other materials. Also in the case of extensive reading vs. intensive reading, 44 percent emphasize the former, 37 percent the latter. The figure suggests certain trends, but the lack of agreement is enough to suggest that teaching emphasis in any given class should be determined on the basis of the needs, interests, and abilities of the children. Teaching emphasis that results in excellent pupil achievement in one case may be inappropriate under other circumstances.

TYPES OF INSTRUCTION

Figure I shows the relative importance attached to six types of instruction by 288 first-grade teachers. Oral reading is given the highest rank; instruction and drill in phonics, the lowest. It is significant, too, that every first-grade teacher reported the use of oral reading and 98 percent the use of drill in word recognition; whereas, for each of the other types, 6 to 11 percent of the teachers reported that they do not give instruction of this kind. This comparison is not intended to suggest that separate periods are provided for the various types of instruction. Oral reading, word study, and one or more types of silent reading are often included in a single class period.

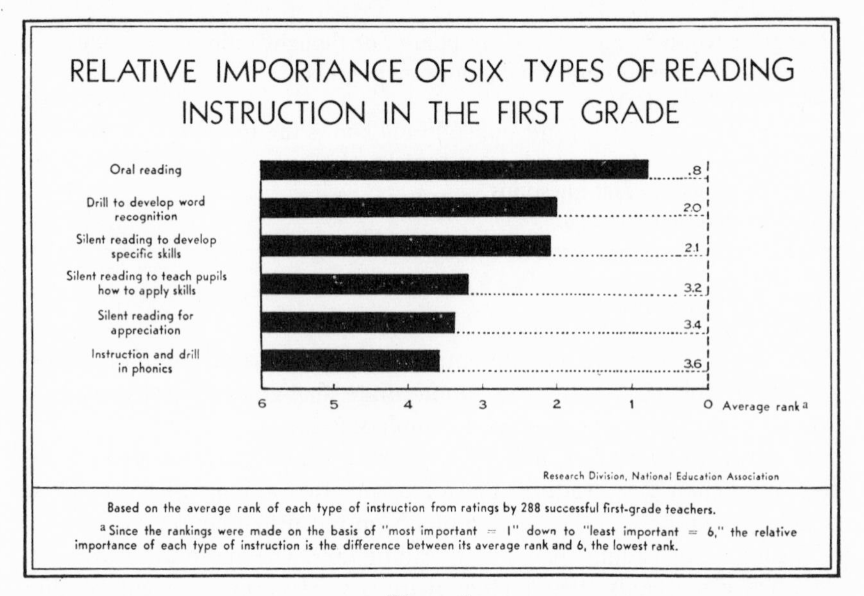

Based on the average rank of each type of instruction from ratings by 288 successful first-grade teachers.

[a] Since the rankings were made on the basis of "most important = 1" down to "least important = 6," the relative importance of each type of instruction is the difference between its average rank and 6, the lowest rank.

Figure 1.

ADAPTING PROCEDURES TO EACH SITUATION

Mention has been made already of the fact that teachers must adapt their practices to the circumstances under which they are working. This is true in setting up objectives and outlining the general plan of instruction; but it is especially true in selecting and applying specific classroom procedures. Success in teaching is not achieved as success in cooking, by following recipes. One group of pupils may learn rapidly when reading is introduced in a certain manner. For another group the same approach may be wholly inappropriate. Procedures should be adapted to the needs of the child, in no case attempting to fit the child to a certain method of teaching. This precaution should be kept clearly in mind in connection with the suggestions on method which follow.

THE APPROACH TO READING

Table 3 shows how 288 successful teachers make the approach to reading. The majority teach pupils first to recognize complete sentences, but nearly a third use short paragraphs as the first unit of recognition. A very few begin with phrases, still fewer with words, and only one with the letters of the alphabet. More than three-fourths teach pupils to read printed symbols first, but only a fifth teach pupils to print before script writing is introduced.

Studies in educational psychology show that words are not recognized by first noting separately each letter, then grasping the meaning. For that reason, the alphabet method of approach is not the natural one. Likewise it has been found that, especially in the very beginning, children recognize whole sentences, and sometimes groups of sentences, more easily than single words or phrases. Sentences are more irregular in general appearance, thus affording more cues to recognition. Moreover, it is easier to associate an idea with a group of symbols—for ex-

TABLE 3. What Pupils Encounter First in Reading

Elements introduced first 1	*Percent of teachers* 2
The first unit of recognition	
Short paragraphs	33.7
Sentences	61.9
Phrases	2.9
Words	1.0
Letters of the alphabet	0.5
Symbols pupils are taught to read first	
Printed symbols	80.3
Script writing	6.7
Both, from the beginning	13.0
Symbols pupils are taught to make first	
Printed symbols	20.7
Script writing	76.4
Both, from the beginning	2.9

Based on questionnaire replies from 288 successful first-grade teachers of reading.

ample, "Close the door, John"—than to associate the meaning of an isolated word such as "door" with the group of letters of which it is composed. Even when teachers have considerable skill in building up a sight vocabulary of isolated words, as some do, there is a tendency for pupils introduced to reading by this method to become word-by-word readers. Their criterion of success is being able to grasp the meaning of each word encountered, instead of being able to get the idea expressed in a sentence. They tend to call out in an expressionless monotone, "The-little-red-hen-found-some-corn," instead of grouping the words into correct thought units "The little red hen found some corn."[8]

It should not be inferred from the foregoing paragraph that pupils do not need to learn the alphabet. Individual letters and their sounds are important, but they are to be learned after the child has made considerable progress in learning to read simple passages. Children who make rapid progress in reading often learn most of the letters and their sounds quite incidentally, requiring a minimum of special teaching. Slow learners require more drill. Teachers should take note of the pupils who need special attention and, at the appropriate time, give whatever drill is necessary for mastery of the alphabet.

Teaching children to read printed materials before they read written sentences is a practice favored not only by the successful teachers who assisted with this study but also by educational psychologists and experts in the field of reading instruction. Moreover, there is considerable evidence that teaching children only to print while in the primary grades, that is, to use *manuscript writing*, results in more rapid progress in reading.[9] Several advantages are claimed for this method of writing, said to have been advocated first by an Englishwoman, M. M. Bridges, in 1899:

1. It is more legible because of simplicity and definiteness of letter form.
2. The beginner learns only one alphabet.
3. It is especially helpful to a child with vision defects.
4. It makes possible more rapid progress in reading, since children do not have to master an additional set of symbols for each word.

[8] See especially: Buswell, Guy T. *Fundamental Reading Habits: A Study of Their* Development. Supplementary Educational Monographs, No. 21. Chicago: University of Chicago Press. 1922. 150 p.

[9] Grill, Erma G. "Manuscript Writing and Its Value to a Sight-Saving Child." *Educational Method* 9: 407–12; April, 1930. Keim, S. Lucia. "The Present Status and Significance of Manuscript Writing." *Journal of Educational Research* 24: 115–26; September, 1931. Long, Howard H., and Mayer, Willa C. "Printing vs. Cursive Writing in Beginning Reading Instruction." *Journal of Educational Research* 24: 350–55; December, 1931. Voorhis, Thelma G. *The Relative Merits of Cursive and Manuscript Writing*. Lincoln School, Research Studies. New York: Teachers College, Columbia University, 1931. 58 p.

5. The motor processes involved in printing words in the same form in which they are encountered in books aid the pupil in word recognition.

It is claimed also that manuscript writing is an aid in spelling, that pupils learn to write in manuscript style more easily than they learn cursive writing, and that it encourages greater neatness. On the other hand, cursive writing is used so generally that pupils must eventually learn to read it and, in nearly all cases, to write in that style. Manuscript writing is slower—at least for many individuals. And finally, there is a certain amount of difficulty involved whenever the transition is made from manuscript to cursive writing. We are concerned here not with the merits of manuscript writing as a system of writing but only with its effect on reading. That this effect is wholesome seems to be an established fact. If manuscript writing is used in the beginning, experimental results thus far reported suggest the fourth grade as an appropriate time to change to cursive writing.[10]

A limited amount of experimentation has also been carried out with reference to the influence of the use of the typewriter on beginning reading.[11] The excellent results in reading obtained in these experiments seem to justify further trial use of this method.

SPECIFIC SUGGESTIONS ON METHOD

During the pre-primer period, children learn to recognize a number of words at sight—at least their own names, the names of other children in the room, the names of certain objects in the classroom and in their immediate environment, and certain action words entering into their play. First of all, they read from the bulletin board, the blackboard, and elsewhere, as needs arise in connection with their work and play. The teacher begins to "talk" to them by printing on the blackboard her greetings, directions, and plans for the day. Later she makes use of a special period for directed reading.

In the first special reading periods, the material used may be either a standard type obtained from a publisher of children's textbooks or material developed by the teacher. For those who develop their own blackboard and chart materials, the following suggestions by Pennell and Cusack should be helpful:

[10] Arnold, Esther W. "The Transition from Manuscript to Cursive Writing." *Elementary School Journal* 33: 616–20; April, 1933.

[11] Spencer, Herbert L. *An Experimental Study Showing the Relative Influences of the Typewriter on Various Phases of Reading Ability Among Elementary-School Pupils.* Doctor's thesis, Universty of Pittsburgh, 1934. Unzicker, Cecilia E. *An Experimental Study of the Effect of the Use of the Typewriter on Beginning Reading.* Contributions to Education, No. 610. New York: Teachers College, Columbia University, 1934. 96 p.

1. The story should be one in which the children are keenly interested.
2. There should be a central idea.
3. There should be a good opening and a good closing sentence.
4. Correct sequence of sentences should be observed.
5. The sentences should be short and of fairly uniform length.
6. The vocabulary should consist largely of words already known to the pupils.
7. Words and phrases should be repeated frequently, but in different situations.
8. Phrases should not be divided at the end of lines.
9. The writing or printing should be large, legible, and bold.
10. The spaces between words should not be too great.[12]

In presenting material to beginners, Hahn recommends a general procedure consisting of four steps: (1) the introductory reading of the whole story, (2) a practice period, (3) rereading and using the story for a specific purpose, and (4) individual and group activities.[13] With reference to the first step she says:

> The introductory reading of the whole story should be accomplished as quickly as possible under the leadership of the teacher who introduces new words and phrases in such a way *that the thought is kept uppermost* in the child's mind *all of the time*. . . . The introductory period is not a drill period. New words and phrases . . . are *introduced* only in order that children may move intelligently thru the story. . . . If the context and the pictures or a question do not bring out the word . . . the teacher supplies it and leads the children skillfully over the difficulties which might otherwise interfere with the understanding of the story. The teacher does not, at this stage, expect the children to master the new words altho some of them may do so.

After the children have read the whole selection silently from beginning to end and have grasped the thought, practice on words and phrases is necessary for many children before they can reread the story fluently by themselves. Sometimes this is given during the same class period as the introductory reading; sometimes in a later period. Games involving show-me-the-word-that-says, actions games, flash cards, and

[12] Adapted from: Pennell, Mary E., and Cusack, Alice M. *The Teaching of Reading from Better Living*. Boston: Houghton Mifflin Co. 1935. p. 192.

[13] Hahn, Julia L. *First Grade Manual To Accompany the Child Development Readers*. Boston: Houghton Mifflin Co., 1935. p. 11–14. For other outlines of procedure see other recently published teaching manuals; also, Pennell, Mary E., and Cusack, Alice M., *op. cit.*, p. 147–259. Parker, Samuel C. "How to Teach Beginning Reading." *Elementary School Journal* 22: 15–30, 104–17, 175–88, and 254–68; September to December, 1921. Buswell, Guy T., *op. cit.*, 150 p.

exercises in identifying words in new arrangements and combinations are among the many types of practice which may be provided. No more practice should be given than the pupils really need.

Following the practice on words and phrases, pupils should be prepared to reread the story for individual or class enjoyment, for the entertainment of others outside the class, or to acquire specific information to be used in carrying out related activities. In this case the reading should be a relatively smooth and independent process.

As a final step, individual or group activities are provided in which the pupil makes use of the vocabulary in new reading situations. The use of workbooks or mimeographed seat work, construction, drawing, dramatization, games, and numerous other activities can be used to supplement the regular reading lesson.

Neither the foregoing method nor any other is equally appropriate on all occasions. Teachers should adapt this plan to their own teaching situations. It is especially important for them to select the devices which they can use most skillfully—devices which are at the same time best adapted to the purposes at hand and to the abilities, needs, and interests of the pupils.

Zirbes[14] points out eight common mistakes in beginning reading, which teachers will do well to avoid:

1. Busy-work remotely related to reading.
2. Beginning too soon, especially with the children of foreign-born parents.
3. Reading in concert as a regular routine.
4. Teaching "the," "in," "of," etc., in isolation.
5. Teaching the A-B-C's to babies who should be playing.
6. Ignoring pupils' current interests for a story *in the book*.
7. One-paragraph reading. Too little continuous silent or oral reading.
8. Stereotype procedure of any kind.

By way of general advice, Meriam[15] suggests that teachers: (1) be informal; (2) develop reading ability through normal activities in which reading functions; (3) watch for good phrases and expressions used by the children and place same on blackboard; (4) write well; (5) regard the identification of each individual word as relatively unimportant; (6) be patient—tell the child what a word is "70 times 7"; and (7) expect slow progress at first.

[14] Zirbes, Laura. "Present Practices in Teaching Reading as They Affect Child Development." *A Better Beginning in Reading for Young Children*. Bulletin of the Association for Childhood Education. Washington, D.C.: Association for Childhood Education, 1932. p. 2–7.

[15] Meriam, Junius L. "Avoiding Difficulties in Learning to Read." *Educational Method* 9: 413–19; April, 1930.

PHONICS

Nearly all authorities in reading agree that children should have a certain amount of practice in word analysis, that is, phonetic training. Without it, they are handicapped in the presence of unfamiliar words and may, on the one hand, depend on the teacher to tell them the new words, or, on the other, resort to random guesses. The issues are: When should phonetic instruction begin? What letter sounds should be taught? What methods should be used? On these questions agreement is less unanimous.

Although in 1925, seventeen of twenty-one systems of reading analyzed by Gates[16] suggested the introduction of phonics within the first two weeks and all of them within the first six, the better practice seems to be to postpone phonetic instruction until considerable progress in reading has been made. The National Committee on Reading suggests that it be delayed "until the child has established the habit of thought-getting, has a reasonable stock of sight words, and has begun to note freely gross similarities and differences in words."[17] Experiments indicate that phonetic training is relatively ineffective during the first half of Grade I.[18] A sight vocabulary of 50 to 100 words is an essential prerequisite.

The selection of the phonetic elements to be taught is a problem that merits the careful study of every primary teacher. The number of sounds that might be taught is legion, but they are far from equal in importance. Many sounds are learned incidentally by nearly all children. Moreover, certain sounds occur much more frequently than others in the words which children encounter. The list of sounds to be taught, therefore, should be selected with care, using the results of the phonetic analyses that have been made.[19] The basic list of phonetic elements

[16] Gates, Arthur J., and others. "Problems in Beginning Reading." *Teachers College Record* 26: 578; March, 1925.

[17] National Society for the Study of Education, *op. cit.*, p. 90.

[18] Sexton, Elmer K., and Herron, John S. "The Newark Phonics Experiment." *Elementary School Journal* 28: 690–701; May, 1928. Garrison, S.C., and Heard, M. T. "An Experimental Study of the Value of Phonics." *Peabody Journal of* Education 9: 9–14; July, 1931.

[19] Important studies of this type are:
Atkins, Ruth E. "An Analysis of the Phonetic Elements in a Basal Reading Vocabulary." *Elementary School Journal* 26: 596–606; April, 1926. Burbank, E. D. "Phonetics in the Elementary Grades for Teachers of Normal Children." *Volta Review* 22: 113–16, 217–20, 274–78, and 323–27; March to June, 1920. Cordts, Anna D. "Facts for Teachers of Phonics." *Elementary English Review* 3: 116–21; April, 1926. Sartorius, Ina C. *Generalizaton in Spelling*. Contributions to Education, No. 472. New York: Teachers College, Columbia University, 1931. 65 p. Vogel, Mabel; Jaycox, Emma; and Washburne, Carleton W. "A Basic List of Phonics for Grades I and II." *Elementary School Journal* 23: 436–43. February,

selected for use in the first grade in Winnetka as a result of the study by Vogel, Jaycox, and Washburne follows:

1. All the short vowel sounds.
2. All simple consonant sounds.
3. The rule for lengthening the vowel before final "e."
4. The phonograms: *ee, ed, ing, er, ea, an, ou, en, ay, oo* (as in good); *oo* (moon), *ar, ow* (cow), *ow* (show), *ill, st, th, sh* and *gr.*

With respect to teaching methods most authorities recommend that teachers: (1) begin phonetic instruction with an analysis of the words in children's sight vocabularies; (2) set aside separate periods for teaching phonics; (3) teach the easiest sounds such as "m" and "s" before the difficult ones such as "b" and "p"; (4) give different children different amounts of phonetic instruction, according to their needs; (5) adopt a definite system of phonics—of which there are several; (6) carefully relate the work in phonics to a rich reading program; and (7) in all phonetic training, deal with words as units, the teacher underlining or covering up parts of words to emphasize phonetic elements.

MATERIALS OF INSTRUCTION IN THE PRIMARY GRADES

Suggestions on evaluating and selecting children's books, a description of the materials in use in the classrooms of 1527 competent teachers, teachers' criticisms of materials being used, and a list of helpful guides to children's literature are given in a later section of this bulletin. For that reason, the discussion here is limited to certain findings from the present questionnaire study: (1) a review of the difficulties reported by a group of successful teachers in providing suitable primary reading materials; and (2) a list of some of the special types of reading material which they find helpful in Grades I and II.

The leading difficulties in providing suitable materials named by 288 first-grade and 260 second-grade teachers are listed below according to frequency of mention:

1. Finding a sufficient amount of easy reading material.
2. Lack of funds to obtain needed materials.
3. Finding materials appropriate for slow learners.
4. Finding materials bearing directly on a particular teaching unit.
5. Problems of administrative routine, such as supplementary readers in use by other teachers when wanted.
6. Finding factual books easy enough for primary children.

1923. Washburne, Carleton W. "The Commonest Syllables." *Journal of Educational Research* 14:199–205; October, 1926. Washburne, Carleton W., and Vogel, Mabel. "A Revised List of Phonics for Grade II." *Elementary School Journal* 28: 771–77; June 1928.

7. Finding beneficial seat work.
8. Finding a variety of material with similar vocabulary.
9. Necessity for making appropriate materials.
10. Finding enough story-book type materials.
11. Finding materials adapted to the interests and abilities of different children.
12. Securing up-to-date materials.

Similarly, the following types of special materials were mentioned as most helpful in first- and second-grade teaching:

1. Workbooks.
2. Seat work, such as, word builders, sentence builders, mimeographed read-and-do exercises, etc.
3. Flash cards—word, phrase, and sentence cards.
4. Reading charts—published charts and experience charts prepared by teachers and pupils.
5. Pupils' booklets.
6. Children's newspapers.
7. Visual aids.
8. Bulletin board displays.
9. Phonetic charts.
10. Games and puzzles.
11. Picture dictionaries.
12. Written directions and action sentences on blackboard.
13. Graphs showing progress of individual pupils or classes.

SPECIAL DIFFICULTIES IN BEGINNING READING

First-grade teachers who participated in this study were asked to list a few of the teaching problems which they had found most difficult during the year just closing and to state briefly what they had done to solve each problem. Table 4 lists the problems mentioned by more than five teachers.

Word-by-word reading stands out as the problem most frequently encountered. To eliminate this tendency, teachers report the following devices: (1) provide phrase drills; (2) have pupils read silently first to get the thought, then orally; (3) mark off, in some way, appropriate thought units; (4) use easy materials; (5) have pupils read, then repeat what was read from memory; (6) have preparatory word study; (7) give pupils a motive for reading—let them read to find out something; (8) commend pupils for reading in a conversational way; (9) emphasize speed; (10) encourage pupils to look ahead, to use a wider eye-voice span; (11) discontinue word flash cards; and (12) compare the good readers to a train which "stops at stations only."

TABLE 4. Problems Especially Troublesome to 288 First-Grade Teachers

Problem	*Number of times mentioned*
1	2
Problems relating to oral reading:	
Word-by-word reading	78
Hesitancy or carelessness in oral reading	21
Mispronunciations	12
Repetition of words or phrases	9
Expression and voice control in oral reading	9
Substitutions—words of same, or similar, meaning	6
Problems relating to word recognition:	
Pupils' inability to figure out new or different words	59
Lack of an adequate sight vocabulary	51
Confusion of similar words	32
Difficulties in recognizing and interpreting abstract words	17
Inability to recognize known words in new situations	16
Reversals	15
Other problems:	
Vocalization	52
Line following	36
Poor comprehension	35
Irregular progress along the line and inaccurate return sweeps of the eyes	25
Eye span too narrow	25
Memorization	20
Lack of interest on the part of pupils	20
Difficult transitions: print to script; charts to books; one type size to another; etc.	19
Pupils read too slowly	13
Language handicaps	12
Span of attention too short	12
Guessing	11
Incorrect interpretation of letters	9
Lack of phonics	8

Several devices were mentioned repeatedly in connection with the different kinds of difficulty in oral reading; for example, (1) extensive practice in both silent and oral reading, (2) the use of easy material, (3) genuine audience situations, (4) reading for a definite purpose,

(5) thorough preparation before reading, (6) training in phonetics, and (7) the correction of faulty habits of English usage. Dramatization was mentioned frequently as particularly helpful in developing good expression and voice control. Accuracy is promoted by word and phrase drills. Repetition can often be eliminated by covering each word as soon as it is called, or if the pupil is reading from the blackboard, by erasing each word as it is read. One teacher tells her pupils that repetition in reading is like "going back home to start over, every time one comes to a traffic light."

A number of teaching devices were also mentioned frequently in connection with the various difficulties centering around word recognition. Extensive reading of easy material, flash-card drills, word games, keeping word lists, and exercises in noting likenesses and differences are among the procedures most often listed. The two devices used most in teaching pupils to cope with new words are drill in getting new words from context, and training and drill in phonics. Special attention to initial and final letters, the use of pictures and picture dictionaries, recognizing known words within longer, unknown words, and the development of pupils' self-confidence are other important methods used in developing accurate and rapid word recognition. The teachers' reports stress the importance of variety in teaching methods in this field, for so much dependence must be placed on repetition that, without variety, vocabulary study is unusually dull.

A problem of method often mentioned was that of eliminating the tendency to interpret letters or words in reverse order, for example, confusing "was" and "saw." This rather common difficulty in the early stages of reading has been thought by some to be associated with left-handedness.[20] Their hypothesis is that the brain centers which control motor responses in left-handed persons are so closely identified with those used in reading that the result is confusion and a tendency to make reversals in reading. Many, however, refuse to accept this explanation. In the most recent and extensive study of the question, involving 136 carefully matched pairs of right- and left-handed children, the latter made the fewest reversals in every test situation provided.[21] Apparently,

[20] Dearborn, Walter F. "Teaching Reading to Non-Readers." *Elementary School Journal* 30: 266–69; December, 1929. Also, Orton, Samuel T. "The 'Sight-Reading' Method of Teaching Reading as a Source of Reading Disability." *Journal of Educational Psychology* 20: 135–43; February, 1929.

[21] Phillips, Albert J. "Relation of Left-Handedness to Reversals in Reading." *Elementary English Review* 11: 97–98, 118; April, 1934. See also, Crider, Blake. "Lack of Cerebral Dominance as a Cause of Reading Disability." *Childhood Education* 10: 238–39, 270; February, 1934.

the difficulty cannot be attributed to left-handedness, but is one experienced in some measure by nearly all children. There are tests to discover what letters or words a pupil reverses and to discover in any given case how serious the difficulty is.[22]

Methods of eliminating reversals in reading mentioned in the questionnaire replies from 288 successful first-grade teachers were: (1) give training in the discrimination of form, size, and color; (2) play games involving left to right responses; (3) increase the amount of phonetic training, with special emphasis on initial letters; (4) cut down on the amount of silent reading, and increase oral reading; (5) teach pupils to do typewriting first, introducing writing later; and (6) provide practice exercises using kinesthetic stimuli to help establish correct recognition. Kinesthetic practice exercises are carried out in the following manner.[23] The troublesome word is written on the blackboard. The pupil traces it, pronouncing it as he does so. This is done several times, until the pupil thinks he can write it from memory. The word is erased. The pupil tries to reproduce it from memory, immediately and at intervals thereafter. Two important elements in exercises of this type should be noted. First, the pupil pronounces the word while tracing over it—not the letters in the word. Second, the pupil reproduces the word from memory, not from copy. Not only reversals in reading but also other difficulties in word recognition can sometimes be corrected by special exercises of this sort.

In eliminating undesirable habits, such as vocalization (lip-movement) or line following, setting up the correct ideal and praise for worthy achievement are of primary importance. Individual progress charts are often used to advantage. To decrease vocalization, some teachers have pupils place fingers on lips, use sentence flash cards, provide more silent reading and less oral reading, or emphasize speed of reading. The use of line markers is by far the most common device used to prevent pupils from pointing out each word. Another simple device to prevent pointing is to have the book held in both hands. The use of line markers, and reading from charts following a pointer, are favorite

[22] Phillips, Albert J., *op. cit.* Also, Teegarden, Lorene. "Tests for the Tendency to Reversal in Reading." *Journal of Educational Research* 27: 81–97; October, 1933.

[23] Orton, Samuel T., *op. cit.* See also, Fernald, Grace M., and Keller, Helen B. "The Effect of Kinaesthetic Factors in the Development of Word Recognition in the Case of Non-Readers." *Journal of Educational Research* 4: 355–77; December, 1921; Keller, Helen B., and Fernald, Grace M. "Remedial Work for Non-Readers." *Problems of the Elementary School Principal in the Light of the Testing Movement.* Second Yearbook. Washington, D.C.: Department of Elementary School Principals, National Education Association, 1923. p. 345–46.

methods of obtaining regular progress along the line and accurate return sweeps from the end of one line to the beginning of the next.

Reading comprehension is improved by (1) having pupils read to find out something definite, (2) silent reading followed by some form of self-expression such as dramatization or drawing, (3) read-and-do exercises, and (4) opportunities for enriched experiences. The last named item is also important in removing language handicaps. Flash-card exercises and exercises in finding words and phrases quickly on the page are widely used in increasing the eye span. Memorization is prevented by presenting the words of familiar stories in a variety of new arrangements and combinations. Interest in reading can be developed, among other ways, by providing an abundance of attractive materials, making reading a pleasant experience, and by making reading necessary for the accomplishment of something the child wishes to do.

Difficulties pertaining to the interpretation of letters in the alphabet may take the form of identifying some over-potent letter with a particular word. For example, the pupil may call every word containing the letter "k," *milk*. Another common difficulty is caused by confusing capital and small letters. A third type is identified with children whose preschool learning has focused their attention too firmly on letters, instead of on ideas and words. Such difficulties usually require exercises in careful observation and much individual instruction.

FIRST-GRADE STANDARDS FOR PROMOTION

Numerous studies have shown that the leading cause of non-promotion in the primary grades—particularly the first—is lack of satisfactory progress in reading. Because of the large percent of failure at that level a few schools are abolishing grade lines in the primary department, classifying pupils according to their achievement but not in grades, and promoting pupils only from the department. Since most schools, however, still classify pupils by grades and continue to fail large numbers of pupils because of reading, the promotion standards set for first-grade pupils merit consideration.

Reed's analysis of these standards in 1927 is one of the best summaries of practice now available.[24] Her findings with respect to the amount of required reading, size of an acceptable reading vocabulary, and the amount of phonetic knowledge expected in each half of the first grade are given in Table 5. For each item the range and average

[24] Reed, Mary M. *An Investigation of Practices in First-Grade Admission and Promotion.* Contributions to Education, No. 290. New York: Teachers College, Columbia University, 1927. 136 p.

TABLE 5. First-Grade Promotion Standards in 155 Cities

REQUIREMENT FOR PROMOTION	AVERAGE		RANGE	
	Low first	*High first*[a]	*Low first*	*High first*[a]
1	*2*	*3*	*4*	*5*
Number of:				
Primers pupils must read	2.31	2.89	0 to 10	0 to 10
First readers pupils must read	1.80	2.51	0 to 5	0 to 15
Supplementary readers pupils must read	2.50	3.50	0 to 12	0 to 15
Words required in the reading vocabulary	168.7	290.0	0 to 850	0 to 1639
Phonograms pupils are expected to know	25.0	26.6	0 to 62	0 to 150
Phonetic families pupils must know	15.0	30.0	0 to 40	0 to 90

SOURCE: Reed, Mary M. *An Investigation of Practices in First-Grade Admission and Promotion.* Contributions to Education. No. 290. New York: Teachers College, Columbia University, 1927. p. 111.

[a] These requirements are in addition to those listed for the low first grade.

amount is indicated. The range begins at zero in every case, because there were always one or more cities having no requirement with respect to each of the respective items.

Selected References

1. Bamberger, Florence E. "Developing Primary Reading Skills." *Normal Instructor and Primary Plans* 38: 22, 66; June, 1929.
2. Bergman, W. G., and Vreeland, W. "Comparative Achievement in Word Recognition Under Two Methods of Teaching Beginning Reading ." *Elementary School Journal* 32: 605–16; April, 1932.
3. Bildersee, Dorothy. *Teaching in the Primary Grades.* New York: D. Appleton and Co., 1932, 332 p.
4. Buswell, Guy T. *Fundamental Reading Habits: A Study of Their Development.* Supplementary Educational Monographs, No. 21. Chicago: University of Chicago Press, 1922, 150 p.
5. Cordts, Anna D. "Facts for Teachers of Phonics." *Elementary English Review* 3: 116–21; April, 1926.
6. Cordts, Anna D. *Word Method of Teaching Phonics.* Boston: Ginn and Co., 1929. 328 p.
7. Gates, Arthur I. *New Methods in Primary Reading.* New York: Teachers College, Columbia University, 1928.

8. Hardy, Marjorie. "Real Learning in the Primary Grades: Learning to Read." *Normal Instructor and Primary Plans* 37: 24, 100–3; April, 1928.
9. Hardy, Marjorie. "Right Attitude Toward Books and Taste in Reading in the Primary School." *Elementary School Journal* 27: 745–50; June, 1927.
10. Huber, Miriam B. "Teaching Beginners to Read—An Integrated Process." *Elementary English Review* 5: 116–18; April, 1928.
11. Meek, Lois H. A *Study of Learning and Retention in Young Children.* Contributions to Education, No. 164. New York: Teachers College, Columbia University, 1925. 96 p.
12 Meriam, Junius L. "Avoiding Difficulties in Learning to Read." *Educational Method* 9: 413–19; April, 1930.
13. Parker, Samuel C. "How to Teach Beginning Reading." *Elementary School Journal* 22: 15–30, 104–17, 175–88, 255–68; September to December, 1921.
14. Pennell, Mary E., and Cusack, Alice M. *The Teaching of Reading for Better Living.* Boston: Houghton Mifflin Co., 1935. 469 p.
15. Sloman, Laura. *Some Primary Methods.* New York: Macmillan Co., 1927. 293 p.
16. Storm, Grace E., and Smith, Nila B. *Reading Activities in the Primary Grades.* Boston: Ginn and Co., 1930, 376 p.
17. Wesley, Marion J. "The Approach to Reading." *Childhood Education* 5: 183–87; December, 1928.

16. Preschool and Kindergarten Experience

DONALD D. DURRELL and
ALICE K. NICHOLSON (1961)

In a society highly dependent on spoken and written words, early education must be concerned with the development of language skills, including preparation for success in beginning reading. Richness of experience and acquisition of desirable habits are the major concern of

---

SOURCE: *NSSE Yearbook* LX, Pt. I (1961), pp. 257–269. Reprinted by permission of the University of Chicago Press.

early education, and these support and are supported by language abilities, both spoken and written. The interaction between experiences and language is constant. Without suitable experience, language is meaningless; without language, experiences are often unrewarding. In early education, both the program of experiences and the growth of language require planning.

Words are symbols for experiences; the richer the experience, the greater the language potential. Language growth, however, is not assured by provision of experiences alone; practice is required for its fullest development. Spoken language is an accepted function of early childhood education. Vocabulary growth, improvement of speech patterns, development of social amenities in speaking, and speech correction are considered a part of the early childhood education program. Less concern is shown for the learning elements related to reading and writing in the early years. Although preschool children usually display an interest in writing, in letters and their names, and in play with word sounds, less attention is paid to the systematic development of these abilities.

An educational program for the early years should be based on a sound philosophy and psychology of childhood. Extreme positions on the nature-nurture controversy have had strong impact on early childhood education. At one extreme it is assumed that maturation is a genetic development primarily; that maturation will "take its course," will not be hurried, and will be little affected by specific training. Schools based upon this premise will provide a safe and stimulating environment in which to store children while nature is at work. At the other extreme, it is assumed that maturation is mainly nurture; that accidental or planned experiences determine later characteristics and achievements of the individual. Schools based upon this premise provide planned learning sequences in various aspects of physical and mental growth. The most acceptable position on the nature-nurture controversy appears to be that physical structure and function are largely genetic but may be modified by environment; that behavioral patterns may be genetic in origin but are highly modifiable; that knowledges and skills result from environment, but their learning may be limited by genetic structure.

This chapter is based upon the assumptions that (*a*) all forms of the communication arts are closely related; (*b*) many experiences necessary for the development of the communication arts must be provided; (*c*) specific instruction is necessary to provide the background skills of reading and writing. An effort will be made to trace briefly the development of the several communication arts through the preschool years.

The First Two Years

The rate of physical growth in the first two years is very rapid. In many instances, half of the adult stature will have been attained shortly after the second birthday. The rate of mental growth is more difficult to ascertain since measures of mental growth during these years are built primarily of sensorimotor items with some symbolic material and a few verbal and social items added in the later months. These tests have limited predictive value, but they do show, according to Munn, "that sensorimotor activities, social responses, and to some extent the elementary symbolic processes, increase in scope during infancy."[1]

There is still much to be learned about the nature of the learner and about how he is affected by learning, Almy warns. However, she does call attention to the cumulative effect that experiences have on the learner.

> Assuming for the moment three infants of equal capacity—one of whom is regularly fed, bathed, and changed but deprived of toys and play, another who is fed, bathed and changed and played with for a few minutes during and following each bath; while the third is continuously played with during all his waking moments—it is likely that each would have a very different repertoire of established responses to bring to a new learning situation.[2]

That growth during this period is rapid must be accepted, especially if one subscribes to the thesis reported by Goodenough that by three years of age, one-half of the adult mental stature may have been attained.[3]

As to knowledge of perceptual development, reliance must be placed on skillful observation and analysis of children's explanations. Subtle changes in perceptual development take place, moving from what is probably a diffused, undifferentiated picture, to transitory interest in details, to abilities to make close discriminations among objects. This growth in perceptual development may result from experiences with embossed pictures in play objects, with different play materials, with pictures and books. Improved visual discrimination leads to more precise perceptions and, in turn, to more precise communication.

Each of the four basic forms of communication—speaking, listening, writing, and reading—is a complex process. The development of one at

[1] Norman L. Munn, *The Evolution and Growth of Human Behavior*, p. 358. Boston: Houghton Mifflin Co., 1955.

[2] Millie Almy, *Child Development*, p. 65. New York: Henry Holt & Co., 1955.

[3] Florence Goodenough, "Measurement of Mental Growth in Childhood," in *Manual of Child Psychology*, p. 478. Edited by Leonard Carmichael. New York: John Wiley & Sons, 1954.

any given stage is dependent upon the development of one or more of the others. Each is often tied closely with emotion and always with experience. Even the earliest experiences relate to communication. As Strickland states, "A baby learns to read before he learns to listen. A mother communicates her feelings and her reactions without words. The baby's reaction clearly indicates his interpretation."[4] From these early reactions to actual speech is a long sequence: listening, various forms of imitating, babbling, gesture, attempts at words, success in single words, a gradually growing vocabulary. Throughout this continuing process, the parent may make a distinct contribution to reading readiness.[5]

Progress in communication is dependent upon mental endowment, maturation, experience, and opportunity for secure relationships with other children and adults, especially with the mother. Considering this last factor, McCarthy cites numerous orphanage studies which show that language growth is impeded when the child lacks close personal contact with the mother.[6] Of concern also is the over-protected child, whose every want is anticipated or whose attempts at vocalization are interpreted. Such a child is allowed neither the opportunity nor the need to develop language. Through trying to push and pull his world, tasting and smelling everything within reach, gaining better control of his body, and communicating with people around him, the normal child usually acquires a few hundred words by his second birthday.

Before Formal Reading

During the years between the second birthday and the age of school entrance, growth in language is usually rapid and constant. The two- or three-word sentence, often imperative in form, is characteristic of the two-year-old. Jargon observed at this age is often left behind at three. Language at three is used more effectively in achieving ends, and there is much less use of primitive communication such as grabbing, kicking, and biting. At four, verbal aggression, bickering, name-calling, fantasy, and play with words are dominant characteristics. Questioning is at a peak, and often attempts are made to pull together scattered bits of information.

In language and concept development, the nursery school can provide exceptional service. The school which encourages speech development

[4] Ruth G. Strickland, "Interrelationships between Language and Reading," *Volta Review*, LX (September, 1958), 334.
[5] Esther Milner, "Study of the Relationship between Reading Readiness in Grade I School Children and Patterns of Parent-Child Relationships," *Child Development*, XXII (June, 1951), 95–112.
[6] Dorothea McCarthy, "Language Development in Children," in *Manual of Child Psychology, op. cit.*, p. 604.

and supports the less verbal children, which provides stimulus for self-expression as well as opportunity for listening, leads the child to new and old concepts in a meaningful fashion. The presentation of good speech patterns and the correction of speech defects builds the child's confidence in verbal communication. The first-hand experiences provided by the nursery school expand the child's knowledge in effective ways. As Read comments:

> We can hardly estimate how modern life limits the intellectual development of children by limiting their first-hand experiences. . . . The results of research that seem to indicate that attendance at nursery school has an effect on the intelligence level of children may be a reflection of the advantages of the larger number of first-hand experiences that are offered at school over the number offered in the modern home.[7]

The development of language is always important to the preschool and kindergarten teacher. She plans situations in which listening is well motivated and has a fund of stories suited to the age group which she teaches. She reads stories aloud, makes up yarns, and has poems on the tip of her tongue, ready for all occasions. Speech is encouraged by "show-and-tell" periods, by impromptu dramatization, by discussion of plans and recent activities, by questions and conversation. Good speech patterns are exhibited and encouraged. Pictures and picture stories are used to stimulate discussion, involving both fact and imagination. Talk is encouraged in play, and in construction and drawing activities. Interest in books is invited by showing pictures in books while reading stories. Fluency and freedom in self-expression in language are considered essential for emotional growth and for social and personal achievement.

Interest in written language is encouraged through dictation to the teacher, who prints on the chalkboard or on large sheets of paper. These include stories told by children, items for a class newspaper, reviews of past activities, plans, and lists, such as names of pupils on teams or in groups, things needed in cooking or home furnishing, and things to take on an excursion. The child is not expected to read these stories or lists but is invited to follow the sweep of the teacher's hand as she reads back the story the class has "written." The positive value of wide and varied experience in the kindergarten have been repeatedly demonstrated.[8, 9]

[7] Katherine H. Read, *The Nursery School*, p. 36. Philadelphia: W. B. Saunders Co., 1955.

[8] Shirley H. Cowin, "Reading Readiness through Kindergarten Experience," *Elementary School Journal*, LII (October, 1951), 96–99.

[9] Rachel S. Sutton, "A Study of Certain Factors Associated with Reading Readiness in the Kindergarten," *Journal of Educational Research*, XLVIII (March, 1955), 531–38.

Most kindergarten teachers will admit these planned speaking and "writing" activities to the classroom. But regarding help in reading or writing words, there is a sharp division of opinion. Speaking and listening are a part of child development, but reading and writing are sometimes not regarded as suitable developmental skills. Some teachers carry their aversion to reading so far as to avoid having printed signs in the classroom; refuse to teach letter names and forms and discourage parents from doing so; and also discourage children's attempts at writing and reading. Apparently writing and reading are thought to be detached from the developmental processes, appearing spontaneously and full-blown "when the child is ready."

Evidence from research shows that interest and ability in written language are a natural part of child development in a literate society. A comprehensive report of the earliest stages of interest in letters is found in the work of Ilg and Ames,[10] who observed that children of thirty-six to forty months may identify some capital letters in an alphabet book or on blocks. The round letters, *O*, *D*, *C*, and *G*, or the vertical letters *T* and *H* may be among the first to interest them. At four years of age the child may recognize salient capital letters and ask for help in writing them. Hildreth notes that most children have learned before school age to recognize some numbers, some letters, and a few word forms.[11] Nicholson found that children entering first grade could tell the names of twelve capital letters and nine lower-case letters. Twelve percent of her population knew the names of all capital letters. The average child could write ten letters.[12]

Hardy, writing for parents, advised that a child is in the first stages of reading when he shows an interest in letters and in alphabet books and blocks, when he pretends to read, and when he asks what a word or a sign says. She advised parents that the best time to help a child is when he is curious and anxious to know: "Children often show an interest in letters before they do in words and sentences. If so, tell them the names of the letters."[13] Gans recommends that a child be shown how to write his name when he requests it, saying, "Why not show the child how to write, much as one shows him how to open a chest drawer, and then give him a chance to explore this new experience."[14]

[10] Frances L. Ilg and Louise B. Ames, "Developmental Trends in Reading Behavior," *Journal of Genetic Psychology*, LXXVI (June, 1950), 291–311.

[11] Gertrude Hildreth, *Learning the Three R's*, p. 141. Minneapolis: Educational Publishers, Inc., 1947.

[12] Alice K. Nicholson, "Background Abilities Related to Reading Success in First Grade," *Journal of Education*, CXL (February, 1958), 7–24.

[13] Charlotte Hardy, "Prepare Your Child for Reading," *Parents' Magazine*, XXV (June, 1950), 36.

[14] Roma Gans, "The Road to Reading," *Child Study*, XXXI (Winter, 1953), p. 8.

It is a common observation that as early as three or four years of age the child scribbles with delight meaningless forms as messages to be sent to friends and relatives.

If child interest is one basis for planning preschool or kindergarten programs, it seems that early aspects of reading and writing should be included for some children. The fact that others may show little interest in these activities might be taken as a clue for extra effort, just as reluctance in speaking or poor ability in catching or in skipping are considered as offering opportunities for helping the child. It is difficult to discover any peculiarity about early abilities related to reading and writing that excludes them from a developmental educational program. While there is an objection to "forcing" the child in language activities, this objection applies equally to all phases of child development, and it is assumed that a good teacher will employ only desirable motivations in all of them.

In discussing early stages of language development, we have been concerned with averages, but individual variations are equally important. The question, "Shall the child in kindergarten be taught to read?" becomes an academic one when the child is already reading.[15] One first-grade child, *writing* to a first-grade friend in October, said, "We won't have reading in our school until December. They don't think we are old enough to read now." She then went on happily to name some books she had been reading. Some children learn to read as early as three, while others at five do not know the names of letters and are unable to remember words which are taught. Obviously, no set program of language development is suitable for all children in any age group. Certainly, it appears undesirable to exclude instruction in reading and writing for those children who show the necessary background and interest.

Word Perception Abilities and Reading Readiness

The basis for reading is spoken language; if a child can understand and use spoken words well, he has demonstrated the capacity for dealing in symbols. Listening comprehension is widely used for determining the level of expectancy in reading. It seems that if a child can handle spoken language, he should be able to learn to read with equal facility. The main requirements for reading and writing, as differentiated from speaking and listening, are the relations between elements of speech and their written counterparts.

It may be that printed words designating objects, ideas, and relationships are easier to learn than spoken words. The written word is fixed

[15] Dolores Durkin, "A Study of Children Who Learned To Read Prior to First Grade," *California Journal of Educational Research*, X (May, 1959), 109–13.

and can be studied at leisure; the spoken word is transient and remains only as an auditory memory. Written words, however, are not direct symbols for objects and ideas; they are symbols for word elements in speech—symbols for symbols—and constitute a secondary relationship rather than a primary one to objects and ideas.

Although a few printed words may be learned as direct symbols for objects, through a "whole word" or a "look-and-say" method, similarities in the visual forms of words quickly lead to confusion. The tie of the written word to the spoken word must be established; the spoken word is the fundamental relationship to the object or idea. Although higher stages of maturity in reading may suppress the relationship to spoken language and the reader may follow ideas without awareness of the words he is reading, the early stages of reading require phonics skills.

One of the essentials for progress in reading is that the child be able to notice separate sounds in spoken words. If he cannot do this, he will be unable to relate the sounds to the printed letters. The ability to repeat words pronounced or to hear difference in spoken words is not adequate; the unit of learning speech is the syllable; the unit of phonetic writing is the sound within the syllable. Many children with excellent diction have never noticed the separate sounds within the individual syllables and, therefore, make little progress in learning to read through instruction in phonics. Learning the sounds of printed letters is a meaningless activity for the child who has never recognized these sounds in spoken words. Some children acquire the ability to identify separate sounds in words without formal training. They may develop power in phonics through "look-and-say" methods of reading. Every repetition of a sight word emphasizes the relationship between the sound and the printed letter, making other words easier to learn.

A second essential for learning to read is the ability to see differences in printed letters and word forms. It requires fairly close perception to notice the differences between *b, d, p,* and *q;* between *m, n, h,* and *u;* between *burn* and *born, from* and *form.* The child who cannot tell letters apart or notice the difference in word form caused by changed letters or letter sequence will have trouble in relating sounds to words.

A third ability is observing the relationship between letter form and the sound of the letter. While some children, as noted above, acquire this relationship without training, most need direct instruction in it. The child who knows the names of letters, even though he has not been taught their sounds, has some basis for word analysis. Since the names of all letters (except *h* and *w*) contain their sounds, the tie between letters and their sounds is partially made. In some cases, spelling the word provides almost as good a clue as does sounding it: for example, *p-e-n, d-e-a-f,* and *t-e-a-m.* The presence of the vowel in the letter name is not too great a handicap in these cases, since the vowel sound follows the initial letter name and precedes the final letter name.

When the relationship between the visual and auditory elements of words has been established, the acquisition of sight vocabulary progresses rapidly. Growth in sight vocabulary, in turn, improves word analysis ability, since each word learned improves the association between sight and sound. Daniels and Diack point out this relationship as follows:

> When there is a consistent relationship between the visual symbol and the sound, the two forms of analysis—aural and visual—are complementary; the eye helps the hear to listen and the ear helps the eye to look.[16]

The importance of ear training and letter knowledge as bases for beginning reading has been demonstrated by Sister Nila,[17] Durrell and Murphy, [18] Gavel,[19] and others. Children making little progress in first-grade reading almost always show deficiencies in these abilities, as do young children coming to reading clinics. Both abilities respond well to instruction, although some children need to be shown through visual and tactile aids the formation of the different speech sounds. The four-year study of Wilson and others[20] called attention to letter knowledges and their importance in the reading program. This study reported that among the first to learn to read and to become the best readers were the first-grade children who knew the most letter forms and sounds. Harrison stressed the importance of letter names and forms as follows: "To try to have children make use of phonics without letting them learn the names of letter forms is like trying to teach them arithmetic without letting them learn the names of number symbols."[21]

There are several levels of ability in letter knowledge, some of which are attained by the time the child reaches first grade, and some of which are not. Nicholson found that matching letter forms and identifying letters in the multiple-choice situation were easy for beginning

[16] J. C. Daniels and Hunter Diack, "The Phonic Word Method," *Reading Teacher*, XIII (October, 1959), 17.

[17] Sister Mary Nila, "Foundations of a Successful Reading Program," *Education*, LXXIII (May, 1953), 543–55.

[18] Donald D. Durrell and Helen A. Murphy, "The Auditory Discrimination Factor in Reading Readiness and Reading Disability," *Education*, LXXIII (May, 1953), 556–60.

[19] Sylvia R. Gavel, "June Reading Achievements of First-Grade Children," *Journal of Education*, CXL (February, 1958), 37–43.

[20] Frank T. Wilson and Others, "Reading Progress in Kindergarten and Primary Grades," *Elementary School Journal*, XXXVIII (February, 1938), 442–49.

[21] M. Lucille Harrison, "Getting Them Ready To Read," *National Education Association Journal*, XL (February, 1951), 106–8.

first-grade children. More difficult were relating letter names to letter forms, naming letters, and writing letters named; capital letters were much more commonly known than lower-case letters.[22] Gavel found that knowledge of letter names at school entrance was a better predictor of June reading achievement than were intelligence quotients or mental ages. Correlations of September tests with June reading achievements were as follows: writing letters dictated, .60; naming capital letters, .58; identifying capitals named, .56; identifying lower-case letters named, .56; naming lower-case letters, .54; intelligence quotients, .45; mental ages, .44.[23] Wilson also found that progress in reading correlated more highly with letter perception ability than with any other items on the tests he used.[24] It should be noted that none of these correlations is high enough to predict accurately an individual's reading achievement.

Reading readiness workbooks from nine commonly used basal reading series were analyzed for frequency of types of exercises by Allen and others. Language development through pictures appeared 367 times; visual discrimination of pictures and nonword forms appeared 179 times; exercises in motor skills appeared 98 times; identification of nonword sounds, 52 times. Practice in letter word forms, and word sounds were less frequent: There were 11 exercises in letter matching, 5 exercises in word outlines, 23 in word matching, and 62 in identification of initial consonants. The same study tested these abilities with measures of high reliability and correlated the results with January reading achievement. The correlations with reading were as follows: language achievement, .38; visual discrimination of nonword forms, .45; motor skills, .17; nonword sounds, .36. Correlations with abilities in word sounds and forms with reading achievement were higher: with auditory perception of sounds in words, .60; with word matching, .55.[25] Goins found similar low correlations between nonword visual perception tests and reading. She found, also, that special training in visual forms had no effect on reading achievement.[26] In view of the low correlations between nonword perceptual abilities and reading, further studies should be undertaken to determine their value in reading readiness. The research

[22] Nicholson, *op. cit.*, pp. 11–15.
[23] Gavel, *op. cit.*, p. 38.
[24] Frank T. Wilson, "Early Achievements in Reading," *Elementary School Journal*, XLII (April, 1942), 609–15.
[25] Ruth J. Allen and Others, "The Relationship of Readiness Factors to January First-Grade Reading Achievement." Unpublished group Master's dissertation, Boston University, 1959.
[26] Jean Turner Goins, *Visual Perceptual Abilities and Early Reading Processes*, p. 57. Chicago: University of Chicago Press, 1958.

evidence suggests that visual and auditory perception related specifically to words would be more effective.

Although the lessons of the reading readiness books may develop desirable abilities such as language fluency, motor skills, and attention to nonword forms and sounds, it is doubtful that they contribute greatly to reading readiness. Since it has long been demonstrated that children bring to first grade oral vocabularies much larger than will be required for reading, it is unlikely that additional language development will improve the child's chances for reading success. Visual discrimination of pictures and objects and auditory discrimination of nonword sounds may improve attention, and they may serve as preparatory training for word forms and sounds, but they appear to fall short of the perceptual type and level required for reading.

There appears to be objection on the part of some teachers of young children to the idea of providing systematic instruction in letters, sounds, and words. Both *systematic* and *instruction* are sometimes considered unacceptable words in preschool and kindergarten. One may "provide opportunity" informally, one may "lead and encourage," but one must not teach. The general idea seems to be that any program of teaching is necessarily *forcing* the child beyond his capacities. It is not necessary to force children to learn letters or sounds within spoken words. There are many opportunities for awakening interest in letters, such as putting signs on buildings children construct, using pictures which have simple identifying words in them, putting labels on pictures or drawings, answering questions about words and letters, assisting children with their early attempts at writing letters and words, providing games in which letters are used. The child's world is full of letters which can be utilized readily: television station call letters, names and brands of foods advertised, highway signs, street signs, newspaper headlines, advertisements, picture books.

Attention to word sounds may also be taught informally. Rhyming words are always enjoyed, and this is one of the beginnings of interest in word sounds. Pictures of objects whose names begin with the same sound may be displayed and named, with attention being called to the similarity of the initial sounds. The same may be done with objects and with children's names. Children enjoy these discoveries, and the activities may be done in the spirit of play.

Writing opportunities also constantly arise. Thank-you notes, invitations, and messages may be dictated by the children and written by the teacher. The daily news, the calendar, the list of ingredients for the applesauce, the shopping list, the cast of characters in the play, reminders of telephone messages—all these and many more can be used to provide interest in writing. Manuscript writing is, of course, used in these activities since it is closer to the print which the children will read.

The beginnings of reading and writing need not be a chore for children. It is not necessary for them to work solely with formal reading readiness workbooks hour after hour. In every aspect of the program, interest should be kept high, meaning emphasized, and delight in learning encouraged.

17. Laying the Foundation for Word Perception

WILLIAM S. GRAY (1957)

The papers presented before the first general session of this conference rightly emphasized the fact that reading is primarily a process of grasping and interpreting meaning. Experience and the results of research show, however, that efficient habits of word perception are essential requisities to fluent, thoughtful reading. It is appropriate, therefore, that we should focus atttention at this time on the problems faced in developing accuracy and independence in word recognition.

The ultimate goal in such efforts is to establish the skills of word perception that characterize independent, self-reliant readers. A good reader perceives most of the words he reads as wholes, often in units of two or three. He knows them so well that he recognizes them instantly at sight. When he meets an unfamiliar word he is able to apply quickly the various word-attack skills essential in recognizing its meaning or pronunciation or both. Any lower level of efficiency in word perception is inadequate.

The nature and scope of the training needed is greatly influenced by the characteristics of our written language. In some languages each

---

SOURCE: *IRA Proceedings* (1957), pp. 83–85. Reprinted by permission of the International Reading Association.

letter has the same sound in all words in which it occurs. In such cases phonics can be used widely and applied easily. Unfortunately in English some letters have several sounds and many of the basic sounds of the language are spelled in various ways.[1]

The reader's task is further complicated by the fact that the sound of a given letter or group of letters is often modified by other letters in a word or by the meaning of the sentence whole. Any system of word attack which relies solely on the slogan, "See this letter, say this sound," is therefore wholly inadequate. Instead, understandings and skills must be acquired which enable the reader to select in given cases the right sound from the various possible alternatives. This is no routine task. It requires the use of many word-attack skills and of all the higher mental processes involved in problem solving.

A sound word perception program should harmonize with the way in which children learn in general to perceive. Experiments made both here and abroad show that, as a rule, they learn to perceive visual forms as wholes, somewhat vaguely at first but gradually in increasing detail. Tachistoscopic studies show that words whose meanings are familiar are recognized far more rapidly and accurately than nonsense syllables or letters in isolation. Other studies show that children who learn to read most rapidly are able to keep in mind a perceptual whole.

These and many other findings favor emphasis on the learning of word wholes at the beginning. This plan has several advantages: It focuses attention on reading as a meaningful process; it enables the child to engage early in rewarding reading activities; and it provides a basic vocabulary that may aid children in identifying the facts and understandings that underlie the various word-attack skills.

Individual differences must also be recognized and provided for. In a summary of research in visual perception, Vernon[2] pointed out that the individual carries with him into each perceptual situation "his characteristic sensory abilities, intelligence, interests and temperamental qualities." Insofar as he may relate any of them to the perceptual act, "his responses will be colored and to some extent determined by these inherent individual qualities." Such findings indicate that general principles underlying the teaching of word perception must always be adapted to individual needs. The common goal sought for all, how-

[1] William A. Craigie, *Problems of Spelling Reform.* S.P.E. Tract No. LVIII. Clarendon Press, 1944. Ernest Horn, "Phonetics and Spelling," *Elementary School Journal*, LVII (May, 1957), 424–32.

[2] M. D. Vernon, *A Further Study of Visual Perception, p.* 255. Cambridge, England: University Press, 1954.

ever, is the understanding and skills involved in efficient word perception.

Promoting Growth in Word Perception

With the foregoing facts and principles in mind, let us consider next the major steps involved in promoting growth in word perception. Four will be discussed.

The first obligation teachers face is to identify the readiness of children for rapid growth in perceiving words and to provide needed training. The ability of children to make essential auditory and visual discriminations can be determined through the use of observation and pertinent tests. Of major importance in providing needed training is a stimulating learning environment which cultivates an inquiring attitude on the part of pupils toward all they see and hear. Furthermore, challenging activities should be provided daily in which visual and auditory discriminations are essential to achieve the ends sought. Further progress may be promoted through the use of well-conceived exercises in readiness workbooks which enlarge the meaning vocabulary of children, promote good thinking and increased command of language, and stimulate a desire to learn to read.

As readiness increases along the lines indicated, steps should be taken to build a sight vocabulary of 50 or more words of high functional value in early reading activities. In doing so the following guiding principles should be observed: The materials read should relate to familiar experiences that are highly interesting to young children; the words involved should be those that are used widely in their daily conversation and should arouse vivid associations; and they should be used a sufficient number of times to insure instant recognition. As the sight vocabulary increases, mere familiarity with the general forms of words is not enough. The skillful teacher soon directs attention to distinguishing features of words so that each attains an identity of its own. In the case of children who learn slowly, specific practice in tracing, writing, typing, or printing words can be provided to advantage. Such activities direct attention not only to the general form of words but to significant details and to their left to right sequence.

As children grow in ability to read very simple material, their interest in reading increases rapidly. At this point reliance on a sight vocabulary is wholly inadequate. The teacher now faces the challenging task of developing ability among children to recognize new words independently and accurately. In this connection she makes use first of clues inherent in four qualities of words, namely their meaning, form, structure, and sound. These sources of help in word perception are referred to as meaning clues, word-form clues, structural analysis, and phonetic analysis.

In developing competence in the use of these aids, four principles should be observed: (1) Pupils should identify the various understandings and skills needed in word attack through the guided study of different types of words that are learned first at sight. (2) On the basis of such experiences, pupils should derive the understandings, or generalizations, that will serve as safe guides in attacking new words. (3) The study of words should be continued as long as new clues to word perception continue to appear in the expanding reading vocabulary which the child encounters. (4) Guidance in the application of the basic facts and understandings thus acquired should be continued until a high level of competence in word attack is acquired.

The final step in equipping children to cope with new or unfamiliar words is training in the use of the dictionary—an art that has been grossly neglected in many schools in the past. Readiness for such training should be provided in the primary grades and systematic guidance in the intelligent and discriminating use of the dictionary should be given in the middle grades.

18. Classroom Help for Children with Beginning Reading Problems

A. STERL ARTLEY (1962)

For the sake of our discussion in this paper, we are placing children and youth with reading handicaps in categories depending on the nature and complexity of their problems.

In the first group are those whose reading problem is only one of a constellation of problems. Usually it is deep-seated, multi-causal, and multi-faceted. Related problems may be neurological, physical, sensory,

---

SOURCE: *The Reading Teacher*, XV (May, 1962), 439–442. Reprinted with the permission of A. Sterl Artley and the International Reading Association.

social, or emotional. Where facilities are available it is not uncommon for several specialists to become involved in both the diagnosis and remediation of the problem. Fortunately, in terms of the total number of retarded readers, the number of children in this group is relatively small.

A somewhat larger group is made up of children whose reading problem, though of varying degrees of severity, is unencumbered with the related problems found in the first classification, or at least stands out as the primary problem. Frequently these are children whose individual instructional needs have been unmet over a prolonged period. Not only has reading growth been at a virtual standstill, but family pressures and the effects of frustration have added complications. These children may be referred to a reading center or to a specially trained reading teacher for diagnosis. Remediation may be carried out in special classes or in summer remedial programs where the services of a specially trained remedial teacher are required.

Reading Difficulties Begin

A third group, a still larger one, is made up of children in the regular classroom who, in terms of specific skill areas, are failing to achieve as well as they should. These are children whose problem is just beginning and who will find themselves eventually in the second group, which we have just described, unless their needs are met through a planned program of instruction. These children and their problems are the responsibility of the regular classroom teacher. It is this group with whom we shall be concerned in this paper.

For the sake of clarification let us describe a few of the children comprising this group. Tom has completed his first grade readiness program but still shows limited ability to detect rhyming words and to indicate other words beginning with a given sound. Helen has been absent from school for a week with an illness and has missed the sequential instruction on several important reading skills. Mark fails to "catch on" to the application of an essential word attack skill. Jane has a persistent confusion between four groups of similar words. Pat runs roughshod over material he is reading orally, getting the meaning through context rather than through accurate recognition of words. Marie's oral reading is accurate, but her voice is high-pitched and she gives little thought to the interpretation of the story. Cathy is a fifth grade transfer pupil who is unable to use the dictionary to get the meaning or pronunciation of words.

One will observe that each child has a particular reading need—we can hardly call it a problem—which on the surface appears quite innocuous, or at the most only annoying. However, these innocuous difficulties have a way of combining and snowballing until we have a major problem which may require specialized services for both diagnosis and remediation. From our clinical experience we have found that the majority of cases referred for diagnosis are not those caused by some obscure emotional problem, an uncorrected visual defect, or an involved neurological problem. Basically, they are an accumulation of unmet reading needs.

Detecting Beginning Problems

To detect and diagnose these incipient problems is one of the primary responsibilities of the teacher. It is at this point that the prevention of major difficulties begins. She must be on constant watch for the child whose reading performance is alerting her to a possible problem.

One of the situations that lends itself to an assessment of needs is the directed reading lesson itself. In fact, every reading lesson should be a diagnostic lesson. It is here that the teacher may observe the application of skills that have been taught. Inability to recognize certain high-frequency words, to read for meaning, to use a familiar sight word to unlock an unknown one, to interpret implied ideas, or to apply a principle of syllabication are symptomatic of a lack of understanding or skill mastery. Both silent and oral reading situations will give the teacher clues to areas where instruction should be modified or adapted to particular children in the group.

Possibly one of the best diagnostic devices that the teacher has available is the practice or workbook. One of the functions of the workbook is to give the child opportunity to practice independently a particular learning or skill that has been taught in the directed reading lesson. Consequently, it will give the teacher an idea as to how effective that instruction has been and the kinds of additional help that a given child may need. If, on a fifteen-item page dealing with the short sounds of vowel letters, a child shows a preponderance of errors, the evidence is quite clear that additional teaching and practice are in order.

If the workbook is to be used to its maximum advantage, every page should be checked by the teacher or by a pupil-helper. If by the teacher, she may give needed reteaching help as the pages are being checked. If a pupil-helper checks the page from a key supplied by the teacher, only those items indicating incorrect responses need to be marked, so that in a free moment the teacher may note pupils who need more help.

The "unit" tests supplied by the publisher of the reading series are designed chiefly as diagnostic instruments. They give an objective measure of each child's readiness for the succeeding level and indicate areas where special guidance is needed. Administering and interpreting the test as recommended by its authors will give an indication regarding the effectiveness of the basic instruction and the adequacy of the day-by-day corrective help.

The personal reading record of each child may also be a means of indicating areas where special guidance is needed. Through individual and group discussions with the children the teacher will be able to get answers to questions such as these: What is the quality of the content being selected for personal reading? Has the child made the discovery that books and magazines are a source of information and pleasure? What is the quality of insight into the motives and behavior of story characters? What types of reactions does he freely make? What is the level of comprehension for main ideas and supporting details? Is the child being frustrated by persistent errors of word attack?

Providing Special Help

Assuming that the teacher is able to identify the specific problem, what action follows? With problems of the type we have been discussing the child seldom needs more than additional teaching or reteaching, directed specifically to the problem at hand. Tom, the boy who needed more work in ear training before introducing the sounds of initial consonants, can profit from activities similar to those that have been suggested in the guidebook of the readiness program. Jane, who was confusing groups of similar words, needs to be shown in one group at a time the features that differentiate one word from the other. This should be followed by practice sentences where the context calls for careful choices between the confused words.

Seldom will it be necessary to use reteaching techniques requiring special training. Excellent suggestions for reteaching and practice will be found in the teacher's manual. In addition, teaching activities and suggestions of materials that may be constructed for practice purposes may be found in such sources as Russell and Karp's *Reading Aids Through the Grades*; Durrell's *Improving Reading Instruction*; and Harris' *How to Increase Reading Ability*.

Pages from workbooks of other series dealing with the skill on which one is working may be used to good advantage in particular instances. If the problem is one of word attack, selected pages from prepared workbooks such as Meighan, Pratt, and Halvorsen's *Phonics We Use* may be useful. Frequently the guidebook to the reading series will suggest activities to be used with children with special needs.

Organizing Special Help Groups

The question of organizing the class or group for additional help is one to be considered. Time is precious to any teacher and she seems never to have enough to do all the things that need to be done. Yet this is not the problem that it appears to be if one organizes special "help" groups made up of those children who require more help. In fact, the meeting of individual needs through "help" groups will provide the opportunity for the teacher to do some of her most effective and rewarding teaching. These groups are made up of the children who evidence the same need; they are designed to deal only with one specific problem, and as soon as that problem is resolved the need for the group no longer exists. Hence, it is temporary in nature.

To be more specific, let us assume that in the directed reading lesson we find two children who need reteaching and additional practice in attacking words where the vowel digraph principle applies. These two children might be called aside for help at a time during the day when the other children are engaged in independent work. Quite possibly one, or at the most several, short sessions are all that will be necessary to help these children over their hurdle.

In many cases the teacher may find that the problem is one that the children may work on together without her direct supervision. For example, several of the children may be having trouble recalling certain sight words. After each child identifies those particular ones that give him trouble, either he or the teacher should write or type the words on halves of 3-by-5 index cards. Meeting in pairs, each child "flashes" to the other his trouble words.

In cases where a problem is more persistent the teacher may need to keep a special group intact over a longer period of time. This may be the case where several children have been absent or where transfers show the need for the development of a particular ability.

Summary

A high percentage of the reading problems that one finds in a typical classroom are a result of the failure of instruction to provide adequately for individual needs. Unless these problems are identified early and individual or small-group help provided, many of these children will experience serious retardation. The time to care most effectively for these cases is when the problem first appears, rather than later when special services may be required for diagnosis and remediation.

IV. Developmental Reading–Basic Skills

What are the basic reading skills? This is a question for which teachers have different answers. Yoakam (19) not only describes with authority and clarity those skills which he feels are basic but he also sets forth valuable suggestions for teaching them. Diagnosis, instruction, and correction based on individual needs are described as essentials in a reading program that would prevent reading disabilities from developing.

Although there is much criticism of the apparent over-dependence of teachers on basal readers for the teaching of basic skills, these books still enjoy wide popularity. One of the fundamental premises of basal reader series centers around systematic control of the sight words introduced. Because of this, the value of the study by Stone and Bartschi (20) becomes evident. They have evolved a list of words based on the five most widely used reading series together with two widely used word lists. The authors of the study do not advocate the teaching of any word list as such, but they do believe that their list constitutes a source that can be used for enrichment or remedial work when coordinated with texts used by pupils.

Vocabulary development is basic to all high-level reading skills. In a 1937 publication, *The Improvement of Reading,* Cole (21) described an ingenious approach to vocabulary development which was completely individualized in nature. Many teachers have found it a very effective method. Their enthusiastic reports substantiate Cole's statement that if a child employs the vocabulary approach she advocates, "His vocabulary will grow considerably faster than by any method of group instruction."

One of the earmarks of a mature reader is his independence in word-attack skills. Without this ability, it is difficult to build a sight vocabulary. How and when these important word-attack skills should be taught is treated with thoroughness by Artley (22).

Phonics! For many years, the most controversial aspect of word attack skill has centered around this subject. Because of its emphasis in the literature, several selections in this chapter are devoted to phonics. Hildreth (23) discusses some misconceptions concerning phonics, and Gates (24) tells how one phonic system—the Carden—affected the reading ability of intermediate-grade children.

A highly significant research study by Clymer (25) indicates that a number of phonic generalizations which we have regarded as sacrosanct for years may be of questionable value. In determining the value of 45 phonic principles (nine were devoted to syllabication), Clymer suggests a minimal level of utility no lower than 75 percent. What principles fail to meet this criterion of worth? How many of these principles do you emphasize in your teaching?

19. How to Cope with Deficiencies in Basic Reading Skills That Block Progress in Learning Activities

GERALD A. YOAKAM (1952)

That there are in basic reading skills serious deficiencies that block learning, especially at the middle-grade and high-school levels is widely recognized. How to cope with these deficiencies is, to a large extent, an unsolved problem. Many children could use reading in learning activi-

SOURCE: Gerald A. Yoakam, *Nature of, and Attack on, Reading Difficulties*, Supplementary Educational Monograph No. 76 (1952), pp. 70–74. Reprinted with the permission of the University of Chicago Press.

ties to greater advantage if it were not for their inability to use basic reading skills effectively. Even at the graduate-school level we find a considerable number of students who read less well than they could were they more effective in their use of basic reading skills.

The Problem Faced

At the root of the difficulty lies some uncertainty about what are basic reading skills and what are the special skills required to read materials of different kinds in an effort to master the facts, principles, and generalizations that constitute the content of reading matter which is intended to inform rather than to entertain. The practice of teaching children to read for general meaning, which has been so common in the past, made no provision for teaching them to read for study purposes and did not provide them with the basic reading skills required in many learning activities. While the situation is now improving through a recent return to systematic teaching of fundamental skills, there are still many persons who remain unconvinced that systematic, sequential development of basic reading skills is essential if the large majority of children are to learn to use reading as a tool for learning. Pupils are now found in the middle and upper grades who have reading difficulties resulting from a lack of systematic development of basic reading skills in the 1930's and early 1940's. This lack occurred because of a mistaken idea that children can learn to read without guidance, instruction, and practice.

In the opinion of the writer, we shall not learn to cope with deficiencies in basic skills that block progress in learning activities until all teachers learn to recognize the importance of basic reading skills and how they function in the reading process. Far too many teachers in the upper levels of our schools have had little or no training in teaching children to read and do not understand how reading ability develops with the maturation of the learner. Too many upper-grade and high-school teachers assume that the child *has learned to read* in the lower grades and that, if children cannot *read to learn* in the middle and upper grades, it is the fault of the teachers at the lower levels. They fail to realize that all teachers who use books in teaching must be teachers of reading if the children under their charge are to use reading as a tool for learning. They must learn to direct the reading of textbooks, reference books, encyclopedias, pamphlets, magazines, newspapers, and other informational materials if the child is to succeed in learning through reading. They must assume responsibility for teaching the new and strange concepts which appear in the content fields and must teach the child how to read for the purposes appropriate to the subject matter with which they are concerned.

Nature and Types of Basic Reading Skills

In order to understand our problem better, it seems necessary that we consider the nature of basic reading skills. Some teachers of basic reading are clear in their minds as to the meaning of the term *basic reading skills.* According to the dictionary, the word *basic* means fundamental. Basic reading skills are fundamental reading skills. But fundamental to what? They are fundamental to all reading of whatever kind. They are the common foundational skills which are used in all types and kinds of reading and without which the reader cannot read. Without these basic skills the child not only will fail to read for enjoyment but will fail to read to learn, which is ordinarily a more difficult matter. All teachers should be able to recognize the presence or the absence of the fundamental skills in the reading of each child and should realize the necessity of dealing with deficiencies in these fundamental skills when they are recognized.

It follows that every teacher should be able to identify basic reading skills. He should learn to recognize the common deficiencies in these skills which are found among inefficient readers. Time does not permit a complete analysis of all the basic reading skills in detail. We shall mention some of the common deficiencies and then attempt to suggest ways of coping with them. Among those that interfere with reading as a tool for learning are the following:

1. Lack of a stock of sight words which the child can recognize automatically without analysis. A reader cannot read fluently without an adequate stock of sight words.
2. Lack of independence in word recognition; inability to attack words that present difficulties, to identify them, to pronounce them, and to associate meaning with them.
3. Inability to use the context in acquiring new meanings and in identifying new words.
4. Lack of ability to recall and use past experience in making meaning out of material being read.
5. Lack of insight into the function of reading and inability to make sense out of printed material.
6. Lack of ability to conceive and accept purposes for reading and to enjoy the acquisition of ideas.
7. Inability to understand the differences between reading for information and reading for amusement and to understand the nature and purpose of historical narrative, expository, and descriptive materials, and the difference between fact and fiction.
8. Lack of ability to read for a variety of purposes and failure to adjust the reading rate and technique to different purposes.

9. Failure to acquire common study skills basic to all kinds of reading, such as ability to locate material; ability to get the main idea; ability to read for details; ability to answer questions; ability to solve problems; ability to evaluate, select, and organize, to outline, summarize, remember, report, and use ideas.

This brief review of deficiencies in basic reading skills is, of course, inadequate and merely suggestive, but many of the items constitute the deficiencies which most often interfere with the success of children in reading for learning. Unless these abilities can be developed among the great majority of children, there is little prospect that the use of reading as a tool for learning can be very much improved in the near future.

Methods of Improving Basic Reading Skills

Having attempted to identify the difficulty, let us now proceed to consider some suggestions on how to cope with it. I shall assume that many of my readers are teachers of the social studies, elementary science, health, and other subject matter, although certainly not by the traditional textbook procedure. Nevertheless, your pupils must read to learn, and you have problems due to their inability to do so. Recognizing that many children now in the middle grades and in junior and senior high schools cannot use basic reading skills effectively, what can you do about it? The suggestions which follow are, of necessity, stated briefly and somewhat dogmatically, but it is my hope that they may help teachers to cope better with the problem of improving the deficiencies in basic reading skills which block progress in learning:

1. Discover how well the children in your classes can or cannot read. Survey their reading abilities. Use analytical reading tests or informal objective tests of your own to locate areas of difficulty. Observe and note signs of difficulty with basic reading skills.

2. Determine the reading capacities of pupils. By the use of either group or individual intelligence tests, find the mental ages of the pupils. Determine whether their reading ages are below, equal to, or better than, their mental ages.

3. Locate those children who because of low capacity will always read at the lower levels.

4. Identify the children whose reading achievement is a year or more below their reading capacities. Note the areas in which they are weak. Give these pupils some remedial instruction aimed at their specific weaknesses.

5. Make a survey of your reading materials. Find the readability levels of your instructional materials. These will generally be above the average comprehension level of your pupils.

6. Search for materials relating to your units of work that have as wide a range of difficulty as the range of reading abilities in your group. Arrange these materials for the use of your pupils and guide them in their use. The use of one of the readability formulas will aid you in finding materials of suitable levels of difficulty. Such materials may be hard to find, but, if you can find them, you will be rewarded.

7. Assemble all the visual materials available that will aid in enriching the experiences of your pupils, teach them new meanings, and add to their understanding. Use such materials to enrich the children's listening vocabularies, develop new concepts, and arouse interest in reading for learning.

8. Use the materials of different levels of difficulty to adjust the reading task to the abilities of your pupils. Some children can read quite well at a fifth-grade level but falter and fail at a seventh-grade level. The intake of ideas must be adjusted to the child's rate of learning.

9. Develop a program of reading instruction based on the specific needs of the children. The purpose of the program should be developmental rather than remedial. Your object is to develop all the basic reading powers to the limits of the child's capacity to learn, not to bring all children to read at the same level of achievement—for the latter is an impossible task. It is possible to teach most children to read better, but it is not possible to teach them all to read at the same level.

10. When assigning reading to be done, direct and guide the children so that each child has a clear idea of what is to be done and how to do it. As a teacher of reading to learn, you are responsible for careful assignment of tasks and for instruction and guidance in how to perform each task. Most of the reading failures and much of the reading retardation that exists today could have been prevented if teachers had learned to take more care in directing the child's learning.

11. Develop new concepts basic to the understanding of new material in advance of their occurrence in material to be read by the child. Make sure that basic concepts are understood before leaving them. Utilize every possible aid to meaning to make the concepts known to the child, including verbal, aural, and visual aids as well as direct contact with processes, institutions, and events.

12. Attack specifically weaknesses in the basic skills of word recognition, or, if you are a teacher in a departmental set-up and do not have responsibility for developing the basic reading skills, confer with the basic reading teacher concerning the weaknesses you observe and arrange specific practice on those skills which are interfering with learning activities.

13. Try to develop insight into, and understanding of, the importance of reading to learn and seek to make such reading significant and

satisfying to the learner. Failure on the part of the child to make sense out of material which should contribute to learning activities leads to the careless, heedless reading often apparent in the curricular fields and to lack of effort on the part of the learner.

14. Abandon the idea of equal achievement by all and seek rather to develop in each child the ability to read as well as he is capable of reading. It is far better that a child read well on some level, even though it is below that of his group, than that he constantly experience frustration due to his inability to cope with material that is too difficult for him to read.

15. Realize that it is your responsibility to aid the child to learn to read for the purposes which are appropriate to the material in each curricular field. There are certain adjustments which children must learn to make to materials of different kinds; and, while as a teacher of basic reading skills, you should teach the child to read for the purposes common to the various fields, as a teacher of social studies you must aid him to read social-studies materials in ways appropriate to that area.

16. The fact, however, that you are a teacher of a special field not wholly responsible for basal reading skills, especially in the departmentalized work of the upper grades and high school does not excuse you from the responsibility of doing all you can to aid children who are deficient in the basic reading skills and do not have any other person to help them. The teacher in the subject areas should be familiar with the essential basic skills of reading and how they operate. At times, special individualized help and even small-group instruction should be given in basic skills, or in a skill that is interfering with a child's progress. As a teacher of social studies or science, you cannot simply shrug your shoulders and blame the teacher lower down in the grades for the shortcomings of the child. You must do what you can to help him when his learning is blocked because of the lack of some needed skill. By asking a child to read aloud the material of his field, you can often discover certain weaknesses in word recognition which can be overcome by appropriate suggestions, guidance, and practice. Deficiencies in basic reading skills must not be allowed to interfere with the child's learning through reading if it is possible by effective teaching to overcome the difficulty.

17. Always adjust the reading task to the ability of the pupils. In light of our knowledge of individual differences, the common assumption of many teachers that all middle- and upper-grade pupils and all high-school students can read and profit from the same textbook must be abandoned. This does not mean, however, that children should not be challenged by attempting to read materials which make heavy demands upon their powers of interpretation, but the task should be one

that is possible for the children to perform if they make the maximum effort. Attempting to have the children read with a maximum effort at all times, however, is unwise. Periods of maximum effort should be interspersed with periods of fluent reading, in which the ideas are achieved with comparative ease.

18. Do not expect that all children can make the same contribution to the unit of work. Let the more able children find, read, assimilate, organize, and report ideas that will enrich the experience of the less able and thus give them the satisfaction of sharing their ideas with others.

19. Observe and appraise the performance of children constantly. Discover weaknesses before they have had the effect of slowing down progress and killing interest. Remedy weaknesses as soon as they are discovered. Prevention of reading disabilities is far better than curing them after the child has experienced unhappiness and frustration caused by his inability to do what is expected of him.

20. A Basic Word List from Basal Readers

DAVID R. STONE and
VILDA BARTSCHI (1963)

Introduction

A review of the literature in the area of word lists for spelling and reading indicates a continuing interest over many years. The more widely used lists have included groups of several types and at several levels. This study is a logical follow-up of many of such studies. Since the basal texts are widely used, often in combination, a list based on "texts in use" gives the teacher a source to be used for enrichment or remedial work, which can be coordinated with any text list by simple checking. Both spelling and reading lists are useful for this purpose.

SOURCE: *Elementary English*, XL (April, 1963), 420–427. Reprinted with the permission of the National Council of Teachers of English and David R. Stone and Vilda Bartschi.

The Ayres (1915) list of 1,000 words was the first carefully comprehensive count of words used in adult writing. Buckingham (1918), Horn (1926), Gates (1935), and Dolch (1936, 1942) developed the basic vocabulary approach. Grade placement of 10,000 words was attempted by Buckingham and Dolch (1936). When checking text series for spelling vocabulary, Betts (1949) discovered little agreement beyond the first 2,000 words, with only limited agreement of about 25 percent in the early grades. A vocabulary survey of "texts in use" was seen in Hackett and Neeley (1936), Betts (1939), and Stone (1942).

Fitzgerald (1938) continued the "frequency" approach to the study of words in the writings of third graders. Thorndike's (1944) monumental study based on the frequency theory developed into *The Teacher's Word Book of 30,000 Words*. This was followed by Rinsland's (1945) list of over 14,000 words used most often in children's writings. The frequency approach was used by Dale and Chall (1948) as part of the procedure for determining readability. Studies in the last ten years have continued to include use of the frequency approach. Fitzgerald (1951) has a basic list of 450, and a list of 350 most useful spelling words. Knepp (1952) combined several frequency and text lists to develop a basic list. Kyte and Neel (1953) have a core vocabulary of around five hundred words. Greene's *The New Iowa Spelling Scale* (1954) gives a graded list of 5,507 words from grades 2–8. Durrell (1956) has a primary list and an intermediate list with reference to Thorndike and Dolch. Hildreth (1956) has a combined word list derived from Rinsland. Fry (1960) developed a useful list of remedial words.

It is clear, of course, that while lists have great supplemental value, they should not be taught as such. Rather they may be used as a core, around which to build meaningful experience. They also may be used to check progress in a program of study.

Procedure

This study was designed to develop a composite list, based on the words introduced in five of the most widely used basal reading series, together with the Dolch (1942) and Fry (1960) lists. The series used were Scott, Foresman and Company, Ginn and Company, Macmillan Company, Houghton Mifflin Company, and D.C. Heath and Company.

The total words introduced in each series, and the percents of the Dolch (1942) two thousand words for spelling in each series are shown in Table 1.

Table I shows that Heath introduces the most new words and Macmillan the least. More Dolch words are used in the Scott Foresman series, and least in the Heath.

TABLE 1. Results of Textbook Studies Comparing New Words and Words on the Dolch Two Thousand Word List in Five Textbook Series

New words	*Scott, Foresman*	*Ginn*	*Macmillan*	*Houghton Mifflin*	*Heath*
1st grade	335	354	235	315	432
2nd grade	544	449	349	531	578
3rd grade	899	682	758	804	873
Total	1778	1485	1342	1650	1883
Words on Dolch list					
1st grade	325	271	201	268	315
2nd grade	442	317	285	349	306
3rd grade	543	407	495	506	184
Total	1310	995	981	1123	805
	74%	67%	73%	68%	43%

Findings

The results are reported here in Table 2 in half-year intervals as 1^0, 1^1, 1^2, 2^1, 2^2, 3^1, and 3^2. Preprimer and primer work have been included in the 1st grade levels. The letter (a) refers to the first 110 Dolch basic words and (b) to the second 110. The (1) refers to the first 100 Fry instant words, and (2) to the second 100.

Each word in the list given below represents its mean grade level placement when all the above sources are considered. The list should tend to refine differences in text materials. It can be used as a basis for comparison with future "word use" studies and for research in phonetics and spelling. It can also serve as a source for enrichment words and remedial words.

TABLE 2. The Basal List

Pre-primer 1^0 word list

a (a) (1)	did (a) (1)	have (a) (1)	like (a) (1)	put (a) (1)	water
and (a) (1)	do (a) (1)	her (a) (1)	little (a) (1)	run (a) (2)	we (a) (1)
are (a) (1)	down (a) (1)	here (a) (1)	look (a) (2)	said (a) (1)	what (a) (1)
away (a) (2)	eat (a) (1)	him (a) (1)	make (a) (1)	the (a) (1)	where (b) (2)
be (a) (1)	for (a) (1)	his (a) (1)	my (a) (1)	then (b) (1)	who (a) (1)
big (a) (2)	fun	house (2)	no (a) (1)	this (a) (1)	will (a) (1)
boat	get (a) (1)	I (a) (1)	not (a) (1)	three (a) (1)	you (a) (1)
but (a) (1)	go (a) (1)	in (a) (1)	of (a) (1)	to (a) (1)	your (a) (1)
can (a) (1)	good (a) (1)	it (a) (1)	one (a) (1)	too (a) (2)	
come (a) (1)	has (a) (1)	know (a) (1)	play (a) (2)	two (a) (1)	

TABLE 2. The Basal List (*cont.*)

Primer 1^1 word list

about (b) (1)	cake	had (a) (1)	mother (2)	saw (a) (2)	they (b) (1)
after (a) (1)	call (a) (2)	he (a) (1)	night	see (a) (1)	time
all (a) (1)	came (a) (2)	hello	now (b)	she (a) (1)	toy
am (a) (2)	could (b) (2)	help (a)	of	so (a) (1)	tree (2)
an (a) (1)	day (1)	how (b) (1)	old (a) (1)	some (a) (1)	up (a) (1)
around (a)	find (b) (2)	hurry	on (a) (1)	stay	us (b) (1)
as (a) (1)	fly (a)	is (a) (1)	other (1)	stop (a)	very (b) (1)
baby	from (a) (1)	jump (a)	over (a) (2)	story	want (b) (2)
back (2)	front	let (b) (2)	pet	street	was (a) (1)
bag	funny (a)	man (1)	ran (a) (2)	take (b) (1)	way (2)
bed	give (a) (1)	may (a) (2)	red (a) (2)	that (a) (1)	went (a)
blue (a)	gone	me (a) (1)	ride (a)	them (b) (1)	when (b) (1)
by (a) (1)	green (a)	milk	sat	there (b) (1)	would (b) (1)
					yes (a)

First reader 1^2 word list

afraid	car	goat	name (2)	side	town
again (b) (1)	cat	got (b) (2)	never (b) (2)	sleep (b)	train
airplane	chair	gray	new (b) (1)	snow	truck
any (b) (1)	children	guess	noise	soon (a) (2)	under (a) (2)
ask (b)	city	heard	nose	stand (2)	wagon
at (a) (1)	cold (a)	hen	or (b) (1)	store	walk (b)
ate (b)	color (2)	hide	out (a) (1)	summer	well (b)
bad	cry	high (2)	please (b) (2)	sun	were (b) (1)
bake	dog	horse	pocket	surprise	wet
ball (2)	door	if (a) (1)	pretty (b) (2)	tell (b) (2)	white (b) (2)
basket	duck	into (a) (2)	pull (b)	than (2)	why (b) (2)
been (b) (1)	far (b)	just (b) (1)	puppy	thank (b)	window
before (b) (1)	fast (a)	laugh (b)	rain	their (b) (1)	with (a) (1)
began	father	light (b)	read (b) (2)	these (b) (2)	work (b) (1)
better (b) (2)	feet	long (b) (1)	ready	think (b) (2)	yellow (a)
black (a) (2)	five (a) (2)	lost	road	thought	
book	flew	more (2)	room	through	
boy (1)	four (b) (2)	morning (2)	sang	together (b)	
brown (a)	garden	much (b)	seen	tomorrow	
buy (a)	girl (2)	must (b) (1)	shall (b) (2)	took	

Reader 2^1 word list

above	animal	aunt	because (a) (2)	birthday	bread
almost	another (2)	balloon	behind	blew	breakfast
along	apart	bear	bell	both (a) (2)	bring (b) (2)
always (b)	apple	beautiful	best (a)	box (2)	bump

Reader 2^1 word list (cont.)

cage
care
carry (a)
catch
chicken
circus
clean (b)
climb
clothes
corn
corner
count
country
cow
cut (b)
dig
dinner
dish
does (b)
dress
each (2)
ear
earth
egg
elephant
else
end (2)
enough
even
ever
every (b)
eye
fall (b)
feed
fell
fence
field
fine
fire
first (b) (2)
fish
floor
flower
follow
food
found (b) (2)
friend (2)
full (b)
game
gave (b)
glad
goodbye
grass
ground
grow (b)
hair
hand (2)
happen
happy
hard
hat
head
hear
hill
hold (b)
hole
home (2)
hop
hot (b)
hungry
hurt (b)
keep (b)
kind (b)
kitchen
kitten
knew
last (2)
late
left (2)
letter
live (b) (2)
loud
low
made (b) (2)
many (b) (1)
men (2)
miss
money
monkey
most
mountain
mouth
music
nap
near (2)
need
nothing
off
once (b)
only (b) (2)
open (b) (2)
our (b) (1)
own (b) (2)
parade
party
pick (b)
place
plant
prize
push
quiet
rabbit
right (b) (2)
rode
roll
rooster
rope
round (b)
same
say (b) (2)
school (2)
sell
sheep
shoe
should (2)
show (b)
sit (b)
six (b)
smell
smile
sound
start (b)
step
still
stood
string
sudden
sure (2)
swim
table
talk
telephone
ten (a)
thing (2)
those (b)
tire
told
trick
uncle
until (2)
wait
warm (b)
watch
wave
which (b) (1)
while (2)
whistle
wind
wish (b) (2)
woman
wonderful
wood
yard
year (2)

Reader 2^2 word list

afternoon
against
air
alone
angry
apron
arm
band
bank
barn
belong
bird
bottom
bought
bright
brother
brought
build
burn
bus
busy
butter
buzz
cabbage
calf
cannot
cap
careful
caught
clown
coat
cook
cover
crawl
cup
dance
dark
dear (2)
deep
different
done (b)
drank
dream
drink (b)
drive
drop
drown
dry
early
earn
engine
face
family
farm
fat
feather
feel
fill
finish
flat
foot
forest
forget
fox
frog
frost
fruit
gate
glass
great
grew
hall
hammer
heavy
held
honey
ice
jar
joke
kept
lady
lamb
land
lay
leaves
leg
life
line
lion
listen

TABLE 2. The Basal List (*cont.*)

Reader 2^2 word list (*cont.*)

lock	paint	real	shore	strong	wall
lot	paper	remember	short	such (2)	wash (b)
luck	park	rest	shovel	supper	wear
lunch	path	ring	shut	swing	wheat
met	pen	river	sign	tail	wheel
middle	people (2)	rock	sing (b)	tall	whole
might	picnic	roof	sister	teacher	wide
mind	picture	row	sir	tent	wife
mine	piece	sad	sky	third	win
minute	pig	salt	slow	threw	wing
mouse	pleasant	sandwich	small (b)	throw	woke
move	point	sea	smart	tie	word
neck	policeman	second	soft	today (b)	wore
nest	pony	seem (2)	sorry	travel	world
nice	poor	send	spring	try (b)	write (b)
nine	present (2)	seven (b)	spot	turn	young
nut	purple	shadow	station	twin	
ocean	queer	shine	stick	use (b) (2)	
owl	quick	ship	stove	village	
pack	race	shook	straight	voice	

Reader 3^1 word list

ago	born	change	danger	farther	grandmother
already	bow	chase	deer	fasten	grocery
also (2)	bowl	cherry	desk	fed	gun
among	branch	chief	dirt	fellow	half
answer	brave	chimney	doll	felt	hang
automobile	break	chocolate	dollar	few	hay
bark	breath	choose	donkey	fifth	heart
bean	brick	chop	drag	finger	hit
beat	bridge	circle	draw (b)	fix	hope
bee	broom	clap	drove	flour	horn
begin	brush	clear	drug	forget	hose
believe	bug	close	drum	fourth	hour
below	bunch	cloth	dug	fresh	hundred
beside	bush	cloud	dust	garage	hung
between	button	course	duty	gentle	hunt
bicycle	cabin	cream	edge	giant	instead
bit	candy	cross	eight (b)	given	interest
bite	card	crow	empty	goes (b)	island
block	cart	crowd	fair	gold	its (a)
board	cave	curtain	fairy	goose	judge
body	cellar	daisy	farmer	grandfather	king

Reader 3^1 word list (cont.)

kite
knee
knife
knock
ladder
lake
large
lazy
leaf
lean
learn
leave (2)
led
lemonade
lie
lift
load
log
love
market
matter
maybe
meal
mean
meet
merry
mild
mile
mill
month
moon

mud
nail
neat
neighbor
nickel
none
north
notice
number
oak
o'clock
office
often
oil
orange
oven
paid
pail
part
pass
past
pasture
paw
pay
peach
peep
pencil
penny
perhaps
pie
pile

pillow
pink
pipe
plan
plenty
plow
pole
pond
porch
pot
potato
pour
promise
proud
queen
quite
radio
ranch
rang
reach
rent
ribbon
rich
ripe
root
rose
rubber
saddle
safe
sail
scare

scratch
scream
seed
sense
sent
set
several
sew
shell
shop
shoulder
sick
sidewalk
sight
silk
silly
silver
since
sled
slide
smoke
smooth
snap
soap
sold
son
song
soup
spend
spread
sprinkle

squirrel
stairs
steam
stir
stone
stool
storm
straw
stretch
stuck
sugar
suit
sunshine
suppose
sweet
taken
tar
taste
tear
tease
teeth
thick
ticket
tight
till
tin
tiny
tool
toward
trade
trap

trip
trouble
true
trunk
turkey
turtle
twelve
twenty
ugly
umbrella
upon (b) (2)
visit
wake
weather
week
whisper
wild
winter
wire
wise
without
wolf
women
won
wooden
yesterday
vet

Reader 3^2 word list

able
accident
ache
act
add
age
agree
ahead
aim
alike
alive

allow
amount
arithmetic
army
arrow
ashes
asleep
attic
awake
bacon
badly

banana
bare
baseball
basement
bath
battle
bay
bead
beast
beauty
became

beg
begun
behave
belt
bend
bent
berry
blame
blanket
blaze
blind

blossom
boil
bone
borrow
boss
bother
bottle
brake
brand
broad
broke

broken
brook
bucket
bud
buggy
built
bull
bullet
bundle
burst
bury

TABLE 2. The Basal List (*cont.*)

Reader 3[2] *word list* (*cont.*)

bushel
butcher
camel
camp
cane
cape
captain
capture
carpet
case
cash
cast
cattle
cause
cent
center
chain
chalk
chance
charm
cheek
cheer
cheese
child
chin
church
class
cloak
clock
closet
clover
club
coach
coal
coast
coffee
collar
colt
cool
copper
cord
cost
cotton
cousin
crack
crazy
creek
creep
crept
crop
crown
crumb
crust
cure
curl
damp
dangerous
dare
dead
delight
die
difference
dim
dime
ditch
doctor
double
dozen
drew
drift
dropped
during
east
easy
either
eleven
enjoy
enter
errand
evening
example
except
excuse
expect
explain
explore
fact
fail
faint
fancy
fault
fear
feast
fifteen
fifty
fight
figure
finally
fit
flag
flame
flight
float
flood
fold
folks
fond
fool
foolish
force
fork
form
forty
fourteen
frame
free
freight
froze
frozen
fur
furniture
gas
gather
geese
gift
glove
golden
grab
grand
grant
grapes
greet
growl
grown
hail
handkerchief
handle
harbor
harvest
hatch
hate
hawk
heat
heel
herd
hero
hid
hire
hoe
hog
hollow
hook
inch
inside
interesting
invite
iron
jail
jelly
job
join
jolly
joy
juice
kettle
key
kick
kill
knot
laid
lamp
language
lap
lately
lead
leader
leather
lend
less
lesson
lettuce
lick
lid
lightning
limb
limp
loaf
lose
lumber
lump
lying
mad
mail
main
manner
marble
march
mark
master
match
meant
measure
melt
mend
mice
mirror
moment
mule
naughty
needle
neither
net
noon
nor
note
notion
obey
odd
offer
onion
order
organ
ought
ourselves
page
pain
pair
palm
paste
pat
patch
peace
pearl
pepper
person
pin
pine
pitch
pitcher
plain
plane
plate
pleasure
pledge
poem
pool
post
pound
praise
prayer
press
price
print
problem
program
prove
pump
pumpkin

Reader 3^3 *word list* (*cont.*)

pure
puzzle
quarter
question
quilt
quit
radish
rag
rail
railroad
raise
rake
rat
rather
rattle
reason
receive
refuse
remainder
repeat
reply
report
respect
return
rice
rid
rob
robin
rotten
rub
rug
rule
sack
sailor
sale
saucer
save
scatter
scissors
scooter
scrip
season
seat
self
serve
settle
shade
shake
shape
share
sharp
shed
sheet
shelf
shirt
shoot
shot
silence
silent
single
sixteen
size
skate
skin
skip
skirt
slap
sleeve
sleigh
slept
slice
slip
slipper
slippery
snake
socks
soil
soldier
sore
south
space
spare
speed
spent
spider
spill
spoil
spoke
spoon
square
squeeze
stable
stack
stalk
stamp
star
stare
state
steal
steel
steep
steer
sting
stockings
stomach
strap
strawberry
stream
strike
struck
study
stuff
supply
sweep
swept
switch
tag
tame
tank
tea
team
tender
test
thief
thin
thirsty
though
thousand
throat
thumb
thunder
tied
timber
tip
toast
tongue
tonight
tooth
torn
towel
tramp
treat
trim
truly
tub
twice
understand
understood
unless
useful
usual
vacation
valentine
valley
view
vine
wade
waste
weak
weave
weed
weigh
welcome
west
whether
whip
whom
whose
wipe
witch
wonder
wool
woolen
worm
worn
worse
worth
wrap
wrong
yell

It will be noted that "basic" and "instant" words are nearly completed by the end of the first half of second grade.

Summary

This study was designed to fill the need of teachers who wonder how various basal series compared in grade placement of words in the first three grades. It provides a composite list based on the word-grade placement in the Dolch list, the Fry list, and these basal series: Scott, Foresman, Ginn, Macmillan, Houghton Mifflin, and Heath. These series have, of course, been based on a variety of use counts. The combination of series has provided the composite list given here.

The words were grouped into half-year levels, with the following distribution at each level: 1^0, 58; 1^1, 79; 1^2, 115; 2^1, 188; 2^2,206; 3^1, 308; 3^2, 505.

A comparison of any text series with the above list will provide information about useful words for enrichment or remedial work.

These kinds of lists should be studied to see if the principle of word attack could be better developed in sequence by rearranging the levels at which some of the words and word groups are first introduced.

Bibliography

Ayres, Leonard P., *A Measuring Scale For Ability in Spelling.* New York: The Russell Sage Foundation, 1915.

Betts, E. A., "A Study of the Vocabularies of First Grade Oral Readers," *Elementary English Review,* 1939, 16, 65–91.

Betts, E. A., *Grade Placement of Words In Eight Recent Spellers.* New York: American Book Company, 1949.

Buckingham, B. R., *Extension of the Ayres Scale.* Bloomington, Illinois: Public School Publishing Company, 1918.

Buckingham, B. R., and E. W. Dolch, *A Combined Word List.* Boston: Ginn and Company, 1936.

Dale, E., and Jeanne S. Chall, "A Formula for Predicting Reading Ability," *Educational Research Bulletin,* 27 (1948), 11–20.

Dolch, E. W., "A Basic Sight Vocabulary," *Elementary School Journal,* 36 (1936), 435.

Dolch, E. W., "Two Thousand Words for Spelling," *Better Spelling.* Champaign, Illinois: Garrard Press, 1942.

Durrell, Donald O., *Improving Reading Instruction.* New York: World Book Company, 1956, 363–366.

Fitzgerald, James A., "The Vocabulary and Spelling Errors of Third Grade Children's Life-Letters," *Elementary School Journal,* 38 (1938), 518–527.

Fry, E. B., "Three Hundred Instant Words," *Elementary English,* 37 (1960), 38–42.

Gates, A. I., *A Reading Vocabulary for the Primary Grades.* New York: Columbia University Press, 1935.

Greene, Harry A., *The New Iowa Spelling Scale,* Bureau of Educational Research and Service, State University of Iowa, Iowa City, Iowa, 1954.

Hackett, J. A., and N. C. Neeley, "The Vocabularies of Twenty-eight First Readers," *Elementary School Journal,* 37 (1937), 344–352.

Hildreth, Gertrude, *Teaching Spelling.* New York: Henry Holt and Company, 1956; "Vocabulary List," 311–342.

Horn, E. A., *A Basic Writing Vocabulary,* University of Iowa Monographs in Education, Series 1, No. 4, 1926.

Knepp, Helen, *Basic Vocabulary Phrases and Sentences for Early Reading Instruction.* Meadville, Pennsylvania: The Keystone View Company, 1952.

Kyte, C. C., and V. A. Neel, *A Core Vocabulary of Spelling Words.* Chicago: University of Chicago Press, 1953.

Rinsland, Henry, *A Basic Vocabulary of Elementary School Children.* New York: Macmillan, 1945.

Stone, Clarence, "A Vocabulary Study Based on 107 Primary Grade Books," *Elementary School Journal,* 42 (1942), 454–455.

Thorndike, E. L., *The Teachers' Wordbook of 30,000 Words,* Third Edition. New York: Bureau of Publications, Teachers College, Columbia University, 1944.

21. Methods of Teaching Vocabulary

LUELLA COLE (1938)

There are relatively few methods of developing vocabulary that are usable with an entire class. For the most part the work in this field is specific and individual. Class time can therefore be used to more purpose if it is spent in the study of different words by each pupil than by drill on the same words for all children.

Group Work

There is, in general, only one point in the procedure at which class instruction is really valuable and efficient. Before the pupils read a story or an assignment, the teacher should look through it and select from six to ten words that might give difficulty. She should present these words to the class and let the pupils study them. Even here, there is some wasted time because a few of the pupils already know the meanings and because there is no way of making certain that those who do not actually learn them. However, the amount of time spent is usually not large and enough learning takes place to pay for the investment of time and effort. At the end of a story, no two pupils will need drill on

---

SOURCE: Luella Cole, *The Improvement of Reading* (New York: Farrar and Rinehart, Inc., 1938), pp. 140–145.

the same words; the situation then calls for individual remedial work—not class instruction.

In the first and second grades of school the teacher can build vocabulary by the use of phonetic drill on word-families. Not every pupil in the room will learn every word, and many pupils will for some time recognize the words only when presented in families and not when a single word from a family is met in context. In the course of time, however, the children do acquire a greater vocabulary by means of such drill than they are likely to get without it. Class rather than individual drill is better when this work is first introduced because the children can help one another with the pronunciation.

In the third and fourth grades, drills in dividing words into syllables and in pronouncing the successive syllables are useful. In the fifth and sixth grades, a study of prefixes and suffixes will contribute to the building of vocabulary, since each prefix and suffix has its own meaning. In the sixth, seventh, and eighth grades, brief exercises in the use of the dictionary are helpful. The chief objection at the present time to such exercises is the fact that in many schools there is no dictionary appropriate for children. Where such a dictionary is available, these exercises—especially if arranged in the form of games—are beneficial in enlarging vocabulary, in training pupils in the actual use of the dictionary, and in building up a habit of using it for reference. These various types of drill will be described more fully in the next chapter, since they are equally valuable in remedial work.

The basic words to be taught are selected automatically for the teacher by the adoption of those books to be used by all pupils in a given grade or class. Any modern series of basic readers has already been checked against the *Teachers' Word Book*. The text in any class immediately determines the extent and content of the necessary vocabulary. Thus the teacher's main problem is not the selection of words. Instead, her chief tasks are, first, to distinguish the essential from the nonessential terms and, second, to make sure that each child learns every essential word. To attain these ends classroom instruction is only partially adequate. The teacher must rely in large measure upon individual training.

Individualized Work

It is not humanly possible for a teacher to be responsible for knowing at all times just which words each child in her class does not know. Yet the efficiency of her teaching depends essentially upon determining exactly this fact. To be sure, the size of the vocabulary for a class as a whole will increase at a moderate rate if the teacher simply presents two or three new words each day and trusts to luck that most of them will be remembered. A far larger vocabulary will, however, be acquired in less time if each child in the room concentrates exclusively on words he does not know. Mastery of vocabulary is a highly specific and individual matter. If one were to test a room of forty children, to determine each child's knowledge of a given 200 words, he would find that no two children had exactly identical vocabularies; it is entirely possible for each of two children in the room to know 79 terms out of the 200 and still not have one word in common. Word knowledge is so individual that no teacher can possibly keep in mind—or for that matter even discover—the exact degree of mastery achieved by each child for any selected number of words.

There is only one really efficient way of individualizing training in word study, and that is to have each pupil keep track of the words he does not know. The procedures involved are simple. The teacher first supplies each child with twenty-five or thirty slips of paper. If she can obtain 5″ by 3″ library cards and cut them in half, these small cards are better than paper slips because they can be handled more easily. She then instructs the pupils to copy each unknown word out of the books they read, writing one word on each card. The cards should be in readiness whenever the pupil is reading anything, no matter what the subject matter of the book may be. Since almost all the words thus recorded will be within a child's understanding as soon as they are pronounced, the teacher should let the pupils get together from time to time in groups of threes, in which each one shows the others the words he does not know. Most of the words that have been collected by all three will be recognized by one child or another. Any remaining words may be looked up in the dictionary if the children are old enough or handed to the teacher for her to explain. After the words are identified, each pupil goes through his own cards, saying each word he can remember over to himself. The cards containing those words he can now identify he puts in one pile; the words he cannot remember he puts in another. The three children in each group now pick up the cards containing words whose meaning they have forgotten and again identify these words for each other. Then each pupil reads through his own cards, once more arranging the words into two piles—those he now knows and those he has not yet learned. This procedure should continue until the pile of unknown words has disappeared.

The frequency of periods devoted to this individualized vocabulary drill should depend upon how rapidly the cards accumulate. Most children cannot handle more than twenty-five cards at once in this way. When the pupils have between twenty and thirty, the teacher should use the reading period for this drill. The cards used at one period are to be kept for a while and reviewed two or three times during the next month. When a pupil can go through a collection of cards easily, fluently, and accurately, he throws them away. Usually, one period a week of word study, carried on in this highly individualistic manner, will develop an adequate reading vocabulary for any intelligent child. In the first place, he knows which words to study. In the second place, he gets a chance to concentrate on those words and no others. In the third place, he is taught the meaning by his own classmates, who are always more effective motivators than an older person. And finally, he can see his own progress. If, for instance, he starts a week with seventeen unknown words and at the end of that time has learned fifteen of them, he knows he is progressing. Every week each child has as his objective the learning of the words he has collected, and at the end of each week he knows just how close to that objective he has come. As a matter of fact, most children will get out their packages of cards and run through them whenever they have a few minutes of leisure. This procedure seems to give them a sense of mastery and, as a consequence, a feeling of great personal satisfaction. Learning words ceases to be monotonous and becomes interesting. Of course, not every child learns every word he has thus selected, but even if he learns half of them his vocabulary will grow considerably faster than by any method of group construction.

It will be noticed that the responsibility both for selecting the words and for learning them is put upon the child rather than the teacher. Her job is to remind him of this responsibility from time to time, by providing him with cards, encouraging him to use them, and setting aside periods for study. She can also help him with definitions when no one in his group recognizes a given word. The responsibility, however, rests essentially on the pupil. This is exactly where it must rest, if vocabulary is to be acquired. No one else can tell a child which words in a story he does not know, but he can list them for himself. No one else can take the responsibility for finding out the meanings, because each child in a room of forty has a different list, and no teacher can teach forty lists simultaneously. Finally, no one can learn the words except the pupil himself. The whole business is thoroughly individualistic.

22. How and When Word Attack Skills Should Be Taught

A. STERL ARTLEY (1956)

Implicit in the title of this paper is the assumption that *word attack skills should be taught.* Concerning this point no one would disagree, regardless of his approach to reading instruction, for basic to interpretation is the ability to perceive the form and meaning of printed symbols. Sparks are struck and intense fires are kindled, however, when one faces the issues of *how* and *when* such word attack skills should be developed.

How Shall Word Attack Skills Be Developed?

Though various questions and problems arise with respect to word perception, the basic issue concerns itself with the psychological process involved in word attack. In brief, shall the approach be one of analyzing known words into their constituent elements which, in turn, the child uses to unlock words, or shall it be one of synthesizing word elements from prior knowledge of their auditory and visual characteristics?

The proponents of the analytic approach contend that their basic position is validated in the tenets of any of the recognized schools of psychology. Thorpe and Schmuller[1] attempt to assemble fundamental learning principles that embody the main features of most of the theories of learning. One of these principles lends direct support to the analytic approach to word attack. It is stated in these words, "Learning proceeds most effectively and tends to be most permanent when the learner is provided with the opportunity of perceiving meaningful relationships among the elements of the goal toward which he is working."[2] In the case of word attack, the "elements of the goal" are the phonic and visual components of the word. For effective learning the learner

[1] Louis P. Thorpe and Allen M. Schmuller. *Contemporary Theories of Learning,* Ch. XIII. New York: The Ronald Press Company, 1954.
[2] *Ibid.,* p. 455.

SOURCE: *Better Reading for Our Times,* I (1956), 75–79. Reprinted with the permission of A. Sterl Artley and the International Reading Association.

must see meaningful relationships among them, yet the constituent parts have meaning only in the context of a word. In the word *city*, for example, each letter bears a meaningful relation to each other letter, and each letter derives its sound value from its position in the word. *C* has the sound of *s* because it precedes *i*, *Y* has the sound of short *i* because it comes at the end of the word. *I* has the short sound because it is in a closed syllable.

For this reason, among others, the proponents of the analytic approach believe that an initial stock of sight words should be built up first. When a sufficient number of these known words follow a particular pattern, phonic or visual, they can be used to develop meaningfully and functionally generalizations or understandings about the way constituent parts function.

Anderson and Dearborn[3] in discussing the psychological rationale of the sight-word method as an approach to initial reading make use of several studies frequently overlooked. They point out that Cattell in 1885 and Erdmann and Dodge in 1898 showed that whereas only a few unrelated letters could be perceived in a given unit of time, familiar words containing two to four times as many letters could be perceived in the same time. The implication of these findings, Dearborn and Anderson point out, was that words efficiently perceived are not seen as a compounding of letters, but in terms of minimal cues or form. This being true, the authors believe that little is gained by teaching the child the letters and sounds as the first step in reading.

In other words, the proponents of the analytic approach contend that efficient reading, both in terms of rate and comprehension, results as the child learns from the outset to give attention to meaning units or word wholes rather than to visual or auditory constituents. Meaning, they insist, is pre-eminent, and nothing should be permitted to interfere with its rapid perception.

It is at this point that those who advocate a vigorous program in word attack before actually initiating reading instruction are most vocal in the defense of their approach. They argue that, although auditory and visual elements are taught before reading is initiated and phonic and structural generalizations are taught deductively rather than inductively from known sight words, this is done to give the young reader control over words he meets and thus is an aid to comprehension.

Whatever force of logic this contention may have, research is not too clear in confirming it. For evidence we can go to the well-known studies

[3] Irving H. Anderson and Walter F. Dearborn. *The Psychology of Teaching Reading*, p. 212f. New York: The Ronald Press Company, 1952.

of Tate,[4] and Agnew,[5] and others. These studies have been reviewed frequently in the literature within the last year, and for the sake of conserving time and space they will not be discussed in detail here. These studies compared approaches to reading emphasizing a strong beginning word attack program (in both cases a phonic approach) with programs stressing a functional and integrated program. They showed the superiority of the students taught through phonics to pronounce unfamiliar words. But though more accurate in word attack they were far less fluent in reading, and they comprehended less well.

In other words, it appears that if one puts emphasis on word attack before the getting of meaning is firmly established, the result will be efficient word attack, but at the expense of meaning—the main purpose of reading. In a sense, in reading like everything else, we get what we want and pay for. If the sole aim of reading instruction is word perception, then a program that gives vigorous attention to structural and phonic elements will give just that. If, on the other hand, the goal is total reading growth with primary emphasis on meaning and interpretation, then the program will need to be one where word attack is closely integrated with other aspects of the program.

In contrast to studies showing the limitations of a program that puts stress too early on word analysis techniques is the more recent one done in Champaign, Illinois, and reported by Henderson.[6] This study, carried out over a three-year period, compares the reading progress of children taught by a program emphasizing a synthetic approach to phonics with children taught in the "traditional manner." The results of this study in grades one, two, and three were consistently in favor of the phonetic groups as measured by standardized tests of word recognition, comprehension, and work-study skills.

It is unfortunate that this study did not clearly differentiate the variable of method from the context of the instructional situation which included the teachers, their enthusiasm for a new approach, and the amount of time spent in planning and organizing the daily work. Consequently, it is extremely difficult to assess the validity of the data presented. In fact, the results of the phonetic approach as reported in grade three are so nearly similar to those reported in a study completed four years prior in the same school system with an integrated approach to

[4] Harry L. Tate. "The Influence of Phonics on Silent Reading in Grade I," *Elementary School Journal*, XXXVII (June, 1937), 752–63.

[5] Donald Agnew. *The Effect of Varied Amounts of Phonetic Training on Primary Reading*, Duke University Research Studies in Education, No. 5. Durham, N. C.: Duke University Press, 1939.

[6] Margaret Henderson. *Progress Report of Reading Study 1952–1955*. Community Unit School District No. 4, Champaign County, Illinois, undated.

word perception that no clear evidence can be found for the superiority of the experimental procedure.

Somewhat closely related to the principle of patterned learning is the principle of motivation which is offered as a validation for the practice of initiating the reading program with *reading* rather than with a program of word analysis. The importance of motivation as a basis for learning is supported by all schools of psychology. The principle is stated by Thorpe and Schmuller in the following words, "Learning proceeds most effectively and tends to be most permanent when the learner is motivated, that is, when he has a stake, as it were, in the activity being undertaken."[7] In lay terms we might rephrase the principle and say that learning proceeds most effectively when the learner sees a close relationship between what he is learning and some felt need or interest.

Those who would advocate the sight-word approach to initial reading stress the close relation of this approach to the principle of motivation. The young child comes to the first grade with the desire to learn to read. To capitalize on this built-in mainspring-to-action, the child needs to begin the reading process through interesting story content rather than through drill on what to him are rote and nonsense elements. Flesch,[8] for example, advocates that first graders analyze some 700 words before reading begins. He proposes a complex synthetic procedure of compounding words through a sequence of learning the names of the letters, the short sounds of the vowels, sounds of consonants, the long sounds of the vowels, and finally the common phonograms. The children are then expected to translate sounds into words which they recite as wholes. Page after page of rote drill material is presented which the children are supposed to digest *before any reading is done.*

Though other synthetic programs differ from this radical approach in the amount of drill material presented and in the technique of presenting it, the basic design is the same—withhold reading until children are able to attack words independently; only then proceed to meaningful reading. It is hard to reconcile this approach to reading with the principle of motivation, for it would be extremely difficult for the child to see any need for or interest in vowels, consonants, diphthongs, and syllables apart from their need in reading. On the contrary, negative attitudes may be built up in the initial stages of reading that condition future progress.

Another recognized educational principle conditioning the word attack program is that learning proceeds most effectively when the learn-

[7] Thorpe and Schmuller, *op. cit.*, p. 451.
[8] Rudolf Flesch, *Why Johnny Can't Read and What You Can Do About It.* New York: Harper and Brothers, 1955.

er's individual method of learning is recognized and utilized. Some children respond better to auditory instruction, others to visual, still others to kinesthetic.

In an effort to determine the teaching method or combination of methods most effective in teaching word perception to various types of individuals, Mills[9] experimented with groups of children taught by a visual, phonic, kinesthetic, and a combination approach. Mills' findings show conclusively that children do learn to recognize words by different methods, and that no one method is superior for all children. For children of low intelligence the phonic method was least effective; for those of average intelligence the kinesthetic method was least effective, while the phonic method showed no statistical significance in either direction. For the superior learner the relative effectiveness of the four approaches was not clearly drawn because these children learned words regardless of the method used. Certainly this study argues strongly for a word attack program that stresses growth in a variety of perception techniques —structural analysis, phonics, word-form analysis, as well as kinesthetic techniques for those who require them.

In the light of the foregoing principles it would appear that the essential features of a sound word attack program would make provision for the following: (1) An adequate balance between word perception and meaning. (2) The development of an initial stock of basic sight words before word analysis is undertaken. (3) The use of an analytic approach to word perception. (4) The development of a variety of word attack techniques.

Of the studies that might be quoted showing the implementation of these principles, only one will be mentioned.

A recently completed study by McDowell[10] compares an extreme phonetic approach with a balanced reading program having a varied word attack program closely integrated with the reading itself. The progress made by pupils having a strictly phonetic program was compared with that of pupils of similar mental ability in classes having the broader reading program. McDowell reports on the basis of standardized test results that the group following the integrated program "reads faster, understands words, comprehends paragraphs, uses the index, and, in general, reads better than the phonetic group." The phonetic group was better in alphabetizing and spelling, the latter having been stressed vigorously from the beginning. In general, he says the children using

[9] Robert E. Mills. "An Evaluation of Techniques for Teaching Word Recognition," *Elementary School Journal,* LVI (January, 1956), 221–25.

[10] Reverend John B. McDowell, "A Report on the Phonetic Method of Teaching Children to Read," *The Catholic Educational Review,* LI (October, 1953), 506–19.

the broader program revealed "a more rounded and harmonious development of reading skills" with nothing sacrificed. Continuing his cogent argument for a balanced reading program, McDowell writes: "Phonics can also serve its purpose in reading as one of the subsidiary word-attack skills. But to overemphasize it is to deny the child many other such skills and to submerge meaning under a barrage of mechanics."[11]

McDowell's study objectifies what reading people have been saying since the publication in 1925 of the Twenty-Fourth Yearbook of the National Society for the Study of Education—that the real danger of an isolated word attack program, be it phonics, word-form, analysis of structure, or whatever, is in over-inflating its importance at the expense of meaning and interpretation, or as McDowell says, submerging "meaning under a barrage of mechanics." As evidenced by this study, word attack skills should be developed within the context of a broad and inclusive reading program that ensures sequential development of all aspects of reading—word perception, comprehension, reaction, and integration.

When Shall Word Attack Abilities Be Developed?

Having considered the *how* of a sound word attack program, the *when* falls into pattern with little difficulty. Perhaps these generalizations will serve as guiding principles:

1. Though use of various types of meaning clues begins at the time reading is initiated, procedures that depend on the analysis of words into either their structural or auditory components should not be undertaken until the child has built up an initial stock of sight words.
2. Analytic procedures (phonics, word-form, structure) should not be initiated until the child has sufficient mental maturity and background of understandings to make instruction meaningful and profitable.
3. Word attack skills should not be developed until a need or readiness for such skills becomes apparent to the learner.

Much of the objective evidence for these generalizations may be found in the studies to which reference has already been made. However, to be more specific several additional studies will be quoted.

The first study to supply evidence as to the proper timing of the word attack program is the almost classic study of Dolch and Bloomster[12] in 1937. To first- and second-grade children tests were given requiring the application of phonic knowledge. The results were then analyzed in terms of the mental ages of the subjects. The authors found that the

[11] *Ibid.*, p. 518.
[12] E. W. Dolch and Maurine Blooster, "Phonic Readiness," *Elementary School Journal*, XXXVIII (November, 1937), 201–205.

mental maturity needed to apply phonic understandings was greater than that needed to acquire sight words. In fact, a mental age of seven seemed to be a prerequisite for achievement in the type of phonic activity involved. However, as others have suggested, this finding does not preclude ear- and eye-training activities on the readiness level.

Other researchers have confirmed Dolch and Bloomster's findings. Sexton and Herron[13] found that the teaching of phonics appears to be of limited value with beginners during the first five months of school. It begins to be of some value during the second five months, and has particular value in the second grade. Consistent findings were also reported by Garrison and Heard.[14]

Assuming the validity of these studies, evidence is relatively clear that the initial stage of reading should concern itself with building phonic readiness and developing a basic stock of sight words, with serious work in phonics, as one method of word attack, coming only as the children are equipped with understandings and maturity to make instruction profitable.

Numerous writers who concern themselves with readiness for initial reading—Monroe, Hildreth, Durrell, Betts, and others—have pointed out the kinds of readiness, both auditory and visual, that equip the child to undertake word analysis. Harris[15] points out that the important aspects of phonic readiness consist of such abilities as hearing differences between words that are alike, being sensitive to rhyming elements, and fusing sounds mentally to form a word.

Moreover, as children enter the second grade and as they progress to new content in social studies, numbers, science, and literature, they will have occasion to meet more and more unfamiliar words. These words create word attack needs involving the use of phonic principles, syllables, prefixes, suffixes, accent, and the like. Understandings and skills involving their use may now be developed functionally and with a minimum of practice *because the need is apparent to the learner.* Although research data are meager on this aspect of the problem, principles in the psychology of learning supply the force of logic to this contention.

[13] Elmer K. Sexton and John S. Herron, "The Newark Phonics Experiment," *Elementary School Journal,* XXVIII (May, 1928), 690–701.
[14] S. C. Garrison and Minnie Taylor Heard, "An Experimental Study of the Value of Phonetics," *Peabody Journal of Education,* IX (July, 1931), 9–14.
[15] Albert J. Harris, *How to Increase Reading Ability,* p. 294. New York: Longmans, Green and Co., 1947.

23. Some Misconceptions Concerning Phonics

GERTRUDE HILDRETH (1957)

Recent controversies over methods of teaching reading indicate that misconceptions concerning phonics and methods of teaching sounding are fairly common. Here are some of the fallacious ideas *commonly* expressed in publications as well as in discussions of reading instruction:

1. Sounding is primarily a process of learning a number of letter elements and letter groups, and then blending these to pronounce words.
2. Teaching words as wholes requires memorization of thousands of separate, unrelated items.
3. Sounding is auditory and the "word method" is visual.
4. The only role of phonics for reading is in building skill for word attack.
5. The chief use of sounding is for oral reading.
6. When a pupil has learned to sound out words, he has mastered the reading trick.
7. Extensive drill on phonics will shorten the time required for learning to read.

Each of these erroneous ideas will be discussed in the following sections.

1. A common fallacy is the assumption that sounding for beginning reading is nothing more than a process of learning the sounds corresponding to separate letters and letter groups, a hundred or more phonograms, then blending these elements to form words. This was the time-honored method beginning with the introduction of the alphabet in ancient times, down through Noah Webster's day and even beyond.

Any words were used for practice in applying sounding and blending, so long as they gave training in pronunciation. This drill was supposed to equip children for reading anything. But methods of learning sound-

---

SOURCE: *Elementary English*, XXXIV (January, 1957), 26–29. Reprinted with the permission of the National Council of Teachers of English and Gertrude Hildreth.

ing for application in reading have changed. Since about 1925 in American schools the older methods of learning sounding for application in reading have changed. The older method of learning phonics by a synthetic process has given way to a more effective method which begins with common words the children understand and enjoy using. The more common sounds that recur in words are first met within the framework of the total word; then through a generalizing process the children learn to identify common recurring sounds in unfamiliar words met in reading. For example, the short *i* sound is first met *within* common words the child already knows and pronounces, e.g., *winter, wings,* or *win.* The long *i* sound might be met first in such words as *ride, slide,* or *hide.* The *ch* phonogram is first learned in familiar words such as *child, chase,* or *choose,* as well as in *watch, catch,* etc.

This intrinsic method of learning sounding becomes an integral part of learning to read instead of a separate skill which may fail in application when the pupil meets an unfamiliar word, or which may later have to be retaught as a skill for reading. The analytic method avoids blending problems, the chief stumbling block with other methods. The older concept of sounding persists in the popular mind because starting with the smallest elements seems more logical than the more subtle process of learning the elements through first becoming familiar with word wholes.

A chief advantage of intrinsic, whole-word sounding is that the process is fully meaningful to the pupils. One child who was drilled on sounds ahead of words kept asking his teacher, "Why must I do it?"

2. The impression is widespread that the "word method" of teaching reading requires the learning of thousands of isolated, unrelated graphic word forms, and that learning words as wholes is like learning Chinese symbols, a sheer memory task. The fact that at maximum maturity the reader may know as many as 20 or 25 thousand words does not mean that he has built up this word bank through isolated drill on each word.

English is a phonetic language, even though it's inconsistent to a considerable degree. Similar letter groups and syllables recur from word to word. The stock in trade of English word structure actually consists of some 800 roots, with the principal roots fewer than 500. It is difficult to find in English any common words, or uncommon ones either, that are not related, e.g., *story, stay, sorry, tray, store, tore,* etc. Other words are even more closely related, e.g., *play, played, plays, playing, playmate, player, playground.* Must each of these seven words be learned as a separate, brand-new item?

These interrelationships among common words, both structurally and phonetically, make possible generalizations about sounds in words which save the pupils from the task of memorizing thousands of words as separate items. A child would be dull, indeed, who would not sense by the time he is seven or so the fact that such words as *each*, *reach*, and *peach* both look and sound alike in some respect; or that there are two "B" sounds and two "R" sounds in the child's name *Barbara*. The brighter children make these generalizations from nursery days.

The teaching of reading in all good schools today takes advantage of these structural and phonetic relationships among words from the time the children themselves show that they are ready to generalize about recurring parts and sounds in words.

3. The critics charge that in the "visual" method the sounds of the words are by-passed. They contend that sounding is auditory; the word method is visual. Common sense alone suggests that all work with words in reading is, *ipso facto*, visual unless one is blind, in which case the tactile sense predominates. How can a child match the letters and letter groups with the sounds that represent them unless he looks intently at the print? As a matter of fact, mature sounding in reading is primarily visual—seeing the sounds in words with only a slight subvocal trace remaining, a sort of vocal echo.

Is the whole word method wholly visual? It cannot be unless the children are deaf. This would suggest that by some magic trick the child is prevented from using his ears during reading lessons. The clang associations between the words the child speaks and hears form the strongest associative link in learning to identify graphic word forms. No thoughtful teacher disregards the aural-oral associations even when showing a child a word such as *puppy* accompanied by a lively picture of the animal. Young children who possess the powers of speech will say "puppy" on sight of the familiar word or whisper it to themselves. Even in so-called silent methods children do extensive articulating because they need the oral crutch. In short, both sounding and the so-called word method are multisensory.

Said Tony's teacher, "We used tracing in his case and by-passed the usual visual and auditory associations." If true, poor Tony was obviously both deaf and blind! Even the educational research workers have made similar fallacious statements when they set out to evaluate the respective merits of the *visual*, the *auditory*, and the *kinaesthetic* method of teaching reading.

4. The justification for teaching phonics is that the skill provides the pupils with a tool for word attack. No one questions this fact; the fallacy lies in assuming that this is the only objective in teaching sounding. Phonics plays another great role in learning to read. Surprising as it seems, phonics is a direct route to building up the stock of words in-

stantly recognized at sight. Every experience in "sounding through" a word makes it more likely that the word will be retained in mind and later recalled by slight clues, visual and oral. The majority of our "sight" words, a full 20 to 25 thousand in the case of the typical adult, are undoubtedly learned in this way, e.g. *memory, electric, abolition, moisture, characteristic, skeleton,* etc. Phonics then is an aid in learning to read. Point 4 should probably be listed as a half-truth rather than a fallacy.

5. The impression is widespread that phonics plays a chief role in oral reading, especially when the context contains new polysyllabic terms, but that sounding plays only a subordinate role in silent reading. On the contrary, the upper elementary grade pupil makes most use of sounding in silent reading, because this is the commonest form of reading beyond the primary period. Sounding is employed constantly by the young reader as soon as he reaches the stage of minimum literacy in order to handle the mushrooming vocabulary in textbooks and other reading materials he uses independently. As pointed out in 3 above, "Silent sounding" rather than fully articulated sounding is the rule in advanced stages, and sounding is reduced to partial clues employed in conjunction with context meaning clues, e.g. *groceries, villain,* etc.

6. Learning to read is assumed to be nothing more than naming letters or learning to pronounce words. As someone put it during the heat of the recent controversy over reading methods, "They can read, even if they don't know what they're reading." A student teacher naïvely inquired, "If you teach reading by phonics, you don't have to bother with meanings, do you?" This sort of comment suggests that reading is a mechanical process of naming words.

Here's a seven-year-old who can pronounce *prevention* and *elucidate,* even *gubernatorial,* but can he read the words, that is, grasp the meaning of these words in context? Not unless the child is the modern counterpart of John Stuart Mill. If the child has learned to sound out words he already knows orally, he can catch the meaning, but this is still far from mastery of the complex skills required in mature reading.

Reading is not a matter of naming one word after another, but of inferring ideas from interrelationships of words in groups. Sounding in context reading does not mean pronouncing each word separately but grasping meanings swiftly through a combination of clues as the eyes sweep over the lines. This combination of sounding and the use of context clues provides the pupils with a double-edged tool for independence in word recognition.

7. Extensive drill on sounding will not shorten the process of learning to read, at least for typical learners, both because learning to read consists of more than sounding words as indicated in point 6 above, and

because learning to use sounding in reading can proceed no faster than total mastery of all the complex skills that make up the reading process.

Learning to read normally requires a period of three to four years even for minimum-level attainments, both because of the complexity of the process, and also because learning to read is dependent, in turn, upon the child's emerging intelligence, his growth in linguistic skills, and new insights gained from common experiences.

Learning the sounding trick for reading is a developmental process allied with, and dependent upon, all the other components of the total reading process. Sounding in reading is a subtle and complex process in itself. Maturity in sounding requires the ability to identify the familiar sounds in new words quickly with minimum vocalization, and to use partial sounding deftly and swiftly in conjunction with context clues. By any system, sounding in reading is perfected only through steady practice during a period of several years.

How can these misconceptions, so widely held even among teachers and educators, be corrected? Only through the concerted effort of leaders who understand the rationale of modern methods; through giving demonstrations, conducting new research studies having functional application to classroom teaching, and through the publication of the findings in terms that are comprehensible to teachers and parents.

24. Results of Teaching a System of Phonics

ARTHUR I. GATES (1961)

This article reports the results of a study of the reading abilities of third-, fourth-, and fifth-grade pupils in a community in which the Carden system of phonics has been used for many years.

We shall use the term phonics to mean any procedure or technique of translating parts (letters, digraphs, etc.) of visible words into sounds and using the sound to work out the recognition and pronunciation of

SOURCE: *The Reading Teacher*, March, 1961, pp. 248–252. Reprinted with the permission of Arthur I. Gates and the International Reading Association.

a word. In this sense some form of phonic training has been employed in American schools for more than a century and is still provided in practically all of them. The methods of developing independent skills in word recognition adopted by most investigators of the teaching of reading during the last quarter century take account of the fact that children, from the beginning, can recognize words as easily as they can recognize letters. Starting children right off to read rather than to labor with letters and letter sounds is believed to be more satisfying and to provide more direction and purpose to teaching the use of phonic and other clues to word recognition, usually introduced soon after the beginning of reading.

Another type of phonics program, first introduced into American schools more than a century ago, began with drill in recognizing and variously manipulating parts of words, usually letters and letter sounds, before words were recognized and read for meaning. In some systems extensive drill on the sounds of isolated letters (singly or in combinations) paralleled meaningful reading of words. In either plan, this type of teaching was based on a formidable program of drill on the sounds of letters and letter combinations organized into some kind of "system" of phonics which was introduced at the beginning of instruction in reading and usually continued through several elementary school grades.

This general type of phonics has been recently championed by several persons, most conspicuously and confidently by a journalist and a college teacher of English. The Carden system is one of the many methods of this type. It begins with drills in naming and sounding the consonants and naming but not sounding the vowels. Later the long sounds of vowels are introduced, followed by the short vowel sounds. Then the consonant blends and an extensive array of other word parts are taught. In the second grade the system introduces a long list of phonic rules along with drill and other efforts to rationalize a host of letter-sound combinations. In the third grade this type of drill tapers off, but it remains as a heavy program of formal phonics through the eighth grade. This system is a very elaborate one, similar in many respects to the Hay-Wingo and other plans of the type popular before and during the period of the Model-T Ford.[1]

Terman and Walcutt[2] state that the Carden system is "flourishing today in a score or two of schools in Long Island, New Jersey, and New York, producing results . . . that far surpass those of ordinary schools,

[1] Julie Hay and Charles E. Wingo, *Reading With Phonics*. (Chicago: Lippincott, 1954, Revised.)

[2] Sibyl Terman and Charles C. Walcutt, *Reading Chaos and Cure*. (New York: McGraw-Hill, 1958), pp. 139–142.

its teachers so enthusiastic that they declare they would resign rather than use another method. . . ." Miss Carden "insists on personally supervising [the] installation [of her system] and training the teachers in any town that adopts it." These writers appear to rate the Carden system as best or at least one of the best of its kind.

This present study involved an analysis of the following data obtained for the pupils in the third-, fourth-, and fifth-grade classes in each of the four schools in a community near New York City:

1. The reading grades of each child in the tests of (a) reading speed, (b) reading vocabulary, and (c) reading comprehension comprising the Gates Reading Survey, and total reading score obtained by combining the three tests.

2. The mental age and intelligence quotient (I.Q.), based on the California Mental Maturity Tests in a majority of cases, and on the S.R.A., the Otis, and other tests in the remainder. The intelligence tests were given at different times over a period of four years.

3. The number of school years during which the child had received instruction by the Carden method, which was taught in the kindergarten and throughout the elementary school. The amount received by each child could therefore vary from a maximum of six years to a minimum of zero years, the latter mainly in the case of transfers from other schools where they were not given Carden training. (The teachers were given considerable freedom to decide whether to give the Carden type of instruction to pupils entering the school in the second or a later grade.)

The Gates tests were given in June 1958, and all other data were computed to that date.

Table 1 shows the actual grade positions and the average reading grades as of June 1958 of those pupils who had received one year or more of instruction in the Carden system.

These data make the Carden system look good; in all three grades the pupils raised on Carden instruction are about a full year ahead of their grade in reading ability. But before we join Terman and Walcutt

TABLE 1. Comparison of Grade Positions and Reading Grades

	N	*Av. No. Years Carden*	*Grade Position*	*Av. Read. Grade*	*Diff.*
Grade 3	91	2.85	3.9	4.86	0.96
Grade 4	80	3.33	4.9	5.97	1.07
Grade 5	72	3.42	5.9	6.88	0.98

in giving unqualified praise to this method, let us take a look at the intellectual level of these children. The average mental ages, converted into mental grades, are shown in Table 2.

In all three grades the average reading grade falls below the mental grade. These children, taught by the Carden method, are not reading quite up to their mental level; they read slightly less well than do children of the same age and intelligence (or scholastic aptitude) in the average American public school. In other words, the A.Q. (Accomplishment Quotient) is less than one hundred.

TABLE 2. Comparison of Mental Grades and Reading Grades

	N	*Mental Grade*	*Read. Grade*	*Diff.*	A.Q.*
Grade 3	91	5.30	4.86	0.44	.92
Grade 4	80	6.10	5.97	0.13	.97
Grade 5	72	7.00	6.88	0.12	.98

* Reading Grade divided by Mental Grade often called the "Accomplishment Quotient."

In this school the Carden reading program certainly did not achieve "such success as to bring tears of pride"[3] to the cheeks of teachers and parents. For a decade the teachers in this school had given the Carden system a fair and competent trial, but the majority gradually came to believe that it was unsatisfactory. One teacher said, "We realized for a long time that our children were not reading as well as youngsters of their intelligence should. The tremendously heavy program of sounding and pronouncing words and drill on rules in the first two grades seems to take the life out of reading for many children. We tried hard to build up new zest for reading in later grades, but many children just never came quite alive again." Instead of "resigning rather than using another method," the teachers in this school requested that the Carden system be replaced by another program. The Carden system was dropped at the end of the 1959–60 school year.[4]

Further analyses of the data were made for several reasons, mainly to determine whether the quantity of Carden training (the number of years devoted to it) bore any relationship to reading achievement. If

[3] Terman and Walcutt, *op. cit.*, p. 142.

[4] Lest someone assume that the writer of this paper or the findings presented in it had something to do with this change, the author wishes to state that neither had any influence whatsoever. The results of the study were not even known to him until September 1960, and he had had no communication and no personal contact with anyone in these schools concerning the Carden or any other reading method until many months after the Carden system had been dropped.

such a relationship did exist, it would be shown by the coefficients of correlation between the two variables.

Intercorrelations of all the variables listed above were computed separately for (1) the entire population of 267 pupils, (2) the 91 pupils in grade 3, (3) the 89 pupils in grade 4, (4) the 87 pupils in grade 5, and those in each of the twelve classes—a total of sixteen intercorrelation tables. All the analyses pointed to the same general conclusions which are indicated in Table 3. This table includes the relevant parts of the table of intercorrelations computed for the total group of 267 pupils.[5]

TABLE 3. Intercorrelations in a Group of 267 Pupils from Grades 3, 4, and 5

Variables	*Carden Method*	*M.A.*	*Reading Speed*	*Reading Vocab.*	*Reading Comp.*	*Total Reading*
Amount Carden Instruction	—	0.02	0.04	0.03	0.03	0.04
Mental Age	0.02	—	0.63	0.62	0.62	0.68
Reading Speed	0.04	0.63	—	0.71	0.72	0.88
Reading Vocabulary	0.03	0.62	0.71	—	0.80	0.92
Reading Comprehension	0.03	0.62	0.72	0.80	—	0.93
Total Reading	0.04	0.68	0.88	0.92	0.93	—

The intercorrelations in Table 3 confirm the generally accepted assumption that a child's intelligence (mental age) is, other things being equal, a powerful determiner of his reading ability. Although mental age is not perfectly measured in this school (since different intelligence tests were used and examinations were scattered over several years), the coefficients with every reading test are substantial. In comparison, the number of years of instruction by the Carden method shows zero correlations with reading ability; the coefficients differ from zero only by chance. In other words, on the average the pupils to whom the Carden method was taught throughout their entire school career were no better readers than those who received half as much Carden training or none at all. Since all the other fifteen tables of intercorrelations confirmed this general finding, only this one will be reproduced in this report.[6]

[5] Including pupils who had received no Carden training and were therefore omitted from Tables 1 and 2.

[6] All the statistical analyses reported in this paper were recommended, made, and scrutinized by Professor Irving Lorge, Director of the Institute of Psychological Research, Teachers College, Columbia University, and his statistical staff.

The Carden method, in and of itself, produced no improvement in reading over and above that obtained by the teachers not using it. The fact that the degree of reading ability developed in these classes was scarcely as great as that produced in pupils of the same mental age in the country at large justifies the suspicion that the Carden system was a handicap rather than a help to these teachers. They expect to do, and the writer predicts they will do, better teaching without it in the future.

As a further check on the findings, another statistical analysis, by means of the method of covariance, was carried out. If the amount of Carden instruction had any appreciable influence in improving reading performance, when the role of intelligence and sampling errors are eliminated, this analysis would have shown it. It did not. The verdict was: Carden method "not significant" in every one of the twelve classes.

These results suggest that when qualified teachers, such as those found in this school, are not teaching Carden phonics, they are giving other forms of instruction which are better. This assumption would account for the fact that the pupils who received, on the average, several years of Carden instruction fell below or, at best, barely equaled the average norms or attainments of pupils of equivalent intelligence, and the further fact that the children taught the method throughout their whole school career were, on the average, equally undistinguished. The variety of insights and techniques of value in developing skills in word recognition and methods of adapting and teaching them to meet the widely differing needs of pupils are described in brief and in detail in many available textbooks, manuals, and articles, and in college teacher-training courses. And good teachers know them today. It seems clear that a formidable, time-consuming program, such as the Carden, would interfere with a good teacher's most effective work by wasting time, dulling interest, and producing an unbalanced array of techniques, including some that are futile or misleading.

But, if it is true, as Terman and Walcutt state, that splendid results have been secured in certain schools using the Carden system, how are we to explain it? The surest way to get good results in teaching reading with any method is to use it in a school which has bright children and able and devoted teachers. There are many such schools in the New York area. It should be noted that Terman and Walcutt present Miss Carden as "a genius," a woman of "infinite patience" whose "abilities in coordinating and organizing a program are dazzling."[7] The findings in this study suggest that what teachers should try to get from Miss Carden is her inspiring personal leadership and not her system of phonics instruction.

[7] Terman and Walcutt, *op. cit.*, p. 142.

The findings of this study do not suggest that teaching phonics is futile or unnecessary. They show merely that the much less complex and less rigid programs employed in most American schools during the past decade produce reading abilities equal to, or somewhat better, than the Carden system in much less time and with less effort. Finally, nothing appearing in the results of this study suggests that we should not try hard to improve instruction in developing word-recognition skills in the future, but the results clearly and emphatically indicate that improvements are most unlikely to be found by searching in the direction taken by the Carden and similar elaborate and unrealistic systems.

25. The Utility of Phonic Generalizations in the Primary Grades

THEODORE CLYMER (1963)

The origins of this study go back to Kenneth, an extraordinary elementary pupil. Prior to my encounter with Kenneth I had completed a reading methods course in a small teachers college which provided a background in the principles of teaching reading as well as a good introduction to techniques. Among these techniques were procedures to develop phonic generalizations and also *the* list (not *a* list) of the most valuable generalizations to develop. (To those of you who might like copies of the list, I am sad to report that somehow through the years it has been lost.)

Difficulties with Kenneth began as the class reviewed phonic generalizations at the start of the school year. Our procedures were like those used in many classrooms: Groups of words were presented, and the class analyzed their likenesses and differences with a view toward deriving a generalization about relationships between certain letters and sounds or the position and pronunciation of vowels.

SOURCE: *The Reading Teacher*, XII (January, 1963), 252–258. Reprinted with the permission of Theodore Clymer and the International Reading Association.

Throughout these exercises, following the dictum of my reading methods teacher, we were careful not to call the generalizations "rules," for all our statements had a number of exceptions. As the class finally formulated a generalization regarding the relationships of letters, letter position, and sounds, such defensive phrasing as "most of the time," "usually," and "often" appeared as protective measures. We also spent time listing some of the exceptions to our generalizations.

At this point Kenneth entered the discussion. While the class was busily engaged in developing the generalization, Kenneth had skimmed his dictionary, locating long lists of exceptions to the generalization. In fact, he often located more exceptions than I could list applications. When I protested—somewhat weakly—that the dictionary contained many unusual words, Kenneth continued his role as an educational scientist. He turned to the basic reader word list in the back of his text and produced nearly similar results. Today, of course, Kenneth's behavior would be rated as "gifted," "talented," or "creative"—although I remember discussing him in other terms as I sat in the teachers' lounge.

As Kenneth had provided a memorable and even a "rich" learning experience for me, he furnished the impetus for a series of studies which will attempt to answer three questions: (1) What phonic generalizations are being taught in basic reading programs for the primary grades? (2) To what extent are these generalizations useful in having a "reasonable" degree of application to words commonly met in primary grade material? (3) Which of the generalizations that stand the test of question 2 can be learned and successfully applied to unknown words by primary children?

What Generalizations Are Taught?

Four widely used sets of readers were selected to determine the phonic generalizations being taught in the primary grades. After a preliminary study of the manuals, workbooks, and readers, the manuals were selected as the source of the generalizations. The manuals presented the generalizations in three ways: (1) statements to be taught to the pupils, (2) statements to be derived by the pupils after inductive teaching, and (3) statements with no clear indication as to what was to be done. Generalizations presented by all three means were included in the analysis.

Five general types of generalizations emerged from the study of the teachers' manuals. These types dealt with (1) vowels, (2) consonants, (3) endings, (4) syllabication, and (5) miscellaneous relationships. Arbitrary decisions were made in assigning some generalizations to one or another of the five types since certain statements might easily be classified under two or more headings.

If we eliminate from our consideration the miscellaneous type of generalization, a total of 121 different statements were located. There were 50 vowel generalizations, 15 consonant generalizations, and 28 generalizations in each of the ending and syllabication groups. In evaluating these figures it should be kept in mind that any statement was considered a separate generalization when its phrasing excluded or included different sets of words than another statement. For example, the generalization, "When there are two vowels side by side, the long sound of the first is heard and the second one is usually silent" and "When *ea* come together in a word, the first letter is long and the second is silent" were counted as two separate generalizations, although the second statement is a special application of the first.

While not directly related to our discussion here, note should be made of the wide variation of grade level of introduction, emphasis, and phrasing of the generalizations. Of the 50 different vowel generalizations, only 11 were common to all four series. None of these 11 was presented initially at the same half-year grade level in all four series. Some series gave a much greater emphasis to the generalizations than did other series. One publisher introduced only 33 of the 121 generalizations, while another presented 68. These comments are not meant to detract from the usefulness of basic materials, but simply to point out some of their differences. These differences do call for careful adjustments in the classroom when pupils are moved from one set of materials to another. The teacher who changes from series X to series Y may need to make some important revisions in his word recognition program. These findings may indicate also the need for further experimentation on emphasis and the developmental aspects of our word recognition program.

Which Generalizations Are Useful?

Forty-five of the generalizations given in the manuals were selected for further study. The selection of these was somewhat arbitrary. The main criterion was to ask, "Is the generalization stated specifically enough so that it can be said to aid or hinder in the pronunciation of a particular word?" An example or two will make our criterion clear. The generalization, "Long *o* makes a sound like its name," is undoubtedly a valuable generalization, but it was not specific enough to meet our criterion. On the other hand, the statement, "When a vowel is in the middle of a one syllable word, the vowel is short," was included because we could judge by reference to a word list how often one syllable words with a vowel in the middle do in fact have a short vowel sound.

Our next problem was to develop a word list on which we could test the generalizations. A reasonable approach seemed to be that of making up a composite list of all the words introduced in the four basic series from which the generalizations were drawn, plus the words from the Gates Reading Vocabulary for the Primary Grades. Once this list of some twenty-six hundred words was prepared, the following steps were taken:

1. The phonetic respelling and the syllabic division of all words were recorded. Webster's *New Collegiate Dictionary* was used as the authority for this information.
2. Each phonic generalization was checked against the words in the composite list to determine (a) the words which were pronounced as the generalization claimed and (b) the words which were exceptions to the generalization.
3. A "percent of utility" was computed for each generalization by dividing the number of words pronounced as the generalization claimed by the total number of words to which the generalization could be expected to apply. For example, if the generalization claimed that "When the letters *oa* are together in a word, *o* always gives its long sound and the *a* is silent," all words containing *oa* were located in the list. The number of these words was the total number of words to which the generalization should apply. Then the phonetic spellings of these words were examined to see how many words containing *oa* actually did have the long *o* followed by the silent *a*. In this case thirty words were located which contained *oa*. Twenty-nine of these were pronounced as the generalization claimed; one was not. The percent of utility became 29/30 or 97. This procedure was followed for all generalizations.

When the percent of utility was completed for each generalization, we set two criteria as to what constituted a "reasonable" degree of application. We have no scientific evidence to demonstrate that these criteria are valid; it can only be said that they seemed reasonable to us.

The first criterion was that the composite word list must contain a minimum of twenty words to which the generalization might apply. Generalizations with lower frequencies of application do not seem to merit instructional time.

The second criterion was a percent of utility of at least 75. To state the matter another way, if the pupil applied the generalization to twenty words, it should aid him in getting the correct pronunciation in fifteen of the twenty words.

The table gives the results of our analysis of the forty-five phonic generalizations. An inspection of the data leaves me somewhat confused as to the value of generalizations. Some time-honored customs in teaching of reading may be in need of revision.

Certain generalizations apply to large numbers of words and are rather constant in providing the correct pronunciation of words. (See, for example, generalizations 19, 35, and 36.)

A group of generalizations seem to be useful only after the pupil can pronounce the word. Generalizations which specify vowel pronunciation in stressed syllables require that the pupil know the pronunciation of the word before he can apply the generalization. (See, for example, generalization 33.) This criticism assumes, of course, that the purpose of a generalization is to help the child unlock the pronunciation of *unknown* words.

The usefulness of certain generalizations depends upon regional pronunciations. While following Webster's markings, generalization 34 is rejected. Midwestern pronunciation makes this generalization rather useful, although we reject it because we used Webster as the authority. Such problems are natural, and we should not hold it against Mr. Webster that he came from New England.

If we adhere to the criteria set up at the beginning of the study, of the forty-five generalizations only eighteen, numbers 5, 8, 10, 16, 20, 21, 22, 23, 25, 28, 29, 30, 31, 32, 40, 41, 44, and 45 are useful. Some of the generalizations which failed to meet our criteria might be useful if stated in different terms or if restricted to certain types of words. We are studying these problems at the present time. We are also examining other generalizations which we did not test in this study.

Conclusion

In evaluating this initial venture in testing the utility of phonic generalizations, it seems quite clear that many generalizations which are commonly taught are of limited value. Certainly the study indicates that we should give careful attention to pointing out the many exceptions to most of the generalizations that we teach. Current "extrinsic" phonics programs which present large numbers of generalizations are open to question on the basis of this study.

This study does not, of course, answer the question of which generalizations primary children can apply in working out the pronunciation of unknown words. The answer to the question of the primary child's ability to apply these and other generalizations will come only through classroom experimentation. Also, this study does not establish the percent of utility required for a generalization to be useful. The percentage suggested here (75) may be too high. Classroom research might reveal that generalizations with lower percentages of utility should be taught

The Utility of Forty-Five Phonic Generalizations

*Generalization	No. of Words Conforming	No. of Exceptions	Percent of Utility
1. When there are two vowels side by side, the long sound of the first one is heard and the second is usually silent.	309 (bead) †	377 (chief) †	45
2. When a vowel is in the middle of a one syllable word, the vowel is short.	408	249	62
middle letter	191 (dress)	84 (scold)	69
one of the middle two letters in a word of four letters	191 (rest)	135 (told)	59
one vowel *within* a word of more than four letters	26 (splash)	30 (fight)	46
3. If the only vowel letter is at the end of a word, the letter usually stands for a long sound.	23 (he)	8 (to)	74
4. When there are two vowels, one of which is final *e*, the first vowel is long and the *e* is silent.	180 (bone)	108 (done)	63
*5. The *r* gives the preceding vowel a sound that is neither long nor short.	484 (horn)	134 (wire)	78
6. The first vowel is usually long and the second silent in the digraphs *ai*, *ea*, *oa*, and *ui*.	179	92	66
ai	43 (nail)	24 (said)	64
ea	101 (bead)	51 (head)	66
oa	34 (boat)	1 (cupboard)	97
ui	1 (suit)	16 (build)	6
7. In the phonogram *ie*, the *i* is silent and the *e* has a long sound.	8 (field)	39 (friend)	17
*8. Words having double *e* usually have the long *e* sound.	85 (seem)	2 (been)	98
9. When words end with silent *e*, the preceding *a* or *i* is long.	164 (cake)	108 (have)	60
*10. In *ay* the *y* is silent and gives *a* its long sound.	36 (play)	10 (always)	78
11. When the letter *i* is followed by the letters *gh*, the *i* usually stands for its long sound and the *gh* is silent.	22 (high)	9 (neighbor)	71
12. When *a* follows *w* in a word, it usually has the sound *a* as in *was*.	15 (watch)	32 (swam)	32
13. When *e* is followed by *w*, the vowel sound is the same as represented by *oo*.	9 (blew)	17 (sew)	35
14. The two letters *ow* make the long *o* sound.	50 (own)	35 (down)	59

*Generalization	No. of Words Conforming	No. of Exceptions	Percent of Utility
15. *W* is sometimes a vowel and follows the vowel digraph rule.	50 (crow)	75 (threw)	40
*16. When *y* is the final letter in a word, it usually has a vowel sound.	169 (dry)	32 (tray)	84
17. When *y* is used as a vowel in words, it sometimes has the sound of long *i*.	29 (fly)	170 (funny)	15
18. The letter *a* has the same sound (ô) when followed by *l*, *w*, and *u*.	61 (all)	65 (canal)	48
19. When *a* is followed by *r* and final *e*, we expect to hear the sound heard in *care*.	9 (dare)	1 (are)	90
*20. When *c* and *h* are next to each other, they make only one sound.	103 (peach)	0	100
*21. *Ch* is usually pronounced as it is in *kitchen*, *catch*, and *chair*, not like *sh*.	99 (catch)	5 (machine)	95
*22. When *c* is followed by *e* or *i*, the sound of *s* is likely to be heard.	66 (cent)	3 (ocean)	96
*23. When the letter *c* is followed by *o* or *a* the sound of *k* is likely to be heard.	143 (camp)	0	100
24. The letter *g* often has a sound similar to that of *j* in jump when it precedes the letter *i* or *e*.	49 (engine)	28 (give)	64
*25. When *ght* is seen in a word, *gh* is silent.	30 (fight)	0	100
26. When a word begins *kn*, the *k* is silent.	10 (knife)	0	100
27. When a word begins with *wr*, the *w* is silent.	8 (write)	0	100
*28. When two of the same consonants are side by side only one is heard.	334 (carry)	3 (suggest)	99
*29. When a word ends in *ck*, it has the same last sound as in *look*.	46 (brick)	0	100
*30. In most two-syllable words, the first syllable is accented.	828 (famous)	143 (polite)	85
*31. If *a*, *in*, *re*, *ex*, *de*, or *be* is the first syllable in a word, it is usually unaccented.	86 (belong)	13 (insect)	87
*32. In most two-syllable words that end in a consonant followed by *y*, the first syllable is accented and the last is unaccented.	101 (baby)	4 (supply)	96

† Words in parentheses are examples—either of words which conform or of exceptions, depending on the column.

* Generalizations marked with an asterisk were found "useful" according to the criteria.

The Utility of Forty-Five Phonic Generalizations (*cont.*)

**Generalization*	*No. of Words Conforming*	*No. of Exceptions*	*Percent of Utility*
33. One vowel letter in an accented syllable has its short sound.	547 (city)	356 (lady)	61
34. When *y* or *ey* is seen in the last syllable that is not accented, the long sound of *e* is heard.	0	157 (baby)	0
35. When *ture* is the final syllable in a word, it is unaccented.	4 (picture)	0	100
36. When *tion* is the final syllable in a word, it is unaccented.	5 (station)	0	100
37. In many two- and three-syllable words, the final *e* lengthens the vowel in the last syllable.	52 (invite)	62 (gasoline)	46
38. If the first vowel sound in a word is followed by two consonants, the first syllable usually ends with the first of the two consonants.	404 (bullet)	159 (singer)	72
39. If the first vowel sound in a word is followed by a single consonant, that consonant usually begins the second syllable.	190 (over)	237 (oven)	44
*40. If the last syllable of a word ends in *le*, the consonant preceding the *le* usually begins the last syllable.	62 (tumble)	2 (buckle)	97
*41. When the first vowel element in a word is followed by *th*, *ch*, or *sh*, these symbols are not broken when the word is divided into syllables and may go with either the first or second syllable.	30 (dishes)	0	100
42. In a word of more than one syllable, the letter *v* usually goes with the preceding vowel to form a syllable.	53 (cover)	20 (clover)	73
43. When a word has only one vowel letter, the vowel sound is likely to be short.	433 (hid)	322 (kind)	57
*44. When there is one *e* in a word that ends in a consonant, the *e* usually has a short sound.	85 (leg)	27 (blew)	76
*45. When the last syllable is the sound *r*, it is unaccented.	188 (butter)	9 (appear)	95

† Words in parentheses are examples—either of words which conform or of exceptions, depending on the column.
* Generalizations marked with an asterisk were found "useful" according to the criteria.

because they encourage children to examine words for sound and letter relationships.

The most disturbing fact to come from the study may be the rather dismal failure of generalization 1 to provide the correct pronunciation even 50 percent of the time. As one teacher remarked when this study was presented to a reading methods class, "Mr. Clymer, for years I've been teaching 'When two vowels go walking, the first one does the talking.' You're ruining the romance in the teaching of reading!"

V. Developmental Reading–Comprehension and Rate

The "heart of the reading task is obtaining appropriate meanings from the printed page."[1] As teachers, we employ reading tests to help evaluate reading comprehension and reading growth. But what do reading comprehension tests really measure? Barbe (26) bemoans the fact that they put a premium on retention of information rather than upon an understanding of what is read. Other indictments involve the facts that comprehension tests reward the fast reader and also fail to measure auding skill. Barbe's article was written in 1958. New reading tests have appeared since that time. Are there any available today that involve "the new type of check on reading comprehension" to which he refers?

Since reading is not a general ability but a composite of specialized skills, it is difficult for the basal reading program to meet the specialized reading demands involved in comprehending material in content fields. Subject matter teachers are obliged to accept the responsibility for much of the training. In effect, every teacher must become a teacher of reading. But do all teachers accept this challenge? Are teachers who are subject matter oriented willing to accept the responsibility for training students to read with greater comprehension in their areas of specialization?

In her article, "Reading in Subject Matter Fields," Smith (27) stresses the responsibility teachers have in helping children read effectively in social studies, science, mathematics, and literature. She delineates the specific skills needed in each of

[1] Albert Harris, *How to Increase Reading Ability* (New York: Longmans, Green and Co., 1961), p. 396.

these areas and in several instances gives special emphasis to the importance of getting children to think for themselves when reacting to the printed page.

Critical reading is an important aspect of reading comprehension in all subject matter areas. All agree that there is a vital need for critical reading. Some writers limit critical reading to detecting propaganda devices; others, however, would include high-level mental processes such as analysis and reasoning. With this in mind, the reader will be interested in the article by Russell (28), "The Prerequisite: Knowing How to Read Critically."

Since pupils are confronted by a great volume and variety of reading tasks, flexibility and speed are needed. However, few reading authorities stress speed reading (many choose to refer to reading speed as rate of comprehension) in the elementary school. Above this level, what is the true value and place of speed reading in the school program? Artley (29) answers this question admirably in his article, "Speed Reading."

When reading speed is discussed, many people automatically think of machines and gadgets. How valuable are tachistoscopes, controlled readers, and pacers in this regard? Are they indispensable? If funds are limited, should machines have a priority? Karlin (30) provides us with some much needed answers by reviewing a number of investigations in which machine-trained groups were compared with those engaged in free, or natural, reading practice.

There is not only historical but practical value in Cole's (31) treatment of the main causes of slow reading. Most of what she wrote in 1938 still remains valid, although present-day writers would place less emphasis on inefficient eye movements as a cause of slow reading.

Certainly there is much about rate of comprehension that we need to understand. This is brought to our attention in a forceful manner by Dechant (32). His article, "Rate of Comprehension—Needed Research," lists enough unanswered questions about rate of reading to keep researchers busy for a long time.

26. Measuring Reading Comprehension

WALTER B. BARBE (1958)

The problem of how to measure comprehension in reading seems to be of major importance for two definite reasons: (1) to determine whether a student understands what is read, and (2) to know what to teach so that comprehension may be improved. In this era of great emphasis on reading problems, attention needs to be turned toward better measurement of reading comprehension.

A definition of comprehension would undoubtedly aid in the measurement; but as with so many such skills, the definition seems to be based upon what the test measures. Almost without exception, standardized reading tests include a section entitled "comprehension," and scores are given to indicate a student's ability in this skill. But unfortunately these scores are often misleading and of little value to the reading teacher who would like to use the scores as a guide for placing children in reading material at their level.

Since some definition of comprehension is essential, perhaps it would be sufficient to say that reading comprehension is understanding the material which is read.

Comprehension or Memory?

One major characteristic of most standardized tests of comprehension is the high value placed upon memory. Instead of measuring how well the student understands what he reads, the test seems to be measuring how well he can remember what he has read. Actually, memory is not a reading skill as such, and would more properly be classified as a facet of intelligence.

It is possible that the reason for the very high correlations which are reported between the results on group reading tests and group intelligence tests may be partially due to the common factor of memory in

SOURCE: *The Clearing House,* XXXII (February, 1958), 343–345. Reprinted by permission of the publisher.

both tests. The place of this factor in a reading test is questionable, and certainly it is unacceptable when disguised with the label "comprehension." (Vocabulary is the main factor common to both reading and intelligence tests, and has been used as one explanation for the high correlation between the two types of scores. The presence of memory items on both types of tests may also be another important reason for the high correlation. In this instance, the inclusion of a memory factor may not be justified.)

There can be no doubt that the existing reading tests are little more than checks on how well the child remembers what he has read, and do little actually to determine the level at which the student understands what he has read.

Quantitative or Qualitative Memory?

The basic problem seems to be whether in the checking of reading comprehension the major concern is over quantitative or qualitative facts. How much? How many? When? Where? These seem to be the usual types of questions on a comprehension check. "Why?" is not a common question, and yet it would surely be a better measure of comprehension than those questions which can be answered from memory without any real understanding. The "why?" type of question is not easily prepared. It leaves a greater chance for ambiguity, because the question cannot be stated or answered in so objective a manner as other questions. The student's background of experience is more likely to influence his response, for the question is asking a reaction to something, rather than a rote repetition of what was read.

The method by which a poor reader explained that he took a reading comprehension check is revealing. His comprehension score was always much higher in silent reading than would be expected. When asked why he apparently could "understand" material read silently (a misuse of the word "understand," brought about by the naïve belief that comprehension and understanding were the same thing) whereas he could not read the same material aloud, he answered, "Oh, when I am supposed to read silently I just look for the numbers and dates in the story. Then when I take the test, I mark the answers which have those numbers in them." Unbelievable? Certainly not; it works.

Why must our reading comprehension tests be so concerned with figures and numbers? One possible explanation is given by Saint-Exupery in *The Little Prince* (Reynal and Hitchcock, Inc.), in which he says, "Grownups love figures. When you tell them that you have made a new friend, they never ask you any questions about essential matters. They never say to you, "What does his voice sound like? What game does he love best? Does he collect butterflies?' Instead, they demand: 'How old is he? How many brothers has he? How much does he weigh? How much money does his father make?' Only from these figures do they think they have learned anything about him."

Regardless of how much we may deny that this is true, a cursory examination of existing standardized reading tests reveals a preponderance of the "how much—how many?" type of question. An improvement would be to include more items requiring the student to understand and use the material which he has read.

Grade Level of Comprehension

Not all reading tests, but certainly many, give a grade level of comprehension in reading. Examining these tests reveals that the level obtained does not necessarily mean that the student comprehends material at that particular level. In many instances it means that he reads at a slow rate and therefore did not finish enough of the material to make a satisfactory score on the comprehension check. Is this poor comprehension? It would hardly seem to be so unless one wished to argue the point that reading comprehension and reading rate cannot be separated. If so, the two scores should never have been separated. Instead of a score in comprehension and a score in other factors in reading, there should have been only a total reading score.

The actual grade level of difficulty of the material which the student can read and understand is what a reading-comprehension grade level should indicate. It should exclude as many other reading factors as possible. It should mean that, given the time, the student can read the material and, without help, understand it. Is this asking too much from a comprehension check? Apparently so, for few tests provide this information.

The grade level at which the child can comprehend material must take into consideration vocabulary, background of experience, concepts, and ability to interpret what the author means.

Oral and Silent Reading Comprehension

Reading teachers know well that children have different levels of comprehension for oral and silent reading. In some instances, a child will be unable to read silently and comprehend what he has read. Actually, the child is very likely unable to figure out a word and so does not systematically cover the material beyond that point. Such a child might also vocalize every word, so that he is actually reading aloud, even though he is supposed to be reading silently. Other children will do exactly the opposite. The emotional pressures of reading aloud make comprehension almost nil. Yet our reading tests usually yield one score on comprehension, with practically no indication of what type of reading was required in order to obtain the comprehension level. It is probably safe to assume that the comprehension score was on material read silently, but there is no assurance the child actually read the material in this manner.

Listening Comprehension

Of value to all teachers working with children in a reading situation would be a measure of listening comprehension of material read to the child. Merely knowing that the child could understand material if he were capable of reading it would be valuable information to all teachers. Group reading tests give absolutely no indication of the actual comprehension level of the child. The comprehension check, therefore, becomes merely another check on the child's ability to use reading skills, but should not be labeled comprehension.

Of practical value to the person working with a child who is having reading difficulties is to know whether the child could understand the material if he were able to read it. In order to determine this, an individual intelligence test is customarily administered to every child receiving assistance in a reading clinic. But the scarcity of reading clinics and the overcrowded conditions in such clinics clearly indicate that the large percentage of reading problems never reach a reading clinic and therefore probably never have the advantage of individual intelligence testing. Therefore, it would seem logical that a test is needed which would indicate how much the child could understand if he were to learn the skills involved in reading. Such a test should be easily developed, for it would probably be nothing more than a carefully graded series of paragraphs which, instead of being read by the child, are read to him. His ability to understand up to a particular level should indicate how well he is capable of understanding material at any particular level, and might have the practical value of allowing classroom teachers to measure accurately the level at which they can hope to raise the child in reading ability, without having to resort to the unrealistic procedure of calling on outside help for every problem.

How About a New Type of Check on Reading Comprehension?

If a new type of reading test were developed which actually measured how well and at what level a child truly comprehended reading material, and at what level the child was capable of comprehending, an entire new era of both achievement testing and teaching might evolve.

Why do teachers place so much importance on dates and figures in their checks of comprehension? Maybe because the same type of question is asked by the people who prepare reading tests and are supposed to know how to measure comprehension in an accurate manner.

It is only too easy to tell teachers that they should check comprehension in a better way, but until someone can show them how, such suggestions will not have any real meaning.

27. Reading in Subject Matter Fields

NILA BANTON SMITH (1965)

The present social revolution and reading in the subject matter fields are mutually interactive. This revolution is ushering in new problems; reading is necessary in coping adequately with these problems.

The kind of reading, however, that will contribute to problem solution is not the kind that is done in pursuing sensational magazines, comic books, and news items on crime and casualty. It is the kind of reading used in delving deeply into social studies, science, mathematics and literature. We have a social, a political and a cultural responsibility in teaching children to read effectually in these fields.

Reading in Social Studies

At the present time, world events are having tremendous impacts upon our lives in the United States. For the average student or adult, the sources of information concerning these events are TV and radio, perhaps with the newspaper running as a poor third. Any interpretations that are given through these media represent the thinking of a commentator, reporter, or editor.

SOURCE: *Educational Leadership*, XXII (March, 1965), 382–385. Reprinted by permission of the Association for Supervision and Curriculum Development and Nila Banton Smith.

We need to place more emphasis upon reading and thinking on the part of the individual himself. It would be helpful if every family would take at least two newspapers, and would, themselves, compare and discuss differing accounts of the same event, in the presence of their children. When the children are old enough to read newspapers, parents should encourage them to read and compare, and join in the family discussion out of which may come generalizations and conclusions based upon family thinking and interpretation. This same procedure might well take place in classrooms with the use of newspapers and magazines brought in by the students.

Maps, globes, and atlases have leapt into new significance in our rapidly changing world. Classrooms and living rooms should be well equipped with these locational references. Both teachers and parents would do well to refer to these facilities when a place has important mention on TV or in newspapers, with children "joining in" or looking up locations themselves when they are able to do so. Encouraging research to extend interest in social studies topics provides functional practice in the use of encyclopedias and other reference books as well as the use of library skills.

The cause and effect pattern of writing is characteristic of social studies content. Every event in history, every geographical change in the earth, has had its cause which in turn has resulted in an effect. It is helpful to students if they are taught to identify this pattern when they encounter it. They may then read for the specific purpose of noting causes and effects, thus having an organizing platform on which to stand while gathering related information.

The ability to make comparisons is needed for effective reading in the social studies field. Much opportunity should be given for making comparisons while pupils are working with social studies.

All pupils, beginning with third grade, should be taught to recognize the basic propaganda tricks in printed materials. These tricks embody use of bad (uncomplimentary) words, glad words, transfer, testimonial, bandwagon technique, plain folks concept, and stacking the cards. Children can be taught at home and in schools to recognize these tricks in advertisements, speeches of politicians, editorials, cartoons, and comments of leaders in some of the foreign countries. It is extremely important that our young people should know when someone is trying to influence their thinking and behavior through printed materials.

Reading in Science

We are living in a highly scientific age. Increasing numbers of people will be working at jobs in science. All of us will be consumers of science and readers of materials involving science. It is of the utmost importance that children be taught special skills needed in the effective reading of content in this subject area. These skills have their roots in the textbooks of elementary school children but appear in increasingly difficult context in high school.

Specialized vocabulary is a significant factor in reading science material. The new words are long, difficult to pronounce, and technical in concept. For teachers working with poor readers, it is suggested that they take a hint from procedures used in teaching reader stories, that is, to clear the way for study of new science content by providing vocabulary work before the students read, both in regard to pronunciation and meanings.

A unique pattern found in science textbooks is the kind of text needed in carrying out an experiment. This pattern usually consists of a set of directions. Every word in this set of directions must be recognized and every direction must be carried out exactly. Those children who have difficulty in reading and following directions should probably have temporary experience in reading the directions orally from the blackboard or book and telling *exactly* what they are going to do before actually following the directions in performing an experiment.

Another type of science text appearing at all levels falls into the *classification pattern* in which living things, objects, materials, elements, gases, liquids, forces, etc. are classified under a common heading, which in turn deals with subdivisions. Students should not read this pattern as they would a story. If a child is taught to identify the classification pattern, he will be able to gear his reading procedure to obtaining the kind of information which is important in this particular pattern—that of grasping the subdivisions and the important characteristics of each.

Another pattern of writing which is particularly characteristic of science, and perhaps the most difficult one to read, is the explanation of a technical process, which usually is accompanied with diagrams necessitating very careful reading of text with continuous reference to diagrams, for example: "How Does the Telephone Work?" This kind of reading requires a doubling of techniques: reading the text and reading the diagram alternately as one feeds into the other. Students need help in learning how to read and understand diagrams, and guidance in adjusting from one to the other while pursuing an explanation.

Still another pattern frequently encountered in science textbooks, but not entirely unique to science, is the *detailed statement-of-facts pattern.* In this pattern the facts are dense, and they frequently embody a definition or a statement of a principle. In reading this pattern, the student is helped greatly if he is taught first of all to find the main idea in each paragraph, then to grasp the details as related to and clustering about this main idea—"as grapes grow out of and cluster about the main stem." Much oral discussion is necessary in developing this skill to a high level. After students have attained some proficiency in analyzing paragraph structure through oral discussion, they will find it helpful to outline science paragraphs heavy in detail.

Reading in Mathematics

Mathematics, like science, is becoming increasingly important in our lives, partly because it is so closely integrated with science, and partly because mathematical concepts must be understood if we live intelligently in our rapidly expanding universe.

Mathematics text is unique in that it embraces types of reading content which differ markedly from narrative reading and from the text of geography, history, and science. It is more compact than text in any of these other fields. It is complicated also by having numerical symbols woven into the sentences along with word symbols.

The most highly specialized pattern of text in mathematics is the short paragraph setting forth a problem situation. Regardless of whether the text is in arithmetic, algebra, or geometry, problems are stated in this format: At the beginning the situation is given, or the condition under which the problem took place is stated; then follows a series of numbers or other mathematical values; and finally the reader is asked or told what to find.

The *reading* of most problems in mathematics involves four different processes: (a) reading the entire problem to grasp the situation as a whole; (b) concentrating on the question or statement at the end that asks or tells what to find; (c) deciding what processes or formulas to use in finding the answer; (d) pulling out the number facts or symbols presented for use in working the problem. After these *reading* activities accompanied with a high degree of reasoning have been completed, then the student is ready to compute the problem mentally or on paper. If a student is having difficulty in mathematics, it would be helpful to explain to him the importance of the *reading* activities which precede computation, and to provide him with special practice on the reading procedures involved, perhaps for a time without working the problems at all.

In addition to problems there are other reading situations in mathematics. At the elementary level pupils must be taught to read calendars, thermometers, time-tables, abbreviations, etc. In the secondary school, students must learn to read exponents, formulas, subscripts, equations, reference tables. The elementary teacher should teach reading as needed in arithmetical situations in the same ways that he teaches it in his basal reading instruction, and the secondary teacher of mathematics might obtain some very good hints from the elementary teacher.

Reading Literature

Interest in reading is the touchstone to all reading activities which contribute to our lives culturally, socially, informatively, and recreationally. Development of interest in reading is of grave import at this time because of the competition of other mass communication agencies, and because of the present unsatisfactory status in the free reading both of students and adults. Literature is a content area which offers an excellent opportunity to develop interest in reading and discrimination in the choice of content.

Having a wide variety of materials available is one of the best ways of nurturing children's interests. Classrooms, libraries and homes should abound in collections of the best in books and magazines.

Parents need counseling about the purchase of books. They should be urged to take the child for whom books are being bought with them and to let him make selection in terms of his own interests. To avoid reading frustration, the parent should be advised to try the book out a little with the child to see whether it is easy enough for him to read. If not, then with his help another book may be selected which is of interest to him but still within the level of his reading maturity.

The enthusiasm of the teacher or parent for books is a strong factor in arousing child interest. Having periods of sharing may help. Supplementing literature with activities in the creative arts also contributes to interest.

At the secondary level different patterns of writing in literature become prominent. These are the *story* (short story or novel), *essay, drama, biography, fable,* and *poetry* of many kinds (ballad, lyric, elegiac, epic, sonnet), some written in rhymed verse, some in free verse, some in blank verse and of many different meters.

Each of these patterns requires a different approach. A student should not read a story, an essay, and a drama in the same way. His purpose is different. He reads a story to enjoy plot, character, and setting; an essay to get the slant of the author as he discusses some aspect of life; a drama to interpret the conversations of the characters involved. Drama is further differentiated in reading in that it is cast in a unique format. Biography and autobiography should be read not merely to follow separate chronological facts but to get a conclusive impression of the person writing it or being written about. Sometimes within the essay or biography the detailed statement-of-facts pattern appears, but this is very light as compared with this pattern which is characteristically used in science.

Interpretation is of the greatest significance in teaching literature. Students must continuously be encouraged to read between and behind the lines to get deeper meanings. Teachers of literature need to ask questions and make remarks during discussion, and formulate assignments for individual or group work which will call forth such thinking activities as: speculating on what happened between events; anticipating what will happen next; making generalizations from details in text; detecting the significance of a statement, passage or selection; making comparisons of characters, events, locales; identifying the purpose of the writer or the motive of characters; associating personal experience with reading context; sensing visual images; and experiencing emotional reactions. Depth reading is an absolute necessity for full and satisfying appreciation.

28. The Prerequisite: Knowing How to Read Critically

DAVID H. RUSSELL (1963)

Censorship usually involves a decision by a person or group about what others should read; ability in critical reading suggests that the individual makes the choice.

We must have competence and established procedures in local districts in dealing with censorship by individuals or in groups, but our first concern is the critical abilities of youth. We want to help young people decide for themselves whether there is communism in *Robin Hood*, pornography in *The Good Earth* or *Drums Along the Mohawk*.

Critical reading does not exist in a vacuum by itself but can be thought of best as closely related to critical thinking.

What is critical thinking? It is best described as essentially a three-factor ability. It includes an attitude factor of questioning and suspended judgment, a conative or functional factor which involves use of methods of logical inquiry and problem solving, and a judgment factor of evaluating in terms of some norm.

SOURCE: *Elementary English*, October, 1963, pp. 579–582. Reprinted with the permission of the National Council of Teachers of English.

The attitude factor, for example, might be represented by, "I'm from Missouri" or "Show me." It means checking on the assumptions of the author—a difficult task, especially in some fiction.

The conative or action factor might include selecting significant words and phrases in a statement, identifying emotion and bias, picking out stereotypes and clichés.

The third, judgment, factor might include distinguishing the relevant and irrelevant, assessing literary merit, and looking for evidence in any conclusion drawn by speaker or writer.

These sound like formidable accomplishments. If they sound difficult to us adults, how can they be started with children? They *are* difficult, slow growing, and yet the need to use them is all around us.

There are four reasons why I believe critical thinking must be stressed from kindergarten through college—why I believe teachers and curriculum committees must give development of abilities in critical thinking a continuous place in the curriculum.

1. The mass media of communication influence us to think and act alike. Conformity, not individuality, is stressed in our listening and much of our reading. The effect of our mass culture is to make little bands of conformists—only the home and the school can help children think for themselves, reject the unworthy, resist the blandishments of the "guy with a bill of goods for sale."

2. High performance on an intelligence test does not guarantee high scores on a test of critical thinking. Good mental ability does not guarantee strong critical thinking abilities. The relationship between general intelligence and critical thinking is positive but not high. Critical thinking abilities are not acquired automatically as a part of general mental growth; specific provisions must be made for their development in all curriculum areas.

3. Attitudes are learned. Youth do not develop a questioning attitude automatically. Teachers and schools have to work to develop the attitude. Such attitudes are learned partly by imitation, for attitudes can be caught as well as taught.

4. Judgment in terms of some norm or standard or consensus implies a background of experience which sometimes the school must supply. Knowledge and experience are prerequisite to critical thinking in the area in which the critical thinking is done. The school must help supply a broad background of experience before problem solving or creative thinking or critical thinking can be attempted. But from the first grade on, let us not stop just with the experience. Teacher and group must discuss, contrast, and compare, and then the teacher moves imperceptibly into questioning and judgment.

Nine Principles

Can the 10-year-old or the 15-year-old really exercise the judgment necessary for evaluating the newspapers, films, or novels he sees? In partial answer, here are nine statements of things we know or believe which have been at least partly verified by research.

1. Some children have acquired abilities in critical thinking before they enter school. I heard one five-year-old say, "*All* the TV ads say they have the best breakfast cereal."
2. Activities in critical thinking begin in the primary grades—not with the "rational" adult.
3. Critical thinking depends less on specific techniques and more on attitude and experience.
4. Part of the attitude factor in critical thinking is the objectivity which comes from the ability to shift perspective—to see one's own behavior and ideas as they might be viewed by others. (This might be part of developing the self-concept, especially crucial in the junior-high years).
5. The experience factor in critical thinking involves considerable participation in the social and linguistic community. A chance to talk things over or to explore the effects of action produces a validation by consensus which is prerequisite to making sound judgments.
6. Although probably not so important as attitude or experience, there are hundreds of skills in the conative or operational phase of critical thinking. These include the ability to read for exact details, to relate cause and effect in a speaker's statement, and to detect a propaganda device.
7. The evaluation phase of critical thinking is closely related to the ability to check one's own thinking against some norm or consensual validation. This means that the child must know the habits and customs of the group, and the school must be aware of possible differences between home and community values.
8. Irrationality in thinking occurs when the challenge to the individual is too severe, when he does not have the resources to meet the questioning of an idea close to the heart of his own personality or philosophy. If we are threatened by a statement or idea, it is hard to consider it unemotionally and critically.
9. Critical thinking about materials which might be labeled "lewd" or "obscene" or "pornographic" by certain censors is probably related to the reader's standards or tastes. Many teachers report success in raising their students' tastes in literature and in cinema. If this is accomplished, the knowledge and attitude might provide the best bulwark against undesirable material.

These nine principles have been partly validated by research. The need for action is indicated.

Action Needed

In English and in other curricular areas, we need greater emphasis on thinking abilities. At least six different thinking abilities can be identified, and one of the most important is critical thinking. Most of the influences of modern life are against such skill, and so the school has a peculiar and unique responsibility for developing it, from the first grade onward.

It is not enough to be *against* communism, sadism, hedonism—we must be *for* the development of skills in critical thinking about any "ism." In our pluralistic culture, there are many extreme voices. We must be able to resist some of the statements of a Senator Joseph McCarthy, a Texas oil millionaire, or a high-riding labor boss. We must be able to decide for ourselves that this writer has something to say but that one is merely filthy.

The ability to examine complex community affairs or personal problems begins in childhood and develops slowly over the years. As a product of our schools, we do not want bulging-jawed squirrels crammed with knowledge. We want not sheep but curious, questioning people; not thoughtless conformity but thoughtful appraisal; not parrotting back but reflecting and judging; not prohibiting but evaluating.

29. Speed Reading: Its Value and Place in a School Program

A. STERL ARTLEY (1963)

Speed reading now vies with phonics and individualized reading for the attention of educators. Many questions have been raised over the desirability of high school courses in rapid reading. Because of the cur-

---

SOURCE: *School and Community*, XLIX (January, 1963), 14–16. Reprinted by permission of the author and publisher.

rent concern over this issue it might be desirable to consider some of these questions.

Does rate of reading have any merit, per se? What part does rate of comprehension play? Rate of reading refers to the number of words that can be read in a given period of time. Rate of comprehension refers to the rate at which material may be comprehended at a specified level in a given period of time. Obviously it is rate of comprehension with which we must be concerned.

Covering material at the rate of 1,000 words per minute while comprehending only 25 percent of the ideas would be of little value. Rate and comprehension should not be divorced.

What is the relation between rate of reading and rate of comprehension? Does the fast reader comprehend more than the slower, or vice versa? It is as much a fiction to assume that the level of comprehension increases as one reads faster as it is to assume that the slow, plodding reader is an efficient comprehender.

Research shows that the coefficients of correlation between the two factors range from practically zero to around .30. Other studies have shown that the relation tends to be higher where easier material is being read, but lower on more difficult material.

Hence, it would be a fallacy to assume that comprehension can be increased if one works on rate alone. Such factors as purpose, background of understanding, and readability of the material must all be taken into consideration when discussing the relation between speed and comprehension.

What factors influence the rate at which one can comprehend? Certain factors within the reader himself affect his rate of comprehension. Intelligence is an obvious one. Familiarity with the content, intensity of interest, level of motivation, and mastery of the skills of reading are others.

On the other hand, certain factors reside in the material. Sentence length and type, vocabulary, organization, and abstractness of the ideas make for ease or difficulty.

In other words, a highly motivated, intelligent person who is a skillful reader, familiar with the content, will be able to read highly readable material faster and with a higher level of comprehension than will his opposite, facing more difficult material.

But the rate at which one *should* read is conditioned by a factor that is even more important than those mentioned above—the purpose for which one reads. Before attempting to read any type of material the reader should always ask himself, "What is my purpose in reading this material?" "What am I supposed to do with the information?" The purpose, then, should dictate the rate.

Reading specialists refer to at least four basic reading purposes, each with its corresponding rate.

First, one may read to locate information, to get the general idea, or to note the organizational pattern. Here the reader *skims.*

Second, he may read to review material that he has covered before, to get the essential features of the story plot, and to discover the main points through which an idea is developed. These purposes may be satisfied by *rapid* reading.

Third, to note supporting details relating to the main ideas, and to sense the emotional and esthetic qualities of a story requires a *normal* rate.

Mastering details for subsequent recall, analyzing the manner of presentation, preparing a detailed summary, and reacting critically to the ideas usually requires a *slow* or study type of reading.

In other words, there are rates of reading, each conditioned by purpose. The efficient reader is one who senses the reading purpose to be satisfied and rapidly adapts his rate accordingly. He has a repertoire of rates readily available which he can use with efficiency and facility.

Is there, then, a standard or expected rate of comprehension for various reading levels—elementary, high school, or adult? No. Because rate of comprehension is conditioned by so many different factors there can be no standard rate or norm for a particular grade or level, unless one specifies the kind of reader, the type of material, and the purpose for which it is being read.

However, it is obvious that with increased age and reading maturity one should expect to find a corresponding increase in the rate of comprehension for materials of similar type, read for similar purposes.

What part do eye-span and eye-movements play in reading? Is not the process of increasing the rate of comprehension largely a matter of training the eyes to move faster and to take in more words at one glance?

Training eye movements and span of perception is only part of the job involved in developing rate of comprehension. True, a reader whose eyes move rhythmically and accurately from line to line, and who is able to take in several words at a glance is a more efficient reader than one who does otherwise.

However, it must be understood that eye-movements do not *cause* efficient reading, they merely *reflect* it. They are the result rather than the cause of whatever kind of reading is done.

In the final analysis the rate at which one can comprehend is the rate at which he can assimilate and organize the ideas. Reading is a thinking process, and the visual component is only a means to that end.

Some reading purposes, like skimming, demand little in the way of a synthesis of ideas. Consequently, one's eyes move along the line of print very rapidly. Other purposes place heavy demands on the mental process of sifting, sorting, and organizing ideas. Eye-movements may be far from rhythmical. One must reread, take time to "think it through," or perhaps organize the ideas into a structured pattern for the purpose of recall. Rather than train eye-movements for efficient comprehension, one should develop the ability to analyze and organize.

Are machines, films, pacers, and tachistoscopic devices essential in increasing rate of comprehension? No, not essential. Their purpose is served chiefly in the development of rhythmical eye-movements, and, as was indicated in the answer to the preceding question, eye-movements reflect rather than cause either good or poor reading.

There are cases, however, where apparatus has motivational value, since young people ordinarily like to work with machines and gadgets. A stop-watch and some easy reading material will be as useful in increasing rate of comprehension as will a machine, and they will certainly do the job much more functionally.

Is it possible to learn to see a "page at a glance" or to read down the center of the page? We have no evidence to show that such feats are possible. On the other hand we have ample evidence to show that this can't be done.

We know from over a half century of research that the eyes can perceive only when they are fixed on a point of reference. They cannot read when in motion. Try it and see.

Moreover, the number of words that one can take in at one fixation has physiological limits amenable to very limited training. It has been shown that at only one half inch to the right and left of the point of fixation the normal eye sees with only 50 percent acuity.

Within these limits 2.5 to 3 words would be as many as one could perceive in one fixation. Hence, any claim for the ability to perceive phenomenal amounts of material at one time does not seem to be substantiated by existing evidence.

Dr. George Spache of the University of Florida estimates that if reading is interpreted as a process of perceiving most of the words on the page, it would be impossible to cover material faster than from 800 to 900 words per minute.

Claims for rates beyond these appear to be for selective reading wherein one omits words, lines, and even paragraphs. Of course, this type of reading is entirely legitimate if the reading purpose demands it.

Would it be advisable to institute a speed-reading course in high school? It must be indicated clearly that speed of comprehension is only one dimension of reading maturity, and possibly not the most important one at that.

Emphasis on speed divorced from other aspects of reading can be justified only for those students who are already efficient readers, as shown by an adequate diagnosis.

Otherwise, attention to rate should be given only within the setting of a broad program of developmental reading involving critical analysis, efficient word perception, vocabulary development, reaction, and the integration of new ideas with past experiences. To give attention to only one aspect of reading would be similar to training a novice carpenter in the use of a power saw only.

Are there some simple but effective methods of improving rate of comprehension that a classroom teacher might use? Yes, there are. Possibly the simplest is simply reminding the student to read faster, but only as fast as he is able to understand what he reads.

One study done with college students, for instance, resulted in an over-all gain of 40 percent in rate as a result of being requested to read faster. The fastest readers with high comprehension scores make an average gain of over 80 percent in words read per minute.

Another suggestion is that of making available reading tasks that permit a rapid rate of comprehension. Many students are slow readers because the nature of their reading assignments has demanded a slow study type of reading.

Assignments that call for locating information, getting the author's "big idea," finding the answer to a specific question give an opportunity to practice rapid comprehension. Caution—don't establish purposes for rapid reading and then check the reader for details.

Use a stop-watch and easy practice materials for "pressure reading." Have each student establish his normal rate of comprehension in terms of words per minute and level of understanding for a given reading purpose.

On each subsequent practice period, using the same type of reading purpose, each student should try to surpass his past record while keeping his level of comprehension uniformly high. Keeping a graph of his gain provides visual evidence of growth as well as motivation.

Additional suggestions may be found in Harris's *How to Increase Reading Ability* (Longmans, Green) and Bond and Tinker's *Reading Difficulties, Their Diagnosis and Correction* (Appleton-Century-Crofts.)

If our present interest in speed of reading will lead to a better understanding of the reading process, of the importance of varying one's rate of reading in the light of purpose, and to the use of techniques and procedures that one can use to improve the quality of comprehension and interpretation at whatever rate of speed is required, then the current emphasis on speed reading will have served a useful purpose.

If, on the contrary, it leads to the indiscriminate introduction of speed classes in high school under the assumption that rate of reading is the end and goal of reading maturity, the movement will have questionable results.

30. Machines and Reading: A Review of Research

ROBERT KARLIN (1958)

The use of mechanical devices in teaching reading has achieved acceptance in several quarters. Their popularity is great in the area of speed or rate of reading. In fact, the general public readily expects the reading "clinic" or "center" to possess these instruments, a situation which has grown out of very favorable reports in the press and popular magazines. Many public schools have either purchased these devices or are seriously considering them in developmental and remedial reading classes.

The Three Categories of Machines

FLASHMETERS

Some flashmeters are called overhead projectors or tachistoscopes. One projects an image on a blackboard or screen for periods of from one or two seconds to perhaps one one-thousandth of a second. The length of projection is controlled by a timing device which is manually set for the appropriate time duration. Glass slides which contain lists of individual words, phrases, sentences, or paragraphs and columns of digits may be purchased or prepared by the user.

A second type is intended for individual use: The viewer releases a timed light which illuminates a printed card that contains a series of

SOURCE: *The Clearing House,* XXXII (February, 1958), 349–352. Reprinted by permission of the publishers.

digits or phrases and sentences. In each instance the viewer records what he sees and then verifies it.

PACERS

The pacer contains a movable screen or bar under which the printed material is placed. The speed at which the screen or bar descends over the printed lines is regulated in terms of a given number of words per minute. Thus, if the reader is able to keep pace with the descending bar or screen, he knows that his rate of reading is equal to the predetermined setting. Specially prepared reading material with corresponding questions is available with some pacers.

FILMS

The third type of device consists of a series of films which are ordinarily designed to be used with sixteen-millimeter projectors. These films permit the viewer to see portions of a line of text in succession; what has preceded it and what is to follow are occluded. The rate at which the text appears is built into the film, and questions accompany each.

Tachistoscopic drills may be found on film which is projected by a machine of a different type.

The first and third types—flashmeters and films—are recommended to the student who desires to increase his perceptual span. It has been suggested that pacers assist the eyes to move more rapidly over the printed lines. All three have been introduced to bring about an increase in reading rate.

Our purpose here is not to evaluate the rationale upon which the design of these instruments is based. Such a discussion would largely be theoretical in nature. Nor is it the purpose of this writer either to exhort or deprecate use of them in reading programs. What is suggested is a dispassionate evaluation of these mechanical devices in terms of existing research. Perhaps some conclusion regarding the desirability of using them may be drawn after such an examination. The literature affords some opportunity to inquire into reading programs which utilized these machines and provides some data that have been obtained under controlled conditions. This review will be limited to investigations that have been undertaken in the last two decades.

A further limitation is the removal from consideration of reports which merely describe the use of mechanical instruments in reading programs. There is no way of knowing to what extent the use of such devices has contributed to reading growth unless there is some control over the variable which can influence the outcomes. Marked improvement in reading rate has been reported for groups which had not received any special training over a given period of time (1), (5), (9), (12).

Results at Four Levels

ELEMENTARY LEVEL

Practically all investigations which deal with machines have been undertaken on the secondary, college, and adult levels. Very few have been initiated in the elementary schools. One study has been reported by Cason (3), whose sample was drawn from the third grade. Fifty-one children were divided into two groups: one received phrasing training without the use of any instrument, while the other was exposed to the same material with the metronoscope (a type of tachistoscope). Equated groups spent an equal amount of time in free library reading. Cason reported no significant differences between the two groups in reading phrases or improving eye movements. Also, there were no clear-cut gains in either programs over those secured through free reading.

SECONDARY LEVEL

Barry and Smith (1) divided 2,166 ninth-grade pupils from the Rochester, New York, public schools into eight groups, each containing above-average, average, and below-average boys and girls. Some groups read only timed articles, others saw only the reading films and answered questions, while still others had some combinations of both. Seven hundred twenty-nine pupils received no special treatment. The investigators found that the gains in reading made without the use of films were similar to those made by the groups that did see films. The group which received no help made as much improvement as did most of the other pupils who received some training.

Blough (2) made available to 324 students of an Indianapolis high school reading training in the form of pacers, films, and specially prepared reading materials. These students participated in fourteen actual teaching sessions. Two hundred eighty-three students served as a control group. The experimental group experienced gains of 24.6 percent in reading rate and 7.5 percent in comprehension, while the control group had gains of 7.5 percent and 3.1 percent, respectively.

Leavell and Wilson (6) tested the relative merits of tachistoscopic and pacer exercises, direct approaches to reading skills through means other than mechanical devices, guided free reading, and a prescribed English course of study. Two hundred ninety sophomores of a Dallas,

Texas, high school participated in the study. The data from one reading test did not favor any specific method within either the normal or superior I.Q. range of students. The results of a second test favored the groups that had tachistoscopic, pacer and tachistoscopic training, the direct approach, and the prescribed course of study over the groups that had pacer training and guided free reading.

COLLEGE LEVEL

Westover (12) divided ninety college freshmen into two equal groups. One was given practice in reading selected exercises; the second read the same content in phrases through a device for controlling eye movements. An additional fifty students received no special exercises in reading. At the end of five weeks, reading tests were administered to all three groups. Westover found that both experimental groups made significant gains in speed of comprehension and rate of reading. However, there was no significant difference between the two. The control group also gained significantly in speed and level of comprehension.

Henry and Lauer (5) evaluated four methods of reading instruction with 274 college students. One group received verbal instruction without definite practice; a second received practice on the metronoscope; a third did practice exercises from mimeographed material, the text for which was the same as that used for the metronoscope; the last group followed self-improvement instructions on texts read at home. The group that did the practice exercises from mimeographed material made the largest percentage gains—18.3 percent—with the home reading group a close second.

One hundred fifty college freshmen, matched for intelligence and reading ability, were divided into three sections by Wedeen (11). Section A read with a pacer, and section B read the same material under stop-watch conditions. Section C received no training. Section A exceeded B in rate but the latter was equal to A in comprehension growth. While the control group made gains in speed and comprehension, these gains were exceeded by both experimental groups.

To three groups of freshmen at the State University of Iowa, Sutherland (9) gave tachistoscopic word and phrase training, films and reading exercises, and no training in reading, respectively. The gains which were made by the films and reading exercises group exceeded those of the tachistoscopic group. The young men and women who did not receive any reading instruction made gains which were statistically significant.

Glock (4) selected 135 college freshmen who needed remedial reading. Some saw phrase reading films, others saw films that used the same text but which exposed two consecutive lines simultaneously, while the rest read the same material in pamphlet form. Glock realized results which showed improvement in rate and rate of comprehension with all three instructional methods. Some teachers obtained better results from one method than from another.

Wooster (13) tested the value of pacer training in a course of effective study. Two groups of six unmatched students each received 345 minutes and 315 minutes, respectively, of pacer training. A third group of forty-eight students served as a control. The investigator did not find any significant differences in rate or comprehension among the three groups.

ADULT LEVEL

Thompson (10) carried out an investigation with 438 officers of the Air Command and Staff School of Air University, Maxwell Air Force Base. The officers were placed through random selection into two experimental groups and one control group. Group I was organized as book-centered. Group II used a pacer to read selections on military subjects, biography, and social studies. Group III did not experience any special reading instruction. On the basis of test results the book-group mean was fifty words a minute faster than the mean of the machine group. Very slight changes in comprehension occurred as a result of training.

Manolakes (8) tested the relative value of tachistoscopic training and pacer training with thirty-four officers of the Marine Corps. Both groups received additional help in vocabulary and comprehension skill. The group which had pacer training alone exceeded the other (pacer and tachistoscope) by 238 words a minute. Both made significant gains in rate of reading.

A mixed group of high-school and college graduates, matched for reading speed, was divided into two sections by Lewis (7). One section received training with the flashmeter and metronoscope and other eye-movement exercises; the other practiced reading timed selections and discussed what it had read. The eye-movement group made an average improvement in speed of 24.7 percent; the practice reading group achieved an increase of 69.1 percent.

Conclusions

From some of these studies it appears that gains in rate of reading can be achieved through the use of a mechanical device. To what extent credit may be given to such a device for such achievement is unknown. Few, if any, of these studies were sufficiently tight to minimize the influences of extraneous variables upon the outcomes.

A second conclusion may be reached: In eleven of the twelve investigations which measured natural reading against machine reading, the groups that received training in the former either equaled or surpassed the machine groups in rate of reading. From these data it can be said that outcomes in speed of reading similar to those achieved through the use of special instruments may be expected from suitable reading instruction which does not includc these same instruments.

Of course, all of the answers have not yet come into the hopper of truth. However, it is reasonable to suggest from what information is presently available that perhaps the monies which might be spent for the purchase of reading machines be used for other purposes.

References

(1) Barry, R. F., and Smith, P. E., "An Experiment in Ninth-Grade Reading Improvement," *Journal of Educational Psychology,* XLV (1954), 407–14.

(2) Blough, Richard, "The Development Reading Laboratory: a Training and Proving Ground for Readers," *Bulletin* of the National Association of Secondary-School Principals, XL (1956), 38–41.

(3) Cason, Eloise B., *Mechanical Methods for Increasing the Speed of Reading.* Columbia University: Teachers College Contributions to Education, No. 878, 1943.

(4) Glock, M. D., "The Effect upon Eye-Movements and Reading Rate at the College Level of Three Methods of Training," *Journal of Educational Psychology,* XL (1949), 93–106.

(5) Henry, L. K., and Lauer, A. R., "A Comparison of Four Methods of Increasing the Reading Speed of College Students," *Proceedings* of the Iowa Academy of Science, XLVI (1939), 273–76.

(6) Leavell, U. W., and Wilston, G. E., "Guided Free Reading Versus Other Methods in High School English," *Peabody Journal of Education,* XXXIII (1956), 272–80.

(7) Lewis, Norman, "An Investigation into Comparable Results Obtained from Two Methods of Increasing Reading Speed Among Adults," *College English,* XI (1949), 152–56.

(8) Manolakes, George, "The Effects of Tachistoscopic Training in an Adult Reading Program," *Journal of Applied Psychology,* XXXVI (1952), 410–12.

(9) Sutherland, Jean, "The Relationship between Perceptual Span and Rate of Reading," *Journal of Educational Psychology,* XXXVII (1946), 373–80.

(10) Thompson, W. C., "A Book-Centered Course Versus a Machine-Centered Course in Adult Reading Improvement," *Journal of Educational Research,* XLIX (1956), 437–45.

(11) Wedeen, S. U., "Mechanical Versus Non-Mechanical Reading Techniques for College Freshmen," *School and Society,* LXXIX (1954), 121–23.

(12) Westover, F. L., *Controlled Eye Movements Versus Practice Exercises in Reading.* Columbia University: Teachers College Contributions to Education, No. 917, 1946.
(13) Wooster, G. F., "An Experimental Study of the Reading-Rate Controller," *Journal of Educational Psychology,* XLV (1954), 421–26.

31. Oral and Silent Reading

LUELLA COLE (1938)

In the first half-year of school, a pupil's fixations are so numerous and the focusing of his eyes so inaccurate that his silent reading is no more rapid than his oral. Moreover, he has a tendency to vocalize words—that is, to pronounce them—whether reading aloud or to himself. The initial stages of reading are, therefore, more or less oral, no matter how the children are taught. By the second grade, however, the eyes can move about twice as fast as the voice. If the children continue to receive intensive drill in oral reading, they develop the eye-movements and the pronouncing habits necessary for reading aloud. By the third or fourth grade these children have a good deal of silent reading to do in the preparation of their lessons. Since their whispering is annoying, the teacher usually succeeds in suppressing it. If she is conscious of the problem involved, she also suppresses most of the lip movement. The matter usually rests at that point. The eye-movements, because they are not visible to the teacher, remain essentially those that accompanied reading aloud. The young oral reader is trained during his first two or three years in school to take short jumps and many of them, and to pronounce each word. In the upper grades he continues doing exactly this, only without noise. Consequently, he is a slow reader and shows the characteristically low comprehension of the person whose speed is inadequate. For these various reasons oral reading should be avoided as much as possible, except at the very beginning. It is useful occasionally for testing purposes. There is, of course, no objection to oral training

SOURCE: Luella Cole, *The Improvement of Reading,* (New York: Farrar and Rinehart, Inc., 1938), pp. 62–68.

in the study of words. Word study is not, however, connected reading. The complete pronunciation of a new word appears to be necessary if it is to be learned, but the complete enunciation of every word in a story is wholly unnecessary for comprehension.

Vocalization

The term *vocalization* refers to any movement of the lips, tongue, or vocal cords. These movements vary all the way from complete pronunciation of every word to a tiny vibration in the throat; this latter is still present in even the best silent reading. Regardless of the method by which a small child learns to read he will at first vocalize to a noticeable extent. The pronunciation of a word is not merely a help in memorizing; if the word is within a child's own speaking vocabulary, he can identify it by its sound. Vocalization is, indeed, a pupil's chief method for getting hold of new words. As he learns to recognize more and more words by their appearance without their sound, he will gradually drop off his speech reactions because they are no longer necessary, unless his spontaneous pronunciation is reinforced by continued drill in oral reading. Anyone, whether child or adult, almost inevitably vocalizes a completely strange word, but a child who has been properly trained in silent reading does not set his speech organs in motion when he is reading familiar material. The less enunciation there is, the better, because vocalization is related inversely to speed.

Use of the voice should, then, be stressed as little as possible—except in word study—for three reasons. First, it slows down the rate markedly, because words can be pronounced about one-fourth as fast as they can be read by the eyes alone. Second, it develops habits of excessive fixation and frequent regression, because the eyes constantly get ahead of the voice. Finally, it interferes with meaning because the unit of pronunciation is a syllable, whereas the unit of meaning, at the very least, is a whole word and is usually a phrase. Complete vocalization often produces more fixations per line than there are words. It keeps the eyes from seeing such a phrase as "my little sister" as a whole because it consists of five separate units of speech, although it is a single unit of meaning. By causing slow and piecemeal reading and by obtruding itself into the reader's attention, vocalization interferes with comprehension.

Word-for-Word Reading

The habit of looking at each word separately may be caused either by excessive training in oral reading or by a too-conscientious attention to details. Some children get the idea that they must look at every word; to omit one would be a sin. Whatever the cause, the habit of plodding word-by-word across a line of print is wholly unnecessary. In the beginning, first-grade children usually do read in exactly this manner. Every word is more or less unfamiliar, and a pupil has no background of experience that can supply any word he fails to see. He must therefore look at every one enough times to recognize it. Soon, however, he should begin to supply words from the context. As soon as he knows that nouns are preceded by the article "the," he can supply this article from experience without looking at it. As soon as he knows that the phrase "not only" will soon be followed by "but also" he can "think" these words without reading them. The good reader can proceed by phrases, not only because he has a wide reading span but because he omits many words, supplying them instead from his previous experience. By the second grade a child will begin to leave out words spontaneously, unless the teacher is insistent that he must read all of them. To be sure, an occasional careless child has to be cautioned to omit fewer words, but in general children tend to read too many words in a sentence rather than too few.

Word-for-word reading is objectionable, not merely because it is slow, but because it inevitably interferes with the acquisition of meaning. Thus the words "in," "the," and "house" each have meanings of their own, but the phrase "in the house" has more meaning than the single words. In this particular instance the meaning of the phrase is the sum total of the meanings of the separate words. There are, however, plenty of phrases whose meaning is not a mere summation of the individual meanings which compose them. Such phrases as "through thick and thin" or "at sixes and sevens" must be read as units or their meaning cannot be understood. Children can learn, by the second grade, to recognize phrases and to read many of them as units. The sooner they achieve this habit, the better—both for their speed and for their comprehension.

Summary

Slow reading may, then, have one or more of three main causes. It may be due to inefficient eye movements, excessive vocalization, or word-for-word reading. These three causes are, of course, interrelated. A child who reads every word as a unit must have many fixations, and he has time to vocalize if he wants to. Excess vocalization leads also to many fixations, and the pupil tends to read syllable-by-syllable—which is even worse than word-for-word. The child with too many fixations usually vocalizes, and the largest unit he sees at once is a word. In general, the three bad habits go together, and it is often impossible to tell for any given child which habit came first, or if all three developed together. From a remedial point of view the chronological sequence does not make much difference.

The typical slow reader is not the victim of a single bad habit, but the possessor of an unfortunate system of habits, each of which reinforces the other. The whole performance is inefficient because it is clumsy and time-consuming. Even if a child becomes as adept as possible with this technique, he never gets the degree of comprehension by which his efforts should be rewarded, because his technique breaks up reading matter into tiny and meaningless units.

Good reading is characterized from the second half of the first grade on by few fixations, few regressions, accurate hitting of a new line, rhythmic movements, little or no vocalizing, and a wide reading span. This method of reading is not a characteristically adult method that can be achieved only after one is grown up. It is merely an alternative method to that used by the slow reader. Any child of normal intelligence can develop either method, depending upon how he is taught. A child who has already acquired one method can learn the other, provided he is given the appropriate drill. The good reader has an efficient combination of muscular habits which function automatically and rhythmically. As a consequence, his attention is free to concentrate upon meaning. There is no reason why better teaching in reading should not develop a greater proportion of children into good readers with good habits from the first. A few pupils will probably always start wrong, but by adequate analysis and remedial work even the child who has made a bad beginning may be re-educated and changed from a slow, plodding, inefficient performer to a good and efficient reader.

Bibliography

1. Buswell, G. T., "Fundamental Reading Habits: A Study of Their Development," *Supplementary Education Monographs*, No. 17, University of Chicago Press, 1922, 150 pp.
2. Center, S. S., and Persens, G. L., *Teaching High School Students to Read*, D. Appleton-Century Company, 1937, 167 pp.
3. Gray, W. S., "Reading," *Survey of the St. Louis Public Schools*, V. 2, St. Louis, Board of Education, 1917.
4. Heilman, J. D., "A Study in the Mechanics of Reading," *Colorado State Teachers College Bulletin*, Series 18, No. 12, Greeley, Colorado, p. 22, 1919.
5. MacCallister, J. M., "Character and Causes of Retardation in Reading Among Pupils of the Seventh and Eighth Grades," *Elementary School Journal*, 31:35–43, 1930.
6. Oberholtzer, E. E., "Testing the Efficiency of Reading in the Grades," *Elementary School Journal*, 15:313–37, 1913.
7. O'Brien, J. A., *Silent Reading*, The Macmillan Company, 1921, 289 pp.

8. O'Brien, J. A., *Reading: Its Psychology and Pedagogy*, D. Appleton-Century Company, 1926, 308 pp.
9. Pressey, S. L., *Diagnostic Reading Tests in Speed, Vocabulary, and Paragraph Meaning*, Public School Publishing Company, Bloomington, Illinois, 1928.
10. Robinson, F. P., "The Role of Eye Movements in Reading with an Evaluation of Techniques for Their Improvement," *University of Iowa Studies*, 39:52 pp., 1933.
11. Tinker, M. A., "Role of Eye Movements in Diagnostic and Remedial Reading," *School and Society*, 22:147–48, 1934.
12. Tinker, M. A., "Diagnosis and Remedial Reading," *Elementary School Journal*, 33:293–307, 1932; 346–58, 1933.

32. Rate of Comprehension—Needed Research

EMERALD DECHANT (1961)

With each bit of research it is becoming increasingly more difficult to speak authoritatively about rate of comprehension. Perhaps this is because we don't understand comprehension. We are not certain what comprehension is, how it may be improved, or how it can be measured accurately.

Rate of reading frequently has been described as rate of comprehension. Perhaps it is better described as speed in grasping the meanings intended by the writer. To read is to comprehend, but one may comprehend at a slow rate or at a relatively more rapid rate.

Thus, rapidity in reading has value in its own right and should be investigated as a separate skill. It is an important asset. There are fast readers, average readers, and slow readers, and it seems more desirable to be a rapid reader than a slow reader.

The superior reader supposedly pushes his eyes across the page as rapidly as his comprehension permits. This may or may not be good. No one can work at top efficiency all the time, and there is no great

SOURCE: *Changing Concepts of Reading Instruction*, VI (1961), 223–225. Reprinted with the permission of Emerald Dechant and the International Reading Association.

necessity in even wanting to. At times slowness is beauty. To read slowly, to think critically, and to feel deeply may be true enrichment.

That many of us read much more slowly than we could is an obvious fact. That others read as rapidly as their comprehension abilities allow may also be true. And for these, rate improvement training is of little value.

Fast readers and slow readers may or may not comprehend well, but sometimes the fast reader comprehends better than the slow reader. This happens when the fast reader is reading approximately as rapidly as his comprehension abilities allow and when the slow reader is reading more slowly than his comprehension allows.

Rate of reading, of course, is not the ultimate goal in reading. The ultimate aim is comprehension according to one's abilities and needs. This means that the good reader is a flexible reader. Rate of reading should always be dependent on the purposes, intelligence, and experience of the reader and upon the difficulty level of the material.

Rate improvement cannot be built on inadequate word identification and word recognition skills. It cannot be built on an experiential background that keeps the reader from understanding what he is reading. And it cannot be built upon immaturity in intellectual development.

On the other hand, there is little doubt that rate of comprehension can be improved. Students and adults who have undertaken some form of rate improvement training do increase their speed and generally will read faster than those who have not had such training.

Advocates of rate improvement programs (no one seriously recommends that only mechanical devices should be used) claim that such programs also may lead to increased accuracy in perception, more accurate and more rapid visual discrimination, wider span of apprehension, better attention and concentration, shorter reaction time, fewer regressions, a decrease in the number and duration of fixations, reduction of vocalization, better comprehension, and general improvement in perceptual skills. Unfortunately, as soon as one attempts to evaluate these claims he is confronted by all sorts of conflicting evidence. The basic facts that the evidence suggests are the following:

1. The visual span (or the amount seen) on the tachistoscope is much wider than the recognition span (the amount seen and understood). Poor readers frequently have a wider visual span than superior readers.

2. The tachistoscopic span is usually wider than the recognition span in normal reading. The fixation span in normal reading is about .65 words for the average eighth grader; 1.06 words for the average twelfth grader; and 1.11 words for the average college student. The tachistoscopic span may include many more words even when exposure time is only one one-hundredth of a second.

3. The perceiver can be taught through tachistoscopic training to "see more" by making greater use of peripheral vision, but no one has demonstrated that this will necessarily increase reading speed or reduce the number and duration of fixations in normal reading. Before his experience on the tachistoscope the reader already sees more than he uses in normal reading even after training.

Tachistoscopic training seems to increase the ability to make quicker mental associations with rapidly changing visual stimuli. It leads to maximum reaction to a minimum of cues and to guessing more accurately what may be only surmised from the context. Unfortunately, in normal reading where all cues can be seen the reader does not seem willing to exert the same physical energy to achieve the same result. Increased muscular tension in a machine program may lead to increased perceptual speed, but how to get the student to exert the same energy in normal reading is another problem.

4. Rate improvement programs, including both machine and book-centered programs, seem to lead to attitudinal and work-habit changes. The student will attack the reading task more aggressively. He will anticipate what is to come and is mentally set to comprehend and to remember. He will demonstrate optimal attention and concentration and may be more active in organizing what he is reading.

Unfortunately, there are many more unanswered questions. So far, we have a better knowledge of *what* is happening, even though this is far from complete, than *why* it is happening. The needs for research are multiple. Here are some:

1. Since regressions are actually fixations in reverse and since the average eighth grader regresses approximately 21 times per 100 words, the average twelfth grader 17 times, and the average college student 15 times, may increase in speed as reported in various studies be mainly the result of a decrease in the number of regressions?

Regressions occur because the reader does not see accurately, has not developed a left-to-right directional attack, or has not learned to coordinate vergence (single vision) and focus (clear vision). Each of these skills can be developed through other means, but perhaps not as easily as through mechanical devices.

The reader also may regress because he lacks confidence in his ability to comprehend; he has developed the habit of checking; or he is not able to follow the trend of thought. Helping the student with these difficulties means essentially two things; building up his confidence in himself and providing for his comprehension needs.

Mechanical devices are motivating. They may even increase comprehension achievement; however, they cannot increase comprehension potential. They merely force the mind to operate on a level approximating its potential.

Persons working with mechanical devices repeatedly have noticed among students an increase in interest in reading and in a desire to improve their reading skills.

It thus frequently is impossible to attribute rate improvements to machines alone. Increased motivation and increased teacher effectiveness may be as significant.

2. Should we choose machine or book-centered programs? What are the relative advantages and disadvantages of each?

3. How can we increase the transfer effects, if there are any, of machine programs? Normal reading is continuous textual and nonrhythmic reading; tachistoscopic reading is almost the opposite. It is rhythmic phraseology. And yet, the good reader is a flexible reader. What are the disadvantages of developing in the reader an inflexible reading attack?

4. How can we determine optimal tachistoscopic exposure time? The average fixation in normal reading is from .22 to .32 seconds. Is there validity in training procedures requiring only .01 seconds of exposure time?

5. What are the transfer effects of numbers in tachistoscopic training? It is almost impossible to perceive more than eight or nine numbers in a series because memory fails, and yet this sequence is shorter than two average words. Numbers must be remembered in exact sequence, and this is much more difficult than remembering words whose exact sequence can be inferred from previous experience. Each number sequence may be different.

As someone has suggested, practicing on digits may increase the ability to watch license plates, but hardly reading ability.

The recognition span on the tachistoscope increases progressively as the student changes from random letters to numbers, to nonsense syllables, to unrelated words, and to meaningful phrases.

6. We need a test with equivalent forms that can be administered before and after tachistoscopic training. Such tests have been developed by Fletcher.[1]

He found that when three equivalent forms were given during the first, second, and last session, most of the gains occurred between the first and second session. The technique of rapid performance on a tachistoscope seems to be acquired rather quickly. What are the implications of this finding?

[1] J. Eugene Fletcher, "Rapid Reading, Perception, and the Tachistoscope," *College of Educational Record*, University of Washington, 25, May, 1959, pp. 52–55.

7. To what degree do the changes in performance as indicated on tachistoscopes, accelerators, controlled readers, and eye cameras reflect in performance changes on standardized tests?

8. How can rate improvement devices best provide for the development of flexibility in reading various materials for various purposes?

9. Individuals who practice on mechanical devices reduce the duration of the fixations (exposure time is reduced) and increase the span (more words are seen), but even before training their tachistoscopic span was wider than their recognition span in normal reading. And, even after training, the recognition span in normal reading is wider than their initial tachistoscopic span. Why? Furthermore, of what relative value is such training?

10. Finally, there are many related questions that constantly perplex the practitioner. For example: How can we develop effective tests of rate of comprehension? How can we determine the student's optimal reading speed on specific materials? We recommend that the rate of reading approximate the student's thinking rate. What is this? And, which rate skills should receive most reinforcement?

VI. Individual Differences

Speaking pedagogically, individual differences, like death and taxes, are always with us. Although first-grade teachers have problems coping with individual differences, we are reminded by Anderson and Dearborn (33) in the opening selection of this chapter that the situation grows worse as one moves into the upper grades. Sixth graders show two and one-half times greater spread in reading skill than do first graders. Even more surprising is this fact: The better the teaching, the greater the range in pupil achievement!

A fairly recent and widely publicized approach to the problem of meeting individual differences centers around individualized reading. According to Stauffer (34), an awareness of the need for individualized instruction in reading dates back to the 1920's. An up-to-date discussion of individual differences is contained in the Twenty-Fourth Yearbook of the National Society for the Study of Education, Part II.

In a more recent article, "Procedures Used in Directing Individualized Reading Instruction," Bond (35) reminds us that reading is a complex process and that children are both alike and different at the same time. He then familiarizes us with dimensions of the problem that must be kept in mind when considering individualized approaches to reading. In closing his article, Bond commends teachers who are not afraid to experiment in their attempt to meet individual needs.

Slow learning children, those whose IQ's generally lie between 75 and 90, constitute a sizable percentage of children in today's schools. Witty (36) provides us with an insight into the nature of the slow learner and makes valuable suggestions as to how his reading needs can be met.

In concerning themselves with individual differences, do teachers make adequate provisions for the more capable student? Whipple (37), editor of a curriculum guide for the Detroit schools, reminds us that a reading program should not overlook the superior student. A. Sterl Artley,[1] co-author of a popular basal series, indicates concern over the tendency of teachers to underestimate the capabilities of gifted pupils. With this in mind, the reader will not want to miss the practical suggestions found in the Whipple material.

Another group of children for whom there is great concern in today's reading programs are the culturally disadvantaged. In the article "Reading Help for the Disadvantaged" (38), the problems faced by teachers who work with these students are nicely itemized. Practical suggestions follow. These involve home visitation, working with parents, interesting pupils in books, and giving the culturally disadvantaged child plenty of love. How do the suggestions and recommendations found in this article differ from those that would be appropriate when teaching all children?

An experimental research study by Carlton and Moore (39) brings to our attention self-selection and self-dramatization of stories as valuable techniques for improving the reading and social adjustment of the culturally disadvantaged.

Teachers who feel that they are groping and not grouping effectively will want to read the article by Clymer (40). He brings to our attention a number of significant points, among which are: (1) There are many ways to group students, none of which produces complete homogeneity; (2) Differences within a grade are much greater than differences between grades; (3) Intraclass grouping is more fruitful than interclass grouping. Clymer provides us with basic questions that should be considered before grouping of any kind is initiated. Helpful, too, are his criteria for inter- and intraclass grouping.

[1] A. Sterl Artley, "Some Musts Ahead in Teaching Reading," *Reading for Today's Children.* Thirty-Fourth Yearbook (Washington: Department of Elementary School Principals, National Education Association, 1955).

33. Individual Differences in Reading Achievement

IRVING H. ANDERSON and
WALTER F. DEARBORN (1952)

Every teacher should have the experience of administering a standardized reading achievement test to her pupils and of making a tabulation or frequency distribution of the results. This exercise would serve to bring forcibly to the teacher's notice the individual differences that exist among the children of any age or grade. The acceptance of the normality of these differences constitutes another foundation stone of the growth philosophy. The student of growth would view the differences in the light of the sources of variation so far discussed in this chapter. The differences are deep-seated, and they cannot be eradicated by training. If anything, the effect of schooling is to increase the variation shown.

Individual differences in reading achievement among children of the same age. Figure 1 presents a fairly typical picture of the differences in reading achievement which occur when children are grouped according to age. This figure has been constructed from the results of standardized reading tests administered to children in the University of Michigan Elementary School. The results are presented separately for each sex. The number of children in the several age groups varies from 47 to 87 for the boys, and from 38 to 81 for the girls. The curved lines running through the figure show the trend of the average results, while the horizontal lines indicate the ranges of achievement.

While the average results increase from age to age, the most notable thing about Figure 1 is the ranges of achievement shown. The variation increases as the age groups become older. At a life age of 132 months, a total difference of more than ten years occurs among the boys. That such differences could exist seems amazing, but the literature abounds with supporting evidence. Variation is the rule in all the school subjects.

SOURCE: *The University of Michigan School of Education Bulletin*, XX (January, 1949), 49–52. Reprinted by permission of Irving H. Anderson.

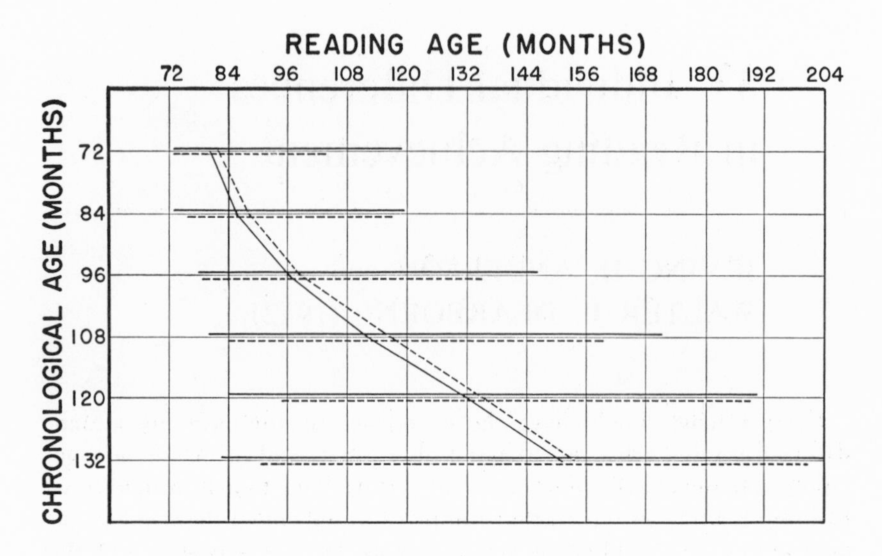

Figure 1. Differences in reading age among children of successive chronological age groups (solid lines, boys; broken lines, girls).

In view of the variations in reading achievement which show up within age groups, it is inevitable that considerable overlapping in performance will occur between groups. Figure 1 shows how it works with reference to range of performance. The two youngest age groups are virtually indistinguishable in terms of this measure. The same may be said for the two oldest age groups. Some overlapping exists throughout all the age groups represented in the figure. There was a boy at age 72 months who had as high a test score as the average child at age 132 months. Another boy at age 96 months achieved a test score which was almost on a par with the performance of the average child at 132 months. It can even be said that there were children among the six-year-old group who read better, according to the tests, than some of the eleven-year-old children.

Incidentally, Figure 1 can be reviewed with profit with reference to sex differences in reading achievement. The figure shows that the girls, on the average, were slightly but consistently superior to the boys, but that the boys were just as consistently more variable. The greater spread among the boys tends to throw more cases of this sex to both extremes, which is in line with the classic doctrine that the greater variability of the male covers both ends of the distribution. The figure clearly shows how much larger in scope the individual differences are than the sex difference. The individual variation leaves small choice between the sexes, except as the boys vary slightly the more. Millard has published a study which brings out many of these same facts. His study was concerned with the relationship between the preadolescent growth cycle in reading and intelligence and sex. He found that the more intelligent pupils of both sexes entered their cycle of development sooner than the less intelligent, but he also discovered that girls tended to enter their cycle earlier than boys. However, wide individual differences in reading achievement were apparent among both boys and girls at all the ages studied. Similar results have been obtained for Negro children by Goodlett and Calloway.

Individual differences in reading achievement among children of the same grade. Since children nowadays tend to be passed along in school in chronological age groups, the differences in reading achievement which are typical of the children of any age are likely to occur when pupils are grouped according to grade. Figure 2 presents a good illustration of this point. This figure has been constructed from the results of a standardized reading test given to all the sixth-grade pupils of the elementary schools of a suburban community near Detroit. The results were converted into grade scores, and the graph shows how these scores were distributed. The distribution is remarkably normal or bell-shaped in appearance. The main talking point again, however, is the variation of the results. The range extends from a grade score of 3.5 to

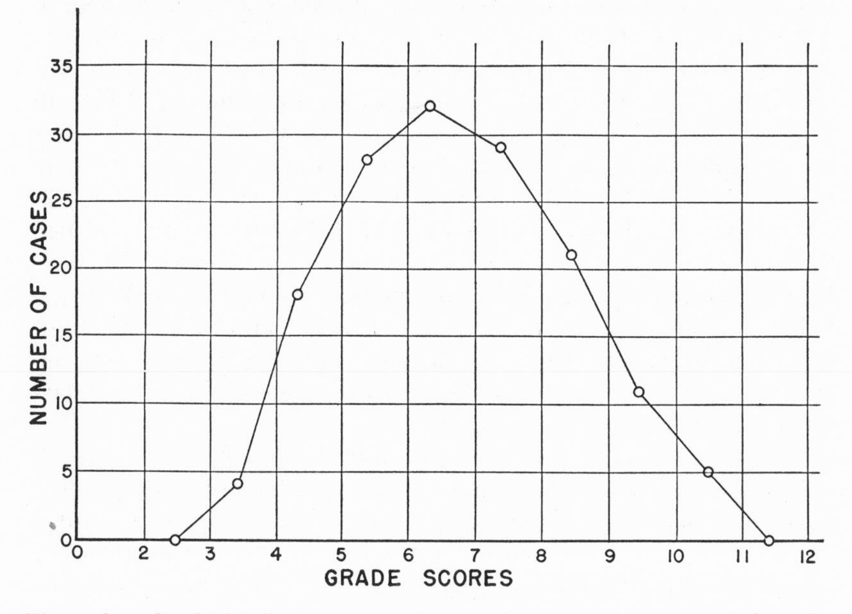

Figure 2. Individual differences in reading grade among a group of sixth-grade children.

one of 10.5, which is a total difference of seven grades. On the basis of similar studies, Betts has reported that fifth-grade pupils may vary in reading achievement from approximately the preprimer to twelfth-grade level. Harris has reported the results of an extensive survey involving 19,063 eighth-grade pupils from the New York City schools, in which the subjects were found to vary in reading achievement from below the third-grade to the college level. Two surveys conducted by the Bureau of Cooperative Research and Field Service of the School of Education, Indiana University, involving 15,206 sixth-grade pupils in 648 schools in Indiana, and 11,424 sophomore students in 243 high schools, revealed extraordinary variation among both groups on the basis of scores on the Iowa Silent Reading Tests. If a variation of three years is taken as reasonable within a grade, 38 per cent of the sixth-grade pupils fell outside this range. Gray reported a survey in which 22 percent of nearly 6,000 ninth-grade students from a Chicago suburb fell below the seventh grade in reading ability, as measured by a standard test. Seventh-grade reading achievement has been suggested by Gray as the minimum requirement for successful high-school work.

The implications of individual differences in reading achievement. To turn now to some of the practical aspects of the matter. The reader-per-grade idea, certainly, is difficult to defend in the light of the variation in reading achievement which is normally present among the children of any age or grade. The use of the same sixth-grade reader, for example, with the group represented in Figure 2, would miss both ends of the distribution. Too many teachers, however, persist in the belief that all children should be brought up to grade each year in reading. In this they are not unlike many parents. It is not unusual to hear a teacher attribute her reading problems to the idea that the children were not brought up to grade the year before. The implication is that the teacher who had the children the year previously was not on the job. It cannot be done. Children do not grow like norms on published tests. In a study of the growth in reading of 28 boys and 28 girls representing a University of Michigan Elementary School population, Olson and Hughes were unable to find a single case whose growth in reading could be described by the line of average development.

The superior pupil is usually able to shift for himself, insofar as reading is concerned. Studies have shown that reading ranks high among the leisure-time activities of bright children, and other work has revealed that the books and magazines which bright children select for their recreational reading possess high literary value. The real losers from the reader-per-grade concept are the children in the low end of the distribution. A case in point was that of a boy of twelve who was placed in the fifth grade but who had not made the expected progress in reading. An examination at the child's school quickly disclosed that the boy had no better than second-grade reading ability. To satisfy his curiosity, the writer asked the lad to go into his room and fetch the book that he held in his hands during the reading period. The youngster quickly returned with the book in hand. It was a fifth-grade reader! The material was obviously too difficult for this pupil. Pressure was nevertheless brought to bear on him to read the material during the reading period. The boy had developed the habit of nervously scratching the side of his head each time he stumbled over a word or caught himself making a mistake. This habit was plainly a reaction to the frustration that he encountered in trying to read material which was too difficult. He had developed other problems as well, including a defeatist complex toward reading. For this child, reading was without any purpose or enjoyment. The distressing part of it is that his case can be endlessly multiplied in schools which follow the practice of assigning a reader per grade, come what may. The children learn to dread reading and to abhor school.

A teacher cannot be a teacher of any one grade alone, but rather must teach all the grades represented in her class. Just because a child sits in a room designated as such and such a grade is no sign that he needs material commonly assigned to that particular grade. Material must be found for every level of attainment, and the interests of all must be satisfied. Meaning or context constitutes the prime requirement for learning to read. This condition cannot be met if half the words are unknown to the child. Bond and Wagner have sized up the evidence correctly in the following passage:

> Another interesting conclusion that may be drawn from the study of any table indicating range of reading ability in any one class . . . is that the teacher is not a teacher of a given grade, but a teacher of many grades. She is not only a teacher of fourth-grade reading, but a teacher of reading of all the grades from the third through the eighth. She is not a teacher of sixth-grade reading, but a teacher of reading of all the grades from the third through the eleventh. It is, therefore, futile to talk about levels of attainment that should be reached by all the children within any given grade. It is far better to know that the children grow at varying rates and that adjustment must be made by the teacher and the school to these individual differences.

The idea that a teacher can be a teacher of one grade alone is an abstraction of the mind. A teacher of a combined third and fourth grade had the right idea when she responded to a query regarding her dilemma: "It makes no difference at all. If you didn't know the children, you couldn't tell who were in the third grade and who in the fourth."

This teacher was taking it all in her stride. She knew that the individual differences which normally occur in each grade would make her two groups practically indistinguishable. Yet teachers have been known to view with alarm the juggling of staff that circumstances occasionally force upon schools. A teacher, for example, who has never taught anything but fourth grade wonders how she will ever be able to manage the third grade which has been thrust upon her in the shuffle. As one teacher protested, "I have always taught fourth grade—I don't know anything about third grade." That such notions could exist is a commentary on the rigidity with which some schools operate their programs. In some schools teachers are virtually forbidden to use any but the reader that is standard for their grade, despite the fact that some of the children might be able to read the whole book at one sitting, not to speak of the rest of the series, while other children might take two or three years and not make any real headway with the material. All the children must somehow be made to utter the words on the last page of the reader before the end of the year, but to allow any of them to go on to the next reader might spoil it for the teacher in the grade to follow. The rest of the curriculum may be just as rigidly prescribed. Some teachers will not stand for it and soon begin looking for another job.

Much abuse has been heaped on modern methods of teaching reading, mainly by parents who are disappointed because their children do not compare favorably in reading achievement with their classmates in school. Similar attacks are made in newspapers and in popular magazines and occasionally even in professional education journals. The plea seems to be for a return to the old alphabet and phonetic methods of teaching reading. Most of this agitation can be put down as a failure to recognize that there is always going to be a low end to the distribution, regardless of the method used. When pupils fail, parents naturally begin looking for excuses. The teacher and her methods constitute an obvious target.

Summary

To attempt an answer now to the parent's query with which this chapter was launched. Reading is still very much taught in the schools. More time is devoted to reading in the primary grades than to any other school subject. Methods have changed, but most authorities in this field agree that the changes have been for the better. No method can get around individual differences. Parents do not expect children to be of the same height or weight. It is equally foolhardy to expect that children will learn to read alike. As Quintilian, who was born in A.D. 35, said "there is in talent an incredible variety, and the forms of mind are not less varied than those of bodies."[1] Children may be delayed in learning to read, even though they have good minds. Reading is an aspect of total growth, and the reason that some intelligent youngsters get off to a slow start is that they are immature in other ways. The same children may eventually develop into excellent readers if parents are willing to bide their time and accept the child as he is. The school has an equal responsibility in this regard. The low end of the distribution presents no special problem to schools which are conducted according to the growth philosophy. Each child is taken wherever he is and given an opportunity to function at that level. Individual differences are taken for granted. Retarded readers are free to select easy books, the advanced may select whatever appeals to them. Olson and Davis have found that under this permissive system, children consume books according to their individual timetables of growth. The practice is a comfortable one for the children as well as for the teachers. The object of the growth philosophy is to promote growth by providing the opportunity. It leaves it to the children to seek experiences which are compatible with their total growth designs.

34. Individualizing Reading Instruction—A Backward Look

RUSSELL G. STAUFFER (1957)

"Is it desirable and practical to carry differentiation still further—to the complete individualization of instruction? This is the issue raised in this volume." Thus wrote Guy M. Whipple in his Editor's Preface to the *Twenty-fourth Yearbook* of the National Society for the Study of Education, Part II, copyright 1923, "Adapting the Schools to Individual Differences." If this quote was not dated, a person unfamiliar with the

[1] Quoted in William Boyd, *The History of Western Education* (London: A. & C. Black, Ltd., 1921), p. 76.

SOURCE: University of Delaware, Reading-Study Center, *Individualized Reading Instruction,* Proceedings of the Thirty-Ninth Annual Education Conference (1957), pp. 3–11.

history of education might readily conclude that it had appeared in a recent periodical or book.

Today individualized instruction seems to be receiving the same amount of attention that was given to grouping in the thirties. Could it be though that our thinking and acting about individualizing instruction runs at least a quarter of a century behind the recommendations of leaders in education? Could it be that the widespread interest in individualized reading instruction and self-selection reflects only what authorities urged many years back? Could it be that we should reread what has already been said about individualizing instruction and then with this perspective examine our current practices? It could be.

It seems almost incredible that our earlier leaders should not only think about methods for improving reading instruction and providing for the widely differing individuals in our schools but also that they should produce in one volume a classic combination of these educational issues. Part I of the *Twenty-fourth Yearbook* of the National Society for the Study of Education is "A Report of the National Committee on Reading." As already stated, Part II is on individual differences.

William S. Gray and Ernest Horn, two of the most highly respected educators on the current scene, were members of both committees, chosen to prepare the two parts of the *Twenty-fourth Yearbook*. The former was also the chairman of the Committee on Reading. Other names appearing on both committees cause the list to read like a specially selected Who's Who in Education. The writings of these people reflect the good judgment of professional individuals genuinely concerned with the improvement of education. As Guy Whipple stated in the Editor's Preface to Part I, the ". . . compilers have kept clearly differentiated what is known, what is merely the best opinion, and what is yet unknown and in urgent need of investigation."

Basic Reasons for Individualizing Instruction

Even though much of the research currently available on human growth and development had not been done when the *Twenty-fourth Yearbook* was written, certain principles emerged that were and still are important for education (Part II, p. 6): (1) No group has yet been found in which the individuals composing it possess equal amounts of any one ability. (2) Performances vary so greatly as to indicate that no single requirement is adequate as a stimulus to a majority of the group. (3) To study the development of a learning process it is absurd to set up as a standard a definite quantity of performance and expect each member of the group to accomplish just that amount and no other.

In addition, the conditions under which children learn produce other differences. All in all, the hierarchy of individuality sets as the first task for education the discovery of the amount of development that has occurred in each student; and, as a second task, the discovery of a means whereby greater ability may be developed.

Coaching the laggards by providing remedial instruction and enriching the curriculum for the bright are simply preliminaries to complete individualized instruction. Furthermore, the issues between individualized instruction and group instruction are really very minor in many respects. What must be kept in mind is that different amounts of time are required by different pupils for the mastery of given skills; that different amounts of practice and reinforcement are needed to develop abilities of different pupils; that different methods yield different results with different people; and that attitudes and interests and motivations further distinguish individuals.

The primary consideration in schools, therefore, should be efficiency of instruction, rather than, as has so often been true, ease of administration. Where efficiency is the order, different attitudes and practices manifest themselves. Such habits as the habit of failure, of half-done work, of working below one's powers, of shirking, are replaced by opposite and more effective habits. As A. A. Sutherland of Los Angeles, California, wrote, "Individual differences among children, while disturbing to a system of education which tries to ignore them, are potentially the means by which human society may progress" (Part II, p. 30).

Attempts at Individualizing Instruction

If Preston Search, formerly Superintendent of Schools in Pueblo, Colorado, and Los Angeles, California, and Frederic Burk, formerly at San Francisco State Normal School, could visit the current scene and note the renewed concern about individualized instruction, they would feel that perhaps at last teachers are ready to break the lock-step in their classes. The lock-step meaning that all pupils in a class as one are required to move forward at the same rate, in the same book, mastering the same amount of material to the same degree of thoroughness. Search is referred to as the first voice in America raised loudly in protest against lock-step methods of teaching. He did so as long ago as 1888. In 1915, Burk's famous "Monograph C" was being widely read and reviewed because it showed the results of two years of work toward individualized instruction.

Mary Ward and others in their section of Part II of the *Twenty-fourth Yearbook* say that for many years Dr. Burk was a student of individual differences and an ardent foe of anything that savored of the lock-step in education. A feature of his plan was that while individual progress was provided for, abundant opportunity was afforded for group work.

It is indeed true that today recommended practices for the teaching of reading go well beyond the "Monograph C" approach. The "home reader" is now the school reader, and reading is taught and tested in school. Reading vocabulary studies initiated then have been extended and refined. As then, "wider opportunity is given for individuals to follow their own tastes" (Part II, p. 70) but at an earlier level. The basic intent of breaking the lock-step is still the same—individualizing instruction.

In Burk's day, the concern was with breaking the lock-step in situations where all pupils in a class were taught as one. Today, in most instances we've broken this pattern, so that in most classrooms a minimum of three groups are identified in each class, and instruction is differentiated for each group. All this does, however, is simply to commit the same errors on a smaller scale from what whole class instruction did on a larger scale. In fact, in some schools this attempt at ability-grouping and homogeneity-seeking is sought after so eagerly that all pupils in grades four, five, and six are reshuffled for reading instruction. This is done so that pupils at the so-called "same level" can be instructed together as a class by a teacher who supposedly has become an expert at teaching skills at a particular level. Study and research as long ago as 1924 showed that the difference between the central tendencies of even the highest and lowest groups is less than the range of abilities within any one group. This may mean that as many as one-fourth of the middle group may make as good a record as the bottom half of the best group.

Also in Burk's day emphasis was shifted to "understanding of the story read, rather than parrot-like repetition in words" (Part II, p. 70). Oral reading in the usual sense was not to be done and as they said, "No child is required to listen to another read and explain what he himself has already read" (Part II, p. 70). Today, the "Round-the-robin oral-reading" performance has been largely eliminated. Now, however, there is strong opposition to the methods so widely practiced in reading instruction that results in "Round-the-robin comprehension." This is the procedure in which the teacher sets the purposes and asks the questions, usually factual in nature, and pupils play back the text, usually verbatim. There is no reflection, no weighing of facts and inferences, no judging and no generalization. The consequence of such reading is a non-thinking, parroting of the text that is even more costly to members of a free society than were the results of the oral reading method.

Later, the Winnetka technique of individual education as directed by Carleton W. Washburne, at one time an associate of Burk's, adapted the "Monograph C" recommendations to a public school system. In the Winnetka technique, instead of varying quality, time was varied. In other words, a child could take as much time as he needed to master a skill, but he had to master it. Some of the things that the teacher did under this system read very much like the so-called new ideas urged under the current drive toward Individualized Reading Instruction. To quote: "The teacher, under this plan, spends her whole time teaching, not listening to recitations. She helps an individual here or a group there; she encourages and supervises. She is about among the children as they work, not at her desk" (Part II, p. 80).

Time was allowed, too, for group and creative activities. Thus, the Winnetka plan allowed not only for flexibility of time but also for different interests and abilities as the curriculum was adapted to individual differences.

At the time Wrightstone was inaugurating the Winnetka plan, Helen Parkhurst started another form of individual instruction known as the Dalton Plan. This plan drew international attention.

Miss Parkhurst said her plan was a sociological rather than a curricular experiment. Its aim was to keep school life from becoming mechanical by socializing the school. It was a vehicle for the curriculum and concentrated more on the life of the school. There were three basic principles: first, the principle of freedom; this meant freedom to work without interruption in order to pursue an interest and to develop concentration. Second, the interaction of group life, or community living, was brought about by having subject laboratories and specialists and by giving the pupils of four or five grades access to a laboratory. And, third, individuals were allowed to budget their time according to their own needs and difficulties. The plan's basic philosophy was to have pupils function as *individual members* of a *social community.*

Of course, the Dalton Plan was applicable only to any part of the school *starting with the fourth grade.* It was supposed that students of that age and stage had sufficient command over the tool subjects (reading, for instance) to work independently and easily. The plan aimed to combine class work, but most important was the training it gave pupils *to handle a job, to manage time,* and *to plan work.*

Other plans are described in the *Twenty-fourth Yearbook,* Part II, but generally two types of plans were presented. One tried to make adjustment for individuals without breaking up the basic class organization; the other provided for strictly individual progress in the common essentials with provision for compensating socialized activities.

Interestingly enough, in the same yearbook the writers provide evidence to show that what they had done might be only half-way measures. But they hoped that the day would soon be at hand when each child would be recognized as a living human being, differing from every other human being in his needs and in the contributions he can make, yet a member of society who must co-ordinate his life with that of his fellow members.

Some of the questions raised and problems to be solved were also listed. What sort of text books and tests should be used? How could schools shift with what they now had? What kind of time schedule should be followed? Should children be kept together in classes, with differentiated assignments? How large should classes be? How could the attitude of teachers be changed so that they could make individual work a success?

In the answering chapters some ideas occur with considerable frequency. Individualized teaching and learning does not mean that it is solitary. The details of the action will have to be, in a large measure, self-directed. In reading there must be an abundance of self-directed, spontaneous reading of books, magazines, and newspapers. "This can have no resemblance to the reading of normal living if great masses of individuals must be assigned the reading at the same time, in class fashion, of the same newspapers, the same magazines, and the same books" (Part II, p. 226). The individual is social-minded and will want to discuss what he reads and profit by the discussion. Small groups, spontaneously formed, are best to stimulate the turning over of ideas in the mind, of seeing their significance and relationships, and otherwise digesting and assimilating them. Teaching must be vigorous, inspiring, and high-minded. Individualized teaching requires a sufficiency of group activities.

There can be no such thing as a uniform standard to be achieved equally by all pupils. Each pupil must be assisted to go as far as he will or as far as he can. To develop necessary skills may require more time and more effort for some pupils than for others. There must be constant measurement. Text books will need to be provided which give sufficient facts, knowledges, and skills. Individualized reading may not be "busy-work or padding." Large classes seriously decrease the advantages of individualized instruction. The teacher is a teacher of children rather than a hearer of lessons. Careful methods of recording progress must be adopted. The good teacher will take the child into partnership and strive to help him help himself. The training of teachers must bring this point of view to prospective teachers.

The recommendations for individualizing the work in a school given by Carleton W. Washburne by way of summary could well be repeated here. Some of the key suggestions are (Part II, p. 271): (1) Select one or a few teachers who are likely to make the experiment a success. Secure their whole-hearted interest and cooperation. (6) Prepare a simple record system to keep track of children's individual progress. (8) Abandon all recitations in the individualized subjects, substituting supervised study and objective tests for the recitations. (10) Keep the parents in close touch with the salient features as these become accomplished facts.

Some of those not listed here are applicable largely in situations where specifically structured plans such as the Winnetka Plan were to be used. The current thinking again about individualized reading instruction skirts the shortcomings of such rigid patterns, but should not skirt the good points.

In his appraisal chapter Kilpatrick looked carefully at only the Dalton Plan and the Winnetka Plan. He pointed to such common features as—acquiring a better sense of responsibility, better time-budgeting, improved social relationships and better self-respect. Indeed, as stated earlier, critics of the time recognized the half-way measures of some of these specific plans, but as implied throughout this review, the critics of today should fully appreciate the values of these plans and go on from there.

Reading Activities in School and Social Life

Thus far, attention has been given almost entirely to Part II of the *Twenty-fourth Yearbook*, "Adapting the Schools to Individual Differences." This, in many ways, might be called the forgotten part of the Yearbook. Now attention needs to be given to the better-known Part I on Reading. As a matter of fact, the subtitle for this section is the title for the first chapter of the Yearbook, Part I. It is used here again because it so well reflects the timely thinking of the Yearbook authors.

The point of view of the Committee was to encourage instruction in reading that would enable pupils to engage effectively in desirable life activities. This was to be accomplished by taking into account the types of reading experiences that people do and should learn to do better. The reading experiences they referred to were activities in modern life as well as in school.

They recognized as the most important change of the first quarter of the twentieth century the enrichment of the course of study whereby wide reading opportunities in many fields replaced a few textbooks. It followed naturally from this that good reading instruction had to provide help in all school activities involving reading. Paralleling this was a clearer recognition that people read for a wide variety of purposes and that the habits employed in reading must be sufficiently sound and the skills sufficiently varied to change with purposes for reading and the kinds of materials used.

This declaration concerning the purposes for which people read and the materials they use to accomplish their purposes led to a better recognition of the value of individualizing instruction. If reading was to enable each reader to participate intelligently in the thought life of the world about him, his thinking powers had to be stimulated by reading so that he could be a well-informed, thinking citizen with desirable interests, standards, tastes, and habits.

World War I had alerted the American people to the large number of non-reading adults. This, along with investigations in reading, led to another conclusion of great significance—one that influenced decidedly the movement toward greater differentiation of instruction—the importance of permanent interests in reading.

If, in the future, reading instruction was not only to teach pupils to read but also to broaden the horizon of the reader, stimulate permanent interests, and foster vigorous use of thinking powers, then instruction would need to be differentiated. Each pupil would need to be stimulated so as to reach his fullest measure of growth. As a matter of fact, one phrase that occurs again and again throughout the *Twenty-fourth Yearbook* report on Reading is "differentiated reading instruction." The Yearbook Committee would have acted fittingly if they had labeled Part I of the Yearbook *Differentiating Reading Instruction* to parallel the excellent title for Part II, *Adapting the Schools to Individual Differences.*

The modern reading program (1924) detailed in Chapter III recognized the need for differentiated instruction at all levels. The section dealing with the initial period of reading instruction begins with a discussion of the wide differences among pupils entering first grade. Children are different in intellect, experience, and interests when they enter school. It is not poor teaching that makes them different as had once been thought. But it is good teaching which capitalizes on the differences and helps each pupil advance according to his best potential. The discussion is climaxed with the following sentence: "In order to provide appropriate instruction for them they must either be taught individually or in groups which are more or less homogeneous" (Part I, p. 32). While many of the essential activities listed are for group instruction using common materals for all in the group, the seed is sown for the individualization of instruction by repeated referrals to the (1) need for instruction in reading with all classroom activities and (2) independent and directed reading to stimulate personal interests and develop permanent habits of reading.

This recognition of the need for differentiated instruction from the very beginning is repeated again and again with increasing clarity and detail at successive levels. In the discussion of the program outlined for the intermediate grades the following two points are made: ". . . the fact cannot be emphasized too vigorously that the essential aims of instruction are attained primarily through wide reading" (Part I, p. 58), and "Each teacher should study the needs of her pupils so carefully and provide appropriate group and individual instruction so effectively that no pupil will reach the end of the sixth grade who has not formed desirable reading attitudes, habits, and skills" (Part I, p. 62).

"Provision for Individual Differences" is the title of Chapter VIII. By devoting a chapter to this method of instruction it may once more be assumed that the Committee did so to show the significance they attached to it. Some of the charges leveled at traditional methods could very easily be thought of as occurring in a 1957 periodical: for instance, "Whole classes are provided with the same articles of reading diet on the same day. Too often the diet is meager and the daily portion insufficient. Freshness and variety are noticeably lacking. Selections are served and rehashed so many times that appetites are systematically dulled" (Part I, p. 227).

Then the report goes on to point out that one of the measures of how effective reading instruction has been is the amount of time which each pupil devotes to reading. By this they meant, reading to satisfy his own purposes, at his own rate, and with appropriate material.

Once again, it is true that to a considerable degree only the seed was being sown for the individualizing of reading instruction. The specifics presented in the eighth chapter are concerned largely with flexible grouping, multiple assignments, and independent work. However, in the paragraph discussing grouping appears the following pertinent statement, "Varying tastes and interests are the bases for the selection of varied materials and also point to the need for an organization of classroom procedures which permits a reasonable amount of choice in the selection of materials" (Part I, p. 229). That this recommendation should foster the self-selection practice and the procedure whereby all pupils are instructed individually is readily perceived.

At the same time the Committee recognized two extreme positions—mass instruction and individual instruction. So they added: ". . . no doubt the best way lies somewhere between the two or in a combination of group and individual work" (Part I, p. 231). What they sought was to have each pupil attain maximum growth with the least amount of waste and the most satisfaction.

Finally, in the last chapter or the summary chapter they direct attention to twelve issues of fundamental importance to a satisfactory program for teaching of reading. The tenth point is: "10. Adequate provision for differences in individual capacities, needs, and tastes" (Part I, p. 306). Another part of this chapter lists problems in urgent need of investigation. The first one listed is *classroom organization*, the sixth is *the relative effectiveness of different teaching procedures*. Much of what has been written in the *Twenty-fourth Yearbook* is necessarily tentative in character, the Committee points out, and represents the Committee's opinion. Before final conclusions can be reached much additional evidence is needed.

In Summary

It seems clear now that a review of the principles and practices stated and outlined in the two parts of the *Twenty-fourth Yearbook* was timely and worthwhile. It should have pointed up a number of things.

Authorities writing in the early twenties and reflecting the experiences and insights accumulated during the nineteenth century and the early part of the twentieth century wrote with amazing discernment, acumen, and farsightedness. The principles they declared are sound and reflect recognition of the role of an individual in a free society, the need for accurate communication, and the need for people schooled in the art of independent thinking, wide reading and considered judgments. The practices they described were as they themselves indicated, half-way measures.

Now then, a quarter of a century later are we about to develop practices that are more than half-way measures? It seems that we are. The flood of reports dealing with how classroom teachers are actually teaching reading indicate that the momentum for individualizing of instruction is increasing. It may be that the quarter century we are now in may provide us with the skills and techniques essential to expert differentiation of instruction.

Lagging behind the recommendations of authorities by a quarter of a century is not too astonishing. Acquiring newer, better practices is by circumstances slow because it involves all the people. Traditions of practices and procedures are not easily put aside. From this we must learn not to be disheartened but to work on courageously and steadily, assured that what we are doing is taking us down the road toward better education.

35. Procedures Used in Directing Individualized Reading Instruction

GUY L. BOND (1957)

It is always a pleasure for me to speak to a conference on reading. It is a special pleasure for me to come to a conference that is considering the fact that youngsters must and will grow differently in regard to reading development.

I want to point out, at the start, that the topic is somewhat bigger, if we consider it in all of its ramifications, than just a description of individualized reading instruction. We must know that the adjustment of materials and methods, to meet the individual differences, is probably the teacher's most difficult task. It is a dilemma that has confronted us from the start of education for all the people. We could trace the whole history of education as attempts to answer this problem. We have, throughout the years, been constantly improving in the ways that we have tried to meet the fact that youngsters will and must grow in reading at different rates and in different ways.

Reading: A Complex Learning

Reading is, as you know, a very difficult learning. It is a complex learning. It is a learning that is cumulative. You must gradually develop the skills and abilities in reading. In fact, all of the major characteristics of a poor reader can be found in a youngster who is starting to learn to read, except that, as he develops reading skills and abilities, he is able to meet more complex materials—materials that call for finer judgments on his part. He is able to meet materials that have an ever-increasing vocabulary load; he is able to differentiate his reading as he develops up through the program so that he can read the materials of

SOURCE: University of Delaware, Reading-Study Center, *Individualized Reading Instruction*, Proceedings of the Thirty-Ninth Annual Education Conference (1957), pp. 42–50.

the various fields of human experience effectively and in ways that are compatible with the purposes for which he is reading those materials.

Learning to read, then, we recognize is difficult. As a matter of fact, it is very fortunate that the youngster, starting to learn to read, doesn't know how difficult it is to learn to read or he would probably give up the attempt, right at the start.

The child learns to read in materials that increase in difficulty gradually and as soon as he becomes comfortable in a preprimer, so that he can read it fluently and well, we put him in a primer or in material of that level of difficulty. He is constantly confronted by a situation in which the problems change as soon as he gains in capability in handling those problems. Therefore, it is no small wonder that youngsters will and must grow at different rates in reading. They learn to read with their eyes, their ears, their energy output, their emotional stamina, their backgrounds of experience, the comfort of their home conditions, their intellectual stature. Every part of the youngster goes into this learning act, and any variation in any of these will make for variation in the rate at which that child learns to read. So, we need not be surprised to find the variation great, at any level. The youngsters entering the first grade come quite differently equipped to start this long job of learning to read what they have ahead of them.

Let us use the fifth grade as an example. We can, in the normal course of events, expect competency in reading to range as much as seven years—from second grade to ninth grade. We should note that the better the instruction in the earlier years, the wider will be the range and the bigger will be the problem of adjusting to the reading capability of those youngsters. At ninth grade, in the normal course of events, the reading capability will range from fifth grade to college freshman. This is the normal thing to expect. Our job is to learn to live with this range in reading ability and to encourage every youngster to grow as well as he is capable of growing and as rapidly as he, as an individual, can gain all of the skills and abilities necessary to grow toward maturity in reading.

The problem we are faced with has certain psychological dimensions. I want to look at them before we start to describe how we may best individualize the reading program. In the first place, I'd like to point out that children are, at any grade level in any class, more alike than they are different. They are different, but they are also alike. They are alike in many important ways. They are alike in that all of them have drives, motives, interests. They all want to succeed in what they are doing. Most of them want to go home and say that things went well in school today. In fact, some of them say that things are going well even when they aren't, or they will make excuses to explain why things don't go so well. Often parents and others who come in contact with the children do not get a completely accurate picture of the problems that the youngster is facing.

Dimensions of a Sound Program

I think that whatever reading program we use, then, must take into account the fact that every youngster must be successful in learning to read; that every youngster should be proud of what he is doing. I think that one important thing that we, as teachers, have to do is to let every youngster have the feeling that he is getting along well in the job of learning to read—not as well as somebody else, maybe, but that every day he is learning and growing. Well, that is just an outgrowth of the first dimension, a dimension of the problem which I happen to think is a very important one.

The second dimension is that children are growing in many ways other than reading and whatever way we take to adjust to reading difficulty, we must know that reading growth is just one of the many changes that is taking place. Therefore, any approach we use must recognize all of the areas of growth of the youngsters. I believe that this dimension, in itself, should make us very cautious about a too drastic failure or acceleration policy. We must remember that the youngsters are growing in many ways. I think that it makes us have to appraise each youngster rather carefully.

The third dimension is that no child's general growth curve in reading is uniform and for different children reading growth does not necessarily follow the same growth pattern nor proceed at the same rate. One youngster of average ability may start to learn to read relatively rapidly. He has good visual perception and good auditory capacities, so he learns some of the initial lessons much more rapidly than any other and brighter youngster, who is not so well equipped in these other respects. But when the instruction gets to be more in the nature of interpreting what is read, and the sensory capacities lose some of their dominance as determiners of success, then the first child may slow down a bit, while the second child, who started out somewhat slowly, may pick up steam as the reading problems demand higher reasoning. This dimension indicates to us that any method of instruction we use must be highly flexible so that we can alter what we are doing for the child as his instructional needs and his reading capacities change.

The fourth dimension is that reading itself is complex. There are marked differences in the reading capacities of a given child. A youngster may be a good reader in one area and relatively poor in another.

He doesn't have a uniform reading profile. He will have low and high points in his reading abilities. This complicates our problem to quite a degree because a youngster, for example, may be a relatively effective reader of science material and a relatively poor reader in some other area. Therefore, programs of grouping according to reading ability would have to consider the kind of reading ability upon which we are going to group. Who will determine whether it will be on the child's ability to read science material, his power of comprehension, or on just what parts of the reading profile would we make that decision? We may need to make our decision according to the subject-matter field involved or we may need to regroup for each new reading situation.

The fifth dimension of the problem is that it changes as we advance up through the curriculum. In the first, second, and third grades, especially in the first and second grades, when the youngster has not gained much independence in word recognition skills, when he is not very adept at grouping words into thought units, when his fluency in reading and his adaptability in reading are not so highly developed as they will be later on, the youngster cannot be relied upon to do as much independent work as can a youngster who is further along in the continuum of reading growth. The fact is, then, that certain adjustments that will work at the high school level, for instance, will not be effective at the primary level. Certain solutions that work well at the primary level may be wasteful at the high school level. The problem changes, then, as we go up through the curriculum.

The sixth dimension is that the methods of adjustment to individual differences must change according to the phase of the reading curriculum being considered. We must alter the way in which we handle the reading and reading instruction in each of the following four areas of the reading curriculum: (1) the basic program, the program wherein we are teaching the reading skills and abilities; (2) reading in the content fields, in which the child reads in order to learn the subject matter; (3) guided literature reading, those reading experiences that relate to the personal development or recreational reading of the youngster; and (4) remedial or corrective reading, those reading experiences that are designed to correct or straighten out confusions in reading. In each of the four phases of the reading curriculum, the solution to the problem of adjusting to individual reading needs is quite different.

The seventh dimension is that the problem changes with any change in school organization—from urban schools to rural schools or from self-contained classrooms to multiple teachers. The problem of how to handle the different instructional needs of the children alters with any change in school organization.

Another dimension is that of time and the fact that there are certain fundamentals of reading instruction that take time. If, for example, we assume an hour for basic reading instruction and if we think of youngsters in a highly individualized program in which there are thirty-five youngsters with thirty-five separate selections to be read, the problem of time becomes a very important element. In this case, the teacher would have less than two minutes with each youngster to introduce the new vocabulary, to establish the purposes for reading. This two minutes must also allow for all of the follow-up instruction, such as the comprehension and word recognition exercises, which would need to be different for each child, since each selection is different. Watching a child read a selection is not, by any stretch of imagination, teaching him how to read.

Teachers Are People

We would like to point out that teachers are people and that their energies are not unlimited. I know because I am a teacher and my energies are not unlimited. There is only a certain amount of energy that I have and sometimes I find that I get tired. So I have to think, in regard to this problem, of the teachers getting ready to present and understanding all of the materials, having read each of the thirty-five selections prior to the time the youngsters read so that she will know where they are likely to get into trouble, be able to build all of the backgrounds, and give readiness experiences so that the youngsters can really read rather than verbalize; so that they can interpret the material. We have to recognize that teachers are people with finite limits to their energy and time, and we must plan ways of adjusting to reading differences in children realistically.

With these dimensions in mind, let us consider solutions to the problem in individualizing reading instruction. We have tried, and I know whole countries that are trying rigorous policies of retardation and acceleration as a means of meeting different rates of growth in reading. We, in America, have rejected this approach. In one country I visited, when I studied how reading was taught in other English-speaking countries, they had a rigorous promotional policy. The promotional policy was such that in a third-grade class I saw seven-year-olds and fourteen-year-olds. That situation defies the psychological dimension that children are growing in many ways other than in reading. Some of the children didn't fit the seats; they couldn't even play together; their interests were quite different. For these reasons, we have rejected such marked retardation and acceleration. But does that mean that we have rejected studying the youngster and seeing if he will be better off in a class coming along than he would be in the class that he was with this year? I don't believe it does, but we are now taking more things into account in making decisions about promotion or non-promotion.

Different Attempts at Differentiating Instruction

We have attempted differentiated assignments and different expected outcomes from youngsters reading the same material as a means of adjustment. The less mature readers read to find specific answers, while the more mature readers read to critically evaluate or to interpret more fully the materials they are reading. We have found that this approach does not fully answer the problem. Differentiated assignments may help to answer the problem when coupled with other methods of individualizing reading instruction.

We have tried ability grouping, assigning children to classes so that they will have more similar reading capabilities than does a typical class. It was indicated in the discussion of dimensions that we must consider upon what basis we will make that decision as to which youngsters will be grouped together. There is no question that ability grouping will lower the range of talent with which we have to work. I do not believe that this approach is as bad as some would have us believe it to be, but I don't think it will do all that other people claim. In other words, I believe that after we get the children grouped, we still have the problem of individualizing their instruction. This is true with any organizational scheme or administrative device for answering the problem.

We have tried fixed groupings within the class. Under this approach, the less mature youngsters could not profit from the enrichment given by the capable readers. In fact, although we have said that we put youngsters together so that they could learn to work together, we have dramatically separated them within the class. We have tried to get around this fault by having them work together in many of the activities, not associated with the reading program, throughout the day and we've done a pretty good job of that. Another difficulty with fixed grouping is that a youngster faultily placed in one of these groups, or a youngster whose growth curve had started to accelerate, would find it difficult to move from one group to another because often moving from one group to another would involve as much as a two-year double promotion. Therefore, we are and we have been looking for other ways of adjusting to individual differences.

Recently we have been using what we call multiple-flexible groupings, groupings wherein we have basic reading instruction given in three or more groups. Then, we have interest groups expanding the topic that the middle group is studying. In this related reading about a topic, the youngsters read individual selections and then share their ideas. When the teacher detects that some youngsters have like problems with regard to reading skills and abilities, she takes these children aside and works with them as a corrective or remedial group, while the rest of the youngsters are working somewhat independently.

We have been working toward more highly individualized programs. We have tried many, many ways of arranging reading instruction so that the children could work together and still have their program somewhat individualized. As was pointed out this afternoon, we are trying new approaches, and that is as it should be. It is with these new approaches that we now want to spend some time. We are not going to look at the problems involved—that comes in another talk later on. What we are going to do is look at one way in which we are now attempting to do this job. It is in the experimental stages as yet. It has been recently labelled the individualized reading program and was defined by the speaker this afternoon as each child reading a different selection according to his interest and stature in reading.

Individualized Programs

This approach takes many forms. First, I would like to say that there can be no question, in my mind at least, that this is a very good way of handling all the experiences that the youngster has with reading other than the systematic instruction in the skills and abilities taught in the basic program. I see individualized reading as an effective way of bringing children and materials together in the personal development or recreational phase of the reading curriculum. Here the youngsters pick books because they are of interest to them, they are at a suitable level of difficulty, and the teacher thinks that they have something to contribute to that youngster's total growth as a person. I do not really believe in a completely free reading program even in recreational reading. I believe in a guided reading program where the youngster is reading books that are suitable to him and will do something for him. He isn't taking just anything he wants to read, but is reading things that should be of some merit to him and will expand his interest and improve his tastes. We just do not have time, in elementary and secondary education, to let the youngster evolve everything. I want to guide and direct his reading so that the evolutionary process is accelerated for him. But, nonetheless, we could readily have every youngster within a class reading a different book in the recreational phase of the reading program. He could even help in the selection of the book he reads. In this literature phase of the reading program, we can either employ individualized reading or we can use a unit arrangement in which the teacher has selected a whole group of books that deal with a given topic, so that there will be some books suited to the poorest readers and some to the best readers within the class. Of course, we want to point out that in the first, second, and third grades, this part of the program is somewhat difficult. But, when the poorest readers are above fourth grade in reading, then there is ample reading material for anything that is worth reading about for even the poorest readers. The high school teachers should note this point rather carefully. We should remember that an independent reader in a third-grade class, the youngster that we lean upon there as a resource worker, is about a fifth-grade reader, and at the high school level, the youngster who is causing us the most serious problem is also about a fifth-grade reader.

There is ample material above the fourth-grade reading level for most topics. But, when you look for material that is below fourth grade in reading difficulty, you will find that tradebook or library writers will not take all of the controls into account that are necessary in order to write simpler material. So we do not find all the material that we would like at these lower levels. I am sure that we will have to have more materials written at the lower levels if we are to go into an individualized reading program. We will need materials written on topics and with interest appeal suited to older children who are less mature in reading ability.

When we consider the second phase of the reading curriculum as those times when the youngsters are using reading as an aid to learning, we find it somewhat easier to use an individualized structure than we do when we are systematically building the skills and abilities in reading. We can organize the subject-matter fields into topics, and we can teach experience units. By having such a series of topics we can teach the subject matter, and at the same time we can adjust the materials to suit the reading capacities of the children, because we are not systematically or in an organized way trying to build the skills and abilities of reading. We are concerned only with using effectively the reading capacities the child has already developed.

Teachers who are attempting to use individualized instruction in the basic reading program (at least out our way) still have groups within their classes in order to get greater homogeneity among the children with whom they are working. The teacher may have a group of children come up to work with her, each child having a book at his own level of reading capability. The teacher watches the youngsters read and when one gets into difficulty, the teacher finds out what the difficulty is and helps to straighten out the confusion. I cannot help but believe that there will be many gaps in the reading program of the children if such a technique is used. Frankly, I have to admit that I am worried about this approach to reading instruction because it is based on the assumption that learning to read is a simple thing requiring only occasional and haphazard instruction. This is far from being true. Reading is a complex learning needing carefully organized and detailed instruction in the skills involved. I do not think the child catches reading skills and abilities by simple exposure as he might catch the measles. I know that he must be taught in a well-ordered sequence of learnings where the teacher does much more than watch him read and correct his errors at the same time as she is watching thirty-five other children. I think we could have quite a debate as to whether the so-called individualized program is the most effective way to handle adjustment to individual differences in reading for basic reading instruction. I don't believe that it is.

I think that in all of our approaches in trying to handle this problem of adjusting to individual differences in reading, we should encourage experimentation. I think that teachers who try new approaches are the ones who are going to learn to be better teachers of reading, and I know the whole profession will gain stature and capability by trying out new and different ways of handling this basic problem that we must solve if every youngster who enters the first grade is going to grow in reading at his own rate and grow comfortably in the job so that he can be proud of what he is doing. It is a hard job. I haven't described how it can be done. I've simply indicated that I am glad that people are experimenting with a wide variety of ways of trying to answer this problem.

36. Needs of Slow-Learning Pupils

PAUL WITTY (1961)

Education is sometimes regarded as a process in which the greatest development of every child is sought, according to his unique nature and needs. One group, often neglected in our schools, is made up primarily of slow-learning children—pupils who are below average in ability, but not retarded enough to be considered mentally handicapped. These pupils are characterized, roughly, by IQ's ranging between 75

SOURCE: *Education*, LXXXI (February, 1961), 331–336.

and 90. In many schools, these pupils constitute about 15 to 18 percent of the class enrollment.

In our efforts to challenge average and superior students adequately, there is an ever-present threat that we shall overlook or neglect the slow-learning pupils. Because of the current emphasis on superior and gifted students, it is especially desirable for us to examine the extent to which slow-learning pupils are being recognized and challenged in every classroom today.

Nature of the Slow Learner

Studies show that the slow-learning pupil usually is not different from other pupils in his physical development, but he may have a slightly greater tendency toward instability. This tendency often is inevitable. The slow learner usually experiences disappointments and frustrations in school because he fails to comprehend materials fully and to make steady progress in learning. Indeed, his learning rate is so slow that by the time he reaches the upper elementary grades his educational status as shown by standard tests usually will be a year or more below the grade standard.

Recognition of these facts may have led Christine Ingram to state: "Satisfactory adjustment in life calls for self-confidence, self-reliance, and independence on the part of the individual. The mentally retarded, because of their inability to compete successfully with other children, tend to lack these essential qualities. It becomes, therefore, the responsibility of the school to provide experiences that will aid this group to become self-confident, self-reliant, independent workers at tasks commensurate with their learning abilities." (3)

Insecurities and anxieties often accompany the slow-learning pupil's growing recognition of his inferiority as he advances from grade to grade. However, the need for safeguarding him from needless anxiety and insecurity exists from the time he enters school. The attitudes of the slow-learning pupil may be influenced deeply by his experiences in the first grade in which his failures lead him to develop grave doubts concerning his own competence and acceptability.

Repeated failure may cause the slow-learning child to resort to compensatory mechanisms. Because of his insecurity, he may be led to exhibit one or a combination of the following reactions: withdrawal, aggression, indifference, lack of interest, nervousness, or marked anxiety. At home, he may reveal a lack of self-confidence and may resort to minor illnesses to receive attention or to avoid regular school attendance.

Care must be taken to insure reliability in appraising the ability of this pupil, since average and superior students who fail in school may exhibit similar behavior. Moreover, it is well to recall that learning rates for slow-learning pupils may vary because of motivational and environmental factors. Careful testing and observation are needed to justify designating pupils as "slow."

Because of the foregoing facts, it is essential at every level of the slow-learning pupil's education for his goals to be attainable. It is essential also for his goals to be raised gradually in order for him to make steady progress.

Building Skills

The educational attainment of the slow-learning pupil should be thoroughly appraised. He often needs help in acquiring the basic habits and skills in all areas, but the need for assistance in reading is usually great and persistent. Accordingly, his reading ability should be evaluated with utmost care. In the primary grades, special consideration should be given to readiness.

The results of standardized oral and silent reading tests may be used to ascertain the child's attainment. Later on, they may be employed to estimate his gains. Data obtained from diagnostic tests also may be helpful. In addition, the nature and amount of the child's reading in books and other sources may be investigated. Study of his rate of reading different types of material also may be pertinent and useful. With such information at hand, it will be possible for the teacher to offer the pupil an opportunity to read materials of appropriate difficulty and suitability.

Steady Reading Gains Possible

If learning goals are adjusted to the slow-learning pupil's educational status and are geared to his rate of learning, the learner's progress usually will be steady. Recognizing his own continuous progress and relatively greater success in school also may contribute to his sense of security and may affect his general mental health favorably.

Within the regular classroom, provision may be made for the slow-learning pupils' acquisition of reading skills by use of multi-level materials. Special help in reading may even be provided throughout the junior and senior high school to satisfy the needs of slow-learning pupils, especially in the area of vocabulary growth.

Study of Interests

It is desirable for the teacher to study the interests of slow-learning pupils. Studies show that these pupils often have meager or narrow interests, in which cases the crucial need is to encourage the development of new or more desirable patterns of interest through enrichment and extension of experience. Visits to near-by airports, farms, and other places of local importance will provide avenues for firsthand experiences which may engender interest.

Interest also may be cultivated through the use of films and filmstrips. The film readers, designed to accompany many films, may be employed successfully with slow-learning pupils, since the film supplies the background necessary for an understanding of each booklet. Experiences of these kinds often stimulate a strong interest in reading.

Observation of pupils during and following experiences of various kinds is one way of detecting worth-while interests or promising avenues for the development of interests. There are other more formal approaches for obtaining pertinent information about the nature and extent of children's interests.

Questionnaires recently have been developed and used in comprehensive studies of children and youth in a research project co-operatively undertaken by Northwestern University and the United States Office of Education, Department of Health, Education, and Welfare. The questionnaires included inquiries concerning the following areas of interest: TV, radio, and movies; play and recreation; reading and vocational and educational pursuits. (4)

Interest inventories, designed to study play activities, fears, wishes, hobbies, preferences, and other or related interests, often yield clues of value in understanding pupils' attitudes and needs. The use of anecdotal records and similar approaches also may enable the teacher to gain further insight into pupil interest. Examination of personal or creative writing may also disclose needs.

The interests characteristic of the slow-learning pupil should be employed. He should be educated not in the shadow of average and superior pupils, but in terms of his own experiences, interests, and concerns. Some slow-learning pupils will be interested in particular vocations; others in the people of various lands; and still others in the exploits and discoveries in space. To satisfy these and other interests, the world of books offers a readily available avenue. In addition to factual presentations, there are narratives, poems, and biographies to satisfy almost every taste, hobby, or interest. (6)

Pupil Needs

We have indicated that, to offer effective instruction, the teacher should have available not only facts about each slow-learning pupil's reading but also information pertaining to his interests. To help guide the pupil in attaining the most rewarding outcomes from reading, findings regarding each pupil's needs are also essential. The study of developmental needs differs somewhat from the study of interests, although similar techniques may be used in both cases. We are searching in our study of needs for evidence of the relative success of each pupil in his adjustment to recurring life demands and situations.

Needs are sometimes referred to as "developmental tasks." According to Robert Havighurst, a developmental task "arises at or about a certain period in the life of an individual, successful achievement of which leads to his happiness and to success with later tasks, while failure leads to unhappiness in the individual, disapproval by society and difficulty with later tasks . . ." (2)

The value of an approach to reading through a concern for need is gradually being acknowledged. This approach is particularly appropriate in the case of the slow-learning pupil because his needs are so frequently blocked or denied. His rehabilitation often appears to depend upon the extent to which his fundamental need for self-respect and self-esteem can be satisfied.

It is recognized, of course, that experience in reading in itself will not lead invariably to the fulfillment of needs. However, if reading is used in association with other activities, it may assist greatly. We must recognize, moreover, that many factors determine the impact of reading upon boys and girls. Thus David Russell wrote: "We must hypothesize that impact of reading is determined by the reader's expectations or set, by his overt purpose for reading, by his conscious or unconscious needs, by the personality traits or patterns which affect much of his conduct, and by combinations of these factors." (7)

It is generally acknowledged that research data on the impact of reading are inadequate and inconclusive. "From the research point of view, however, the effects of reading are an uncharted wasteland in an otherwise well-mapped territory." (7)

Nevertheless, there is, it seems, justification for recommending an approach to reading through a concern for the interests and needs of the slow-learning pupil. For case-studies do show that such reading often has a desirable effect upon the mental health and well-being of the pupil. (9)

Reading and Developmental Needs

In the Northwestern University Psycho-Educational Clinic, books have been employed for many years to aid children in making desirable personal and social adjustments.

A list of needs that characterize children at various levels has been drawn up, including, for example, understanding oneself better; adjusting to one's peers or associates; understanding and participating effectively in family life; achieving an understanding of, and an acceptable personal choice of, occupation and other needs. Books which may contribute to the fulfillment of each need often are suggested from a list of appropriate titles. Stories may be selected which provide the adolescent with an opportunity for appropriate identification and also with an opportunity to attain a better understanding of himself. Case-studies have revealed remarkable gains made by slow-learning pupils whose reading has been guided by this approach.

The clinic's list is only one of several such lists which have been compiled during the past decade. An excellent bibliography of this type was published as a supplement to the *Chicago Schools Journal*. (5) This bibliography contains annotated references for books arranged under seventy-eight headings.

Developmental Reading Aims

For the slow-learning pupil, a developmental reading program appears especially desirable. Such a program recognizes the value of continuous systematic instruction, utilization of interests, fulfillment of developmental needs, and the relationship of experience in reading to other types of worth-while activity. By this four-fold approach, steady growth in reading skills is made possible, and the attainment of basic human satisfactions is facilitated.

One aim of this program is to lead the slow learner to become like other pupils, independent in using the library and other resources for satisfying his interests and fulfilling his varied and changing needs. This objective will be achieved if the student is enabled to enjoy reading and the results of reading.

He usually will enjoy reading if he acquires a reasonable command of silent and oral reading skills. He can acquire these skills through an efficient, systematic program of reading instruction and guidance throughout the course of his education.

The slow-learning pupil will enjoy the results of reading when reading experience is associated with his interests and needs. Accordingly, slow-learning pupils may become skillful, independent readers on their own levels and may continue to extend their understandings and satisfactions throughout their lives by reading.

Importance of the Teacher

Perhaps the most significant single factor in determining the success of efforts with the slow-learning child is the teacher.

A major responsibility of the teacher of the slow-learning pupil is to provide a classroom atmosphere in which success, security, understanding, mutual respect, and opportunity to attain worthy educational goals are pervasive. In such an atmosphere the teacher will be prepared to direct children's development in such a way that their emotional life will yield the maximum of human satisfactions and values.

In all classrooms the mental health of the teacher is obviously a most important consideration. (8) In a quest for mental health the teacher will find many sources of help, not the least of which will be the satisfactions derived from observing the growth and progress of all types of pupils. Especially great will be the satisfaction experienced by the teacher who observes, in the case of slow-learning pupils, conspicuous gains in self-confidence, self-respect, and general mental health as well as in academic attainment.

References

1. Brooks, Alice R. "Integrating Books and Reading with Adolescent Tasks," *The School Review*, Vol. 43, pp. 211–219.
2. Havighurst, Robert J. *Developmental Tasks and Education* (Chicago: University of Chicago Press, 1948).
3. Ingram, Christine. *Education of the Slow-Learning Child* (2d. ed.; New York: The Ronald Press, 1953).
4. *The Interests of Children and Youth* (Washington, D.C., U.S. Office of Education, 1959).
5. LaPlante, Effie, and O'Donnell, Thelma. "Developmental Values through Books." *Supplement to Chicago Schools Journal* (March and April, 1950).
6. Larrick, Nancy. A *Teacher's Guide to Children's Books* (Columbus, Ohio: Charles E. Merrill Books, Inc., 1960).
7. Russell, David. "Some Research on the Impact of Reading," *The English Journal* (October, 1958).
8. Witty, Paul (Chairman). *Mental Health in Modern Education,* Fifty-fourth Yearbook, Part II, of the National Society for the Study of Education (Chicago: University of Chicago Press (Distributor), 1955).
9. Witty, Paul. "Promoting Growth and Development through Reading," *Elementary English* (December, 1950).

37. Reading Instruction for Children of Superior Ability

GERTRUDE WHIPPLE (1953)

In planning a reading program for the children of a class, the teacher finds a very important and challenging responsibility in providing opportunities for the superior pupils. The term "superior" includes roughly up to 15 or 20 percent of the more able students in the average school; about 2 percent of the school population are considered "gifted" or perhaps "genius." It is important to study and develop superior learners for many reasons, but especially because they should be prepared to provide sound leadership for our people. Education in a democracy implies the development of the gifted individual, and reading is a valuable means to this end.

The growth of the superior child, like that of other children, is influenced by maturation. The natural process which brings about growth in the child's height and weight and produces other physical changes also causes him to learn. As the farmer knows that he does not make the corn grow and that all he can do is to provide favorable conditions for its growth, so the teacher should know that his most important function in serving the child is to provide the most favorable conditions and opportunities for individual development and learning.

We need to remember, too, that growth throughout childhood is not uniform but occurs in cycles and that each child is unique in his pattern of maturation. It has been found that children differ so much in their inborn natures that no one sequence of steps or experiences will be equally effective with all. It is known that boys and girls who know very little at birth gradually become men and women and that during this process they inevitably learn. Learning, then, can be considered a natural by-product of experiencing. As teachers guide the natural process of growth, true learning takes place. As Dr. Stuart Courtis points out in this article, "New Understanding of Learning," we need to place chil-

SOURCE: Gertrude Whipple, *Curriculum Guide in Reading* (Detroit: Board of Education, 1953), pp. 39–47. Copyright 1953. Reprinted by permission of the author and the publisher.

dren in situations where they will be stimulated by their own purposes. Then if the teacher supplies them with materials and demonstrations of how to use these materials and assists them in every way possible to achieve their purposes, they will acquire intellectual power just as they grew into power to walk. True learning is a maturation process. It is being discovered that learning to read, to write, and to figure is just as inevitable as learning to creep, to walk, and to talk.

In working, then, with children who achieve outstandingly, the teacher finds it unnecessary to give help in the same way as to children of lesser achievement, but finds instead a golden opportunity to free these gifted children from many restrictions, to enrich their learning in ways which will bring them new power, and to assist them in developing their own life purposes.

Characteristics of Superior Learners

How can the teacher select the children of superior ability? What are the signs of superiority? To find the gifted pupils, the teacher will first consult his initial survey. He will also note indications of superior intelligence in his day by day work with the children. Perhaps he will find unusual powers of concentration or an ambition to excel. A fine command of language and superior reading powers are indications too. Gifted children are often equipped with a keen sense of humor and independence of judgment as well as exceptional powers of observation. The endless questions asked by the superior child usually mean that he has interest in many things about him and that he has a great desire to learn and is alert beyond his years. His answers are usually to the point; he writes fine examination papers and often gets high school marks. Probably the outstanding indication of superiority is that of original or creative thinking.

The teacher ought also to watch for children who do not show these characteristics but who, if offered certain motivation, will emerge with superior achievement.

What are the mental processes which superior children use to a greater degree than do other children? In planning instruction, it is important to consider the potentialities of superior learners. The superior learner has a surplus of mental age beyond his chronological, or life, age. This mental surplus continues to increase as the child grows older.

All pupils tend to learn by complex associative methods rather than by simple direct rote drill. But superior pupils are able to make many mental connections which put meaning into what they learn. By taking advantage of the countless possibilities of associative learning, the teacher may provide much enrichment for the gifted pupil.

Superior children, though interested in a fair number of concrete examples, are much better able than other children to grasp abstract or generalized rules. Superior children are capable of creative thinking and require little if any drill in order to remember what is understood. They are interested in long-time planning rather than day-to-day assignments. They are able to plan and carry out projects by themselves. Often they possess much energy and enthusiasm. They also have powers of self criticism, are aware of pitfalls and errors, and usually know how to correct them.

Superior children are curious about the world. They wish to know about people other than themselves, to learn ideas different from their own, and to learn about other countries and civilizations. If properly guided, superior children tend to develop and cultivate comparatively unselfish and social points of view. They enrich their own thinking by making comparisons between the activities and lives of people around them and ways of living elsewhere, while slow learners find difficulty in comprehending things remote from their specific area.

In summary, the degree to which a child is able to use the following processes is an indication of his superiority of thinking: (1) descriptive and observational powers; (2) powers of generalization involving ability to analyze and organize ideas and to associate them in new ways; (3) powers of insight; (4) ability to apply and use principles learned; (5) creative and appreciative powers as in invention, original writings, music, art, etc.

Creativity, the highest form of thinking, usually combines these processes. A teacher may judge the effectiveness and quality of his teaching of superior children by the extent to which they use these higher mental processes.

The Superior Learner as a Person

For the superior pupil, enrichment of the curriculum is usually better than special promotion. In some instances, a gifted child who is large for his age and socially well adjusted will benefit by being accelerated and placed with older pupils. But usually it is better to broaden the superior child's learning instead of accelerating it, because he is then more likely to attain satisfactory social and emotional adjustment. It is important that superior children be well-rounded and well-adjusted.

The attitude of the superior individual toward other children is of major concern. An arrogant attitude toward other children on the part of the gifted child is decidedly harmful to him as well as detrimental to the slow or average child, and care ought to be taken to prevent such a development. The child should learn that he must often defer to others and that others besides him must sometimes be first or best. He should learn patience and respect for the rights of others. For this reason, he requires opportunities to work with others; it is better to adjust the reading program within mixed or heterogeneous groups than to segregate superior children.

The solution of any problem of the superior reader requires insight into his personal needs as well as his reading needs. The basic principles of adjustment which apply to normal children are applicable to the gifted pupil. No good plan for reading can be carried out until the teacher knows his pupils well. This study requires time, effort, interest, and proper evaluation. A knowledge of a number of contributing factors will give the teacher many essential leads in satisfying the needs of the gifted child as well as those of the average or slow child. The following contributing factors are important: (1) the economic and health conditions of the child and his family; (2) the educational and cultural atmosphere of the home; (3) attitudes of parents or other members of the family; (4) emotional problems, if present; (5) outside interests, activities, hobbies; (6) schedules for both recreation and chores; (7) neighborhood conditions; (8) community opportunities; (9) the movies, comics, and radio and television programs which the child selects and talks about in his free moments; (10) his choice of free reading; (11) his degree of security.

General Organization of the Reading Activities for the Superior Learner

It is considered undesirable to place gifted children in an independent group, leaving them to learn by trial and error. Rather, the guidance of superior children in their reading activities is essential and ought to be just as detailed and helpful as guidance of the retarded children. Adjustment of the reading program should provide purposeful individual assignments in reading, enrichment at advanced levels of work, guidance in library reading, individual or small group discussions relating to special projects, and some kind of follow-up to see that each teacher concerned is informed of the child's unusual potentialities. If possible, advice may also be given to his parents regarding the cultivation of the child's special talents.

The superior reader should participate in the current reading unit and in the discussion of materials read. The child should have the opportunity to participate in the reading units underway so that he may derive the values that come from group discussions, group pooling of ideas, group thinking, etc. He should be given the opportunity to profit from the experiences and insights of his classmates, to check the validity of his own thinking in the light of group thinking, to learn to formulate and express ideas in a social situation, and to grow in ability to cooperate with others in various activities.

Children of the same chronological age group usually have common social needs which can best be met in large group activities. The superior as well as the average and retarded pupils experience social needs and drives. For this reason, there is an advantage in having the entire class work together at times. The entire class participates in the introduction of a reading unit and sometimes in reporting and interpreting what is read. Occasionally the superior readers who complete their own reading will be called upon to give special help to a small group of children who are less able in reading. During discussion periods, the teacher provides for individual differences within the group by adapting his questions to the abilities of the individual children. The superior pupil is asked questions which challenge his ability to think, to analyze, to examine critically, and to interpret.

Superior pupils ought to do some of their reading from basal readers. The basal readers supply interesting content which can be used to further the child's ability to react at a high level of interpretation. In fact, the reading of such materials increases the child's enjoyment and assists him in acquiring speed and facility. It must be kept in mind, however, that the superior pupil should be expected to make more subtle interpretations than the average pupil. The superior pupils should see the implied meanings as well as those that are stated. In class discussions, questions involving critical reactions, difficult judgments, abstractions, and subtle inferences are directed toward the superior pupil. He should also be encouraged to extend the ideas acquired in basal reading with a variety of supplementary reading activities. He may be encouraged to report relevant incidents and facts gleaned from the wide reading of more difficult books than the average child uses.

Ample time is provided for the superior reader to engage in reading motivated by his own interests and curiosities. During regularly scheduled library periods and at free times throughout the day, the superior reader ought to have the opportunity to read materials that will enrich his experience and interests, satisfy his present needs and curiosities, and help him to develop good work habits. He should not be allowed merely to satisfy some minimum requirements and then to fritter away his time. To meet both the personal and the social needs of the superior reader, we ought to provide reading for different purposes many types of material at various levels of difficulty.

The superior as well as the poor readers need careful diagnostic study when they meet difficulties or fail to achieve up to their capacities.

Sometimes a gifted pupil becomes a remedial-reading case. Such a pupil can ordinarily be provided with special guidance and practice during the course of his regular reading activities. Using the results of the initial survey in reading, the teacher may identify such pupils. They may then be given attention in small groups containing children of similar reading achievement.

Specific Methods of Teaching

Superior learners should carry on a variety of activities which will contribute to the work and interests of all the children. In projects which concern the whole class they should be working as members of a group concerned with common problems. They can contribute to the group work their creative powers, their initiative, their independence, and their ability to make plans and carry these out.

Enrichment in reading for the superior child calls for many different teaching procedures. In later elementary grades, gifted children will have the mental powers and reading skills of average high school pupils or better. But because these gifted children have not had sufficient experience in reading, it is unwise to expose them to all the types of reading suitable for their achievement levels. Many of these types ought to be reserved for later years when the children are capable of understanding the true meaning of the materials.

Devices and procedures which teachers find effective in enriching the program for superior children without drawing on unduly advanced materials are:

1. Carrying out individual activities
2. Engaging in wide reference reading for background or specific use such as answering an important question raised in class
3. Assembling library materials for use by the group
4. Reading items submitted for the school newspaper and selecting those to be included
5. Directing choral speaking at times
6. Writing radio scripts based on reading
7. Acting occasionally as leader in preparing a dramatic presentation
8. Reporting on a field trip related to a reading theme
9. Preparing a book talk
10. Finding information for a special program on holidays or important personages
11. Making a dictionary containing words related to the reading unit
12. Making a record of "Books I Want to Read," keeping it active in a notebook, adding and checking off books of interest as they are read

13. Reading to learn using advanced skills. The *Reader's Digest Workbooks* have articles of great interest followed by exercises designed to develop many of these skills. The *Weekly Reader* is a good medium upon which critical reading and discussion of current news can be based. *Uncle Ray's Magazine* brings much material of high interest for good readers.
14. Building up richer word meanings through vocabulary and dictionary study
15. Making a collection of poems on the unit
16. Making a movie strip or slides on some topic read about during the unit
17. Assembling exhibits on a unit; preparing labels for each article
18. Writing a short play using information gained through reading
19. Making a list of questions for the group to use in a panel discussion
20. Keeping a bibliography of books read on the unit
21. Making a meaningful classroom border with written explanations for the unit at hand
22. Preparing bulletin boards on the unit or on special days
23. Practicing good citizenship by helping a slow child in reading
24. Exploring sources of free and inexpensive materials, such as posters, pictures, pamphlets, and maps, and being responsible for obtaining and filing these materials for use as they arrive
25. Building, organizing, and keeping up a picture file for permanent use in the classroom
26. Making a carefully organized scrapbook on a theme related to wide reading

A library corner in a classroom, which provides for various interests and abilities, is essential. The children should find there picture books, science books and pictures, historical books, biographies, and every other kind of reading materials that can be obtained. Children should be given opportunities to consult and read these books and to have happy, friendly discussion of their interests and choices.

Superior children, especially, should be encouraged to use the school and public library. A trip to a library to arrange for library cards and to introduce children to library procedure and to a wealth of fine reading material is especially pleasant, profitable, and stimulating to the superior reader. The library habit may be fixed for life by means of happy experiences there.

It is worthwhile to aid the superior child in the selection of books specifically bearing on a problem at hand and also to give him help in efficiently locating reading material. Guidance of superior children in the development of good study habits is necessary to prevent superficial or careless work. Such guidance should: (1) acquaint him with authors; (2) acquaint him with library card catalogs and reference books and how to use them; (3) teach him the printed parts of a book; (4) teach him where to watch for new titles of books in the newspapers and magazines; (5) teach him to read good magazines suited to his age level; (6) encourage him to start his own library.

Superior children ought to be encouraged to read in many subject-matter areas. It is worthwhile to direct their reading into many subject-matter fields—to poetry, folk-lore, mythology, social studies, history, geography, art, music. A gifted child's experience may be enriched by directing his reading and observation into the field of science.

Research type reading as well as wide background reading qualifies the child of superior reading ability as a resource person for his group or class. The superior learner is capable of helping other children in the group to find answers to the countless questions which their active minds suggest. He should be given instruction in advanced reading techniques such as outlining and note-taking.

Summary

The classroom teacher, then, who recognizes superiority in a child, will find it necessary to understand in what ways he is gifted and how his superior intelligence can function in learning situations. The teacher will make provision and adjustment within the limitations of the classroom to foster the child's superior gifts by enrichment rather than acceleration. The teacher will give the child definite guidance and instruction rather than allow him to learn by trial and error. The teacher will study the child's individual needs as a person as well as a learner. While giving him as much individual development as possible, the teacher will not deprive the child of the benefit of working with his group, of cooperation, of group thinking, and of all the other values derived from contributing and participating in a social situation. The aim for the superior as well as the average and less able child is that of personal development and enrichment toward a well-rounded life.

38. Reading Help for the Disadvantaged

(1966)

Who are the disadvantaged—and why must teachers be concerned with their problems? They are children who are born or grow up with a deficient cultural background. They make up 70 percent of the students in large industrial cities. As the middle class runs to the suburbs, and as the poor continue to rush to the cities, we can expect to have many schools made up almost entirely of the culturally different.

As a result, more and more teachers are finding themselves confronted with many unique problems involved in teaching disadvantaged youngsters to read, and in enlisting the parents' help, which is important but sometimes difficult to obtain. Four major problems usually confront teachers of disadvantaged youngsters: (1) Students have little or no reading readiness. (2) Students have little or no motivation to read. (3) Parents often act hostile and disinterested. (4) Teachers must learn to know and understand an "alien" way of life.

New PR Problems

The familiar public relations problems found in suburban schools have a new face in big-city schools, and in schools in some poor rural areas. For example, the teacher who tries to involve parents in helping their children learn may find nothing but hostility in many cases. Teachers realize that the parents are interested in their child's welfare; that negative parent attitudes usually mean anxiety, fear, or distrust of authority figures such as teachers. Here are some of the ways in which teachers are coping with suspicion and seeming disinterest on the part of disadvantaged parents.

1. On home visitations, they try to break down fear and distrust by showing natural acceptance and noncritical feelings toward parents and their children—even if the home background, clothing, and language

---

SOURCE: *High Points*, XLVIII (March, 1966), 51–54. This selection originally appeared in *NEA Newsletter*, December 1965, under the title *It Starts in the Classroom.*

are strange and even repulsive to the middle-class teacher's sensibilities.

2. Parents are told, in simple easy-to-understand terms, what their child is doing in school—especially in reading—and why he is doing it.

3. When the teacher suggests ways the parents can help, the ways must be realistic. If they are asked to read to their child, either the teacher provides suitable books or tells the parent where the nearest library is and how to use it. (The teacher, in situations like this, is tactful—never giving parents any cause to feel embarrassed about their background or educational shortcomings.)

More Parent Approaches

4. Many working-class parents do not feel comfortable in school functions, such as open houses or PTA meetings. They are just as interested in their children as other parents, but they feel more at ease with a smaller group in an informal atmosphere. Formal presentations by school officials will not motivate them to attend school meetings. Every attempt should be made to break down the "big group-with-speaker" events into small, friendly discussion groups.

5. Group parent-teacher conterences can sometimes be held in the parents' home—perhaps with several other parents. In this informal setting, suggestions of ways parents can help their children learn to read, write, and spell will be more acceptable. This also offers the fringe benefit of getting other members of the family—grandparents, brothers, and sisters—interested in helping.

Getting Them Interested in Books

Children from disadvantaged homes usually have little interest in books or reading. They are not accustomed to books. Also, the subject matter of many books used in school has little connection with real life, as these children live and see it. Margaret Rowe, teacher of primary grades in Taft School (Ely, Nevada) has found that the following techniques spark their interest in books and reading.

1. When first reading aloud to the class, choose the books very carefully. These children don't know how to listen. They are unable to relate to the characters and situations most middle-class children love. They are not used to hearing stories, and their interest must be captured by a planned campaign.

2. The themes that grab their interest and hold it are based on the old human problems of, for instance, triumph over brothers or sisters (the younger brother stories, many of the "Jack" tales); scapegoats and fools who ultimately triumph; bumbling characters, animals or humans who are the victims of jokes played by slyer companions.

3. Use folk tales and legends in editions with simple vocabulary, adapted for silent reading by first- and second-graders. Read these stories with the book facing the class, so the children in front can follow the printed story and the others can see the pictures while you read.

4. After the story, distribute lumps of clay. Encourage each child to form a character, a tree, or some object in the story. After no more than 10 minutes, assemble the figures on a shelf, with colored paper beneath and behind them.

5. Ask a volunteer to print the title of the story for the display. Occasionally, another will make a crayon picture of the display.

6. Vary the activities by letting a member of the group start telling the story which was read the day before. Others can pick up the story at different points, and finish telling it.

7. These story-time activities can be carried on with a group of non-reading, "unbooked" children, while others in the class are busy with free selection of reading from the classroom bookshelf. Soon the non-readers (children who can or can't read, but never voluntarily turn the pages of a book) are begging to take home the books that have been read to them, to read again and share with younger children in the family.

How About "Compensatory Programs"?

Failure in school breeds more failure in school. By the time many children reach seventh grade or high school, they have had so little success that they are psychological drop-outs unless they receive special help. This special help is compensatory education. Few teachers are without at least some students who need such help. Many teachers find that all their students fall into this category. In most cases, these students' basic and most serious lack is the ability to read. The following programs, projects, and activities are used by teachers and others to help students build readiness for reading, interest in reading, and greater skill in reading.

1. For many, many high school students, remedial reading or reading about particular jobs and job training can be more beneficial than reading Shakespeare or Sir Walter Scott.

2. Students who are involved in job training can be motivated to build reading vocabulary if the words used are those used in their work.

3. Field trips to zoos, parks, and public libraries give students something to talk about and write about in the classroom. Many have never seen a live animal, have never visited the library which may be in walking distance of where they live.

4. Tutoring younger students in reading or arithmetic can sometimes be done by high school or college students in the community.

5. Project Head Start gives preschool children from disadvantaged homes the opportunity to take part in play activities that build reading and school "readiness." School programs that follow should be closely related to these activities. To do something at the early stage that is not complemented in the primary grades may cause the child to retreat to where he was before, according to Martin Deutsch, director of the Institute for Developmental Studies, New York Medical College.

6. Opportunities are made for the student to display and build on the talents he has. A student with limited ability to read may have high ability to repair an automobile. To build his self-esteem, the teacher may ask him to point out on a chart the various parts of an automobile. The student might then ask other members of the class to write names of the various parts on the blackboard as he names them.

Love 'Em or Leave 'Em

It is generally agreed by men and women who work with the disadvantaged that the most important ingredient for success is teacher attitude. Teachers who feel that disadvantaged children are stupid, or who cannot like them because they are shabby, dirty, smelly, or use shocking language should not be working with them.

Youngsters from poor backgrounds are unusually sensitive to nonverbal clues in the behavior of others. They are quick to sense phoniness —teachers who say one thing but feel another. "The prime mover of working with disadvantaged children must be love of all children, including the 'unlovely,' " says Betty Dickinson, resource teacher at Ellis School, Rockford, Ill. "Without this love, the teacher should not be allowed the privilege of working in this area of teaching. This love guides a teacher to empathy and constant efforts to understand a way of life very different from his or her own experience."

39. Culturally Disadvantaged Children Can Be Helped

LESSIE CARLTON and
ROBERT H. MOORE (1966)

People often assume that culturally disadvantaged children cannot make normal progress in school unless conditions in their homes are improved. We believe that this assumption is false, that the school can bring about normal learning progress by providing effective learning experiences, developing a favorable classroom climate, and fostering positive self-concepts.

To determine the validity of this belief, we conducted a study (and a recent corroborative follow-up) in which teachers of culturally disadvantaged elementary children used self-selection and self-directive dramatization of stories by pupils to teach reading.

Classes in each of the first four grades of a school in a very old area of Joliet, Illinois, made up the experimental group. Of the total school population of about 500 children, 85 percent were Negro and 5 percent Puerto Rican and Mexican. Children moved in and out of the community often, and very few school records were available. The economic level of the community was low, and pupils frequently came to school crying because of cold and hunger. Since the school had no lunch program, many children remained hungry all day.

We found most of the children to be emotionally unstable. They talked incessantly, but rarely to anyone in particular. If a pencil fell on the floor, they would often shout "Thief!" and accuse someone of taking it. They hit each other. They tattled. They moved continuously.

Although we recognized the possibility of obtaining inaccurate results, we administered reading achievement and mental maturity tests to all the children in both the experimental and the control groups. A large percentage in both groups had low intelligence-quotient scores,

---

SOURCE: *NEA Journal*, September, 1966, pp. 13–14. Reprinted by permission of the authors and publisher. Published originally as Research Project G-190 by the U. S. Office of Education.

and the majority were much below their grade level in reading achievement.

Three women and one man taught the experimental groups. All four had studied the techniques of self-directive dramatization, and two had taken part in a similar study with classes made up largely of middle-class white children. One teacher had taught two years in a school which used basal reading books and three reading groups. Another was a beginning teacher.

The teachers of the control group had more experience teaching the culturally disadvantaged than the teachers of the experimental group and had been in their present positions longer but they had not studied techniques of self-directive dramatization. During the study, they gave reading instruction chiefly through the traditional use of a basal reader and mainly in formal whole-class or small-group instruction. No special teachers worked with either the experimental or the control group.

Matches for each pupil in the experimental group were selected from other classes in the same school and from classes in another elementary school with a population of similar racial makeup and socioeconomic level.

To provide for the needs and desires of all the children in the experimental group, books on many different reading levels were made available in the classroom. As a preliminary step to self-directive dramatization, the children selected their own stories and read alone. Gradually they began to work in pairs and in small groups and to take turns reading to each other.

The groups were formed according to each child's preference for a story to read and dramatize. After the children in a particular group had read the story cooperatively, they agreed upon which character each would portray in the complete dramatization. Generally the groups selected different stories and stories on different reading levels. The groups all read their stories at the same time but took turns in dramatizing them. The dramatizations were spontaneous and completely unrehearsed.

Self-directive dramatization was employed in this study not only to find out what gains children would make in reading but also to see if pupils' self-concepts would change. We assumed that a change from a negative to a positive self-concept would contribute to progress in reading.

On the supposition that a child's behavior reflects his concept of himself, we made up a check-list of thirty-one questions dealing with different behaviors. Before the beginning of self-directive dramatization, teachers of the experimental group observed each child in relation to these questions and recorded the observations. At the end of the year, teachers checked the questions again to see what gains each child had made.

Typical checklist questions were: (1) Does the pupil refuse to do things because he thinks he does not do them well enough? (2) Does he try to have the attention of the teacher at all times? (3) Does he often fail to finish what he starts? (4) Does he do things to attract attention—make faces, talk loudly, try to "steal the show"? (5) Does he show signs of being jealous (of a child's new clothes or praise given another pupil, for example)?

The number of checks before and after the use of self-directive dramatization in the classroom led to the inference that desirable changes did occur in the self-concept of the pupils. The following are the number of checks for the children of each grade before and after the self-directive dramatization.

	Grade 1	*Grade 2*	*Grade 3*	*Grade 4*
Before	519	480	318	558
After	204	82	104	105

After participating in self-directive dramatization, many of the children were able to sit together without hitting each other. Intermittently, they still talked at the same time, but not excitedly and unceasingly. They were also a bit more willing to take turns. In various ways, they showed that they felt more kindly not only toward their classmates but also toward the adults who worked with them. One child wrote this letter to us:

"You are kind to us. Our teacher is kind to us. You bring us books that we like. Be careful on the highway when you come back to see us."

Children who had refused to have anything to do with reading at the beginning of the school year now often preferred reading to going outside to play, especially if they could find someone to sit near them and listen to them read. This was a great change from the early part of the school year when a boy threatened one of the investigators with his fists for offering to help him read.

Now, too, the children talked with visitors or strangers who came to the school. They smiled occasionally and had lost much of their look of fear, hostility, or suspicion.

In all four experimental groups, the mean gains in reading exceeded those of the control groups. In addition, the gains of all the experimental groups were greater than would be considered "normal" for the length of time involved. For example, the first graders in the experimental group gained more than one year in reading over a period of about three-and-one-half months. The gains for the other grades were made over a seven-and-one-half month period.

The first two columns of the table below show the mean reading grade scores for each grade of the experimental group before and after the experiment; the last two columns show the mean gains of the experimental and control groups.

	MEAN FOR EACH GRADE OF EXPERIMENTAL GROUP		GAIN OF EXPERIMENTAL GROUP	GAIN OF CONTROL GROUP
	Before	*After*		
Grade 1	0.58	1.71	1.13	0.24
Grade 2	1.26	3.13	1.87	1.25
Grade 3	2.17	3.35	1.18	0.79
Grade 4	3.39	4.24	0.85	0.43

The results of the reading tests seem to confirm our belief that culturally disadvantaged children can learn if good teachers supplied with appropriate materials employ the best possible methods of teaching.

Among these methods, self-directed dramatization seems to be particularly effective for a number of reasons. On the basis of the study, we feel that it can contribute to the improvement of self-concept of pupils and can help develop their skills in reading. It provides pupils with a chance to express themselves in the guise of somebody else and gives them a chance for physical activity—almost a necessity, because these deprived youngsters are inclined to be excitable, restless, and unable to concentrate on desk work for any length of time.

In short, our study suggests that the technique of self-selection and self-directive dramatization of stories may prove to be a major means of upgrading the educational level and improving the personal and social adjustment of culturally disadvantaged pupils.

40. Criteria for Grouping for Reading Instruction

THEODORE CLYMER (1966)

Until quite recently most schools followed the practice of placing students in heterogeneously grouped classes and providing these students with the best curriculum possible. Currently we have had a rash of solutions to the question of "How shall we group our students?" Most of these solutions are reincarnations of specters which were put to rest years ago in education's graveyard. But, unfortunately, many of them have come back to haunt us. The only startling new method for grouping children was suggested during a P.T.A. meeting when a mother asked the writer, "What do you think of this new method of 'homogenized grouping'?"

Of solutions, there is no shortage. We need only turn to our weekly news magazine, read the letters to the editor in the local paper, listen to the retired military expert, or even study with a professor of education—and all will offer solutions to the dilemmas we face. Before we can critically evaluate any of these suggested solutions, we must be aware of at least four basic areas of information concerning the psychology of individual differences.

The Psychology of Individual Difference

The first of these areas is the range of individual differences in reading ability found in any heterogeneously grouped classroom. The range of ability—that is, the spread from the best reader to the poorest reader—is two-thirds of the chronological age of the usual child in that classroom. An illustration will make this clear. As children in a fourth-grade classroom are about nine years old, we take two-thirds of nine and find that the spread at Grade IV is six years. Usually half of this spread is above grade level and half below. So in our hypothetical fourth grade

SOURCE: *Proceedings of the Annual Conference on Reading,* XXI (December 1959), 43–48. Reprinted by permission of the University of Chicago Press.

we would expect to find some students reading as low as first-grade level and others as high as seventh grade. This technique ignores the 2 percent of the population at either extreme.

In evaluating any suggested plan of grouping children, a second factor must be considered. This is the frustrating domain of trait differences. When we talked of the range of reading ability, we were speaking of differences in reading ability among a group of individuals. Trait differences refer to the differing abilities of a single person. Trait differences occur because abilities are *not* perfectly correlated. The pupil highest in spelling is not necessarily highest in arithmetical computation or reading. These trait differences are much greater than is generally assumed. Years ago, Clark Hull presented data which showed that trait differences are 80 percent of individual differences.[1] This means, for example, that when children are assigned to an A, B, or C group on the basis of intelligence (in the 1920's we called these groups the X, Y, Z groups), the groups will differ in intelligence; but when the groups are examined for reading or arithmetic ability, nearly a complete range will be found *within* the A, B, or C group.

The impact of trait differences on any plan of grouping must be acknowledged. Trait differences are not philosophical considerations but practical, empirical facts which, although upsetting to many current advocates of grouping, cannot be denied.

The third major consideration for grouping concerns grade standards and the difference between grade levels. From that black day when the concept of grade levels was imported from Europe until the present, teachers, administrators, and parents have been hypnotized by grade standards and the differences between grade levels. We have unfairly exaggerated the difference between one grade level and another and have minimized the differences of pupils within any grade level. There is really little difference between an average college freshman and sophomore in reading ability, or between an average fourth grader and fifth grader. Harris illustrated this point when he presented median rate of reading for various grade levels as determined from standardized tests.[2] His data showed that, for the tests he considered, a student read 206 words per minute to achieve a sixth-grade score. To obtain a seventh-grade score, 215 words per minute were required. When we say, "I have a sixth grader, but he's not really ready for the seventh grade," if

[1] Clark L. Hull, "Variability in Amount of Different Traits Possessed by the Individual," *Journal of Educational Psychology*, XVII (February, 1927), 97–106.
[2] Albert J. Harris, *How To Increase Reading Ability*, p. 508. New York: Longmans, Green & Co., 1956 (3d ed.).

it is rate of reading we are concerned with, he will need to improve little to achieve the seventh-grade standard if he is an average sixth-grade student. Harris' data showed less than a fifty words per minute increase from sixth to ninth grade.

This discussion does not suggest that there is lack of progress in reading skill from one grade to another but indicates that we have overemphasized differences between grade levels. The difference between the average reading score of the top quarter and bottom quarter of an intermediate class is two to four times as great as the difference between the average score of two successive grades. In other words, differences within a grade are much greater than the difference between grades.

Assigning children to "combination" or "split" grades is sometimes a puzzling problem which calls for a good understanding of differences within and between grades. More than one principal has been surprised when he assigned average sixth graders and superior fifth graders to a combination grade only to discover that the superior fifth-grade students achieved academically far beyond the average sixth-grade students.

A fourth set of implications for grouping grows out of the effects of good teaching on individual differences. Nearly everyone who has ever been a teacher has asked about at least one group of pupils, "I wonder what these students did all last year." Implicit in such questions is the belief that, if the previous teachers had done an adequate job, the range of ability would be lessened and the pupils would be more uniform in their achievements.

Serious reflection reveals that when curriculum goals are unlimited, good teaching will increase rather than decrease individual differences. Good teaching results in the slower pupils' moving ahead substantially, but the better pupils will move ahead even more. The net result of good teaching is growth for all—but greater growth for the capable, and hence greater spread. Any plan for grouping which aims to reduce differences is bound to fail if unlimited curriculum goals are maintained.

Questions to Be Asked in Grouping

Before turning to the specific criteria of grouping, we should keep in mind a series of questions which must be asked in setting up groups for reading instruction. Among the many questions which could be considered, the following eight questions centered in five areas seem particularly important:[3]

[3] Questions 1, 2, 3, and 8 are adapted from Philip E. Vernon, "Education and the Psychology of Individual Differences," *Harvard Educational Review*, XXVIII (Spring, 1958), 91–104.

The criteria

1. Is the criterion of major importance in educational progress?
2. Can the criterion be accurately measured?
3. Is the criterion stable and constant enough to be useful?

The learner

4. Do the groups formed on the basis of the criterion learn more efficiently?

The teacher

5. Do the groups formed on the basis of the criterion increase the teacher's effectiveness?
6. Does the method of grouping accept individual differences among teachers?

The administrator

7. Is the method of grouping administratively possible?

The public

8. Is the method of grouping socially acceptable?

For any criterion of grouping, these questions will seldom be answered with a definite "Yes" or "No." More often we will have to ask, "To what degree is the answer 'Yes' or 'No'?"

In the space available only a few of the above questions can be developed further. Questions 4, 5 and 6 deserve special attention. Unless the method of grouping increases the learner's effectiveness and the teachers and yet fail for other teachers. The techniques of grouping strate any dramatic superiority of one method of grouping over another in terms of pupil academic growth.

Question 6 raises an important and neglected aspect of grouping. Some methods of grouping might be highly successful for certain teachers and yet fail for other teachers. The techniques of grouping involved in the so-called individualized method of teaching reading are an illustration. A few highly talented teachers are successful in using this plan—but many, or even most, teachers find this method of grouping an impossibly complex undertaking.

Occasionally a teacher will develop a technique or plan of grouping which is highly successful. On the basis of the success of the technique for this one teacher, supervisors and administrators may encourage—even require—other teachers to adopt the same technique. Since we claim to accept individual differences among our students, then how soon will we apply a similar philosophy to teachers?

Criteria for Interclass Grouping

Many criteria are currently being applied in making decisions on the students to be assigned to certain classrooms or classes. If three first-grade rooms are to be formed in an elementary school, how shall students be assigned to these classrooms? When two sections of senior English are offered, should certain types of students be channeled into each section? To answer these and many others, the following criteria are sometimes applied:

INTELLIGENCE

Any attempt to achieve homogeneous groups by use of intelligence measures is doomed to failure. The earlier discussion of trait differences is particularly pertinent here. In those schools considering grouping by intelligence tests, two suggestions can be made. Set up a two-way table with three levels of intelligence on one axis and three levels of reading achievement on the other axis. This would produce a table of nine cells. Then, on the basis of test data, place each student in his appropriate cell. The results will be disappointing, for reading and intelligence are far from being perfectly related—even when the "intelligence" test requires reading tasks to demonstrate ability.

The second suggestion is to repeat a different form of the same intelligence test to part of the student body to check the reliability of the M.A. or I.Q. scores. Changes in I.Q. scores of fifteen points from first to second testing will not be uncommon; changes of twenty points will not be rare.

AGE

The legal admission age to the kindergarten or first grade has received a good deal of attention. Some research suggests that children who are older as they enter school achieve more—but this difference does not appear until the intermediate grades. Many first-grade teachers believe they could eliminate several problems by requiring that children be older as they enter school. There seems, however, to be no significant difference in percentage of disabilities in Sweden, where children enter the first grade at about seven years, and sections of the British Isles, where formal reading instruction often begins at five years of age.

SEX

Since boys develop physically more slowly than girls and as a group are less ready for reading at the first grade, the suggestion has been made that boys should be a year older than girls as they enter school. Three fallacies are evident in such reasoning. First, physical development has almost no relationship to early success in reading. Second, passage of time does not automatically increase readiness. Third, while boys *as a group* are less ready than girls *as a group*, there is nearly complete overlap of the boys' and girls' distribution of readiness. Many boys are more ready than many girls.

ACHIEVEMENT

Academic accomplishment is used in interclass grouping in two ways —for promotion from one grade level to another and for assigning students to multiple sections of a class or classroom. On both academic and personality development the research evidence favors promotion.

British schools have a long history of assigning elementary-age students to one of three "streams" on the basis of achievement, a plan being suggested for American schools. In a recent carefully designed study, Rudd compared a group of students who were "streamed" with an equivalent group who were not "streamed."[4] On the basis of a year's study, he concluded that the "streamed" groups did not achieve more than the "non-streamed" groups. More aggressive behavior was noted in the "streamed" group, probably indicating more personal tensions for this group of students.

INTEREST OR VOCATIONAL GOAL

While we would not expect elementary-age students to make curriculum choices on the basis of interest or vocational goal, at the secondary and college level students are offered such choices. High schools large enough to provide such choices as vocational and college preparatory English find that a careful guidance program backed by a good series of psychological and achievement tests will enable students to be grouped effectively into classes where achievement, ability, and interest are somewhat more homogeneous. Philosophical and practical considerations suggest that students participate in such decisions rather than being assigned to a section the school deemed advisable.

We can say with assurance that at the elementary level most criteria for interclass grouping should be viewed with a good deal of skepticism. At the secondary and college level, where multiple criteria can be applied—and when the student is mature enough to participate in the decision and eventual academic status can be more adequately evaluated —*some* increase in homogeneity can be expected.

[4] W. G. A. Rudd, "The Psychological Effects of Streaming by Attainment," *British Journal of Educational Psychology*, XXVIII (February, 1958), 47–60.

Criteria for Intraclass Grouping

No matter how children are assigned to a class—whether by an alphabetical listing or by an exacting analysis of reading ability—the success or failure of the reading program rests with the classroom teacher and the intraclass grouping that is done. No technique of interclass grouping can produce a classroom of students who can be treated alike. This is as true in the kindergarten as it is in the graduate school.

Commonly applied criteria for intraclass grouping include at least the following:

GENERAL ACHIEVEMENT

Most teachers form their reading groups for instructional purposes on the basis of reading ability. Teachers provide differentiated instruction to meet the individual differences of the class group in two to four groups, as a rule.

ACHIEVEMENT IN SPECIAL SKILLS

Because students, even those with similar general reading achievement, vary widely in their ability in special skills in reading—such as word recognition, speed, study skills, vocabulary development—other groupings will be required. In these groups, students with special problems meet with the teacher for special instruction and carry out appropriate assignments. The members of a special skill instructional group are often drawn from more than one general reading group.

SOCIAL NEEDS

A first-grade child who read at beginning fourth-grade level expressed his social needs when he asked his teacher if he could join a reading group. He said, "I can read, you know; but I do like to work with my friends."

Occasionally a child will respond well to working with a group because he finds it a challenge or because his friends are working in the group. Such social needs should be recognized as one factor influencing grouping.

BACKGROUND

Both the teacher's and the students' backgrounds will influence the grouping procedures used. In developing instructional groups within a class, the teacher must move slowly by a very carefully planned program or the result is chaos. Many inexperienced teachers are discouraged by initial experiences in grouping because they tried to do too much too soon.

The student's previous experience with instructional groups will be another major factor to be considered. Students who have been grouped in previous grades fit into instructional groups easily and rapidly because they accept the idea of different assignments within a classroom and because they have learned the routines of a grouped classroom. When such a background is lacking, a slow, carefully developed introduction to group work must be carried out.

Summary

This discussion of criteria of grouping for reading instruction suggests that much of the current interest in interclass grouping is based on false hopes. We have not found a method of assigning children to produce homogeneous classes. The interclass grouping may help some, particularly at the high school and college level—but the real solution to our problem must be met by the classroom teacher with intraclass grouping.

We began our discussion by suggesting that many of the current proposals of interclass grouping were specters which were disinterred from education's graveyard. Before we put these specters back into the curriculum, we must ask an important question: "Are we willing to pay the funeral expenses a second time?"

VII. Methods and Materials

It's incredible that in his second report to the Massachusetts Board of Education in 1838, Horace Mann (41) emphasized the whole word approach to the teaching of reading. He also stressed reading aloud to children and the importance of teaching beginners meaningful words only. Statements like "the foundation of the habit should be laid, in the reading of the very first lesson, of regarding words as the names of things; as belonging to something, and as nothing by themselves," suggest a profound awareness of semantics long before the world heard of Korzybski or Hayakawa. What other ideas can the reader find in Mann's writing that mark him as someone 100 years ahead of his time?

In the 1940's much attention was given to the Non-Oral Method of teaching reading. McDade, the father of the method, contended that use of the speech organs in early silent reading resulted in lip movements and subvocalization which later plagued adult readers. His method, therefore, involved developing meaningful responses to printed symbols that were free of accompanying speech. When the reader peruses Buswell's (42) appraisal of the Non-Oral Method, it might be wise to keep in mind McKee's statement ". . . there is good reason to believe, therefore, that in order to understand the meaning of a given sentence, the young child must reconstruct in his mind the intonations that he would hear if someone spoke or read the sentence to him meaningfully or if he himself spoke the sentence."[1] In this same vein Harris writes that "the Non-Oral

[1] Paul McKee *et al.*, Teachers' Manual for *With Jack and Janet* (Boston: Houghton Mifflin, 1949), p. 5.

Method tries to eliminate the natural advantages that the normal child has over the deaf and dumb."[2]

There are many approaches to the teaching of reading as carried on in the elementary schools of the United States today. Olson (43) familiarizes us with a number of these. Included in his discussion are the basal reading series, the phonic approach, the language experience approach, initial teaching alphabet, and linguistics.

Of the many approaches to the teaching of beginning reading, none surpasses the basal reader in popularity. Millions of copies are used in the United States. Exactly how they are used was studied by Staiger (44) through the use of a questionnaire that elicited responses from schools in 49 states, including Hawaii.

Confronted by numerous renowned reading specialists, each of whom advocates a different method, what is the teacher to do? Schubert (45) tries to answer this question. Additional assistance is provided by Mills (46) in his article, "An Evaluation of Techniques for Teaching Word Recognition." What contribution to learning is made by the kind of test Mills describes?

Any teacher who has worked with slow learners or reading disability cases, knows how important it is to use easy-to-read and interesting books. Chall (47) provides us with specific suggestions and materials relevant to this problem. What needs are these materials designed to meet?

[2] Albert J. Harris, *How to Increase Reading Ability* (New York: Longmans, Green and Co., 1956), p. 82.

41. Second Report to the Massachusetts Board of Education

HORACE MANN (1838)

If then, in learning, all wills and desires, all costs, labors, efforts, of other, are dependant at last, upon the will of the learner, the first requisite is the existence in his mind of a desire to learn. Children, who spend six months in learning the alphabet, will, on the playground, in a single half day or moonlight evening, learn the intricacies of a game or sport,—where to stand, when to run, what to say, how to count, and what are the laws and the ethics of the game,—the whole requiring more intellectual effort than would suffice to learn half a dozen alphabets. So of the recitation of verses, mingled with action, and of juvenile games, played in the chimney corner. And the reason is, that for the one, there is desire; while against the other, there is repugnance. The teacher, in one case, is rolling a weight up hill, in the other, down; for gravitation is not more to the motions of a heavy body, than desire is to the efficiency of the intellect. Until a desire to learn exists within the child, some foreign force must constantly be supplied to keep him agoing; but from the moment that a desire is excited, he is self-motive, and goes alone.

Perhaps the best way of inspiring a young child with a desire of learning to read is, to read to him, with proper intervals, some interesting story, perfectly intelligible, yet as full of suggestion as of communication; for the pleasure of discovering is always greater than that of perceiving. Care should be taken, however, to leave off, before the ardor of curiosity cools. He should go away longing, not loathing. After the appetite has become keen,—and nature supplies the zest,—the child can be made to understand how he can procure this enjoyment for himself. The motive of affection also may properly be appealed to, that is, a request to learn in order to please the teacher; but this should never be pressed so far as to jeopard its existence, for it is a feeling more pre-

---

SOURCE: Lawrence C. Cremin, ed., *The Republic and the School* (New York: Teachers College Press, 1957), pp. 38–43.

cious than all knowledge. The process of learning words and letters is toilsome, and progress will be slow, unless a motive is inspired before instruction is attempted; and if three months are allowed to teach a child his letters, there is greater probability, that the work will be done at the end of the time, even though ten weeks of it should be spent in gaining his voluntary co-operation, during the residue of the time. A desire of learning is better than all external opportunities, because it will find or make opportunities, and then improve them. . . .

When a motive to learn exists, the first practical question respects the order in which letters and words are to be taught; i.e. whether letters, taken separately, as in the alphabet, shall be taught before words, or whether monosyllabic and familiar words shall be taught before letters. In those who learnt, and have since taught, in the former mode, and have never heard of any other, this suggestion may excite surprise. The mode of teaching words first, however, is not mere theory; nor is it new. It has now been practised for some time in the primary schools of the city of Boston,—in which there are four or five thousand children, —and it is found to succeed better than the old mode. In other places in this country, and in some parts of Europe, where education is successfully conducted, the practice of teaching words first, and letters subsequently, is now established. Having no personal experience, I shall venture no affirmation upon this point; but will only submit a few remarks for the consideration of those, who wish, before countenancing the plan, to examine the reasons on which it is founded.

During the first year of a child's life, he perceives, thinks, and acquires something of a store of ideas, without any reference to words or letters. After this, the wonderful faculty of language begins to develop itself. Children then utter words,—the names of objects around them,—as whole sounds, and without any conception of the letters of which those words are composed. In speaking the word "apple," for instance, young children think no more of the Roman letters, which spell it, than, in eating the fruit, they think of the chemical ingredients,—the oxygen, hydrogen, and carbon,—which compose it. Hence, presenting them with the alphabet, is giving them what they never saw, heard, or thought of before. It is as new as algebra, and to the eye, not very unlike it. But printed names of known things are the signs of sounds which their ears have been accustomed to hear, and their organs of speech to utter, and which may excite agreeable feelings and associations, by reminding them of the objects named. When put to learning the letters of the alphabet first, the child has no acquaintance with them, either by the eye, the ear, the tongue, or the mind; but if put to learning familiar words first, he already knows them by the ear, the tongue, and the mind, while his eye only is unacquainted with them. He is thus introduced to a stranger, through the medium of old acquaintances. It can hardly be doubted, therefore, that a child would learn to name any twenty-six familiar words, much sooner than the twenty-six unknown, unheard and unthought of letters of the alphabet.

For another reason, the rapidity of acquisition will be greater, if words are taught before letters. To learn the words signifying objects, qualities, actions, with which the child is familiar, turns his attention to those objects, if present, or revives the idea of them, if absent, and thus they may be made the source of great interest and pleasure. We all know, that the ease with which any thing is learned and the length of time it is remembered, are in the direct ratio of the vividness of the pleasurable emotions, which enliven the acquisition. . . .

But one thing should be insisted upon, *from* the beginning, and especially *at* the beginning. No word should be taught, whose meaning is not understood. The teacher should not count out words, faster than ideas. The foundation of the habit should be laid, in the reading of the very first lesson, of regarding words as the names of things; as belonging to something else, and as nothing by themselves. They should be looked at, as a medium, and not as an end. It is as senseless for a child to stop at the sign of the printed word, in reading, as it would be to stop at the sound of the spoken word, in conversation. What child would not repel the intercourse of a person, who spoke to him only words, of which he knew nothing? No personal charms would be long sufficient to compensate for speaking to a child, in an unknown tongue. How is it possible then, that an active-minded child should not disdain the dreary pages of a book, which awaken no thought or emotion within him;—which are neither beauty to the eye, nor music to the ear, nor sense to the understanding? As reading is usually taught, the child does not come into communication with his lesson, by any one of all his faculties. When a child looks into a mirror, or at a picture where the perspective is strikingly marked, he will reach around to look behind the mirror, or behind the picture, in hope of finding the objects in the place where they appear to be. He cares nothing for the mirror, nor for the canvas;—his mind is with the things presented to his senses. In reading, the page should be only as the mirror or picture, through which objects are beheld. Thus there would be far more delight in looking at the former, than at the latter; because words can present more circumstances of variety, beauty, life, amplitude, than any reflecting surface or dead picture. Should we not revolt at the tyranny of being obliged to pore, day after day, upon the outer darkness of a Chinese manuscript? But if the words are not understood, the more regular formation of the Chinese characters gives them a decided advantage over our own letters. Give a child two glasses, precisely similar in every respect, except that one shall be opaque, the other a magnifier. Through the former nothing can be seen, and it therefore degenerates into a bauble; but the latter seems to create a thousand new and brilliant objects, and hence he is enamored of its quality. There is precisely the same difference in the presentation of words. Yet we punish children, because they do not master words, without any regard to their being understood.

But how can this plan be executed? In this way. During the first year of a child's life, before the faculty of speech is developed,—before he has ever uttered a word—he has obtained a considerable stock of ideas, respecting objects, qualities and motions. During the next year or two and before it is usual to teach letters, he is employed through every waking hour, both in learning the words, expressive of known phenomena and also in acquiring a knowledge of new things and events; so that before the age of four or even three years, the items of his inventory of elementary knowledge swell to thousands. In his memory, are not merely playthings, but catalogues of furniture, food, dress, insects, animals, vehicles objects in natural scenery, divisions of time, and so forth, with various motions and appearances, belonging to them all. Numbers, sounds, events, feelings, also come into the list. This is a stock not readily exhausted. By first teaching the names or phrases expressive of these, the substance is always present to his mind, and the words are mere signs or incidents; and a habit is formed of always keeping the mind, in after-life, intent upon things and their relations, —a habit of inestimable value and the only foundation of intellectual greatness. . . .

Reading is divisible into two parts. It consists of the *mechanical*, and the *mental*. The mechanical part is the utterance of the articulate sounds of a language, on inspecting its written or printed signs. It is called mechanical, because the operation closely resembles that of a machine, which may receive the best of materials and run through a thousand parcels of them every year;—the machine itself remaining just as bare and naked at the end of the year, as it was at the beginning. On the other hand, one portion of the mental part of reading consists in a reproduction in the mind of the reader of whatever was in the mind of the author; so that whether the author describes atoms or worlds, narrates the history of individuals or nations, kindles into sublimity, or melts in pathos,—whatever was in the author's mind starts into sudden existence in the reader's mind, as nearly as their different mental constitutions will allow. An example of the purely mechanical part is exhibited in reading a foreign language, no word of which is understood; as in the case of Milton's daughters, who read the dead languages to their blind father;—they, with eyes, seeing nothing but black marks upon white paper, he, without eyes, surveying material and spiritual worlds, —at once charmed by their beauties, and instructed by their wisdom.

With the mental part, then, reading becomes the noblest instrument of wisdom; without it, it is the most despicable part of folly and worthlessness. Beforehand, it would seem quite as incredible, that any person should compel children to go through with the barren forms of reading, without ideas; as to make them perform all the motions of eating, without food. The body would not dwindle under the latter, more certainly, than the mind, under the former. The inevitable consequences are, that all the delight of acquisition is foregone; the reward which nature bestows upon the activity of the faculties is forfeited,—a reward which is richer than all prizes and more efficient than all chastisement;—and an inveterate habit is formed of dissociating thought and language. "Understandest thou what thou readest?" therefore, is a question quite as apposite when put by a teacher to a child in his horn book, as when asked by an Apostle of the ambassador of a Queen. . . .

42. An Appraisal of the Non-Oral Method of Teaching Reading

GUY T. BUSWELL (1945)

During the ten-year period from 1935 to 1945 the Chicago public schools have carried on an unusual experiment in the teaching of reading—unusual in the nature of the method employed and unusual, for public-school systems, both in the scope of the experimentation and in the length of time during which the administration made possible the conditions for carrying on the experiment. This new method of teaching

SOURCE: Guy T. Buswell, "An Appraisal of the Non-Oral Method of Teaching Reading," Supplementary Educational Monograph No. 61, 1945, pp. 51–57. Reprinted by permission of the University of Chicago Press.

reading was begun in one class in the autumn of 1935. In 1936 eleven classrooms introduced the method. By 1939 there were 470 rooms in the Chicago schools which were employing this method, and in the autumn of 1944 it was being tried in 137 of the 346 elementary schools in the city. All told, more than seventy thousand pupils have been taught reading in these experimental classes since 1935.

The new method which has been used in these classes has been officially designated as "non-oral reading." The essential characteristic of this method of teaching reading is that it proceeds by direct association between the visual symbol and the meaning, without the intervention of either the oral pronunciation of the words or the inner subvocalization of the words. Since many persons, when reading silently, still carry on a process of subvocalizing the words, the resulting process is silent only in the sense that it is noiseless; in other respects the reading process is no different from that employed in oral reading. Hence this new non-oral reading should be contrasted with both oral reading and much that commonly passes as silent reading. The non-oral method is an attempt to reach the same goal of reading proficiency toward which all silent-reading methods strive, with varying degrees of success.

While this report is, in the main, a report of the non-oral reading experiment in the city of Chicago, the issues involved are by no means peculiar to Chicago but are of the widest possible significance. The problem itself is not new. When Horace Mann was secretary of the Board of Education of Massachusetts, he gave considerable space in one of his reports to a criticism of the teaching of oral reading at that time, which, he said, resulted in the exercise of the vocal organs on the empty air without developing a corresponding sense of the meaning of what was read. In spite of Horace Mann's vigorous attack on the oral reading of his time, no fundamental changes in methodology were made in American public schools until about the year 1915. During the decade from 1915 to 1925 a sweeping reform spread all over the country and resulted in a substitution of silent-reading methods for oral-reading methods. It is doubtful whether American education has ever witnessed a more significant reform than this silent-reading movement, which was so effective that at the present time the major teaching of reading in the elementary school employs far more silent reading than it employed during the earlier period, and in most elementary schools the proportion of reading experience now is much greater for silent reading than for oral reading. While this silent-reading reform appears on the surface to be far reaching in effect, a closer analysis of the outcomes of the movement indicates that the change was more superficial than many of its advocates presume. It was superficial in the sense that silent reading may be carried on, and in many cases is carried on, by exactly the same psychological process as oral reading, except for the fact that there is no oral vocalization of the words. For many silent readers, subvocalization, or, as it is commonly called, "inner speech," accompanies reading.

The Non-Oral Method in Chicago

The non-oral reading experiment in Chicago was initiated by James E. McDade, who was at that time assistant superintendent of schools in Chicago. The experiment was limited to Grades I and II of the elementary school. In the experimental classes all instruction in oral reading was postponed until Grade III or later. During the first two years no oral reading was permitted at any time. There was a great deal of oral language work, but this was purposely carried on entirely separately from the classes in reading. The essential purpose of the reading method was to enable children to get the meaning of the printed page directly from the visual symbols without the intervention of oral pronunciation and without the employment of inner speech. Consequently, instruction was carried on through picture dictionaries, through pantomime activities, and through other ingenious ways by which the meaning of words might be made clear without use of oral pronunciation. Reading achievement was measured by the responses of children to what was read rather than by their oral pronunciation of the words.

The materials for the experiment had to be constructed by the teachers, since no ready-made supply was available. Manuscript writing was used in all blackboard work. The pupils participated in the preparation of much of the material needed, thereby obtaining training in art, handwriting, and composition as well as in reading. Throughout the experiment the objective was to enable the children to think the meaning without saying the words.

The non-oral method makes no claim that oral reading should be abandoned in the school but recommends only that it not be used until the essential reading attitude, that of thinking meaning in response to visual perception of words, has first been established. Furthermore, the advocates of the non-oral method are in no sense antagonistic to the *teaching of oral language*. On the contrary, the method makes much use of oral language, but only in situations separate from the activity of reading.

One other distinction should be made clear. By its name the non-oral method seems to be contrasted only with oral reading. In this report the two procedures that are compared will be called the "oral" and the "non-oral" methods. However, it must be understood clearly that what is called "oral reading" in this report is the combination of oral and silent reading in Grades I and II as it is conventionally carried on in most American schools. Where oral reading is taught from the beginning along with silent reading, the silent-reading process generally takes on all the characteristics of oral reading except the sound of the voice, which is subdued into subvocalization or inner speech. Non-oral reading is, by definition, silent reading in which there is no subvocalization or inner speech. The crucial question is whether this definition is realized in fact.

The Evaluation Study

The problem of this study is to determine whether pupils taught by the non-oral reading method are able to read better, both rate and comprehension being considered, than are pupils taught by the usual method of combining oral with silent reading. The non-oral method was used only in Grades I and II. However, it was decided to base the evaluation on the reading of children in Grade VI so that the more permanent effects of the method of teaching could be measured.

The data for the study were derived from tests given to 1,699 sixth-grade pupils in 32 public schools in Chicago. The schools were selected to give a fair sample of economic, racial, and geographic factors. Tests were given to all pupils in Grade VI of the schools used. However, data were used only for pupils who had attended Chicago public schools throughout the entire six-year period and who had used either the oral or the non-oral method consistently in both Grades I and II. Four hundred and seven cases were excluded for not meeting the first of these conditions and 131 for the second. Furthermore, 43 cases had to be dropped because of incomplete data or because of errors in testing. After these eliminations had been made, there remained 1,118 cases, of which 523 had been taught by the oral method and 595 by the non-oral method. From these cases, two matched groups were selected, paired according to the following three criteria: (1) cases were matched within five points according to intelligence quotient; (2) chronological age was kept within a difference of one year; and (3) skipping or repeating grades was held to a difference of one semester. The 930 pupils (465 matched pairs) who met these conditions constituted the principal group used in the study.

Two standardized reading tests were combined into a single battery affording a fifteen-minute sample of reading. The tests used were Part I of the Intermediate Division of the Diagnostic Examination of Silent Reading Abilities by Van Wagenen and Dvorak and the paragraph test from the Nelson Silent Reading Test for Grades III-IX. All tests were administered by the writer and were scored by his research assistants.

Results of the Tests

The mean score of the group which had been taught by the conventional oral reading method in Grades I and II was 34.0, while the score for the group which had been taught by the non-oral method in Grades I and II was 36.0. The standard deviations for the two distributions were 11.4 and 12.1, respectively.

A somewhat more satisfactory method of comparison, which takes more specific account of the pairing of cases, gives the amount of difference between the reading scores of the 465 matched pairs of pupils. In 17 cases there was no difference between the scores, the deviation being zero. There were 195 pairs in which the oral score was higher than the non-oral, and 253 pairs in which the non-oral score was higher than the oral score. The mean difference in the scores, which takes account of the amount as well as of the direction of the difference, was 1.8 in favor of the non-oral method. However, the standard deviation of the difference was 5.5, giving a critical ratio of only 0.3, which indicates that the difference of 1.8 is not statistically significant. Further analysis of the situation will help in interpreting the effectiveness of the two methods.

Theoretically, the basic difference between the two methods of teaching reading is the assumption that pupils taught by the non-oral method will make a direct association between the visual perception of the word and the meaning, whereas by the usual method of oral-silent reading the association is indirect and involves subvocalization or inner speech as a part of the process. The most objective evidence of inner speech in silent reading is the presence of lip-movement. The absence of lip-movement is no guaranty that there is no inner speech, since it is quite possible to read silently with a consciousness of inner speech and yet suppress completely all movements of lip and throat. However, where there is lip-movement, the presence of inner speech is incontrovertible. Consequently, while a tabulation of lip-movement can in no sense be considered a complete record of the number of pupils who read with subvocalization, it must be admitted that, wherever lip-movement is observed, subvocalization is going on. Theoretically, there should be no lip-movement in non-oral reading; therefore a comparison of the lip-movements of the two groups should provide data of significance. Since lip-movement is an indication of the method by which one reads, without regard to the rate or the comprehension that results, it is valid to make a comparison on this point between all cases available for matching. Since records of lip-movement were taken in only seventeen of the thirty-two schools, it is desirable to secure as many cases as possible for the comparison. Consequently all cases available for matching were used —a total of 351 cases for the oral group and 237 cases for the non-oral group. In the oral group there were 75 cases, or 21 percent of the total, showing lip-movement; in the non-oral group there were 41 cases, or 17 percent of the total, showing lip-movement. Again the difference is in favor of the non-oral group, although it is not so great as one might expect in view of the theoretical assumptions underlying the method. Since there is no possible defense of lip-movement in silent reading, both the oral and the non-oral methods fall short of their objectives in this respect, but the non-oral group approaches its goal more nearly than does the oral group.

Although, in the matching of the cases for the 465 pairs of pupils, the number of semesters skipped or repeated was used as one of the criteria for matching, the amount of skipping or repeating was found to be quite different for the two groups. Since ability to read is one of the important factors in progress through school, some special consideration will be given to this factor. Satisfactory data as to number of grades skipped or repeated were available for all except four of the 523 oral cases and all but two of the 595 non-oral cases.

There were 91.7 percent of the oral group and 86.2 percent of the non-oral group who had skipped no semesters. One or more semesters had been skipped by 8.3 percent of the oral group and by 13.8 percent of the non-oral group. However, 26.8 percent of the oral group had repeated one or more semesters, while only 13.7 percent of the non-oral group had repeated. Of those repeating two or more semesters, the percentage was 11.1 for the oral group as compared with 3.9 for the non-oral group.

The classification of these pupils into oral or non-oral methods was done at the time they entered Grade I, so there was no possible chance to predict at that time who would be the repeaters or the pupils to be accelerated. Intelligence tests were not given until a later time, and, as has already been shown, the two groups of matched cases were equalized in terms of mental ability. The difference in the percentage of children skipping or repeating grades in the two methods is large and is statistically significant. With other factors controlled, it is apparent that pupils taught by the non-oral method have acquired a technique which has enabled them to progress in school more satisfactorily than those who were taught by the oral method. Furthermore, it should be remembered that the data on skipping and repeating covered the entire school period through the first five grades and into Grade VI and are not limited to Grades I and II, where the non-oral method of reading was taught.

Summary of Findings and Conclusion

The eight principal factors covered by the study are listed in Table 1. As will be seen, the difference between the two groups are in most cases small and in some cases are not statistically significant. However, the general consistency of the direction of the differences, which in every case favors the non-oral method, should be observed. In a few of the cases the differences are large and are significant in themselves. For example, nearly twice as many pupils taught by the non-oral method were accelerated in their school progress by one or more semesters during the period from Grade I to Grade VI. Likewise, the frequency of retardation by one or more semesters was only half as great for those taught by the non-oral method as for those taught by the oral method. In the case of lip-movement, the difference in the percentages of children who gave this evidence of subvocalization is statistically significant. A comparison of the mean reading scores, which takes into account the amount of the difference as well as the direction of the difference, shows a difference between the means for the two groups which is not statistically significant. However, when the direction of the difference is taken pair by pair, the non-oral cases had the higher scores in 253 cases as compared with 195 for the oral group. When cases with low intelligence quotients were compared with cases with low intelligence quotients, and high with high, the results were not statistically significant but again were slightly in favor of the non-oral group.

TABLE 1. Summary Comparison of Oral and Non-Oral Matched Groups in Grade VI

Factor Compared	*Oral Group*	*Non-Oral Group*
Mean reading score	34.0	36.0
Mean difference in reading score of matched pairs		1.8
Number of paired groups making higher reading score	195	253
Percentage of pupils showing lip-movement	21.0	17.0
Percentage of pupils who skipped one or more semesters	8.3	13.8
Percentage of pupils who repeated one or more semesters	26.8	13.7
Mean reading score of pupils with low intelligence quotients	22.8	23.7
Mean reading score of pupils with high intelligence quotients	45.2	46.1

General Conclusion

In view of all the evidence and of all the factors relating to the situation, the writer's judgment is that the non-oral method possesses certain values which justify a continuation of its use. There is no evidence whatever that the non-oral method is less effective than the prevailing method of teaching reading, and there are several indications that it has values that give promise of a definite improvement in the teaching of reading.

The advocates of non-oral reading have made a contribution by pointing out that silent reading may be silent in that there is no articulation whatever, or that it may be no different from oral reading except that the sound is suppressed. The essence of the distinction between superior reading and the kind of reading commonly done is exactly at this point. Reading can be made a far more efficient process than it has so far been made in the schools. Essentially, reading is a process of comprehension, of thinking meanings, not a process of saying words. It is not necessary to say the words in order to get the meaning. The saying of the words takes so much time, whether done orally or subvocally, that the possible efficiency of the reading process is lost. The really superior readers who are occasionally found both within and without our schools are those individuals who have learned to read without the restrictions of subvocalization. This point is of first-rate importance. The load of education in high school and college would be immeasurably relieved if, in the elementary school, pupils could be given a method of reading which would free them from the necessity of subvocalization.

Clarity in regard to the mental processes involved in reading and in oral language is particularly important at the present time because of the emphasis on an integrated and articulated language-arts program. Some of the difficulty is caused by a slovenly use of the word "integration." Integration means relating in some intelligent fashion; it necessitates seeing relationships; it demands some kind of organization. Some persons seem to have the idea that integration means an indiscriminate and incidental mixing of whatever education deals with. The only possible result is a mess. Integration in the language-arts program possesses immense possibilities and implies an understanding of learning processes which in some combinations will support one another and in other combinations will work directly against one another. There is a difference between relating and mixing. Oral and silent reading should be related but not mixed.

The non-oral method is not a fad. It is a logical next step in the evolution of the teaching of reading. The schools of Chicago have done the profession a service in emphasizing this distinction in process. The experiment reported in this paper has not solved the problem, but it has indicated some of the difficulties to be overcome and has furnished some promising leads. Continued study and experimentation might eventuate not merely in a small improvement in reading efficiency but in an improvement comparable in significance to the break from the alphabet method, from teaching reading and spelling in combination, and from the use of oral reading as the basic method with a single book to a grade. The program ahead should be one of experiment, not of argument.

43. Reading: The Approaches We Use

ARTHUR V. OLSON (1965)

Never before has there been such a profusion of materials for teaching reading. With the advent of the "space race" and the resulting emphasis upon education, the public has placed the entire educational system under careful scrutiny. Since reading skills are the key to knowledge, it is obvious why the public has such an interest in the way reading is taught and the outcomes of progress in that field.

Without the skill of reading, a child cannot make satisfactory progress in our schools. Not all of our children learn to read. We know that this is true, but the failure of some children is not easily explained. It may be because of low intelligence, emotional problems, poor teaching, physical problems, moving from town to town continuously without establishing roots, or poor home environment—any one or a combination of these factors. Because of the inability to point to a single factor for reading failure, many approaches and panaceas have been offered to educators within the last few years. As a result of the interest by the general public and the misunderstandings concerning the teaching of reading, it is important that those directly responsible for the curriculum be as informed as possible.

The reading controversy centers not on any claim that we are not teaching the reading skills but on the question of how we can teach the reading skills so that more children will be able to find success in school.

SOURCE: *The Clearing House*, XXXIX (January, 1965), 259–264. Reprinted by permission of the publisher.

Several approaches are in use. The most common is the basal reading approach; second is the basal reading approach used in conjunction with experience charts; third is phonics programs; fourth is reading programs based upon the language experience of the child.[1] These four approaches are the ones which have the greatest frequency of use in our public schools. Two others, however, are worth mentioning: the initial teaching alphabet and the linguistic approach.

The Basal Reading Approach

This approach is the one most commonly used throughout the United States at the present time. There are several series of readers on the market, each of which provides textbook material, workbooks, and supplementary materials for the students, and manuals and guides for the teacher. Usually the basal readers provide instruction from reading readiness up through grade six, and in many cases through grade eight.

The vocabulary is carefully controlled from book to book, primarily in grades one through three, with careful development of a sequential program and balanced skills. Within the last few years the basal readers have come through many an extensive change. The vocabulary has been enriched in many cases to meet the individual needs, the content has been changed somewhat by the introduction of stories written by well-known children's authors and authors of adult material. Much supplementary material for classroom use has also been introduced.

The basal readers are used by thousands of teachers throughout the United States with a great deal of success. Until a new teacher becomes thoroughly acquainted with the reading program, it is inadvisable for her to try to develop a reading program on her own. The material which is in the basal reader has been developed through years of study and many years of experience by classroom teachers. Because most of the material has been experimented with in many types of situations, the teacher's guide provides a valuable resource for the teacher in providing interest and productive activities for her class. Even for the teacher who has a great many years of experience and a good grasp of the skills which make up reading, the basal reader still offers a valuable source of material for devising a skills program. The teacher may feel that she wants to use the material in a variety of ways. She may want it used as a part of an enrichment program or an individualized reading program, or to supplement other basal readers. In any case, it should be useful to the teacher as a guide for checking on the skill to be developed.

In some cases the basal reader has not been used as it was intended. The basal reader is not a total and complete program by itself. It is

[1] Mary C. Austin and Coleman Marrison, *The First R*. New York: The Macmillan Company, 1963.

merely a part of the total program. It is impossible to teach through the basal reader all of the skills which are needed. Most of the content is story material. Since this is true, many of the skills that we teach, such as finding main ideas, organization, sequence, study skills, and others, must be taught in the content area as well. The basal reader, although it does have a number on the outside cover, is intended to meet the different instructional levels of all the children in every class. Because of the wide range of ability which we have in our classrooms, it is impossible to take care of all of the instructional needs through one book. A teacher must use other books within the same series for the children below and above the instructional level of the grade, or she may use a co-basal series.

Since reading is a sequential development of skills, there is no such thing as having children cover all pages in a certain reader by the end of the year. The statement has been made by some experts in the field of reading that as many as 30 percent of our children are reading at the frustration level. If this is true, we are not doing our job.

The teacher's guide was never meant as a detailed prescription to be followed exactly in all aspects for all children. We know full well that some children are going to need more development in some skills than in others. There are also going to be some children who do not need the drills or some of the skills which are taught.

One of the most important criticisms that have come out of the basal reading program is directed against the teacher's use of the workbooks. If workbooks are used indiscriminately with all children, they have little value in developing needed skills. If the teacher fails to check the workbook activities with the children so they know the progress they are making and the errors they are making, the material is being grossly misused. The value of the material lies in the information it can give the teacher about the application of the skills. It has never been intended as a testing situation or as a busy-work activity.

In many of the activities involving the basal reader, directions must be given to the children. As this is to be a learning situation, the experience that a child is going to need to bring to the reading must be developed before, and the teacher's guidance through the material is mandatory.

The basal reading programs which are most commonly used in our public schools are as follows:

Alice and Jerry Basic Readers, Mabel O'Donnel, and others. New York: Harper & Row, Publishers.

Betts Basic Readers, Emmett Betts, and others. New York: American Book Co.

Developmental Reading Series, Guy Bond, and others. Chicago: Lyons and Carnahan.

Ginn Basic Readers, David Russell, and others. Boston: Ginn and Company.

Macmillan Readers, Arthur Gates, and others. New York: The Macmillan Company.

New Basic Readers, Curriculum Foundation Series, Marion Monroe, and others. Chicago: Scott, Foresman & Co.

Reading for Interest Series, Paul Witty, and others. Boston: D. C. Heath & Co.

Reading for Meaning Series, Paul McKee, and others. Boston: Houghton Mifflin Co.

Sheldon Basic Readers, William D. Sheldon, and others. Boston: Allyn and Bacon, Inc.

Winston Basic Readers, Russell G. Stauffer, and others. New York: Holt, Rinehart and Winston, Inc.

The Basal Reading Approach Used in Conjunction with Experience Charts

Charts based upon the real experiences of children provide available reading material for the beginning stages of reading instruction and for later development. The preparation of the charts involves very specific techniques which can be mastered easily by any interested teacher. The charts can usually be divided into two general categories: (1) charts made by the teacher from the dictation of the students, and (2) practice charts made by the children with the aid of the teacher.

The function of the first type of chart is to give the children the experience of seeing their own spoken words converted into printed symbols. The emphasis is not upon reading the chart but upon noticing the fact that words can be written down and the process by which we do write words—primarily left to right, return sweep to the next line, and left to right again.

There will be some children who have advanced in reading maturity and who will probably be able to read some of the words just from seeing the material written. There may be some children who will even want to learn to read the whole chart by themselves.

The second kind of chart, the practice chart, is prepared primarily to give actual practice in reading and writing. In developing this, the teacher will try to guide the children into making simple sentences, with the vocabulary load closely related to those they will find in their reading material. Because these charts will be ones in which the children have a direct and immediate interest, the material will often provide a welcome change from that which they find in their basal reader.

Even as the children progress through the grades, the experience charts will be of value in helping them to summarize their ideas of materials that they have read in the content areas. It will also afford them the opportunity of having more experiences with the vocabulary that they are trying to learn.

The Phonics Approach

Of all the issues in reading instruction, none has received more attention or aroused more discussion and misunderstanding than phonics. Not only are teachers interested in the role of phonics, but parents have looked upon it as an answer to all the reading problems.

The advocates of this approach believe that phonics (sounds as they apply to reading) should be introduced either before a sight vocabulary is established or on a parallel with the beginning basal reader. They reject the "whole word" approach, because they believe the child first sees the word as individual letters and then the larger unit of the word as a whole.

Among the proponents of the "phonics-first approach" there is little consensus of opinion regarding the proper method of teaching. Each approach establishes a step-by-step sequence which the authors warn must be followed if the child is to read. They emphasize that learning phonics is a memorization process that can only be mastered by repetitive drill. Their material consists of workbooks containing page after page of isolated words and phonic elements.

One phonic system calls for learning the names of all 26 letters of the alphabet on the first day of instruction. Another emphasizes a letter-by-letter approach to reading, with the emphasis upon the sound of each separate letter. Others teach all of the vowel sounds first (long and short), followed by the consonants, while some teach only the long or short vowel sounds first. The teaching of blends, vowels or consonant digraphs, and dipthongs varies to a greater extent even than some of the other elements in the various materials. In some cases, only selected elements are taught, and others are ignored. In most of the material, there is little, if any, effort to help children evolve or understand phonic principles or to aid them in arriving at useful generalizations.

There is no evidence as to the value of many of the phonics programs now available to our schools except the opinions and prejudices of their authors. There is little consensus of opinion as to appropriate methods in the phonics approach, and serious doubts should be raised about the use of most phonics materials either in isolation or in conjunction with basal readers.

If the school is pressured into using a phonics program, it should be used on a very limited basis, rather than school wide, and it should be evaluated under the best research conditions possible. Wholesale adoption can only result in confusion, more problems, and no indication as to the worth of the material.

The Language Experience Approach[2]

The language experience approach was developed in San Diego County, California, under the direction of R. Van Allen, curriculum director for the county school system. This approach attempts to integrate the communication skills of speaking, writing, reading, and listening.

In simplest terms, the approach can be thought of in the following manner. What a child thinks about he can talk about; what he can talk about he can write, or the teacher can write for him. What he writes he can read; he can read what he writes and what others write. What he has to say and write is as important to him as what other people have written for him to read.

From the very beginning of the school year, the children are encouraged to express themselves through speaking, writing, painting, and so forth. The teacher works with individual children and with small groups of children, helping them to write down "talk." Reading skills are taught informally by the teacher's talking to the children about the words, names of letters, beginning sounds, ending sounds, sounds in between.

The language experience approach seems to have some merit for beginning reading instruction. It does seem to develop an interest in reading, there is an integration of the language arts and other communication skills, the children understand that reading is an important form of communication, and the approach does encourage creative expression.

Certain aspects of the approach are open to careful questioning. A teacher using this approach would have to be well aware of the development of reading skills, to be sure that the children were getting a balanced and sound program. There would be some danger of continual misspelling, poor expression, and punctuation errors if the teacher, fearing to hamper creativity, failed to correct errors. It is also possible that memorization of written material may be mistaken for reading.

The Initial Teaching Alphabet[3]

The i/t/a was developed in England by Sir James Pitman for use in teaching beginning readers. In this alphabet, there are 44 symbols in-

[2] Doris May Lee and R. Van Allen, *Learning to Read Through Experience*. New York: Appleton-Century-Crofts, Inc., 1963.
[3] John Downing, *The Initial Teaching Alphabet*. New York: The Macmillan Company, 1964.

stead of our 26-letter alphabet. These symbols represent all of the sounds in the English language and are consistent in that a given symbol represents the same sound each time it is encountered. In traditional orthography, the 26 letters, individually or in combination, can represent upwards of 2,000 sounds.

The i/t/a, derived from the Augmented Roman Alphabet, is not designed as a continuing method. It is devised for use during the first 15 months of formal reading instruction. This method is in its fourth year of a five-year research study in England, with concurrent research projects in the United States. The largest of these involves 46 first grade classrooms in Bethlehem, Pennsylvania, and is sponsored by a research grant from the Ford Foundation and directed by Dr. Albert J. Mazurkiewicz of the i/t/a study center at Lehigh University.

Supporters of i/t/a claim that children using it can learn to read in much less time than those using traditional orthography. The studies have not been in progress for a sufficient length of time, however, to determine if wholesale adoption is justified. There is still the unanswered question of transition to regular print after the initial teaching period and the possible affect upon later spelling and speed of reading.

Sir James Pitman is more than aware of these problems and warns that the i/t/a method is only in the first stage of a long-term research investigation.

The Linguistics Approach[4]

The science of linguistics has aroused much interest in the last few years as a possible aid in improving reading competencies. Linguistics, because it is a complicated science, has resulted in misunderstanding, confusion, and hastily constructed material when applied to reading. The fact remains, however, that its application to reading is evolving.

The contribution of the science of linguistics to reading has come primarily from the descriptive linguists. They believe that, in reading, the child must be able to respond to the language signals as represented by written symbols (words) in the same way that he responds to the patterns of auditory shapes. The key to an understanding of descriptive linguistics is in the concept of "pattern." It is argued that some of our reading failures are due to the obvious differences between the patterns of speech of children and the patterns we ask them to read. Much of the child's reading material is in a pattern that is unreal to him. It is imperative that a child have sentence sense, that is, that he should possess a knowledge of word arrangement and corresponding word function.

[4] Carl E. Lefevre, *Linguistics and the Teaching of Reading.* New York: McGraw-Hill Book Company, 1964.

At the present time, there is some confusion regarding where to start beginning readers. Some would have the child begin with the smaller units in structural analysis, such as the phoneme (elemental speech sound), morpheme (the smallest unit with a meaning), word, and grapheme (letter symbol for a phoneme). Others would have us start with the simple sentence first. At the present time the concepts in linguistics, as they apply to the development of reading skills, are not well enough defined or established to arouse more than curiosity and a "wait and see" attitude.

Summary

The approaches used in teaching reading are many, and the problem of selecting the approach that will be most successful with all of our children is still solved by an educated trial-and-error method. There is probably no one approach that meets the needs of all. For most students, the basal reader has to be supplemented with more work in study skills, word recognition skills, comprehension skills, or other skill development areas. None of the approaches mentioned solves all the reading problems. The one thing we are sure of, however, is that an eclectic approach, taught by an intelligent teacher, supported by knowledgeable administration, is a prerequisite to good reading instruction.

44. How Are Basal Readers Used?

RALPH C. STAIGER (1958)

Millions of copies of basal readers are being used in schools throughout the country. In order to collect information on the attitudes of school people toward some aspects of basal reader use, a questionnaire was sent to teachers, supervisors, consultants, and superintendents in many different types of schools in all 48 states and Hawaii in January of 1957. The findings are reported in this article.

Since the sample of schools was not a random one, it would be unsound to conclude that these proportions are truly representative of

---

SOURCE: *Elementary English,* January 1958, pp. 44–46. Reprinted with the permission of the National Council of Teachers of English and Ralph C. Staiger.

practices throughout the country. A sample of 474 responses from all 48 states and Hawaii, however, can be a useful indicator of practices.

The questionnaire was designed to offer as little resistance as possible to the respondent. It contained eleven questions, ten of which could be answered by check marks. A stamped self-addressed envelope was included. 615 questionnaires were mailed and 474 or 77.07% were returned. This was considered an adequate return.

The questionnaire read as follows:

1. Which plan do you use? (a) One series of readers basally (b) Two series of readers cobasally (c) Three series of readers cobasally (d) More than three series of readers for basal instruction (e) No basal readers (f) Other.
2. Which series do you use in your basal program?
3. When a reading group changes from one series to another, when is the change usually made? (a) At any opportune time (b) After the preprimers (c) After the primer (d) After the first reader (e) After the 2–1 or 2–2 readers (f) After the 3–1 or 3–2 readers (g) Other.
4. Who decides whether a pupil or group changes from one series to another, if a change is made? (a) Teacher alone (b) Teacher and supervisor or consultant (c) Consultant alone (d) Administrator alone (e) Other.
5. Do you use for supplementary reading the basal readers of any publishers other than the above?
6. At the primary grade level, are you satisfied with the two-level (2^1–2^2, 3^1–3^2) editions of the readers?
7. At the intermediate grade level, do you believe that two-level readers (4^1–4^2, 5^1–5^2, 6^1–6^2) are desirable?
8. Did or will the additional expenditure involved in two-level readers influence your adopting them in the primary grades?
9. Did or will the additional expenditure involved in two-level readers influence your adopting them in the intermediate grades?
10. Do you encourage use of the workbook which accompanies the basal reader?
11. How do you recommend use of the teacher's manual? (a) As the prescribed course of study (b) As a guide (c) Useful occasionally (d) Rarely useful (e) Other.

Results

PLAN USED

Of the 474 schools in this sample, 69% reported using one series of readers basally. Comments made on the questionnaire indicated that 17.7% of these were varying their procedures so that it was doubtful whether a one-series plan was actually being used. Some of the variations mentioned included different series at the primary and intermediate levels, varying practices in the different schools of one community, or even in different classrooms of one school, and the experimental use of a cobasal series in some classes. Eight percent of the single basal users took the trouble to specify that supplementary readers were an important part of their reading program.

That two series of readers were used cobasally was reported by 20.0% of the schools; 5.7% used three series cobasally, 5.1% used more than three series. We must be careful to interpret the data collected in the light of the foregoing findings, for the sample appears heavily loaded with single basal series schools.

PUBLISHERS

The materials used by the schools queried were many and varied, and all of the major publishers were reported, sometimes as single basal adoptions and usually in combination with other materials. Being used as single basic readers were the series of Ginn and Company, Houghton Mifflin and Company, Lyons and Carnahan and Company, Macmillan and Company, Row, Peterson and Company, Scott Foresman and Company, and Silver Burdett and Company. Twenty-nine other combinations were represented, including two, three, four, five, and six series combinations. In these groups were represented the readers of the American Book Company, D. C. Heath and Company, Laidlaw and Company, and the Winston Company, in addition to the readers listed above.

CHANGING SERIES

Teachers sometimes find that a group of pupils need additional instruction at a given level. When a shift is made from one series to another by a reading group within a classroom, the data showed that no particular level is favored for making the change. 40.1% of the respondents indicated that such changes were made at any opportune time, no matter at what level the pupils are reading. The schools which use only one series cannot make such a shift, and therefore 33.1% of the responses showed that no change is made. Other responses showed that 4.6% of the schools favored changing after the pre-primer level; 4.0% after the primer, 3.8% after the first reader; 2.5% after the 2–1 or 2–2 readers, and 5.5% after the 3–1 or 3–2 readers.

DECISION TO CHANGE

The decision to change a pupil or group from one series to another was apparently considered important enough to warrant the teacher's consulting with a supervisor, principal, or consultant in 51.5% of the schools responding. The teacher alone made the decision in 17.7% of the schools. In no case did the consultant or the administrator alone make the decision.

Perhaps it would be well to recall that most of the returns were from principals and supervisors, and so might be colored according to their beliefs. It is possible that in practice more such decisions are made by the teacher than these results indicate.

SUPPLEMENTARY READING

An overwhelming proportion of the responses indicated that the basal readers of publishers other than those adopted were used for supplementary reading. Only 5.4% of the respondents said that this was not common practice, while 92.5% approved of using basal readers for supplementary reading.

TWO-LEVEL READERS

Two-level editions of second and third readers have been on the market for several years. Apparently they have been accepted by a majority of school people, for 89.9% of the returns indicated satisfaction with the two-level plan at the primary level, while 5.3% did not approve. A small number suggested the need for additional in-between books, even though this question was not asked. When the subject of the increased cost of two-level readers was considered, 85.9% of the returns indicated that cost did not influence their adoption in the primary grades.

One relatively new development in basal readers has been two-level readers at the intermediate grade level (4–1, 4–2, 5–1, 5–2, 6–1, 6–2). Opinions on the desirability of these books were 63.7% in favor, 27.2% opposed, with the remainder not answering directly. Opinions on the influence of the cost factor were somewhat different from those toward the primary level materials; 23.5% believed that the additional expenditure would influence their adoption, while 69.8% did not believe that cost would be a factor.

WORKBOOKS

Workbooks which accompany basal reading programs constitute an important feature of the program, according to publishers. Single basal users are more likely to make use of this part of the program, for 91.4% of single basal reader schools reported using workbooks, while 76.3% of cobasal schools and 49.0% of tribasal and other schools use workbooks. Many of the affirmative answers specified that correct use of a workbook was important to its educational value.

MANUALS

Teachers manuals are used in different ways in different schools. In 15.0% of the returns it was reported that the manuals are recommended as a prescribed course of study, while 68.1% of the returns recommended the manuals as guides. Their usefulness for inexperienced teachers was indicated in some of the responses. Other returns showed that they are recommended both as a guide and as a course of study. This accounted for 9.9% of the returns. Less than one percent of the responses suggested that the guides were useful only occasionally.

Conclusions

Although it is recognized that the samplying of 474 schools cannot be considered truly representative of all schools, the following conclusions appear valid.

1. While many schools adhere to the single basal series plan, a considerable number are making use of books in other series. These are used as cobasal readers, to be used in conjunction with the basal series, or as supplementary readers, to give pupils additional practice in reading. The great majority of schools use basal readers for some supplementary reading.

2. When more than one series of readers is used for basal instruction, the change is made when it will benefit the needs of the child rather than at any predetermined reader level.

3. The change from one series to another is usually made after the teacher has conferred with a supervisor or principal, although in many cases the teacher alone makes the decision.

4. Two-level readers in the primary grades have won widespread acceptance. At the intermediate grade level they are not so well accepted, although many school people think they are desirable. The additional cost of these materials, while taken into consideration in many cases, has not prevented them from being adopted in most schools.

5. The workbooks which accompany basal readers are more likely to be used when a school adopts a single basal reading series. The likelihood of workbooks being used when two or three series of readers are used is considerably less. The greater the number of basal readers used for instruction, the less likely the students are to use the accompanying workbook.

6. Teachers manuals have been accepted by most school personnel as an aid to teachers. While some schools use the manuals as the prescribed course of study, most consider them a guide.

45. Whose Brand of Reading Methods Is the "Best Buy"?

DELWYN G. SCHUBERT (1953)

When the numerous methods and techniques of teaching reading to the disabled reader are pondered, many teachers are in a quandary. Each specialist—Gates, Monroe, Dolch, Fernald, etc., all renowned in the reading field—advocates a different method. What is the answer? What should be used? Is there a best method?

Basically, there are three methods for teaching words to disabled readers: the visual, the phonic, and the kinaesthetic. There is no best method *per se*. Only when a remedial program is based on individual needs can any method be cited as superior.

For example, Marion Monroe[1] tells of a seven-year-old boy who suffered from a severe reading disability of a neurological origin. No matter how hard the child tried, he was unable to remember words when the usual sight method was employed. As soon as the cause was uncovered, he was taught by tracing large models of words while saying them out loud. This was a kinaesthetic approach. And it worked! Soon he was able to recognize words and began to show definite and competent progress.

Bond's research[2] shows that children suffering from hearing losses are at a marked disadvantage in learning to read when a purely phonetic method is employed. On the other hand, he found that the look and say method does not penalize the child who has an auditory loss. It is evident that if a child suffers from auditory or visual deficiencies, it is wise to choose a method of instruction that minimizes the handicap as much as possible.

[1] M. Monroe, *Growing Into Reading*. Scott, Foresman and Company, Chicago, 1951, pp. 63–65.
[2] G. L. Bond, *The Auditory and Speech Characteristics of Poor Readers* (Teachers College Contributions to Education, No. 657). Teachers College, Columbia University, New York, 1935.

SOURCE: *The Clearing House*, XXVII (January, 1953), 266–267. Reprinted by permission of the publisher.

It is a mistake to assume that just because children are free from discernible sensory impairments that they will learn as easily when one method is employed as another. Any teacher can convince himself of the falsity of this belief by checking the auditory and visual memory spans of a group of children. Not infrequently does one find that students with fine visual memories have much poorer auditory memories or vice versa. For seemingly inexplicable reasons some children have great difficulty in making visual associations but show excellent phonic aptitude. In such cases, Monroe's phonetic approach of blending and forming word elements into whole words is to be recommended.

For the child who is adept at making visual associations but shows ineptitude when phonetic approaches are employed, Gates' method of stressing the general configuration of words as a basis for recognition is appropriate. Since it is not possible to tell which method will work best in an individual case, the teacher must be flexible and versatile. If Harry doesn't respond favorably to one method, another method must be tried.

In final analysis, if there is a best method, we are forced to term it an eclectic one. When an individual method is used to the exclusion of others, some children are doomed to failure regardless of how sincere, competent, and enthusiastic the teacher. Today many teachers use the popular flash method. It is true that most children learn easily and quickly when this method is employed. But still there are needless fatalities. The number of failures could be reduced markedly were the teacher to use several avenues of approach so that the student could choose the particular method or combination of methods that seem to be best suited to his individual needs.

46. An Evaluation of the Techniques for Teaching Word Recognition

ROBERT E. MILLS (1956)

The teaching of reading has seen the championing of various methods as the most effective for the teaching of word-recognition skills. Reading authorities have used empirical data and their own opinions to promote particular brands of reading without enough objective research data to validate their assertions. Schubert summarizes our present predicament when he comments:

> When the numerous methods and techniques of teaching reading to the disabled reader are pondered, many teachers are in a quandary. Each specialist—Gates, Monroe, Dolch, Fernald, etc., all renowned in the reading field—advocates a different method (4).

Much of the difficulty in determining appropriate methods for the teaching of word recognition comes from confusing the particular reading skill of word recognition with general reading achievement, which involves not only word recognition but also comprehension, generalizing, inferring meanings, and the like. Phonics, visual analysis of words, and kinesthetic tracings are techniques which have been developed and used for the specific purpose of aiding the child to identify and recognize the printed symbol. Only after the child has a certain degree of competency in word-recognition skills is he able to read. That is, *the act of reading is different from the act of identifying or recognizing words.* As Dolch might state it, the child has to have a certain number of "bricks" available before the "house" can take shape:

> We may say that the understanding of words in reading is basic because without understanding of word meanings there can be no reading. Words are to reading matter what bricks are to a house. When you look at the house you do not think of the bricks; but without the bricks there would be no house (1).

SOURCE: *Elementary School Journal,* LVI (January, 1956), 221–225. Reprinted by permission of the University of Chicago Press.

It is the problem of helping the child secure the "bricks" (words) that has been of concern. Yet most of the researchers have used complicated measures of eye fixations, sentence- and paragraph-comprehension tests, and speed of reading in an attempt to ascertain the relative efficiency of a particular method of teaching word recognition. Promotion of generalized plans for developmental reading, such as the "intrinsic method" or the "non-oral method," has become confused with the specific methods of teaching word recognition, namely, the visual or look-and-say, the phonic or auditory, the kinesthetic or tracing, and combinations of these three.

Among the three basic methods there are no clear delineations. Phonic, visual, and kinesthetic elements are involved in all printed symbols of our language. Thus, when we speak of a phonic method, we are simply indicating that stress is being given to the auditory characteristics of the word and that this stress becomes the differential between the various methods.

Purpose and Subjects of This Study

The basic purpose of the study reported in this article was to determine the teaching method or combination of methods most effective in teaching word recognition to various types of individuals.

The subjects were thirty-nine boys and nineteen girls in Grades II–IV of five public schools in Pasco County, Florida. These subjects were divided into nine classifications for purposes of treatment. Each of the three age levels was divided into three groups of intelligence levels (low, 65–80; average, 85–100; and high, 105–20) as determined by the Wechsler Intelligence Scale for Children.

Procedures Used

A test instrument, the Learning Methods Test (3), was specifically devised by the author for this study. Basically this test is a series of standard teaching lessons, accompanied by tests to determine the efficiency of the various methods for different children. Harris and Roswell (2) have suggested such procedures but with an informal manner of presentation, teaching procedures, and testing. Here we have attempted to standardize an instrument for the specific purpose of determining the most effective method for teaching word recognition to the individual pupil.

The materials for this test consist of four sets of graded picture-word cards; a manual of directions, which provides specific instructions for the four fifteen-minute teaching lessons, each of which stresses a different method (visual, phonic, kinesthetic, or a combination); and record forms.

In order to determine the appropriate level of words to be used in the Learning Methods Test, a pretest of word recognition was necessary. The picture-word cards were administered to obtain forty words that the child could not recognize in five seconds of exposure time. These words were to be used later in the four learning-methods situations. For example, if forty words from the first-grade cards could not be found that the subject did not know, then no words from the first-grade level were used. Instead, a check was made to find forty unknown words on the second-grade level.

The cards were first presented to the child with the word side up. If at the end of five seconds the subject had not responded correctly to the word, this "unknown" word then became one of the training and test words. This process was continued until all the cards on that particular level had been administered. From these unknown words, forty cards were selected at random by shuffling the stack thoroughly and then counting off the first forty cards.

A systematic rotation procedure was used for the order of presentation of the teaching methods. If the visual method was used as the first teaching method with Subject A, then Subject B was presented with the phonic method as the first procedure, and so on.

The pretest and the first fifteen-minute lesson on ten words were administered on the first day. Twenty-four hours later a delayed-recall test was administered to the subject as a check of his recognition of the ten words taught him the preceding day. The total number of correct responses on this delayed-recall test was recorded as his score for that particular method and became a part of the data for this study.

On the same day as the delayed-recall test for the first training session (the second day), a second fifteen-minute lesson using a different method was presented to the subject. This process of individualized lessons and testing at twenty-four-hour intervals was continued on consecutive days until all four teaching methods had been utilized. On the fifth day the delayed-recall test for the fourth lesson was administered. Thus each subject had four scores ranging from 0 to 10 for each method.

This study was concerned with four basic methods of teaching word recognition: the visual, the phonic, the kinesthetic, and a combination of the three. In order to obtain specific techniques or steps that would be typical of a particular method of teaching word recognition, six activities were selected for each method on the basis of frequency of mention in the literature. For each method these specific teaching activities were outlined in the manual of directions for the Learning Methods Test. These standard teaching procedures were used so that each subject would have the same variety of activities for each method and in the same order as every other subject.

Treatment of Pertinent Variables

Because of the many variables of great importance in attempting to evaluate techniques of teaching word recognition, it was necessary to limit the number of variables treated in the research design to those that other research and empirical data indicated as being most significant, namely, sex, chronological age, reading level, and intelligence.

An attempt was made to control the other important variables in the following manner. The teacher variable was controlled by employing only one teacher, the author, to do all the testing and teaching both for the standardizing of the Learning Methods Test and for collecting the data for this study. The race variable was controlled by using only subjects from the white race. A further control of note was that no child from a bilingual home was used as a subject. Visual and hearing efficiency were controlled through administering the telebinocular and audiometer tests; only children who fell in the normal range on both these tests were used as subjects. Reading-achievement level was controlled by the items on the Learning Methods Test. Grade placement was controlled by having all subjects in the seven-year-old group from the second grades, eight-year-olds from the third grades, and nine-year-olds from the fourth grades. Geographical distribution of subjects was confined to a radius of thirty-five miles, with all subjects residing in Pasco County, Florida. This, of course, limits the generalizations that can be made from the findings of this study.

A special research design employing the *t* test was used to determine the significance of the sex variable. Twenty-four pairs of boys and girls, matched in relation to chronological age, reading level, and intelligence, were used. The results of the *t* test indicated that there were no significant differences at the 5 percent level of confidence between the two sexes for any of the four methods. However, the girls tended to score higher on all four methods than did the boys: the girls had a total mean score of 6.39 compared with the boys' total mean score of 5.60. Since there were no significant differences, both boys and girls were used for the study.

Statistical Results

Table 1 indicates means and standard deviations of delayed-recall scores obtained on the Learning Methods Test for all fifty-eight subjects. Because of the high standard deviations for certain groups, a test for the homogeneity of variance was run; the corrected chi square was not significant. Therefore the hypothesis of random sampling from a population with a common variance was accepted.

TABLE 1. Mean Scores and Standard Deviations of 58 Pupils in Grades II–IV on Delayed-Recall Tests of Word Recognition Taught by Four Methods

	LOW INTELLIGENCE (65–80)		AVERAGE INTELLIGENCE (85–100)		HIGH INTELLIGENCE (105–20)		ALL GROUPS	
Age Group and Method	*Mean*	*Standard Deviation*	*Mean*	*Standard Deviation*	*Mean*	*Standard Deviation*	*Mean*	*Standard Deviation*
Seven-year-olds:	5 pupils		5 pupils		5 pupils		15 pupils	
Visual	4.0	3.24	7.6	1.14	9.6	0.55	7.1	3.03
Phonic	1.8	3.03	5.2	1.92	8.8	1.10	5.3	3.58
Kinesthetic	4.0	2.86	4.8	2.49	6.4	2.51	5.1	2.63
Combination	3.2	2.77	7.8	1.79	8.6	1.14	6.5	3.09
All methods	..	...	..	...	..	...	6.0	3.14
Eight-year-olds:	5 pupils		6 pupils		5 pupils		16 pupils	
Visual	2.4	1.34	7.5	1.64	9.2	.84	6.4	3.16
Phonic	1.8	.45	7.2	1.94	9.0	1.22	6.1	3.33
Kinesthetic	6.0	.71	7.3	1.96	9.2	1.10	7.5	1.86
Combination	3.8	.84	8.3	.81	9.6	.55	7.3	2.60
All methods	..	...	..	...	..	...	6.8	2.80
Nine-year-olds:	9 pupils		12 pupils		6 pupils		27 pupils	
Visual	6.0	2.78	8.1	1.57	9.2	1.60	7.6	2.34
Phonic	5.1	3.10	7.1	1.97	8.7	1.21	6.8	2.59
Kinesthetic	5.9	2.20	5.9	1.97	8.2	2.14	6.4	2.22
Combination	6.0	3.04	7.4	1.38	9.0	2.04	7.3	2.38
All methods	..	...	..	...	..	...	7.0	2.40
All subjects:	19 pupils		23 pupils		16 pupils		58 pupils	
Visual	4.5	2.93	7.8	1.47	9.3	1.08	7.2	2.77
Phonic	3.4	3.04	6.7	2.03	8.8	1.11	6.2	3.89
Kinesthetic	5.4	2.19	6.0	2.18	7.9	2.20	6.4	2.38
Combination	4.7	2.77	7.7	1.36	9.1	1.39	7.1	2.61
All methods	4.5	2.80	7.1	1.92	8.8	1.57	6.7	2.74

An analysis-of-variance design was used to determine whether the means of the thirty-six groups differed significantly. (Unequal numbers of cases were used, but there was a minimum of five subjects for each of the thirty-six cells in the factorial design.) The following is a summary of this analysis of variance.

Significant at the 1 percent level of confidence were intelligence interacting with method, chronological age interacting with intelligence, and intelligence as a main effect. The interaction of chronological age with method was found to be significant at the 5 percent level of confidence. The interaction of age with intelligence was not of direct importance to this methodology study and, therefore, was not further analyzed. As would be expected, intelligence proved to be the most significant factor in determining the number of words learned in a fifteen-minute teaching lesson.

After it was found that the over-all F's were significant for the intelligence-method interaction and the age-method interaction, the *t* technique was used to test the significance of the difference between any two of the group means. Using the 5 percent level of confidence, the conclusions stated below were reached as a result of this treatment of the data.

Conclusions

The study showed conclusively that different children learn to recognize words more efficiently by different teaching methods and that no one method is best for all children. Some conclusions about the effectiveness or the ineffectiveness of specific teaching methods were drawn for certain types of children.

1. *Children of low intelligence.* The phonic method is least effective for this group. The kinesthetic method is best in the greatest number of cases, but it is not statistically better than the visual and the combination methods.

2. *Children of average intelligence.* For the majority of cases in this group the kinesthetic method is the least effective. The phonic method showed no statistical significance in either direction. The combination and the visual methods proved to be about equally good for this group of average intelligence.

3. *Children of high intelligence.* In this group we are restricted in any conclusions we can draw about the relative effectiveness of methods because all subjects tended to learn words readily regardless of the teaching method used. However, the visual method did prove superior to the kinesthetic method for this group.

4. *Seven-year-olds.* The visual method appeared to be best and the kinesthetic method appeared to be the poorest. The other two methods seemed to be neither consistently effective nor ineffective in working with this group.

5. *Eight-year-olds.* The kinesthetic method proved to be best for this age group; it is significantly better than the phonic and somewhat better than the other two. This finding may have some possible relation to the fact that eight-year-olds are usually just becoming proficient in handwriting and show a great deal of interest in related activities.

6. *Nine-year-olds.* No one of the four methods was outstandingly effective or ineffective. The visual method did tend to be better than the kinesthetic method for this group of older children.

7. In general, the higher the intelligence, the more readily children learn words. However, there is no consistent relation between age and a child's readiness to learn words for the three age groups studied. This

finding has implications for present school practices where chronological age is all too often used as the major criterion in deciding when a child is ready to learn words.

Summary

In any study involving the dynamics of children, some variables are always neglected because of their infinite number and complexity and because of the limitations of research facilities. Therefore more research is needed in this area to validate present findings and to explore other important variables not adequately treated in past research. From this study evolve recommendations of practical application to classroom teachers and remedial-reading clinicians. These include the following:

1. Because different children learn to recognize words most efficiently by different teaching methods, the classroom teacher must be aware of these individual differences when he applies group-instruction techniques. Our research indicates the need for the teacher to familiarize himself with all the various techniques and to be versatile in the use of these if he is to teach *all* the children.
2. In individual cases of failure to make the expected growth in word-recognition skills, our research indicates the need for a diagnostic study of the child to determine the most appropriate method for the particular individual.

In summary, it is believed that this study has far-reaching implications for all those interested in how children learn to recognize words. We have theorized about individual differences for decades, but we have done little to apply this theory in teaching practice. This research indicates the need for the concentration of energies on finding out *which* method is best for *which* children rather than developing a recipe or "a best method" that will serve for all children all the time.

References

1. Dolch, Edward W. "The Use of Vocabulary Lists in Predicting Readability and in Developing Reading Materials," *Elementary English,* XXVI (March, 1949), 142–49.
2. Harris, A. J., and Roswell, Florence G. "Clinical Diagnosis of Reading Disability," *Journal of Psychology,* XXXVI (June, 1953), 323–40.
3. Mills, Robert E. The Learning Methods Test. Gainesville, Florida: Reading Laboratory and Clinic, University of Florida, 1954.
4. Schubert, Delwyn G. "Whose Brand of Reading Methods Is the 'Best Buy'?" *Clearing House,* XXVII (January, 1953), 266–67.

47. Locating, Introducing and Using Easy-to-Read, High-Interest Reading Matter

JEANNE S. CHALL (1957)

It is over 20 years since Edward L. Thorndike[1] analyzed supplementary books recommended for fourth, fifth, and sixth graders and concluded they were too hard for the majority. Subsequently he set up vocabulary specifications for children of average ability and below, and adapted the books to these specifications. He was criticized by many, but in spite of the criticism, these books[2] are still used in clinics and schools. His study also marked the beginning of a concerted effort to provide interesting reading material for poor readers.

Were we to repeat his study today, we would probably find a more encouraging situation. For junior and senior high school students reading at intermediate levels, there is a considerable choice of suitable books. For retarded readers still struggling through first, second, and third grade levels, however, the supply of books on their maturity level is still extremely low. For them the situation is a familiar one: what they want to read, they cannot—what they can read, they will not. The disparity between their social maturity and their reading ability makes the choice of a book almost as delicate as international diplomacy. If interest takes priority, we risk exposing them to further failure. If reading ease is the major criterion, we risk offending their self-respect.

The remainder of this paper will consider ways to avoid the dilemma by suggesting ways of making available to the reading disability case, the slow learner, and the mentally retarded, books that they can and will want to read.

[1] Edward L. Thorndike, "Improving the Ability to Read." *Teachers College Record*, XXXVI (October, November, December, 1934), 1–19; 123–44; 229–41. Bureau of Publications, Teachers College, Columbia University, 1935.
[2] The Thorndike Library, published by Appleton Century.

SOURCE: *Reading in Action*, II (1957), 54–57. Reprinted with the permission of Jeanne S. Chall and the International Reading Association.

Defining the Easy-to-Read Book

In general, an easy-to-read book is one that can be read by a given reader without undue frustration. By convention, we use reading grade levels to evaluate both books and readers. Thus, a book is easy to read for a youngster with third grade reading ability if it is written on a third grade reading level. However, his interest in the subject matter, his previous knowledge of the subject, his purpose, and the amount of help he will receive while reading the book should also be considered. If the reader is highly interested in the content or is informed on the subject, or reads it with the help of a sympathetic teacher, he may find it "easy" even if it is on a fourth or fifth grade level. If he reads it at home, it should probably be somewhat below his reading level. If he is intelligent and striving, it could be harder. If he is easily upset by failure, it probably should be below his reading level. There are no hard and fast rules here.

What Is High Interest?

High interest is not so easily defined or measured. It involves two main aspects. The first has to do with the over-all maturity of the book —its content, style, illustrations, print, and size. Children know, even if we do not, when a book is babyish. They also know what kinds of books their friends are reading. They know that reading books of adventure, mystery, biography, and science are signs of growing up, and there is something childish about reading fairy tales at the age of 12. High interest can refer to a book that is more mature in content, treatment, and physical makeup than the level of reading needed to cope with it.

The other aspect of interest has to do with whether the book is interesting or dull, irrespective of its maturity. Nursery rhymes and fairy tales are interesting, even if we do outgrow them. A book can be dull for an airplane enthusiast even if it is about airplanes. Here, the skill of the author in making his subject lively and moving is important. Illustrations help. This kind of high interest is even more elusive than the first and although all writers try to achieve it, not all succeed.

The books for poor readers should be high on both types of interest. The content should be mature, i.e., on a par with chronological age, and the treatment should be exciting.

Locating Materials

Where can easy books of high interest be located? There are two major sources: (1) the growing numbers of books specially written or rewritten for retarded readers and adults of limited literacy, and (2) the trade books, textbooks, and magazines published for the normal reader.

The specially adapted materials have in the past been frowned upon as distortions of the original author's intent and style. However, they continue to grow in popularity and are the very backbone of remedial programs. The U. S. Government Printing Office has sponsored such materials[3] for servicemen of limited reading ability. Recently Dr. Seuss, the gifted author of children's books, felt the need of the poor reader and wrote an easy-to-read book.

For the older child still on primary levels, books that come to mind are *Bucky Button, Cowboy Sam,*[4] *I Know a Story* and *It Happened One Day,*[5] *Straight Up,*[6] the *Disney Series,*[7] the Dolch *Basic Vocabulary and Pleasure Reading Series.*[8] There are others, but on the whole, the supply is still too meager. We need more books at the first, second, and third grade levels of higher maturity level than even those mentioned for children who first begin to read at the age of 8 or 10. To read about the antics of six-year-olds at the age of 8 or 10 adds insult to the already existing injury!

For the retarded reader at intermediate levels there is a much wider choice—*The Teen Age Tales,*[9] the *Reader's Digest Skill Builders,*[10] the *new Reading Laboratory,*[11] the *American Adventure Series,*[12] and numerous adapted classics.

There is an even greater selection of easy-to-read books of high interest trade books, of which only a few can be mentioned: *The Childhood of Famous Americans* series,[13] *The Landmark Books* and *Allabout Books.*[14] Complete listings can be found in the recent compilations of:

Helen Blair Sullivan and Louise E. Tolman, "High Interest-Low Vocabulary Reading Materials. A Selected Booklist." *Journal of Education,* Vol. 139 (December, 1956), p. 1–132.

George Spache, *Good Books for Poor Readers,* Gainesville, Florida: University of Florida, 1954.

[3] Edgar Dale, *Stories for Today,* Washington, D. C.: Government Printing Office, a reader for servicemen written at fourth grade level.
[4] Chicago: Benefic Press.
[5] Evanston, Illinois: Row, Peterson & Co.
[6] New York: The Macmillan Co.
[7] Boston: D. C. Heath.
[8] Champaign, Illinois: Garrard Press.
[9] Boston: D. C. Heath.
[10] Pleasantville, N. Y.
[11] Chicago: Science Research Associates.
[12] Chicago: Wheeler.
[13] Indianapolis, Ind.: Bobbs-Merrill.
[14] New York: Random House.

J. T. Hunt, "Easy and Interesting Fiction for the Handicapped Reader," *High School Journal,* Vol. 39 (April, 1956), p. 378–85.

Cloy S. Hobson and Oscar M. Hough, "Materials for the Retarded Reader," issued by Adel F. Throckmorton, State Superintendent of Public Instruction, Topeka, Kansas, 1954.

Viola Wallace, *Books for Adult Beginners,* Grades I to VII. Chicago: American Library Association, 1954.

Ruth Strang, Margaret Scoggin, and Christine Gilbert, *Gateways to Readable Books,* New York: H. W. Wilson Co., 1952 (revised).

Regular book lists compiled for librarians and teachers, and those distributed by publishers are less helpful for remedial teaching. They give only broad age or grade designations—often a combination of maturity of content and reading difficulty. It is usually of little aid for our purposes to know that a book is for ages 6 to 9, or 8 to 12. Perhaps in the near future, publishers will give us more useful estimates of reading and interest levels than they now provide.

Evaluating Materials

With the tremendous numbers of books published each day, lists soon become dated. It would be well to be able to judge books for ourselves. The following criteria are offered to aid in evaluation:

Reading level. This can be estimated in various ways. First, if time and money permit, apply a suitable readability formula. If this cannot be done, try the book out on the reader. For the primary reading levels, if a reader makes about five or fewer significant word recognition errors per 100 running words, it is probably right for him. But this should not be interpreted literally. If the child is to read it alone, fewer errors may be appropriate.

Interest level. Only judgment can be used to evaluate interest level since no formula comparable to a readability formula exists. The things to consider in judging interest level are:

1. Subject matter. For a rough estimate of the content that appeals to different age groups, we can use the general findings of psychological studies of children's interests. These are summarized in most textbooks on reading instruction. However, it is well to remember that these findings are based on the books that were available at the time the studies were made. More recently, as interesting books on science and history are published for younger readers, they have taken to them as avidly as to the older animal stories and fairy tales.

2. General style and treatment. The less mature books tend to personify animals and machines. They often present information through young children. For older children with low reading ability, a straight-

forward treatment is preferred. The writing should not talk down, nor oversimplify or overexplain.

3. Physical makeup. For poor readers, the illustrations of children should be of children close to their age, not of children younger than themselves. The shape of the books should not be of the pre-school outsize kind, but should resemble the shape and size of books read by other children of their age.

4. Size of type. The smaller the print, the more mature the book appears. The poor reader is especially sensitive to a book that looks childish because of its over-large type. Unfortunately, many publishers have in the past worked on the assumption that the major criterion of an easy book is large type. Often the vocabulary is at intermediate grade reading level and the print is at first-grade level. What we need for the poor reader are books of first-grade vocabulary level and fourth-grade print.

5. Length: A book or story should be brief. For the poor reader to complete a book of 100 to 200 pages is often equal to our reading Gibbon's *Decline and Fall of the Roman Empire.*

And last, but of great importance, the book should be interesting. It should have something to tell, and tell it with humor, excitement, and vitality.

Introducing and Using Easy-to-Read Books

As with books for more able readers, easy-to-read books should be introduced with zest and enthusiasm by the teacher. Attractive jackets and plastic covers help greatly. They should be made available to all children in a class, whether they are good or poor readers. In a recent study where we introduced easy-to-read materials in a sixth-grade classroom library, the better readers appropriated them first. This added to the prestige of the books and took away from them any taint of their "easiness."

A question that often occurs is: "Should the children be informed of the reading level of such books?" This depends upon the maturity of the pupils and how the reading level is explained. However, whether or not the reading level is made known to the pupils, it should be made known to the teacher, and preferably somewhere in the book. Thus, she can lead the children to the books they can read. The children can also find their own books more easily if some evidence of difficulty is available. A reading grade level is usually not preferred because of its associations with over-all maturity. At our clinic, we have used letter designations instead of grade numbers. The new Reading Laboratory uses color for reading levels.

In summary: within the past twenty years there has been a growing awareness of the needs of the poor reader by providing him with easy-to-read books of high interest. The teacher may find such books by consulting various reading lists and by evaluating books according to the criteria outlined. It is suggested that books for poor readers have the same content, format, and treatment as those for good readers of the same age. Such uniformity will help bridge the psychological gap which often exists between the poor reader and his more successful contemporaries.

VIII. Diagnosis and Correction of Reading Problems

Who needs help in reading? Who are disabled readers? How may they be identified? In the opening selection of this chapter, Austin (48) provides us with needed guidelines for identifying readers who need assistance.

Reading disability, according to Schubert (49), stems from many causes. Just as it is essential for a physician to uncover the causes of a patient's difficulty in order to effect a cure, locating and understanding the causes of reading failure is fundamental to diagnosis.

Rosenbloom (50), an optometrist, who for years has had an interest in visual difficulty as it relates to learning, discusses visual diagnosis, an area of great importance. Many teachers fail to realize that 25–50 percent of our school population is in need of visual attention. Are you, as a teacher, sensitive to the symptoms of visual defects? How much confidence can be placed in the Snellen Chart? What better visual screening devices are now available?

The importance of understanding emotional disturbances in connection with reading disability is evident when one considers how often disabled readers demonstrate personality maladjustment. Some children enter school with emotional problems that stem from a variety of physical and/or environmental causes. Other children become disturbed emotionally because of reading failure and the constant frustration that results. Schubert (51), in his article, "Reading and Personality Problems," highlights emotional disturbances as causes of reading failure; Sherman (52) places emphasis on the emotional disturbances resulting from reading failure, contending that "no other inadequacy creates as great a sense of frustration and failure as a reading difficulty." How can a teacher be sure that a child's emotional disturbance predated or followed his reading difficulty? How may the school psychologist assist the teacher in dealing with emotionally disturbed children?

Although we may hesitate to admit that the school is responsible for certain reading problems, there is strong evidence that this is often the case. In his book, *Teacher's Guide for Remedial Reading,* Kottmeyer states, "The plain fact of the matter is that poor teaching or poor learning conditions are probably responsible for more reading disability than all the other investigated causes put together."[1] In addition to poor teaching, of course, many other educational factors are involved.

A good diagnosis illuminates paths of remediation for the teacher. A sound diagnosis not only reveals the seriousness of the reading problem, but it helps clarify the nature of the disability. The exact depth of a diagnostic study depends not only on the seriousness of the problem but also on the number and kinds of specialists available as well as the diagnostic equipment employed. A staff of experts in a reading clinic can do more detailed diagnostic work than a remedial teacher working alone. By the same token, a full-time reading specialist can do more probing into the causes of reading disability than a classroom teacher.

The various degrees and types of diagnoses are represented in the articles by Sheldon, Monroe, and Robinson. Sheldon (53) treats the subject on a classroom level; Monroe (54) considers the implications of diagnosis on a remedial level; and Robinson (55) describes diagnosis as it might take place in a clinical setting.

As early as 1922, Gray (56) enunciated a series of principles for remedial teachers in a monograph under the heading "Suggestions Concerning Remedial Instruction." For a more recent enunciation of the basic principles of remedial instruction we are indebted to Bond and Tinker (57). How many of these principles are as applicable to the classroom as they are to a reading clinic?

[1] William Kottmeyer, *Teacher's Guide for Remedial Reading* (St. Louis: Webster Publishing Company, 1959), p. 16.

48. Identifying Readers Who Need Corrective Instruction

MARY C. AUSTIN (1953)

Reading retardation continues to be one of the most persistent problems at all levels from the primary grades through the university. Surveys during the past three decades have disclosed the wide range in reading ability and the large amount of reading retardation in any one grade. It is not unusual to find reading achievement within a class varying from three to ten years or more, with the range tending to increase as the pupils advance through school. Numerous investigators have estimated that from 5 to 40 percent of the school population are retarded in reading and should receive corrective instruction.

Classroom teachers, administrators, and supervisors are vitally concerned with the importance of providing for individual differences. To meet reading needs, many modern schools are now providing three kinds of reading programs: developmental, corrective, and remedial. The *developmental* program provides for the majority of readers who are making satisfactory progress in elementary and secondary schools and colleges. *Corrective reading* refers to the type of organization required by nonreaders and retarded readers whose difficulties are relatively mild and uncomplicated by emotional problems. Individuals receiving this type of guidance usually show improvement in reading when systematic instruction is initiated at their instructional levels. Three groups of individuals who respond to corrective reading are mentioned later in this paper. The term *remedial reading,* which is used rather loosely to refer to any specialized reading assistance, should be reserved to designate specifically the type of program required by retarded readers who have varying degrees of difficulty in the association and retention of meaning with printed symbols, especially when a visual-auditory approach is used in teaching reading.

Because of the magnitude of the problem, school workers are reexamining their methods of identifying retarded readers in order to lo-

---

SOURCE: Mary Austin, "Identifying Readers Who Need Corrective Instruction," Supplementary Educational Monograph No. 79, 1953, pp. 19–25. Reprinted by permission of the University of Chicago Press.

cate those individuals who will profit most from special reading instruction. Classroom teachers, as well as remedial-reading specialists, are attempting to answer these four questions: (1) What is meant by the term *reading retardation?* (2) What procedures are used for selecting the pupil in need of corrective-reading instruction? (3) At what point of retardation should pupils be referred for special help in reading? (4) How shall we distinguish between classroom and clinical problems?

Despite the fact that retardation has been the subject of much study and discussion, there seems to be no generally accepted definition of a retarded reader. Furthermore, some authorities differentiate between retarded readers and reading-disability cases. When this distinction is made, the *retarded readers* are usually those whose reading is below expectancy for their chronological age and grade, and *reading-disability cases* are those pupils whose reading is also well below their intellectual level.

Surveys of present practice indicate that many teachers commonly define reading retardation in terms of the discrepancy between mental age and reading age. When the reading age is conspicuously below the mental age, the pupil is regarded as having difficulty in reading. Moreover, when this concept of reading retardation is accepted, the mental age is assumed to be the level at which an individual can be expected to achieve in reading. From the standpoint of the school, this concept of retardation is practical because it is easily understood by teachers and is based on information usually available in the school system.

On the other hand, several authorities question a definition of reading retardation which merely compares the pupil's mental maturity with his present success in reading. In light of the current knowledge of child development, reading achievement is thought to be one aspect of the total growth of an individual. For this reason, expectancy of achievement in reading appears to be dependent upon a number of factors, including intelligence, emotional well-being, physical development, the nature of the instructional program, and the individual's general level of achievement in other areas. Therefore, a study of retardation in reading should involve, insofar as possible, an appraisal of the whole child. Certainly most people would agree that to provide special training in reading and to ignore the lack of maturity in other growth areas is a waste of time. In addition, feelings of distaste for reading may result and spread to other school activities formerly enjoyed by the child.

Frequently retardation in reading is confused with general mental retardation. While reading retardation has been found at *all* levels of intelligence, some investigators have revealed that as many as 80 percent of the retarded readers possess average or above-average intelligence.

Retardation also exists at all levels of reading achievement. In many school situations, when intelligence is evaluated in relation to reading accomplishment, the extent of retardation among pupils who are reading at or above their assigned grade levels appears to be as high as among children who are reading at or below grade average. It is also true that children who are not achieving up to grade level may not be retarded if their achievement closely approximates their intellectual status.

For the purpose of this discussion, a retarded reader should be regarded as the individual whose reading achievement falls significantly below his capacity for reading. *Capacity* for reading in its broadest connotation, as used here, includes the pupil's physical, emotional, and social development, as well as his mental maturity. Several common methods of identifying a retarded reader are described in the following section of this paper. It must be recognized, however, that the applicability of these procedures to different school situations will vary.

The traditional practice of many teachers who were planning to select a small number of pupils for special instruction in reading was to choose the poorest readers in the classroom. Obviously, if a fifth-grade pupil could read only second-grade materials or was in the lowest tenth of his class group on the basis of national norms for a standardized reading test, he must have a reading problem. There was little doubt in the thinking of many teachers as to the need for a specialized program without further delay or diagnosis.

All too often the procedure for identifying the individual in need of special help was to make a comparison of the pupil's reading ability in relation to one or more external standards. Typical examples of these external standards include (1) "evaluating the child's reading on the basis of teacher or parent expectancy," (2) comparing his reading ability with the accomplishment of his grade or class group, (3) ascertaining his success in relation to the norms on a standardized test, or (4) "determining the presence or the absence of the ability to read at all."[1] Each of these selection procedures tends to ignore the general maturation of the individual.

Fortunately, teachers are recognizing the need for procedures of selection which compare what the pupil is doing in reading with various other indices of his achievement and, from this comparison, evaluating whether the reading is significantly lower than accomplishments in other areas. From this point of view, five procedures might be suggested as valuable in varying degrees for identifying the individual who would profit from specialized training in reading: (1) the discrepancy between

[1] Virgil E. Herrick, "Selecting the Child in Need of Special Reading Instruction," *Elementary School Journal*, XL (February, 1940), 425.

mental age and reading age, (2) the Monroe reading index, (3) the informal reading inventory, (4) Olson and Hughes's "split-growth" analysis, and (5) the case-study technique.

THE DISCREPANCY BETWEEN MENTAL AGE AND READING AGE

The purpose of this technique is to compare the child's capacity for reading (determined by the mental age obtained from an intelligence test) with his present reading success (obtained from a reading-achievement test) and to decide upon the basis of this comparison whether the child should receive special reading instruction. Harris[2] has suggested that, because most good tests of intelligence and of reading have probable errors of measurement ranging between two and six months, an individual's reading ability should be at least six months below his intelligence level before one can be reasonably confident that his reading is definitely below expectation. As a general guide Harris indicates that children may be selected for special reading instruction when the difference between reading age and mental age is at least six months in the primary grades, nine months for children in Grades IV and V, or a year for pupils above Grade V.

The results of reading tests, however, are merely suggestive of an individual's true reading status. Teachers should interpret the results of these tests as being indicative of the level at which the pupil experiences difficulty. Actually, the child's instructional level may be one or more grades below the achievement level obtained from standardized tests. This fact must be taken into consideration by those who decide to use standardized reading-test data for comparison with the results of intelligence tests in identifying retarded readers.

Although, as previously stated, the use of this technique is practical for schools, it may be questioned whether judgments based on two tests are valid. A second objection may be made to the narrowness of the selection procedure, since other developmental areas are not considered.

THE MONROE READING INDEX

Marion Monroe has devised a single index of reading ability using an average of chronological age, mental age, and achievement in arithmetic computation, and she compares this combination with the child's reading age. A reading index of 1.00 indicates a harmonious relationship among the various areas. Indices above 1.00 represent special abilities in reading, and those below .80 indicate severe disabilities.[3]

[2] Albert J. Harris, *How To Increase Reading Ability*, pp. 199–200. New York: Longmans, Green & Co., 1947.

[3] Marion Monroe, *Children Who Cannot Read*, pp. 14–15. Chicago: University of Chicago Press, 1932.

The Monroe reading index is an improvement over the preceding selection technique. The introduction of chronological age and the arithmetic-computation age broadens the base for comparison by including two ears of development not so easily influenced by reading difficulties as are the results of reading and mental-maturity tests.

THE INFORMAL READING INVENTORY

A number of teachers are finding it effective to appraise the pupil's reading levels and needs by using sets of graded readers which include materials *below* and *above* as well as *at* the grade placement level obtained for the individual on a standardized test. This type of inventory, as described by Betts,[4] enables the teacher to estimate the *independent*, the *instructional*, and the *frustration* reading levels. In addition, specific needs at the instructional level may be evaluated. It is also possible to appraise a *hearing-comprehension* level by reading to the pupil at successively higher levels. Hearing comprehension, determined in this manner, provides a fairly satisfactory index to reading capacity, according to Betts. The amount of retardation in reading may then be estimated by noting the disparity between the probable capacity level and the instructional level.

It is often desirable to have the pupil read different types of materials at various grade levels before reaching a conclusion about his reading status. The child who reads social-studies materials poorly may do much better when confronted with science materials, or vice versa.

An informal reading inventory has the particular merit of giving the teacher direct evidence regarding achievement and need in terms of available instructional material. Observation of the pupil as he reads orally and silently provides clues for adapting instruction to his specific difficulties.

THE "SPLIT-GROWTH" CONCEPT

The research of Olson and Hughes has featured longitudinal studies of the development of the same group of children over a period of years, including height, weight, dentition, strength of grip, ossification of wrist bones, mental growth, and school achievement.[5] The average of these ages is labeled the individual's "organismic age," and it may be compared with the pupil's reading age in regard to a single point in growth (cross-sectional view) and longitudinally as to direction and rate of growth

[4] E. A. Betts, *Foundations of Reading Instruction*, pp. 438–88. New York: American Book Co., 1946.

[5] *a*) Willard C. Olson, *Child Development*, pp. 163–91. Boston: D. C. Heath & Co., 1949.

b) W. C. Olson and B. O. Hughes, "Concepts of Growth—Their Significance to Teachers," *Childhood Education*, XXI (October, 1944), 53–63.

over a period of time. These studies reveal that reading is as much an aspect of growth as are the other measures of the organismic age. In addition, the measurements manifest some unity when viewed as a whole; reading shows the same tendency toward unified organization and consistency with the complete pattern of total development.

The "split-growth" technique can be helpful in identifying children who will profit from special reading instruction because it provides both a cross-sectional and a longitudinal approach. Undoubtedly there are pupils whose retardation in reading is influenced by a retarded pattern of total growth. The reading age might be lower than the other developmental areas when examined at a single point, but further examination of the growth pattern over a period of time might reveal that the child probably should not be chosen for intensive instruction in reading if his present achievement is in agreement with other phases of his development. On the other hand, if this longitudinal examination of growth in reading should indicate that reading is falling significantly behind—"splitting" away from—the other areas which are proceeding harmoniously, remedial reading might be of value.

Although the advantages in using the "split-growth" technique and the previously discussed procedures are obvious, the methods may be seriously criticized because they tend to ignore personality and the importance of understanding the whole child.

THE CASE-STUDY APPROACH

Research has indicated that there is no one universal cause of reading retardation. The reading problems of each individual are frequently characterized by a constellation of difficulties. In order to provide an understanding of the interrelationships among the various causal areas, the case-study approach investigates and evaluates the pupil's physical, intellectual, emotional, social, and educational development as shown by reports of parents, teachers, and pupil. The "split-growth" technique and the Monroe reading index may be included as part of the total study.

The major advantages of the case-study procedure are not only that it makes possible a cross-sectional and longitudinal analysis but that it also presents information which helps interpret each stage of the child's development and suggests probably helpful teaching techniques. Furthermore, the analysis affords a basis for predicting probable progress. A number of good books, such as those by Prescott,[6] Strang,[7] and Torger-

[6] *Helping Teachers Understand Children*. By the Staff of the Division on Child Development and Teacher Personnel. Prepared for the Commission on Teacher Education. Washington: American Council on Education, 1945.

[7] Ruth Strang, *The Role of the Teacher in Personnel Work*. New York: Bureau of Publications, Teachers College, Columbia University, 1946 (revised).

son,[8] are available to help teachers understand children through the case-study approach.

Probably no teacher has the time to make complete case studies for the number of pupils needing special instruction in reading. However, the making of one or two case studies of children in a single class gives the teacher an understanding of a particular child and his needs and also helps the instructor to be more sensitive to the needs of the whole group of children.

Critical Point of Referral

The difficulty of establishing a critical point of referral for corrective-reading instruction is another important aspect of the problem to be determined. Reading retardation has been described in terms of a continuum, ranging from nonreaders with an extreme type of associative learning disability to relatively mild problems. Obviously the children with the most persistent difficulties should receive immediate study. However, it is equally important that the difficulties of the less severely handicapped be detected as early as possible so that carefully planned instruction may prevent a major problem from arising. The question for the latter group remains. At what point shall the individual be given special help and when should he be permitted to continue his various activities without additional assistance? Actually there cannot be any one general answer to this problem. Each school must determine its own point for referral based on what is practical in terms of its educational philosophy, its personnel, the number of retarded readers, and the best information available at the time the judgment is made.

Classroom and Clinical Problems

CLASSROOM PROBLEMS

Having identified the retarded readers in a class, the teacher must plan to provide effective reading instruction. Often children with minor difficulties in reading will show marked improvement in small groups when the classroom instruction is adapted to their level of achievement, interests, and strengths and weaknesses by a teacher whose relationship with the group is one of sympathetic, friendly concern. In most instances special help in reading is a common-sense procedure and, except for clinical problems, may be carried out by any good classroom teacher who has had some additional professional preparation.

[8] Theodore L. Torgerson, *Studying Children: Diagnostic and Remedial Procedures in Teaching*. New York: Dryden Press, 1947.

Betts[9] has described three groups of individuals who will profit from corrective reading in the classroom: (1) pupils with language deficiencies; (2) those with experience deficiencies, resulting in significantly higher levels of verbal ability, or language facility, than conceptual background; and (3) those with specific difficulties, such as inability to adjust rate to the purpose of the material.

Undoubtedly, the teacher recognizes almost immediately the reader who has a language-skill deficiency. The poor reader gives evidence of this difficulty through his inability to attack new words. His difficulty is characterized by such symptoms as word-by-word reading, mispronunciations, insertions, substitutions, omissions, vocalization, regressions, pointing with the finger, tensions and the like. These faulty habits and the inability to cope with new words can usually be eliminated by a corrective program that begins with the reader's instructional level and provides systematic guidance in word-analysis techniques.

The second group of readers includes those whose language facility is greater than their experiences. These individuals may pronounce words with unusual ease. Their reading may be rhythmical and their comprehension-test scores may be satisfactory, but they cannot reconstruct the experience behind the symbols. They are verbalizers who have failed to associate precise meanings with symbols. For them, the corrective-reading program must emphasize reading as a thinking process from which meaning is to be obtained. Opportunities must also be provided for the development of meaningful concepts.

For retarded readers who will receive special assistance in reading in the classroom, these questions, require attention: Is the pupil ready for systematic guidance in reading? What is his present instructional level? What is his intellectual level? Is there a visual problem or a hearing impairment? How does the child feel about his problem? What are his chief interests?

CLINICAL PROBLEMS

A small percent of the school population experiences such severe difficulty in reading that progress cannot be made in the average classroom. Additional information must be obtained to give a more complete picture of the child's difficulties. Robinson[10] found that children who are seriously retarded in reading also present many physical, intellectual, social, and emotional problems and that retardation in reading usually

[9] E. A. Betts, "Factors in Reading Disabilities," *Education*, LXXII (May, 1952), 626–27.

[10] Helen M. Robinson, *Why Pupils Fail in Reading*, p. 220. Chicago: University of Chicago Press, 1946.

tends to increase in seriousness in proportion as the number of anomalies increase. Referral to a reading center or child-study clinic is often made for a more detailed study of the individual's difficulties.

In the more extreme reading problems, Betts[11] has suggested that these questions and others should be answered: What developmental factors have contributed to the disability? What is the relationship between nonverbal and verbal intelligence scores? Does oral rereading following silent reading improve rhythm? What is the relationship between hearing comprehension and visual, or reading, comprehension? Is there confusion in "central" dominance? In what type of emotional climate has the child lived? What is the relationship between associative learning test scores? What are the relationships between memory test scores?

In conclusion, the early identification of the retarded reader is crucial. The introduction of corrective and remedial techniques in time to prevent the establishment of poor habits, confusions, and inadequacies will subsequently help to prevent not only failures in school but also the development of undesirable behavior tendencies that are primarily caused by educational maladjustment.

[11] Emmett Albert Betts, "Corrective and Remedial Cases: Analysis and Follow Up," *Elementary English*, XXIV (March, 1947), 147.

49. Know the Cause Before Applying the Cure

DELWYN G. SCHUBERT (1952)

When someone visits a doctor and complains of chills and muscular aches, he isn't plunged into a tub of ice water to break his fever or given rubbing liniment to assuage his pain. A physician knows too well that the elimination of symptoms does not cure a disease. If he finds a syndrome that indicates bacterial invasion, sulfa drugs or penicillin may be prescribed to attack the infection at its source and thereby restore good

SOURCE: *College English*, XIII (April, 1952), 394–395. Reprinted with the permission of the National Council of Teachers of English and Delwyn G. Schubert.

health. Careful diagnosis of basic causal factors, it is important to note, always precedes treatment. The same is equally true of remedial reading.

A perusal of the literature on reading reveals that all to often remedial work parallels the ice-water and rubbing-liniment analogy. Methods, techniques, and gadgets are employed that concern themselves primarily with manifestations of reading sickness rather than with the amelioration of causal factors.

In working with retarded college readers, the writer has been impressed by the ease with which marked improvements take place when attention is focused on amenable causal factors. The following cases serve as illustrations.

Mrs. X., an attractive woman of thirty-five, entered the reading clinic with scores below the twentieth percentile on a standardized reading test. During the administration of the California Test of Mental Maturity (one of a battery of tests given for diagnostic purposes), Mrs. X. put her head on her arms and began to sob audibly. Through an interview which was scheduled the following day, certain facts were uncovered. Mrs. X. had a Master's degree from a well-known eastern university. She had been a fine student and a voracious reader. Recently, however, along with a number of reverses, her husband divorced her and remarried "a more intelligent woman." The divorce and her husband's remarriage were a tremendous blow to her ego. She spoke freely of being dumb and incapable of coping with college work because of "mental deterioration." At this point it was evident to the writer that reading retardation was just one exemplification of a complete lack of confidence. Something had to be done to restore it. After a few meetings during which Mrs. X. was encouraged to talk about herself, the writer induced her to take a "short and enjoyable test." With adequate praise and reassurance, the Wechsler Bellevue Intelligence Test was given without the subject demonstrating any emotional instability. Evaluation revealed an intelligence quotient of 135 for the full scale. Mrs. X. was informed of her achievement and told that the test proved conclusively that she had the ability to handle college work and need have no fear of any testing situation. A few additional interviews followed. When Mrs. X.'s self-confidence seemed fully restored, she was given the Minnesota Reading Tests. Scores for speed, vocabulary, and comprehension all exceeded the eightieth percentile. Mrs. X. no longer was a disabled reader.

Informal and standardized tests showed that Mr. M. was an accurate but extremely slow reader. Rate of comprehension scores ran consistently between 170 and 180 words per minute for all kinds of materials. No visual, auditory, mental, or emotional factors seemed related to his retardation. Through an interview with Mr. M., however, the writer learned that he had studied law for several years. His professors had stressed, at all times, the importance of slow, detailed reading. Here was a possible answer! It was apparent that this kind of reading over a long period of time could have brought about a habituation to a slow rate of reading. With this in mind, remediation centered around Mr. M.'s reading easy materials under the pressure of time. Supplementary training involved tachistoscopic phrase and sentence drill. The results were most gratifying. Within a few weeks (a summer session was involved) Mr. M. had more than doubled his reading speed without any loss in comprehension.

A forty-six-year-old woman, Mrs. T., read slowly and inefficiently. She suffered from intermittent headaches and reported a "tendency for letters to run together at times." A syndrome of visual difficulty seemed evident. The Keystone Visual Survey Tests showed that Mrs. T. was decidedly farsighted. A plus lens test with the Snellen Chart indicated that her hyperopia undoubtedly was interfering with reading. She was told to visit a specialist immediately. But Mrs. T. appeared day after day without glasses. When questioned, she admitted visiting no specialist because "he might want me to wear glasses, and they would make me look old." The writer argued and pleaded. A few weeks before the term ended Mrs. T. began to wear glasses. Her oculist had diagnosed the condition as presbyopia (farsightedness due to an age factor). Relief was immediate. Mrs. T.'s headaches disappeared and reading became enjoyable. Improvement was sufficient to enable Mrs. T. to meet the reading standards set up by the college for admission to directed teaching.

These cases serve to show the importance of uncovering and dealing directly with the causes of reading retardation. The indiscriminate use of techniques and devices hardly ever achieves gratifying results and can in some instances do definite harm. In Mrs. X.'s case, for example, an emphasis on increased reading speed and comprehension would have only intensified her lack of self-confidence. Without glasses, Mrs. T. could experience only more frequent headaches and discomfort from reading drill.

When proper diagnosis precedes prescription, the remedy most always is effective. Applying techniques indiscriminately puts a teacher professionally in the bracket of a physician in the dark ages, when the patient was bled for any and all symptoms of illness.

50. A Critical Evaluation of Visual Diagnostic Materials[1]

ALFRED A. ROSENBLOOM, JR. (1955)

Our modern concept of vision is quite different from the concept of twenty or thirty years ago. Formerly we were concerned primarily with the keenness of vision and the use of both eyes in the act of seeing. We asked such questions as, "Does the child see clearly at distance?" "Does he use both eyes together?" "Does he need glasses?" As important as these considerations are in caring for the vision of the child, we know that they constitute only a small sector of the knowledge needed to determine whether the child is visually efficient. Today our question is, "Do the child's visual and perceptual processes operate effectively so that meaning can be obtained from the printed page?"[2] Sir William Osler once said, "The value of experience is not in seeing much, but in seeing wisely." Do our children possess this priceless ability? We have real reason to wonder.

Various school surveys have revealed that one-fourth to one-half of our school population needs visual care. A prominent consideration in the reading-readiness program concerns the child's physical well-being, of which visual efficiency is an important factor. Acknowledging the desirability of the refractionist's recommendation that all children have a complete visual examination before entering school, we must recognize the fact that at the present time this is neither practical nor economically sound. How are we to meet the problem of identifying that one-fourth to one-half of our school population who will need visual care?

Although it is not possible to examine all children, it is possible, by means of visual screening tests, to identify those children who are most

[1] Address presented on November 26, 1954, at the annual meeting of the National Association for Remedial Teaching held in Detroit.

[2] Marguerite Eberl, "Visual Training and Reading," *Clinical Studies in Reading. II*, p. 242. Supplementary Educational Monographs, No. 77. Chicago: University of Chicago Press, 1953.

SOURCE: *Elementary School Journal*, LVI (September, 1955), 27–31. Reprinted by permission of the University of Chicago Press.

likely to need visual care. Visual screening is *not* a visual examination. Visual screening is *not* designed to help the teacher or school nurse to diagnose the visual problem. The purpose of visual screening is *not* to define the defect. Visual screening is a means of identifying children with visual difficulties who should be referred for visual examinations. It provides little more than a rough over-all estimate of visual function.

Visual screening tests are considered to be diagnostic tests. Yet, strictly speaking, there is no such thing as a diagnostic test. A test cannot diagnose: it can only provide factual information about the functioning of the individual in the specific test situation. In any critical appraisal of visual function, several questions should be considered: What visual characteristics do refractionists consider important? Which visual characteristics do screening tests evaluate? How reliable and valid are visual screening tests? How should the findings be interpreted for selecting referral cases? What problems and limitations does visual screening present?

Visual Characteristics Considered Important

In order to be reasonably sure that the child is visually ready for reading, the refractionist must be able to answer the following questions in the affirmative: (1) Can the child see clearly and distinctly at all working distances? (2) Can he fuse the impressions of each eye into a single image at all working distances? (3) Do the functions of seeing clearly and seeing singly have sufficient co-ordination to enable the child to continue efficiently his visual tasks? (4) Does he possess sufficient fusional and accommodative reserves to maintain sustained visual concentration? (5) Is the child free from any disease of the eyes which would interfere with normal visual functioning?

Characteristics Evaluated by Screening Tests

Although the number of subtests in the screening batteries vary, the following tests of visual characteristics are included in one or more of the screening devices:

1. Tests of visual acuity or keenness of vision for each eye and both eyes at far and near points. Such tests measure clearness of vision.
2. Tests of fusion measure the ability to combine the images from each eye into a single impression.
3. Lateral and vertical phoria tests at far and near point determine the balance or positional co-ordination between the two eyes.
4. Tests of depth perception determine the ability to perceive size and distance relationships. Thus phoria and depth tests are considered to be measures of binocular co-ordination.

5. Tests for hyperopia and myopia, using convex and concave lenses, provide a gross measure of refractive deviation from normal.

6. Tests of color perception are designed to determine manifest deviations from standard color vision.

Among the screening tests used in schools today, the most common is one designed in 1863 by a man named Snellen. The Snellen chart is adequate within the limited sphere of determining clearness of vision at twenty feet or far point only; it gives us no information concerning the many additional skills necessary for efficient seeing. Thus such an examination identifies for referral mostly children who are nearsighted. It may be of particular interest to those concerned with reading problems to note that research studies indicate that nearsighted children tend to be the better readers.

In addition to the limitation of testing only for clearness of vision at far point, the Snellen chart has other weaknesses. Research[3] has indicated that it is not possible to predict accurately near acuity from far-point measurement. Therefore a correction for myopia established by an examination based upon looking at a chart from a distance rarely makes the child more comfortable or efficient at a near-point task such as reading. A second weakness is the deceptive impression it creates; in the case of those children whom the Snellen chart fails to identify for referral, the tested visual performance is apparently 100 percent efficient. This is the real tragedy of the use of the Snellen test! Not only are the inadequacies of the Snellen chart apparent to refractionists, but also educators themselves have advocated replacing this test by more efficient screening devices.

Admitting the inadequacies of the Snellen chart, have we any other screening devices that are more adequate? Although the commercial instruments available vary widely in the nature and number of their subtests, any one of these is more effective as a means of identifying children with visual problems than is the Snellen test. In a research study reported in *Clinical Studies in Reading. II*, Robinson and Huelsman[4] have graphically presented a comparison of these subtests. In addition to the most widely known commercial batteries, there are several tests that deserve mention as accessory visual screening procedures. Recent research studies[5] have indicated that the Spache Binocular Reading Test

[3] Helen M. Robinson, "An Analysis of Four Visual Screening Tests at Grades Four and Seven," *American Journal of Optometry and Archives of American Academy of Optometry*, XXX (April, 1953), 180.

[4] Helen M. Robinson and Charles B. Huelsman, Jr., "Visual Efficiency and Progress in Learning To Read," *Clinical Studies in Reading. II*, p. 41. Supplementary Educational Monographs, No. 77. Chicago: University of Chicago Press, 1953.

[5] *a*) Helen M. Robinson, "Visual Efficiency and Reading," in Staff of the Reading Clinics of the University of Chicago, *Clinical Studies in Reading. I*, p. 112. Sup-

and the Keystone Hand-Eye Co-ordination Test are good measures of suppression. Since none of the commercial batteries include a near-depth test, the Wirt Stereotest can be used to screen this function.

Reliability and Validity of Visual Screening Tests

The efficiency of a screening procedure depends upon the reliability and the validity of its component parts. What data do we have that may serve as a criterion for evaluating these screening procedures? Reliability data are available for the Eames Eye Test, but there are no comparable data for the Massachusetts or Keystone batteries. Recent research conducted by Robinson[6] provides reliability data on the Ortho-Rater test battery. Although further research is needed, available data seem to suggest that the Eames Eye Test and the Ortho-Rater batteries are reliable screening tests.

Despite the fact that we do not use screening tests to diagnose visual problems, it is nevertheless important to know the validity of each subtest. In the reliability study previously cited,[7] the validity of the findings of four screening tests was checked against the findings of two professional refractionists. The comparison indicates that agreement between screening tests and professional judgment is highest for the Ortho-Rater and Massachusetts batteries; is considerably lower, although still statistically significant, for the Keystone battery and insignificant for the Eames Eye Test.

When considering the question of validity, it must be remembered that the accuracy with which children are identified for visual care depends, in part, on the test standards for passing and failing. In most screening tests the norms are based on children of different ages without consideration of the developmental nature of vision. The research studies of Gesell and his associates[8] have established without question the importance of this consideration.

Even when great care is used in selecting children to refer for eye examinations, experience has shown that some appear to have no visual problems. The amount of over-referral is sometimes interpreted as an

---

plementary Educational Monographs, No. 68. Chicago: University of Chicago Press, 1949.

b) Alfred A. Rosenbloom, Jr., "Aniseikonia among Good and Poor Readers," p. 45. Unpublished Master's thesis, University of Chicago, 1953.

[6] Helen M. Robinson, "An Analysis of Four Visual Screening Tests at Grades Four and Seven," *American Journal of Optometry and Archives of American Academy of Optometry*, XXX (April, 1953), 185.

[7] *Ibid.*, p. 184.

[8] Arnold Gesell, "Vision and Reading from the Standpoint of Child Development," *Clinical Studies in Reading. II*, p. 130. Supplementary Educational Monographs, No. 77. Chicago: University of Chicago Press, 1953.

adverse reflection on visual screening. Such a conclusion is not necessarily well founded. Over-referral may be the result of a number of factors, two of the most important being (1) lack of agreement among refractionists as to the relative importance of the visual functions tested and (2) the establishment of excessively high standards for passing or failing.

At our present level of development of visual screening procedures, it is understandable that such factors should exert an influence. On the one hand, high standards are desirable in view of the stated purpose of the test. On the other hand, we cannot expect complete standardization of opinion among refractionists. Professional judgment may dictate to some the desirability of prescribing a small correction for reading, while others may consider that such a small correction is not advisable. There are differences in opinion regarding the nature and importance of certain refractive test procedures at the reading distance. Some practitioners consider visual acuity at far point only and are not concerned with tests at the reading distance.

It is equally true that some children needing visual care may pass the screening test. This is the problem of under-referral. Under-referral may also be the result of a number of factors, two of the most important being (1) the acceptance of excessively low standards for passing or failing and (2) inclusion of too few tests within the screening battery. Unfortunately those children who are not identified through screening devices do not receive the needed visual care until more severe symptoms become manifest. The awareness of this type of screening error should enter into any thorough evaluation of the effectiveness of school vision practices.

The problems of both over-referral and under-referral indicate an area in which further research is needed. One of the problems within this area that remains to be definitively answered is that of the nature and the number of visual functions which need to be tested in order to determine visual efficiency. A closely allied problem is that of reaching a decision concerning the critical point which constitutes passing or failure on a visual screening test. To meet this problem, consideration will have to be given, on the one hand, to the visual characteristics of children at various stages of development. On the other hand, it will involve reaching a compromise satisfactory to most refractionists that will keep both under-referral and over-referral at a minimum.

Interpreting Test Findings

A question which concerns many people who administer visual screening tests is that of the interpretation of the results for referral. Where the tests are clearly passed or failed, there is no question regarding recommendations. However, if only one or two subtests are marked doubtful or failing, the interpretation of the tests for such borderline cases becomes difficult. It is advisable to recheck any child within a week after administering the original battery before a final interpretation is made. Sometimes a recheck will show that some misunderstanding or error occurred in the first testing or, perhaps, that some unsatisfactory physical situation contributed to the failure. In the reliability study by Robinson,[9] some of the results were higher on the second test. This suggests that practice might improve the scores and points to the desirability of repeating the test battery for pupils who secure questionable ratings.

If upon retest only one subtest is failed, referral would depend in large measure on the test failed. Research suggests that the tests made at the reading distance usually are more important to the visual efficiency of the retarded reader than are the distance tests. Referrals rarely are made because of failure on the color test only. On the other hand, failure on the visual-acuity test at near point would constitute an important reason for referral. If both fusion and phoria tests are failed at near point, this is more significant for referral than the child's failure on either test alone. An additional problem of referral is that of the varying degree of facility in administering visual screening tests. The experience of the test administrator will also influence his evaluation of the over-all profile of visual performance.

Problems and Limitations in Visual Screening

Visual screening presents several limitations. Certainly the brief nature of the visual screening tests does not make real demands on vision, and, as a consequence, the tests often do not reveal faulty visual function. Visual screening tests do not identify every child who has a visual problem, for they are inadequate in identifying certain less common visual difficulties, such as aniseikonia, incipient myopia where acuity is normal, intermittent strabismus, and peripheral and central defects of the visual field.

In considering the limitations of screening tests, it should be recognized that visual screening results tend to be like certain educational tests in that there is no single correct answer. The findings must be evaluated in terms of the whole child—his physiological and psychological self as well as the nature of his visual performance. Visual screening tests are not really diagnostic tests. Rather, they provide a means of obtaining a limited behavioral sample under selected and somewhat artificial test conditions.

[9] Helen M. Robinson, "An Analysis of Four Visual Screening Tests at Grades Four and Seven," *American Journal of Optometry and Archives of American Academy of Optometry,* XXX (April, 1953), 185.

Recognizing these limitations, as well as the fact that many schools have no visual screening programs, recent studies have been conducted to determine the accuracy with which a check list of visual symptoms can be used to identify pupils needing professional visual care. A research study by Knox[10] reports observations carried out at the third-grade level. This study shows that a classroom teacher who knows how to use a carefully selected check list of visual symptoms and how to observe critically for such symptoms can provide supplemental information valuable in the accurate identification of children needing visual care. This is an important area for further research. Teachers must know not only what characteristics to observe but also the proper methods of observing them. Neither observation of symptoms nor visual screening tests alone will identify all pupils needing visual care, but a combination of the two is more likely to be accurate.

In the field of remedial instruction, both refractionists and educators face challenging problems. As refractionists, we are grateful to educators for the assistance and cooperation that they have given us in identifying children with visual problems. We recognize the problems that are still unsolved. In the realm of providing greater reliability, refractionists need to refine their test selection, to improve standardized conditions of testing, and to reduce factors dependent upon examiner variability. In the realm of providing greater validity, moreover, there is a great need for the determination of uniformly acceptable standards to serve as criteria in judging validity of screening batteries.

We recognize clearly that our task is one of providing the best visual care for our children. We look to educators to teach all children all the varied and complex reading skills they need. Improving reading is truly a co-operative undertaking. Each of us has a vital share in the task of insuring that every child will have an equal opportunity to fulfill his maximum educational potentiality.

[10] Gertrude E. Knox, "Classroom Symptoms of Visual Difficulty," *Clinical Studies in Reading. II*, pp. 97–101. Supplementary Educational Monographs, No. 77. Chicago: University of Chicago Press, 1953.

51. Understanding and Handling Reading–Personality Problems

DELWYN G. SCHUBERT (1960)

Research is equivocal as to the exact relationship between personality maladjustment and reading. Nevertheless, the majority of studies dealing with the problem show that there is a relationship, even though these studies differ as to its degree.

Consensus has it that most personality maladjustment found among disabled readers follows reading failures and results from the consequent frustration, anxiety, and feelings of inferiority experienced by the child. In certain cases, however, maladjustment obviously pre-dates entrance to the first grade. When this is true, reading failure appears to be a manifestation or concomitant of more basic emotional problems—problems which make concentration on school work difficult or impossible. Causative factors of such emotional problems may be physical or environmental.

Causes of Emotional Disturbances

A child who is labeled "lard," "fats," "slats," or "beanpole" because of his physical stature is subjected to emotional stress. Worse still is the emotional scarring suffered by the youngster born with crooked teeth, facial birthmarks, or strabismus. These conditions, and many others, can have an adverse effect on the emotional health of a child.

Those of us who have sat through a movie when the picture was out of focus can appreciate the emotional disturbance children with visual defects experience when they constantly have to contend with distorted images. And all of us have heard, on occasions, a defective sound track that proved intolerable after only a few minutes of unintelligibility. Think of what the auditorily impaired child experiences.

Endocrinologists tell us that hyperthyroidism frequently manifests itself in nervousness and emotional instability. Similarly, it is not unu-

---

SOURCE: *Elementary English*, December, 1960, pp. 537–540. Reprinted with the permission of the National Council of Teachers of English and Delwyn G. Schubert.

sual to find irritability and irascibility accompanying brain damage. And certainly a child suffering from undernourishment, lack of rest, chronic infections, etc., finds nothing in his poor health to improve his disposition.

Many emotionally disturbed children are victims of unfortunate home conditions. A child may be rejected because he was unwanted. Such a child may fail in reading as a means of securing attention from parents who otherwise are indifferent to him. On the other hand, a child may be the victim of oversolicitousness. Since busy teachers aren't able to give undivided attention to a child whose parents never had him assume any responsibility, reading failure is inevitable. Certain children don't want to learn how to read since they realize that learning how to read is associated closely with growing up. And the last thing they want to do is grow up.

Youngsters who come from broken homes or homes in which dissension and inconsistent discipline run rife are in a perpetual state of emotional turmoil. Very often unwitting parents subject children to invidious comparison. If a child is forced to compete with a superior sibling or neighborhood prodigy, he frequently develops feeling of inferiority resulting in a give-up or submissive attitude which spells defeat before he begins.

Teachers, too, may be guilty of some of the same shortcomings characterizing parents. They may reject certain children or make unfavorable comparisons between brothers and sisters. Teachers who make sarcastic remarks such as "How can you be so stupid?" and "I don't know why I waste time on you" may have traumatic effects on a child. An unpleasant teaching personality accompanied by uninspired teaching and the use of deadening drills have driven many children into maladjustment. Other children suffer maladjustment because they are forced into reading before they have the requisite readiness. A poor start doesn't augur well for future mental health.

Detecting and Understanding the Emotionally Disturbed Reader

Methods and techniques for studying emotionally disturbed readers are many and varied. The most simple and practical way is through daily contact and observation. In this connection, a list of symptoms of emotional disturbances may be helpful. However, when using such a list it must be remembered that we are encountering a "whole person." Each of the symptoms must be considered in light of the total personality of the individual: (1) tics, twitchings; (2) psychosomatic illness (dizziness, nausea, or headaches); (3) apathy, excessive daydreaming, fantasy; (4) enuresis after the age of three, nail-biting, thumbsucking;

(5) excitability, hyperactivity, uncontrolled emotionality; (6) morbid fears or phobias; (7) insomnia, nightmares, somnambulism; (8) self-consciousness, stuttering; (9) depression, guilt feelings; (10) suspiciousness, tenseness, anxiety; (11) fighting, stealing, bullying, and other anti-social behavior.

When a teacher is dealing with an emotionally disturbed reader it is essential that she win him over as a friend. Once she has established rapport with the child she can talk to him about his likes, dislikes, loves, fears, and hates. In an indirect way she can get the child to provide information helpful in answering questions such as the following: What is the child's attitude toward his parents, brothers, and sisters? Does he feel he is a failure? Does he feel he is stupid? Is the child afraid of anything or anyone? Is his sleep disturbed by bad dreams?

One of Paul Witty's questionnaires[1] includes a question which frequently elicits information that helps to uncover causes of emotional disturbance: "If you could have one wish which might come true, what would be your wish?" Helpful information can be obtained from older students by asking them to respond in writing to topics such as "What Bothers Me" and "Things I Worry About."

Paper and pencil tests are available to teachers who wish to supplement their subjective judgment of children's personality patterns. These include: Mental Health Analysis Test,[2] California Test of Personality,[3] and Aspects of Personality.[4] Teachers who use such tests should realize that a child may answer the questions involved in a way he feels will be pleasing to the examiner. Then, too, the fact that the child is a poor reader may give rise to misinterpretations of the questions. Reading the questions aloud for the youngster isn't a good idea either since this practice will invalidate test results.

Clinical psychologists often employ projective tests when studying children. Projective tests are based on the knowledge than an individual reacts to an unstructured situation in terms of his own needs, values, and conflicts. Such tests include: The Blacky Pictures,[5] Children's Apperception Test,[6] Rorschach,[7] and Thematic Apperception Tests.[8]

Some projective techniques have been used in classrooms by having children complete unfinished sentences and stories, draw pictures of their families, and paint pictures. Elizabeth Graves has developed an

[1] P. Witty and D. Kopel, *Reading and the Educative Process*. New York, N. Y., Ginn and Company, 1939, p. 339.
[2] California Test Bureau, 5916 Hollywood Blvd., Hollywood, Calif.
[3] *Ibid.*
[4] *Ibid.*
[5] *Ibid.*
[6] *Ibid.*
[7] *Ibid.*
[8] *Ibid.*

interesting sentence completion test that would be especially helpful on the junior and senior high school level.[9] Paula Elkisch has evolved a number of criteria that would prove helpful to a teacher who is studying the emotional needs of children through their paintings and drawings.[10]

Helping the Emotionally Disturbed Reader

No one has greater social stimulus value in the schoolroom than the teacher. And it follows that the successful teacher of emotionally disturbed children must demonstrate emotional balance and poise in her own behavior. Only the well-adjusted teacher can create an atmosphere of acceptance and encouragement that is basic to the rehabilitation of a disturbed child.

Specific recommendations for personality therapy with retarded readers are as follows:

1. Probe carefully for the cause or causes (physical or environmental) of the child's emotional disturbance. Eliminate or ameliorate these whenever possible. Also (a) check on the sleeping and eating habits of the child; (b) encourage the parents to take the child to a medical specialist who is aware of the interrelationships between reading failure and specific physical difficulties; (c) orient the parents as to what constitutes a good emotional climate in the home.
2. Avoid frustrating the child by exposing him to material that is too difficult. Remember that interest and motivation—prime catalysts in the learning process—do not function when the organism is frustrated.
3. Help the child secure ego recognition by experiencing success in non-reading pursuits such as drawing, music, sports, etc. This should be done in moderation so as not to obviate the need for achievement and recognition in reading.
4. Use audio-visual approaches with the child so as to provide other avenues of learning for him until repairs can be made on his "reading road."
5. Provide the child with opportunities that give vent to pent-up emotions through play, art work, music, etc.
6. Help the child develop a mentally hygienic outlook by not taking life too seriously. Show him that we all make mistakes and that many times they're very funny.
7. Establish a tutoring-counseling relationship with the child if possible. If you can take time to listen to a child's troubles sympathetically

[9] C. M. McCullough, R. M. Strang, and A. E. Traxler, *Problems in the Improvement of Reading*. New York, McGraw-Hill, 1955, pp. 250–1.
[10] P. Elkisch, "Children's Drawings in a Projective Technique," *Psychological Monographs*, No. 266, Vol. 58, 1945.

and understandingly, so that the child can be sure of receiving encouragement and support rather than reprimand, emotional blocks to learning begin to atrophy.

8. Praise and reassure the child whenever possible. Keep from him any feelings of disappointment and anxiety you may experience.

9. Don't embarrass the child in oral reading situations by forcing him to read materials "cold." Make such experiences build his feelings of self-worth by choosing materials carefully and by giving him sufficient help before he reads aloud.

10. Employ a reading game at each session so that the child associates reading with something that is fun. This will help dissipate negative feelings about reading.

11. Help the child develop those interests, hobbies, and skills on which the group puts a premium. This will encourage group acceptance of him and will develop a sense of belonging that is essential to his mental health.

Teachers employing principles and suggestions such as the foregoing can do a great deal to help the emotionally disturbed reader. But, above all, they should remember that nothing can or ever will supplant the magical power of the teacher who is genuinely interested in children and capable of instilling in them a feeling of confidence and self-worth.

52. Psychiatric Insights into Reading Problems

MANDEL SHERMAN (1949)

Clinical psychologists and psychiatrists are becoming increasingly interested in the problem of reading defects because a noticeable proportion of poor readers develop emotional tensions and conflicts. Any type of deficiency tends to create a feeling of inferiority and inadequacy. In this pattern the person tends, at first, to rationalize his deficiency in terms of the unimportance of the problem or in terms of some un-

SOURCE: Mandel Sherman, "Psychiatric Insights into Reading Problems," Elementary Educational Monograph No. 68, 1949, pp. 130–132. Reprinted by permission of the University of Chicago Press.

avoidable cause which may indicate that he is not at fault. A person may rationalize his poor athletic ability by emphasizing his academic interests. Another person may rationalize his poor scholarship by pointing to the successes of those who have had little schooling. In these and other ways most individuals can rationalize, with some degree of satisfaction, their inadequacies or defects. The poor reader, however, usually has much more difficulty in rationalizing, because every phase of his academic career and his other adjustments is directly or indirectly affected by his defective reading ability.

Psychiatrists have observed that no other inadequacy creates as great a sense of frustration and failure as a reading difficulty. This is partly due to the fact that everyone is expected to be able to read adequately in order to advance in his schooling. Reading is also considered a criterion, in the cultural sense, of an individual's mental ability. If a person is deficient in some academic subject such as arithmetic or geography he can avoid facing his inadequacy by avoiding those subjects. But a person's reading defect cannot be easily circumvented. His disability is brought to his attention, not only when he attends school, but in almost every other situation. He finds himself culturally in an inferior position because he cannot read books as ably as others, nor in some cases can he even read the newspapers with a semblance of competence. In one sense, therefore, the person with a serious reading defect finds himself in the same cultural position as the illiterate. He is reputationally classified by his fellow-men either as an inferior individual or as a queer person. As he grows older he is less able to rationalize the defect or to avoid the conflict associated with his deficiency and therefore accumulates further and further frustration.

The emotional disturbances of the poor reader are important not only from the standpoint of mental health but also because they increasingly interfere with reading ability. The conflicts, the sense of inferiority, and the resulting emotional confusion create critical barriers from which the individual is often forced to withdraw. The consequent emotional blocking may be so intense that the individual becomes totally disinterested in reading or in improving his ability to read. He may then refuse to attempt to read material which would otherwise be within the scope of his ability. His antagonism to reading and his withdrawal are further intensified as pressure is placed upon him to read and to learn further.

Emotional blocking and antagonism to reading often develop in the school child who is forced by his teacher to read aloud in the classroom in spite of his inability to read well. Many teachers believe that continued pressure may in some way overcome the pupil's blocking and his lack of motivation. Experience has shown that, on the contrary, such continued stress actually increases the emotional turmoil of the pupil and also fixates his blocking. When pressure is haphazardly used to create effort and motivation, a vicious cycle often develops. The pressure creates a greater degree of emotional turmoil, and, in turn, the emotional turmoil creates a greater degree of blocking and, therefore, prevents any real improvement in reading ability.

The defensive reactions of the poor reader are the most significant factors in his failures in school. No person can permanently maintain an attitude of inferiority. In time he either rationalizes his inferiority or, if he cannot do so, he develops some defensive mechanism. This often occurs in the poor reader who finds himself in an inferior and reputationally undesirable situation in the school. As a consequence he becomes defensive against most educational procedures. Not only does he dislike any academic work of which reading is a part, but he also begins to be critical about all other phases of his education. In consequence, pupils who are of normal or even superior intelligence may fail in subjects which do not involve a high level of reading ability. Their critical attitude toward the other pupils and especially toward their parents and teachers further intensifies the defenses which they bring to bear upon the problem. Observant teachers have noticed how variable the attainment of these emotionally disturbed pupils may be. On occasion, when they feel secure, when they feel more confident in themselves, their level of attainment is much higher than when they feel self-critical and unable to respond to the demands of the teacher. It is thus exceedingly important to give the poor reader a sense of accomplishment in some other area. It is also very important not to allow a reputation of inadequacy or deficiency to be recognized by the other pupils. When the poor reader is convinced that he has a poor reputation as a student his defensive reactions are likely to increase and his antagonism to education may become permanent.

The nature of the therapy for a reading defect must be determined only after the personality of the student is carefully evaluated. The treatment depends, in part, on whether his emotional problems are the basis of the deficiency or whether they are merely correlates of the reading defect. In all cases of emotional disturbance, the treatment must be directed, at least in part, toward the cure of the emotional disorder. The teacher, as well as the reading specialist, must direct her attention to the reorientation of the emotional turmoil of the pupil and only secondarily to the techniques of reading. His basic conflicts must be discovered and functionally solved.

The competitive situation in the classroom must be reduced. If the pupil has a sense of inferiority and believes that others have recognized his inadequacy, he should not be exposed to further comparisons between himself and his fellow-students. Although he should learn to accept his reading deficiency temporarily, he must not consider it inevitable or a sign of some general inferiority. He can be taught to regard it as an inadequacy no more serious than the ineptitude of a person who cannot learn the technique of a musical instrument or some athletic activity. His sense of efficiency can be increased by giving him special training in an area in which he can excel. His feeling of frustration in the field of reading will thus be reduced by his compensatory excellence in some other field of endeavor. If he can distinguish himself in some skill or activity, he will not only feel more competent personally but will also attain a reputation among his fellow-students which may mitigate against the knowledge that he is inadequate in reading.

The reduction in his sense of personal inadequacy and the decrease of frustration to which he had been previously exposed will in most cases increase his motivation and his ability to read. It is of first importance that the poor reader does not consider his condition critical or so serious that he begins to feel hopeless about his future.

Capable treatment of a reading deficiency involves a reduction of the individual's negative attitude toward his inadequacy. The teacher can do a great deal in this respect by decreasing the emphasis upon the defect as such and increasing the individual's motivation in the meaningfulness of the material he reads. This has been accomplished in a large measure by the reading material which has recently been published for poor readers. Meaningful and important reading has been provided at a level that poor readers can comprehend. They no longer need to read books which are below their level of intelligence. More can be done by interesting these poor readers in the importance of what they read than by stressing the mechanics of reading.

In attempting to alter the attitudes of the non-reader toward his continued efforts to learn to read, it is important to create a certain degree of nonchalance. This does not mean the individual's motivation should be reduced. On the contrary, a casual and confident attitude will actually increase his motivation to improve his capacity. If the poor reader can develop such an attitude he will not create mental crises whenever he reads. In addition to encouraging a casual approach, the teacher must give the pupil assurance by accepting him in spite of his defect. She can establish a feeling that he is basically no different from any other pupil except that he has a given problem of reading in the same way that other pupils have other special problems.

Instead of motivating him by investing him with a sense of fear in regard to his future she can stimulate a great deal of motivation by giving him the assurance that his progress may be just as effective as the progress of any other pupil in the school. Providing the pupil with an assurance of his worth and a sense of security will eliminate the crises with which he is continually involved when he thinks about his failures. His neurotic self-evaluations can also be reduced, and in their place he will be more able to develop a sense of personal dignity and a sense of optimism for the future.

The teacher must, of course, recognize that some poor readers have emotional disturbances which need special treatment by the psychotherapist. The demands upon the teacher are not eliminated, however, even when a pupil requires psychiatric treatment. Her functions are even greater, for she must deal not only with the usual problems of the non-reader but with the special problems in cooperation with the psychiatrist.

53. Specific Principles Essential to Classroom Diagnosis

WILLIAM D. SHELDON (1960)

The classroom teacher usually recognizes that children vary in reading skills and in their ability to learn to read. Although most teachers are familiar with various tests and ways of assessing reading status, they also need to understand certain basic principles of diagnosis and how to apply these principles in the classroom.

Specific Principles of Diagnosis

The following specific principles of diagnosis need to be understood by each teacher:

1. Diagnosis is an essential aspect of teaching and a preliminary step to sound instruction.
2. Diagnosis should be continuous, because child growth in reading depends upon the sequential development of skills, which is promoted through the teacher's knowledge of each child's progress.

SOURCE: *The Reading Teacher,* XIV (September, 1960), 2–8. Reprinted with the permission of William D. Sheldon and the International Reading Association.

3. Diagnosis is an individual task and reflects the fact that each child is different.

4. Diagnosis of reading status demands far more than an assessment of reading, because reading difficulties are symptomatic of many causative factors.

5. Because reading is but one aspect of language, teachers must understand the listening, speaking, and writing status of children to fully understand their reading abilities.

6. Because the instruments of diagnosis have not been perfected, the limitation of each instrument must be thoroughly understood.

After considering the principles of sound diagnostic procedures many teachers throw up their hands in despair and say that they cannot diagnose. They suggest that diagnosis is beyond them. It is our contention that teachers can and must diagnose if an analysis of reading problems is to be accomplished (14). We shall consider each principle and develop ways in which the principles can be applied in practice by every teacher.

Diagnosis an Essential Preliminary

Diagnosis is an essential aspect of teaching and is a preliminary step to sound instruction. Diagnosis as a first step in lesson planning suggests two things:

1. Lessons in reading must be planned with a specific understanding of each child's limitations in reading in mind. This means that formal and informal tests are needed to pinpoint the actual level on which each child can profit from instruction.

2. As teachers gain precision in evaluating the reading status of children, instruction will tend to become more specific, and instructional groups will be limited in size. Specific teaching means that provision will be made within each lesson for the reintroduction in a new context of words not mastered in previous lessons or a reemphasis on the learning of an analytic skill which is not applied properly in new lessons. There is also considerable flexibility in such teaching. Instead of following completely a pre-planned lesson, teachers adjust to pupils' learning of each new skill and provide for more review of difficult skills than would ordinarily be provided to more able readers.

For the ordinary child whose reading is developing in a more or less normal manner, four aspects of reading must be assessed:

1. *Understanding of concepts* related to each specific lesson. Teachers can assess concept development by giving each child an opportunity to discuss the new ideas in a lesson. It is especially important that pupils be allowed to relate the new ideas to their own understanding by re-

counting experiences they have had which are similar to those in the story. Sometimes children indicate their understanding of concepts by supplying synonyms for the word or phrase which has fixed the concept.

2. *Understanding of specific meanings* of known words as used in the new lesson and a clear understanding of new words met for the first time in the lesson. An accurate understanding of word meaning is basic to good comprehension. It is particularly important for teachers to explain words which have a different meaning in a new context. Arousing the curiosity of children about specific word meaning contributes also to the development of critical thinking in reading.

3. *Ability to attack new words* through one of the analytic techniques. Most reading lessons develop an eclectic approach to word analysis. This means that whenever opportunities for using phonetic or structural analysis or contextual clues arise, teachers should lead children to use the varied analytic skills. In so doing teachers increase skill and flexibility in word analysis. For more mature readers it is wise to encourage whenever appropriate the use of glossaries and dictionaries in analyzing new words.

4. *Ability to comprehend* the material read and to answer questions about it. It is important that a constant check be made of the pupils' understanding of what they read. Such aspects of comprehension as understanding the main idea and related details, interpreting the author's meaning, and reacting critically to what is read must be developed in daily instruction.

In summary then, the first principle of diagnosis is recognized when teachers plan their daily lessons to meet the reading needs of each child in a precise manner.

Diagnosis Continuous

Diagnosis should be continuous, because child growth in reading depends upon the sequential development of skills, which is promoted through the teacher's knowledge of each child's progress. Continuous diagnosis indicates a need for evaluating children carefully before instruction begins and then continuing the diagnosis on a daily, weekly, and term basis. First steps in diagnosis can involve the rather routine practice of studying the records which previous teachers have made on each child. At the first-grade level scores from reading readiness tests are usually available. Also of value in the appraisal of each pupil are measures of mental maturity. Often the most important contributions to first-grade teachers is the knowledge obtained from the written comments of kindergarten teachers concerning the observed over-all learning status and capacities of each child.

The next step in diagnosis involves careful and studious reaction to each child as first lessons are taught. When children find new concepts difficult to deal with in their reading, stumble over words taught in previous lessons, fail to isolate a simple main idea or detail, then the sensitive teacher is aware in general of the need for instructing the children in less difficult material. Sometimes children have specific problems which can be resolved by careful reteaching. Careful diagnosis during initial teaching is of the greatest importance. It is our contention that poor reading is actually encouraged when teachers instruct children on too difficult a level. Many reading specialists feel that if each child were taught on his instructional level, with this instructional level frequently reassessed, reading failures would be reduced substantially and children would enjoy reading.

While teachers can do a day-by-day diagnosis during actual teaching by listening to children read and connecting their written reactions to reading, it is also important that more elaborate periodic checks be made of progress. Certainly no book or reading level should be deemed mastered until a thorough check is made of vocabulary studied, word analysis skills learned, and comprehension of materials is assessed. This testing or evaluation is best done through informal tests which are based on the books read and the lessons taught.

For example, after a certain book is read, a check could be made of each child's recognition of every fifth new word in the book. A short test of the child's ability to actually apply newly learned word-analysis skills can be made from the skills taught in the lesson. The recognition of the silent letters in vowel digraphs might be reviewed, or the ability to note differences between long and short vowels can be checked. If a new rule of syllabication has been taught, a check can be made of it in practice.

A more elaborate diagnosis can be made at the end of a term. The instruments used can consist of teacher-made tests based on actual materials read, informal inventories such as those described by Betts (2), Dolch (5), Harris (8), and others. Formal inventories such as the Durrell Analysis of Reading Difficulty (6), McKee's Phonetic Inventory (12), and other tests of this type can be used. An even more formal assessment can be made by the use of standardized reading tests, which, although limited in terms of the diagnosis of individuals, have certain values as gross gauges of progress.

Diagnosis an Individual Task

Diagnosis is an individual task and reflects the fact that each child is different. To diagnose, the teacher must consider the individual child.

This means that time must be set aside for diagnosis both during the daily lesson and at the end of such time periods as those suggested above. Informal reading inventories such as those suggested by Betts (2), can be the most important diagnostic instruments in the classroom teacher's kit.

The informal inventory can be constructed by selecting passages from graded reading books which have not been read by children prior to the testing. Two selections of 100–150 words in length can be selected from each reader, or a selection can be written using the vocabulary of specific readers. One selection is used to test oral reading while the other is used as a measure of silent reading. Teachers note the kinds of errors children make while reading orally and use the errors as a guide for corrective instruction. Such errors as omissions, substitutions, reversals, repetitions, ignoring punctuation, and incorrect phrasing are all noted during oral reading.

Comprehension of the materials read silently is measured through questions asked following the reading. These questions demand an understanding of the main idea, related details, the sequence of ideas, and the understanding of ideas not directly stated by the writer.

Teachers can receive from the suggested references some guidance in evaluating the level on which children read. However, the decision as to whether a child is frustrated by what he reads, is not challenged by the material, or needs instruction to read successfully is left up to the judgment of the teacher.

Diagnosis More than Reading Assessment

Diagnosis of reading status demands far more than an assessment of reading, because reading problems are symptomatic of many causative factors. It is important that classroom teachers realize that many resources outside the classroom are needed for a complete assessment of children. Teachers need to know the nature of the reading problem if children are showing signs of distress during reading instruction. An ability to classify readers as corrective or remedial, as differentiated from the normal or developmental, can be strengthened through reading (1, 8, 9, 15).

Kress (11) describes the child with a corrective problem as one who "may be retarded in reading anywhere from a few months to several years below his expected grade level of achievement, as estimated by an individual intelligence test. For this child, the principal deterring factor, which inhibits progress in reading, is the inability of his classroom teacher to instruct the child on a level within his present range of word recognition and comprehension skills. The child's problem may involve inadequacies in experience background, concept development, word recognition, and/or word comprehension, but there is no basic neurological or psychological learning difficulty present.

"The remedial reader is quite a different type of learning problem. If the difficulty is identified early, the extent of retardation in reading may be no greater than that found in mild corrective problems. However, the child with a remedial problem, in addition to being faced with the same inhibiting factor as found in the corrective category, is handicapped by a basic neurological or psychological difficulty.

"A child in this category has an associative learning problem. When the usual teaching techniques are employed, the child cannot relate meaning from his own experience background to the symbols-words which he is trying to learn."

A teacher is well on his way to sophistication in diagnosis when he recognizes that a child has serious problems needing corrective or remedial treatment rather than a simple problem which would respond to more carefully presented developmental lessons. While the teacher might not know how to diagnose the more serious difficulties nor know how to treat them, he should be able to recognize when children have serious problems.

Classroom teachers can look to the school physician and psychologist to provide help in the diagnosis of general health and emotional status. A thorough diagnosis by experienced clinicians can also provide more clues of the child's intellectual and neurological status. The classroom teacher is not expected to perform the diagnostic functions of the physician, psychologist, or neurologist, but we can expect the teacher to be well enough acquainted with children to know when the severity of a reading problem warrants a more complex diagnosis than he can provide.

Reading and Language Arts

Because reading is but one aspect of language, teachers must understand the listening, speaking, and writing status of children to fully understand their reading abilities. The relationship among the various language arts must be thoroughly understood by teachers before they can fully appreciate the child's problem in reading. Corrective or remedial reading instruction is a questionable procedure when the basic problem of a child is his inability to listen adequately or speak our language with fluency.

It is probable that the isolated teaching and diagnosis of reading has been due to the emphasis upon reading instruction that has not taken into full consideration the place of reading in the development of language. Certainly a meager listening and speaking background will account for much of the difficulty children have in reading. An inability to write adequately is also related to a general language problem. Certainly an understanding of the structure of our language gained through both listening and reading will be reflected in the child's ability to write in a correct manner.

Teachers should make a special effort to assess the listening abilities of children. The assessment can be made through informal means, such as reading to children and then observing their reactions. If a child can re-tell or dramatize a story which has been read to him we can gain some appreciation of his ability to listen. The teacher might also give commands or directions and observe the child's ability to respond. A more formal assessment of listening ability can be obtained through the STEP Listening Test (4). Early primary teachers have been provided many excellent measures of listening through lessons found in so-called readiness booklets.

It is of first importance that teachers of bilingual children, or children who come from deprived homes, study the listening ability of children to make sure that the words introduced in reading are part of the listening vocabulary.

Speaking ability can be determined through daily contact with children. However, a word of caution is in order here. It has been our experience that a few children often monopolize the speaking opportunities in a group or class. Records kept by teachers of the conversation of children in their classes frequently reveal that relatively few children monopolize these discussions. An informal assessment of speaking ability has been devised by Sylvia Jones (10). She has selected a series of colorful, action-filled pictures of scenes with which most first-grade children are familiar. Mrs. Jones has given these pictures (6) to individual children and asked them to tell her about the pictures. The notes of what each child has said not only indicate the fluency of the children but the wide range of their concepts, vocabulary, and general understanding.

Informal tests of writing are also needed to round out the understanding of the general language skills of children. A knowledge of the listening, speaking, and writing ability of children will not only give teachers a better understanding of the reasons for reading disabilities, but will also serve to focus attention on the fact that reading cannot be taught in isolation. Reading must be presented in a general language development setting.

Limitations of Diagnostic Tests

Because the instruments of diagnosis have not been perfected, the limitation of each instrument must be thoroughly understood. It is recommended that teachers study the tests they use to assess the status of children in order to become fully aware of uses and limitations of the tests. If a test has been reviewed in Buros' *Mental Measurement Yearbook* (3), then it is helpful to read the critique of the test in this volume. The more sophisticated test expert often pinpoints limitations of tests and indicates strengths or weaknesses not always obvious to the teacher.

In using informal inventories in which comprehension is checked by rather simple questions of detail, it is interesting to discover how many questions children answer correctly without fully understanding the material.

The range of scores which can be obtained by giving two or three different reading or intelligence tests to the same child should also be noted (13). Some teachers have discovered that certain formal reading tests have a limited ceiling and are not adequate as a measuring instrument for the more able children in a class. Teachers have found that other tests yield reading scores which might represent a grade placement one or two years higher than that on which children can read with understanding.

It is important that teachers become well acquainted with the formal and informal tests used in the assessment of children. The limitations of tests should be understood in terms of the children being tested. Teacher judgment also needs critical examination. If tests measure inadequately, it is the teacher who must detect the inadequacy, and it is the teacher who must provide a further measure of skill.

If children are to be properly taught they must be diagnosed accurately. Teachers can diagnose the reading status of their children to a limited degree by adhering to a few basic principles. When the limited diagnostic ability of teachers needs supplementing, then teachers must be well enough informed to call in the necessary help in order to obtain a more accurate estimate.

References

1. Betts, E. A. *Foundations of Reading Instruction*. New York: American Book Co., 1956.
2. Betts, Emmett A. *The American Adventure Series Handbook*. Chicago: Wheeler Publishing Co., 1956.
3. Buros, Oscar (ed.). *Fifth Mental Measurement Yearbook*. Highland Park, N.J., The Gryphon Press, 1959.
4. *Cooperative Sequential Tests of Educational Progress, Listening*. Princeton: Cooperative Test Division, Educational Testing Service, 1957.
5. Dolch, Edward A. "Testing Reading With a Book," *Elementary English*, XXVIII, No. 3 (March, 1951), 124–125.

6. Durrell, Donald D. *Durrell Analysis of Reading Difficulty* (New Edition). Yonkers: World Book Co., 1955.
7. Durrell, D. D. *Improvement of Basic Reading Abilities.* Yonkers: World Book Co., 1940.
8. Harris, Albert J. *How to Increase Reading Ability,* 3rd ed. New York: Longmans, Green, 1956.
9. Johnson, Marjorie S. "Factors Related to Disability in Reading," *The Journal of Experimental Education,* XXVI (Sept., 1957), 1–26.
10. Jones, Sylvia. "A Sampling of the Vocabulary of Fourteen First Grade Children" (Unpublished study), Syracuse University Reading Center.
11. Kress, Roy A. "When Is Remedial Reading Essential," *Education,* 80 (May, 1960), 540–544.
12. McKee, Paul. *The McKee Inventory of Phonetic Skill.* Boston: Houghton, Mifflin.
13. Sheldon, W. D., and Manolakes, George. "A Comparison of the Stanford-Binet, Revised Form L, and the California Test of Mental Maturity (S-Form)," *The Journal of Educational Psychology,* 45 (Dec., 1954), 499–504.
14. Sheldon, W. D. "Teachers Must Diagnose," *Education,* 78 (May, 1958), 1–2.
15. Stauffer, Russell G. "Reading Retardation and Associative Learning Disabilities," *Elementary English,* 26 (March, 1949), 150–157.

54. General Principles of Diagnosis of Reading Disabilities

MARION MONROE (1937)

To be effective, remedial instruction in reading must be preceded by careful diagnosis. The remedial teacher must first discover the nature of the child's difficulty, search for causes and then set up a specific program to treatment that will either remove the causes, or if that is impossible, will at least enable the child to read as well as his limitations permit. The very complexity of the reading process makes diagnosis

SOURCE: Marion Monroe, *Remedial Reading* (Boston: Houghton Mifflin Company, 1937), pp. 12–17. Reprinted by permission of the publisher.

difficult. So many conditions and factors which affect reading have been brought to light by recent investigations with such divergent interpretations that the remedial reading teacher may find herself in a state of uncertainty and confusion in trying to reconcile conflicting theories and points of view. A few general principles of procedure and a classification of causes may assist the teacher in making a diagnosis of the difficulties of children who cannot read.

Multiple Causation of Reading Disabilities

Reading disabilities are usually the result of several contributing factors rather than one isolated cause. Studies of the causes of reading disabilities reveal no clear-cut factors which occur only in poor readers and never in good readers. Some children who possess the impeding factors appear to be able to read in spite of them. For example, poor vision occurs as a factor in a certain percentage of reading-disability cases and undoubtedly impedes reading; yet some good readers are found who also have poor vision. A similar state of affairs occurs in the studies of almost every discovered cause of reading disability. A few good readers are found who have poor vision, poor hearing, emotional instability, who come from environments detrimental to reading, and who have had inferior teaching. Even among mental defectives are found occasional children who have acquired a glib skill in the mechanics of reading even though unable to comprehend much of the content read. We may conclude that in most cases, one factor alone is not sufficient to inhibit the act of reading, if compensating abilities are present and if the child's reaction to the difficulty is a favorable one. This fact should not, however, serve to minimize the importance of any difficulty. Occasionally a simple difficulty, so easily overcome in the majority of cases as to appear unimportant, may be the direct reason for setting up in a certain child a number of emotional inhibitions to further learning. The reading diagnostician must, therefore, investigate each case with the hope of locating as many contributing factors as possible, study the interrelationships of these factors and weigh their importance in the light of the child's reactions to the difficulties. Individuals vary greatly in their experiences and in the number and combinations of factors contributing to the problem: only a thorough acquaintance with each child can lead to a complete understanding of his reading disability.

It is not essential, however, for every cause to be located before beginning remedial work. This would delay the remedial instruction unnecessarily. A first "working-hypothesis" may be set up after the initial tests and the remedial teacher may begin treatment with those factors which are best understood. The diagnosis then continues as the remedial work gives further opportunities for observation and testing of hypotheses, and opens new leads for investigation. Diagnosis and treatment, therefore, go hand in hand—the treatment being based on the first tentative diagnosis, and the diagnosis being modified or confirmed on the basis of the outcomes of remedial instruction.

Diagnostic Procedures

The diagnosis of reading disabilities should contain two types of analysis: (1) *descriptive and* (2) *causative.* In the descriptive analysis the examiner details as completely as possible the nature of the child's reading disability. Both subjective observation and objective test data are included in this type of analysis. The descriptive analysis should answer the following questions:

a. What reading level has this child reached? This question is answered by data from standardized reading tests, usually in terms of reading grade, and varies from total non-reading to almost any grade level of reading.

b. How far below expectation is this reading level? This question is answered by comparing the child's reading-grade with his actual grade placement, his chronological age, his mental age, the number of years he has attended school, and his achievements in other non-reading subjects. Here again almost any degree of retardation may be present. This relationship between reading and other abilities may be expressed as a reading index or an achievement quotient.

c. Are all types of reading equally retarded? This question is answered by comparing grade scores on different types of reading tests: that is, oral, silent, word-recognition, vocabulary, reading for particular types of comprehension, reading rate, etc. Many variations may be found: the accurate oral reader who gets no meaning from his reading; the speedy silent reader who stumbles orally; the generally poor reader in all types; or the child who is up to grade in the mechanics of reading but who lacks interest or desire to read.

d. What are the particular characteristics of the child's reading? This question is answered by analysis and description of his reading errors, the most frequent types, how his errors compare with typical errors at his own reading level, how his eyes move in reading across the page, how he articulates and phrases in oral reading, what mannerisms and peculiarities he shows while reading, and what methods of self-help he employs (such as spelling, sounding, pointing, etc.). Photographs of eye-movements assist in analyzing the characteristics of his reading.

e. How does the child respond to his reading difficulty? This question is answered by a description of his reactions to reading such as aggressive dislike, withdrawal, compensatory activities, discouragement, apathy, etc. The examiner tries to discover what the reading disability means to the child in his social relationships.

f. What is the child like as an individual, apart from reading? This question is answered by a general description of the child, his personality, his physical appearance and physical condition, his social response, his spontaneous language and comments. The examiner tries to discover the interests and motivating drives in his behavior.

g. What have been this child's experiences? This question is answered by conversation with the parents and teachers in which the examiner obtains a personal, social, and school history of the child. Family relationships are often helpful in understanding the child's difficulty, particularly if he is compared unfavorably with siblings, or if he feels insecure in his personal relationships.

From the descriptive analysis of the child the examiner forms his opinion as to what are the causal factors in the disability. The questions now to be answered are: *Why has this child failed to learn to read? Why does he show these particular characteristics and mannerisms in reading and why has he chosen these particular reactions to failure?* The examiner now is set searching for reasons and explanations. Perhaps it will not be possible to answer these questions for every case. Researches on reading disabilities are fairly recent; most of our knowledge in this field dates within the past ten or fifteen years. Some of the causes of reading disabilities have already received fairly intensive and critical study; others have been merely suggested as possibilities from case studies without having been put to experimental tests. Still other causes, as yet unrecognized, may come to light with increased knowledge. Granting the limitations of our present knowledge, the examiner will find it helpful to state the causes of the difficulties in so far as can be determined.

55. Clinical Procedures in Diagnosing Seriously Retarded Readers

HELEN M. ROBINSON (1956)

The major function of the service provided by reading clinics is to assist children and/or adults to make very rapid progress in reading. The first step in this program is to secure a diagnosis of each person's reading. The purpose of the diagnosis is to learn as much as possible about the retarded reader: his capacity to read, his special strengths and weaknesses in reading, his interests, and his personal reactions to past instruction. The goal of the diagnosis is to make a prognosis and to arrive at sound recommendations for remedial therapy.

Clinical diagnosis requires varying amounts of time, depending on the complexity of the problems involved and the organization and facilities of the clinic. In our reading clinic, we follow an outline or plan for the diagnosis of all retarded readers.

Diagnostic Plan

Since we accept referrals from the elementary school, high school, college, and adult population, our diagnostic plan must be sufficiently flexible to meet the needs of a wide range of age and achievement levels.

The specific steps in the diagnosis follow:

First, secure as much information as possible about the person and record it on a case history blank. Second, obtain the most accurate measure possible of the level at which the person should be able to read. Third, administer a standardized reading survey test with diagnostic features to determine the general level of reading achievement. Both oral and silent reading should be appraised. Fourth, analyze the data secured in the three preceding steps to determine whether the person has a reading problem and the extent of the retardation. If not, guidance is now given to parents, client, and the school concerning other

---

SOURCE: *Proceedings of the International Reading Association*, 1956, pp. 152–156. Reprinted with the permission of Helen M. Robinson and the International Reading Association.

services or procedures which may be useful. If a reading problem is manifested, the next steps are taken.

Fifth, a detailed analysis of the nature of the reading problem is made. Sixth, an attempt is made to identify factors which may be inhibiting reading progress. For example, visual and auditory efficiency, and personal and emotional problems are factors given careful consideration.

The seventh step is to collate all of the data secured and to interpret the results as accurately as possible.

The last step is to make appropriate recommendations for remedial therapy. In addition to the most useful procedures to follow, materials for teaching reading are suggested. In addition, referral to other specialists may be made if the screening procedures suggest the need for such examination.

Following the diagnosis, a report is written to the referral agency and/or to the parents. If the referral agency is a professional one, such as a school, or a child guidance clinic, the results of all tests are given. On the other hand, if the report is to parents, results of tests are interpreted in relation to the reading difficulty.

The Case History

At the time the diagnostic appointment is made, the parents of children are asked to have the school send directly to us pertinent information about the pupil. We are anxious to secure scores on intelligence and achievement tests, health records, attendance records, a summary of the problems the pupil has exhibited in school and the procedures used in attempting to solve them, and the kinds of co-operation the parents have given the school.

One or both of the parents usually accompany children of elementary or high school age. The clinician talks with the parent for approximately a half-hour while the pupil is engaged in other activities. Usually the clinician asks the parent to tell all about when and how the reading problem began and what steps have already been taken to remedy the difficulty. When the parents relate this information, it is possible to learn a great deal about significant attitudes often not elicited by direct questions and answers. An accepting attitude on the part of the clinician is essential to encourage parents to talk freely rather than to attempt to express only acceptable attitudes. At times, it may be necessary to ask other leading questions, such as "What was he like before he went to school?", "How did he feel about having tutoring after school?", and "Why was he asked to repeat the grade?" In addition, certain factual data must be secured, such as birth history, diseases or accidents, and ages of walking and talking.

Whenever the data are available, we ask for reports from recent medical or visual examinations, child guidance or speech clinics, psychiatrists, social workers, or any agency with which the child has had contact.

If the examinee is a college student or an adult, he usually gives the history. In this instance emphasis is placed upon his experiences and how he has reacted to them. We are also concerned with his interests and hobbies, his hopes and personal expectations.

When the history data are assembled, the real test of clinical skill is interpreting these data accurately—that is, to detect bias and error, to determine which statements represent fact as opposed to wishful thinking, or if some are made to impress the examiner. From this analysis, a general picture of the examinee, in his school and social setting, begins to emerge.

Reading Capacity and Achievement

Prior to testing, it is essential to establish rapport with the subject. If this is an older student, the relationship is established while the case history is being taken. When the parents have given the background data, a conference with the pupil is essential to be certain that he is ready to accept testing. This requires varying amounts of time, depending on the pupil.

At present there are no really valid measures of reading capacity for an individual of any age, although individual intelligence tests have been widely used for this purpose. The Stanford-Binet (Houghton-Mifflin) for pupils under the age of sixteen years should be supplemented by a non-verbal battery to secure a fair estimate of level of intelligence. Recently we have been using the Wechsler Intelligence Scale for Children (Psychological Corporation, New York) which yields both a verbal and performance intelligence quotient. While the verbal score seems to be most closely related to reading achievement, the performance score is very useful for children with language problems. For high school and college ages, the Wechsler-Bellevue Intelligence Scale for Adolescents and Adults (Psychological Corporation, New York) is used most frequently.

If one of the foregoing intelligence tests is chosen as a measure of reading capacity, the results must be interpreted with care, because there is far from a point-for-point relationship between intelligence and reading achievement in the general population. Furthermore, experience shows that following successful remedial instruction, the intelligence quotient is often increased.

Reading achievement may be assessed by standardized or informal tests. In most instances, a survey test with diagnostic features is chosen.

At the elementary reading levels, the Chicago Reading Tests (E. M. Hale & Company), the California Reading Tests (California Test Bureau), and the Gates Survey Test (Bureau of Publications, Teachers College, Columbia University) are most often used. For high school and college levels, the Cooperative English Test: Reading Comprehension (Educational Testing Service) is preferred, but the Nelson-Denny Reading Test (Houghton-Mifflin) or the Iowa Silent Reading Test (World Book Company) may be used.

Since some children become "test-wise," or obviously guess at the answers to questions, informal tests may be needed. Silent and oral reading of a short selection from each of several graded readers often offers considerable assistance in determining the stage of reading growth which the pupil has attained.

Most severely retarded readers will be characterized by mental ages from two to five years beyond their reading achievement levels. In case mental ability and reading achievement are not so widely separated, reading clinics usually consider many other factors in deciding whether to continue the diagnosis.

Analysis of the Reading Problem

The majority of retarded readers who score at fourth grade or below have a major problem in word recognition which is basic to the difficulty, regardless of the age or grade placement. Among those cases, it is essential to explore the range of sight and meaning vocabulary and the efficiency of all word-attack skills.

To estimate the sight vocabulary, the Dolch Picture-Word Cards (Garrard Press) may be used as a test. Should these words be recognized instantly, additional words from the list of new words used in a basal reading series may be used for more detailed testing if necessary.

In our Reading Clinic, the knowledge of phonics and structural analysis is usually evaluated by using an unpublished phonetic skills test which was developed by a former member of our staff. For this test, the elements and principles are checked in nonsense syllables and words so that neither meaning nor sight vocabulary may be used as an adjunct. However, the application of phonetic skills and principles is also observed in the formal and informal oral reading tests.

Whenever it is appropriate, the use of the dictionary is observed as the pupil looks up an unknown word or two from the materials he has read in the informal test.

If a pupil recognizes only a few words, it is important to determine whether he is likely to learn more readily by one method than others. For this purpose, both visual and auditory discrimination tests are administered. The visual discrimination tests we use are unpublished and only in experimental form. The auditory discrimination test was developed by Dr. Joseph Wepman, speech specialist at the University of Chicago.

If the major reading difficulty is primarily in the area of vocabulary or word meanings, only a few tests are available with diagnostic features. The Diagnostic Reading Tests for Grades 7–13 include a section on vocabulary which is subdivided into general, English, mathematics, science, and social studies. The Michigan Vocabulary Profile Test (World Book Company) for Grade 9 through the senior year of college includes the following areas: human relations, commerce, government, physical science, biological science, mathematics, fine arts, and sports.

In many instances vocabulary problems become evident in oral reading, and in the comprehension sections of other tests. This informal appraisal is exceedingly useful to the diagnostician.

Special difficulty in comprehension can be examined two ways: first, in relation to the different areas of understanding, and second, according to the ability to comprehend what is read in various subject areas. Although research supports the hypothesis that comprehension is a unitary ability among average high school and college students, experience shows that those with difficulty in this area may have specialized problems. In order to ascertain the specific weaknesses, the clinician may examine the types of errors made on questions answered in the survey test, calling for different abilities such as getting facts, main ideas, etc. In addition, it may be useful to administer an untimed test such as Part III of the Analytic Reading Scales (Van Wagenen Psycho-Educational Research Laboratories, Minneapolis). Although questions about the validity of the separate parts have been raised, experience with these scales reveals that the results may be indicative of the kinds of remedial instruction needed.

For students who are receiving their terminal education, the SRA Reading Record (Science Research Associates) samples many of the kinds of reading activities used most frequently outside the schools.

In the content areas, informal testing is usually required, since diagnostic standardized tests have not proved to be useful so far.

Two types of reading rates should be tested, since we hope that students may be flexible in adapting their rate to the difficulty of the materials. For this purpose, Part I of the Analytic Reading Scales offers a measure of rate of reading materials at about the fourth-grade level of difficulty. In order to make a comparison we frequently use the adaptation of the Van Wagenen-Dvorak Diagnostic Examination of Silent

Reading Abilities (unpublished) developed by Dr. Guy T. Buswell. Since the time is recorded for reading each of the twelve paragraphs, written at varying levels of difficulty, it is possible to determine the range in reading rates when they are accompanied by the comprehension questions of disparate types.

Students who rank relatively high in word-recognition, vocabulary, and comprehension, and relatively low in rates of reading are usually asked to read selections before an eye-movement camera. The film yields information on the maturity of reading habits. The symptoms exhibited may be useful in prescribing remedial therapy.

Oral reading may be evaluated and analyzed by using the Standardized Oral Reading Paragraphs (Public School Publishing Co.) or the Gilmore Oral Reading Test (World Book Co.). It is also helpful to use informal materials. The results of the tests in grade scores are of less value diagnostically than the analysis of performance and a check list of observed behavior. An excellent source suggesting characteristics to be observed is in the record booklet for the Durrell Analysis of Reading Difficulty (World Book Co.).

It is essential to remember that reading retardation is usually characterized by problems in more than one of the areas outlined in the preceding paragraphs. These areas have been discussed separately only because each must be considered in the diagnosis.

Inhibiting Factors

Research reveals that it is usually impossible to specify the causes of severe reading retardation without fairly detailed data accumulated from the time the pupil enters school. Nevertheless, it is essential to identify any difficulties which may be interfering with reading progress at the time remedial instruction is initiated.

One of the factors considered is visual inefficiency, which appears frequently. The Ortho-Rater Tests of Visual Efficiency (Bausch and Lomb Optical Company) are usually administered to all students. If there is doubt about the need for referral to a refractionist, the test is repeated at a later time. When parts of the battery other than the acuity tests are failed, the Spache Binocular Reading Test (Keystone View Co.) and the Hand-Eye Co-ordination Test (Keystone View Co.) are used. Report forms are given to the parents for the refractionist to fill in and return to the Clinic whenever a referral is made.

Hearing is screened by use of the Maico Audiometer. This permits appraisal of auditory acuity over a wide range of sound frequencies. Students who fail parts of this test are referred to an otolaryngologist.

Personal adjustment is appraised informally in most cases. The diagnostician is sensitive to behavior and attitudes which often interfere with learning to read. In cases where it seems necessary, one of the projective tests, usually the Rorschach (Grune and Stratton, Inc.) is administered. Except in extreme cases, it is exceedingly difficult to determine whether the emotional problem is of such nature and severity that it will interfere with learning to read. Frequently the pupil is accepted for tutoring on a trial basis before a final decision can be made. Maladjusted pupils are referred for psychotherapy and often return at a later time for reading instruction.

Careful observations are made to detect obvious symptoms of hypothyroidism, and special attention is given to any indications, in the history or performance, of brain damage. If the latter is suspected, differential diagnosis is made by a medical psychologist on our campus.

Speech problems are fairly infrequent among the pupils who come to our clinic, but are always referred to a speech correctionist, and very often, the corrective therapy in speech and reading are coordinated.

Interpretation and Recommendations

Since a test is administered only when it is anticipated that the results will supply specific information needed by the examiner, the last and most exacting step in diagnosis is to collate the results and interpret them. The scores on tests are examined critically in relation to performance on items within the tests and to observations of the behavior and attitudes of the examinee. Such a task requires considerable experience in test interpretation and a great deal of insight into how children learn to read.

The recommendations are concerned with the level at which instruction should begin; the methods which are most likely to be successful; the materials which are appropriate for use and, at the same time, in close harmony with the interests of the pupil. Finally suggestions are offered for dealing with special problems in inter-personal relationships.

Concluding Statement

The plan for a reading diagnosis outlined in this paper includes eight steps. By selecting appropriate devices for measurement, or techniques for observation, this plan may be applied to most severely retarded readers. The data secured and properly interpreted serves as a starting point for remedial therapy. In addition, diagnosis must be continuous during the period of remedial instruction.

56. Remedial Cases in Reading: Their Diagnosis and Treatment

WILLIAM S. GRAY (1922)

Summary of Causes

Difficulties in practically all phases of reading are due to a wide variety of causes. Those which were of most significance in the cases reported in this chapter may be summarized briefly as follows: (1) low native intelligence, inadequate language habits, and lack of general experience; (2) little or no interest in reading, a careless, indifferent attitude toward school work, and ineffective attention and application; (3) inadequate attention to the content, difficulties in the mechanics of reading, ineffective rates of reading, an inadequate meaning vocabulary, failure to think independently about the content, and inability to picture unfamiliar situations; (4) poor home environment, distracting social influences, and inadequate parental supervision; and (5) inadequate or inappropriate reading materials and poor instruction. The list is a relatively long one and includes many of the causes mentioned in earlier chapters. It is apparent that the teacher who attempts to determine the causes of failure in an individual case must canvass various possible explanations systematically before reaching final conclusions and planning remedial instruction.

CONCLUSIONS CONCERNING REMEDIAL INSTRUCTION

The following specific suggestions concerning remedial instruction are based on the study of cases reported in this chapter. (1) Individual instruction is preferable. (2) The confidence and co-operation of the pupil must be secured. (3) Keen interest must be aroused in reading through the use of material directly related to the pupil's interests. (4) The first selections must be simple enough to enable the pupil to read with a fair degree of success. (5) Specific problems should be assigned to direct his

---

SOURCE: William Gray, "Remedial Cases in Reading: Their Diagnosis and Treatment," Supplementary Educational Monograph No. 22, 1922, pp. 185–187. Reprinted by permission of the University of Chicago Press.

attention to the important points. (6) These problems should increase in difficulty as his power of interpretation develops. (7) The problems which are assigned must vary in order to include all important phases of interpretation. (8) In connection with training in interpretation, he must be given exercises to promote rapid and accurate recognition of individual words and words in groups. (9) Drill exercises to increase his span of recognition and to establish regular eye-movements should also be given. (10) Exercises must be included to assist the pupil in reading rapidly as well as thoughtfully. (11) As soon as the pupil has made some progress in accurate interpretation and in the mechanics of reading, he should be assigned types of exercises which require independent thinking. (12) He should also be encouraged to read as much as possible outside of class in order to secure a large amount of practice in reading which is necessary in establishing fluent habits. (13) Remedial instruction should not be discontinued until pupils have substituted good habits for poor ones in all phases of reading and can read content subjects rapidly, intelligently, and independently.

Remedial instruction for pupils who are weak in most phases of reading must be both comprehensive and specific. A well-balanced program should be adopted which provides adequate training in each phase in which weakness is discovered. As a rule, training should be carried on simultaneously along all lines, although major emphasis may be placed at any time on a given phase in which serious difficulty is encountered. As training continues, the most important need of a pupil may change and the emphasis in instruction must be shifted. For example, a pupil who is weak in all phases of reading may need first of all exercises which direct his attention to the content in order to aid him in both interpretation and recognition. As he overcomes his difficulties in the interpretation of simple passages, it may be necessary to emphasize in turn each of the following: the interpretation of passages of a problematic type, increasing his rate of silent reading, or developing independence in the recognition of polysyllabic words. The remedial teacher must study the pupil's needs continuously, and must supplement a well-balanced program of reading instruction with specific emphasis from time to time on particular phases of reading which require immediate attention.

57. Basic Principles of Remedial Instruction

GUY L. BOND and MILES A. TINKER (1967)

The complexity of the reading act, the nature of reading difficulties, and the many characteristics of child growth and development that have a bearing on reading success make it clear that no two cases of disability are exactly alike. Four detailed aspects of this general fact have also been shown; no two cases of reading disability result from the same set of circumstances, no two have exactly the same reading patterns, no two cases have the same instructional needs, and no two can be treated in exactly the same manner. Every child is different in many ways from every other child. Because his difficulties in reading stem from a wide variety of causes, the diagnosis of his case involves a study of the child to find out his instructional needs and everything else that may influence a remedial program for him.

The remedial teacher studies the diagnostic findings and then arranges a learning situation that will enable the child henceforth to grow in reading at an accelerated rate. The remedial teacher's problem is to appraise materials and methods in order to select the combination that will best suit a given disabled reader. The many kinds of reading confusions children manifest indicate that no two disabilities will be corrected exactly the same way. Nonetheless, there are some basic principles underlying remedial instruction irrespective of the specific nature of a particular reading disability. There are certain common elements among corrective programs, whether we are treating a comprehension case, a problem of word recognition, or an oral reading limitation.

Among the more important general categories of basic principles underlying treatment of disabled reading are the following:

SOURCE: Guy L. Bond and Miles A. Tinker, *Reading Difficulties: Their Diagnosis and Correction*, 2d ed. (New York: Meredith Publishing Company, 1967), pp. 241–266. All numbered references appearing in the original text have been deleted.

1. Treatment must be based on an understanding of the child's instructional needs.
2. Remedial programs must be highly individualized.
3. Remedial instruction must be organized instruction.
4. The reading processes must be made meaningful to the learner.
5. Consideration of the child's personal worth is necessary.
6. The reading program must be encouraging to the child.
7. Materials and exercises must be suitable to the child's reading ability and instructional needs.
8. Sound teaching procedures must be employed.
9. A carefully designed follow-up program is necessary.

Treatment Must Be Based on an Understanding of the Child's Instructional Needs

The remedial program must be designed to emphasize those phases of reading growth that will enable the disabled reader to grow rapidly and solidly. The program designed for each child must be based on a diagnosis of his instructional needs. The purpose of the diagnosis is to obtain information about each child that is necessary in order to formulate a remedial program suited to him. Watkins has shown that the child who is in trouble in reading often has an unequal profile showing an unfortunate pattern of reading skills and abilities. Some phases of reading will be well learned while other phases will be developed poorly. Still other phases may have been overemphasized to the point that they restrict the child's development in reading. The diagnosis must ferret out these inconsistencies in the child's attack on reading.

The child having difficulty in reading will show irregular performances. He may have a large sight vocabulary but he is unable to phrase well. He may be high in word recognition but low in comprehension. A reading diagnosis is designed to locate the inconsistencies that preclude rapid and effective growth in reading. The diagnosis is designed to locate essential areas of growth that have been neglected, those that have been faultily learned, or those that have been overemphasized. It is impractical to start a remedial program in reading until the nature of the instruction needed by the disabled reader has been established. Otherwise, the program may stress areas already overemphasized or omit areas needing attention or perhaps underemphasize such areas.

The remedial program must be based on more than an understanding of the child's reading needs. It must also be based on the child's characteristics. The child who is hard-of-hearing needs a different approach to reading than does his counterpart with normal hearing. The child with poor vision needs marked adjustments in methods and, if his limitation is severe enough, in materials also. The child who is a slow learner needs modified methods and so does the child who is emotionally disturbed. The modifications of instruction for such children will be discussed in a later chapter.

Inasmuch as each case is different, there can be no "bag of tricks," nor can there be a universal approach which will lead to the solution of disabled readers' problems. Many times, remedial training suited to one child would be detrimental to another. If, for example, a remedial program has been planned to develop more adequate phrasing, the child might well be required to do considerable prepared oral reading in order to help him to read in thought units. This same recommendation would do serious harm to the youngster who is already overvocalizing in his silent reading. It would exaggerate the faulty habit he had acquired and increase his disability. To sum up, every remedial program must be made on the basis of a thorough appraisal of the child's instructional needs, his strengths and weaknesses, and the environment in which correction is to take place.

CLEARLY FORMULATE THE REMEDIAL PROGRAM

After the diagnosis has shown the kind of instruction that is needed, the remedial program should be carefully planned. This requires writing down what is to be done for each case. This must be done because it is too difficult to remember each child, his needs, the level of his attainments, and his limitations with the exactness that is necessary in order to conduct an effective corrective program. The written case report should indicate the nature of the disability and the type of exercises recommended to correct the difficulty. It should identify the level of material that is to be used. The written report should state any physical or sensory characteristics of the child that need to be corrected or for which the program needs to be modified. Any indication of faulty personal adjustment or unfortunate environmental conditions should be included. The child's interests, hobbies, and attitudes should become part of the written record. Most important, this record should include a description of the remedial program recommended and the type of material and exercises to be used.

THE REMEDIAL PROGRAM SHOULD BE MODIFIED AS NEEDED

The original plan of remedial work is not to be considered a permanent scheme of instruction. It will need to be modified from time to time as the child progresses in reading. Often a child who is having difficulty in learning changes rapidly in respect to his instructional needs. The better the diagnosis and the more successful the remedial work, the more rapidly will the child's needs change. One disabled reader, for example, may have failed to build analytical word-recognition techniques but is depending on sight vocabulary and context clues as his means of recognizing new words. He would be given remedial work designed to teach him the analytical techniques. After a time, he may develop considerable skill in word study, but he may not make a corresponding gain in rate of reading. His problem would no longer be one of developing word analysis. In fact, emphasis on this phase of the program might become detrimental to his future reading growth. The use of larger word elements and other more rapid word-recognition techniques and further building of sight vocabulary would be advisable. As the problem changes, so must the program of remediation be modified in order to meet the new reading needs of the child.

Inasmuch as the child's instructional needs change rapidly, it is unwise to set him into a remedial program that resembles the production line in a factory. Such a program assumes that once a given child's level of reading performance is identified, all that is needed is to put him through a set of exercises uniform for all children. There is no single method suited to all children even in the developmental reading program. The disabled reader whose needs change rapidly as his limitations are corrected, is in dire need of a program that readily adjusts to every change in his reading pattern. To achieve success, a remedial program must be based upon a continuous diagnosis and it must be modified as the child's instructional needs change.

In some instances, the original program for remediation does not result in improvement. When this occurs, a re-evaluation of the diagnosis and perhaps additions to the diagnosis are in order. A somewhat altered approach to instruction may be necessary to bring success.

A VARIETY OF REMEDIAL TECHNIQUES SHOULD BE USED

There is an unfortunate tendency, once a form of remedial instruction has been prescribed, to stick to the use of that specific type of exercise to overcome a known deficiency. Basing a remedial program upon a diagnosis does not imply that a given exercise can be used until the child's reading disability is corrected. There are many ways to develop each of the skills and abilities in reading. An effective remedial program will use a variety of teaching techniques and instructional procedures.

Many sources of help describing teaching techniques are available to the remedial teacher. Professional books on remedial instruction in reading give suggestions for correcting specific types of reading retardation. Russell and Karp have compiled a helpful group of remedial techniques. Manuals and workbooks accompanying basal reading programs are the most fruitful source of teaching techniques. The exercises suggested for teaching the skills and abilities when first introduced in such manuals and workbooks are the sort of things that prove beneficial for remedial programs. If, for example, a fifth-grade child has difficulty with finding root words in affixed words, the teacher can find many and varied exercises in second- and third-grade manuals to teach this skill. The remedial teacher could have the child start with exercises which have simple variant endings on words, such as *walked* or *looking*. As the child improves, the exercises can be increased in difficulty up to those found in fourth- or fifth-grade manuals or workbooks which involve words with prefixes and suffixes, such as *unlikely* or *reworkable*. Teachers' manuals and workbooks accompanying basal readers give exercises and suggested activities that may be used to teach all skills and abilities in reading. The newer basic series of books have lists of these exercises with page references. As she examines the teaching techniques suggested in such materials, the remedial teacher can accumulate a variety of exercises for each of the important types of disabilities. She can keep the program dynamic and interesting to the child by using a variety of teaching techniques and at the same time be sure that the instruction emphasizes the skill development that is needed.

In attempting to use a variety of teaching methods and techniques, care must be taken that the teaching approaches do not confuse the child. The directions given him should be simple, and the teaching techniques should not be changed too often. The exercises should be as nearly like the reading act as possible. Artificial or isolated drills should be avoided. The child should not have to spend time learning complicated procedures or directions. Enough variety should be introduced, however, to keep the program stimulating.

An effective and interesting teaching technique should not be used too long nor so often that it loses its value. A fifth-grade child, for example, may be weak in visualizing what is read. For him, the remedial work is planned to emphasize the ability to form sensory impressions and to stimulate the imagination. The teaching techniques used have him read a story and then draw some illustrations for it. This is an effective means of getting this particular child to visualize as he reads. But remember, if he should have to draw pictures of what he reads every day, he may decide that he would rather not read at all. Variety could be introduced by visualizing for different purposes. At one time, pictures for a play television show might be made; at another time, the child might describe how furniture could be arranged for a creative dramatic presentation; at another time, he might read and tell how he thought the scene of a story looked. All of these purposes would require visualization of what is read.

Basing treatment upon an understanding of the child's instructional needs means that the remedial program is planned after a thorough diagnosis has been made. It does not mean that the program becomes fixed or that further study of the child is unnecessary. It is true that if the basic principles of remedial instruction discussed in this chapter are followed, approximately 65 percent of disabled readers will improve even without diagnosis. However, there will remain somewhere around 35 percent of disabled readers who will not get along well. Aside from those children who are described as cases of simple retardation, there is no way of knowing which children will be among the successful and which will be among the 35 percent for whom the remedial work will fail. Whichever children the failures happen to be, they will probably become even more stubborn cases than they were before the remedial instruction started. Those children who did improve without a diagnosis would have improved even more rapidly if the remedial program had been designed to meet their specific needs. Mass training by common methods is unfortunate even if given the label of remedial instruction.

The reason most programs that attempt to correct reading disability meet with some degree of success is because the children are treated individually and many desirable adjustments are made. Even artificial programs, which are basically poor, will demonstrate a modicum of success if they are given by an enthusiastic teacher because they are given to individual children. Well-rounded remedial programs based on careful and continuous diagnosis, using a variety of teaching techniques and taught by an equally enthusiastic teacher, will give far better results.

Remedial Programs Must Be Highly Individualized

The disabled reader is one who has failed to respond to reading programs that are designed to meet the instructional needs and characteristics of the majority of children. The onset of reading disability is usually gradual. The child who becomes a disabled reader gets into a moderate degree of difficulty, misses some instruction, or in some way falls behind or gets confused. The reading curriculum and the class itself go on, while the child is left farther behind. Soon he finds himself hopelessly out of things. He can no longer read well enough to keep up with his group. He may develop an aversion to reading and he is quite likely to develop unfortunate reading habits. All of these things accumulate until it is apparent to the teacher that the child has become a disabled reader.

He has not learned the skills and abilities essential to effective reading. Faulty habits and unfortunate modes of reading have become established. He is developing or has already developed an attitude of dislike and antagonism toward reading, and his sense of defeat mounts higher and higher.

Such a child's difficulty has been brought about gradually through his failure to progress in the usual fashion. The teacher, confronted with thirty-five other children, at first failed to see the child's need or could not take the time to adjust the instruction to his requirements. The child thus developed an abnormal and unfortunate variation in his reading skills and abilities.

A program designed to treat reading disabilities is based on the assumption that children learn differently and need programs that meet their individual requirements. Such programs must be based on a recognition of a particular child's physical and mental characteristics and must be designed individually to be efficient in overcoming his difficulties.

THE REMEDIAL PROGRAM SHOULD BE IN KEEPING WITH THE CHILD'S CHARACTERISTICS

The expected outcomes of instruction and the methods used in achieving these outcomes will need to conform to the child's characteristics. If the child is lacking in general intelligence, he can neither be expected to reach the ultimate stature in reading of children of greater mental capability nor can he be expected to progress as rapidly. The remedial teacher will be wise to modify the outcomes of the program. The prognosis for rate of gain is usually directly proportional to the general intelligence of the child. In addition to lowering the results she expects, the remedial teacher would be wise to modify the methods of instruction also to meet the slow-learning child's needs. Such children need more concrete experiences, more carefully given directions, and more emphasis on repetition and drill than do children of higher intelligence.

If a child has poor vision or poor hearing, modifications in methods will need to be made. Such limitations make learning to read more difficult but in no way preclude the child from achieving. Deaf children have been taught to read about as effectively as their contemporaries with normal hearing when methods of instruction were adjusted to their needs. Children with marked visual defects have learned to read well, but they are more likely to get into difficulty. The disabled reader with lesser degrees of sensory handicaps can be taught more efficiently if his limitations are known and modifications in methods of instruction are made. The nature of the adjustments in methods that have proven helpful will be discussed fully later in this book.

REMEDIAL INSTRUCTION SHOULD BE SPECIFIC, NOT GENERAL

The remedial teacher should focus instruction upon the specific reading needs of the child. The diagnosis has usually indicated that there is something specifically wrong with the pattern of the child's reading performance. One child, for example, may have learned to read with speed but falls short of the accuracy required in certain situations. Such a child should be given material to read that has factual content and he should read it for purposes that demand the exact recall of those facts. Another child may be so overconcerned with detail that he reads extremely slowly, looking for more facts than the author wrote. He becomes so concerned with the detail that he cannot understand the author's over-all intent. The teacher, in this latter case, would be specifically endeavoring to make the child less compulsive so that the rate of reading and its outcomes can become compatible with the purposes of this particular reading.

The principle that remedial instruction should be specific and not general means that the remedial teacher should emphasize those phases of reading development that will correct the child's reading limitation. It does not mean that just one type of exercise should be employed nor does it mean that a specific skill or ability should be isolated and receive drill. In the case of a disabled reader who has an insufficient knowledge of the larger visual and structural elements used in word recognition, the teacher would be making an error if she used a method that gave isolated drill on word elements. A more effective procedure would be to have the child read a basal reader at the proper level of difficulty. He would read for the purposes suggested in the manual, but when he encountered a word-recognition problem, the teacher would help him by emphasizing the larger elements in the word. When the exercises given in the manual for developing basic skills and abilities were studied, the remedial teacher would have this child do the ones that gave him experience in using the larger visual and structural parts of the words. The teacher could construct some additional exercises that would provide experiences with the larger elements in words the child already knew so that he could learn to use these in recognizing new words. Types of exercises suggested in manuals of other basic reading series using vocabulary known to the child could also be used in constructing these teacher-made materials.

The workbook exercises accompanying the basic reader should be used. The disabled reader may need to have certain pages selected for him so that he does not have to do all the exercises. This must be done, because the child has an uneven profile and he may have emphasized one phase of reading instruction to the detriment of another. The child who needs a greater knowledge of large visual and structural elements may have failed to develop them because he had overemphasized phonetic letter-by-letter sounding in word recognition. Such a child should avoid for the time being the exercises that teach the knowledge of letter sounds.

Children have been given remedial instruction by various procedures at the University of Minnesota Psycho-educational Clinic. Children who were taught by using a regular developmental reading program, modified to emphasize those skills in which a given child needed further training and to minimize those which he had overemphasized, showed far greater gains than did the children who were taught by isolated drill exercises. It is to be concluded that remedial training is best done in nicely controlled reading programs such as are found in basic readers, but with modifications to meet the instructional needs of each child.

REMEDIAL INSTRUCTION SHOULD BE ENERGETIC

Growth in reading presupposes an energetic learner. Of course, the child must learn to read by reading. He must attack the printed page vigorously and often if he is to succeed. A fatigued child cannot be expected to make gains during the remedial period. Therefore, the length of the period for remedial instruction should be such that concentrated work is possible. The disabled reader frequently finds it difficult to attend to reading for any considerable length of time. His lack of attention may be due to a variety of causes. In one case it may be lack of physical stamina, while in another it may be that he is not getting enough sleep at night, or it may be that his emotional reactions to reading sap his vitality. His inattention or lack of vigor may be due to habits of escaping from an unsuccessful and uncomfortable situation. Whatever the cause, most children if properly motivated can apply themselves to the reading situation at least for a short period of time. Obviously, if the lack of attention and vigor result from a condition that can be corrected, the correction should be made. In any case, the length of the remedial reading period should be adjusted so that an energetic attack can be maintained.

Frequently it is necessary to divide the remedial sessions into short periods. The child may work with the remedial teacher for a period of forty-five minutes. At the start of the remedial training, it may be necessary to have him read from a basic reader for only ten minutes for specific purposes and then have him use the results of his reading in some creative activity, such as drawing, constructing, modeling, discussing, or the like. Then the child might work on some skill development exercises which emphasize the training he needs. These exercises might entail rereading the material he read at the first part of the session or they may be word-recognition drill on new words introduced in the basic reader. Finally, the child might be asked to tell about the book he has been reading independently. As he gains in reading growth, the length of concentrated reading time should be increased. Soon the child who has no physical limitation will be reading longer without interruption. When this is so, the use of creative activities can be less frequent. Then the child can read for several days during the remedial periods before he utilizes the results of reading. He will still need to discuss what he has read and do the exercises suited to him as suggested in the manual or as found in the workbook.

Remedial Instruction Must Be Organized Instruction

Reading instruction in both the developmental and remedial aspects must be well organized. The skills and abilities grow gradually as the child meets more complex applications of each. There is a tendency for remedial teachers to neglect the sequences involved in teaching the child each of the basic areas. In word recognition, remedial work is often erroneously given in one phase before the child has developed the learning that should precede it. The child may, for example, lack ability to break words into syllables, so the remedial teacher gives him exercises to develop that skill. A study of the sequence in word-recognition techniques might show that the child had many other learnings to master before he could be expected to be successful in this relatively mature approach to word recognition.

In order that growth in word recognition may develop smoothly, with no undue burden upon the learner who is already in difficulty, a gradual, orderly sequence must be maintained. Such organization is necessary so that there will be no omissions in developing the essential skills, so that there will be little chance for overemphasis, and so that new skills are introduced to the child when he has the necessary prerequisites for learning them. In learning to recognize words, the child should first establish the habit of left-to-right orientation before he is allowed to employ any detailed analytical attacks. He should also learn to recognize word wholes when he knows them, rather than to employ analysis; to use the context and initial elements before he is encouraged to attend to variant endings; and to form the habit of viewing the word systematically from start to finish before he is required to visually separate the words into syllables.

The child who is in confusion in reading requires even more systematic instruction than does the child who is learning without difficulty. The remedial teacher must either be completely aware what sequence of learning is desirable in all the areas of reading growth or she must use the basal reading material in which the orderly development of skills has been carefully planned. The remedial teacher cannot afford to use haphazard approaches. She must follow the sequence and explain carefully each new step in it. Therefore, the most successful remedial teachers find it expedient to use basic reading programs, modified to fit the child's specific needs, whatever they may be.

The Reading Processes Must Be Made Meaningful to the Learner

One reason why the disabled reader is in difficulty is because he does not understand the processes involved in being a good reader. The remedial teacher has the responsibility not only for maintaining orderly sequences of skill development but also for making the steps involved meaningful to the child. The teacher should not only teach the child to use context clues in word recognition, but also she should let the child see how helpful such an aid to word recognition can be. The teacher should show the child how to organize the material he reads for effective retention. She should, in addition, let the child understand why such an organization is effective. The child should be led to understand the importance of reading certain material carefully with attention to detail, while other material can be read rapidly to understand the general ideas it advances.

If the remedial teacher expects the child to retain a knowledge of word elements, it is important for her to show him how much they will aid him in recognizing new words. For too long, many remedial teachers have felt that if the child is stimulated to read material at the correct level of difficulty he will automatically develop the needed skills. This point of view can be seriously questioned. A more reasonable assumption is that the child should be shown how to go about his reading and how much use he can make of each added reading accomplishment. Suppose a child, for example, has learned by rote to pronounce prefixed words. How much better it would have been to point out to him the prefixes in those words and show him how they change the meaning of the root words.

The remedial teacher will find that making the processes of reading meaningful to the learner helps to solve his reading confusions. Drill on isolated parts of words is not as effective as is a meaningful approach to reading. Modern developmental reading programs are planned to enable the child to develop the needed skills and abilities and to understand the usefulness of each. The remedial program should be concerned even more with making reading processes meaningful to the child. The day has long since passed when it was assumed that if we but interested the child in reading, he would effectively go ahead on his own to develop skills of which he was unaware.

Consideration of the Child's Personal Worth Is Necessary

The disabled reader frequently feels insecure and defeated in school. Any remedial program designed to treat reading disabilities must make the child feel his successes from the start. It must also take into account the child's sense of personal worth. The child who is in serious trouble in reading is often antagonistic toward reading and thoroughly dislikes it. He would like to wake up some morning knowing how to read, but he believes there is something wrong with him that precludes his learning to read. Frequently he thinks that he is mentally incapable of learning or that he has some other defect. Often he has a poor estimate of himself as a person.

Remedial programs should consider the fact that the disabled reader builds a barrier between himself and all reading instruction. One of the first tasks of a remedial teacher is to gain the child's confidence. Resistance to the remedial program will be magnified if the child is classified in any unfortunate way. Whenever the remedial work is to be done by the classroom teacher, the child should be a working member of that class. He should be able to enter into the various activities even though his part in them is meager.

If it is necessary to give a child remedial training in the school reading center, great care must be taken when the work starts. Remedial programs should be considered a privilege and should be entered voluntarily. When the remedial groups are made up, it is strategic to include in them the brightest children who are disabled readers. These children are known to be bright and capable in other areas of the school curriculum and so the other children will see that the program is for able children who are having some specific difficulty. Another reason for selecting the more able children to start with, is that in their instances there is a greater chance for rapid improvement. This will enable the program to get off to a good start and will make it possible to do the most service to the greatest number. Besides, such an approach will place the remedial work in its proper perspective of being special instruction in reading rather than a class designed for the mentally inept.

In many schools, cases are selected for remedial work by sending the four or five poorest readers from each room to the reading center. This is an unfortunate practice. As has been previously explained, the poorest readers in the room are not necessarily the children who will profit from remedial instruction in reading. Many such children are essentially slow learners. They are not disabled readers. Only children who are properly classified as reading disability cases should be sent to the school reading center for remedial instruction. Another tendency is to refer disciplinary and delinquent children to the reading center for individual work or for work in the smaller group. While it is true that many delinquent and disciplinary cases are poor readers, it is unwise to give the remedial teacher too large a number of these children at any one time. The correction of reading disability is a difficult task and if too many kinds of problems are concentrated in any one group, the teacher cannot hope to be successful. Also, the reading center will acquire a reputation as a place for misfits.

In general, it is desirable to inaugurate remedial work with children who have the following characteristics: (1) general intelligence of over 90 as measured by suitable tests; (2) children who have asked to be admitted after the work has been discussed with them; (3) children whose parents have requested such service; (4) children who are classified as having reading disability as their major problem; (5) not too great a proportion of children with behavior problems at any one time.

Frequently the disabled reader is emotionally tense or insecure. He has had no real opportunity to gain confidence in himself because most of the school day involves reading. For some time he has been much less effective in school work than his intellectual level would indicate that he should be. Such a child may become submissive or demanding, aggressive or withdrawn, or show his basic insecurity in a variety of ways. He may develop attitudes of indifference, dislike, or rejection. He may resist help, display few interests, and be antagonistic toward reading instruction. Remedial reading programs must overcome these unfortunate attitudes and compensatory modes of behavior. One of the first responsibilities of the remedial teacher is to develop in the child a need for learning to read. The second is to gain the child's confidence to such a degree that he will know a personal interest is being taken in him and that now his reading problem is going to be solved. A direct attack on the reading problem by a businesslike, considerate adult will do much to overcome tensions and faulty attitudes. When a child recognizes that an interest is taken in him and his problem, it will give him the much-needed sense of personal worth and the confidence in himself that he has hitherto lacked.

The Reading Program Must Be Encouraging to the Child

Most disabled readers are discouraged about their failure to learn to read. They frequently think that they cannot learn. This lack of confidence in their ability to learn is detrimental to possible reading growth.

The effective learner is a confident and purposeful learner, one who has a desire to learn and finds pleasure in working toward his goal. In order that a child may go ahead rapidly in learning to read, it is necessary for him to know that he can learn and to see that he is progressing satisfactorily.

There are several principles underlying remedial instruction that give the child this sense of confidence he needs. The following principles will help to give the child the necessary encouragement:

1. The teacher must be optimistic.
2. The child needs group as well as individual work.
3. The child's successes should be emphasized.
4. A positive approach should be used in pointing out errors.
5. His growth in reading should be pointed out to the child.
6. Remedial programs should not be substituted for enjoyable activities.
7. Remedial programs must be pleasant and free from undue pressures.

THE TEACHER MUST BE OPTIMISTIC

A teacher who would help a child to overcome a reading disabilty should be a buoyant, energetic person. She must make the child sense her confidence in him. At times, the problems involved in correcting a complex reading disability may seem to her to entail almost insurmountable teaching problems. Nevertheless, the teacher must approach each disabled reader showing that she knows he will learn to read. Such an attitude is an outgrowth of a thorough understanding of the instructional needs of the child, that is, a sound diagnosis, and of having the remedial program planned well enough in advance so that the general nature of remedial instruction is clearly in mind. In addition, the teacher gains immediate confidence through knowing exactly what is going to be undertaken during each remedial lesson. A well-prepared teacher who knows exactly where each session is going will instill confidence in the child. With this preparation, progress in reading ordinarily takes place.

The teacher may well be optimistic, because the vast majority of reading disability cases do show immediate gains from remedial instruction. If the child's reading problem and his characteristics have been carefully appraised and if the program has been carefully formulated, success is almost assured. Of course, the teacher's confidence may sometimes, and from time to time, be shaken. There are periods during the corrective treatment of practically every remedial case when there is little evidence of new growth. But all the same, confidence in the child's ultimate success must be maintained even when things do not appear to be going well. Under some circumstances the remedial program should be restudied and the diagnosis reviewed, but all this need not lessen confidence in the child's ultimate success.

THE CHILD NEEDS GROUP AS WELL AS INDIVIDUAL WORK

The disabled reader needs to share experiences with other children just as much as, or even more than, the child whose growth in reading is normal. Not only should his classroom work be organized so that he can participate in some of the important activities with which the class is concerning itself, but also it is beneficial for the child who is in difficulty to see that there are other children who are having similar difficulties. It is therefore recommended that whenever it is possible to have disabled readers work in groups, this should be undertaken. Much good can be gained by the disabled reader in seeing other children right around him who are in a like difficulty, and who are making progress in overcoming it. It is sometimes assumed that remedial reading instruction is a formal procedure in which the child is separated from other children and drilled until his disability is corrected. Such instruction is most unwise. It is a boost to the child to know that there are other children who are learning to read and who are able to use their newly gained proficiencies in group situations.

The summer program of the University of Minnesota Psycho-educational Clinic provides a good illustration of how both individual and group remedial work can be made available to the child. Of course, in the school reading center or in the typical reading clinic, slight modifications would have to be made. The children who come to the summer reading clinic at the University of Minnesota are, for the most part, extremely disabled readers. The great majority of them would be described as complex or limiting disability cases. The most successful approach that we have been able to devise for these children has been to separate them into groups or classes of about 15 to 20 children. They work with a classroom teacher for an entire morning. In the classroom work, there is a regular unit of instruction, using topics to be found in readers and selected so as to be at the reading level at which the greatest number in the class can read comfortably. These topics are supplemented by additional reference books in the room. For some of the children, picture books or pictures in books which supply information are used. In addition to the unit the children are reading about, there is group instruction using basal material at the appropriate level for each group within the class. Then for a period of from a half hour to an hour every day, each child is withdrawn from the class, either in small groups of four or five or for individual instruction, whichever is deemed best from the nature of the case. In this situation, the children are given remedial instruction designed to overcome their specific remedial problems. Children in the same major classification of disability form the small groups. Children who do not fit into any groups are handled individually. In a typical school reading center, the remedial reading teacher would not have additional personnel to handle small groups. Therefore the modification recommended for the school reading center would be to have those children who were less seriously retarded or who constituted a very similar type of disability, such as the slow readers, brought together for instruction in relatively large groups. Those children with more complex disabilities could be handled in smaller sections. Such group sessions could be conducted during the morning. Then the remedial teacher would be free in the afternoon to handle smaller groups or work with certain individual children whom she had observed during the morning sessions were in need of additional help.

THE CHILD'S SUCCESSES SHOULD BE EMPHASIZED

In order that the remedial program may be encouraging to the child, his successes rather than his mistakes should be emphasized. Teachers have a tendency to point out errors to children rather than to make them feel that for the most part they are doing particularly well. A child whose errors are continually focused upon may become overwhelmed by a sense of defeat. A wise teacher will start the child in a remedial program that is somewhat easy for him so that his successful performance will be immediately apparent. As he gains confidence, the difficulty of the reading situations may be increased. The teacher should always be quick to recognize when the child has put forth a real effort and has done something well. Many times, particularly at the start, recognition will have to be given for activities related to the reading rather than the reading itself. Gradually the teacher will find increased opportunities to give praise for the actual reading that is well done. At all times it should be remembered that the effectiveness of remedial instruction depends in no small measure upon the child's gain in confidence. This gain in confidence is brought about through successful experiences with reading which in the past had caused the child so much difficulty.

A POSITIVE APPROACH SHOULD BE USED IN POINTING OUT ERRORS

The emphasis upon success does not mean that errors are to be altogether overlooked. The faulty reading of a child must of course be brought to his attention. Errors in word recognition must be pointed out. Faulty habits in reading which limit his speed must be recognized by him before they can be corrected. Sometimes it is necessary to demand greater exactness in reading on the part of the child. While it is true that the teacher must point out the child's mistakes, she must at all times indicate that the child is improving and that for the most part he is really doing well. If, for example, a child should call the word *house, horse* in the sentence "The dog ran up to the house," the teacher should point out to him that he had the sentence nearly correct, but that in order to be exactly right he should have looked at the center part of the last word a little more carefully. As a matter of fact, the child did recognize most of the words in the sentence. He made an error that indicated that he was using the context well and that his error was a very slight one indeed. The words *house* and *horse* do look much alike.

In a comprehension lesson, the child may give the wrong answer to a question. Instead of saying that the answer is wrong and calling on another child in the group, it would be far better for the teacher to say, "Let's see what the book says about this" and then find out wherein the child made his error. It will frequently be found that he did not understand the meaning of a word or that he failed to notice a key word such as *not*, or that he had not grouped the words into proper thought units. Whatever the cause of his error, it should be located and the child should be shown the correct way to read the passage. The attitude of the teacher should be not one of pointing out errors but one of helping the child learn to read.

GROWTH IN READING SHOULD BE DEMONSTRATED TO THE CHILD

The disabled reader needs to have his growth demonstrated to him. There are many ways in which reading growth can be shown. The diagnostician has isolated the child's needs in this regard and indicated the amount of emphasis that should be given. It will be recalled that the method for demonstrating the progress of the child to him depends upon the nature of the reading problem. If, for example, the child is trying to develop a sight vocabulary, he could make a picture dictionary of the words he was trying to learn. As the dictionary became larger, the child would recognize that he had increased his sight vocabulary. The child who is working on accuracy of comprehension could develop a bar chart (Fig. 1) in which he would indicate his level of percent of accuracy on successive periods. If such a child failed to gain over the period of a week, the teacher could simplify the material or ask more general questions so that accuracy would increase. Then, as the child gained confidence, the difficulty of the material could be gradually increased again. It is a good plan for the child to go back, from time to time, and reread something that he has read previously. He will discover that material that was difficult for him a short while ago is now relatively easy for him

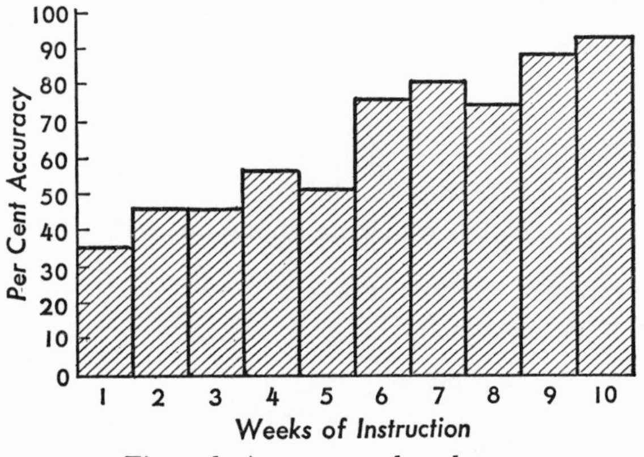

Figure 1. An accuracy bar chart.

to read. This will be especially true if the teacher takes time to develop the necessary readiness prior to the reading.

Whatever the nature of the difficulty, it is important for the remedial program to be organized to demonstrate to the child that he is progressing toward his goal of better reading. The child who has been in difficulty for a long time needs whatever encouragement can be given him. He needs not only to be in a comfortable learning situation, but also to see that he is making effective advancement in reading.

REMEDIAL PROGRAMS SHOULD NOT BE SUBSTITUTED FOR ENJOYABLE ACTIVITIES

The remedial teacher must so organize the periods of instruction that children are not required to come for training at a time that competes with other activities of great importance to them. For example, it is a frequent practice to have children come to a clinic for remedial instruction after school. This is a decidedly unfortunate time for a boy who enjoys outdoor sports with his friends, and who finds this the only time that such outdoor games are played in his neighborhood. In scheduling summer reading programs, it is wise to delay their start until a week or so after school is out and the children have found that they have time that they do not know what to do with. Even then the better scheduling time for classes is probably in the morning, because the majority of things that the child likes to do, such as going swimming or playing baseball, are done in the afternoon.

The busy classroom teacher frequently finds it difficult to give an individual child attention he needs when the class is in session. She may therefore select recess time or the time in which other children have their hobby clubs, or are in the auditorium viewing a movie, for helping a child with his reading. Such a practice is understandable but is unfortunate for the correction of a reading disability. A better time would be to work with the children needing re-education while the rest of the children are busily engaged in studying or reading independently. Whatever time is used for giving remedial help, it is important that it does not conflict with activities which are important to the child.

REMEDIAL PROGRAMS MUST BE PLEASANT AND FREE FROM UNDUE PRESSURES

An effective remedial program must be one that is satisfying to the child, makes him feel that he is getting along well, and keeps at a minimum any anxiety which he feels about his reading progress. The teacher's responsibility in encouraging the child to read energetically is indeed great. She should neither unduly hurry the child nor allow him to dawdle; she should be sure the child is working hard and yet avoid putting undue pressure on him. Most children, in fact practically all children, can be expected to work intently in developing reading ability. This is especially true if the reading materials are at the right level, if the child is properly motivated, and if he is reading for purposes that are real to him. There should always be a friendly atmosphere, but an atmosphere that keeps uppermost the point of view that the child is there to learn to read.

Materials and Exercises Must Be Suitable to the Child's Reading Ability and Instructional Needs

The selection of appropriate material for remedial work in reading is one of the most important problems the remedial teacher has to solve. Some teachers feel that the most important element in the problem is that the material should deal with a subject in which the child is interested. Others feel that the level of difficulty of the material is of even greater importance. Still others believe that having the type of material that is compatible with the nature of the remedial instruction is of paramount importance. There can be no doubt that all three of these elements enter into the selection of appropriate material for remedial instruction. Without trying to decide here between them, we may conclude that the more important considerations in selecting material are:

1. The materials must be suitable in level of difficulty.
2. The materials must be suitable in type.
3. The materials must be at the appropriate level of interest and format.
4. The materials must be abundant.

THE MATERIALS MUST BE SUITABLE IN LEVEL OF DIFFICULTY

The child grows in reading by reading; therefore the material that is used for remedial instruction should be of a difficulty level that enables the child to read comfortably and with enjoyment. The diagnostician will have suggested the level of difficulty of the material the child could be expected to read. The remedial teacher must pick out materials at that level to suit the child. The difficulty of material can be judged in many ways. Readability formulas, such as the Lorge formula, the formula of Dale-Chall, and that of Spache have proven useful in estimating the reading level of materials. Most of the basic readers are carefully graded and indicate the level of reading maturity necessary for their use. In general, of course, books of second-grade level are suitable to the child whose skills are of second-grade maturity. Third-grade books are suitable for the child whose basic skill development is approximately that of a third-grade child. Ungraded books can be estimated by a formula or by using a basic reading series as a difficulty rating scale. The difficulty of an ungraded library book may be judged by comparing it with the various grade levels of a basic reader. For example, a library book can be compared with a third-grade reader. If it is judged to be harder, it may then be compared with a fourth-grade reader, and so forth, until the approximate level of difficulty can be estimated. In making the judgment, the teacher should look at the number of unusual words it contains, the length of its sentences, the number of prepositional phrases, the number of unusual word orders, the complexity of the ideas it includes. In judging level of difficulty, it is important that the remedial teacher remember that the results of standardized survey tests tend to give an overestimation of the skill development of a reading disability case. Therefore, it is usually wise to start remedial instruction with material that is somewhat lower than the child's general reading score as indicated by standardized tests.

The difficulty of the material that is suitable for remedial instruction will vary somewhat with the nature of the child's disability. The teacher should modify the general estimate of level of difficulty according to the outcomes of instruction to be achieved by the use of that material. For example, if the child's major problem is one of developing sight vocabulary, the material should be relatively easy with few new words being introduced. Those that are introduced should be used often in the material. For such a child, a relatively easy level in a basic reading program would be desirable. On the other hand, for the child who is trying to analyze words effectively, a higher concentration of new vocabulary would be desirable. The child could well afford to meet one new word in approximately every 20 running words. This would give him an opportunity to employ the techniques of word analysis that he needs to develop and at the same time it will enable him to maintain the thought of the passage so that context clues can be used as a means of checking the accuracy of his word recognition.

A child who is trying to increase his speed of comprehension, should use material that is for him definitely easy. Such material would have few if any word-recognition problems for him. On the other hand, the child who is trying to increase his power of comprehension should use material with which he must tussle, but he must have a reasonable chance of successfully comprehending the material.

THE MATERIALS MUST BE SUITABLE IN TYPE

It is often said that any kind of material that is suitable for teaching reading in the first place is suitable for remedial instruction. While this is true, it is important to recognize that the material must be nicely selected to meet the child's instructional needs. The type of material that is suitable for one kind of disability is not necessarily suitable for another. If the child's major problem is that of increasing his speed of reading, the most suitable material would be short stories whose plots unfold rapidly. The material should not only be easy in regard to reading difficulty, but the nature of the content should be such that the child can read it to gain a general impression or the general significance of the story. If, on the other hand, the child's problem is one in the word-recognition area, a basic reader along with the exercises found in the manuals and the workbooks related to the word-recognition problem would be the most desirable type of reading material to use. If the child's problem is in the comprehension area and it is desired to increase his accuracy in reading, material in science or in social studies that has considerable factual information should be used. In every instance, the material should be at the appropriate level of difficulty, but also in every instance, the material should be of a type that is appropriate to the outcomes of reading expected.

THE MATERIALS MUST BE AT THE APPROPRIATE LEVEL OF INTEREST AND FORMAT

A relatively mature and intelligent 12-year-old will usually not find first- and second-grade material interesting, nor will he find the format very attractive. Such a child with second-grade reading ability must nevertheless use material that he can read. The problem facing the remedial teacher in this respect is very great. The second-grade book is designed for a child who is 7 or 8 years of age. The pictures in it are of small children and its print looks large and juvenile. The topics dealt with in the book are appropriate to the 7- or 8-year-old and not to a 12-year-old. Therefore, many books that are used for remedial reading instruction lose some of their value because they lack interest and have the wrong format. In such a case, however, there can be no compromise with the need for using material that is at the suitable level of difficulty. The problem resolves itself, then, into how to find material that is of a suitable level of difficulty and is as appealing as possible to a child of more mature age.

An increasingly large number of books suitable for remedial work are being developed. There are those books that are primarily designed for the less capable reader. They include such useful books as *The Cowboy Sam Series, The Deep-Sea Adventure Series, Everyreader Series, The Morgan Bay Mysteries*, and *Interesting Reading Series*.

There has been an increase, happily, in the amount of published material designed to give effective aid in developing the skills of disabled readers who are diagnosed as having specific instructional needs. Such materials as are found in *The Macmillan Reading Spectrum, Classroom Reading Clinic*, and *The S.R.A. Reading Laboratories* are suitable for correcting some of the deficiencies in skills of disabled readers.

Phonetically regular materials and certain word-recognition skill books are useful for children who are found to be unable to progress at a normal pace toward satisfactory proficiency in word recognition. Such series as *Phonetic Reader Series, Breaking the Sound Barrier, Eye and Ear Fun, and Phonics We Use* will prove helpful in this respect when used judiciously.

A new type of material that appears to have merit for use with disabled readers is programmed learning material. An example of reading exercise material of this kind is *Programmed Reading*. Other organized learning programs should be forthcoming shortly.

Basic reading programs are being developed that have parallel readers, such as the Regular and Classmate Editions of the *Developmental Reading Series*. In this series of readers, there are two editions which are alike in all important respects. They have the same covers, the same titles, pictures, content, and interest level. The difference lies in the fact that the classmate edition is written with a smaller vocabulary load, shorter paragraphs, simpler sentences, and fewer words per page. The classmate editions are considerably easier in reading difficulty than are the regular editions. The sixth-grade book in the regular edition requires sixth-grade reading ability, whereas the same stories can be read in the classmate edition by children who have only third-grade reading ability.

The workbooks that accompany basic readers are also suitable material. The workbooks look considerably more mature than the basic readers they accompany. The pictures are in black and white. The drill exercises give no indication of the maturity level of the children who are expected to read them. There are many lists of books that are suitable for use in remedial work. Many of these lists indicate the level of reading maturity which is required to read the books and also indicate the maximum age of a child who will enjoy reading the material.

THE MATERIALS MUST BE ABUNDANT

In selecting material for remedial work, the first and most important consideration is that it must be of the proper level of difficulty. The second is that it should be appropriate in type. The third is that it should be interesting in format and meet the interest level of the child. Another consideration in securing materials to be used in remedial reading is that they should be abundant. There should be a wide variety of material meeting many interests and at various levels of difficulty. For any one child, there should be ample material suitable for him to read. There should be material for his remedial instruction and also material for his independent reading. The independent reading for a remedial reading case should be considerably easier than that used in giving him remedial instruction. The material for independent reading needs to be on a wide variety of topics because the children will have a wide variety of interests. The material that the child is to read independently should fulfill an existing interest which the child already has, while the material that is used for instructional purposes must be such that he can be motivated to take an interest in reading.

Sound Teaching Procedures Must Be Employed

During the entire discussion of principles for treatment of reading difficulties, it has been implied that remedial instruction is the application of sound teaching procedures directed toward the specific needs of the child. Instruction in remedial reading is not unusual in character, nor is it necessary to use expensive and artificial equipment. The skills and abilities should be emphasized in actual reading situations free from isolated drill. Sound teaching procedures such as those used for introducing the reading skills and abilities in the first place should be used. The materials best suited to remedial instruction are those that are best for the developmental program.

The difference between remedial instruction and the developmental program is in the extent of individualization and in the study of the child rather than in the uniqueness of the methods or materials it employs. There are certain principles of reading instruction that are sometimes neglected in remedial work. Readiness should be carefully built for every topic and every selection to be read by the disabled reader.

This includes the creation of interest in, the development of background for, and the introduction of new words for each selection the child reads. The child who is in difficulty in reading, just as much as other children who are not, should have the purposes for reading well understood before the reading is done. He should also use the results of his reading in a creative enterprise of one sort or another. If, for example, he has read a selection about flood control to find what techniques are used, it would be important for him to make a diagram of a river bed illustrating what he had learned, just as it would be for children in the developmental reading program. Seeing that children use the results of their reading is a good procedure for all children. It becomes an essential practice, though an often neglected one, for children who are in difficulty in reading. The form of use to which the results of reading are put may be a discussion, a picture drawn, a chart made, a map planned, or any one of many such enterprises. The relative amount of time devoted to these things should be small, however, and above all, the creative work should be the child's own.

Consideration must be given to the learning environment of the child both in and out of school. Whether the remedial work is done in the classroom, the school reading center, or the clinic, only a small segment of the child's reading is done during the corrective lessons. If the remedial program is to be successful, the rest of the child's reading day must be adjusted to his needs and reading capabilities. The effective work of the remedial periods can be destroyed if unfortunate demands or pressures are placed upon the child either in school or at home. As has been stated earlier, both the classroom teacher and the parents will be willing to co-operate if they are given an understanding of the child's reading problem. The parents are often endeavoring to help the child with his reading, and this is as it should be, but the remedial teacher should consult with them so that their work will be of the greatest benefit to the child. Bond and Wagner show many ways in which parents can help a child to grow in reading.

The remedial teacher will find it helpful to keep a cumulative account of the child's progress. The record should include the books read, the type of exercises used and the success of each, any charts used to show the child his progress, and the results of periodic tests. In this connection, any indications of fields of interests and anecdotal accounts of the child's reactions to the remedial program will be a help. By studying this record, the teacher can compare periods of rapid growth with the type of exercises used and books read at those times. A study of past records will recall to the teacher those approaches that were successful with other similar cases. The teacher can assemble a file of such folders, arranged according to the specific problem involved.

A Carefully Designed Follow-Up Program Is Necessary

When the child has made sufficient progress to permit his release from the concentrated remedial program, he should gradually be put into situations where he must rely to an increasing extent on his own resources. All such children should be carefully followed up by the classroom teacher. For many, continued reinforcements by means of further remedial help are most important. In a study of the long-term effects of remedial reading instruction, Balow found that continued remedial training, amounting to a long-term treatment rather than a short-course, is desirable. He concludes that concentrated remedial work gives remarkable results, but that "severe reading disability is probably best considered a relatively chronic illness needing long-term treatment rather than the short course typically organized in current programs.

Many of the children with less severe reading difficulties may be able to make the adjustment into regular classroom work. Even these children may become discouraged again if their work does not go well after they finish remedial instruction. Any indications of loss of interest or of confusions in learning should get immediate attention by the classroom teacher during the readjustment period.

Summary

Although the remedial work for each disabled reader must be different in certain respects, there are some common elements among the corrective programs. The remedial program must be designed to emphasize the child's instructional needs as shown by the diagnosis, and therefore there can be no universal approach in all cases. The remedial program for each reading case must be carefully planned and what is to be done should be written down. It will be necessary to modify the program from time to time in order to keep abreast of the child's changing instructional needs. Even though the program is well planned to give emphasis on overcoming a specific disability, a variety of remedial techniques should be used. The remedial teacher will find manuals and workbooks that accompany basal reading programs the most fruitful source of teaching techniques.

Remedial reading programs must be highly individualized and they must be designed in keeping with the child's instructional needs and characteristics. It is necessary to modify the approaches to reading in order to adjust to such limitation as poor hearing or poor vision. Remedial instruction should not drill upon one specific skill or ability in isolation, but should provide new experience in whatever skills are needed in connection with purposeful reading. The length of remedial sessions should be so planned that the child will not become fatigued or inattentive.

Reading instruction for the disabled reader must be well organized in order that skills and abilities may be developed smoothly with no undue burden for the child, with little chance for overemphasis, and with no omissions of essential learnings. The teacher should not only maintain an orderly sequence of skill development but also should make the steps involved meaningful to the child.

The remedial reading program must be encouraging to the child, since much of his trouble arose because he had lost confidence in his ability to learn. The teacher should be optimistic; the child's successes should be emphasized; and his progress should be demonstrated to him. Materials must be suitable to the child's reading abilities and instructional needs; they should be suitable in level of difficulty and type of content; they should be as nearly as possible appropriate in level of interest; and they should look "mature" to the child. The materials used for remedial instruction must be of such difficulty that the child can read them and of such maturity that he will be motivated to read them. There can be no compromise with the difficulty level of the material because the child will not be interested in reading material he cannot read, no matter how attractive the subject matter. In all remedial work, sound teaching procedures should be used and artificial devices and isolated drill should be avoided.

Selected Readings

Blair, G. M., *Diagnostic and remedial teaching,* rev. ed. New York: Macmillan, 1956, Chap. 4.

Bond, G. L., and Wagner, E. B., *Child growth in reading.* Chicago: Lyons & Carnahan, 1955, Chap. 11.

Bond, G. L., and Wagner, E. B., *Teaching the child to read,* 4th ed. New York: Macmillan, 1966, Chap. 16.

Brueckner, L. J., and Bond, G. L., *Diagnosis and treatment of learning difficulties.* New York: Appleton-Century-Crofts, 1955, Chap. 5.

Durrell, Donald D., *Improving reading instruction.* New York: Harcourt, Brace & World, 1956, Chap. 14.

Gates, Arthur I., *The improvement of reading,* 3rd ed. New York: Macmillan, 1947, Chap. 5.

Harris, Albert J., *How to increase reading ability,* 4th ed. New York: McKay, 1961.

Kottmeyer, William, *Teacher's guide for remedial reading.* St. Louis: Webster, 1959.

Tinker, Miles A., and McCullough, C. M., *Teaching elementary reading,* 2nd ed. New York: Appleton-Century-Crofts, 1962, Chap. 12.

IX. Evaluating the Reading Program

The importance of evaluation cannot be overemphasized. As Ross stated it: "Without some form of evaluation everything about education becomes a matter of blindly hoping all is well."[1]

Meaningful evaluation, according to Tyler (58), is not possible without clearly defined objectives. And these are hard to come by. It is true that most teachers have broad, general ideas that are designed to serve as goals or guides. But for evaluative purposes, goals must be specifically defined. Teachers must be able to answer questions such as these: "What are we trying to help students acquire? What abilities, skills, attitudes, habits, etc. do students need if they are to profit from their reading?" Could you, as a teacher, answer questions such as these?

All teachers want to do a good job of teaching reading. How can they evaluate their teaching efficiency? Letton (59) is helpful in this regard. She gives us some practical, informal ways for measuring the oral and silent reading skill of our pupils. To assist teachers in measuring reading comprehension, Letton describes five levels or types of questions that can be employed. These are: factual, reorganizational, inferential, interpretive, and evaluative. She also tells us how teachers can secure the help of parents in evaluating the reading interests and attitudes of pupils.

An awareness of the necessity for evaluating pupils' reading needs and levels of achievement has been with us for a long

[1] C. C. Ross, *Measurement in Today's Schools* (Englewood Cliffs, N. J.: Prentice-Hall, Inc., 1947), p. 490.

time. In 1935, a research bulletin of the National Education Association devoted space to the subject, "Determining Reading Achievement" (60). Not only did the study deal with teachers' reactions to various aspects of testing but it reported the percentage of teachers who had not formulated definite goals and standards relevant to pupils' reading achievement. In this regard, how do you think today's teachers compare with teachers in the 1930's?

In order to determine the achievement levels of students in regard to clearly defined goals, formal testing is necessary. Torgerson (61) tells us what, in general, constitutes an adequate testing program. He describes the need and value of objective testing in our schools. Questions such as the following are answered: How may reading tests be used to determine growth in reading? How may they be used to discover individual reading difficulties?

Unfortunately, standardized reading tests have many limitations. Traxler (62) sets forth the limitations as well as the values of standardized reading tests. He points out that if reading is an associative thinking process, what are we measuring when we probe the ability to think about reading material? Reading ability or intelligence? This is only one of several problems inherent in reading tests and testing. What other pertinent limitations of standardized reading tests are raised by Traxler?

58. The Essential Aspects of Evaluation

RALPH W. TYLER (1958)

Over the past quarter of a century the term "evaluation" has been used with increasing frequency, until today it is the most common word used in referring to educational appraisal. Also, during those twenty-five years, there has developed an increasingly articulated conception of the nature of educational evaluation and the procedure involved. In reviewing this history of evaluation, I find four distinguishable phases.

Educational Values and Objectives

The selection of the term "evaluation" has largely arisen from dissatisfaction with the direction that the so-called scientific movement in education had taken. The products of learning were being "measured" by tests which reflected the content of teaching materials but which were not built on a systematic analysis of the educational values to which good schools were dedicated. For example, reading tests of that time were constructed on detailed analyses of vocabulary and of the percentages of pupils answering questions correctly, but without systematic examination of the major educational values sought in the teaching of reading. As a result, most test items required only simple comprehension of reading passages or an unanalyzed mixture of pupil responses. Experienced teachers were sure that a number of values in addition to "plain sense comprehension" of reading passages could be and often were achieved in the teaching of reading. Interpretation of reading materials, for example, was much more than straightforward comprehension. Lifelong reading interests and sensitive responses to poetry are two illustrations of values which loom large in a reading program. These were minimally reflected in educational appraisals of that time.

Out of this background, the term "evaluation" meant a procedure for appraising the educational values actually developing in an educational

SOURCE: *Proceedings of the Annual Conference on Reading,* XX (December, 1958), 4–9. Reprinted by permission of the University of Chicago Press.

program. The first step in working out a plan of evaluation in the Eight-Year Study, begun in 1933, was to identify the values which teachers were attempting to reach; that is, we sought early in the study to find out what educational objectives were aimed at in order to plan appraisals to find out how far they were being attained.

To say that evaluation should begin with the educational objectives is simple enough, but to obtain a list of objectives clearly enough defined to guide the construction of means of appraisal is not easy. Many teachers have not stated their objectives; in fact, some which they consider most important may not have been explicitly formulated in their own minds. Hence, the listing of objectives requires a good deal of thought and discussion guided by such questions as: What are we trying to help students acquire in and through our reading program? What abilities, skills, knowledge, attitudes, interests, habits, and the like do students need to get the most out of reading? Which of these can we develop through our reading program? Why are we using these materials or these procedures in reading? Do they suggest certain results or objectives that we are or ought to be aiming at? These are simply different ways of reminding ourselves of possible objectives, but often several different questions are needed to stimulate teachers and students of education to reflect upon their own experiences and purposes.

A second problem in getting objectives useful in guiding evaluation is the difficulty of defining objectives clearly. The purposes or objectives of education are to help the student acquire ways of behaving, that is, ways of thinking, feeling, and acting, which he has not previously followed. Thus, a child may develop a mode of attacking unfamiliar words which he has not previously used, or a pupil may acquire an interest in reading science periodicals which he had not previously had, or a college student may develop a way of interpreting and responding to poetry which is new to him. These are a few random illustrations of the varied kinds of behavior which teachers may seek to develop in and through reading. If an evaluation is to be made, we need to know what kinds of student behavior we are looking for; hence our objectives need to be defined in terms of student behavior. When we talk about comprehension as a reading objective, what kind of behavior is involved and with what kind of reading materials? Such a definition provides a set of specifications for an appraisal of reading comprehension.

We discovered in the early days of evaluation that skills and abilities were easier to define than such objectives as interests and appreciations. Working over the years with teachers, we have found some fairly common agreements in defining some of these less tangible objectives. Interest in reading, for example, is often defined in terms of the following behavior: "The student likes to read. He gets satisfaction in reading. When he has free time, he often chooses voluntarily to spend time in reading." Usually teachers are concerned not only that students become interested in reading but that they become interested in reading many types of books and magazines and that the content of the reading they choose voluntarily shows increased complexity and maturity as time goes on. Such definitions of objectives in terms of behavior make it possible to plan appraisals based on the important educational objectives. This was a first significant phase of the development of evaluation.

The Nature of Educational Tests

Since the purpose of educational appraisal is to find out how far each of the important educational objectives is actually being realized, means for describing or measuring actual student behavior are essential. Without real evidence of what students are learning, we tend to rely heavily on our own preconceptions, and our temperaments, optimistic, skeptical, or pessimistic as they may be, will largely color our conclusions.

However, twenty-five years ago the prevailing conception of educational tests was a paper-and-pencil device, usually consisting of true-false or multiple-choice items. These devices could provide evidence of the amount of information the student could recall and could indicate, too, his facility in manipulating mathematical expressions and his ability to comprehend reading passages. But they were not relevant to some other important objectives. They did not provide evidence of habits, attitudes, interests, and appreciations. Few exercises required depth of understanding or interpretation. As we sought to develop means for evaluation, it became clear that we must broaden the concept of an educational test. We now think of an educational test as a series of situations which call forth from the student the kind of behavior defined in the objective and permit a record to be made of the student's actual behavior. A test of reading interpretation should consist of a series of situations in which the student is stimulated to read and to interpret what he is reading and in which a record can be made of the student's interpretations. A test of reading interests should consist of a series of situations in which the student is free to choose activities and a record can be made of the extent to which he freely chooses to read.

This conception of an educational test makes possible the use of a variety of testing devices; not only can paper-and-pencil exercises be used, but also such procedures as observation, interview, questionnaire, samples of products made, and records obtained in other connections may serve as evaluation devices. To appraise habits, observation may be employed or, under certain circumstances, questionnaires may be useful.

To appraise appreciation of literature, interviews focused on the student's responses to his reading, and his feelings and judgments are sometmes helpful. Records of book circulation in the library may sometimes provide evidence of reading habits and interests. Hence, although the realization that comprehensive educational evaluation requires evidence about several important objectives made the task seem more difficult, the further recognition that a variety of appraisal methods could be used encouraged us in the work.

The accepted criteria by which to judge measuring devices—validity, objectivity, and reliability—were not abandoned in the development of evaluation, but they were redefined in terms appropriate for the broader conception of educational measurement. Validity, the requirement that a measuring device actually measures that which it purports to measure, is still the most important criterion. However, in terms of evaluation this means that the testing device should actually obtain a sample of the kind of behavior stated in the objective with reference to the content implied by the objective, or the device must be shown to appraise behavior that is highly correlated with the behavior stated in the objective. Furthermore, the content of the test should be appropriate to the objective: that is, the reading passages used and the new words involved should be appropriate to the definition of the objective aimed at with this pupil. This conception of validity is central to evaluation and is quite different from coefficients of validity derived from internal homogeneity of items.

Objectivity is also an essential criterion of a satisfactory evaluation device. All appraisal involves human judgments: the kind of behavior to be appraised, the units of measure to be used and their definition, those involved in the comparison of the pupil's reactions with the measuring standards, and those required in the interpretation of the measures. In this sense, subjectivity can never be eliminated in appraisal. But, as in physical measurements, purely individual idiosyncrasies in judgments can be greatly reduced, and the appraisal made by one set of judges can be very similar to the appraisal made by another set. This increase in objectivity is made possible by agreeing on objectives, by clearly defining the objectives, by constructing devices that more clearly and adequately give records of the kind of behavior thus defined, by agreeing on the units of measurement or the categories of description to be used, by training judges in the use of the devices, by employing methods for analyzing responses which are consistent with the objectives, and by checking interpretations through further empirical studies.

Reliability is also an important criterion for an evaluation device. An evaluation instrument is unreliable when the results obtained from it vary markedly from those obtained from similar devices. Unreliability arises from the fact that any appraisal can include only a sample of a student's behavior. A vocabulary test could not include all the words a pupil might know. A comprehension test could not include all the reading passages a student might be able to read. A test of habits could not cover every minute of the student's life. Hence, conclusions are drawn from a sample of situations in which the student reacts. To assure a reliable test, samples of behavior should be included which involve the known variations likely to influence the student's reactions; that is, the test should include a representative sample of situations which evoke the desired behavior. Furthermore, to assure a reliable test, the size of the sample, the number of exercises, or the time intervals involved should be large enough to cover variations attributable to unknown or chance factors; that is, the sample should be adequate. The usual coefficient of reliability is an estimate of the adequacy of the sample, but it does not provide an estimate of its representativeness. Representativeness can be assured only through the selection of situations or test exercises.

Evaluating Characteristics of Learners

As we began to appraise student learning in the Eight-Year Study and to observe the varied effects of different procedures, materials, teaching personalities, and the like, it became clear to us that the educational effects in many cases appeared to be related to a number of the students' characteristics. A free reading program in the ninth grade which showed great influence on the quality of reading interests in one school seemed to have much less effect on the quality of interests in another school. Yet the appraisal of mental ability revealed no appreciable differences in the distribution of these scores. Similar findings in important areas led us to recognize the need for evaluating a number of student characteristics if we were to understand and report the values of various kinds of educational experience. Instructional procedures, materials, and principles of curriculum organization were often effective for students with certain characteristics and not for others. Hence, the conception of evaluation developed to include the evaluation of the learners' characteristics as well as the outcomes of the learning. Among the significant characteristics, in addition to age, sex, and mental test score, were social class, educational and occupational goals, cultural level of the home, parents' attitude toward importance of education, interests, types of motivation, social acceptance by peers, physical growth, and work experience.

Probably the number of characteristics relevant to planning a comprehensive reading program is greater than for any other school subject.

Hence, it is necessary in developing a plan for evaluating reading to select those characteristics of students which are likely to have most influence in determining the kinds of reading programs to provide. Without an evaluation of the learners' characteristics, important information is not available on which to plan educational programs and with which to interpret the results.

Assessing the Conditions of Learning

When the Eight-Year Study began, it was commonly assumed that curricular plans, teaching methods, and instructional materials were in themselves clearly defined factors which could be assessed in terms of their effectiveness producing desired learning in the students. Educational experiments had been conducted comparing the "laboratory method" of science instruction with the "lecture-demonstration method," comparing "large-class instruction" with "small-class instruction," comparing the "reading method" of language instruction with the "grammar translation method," and so on. Often several investigations of the same "methods" yielded quite different results. In the Eight-Year Study several schools explored such innovations as "pupil-teacher planning" and the "core curriculum." As we observed the developments in different schools of what was thought to be the same innovation, and as we talked with teachers about them, we began to realize that a phrase like "pupil-teacher planning" takes on concrete meaning in terms of the way in which such an innovation is conceived, developed, and actually carried on by the teacher. We sometimes found as much variability in results obtained among classes purportedly using the same "method" as we found among several different "methods."

It is clear that educational evaluation should include an assessment of the conditions of learning if the results of appraising what the students are learning are to be understood. This assessment will usually include descriptions of some conditions of learning and also more precise appraisals, depending on the ease of assessing the particular condition. What conditions of learning should be assessed depends to some extent on which ones appear to be critical for the educational program under study. Generally, a description or appraisal of the following conditions of learning will give a very useful picture of the teaching methods, materials, organization, and the like: (1) Student motivation; (2) Recognition by the student of the need to learn new behavior; (3) Guidance in developing new behavior; (4) Availability of appropriate materials to practice the kind of behavior to be learned; (5) Time for effective learning; (6) satisfaction obtained by the student from the desired behavior; (7) provision for sequential practice with learning experiences provided from day to day; (8) student standards of performance which for them are high but attainable; (9) valid and practical means for the student to judge his performance.

Conditions for learning, such as the foregoing, provide a more useful way of describing teaching procedues than a description in terms of the proportion of lecture, discussion, small-group activity, and the like. It is possible for creative teachers to get results by a variety of procedures. But, whatever methods they use or however they stimulate reactions, their effectiveness can be more clearly understood by examining the teaching in terms of the extent to which the conditions of learning are provided.

What Is Evaluation?

In the light of the history of the past quarter of a century, evaluation is seen as a growing conception. Used as a term to cover the process of appraising the results of learning, it has developed into a process involving educational objectives, educational tests and measurements, the appraisal of the learner's characteristics, and the assessment of learning conditions. I believe that the conception will continue to grow as we identify other important areas which must be described or assessed if we are to understand education more fully, and more wisely guide the learning of our students.

59. Evaluating the Effectiveness of Teaching Reading

MILDRED C. LETTON (1958)

The evaluation of the effectiveness of teaching reading goes on continuously throughout the school year, with the classroom teacher judging the day-to-day progress of pupils, as well as measuring growth in reading at the end of specific units of study or at other regular intervals. This evaluation is likely to be informal, as developed by the teacher or as suggested by the teachers' guides of basal reading series. Appraising

---

SOURCE: *Proceedings of the Annual Conference on Reading*, XX (December, 1958), 76–82. Reprinted by permission of the University of Chicago Press.

the effectiveness of teaching reading makes it possible for the classroom teacher to locate the strengths and weaknesses of his group; to note the strengths and weaknesses of individuals; to appraise the proportion of emphasis between the skills program and the program for developing reading interests, attitudes, and appreciation; to determine the value of different methods of teaching particular reading skills; and to ascertain the effectiveness of the sequential plan and the results of depth instruction at each grade level.

Needless to say, one cannot evaluate the effectiveness of his methods of teaching reading unless he recognizes his goals. The effective teacher needs to know *every* day, for *every* reading class, what his objectives are, why he is presenting this material, and how he will determine whether pupils have attained the goals which he had in mind for the lesson or the unit. Through such evaluation the teacher can judge, at any point, where any pupil is along the road to more effective reading.

There are two major aspects of reading in which the classroom teacher is most often interested. First, he wishes to evaluate the effectiveness of teaching reading *skills,* both oral and silent. Second, he wants to appraise the reading interests and attitudes of his pupils.

Effectiveness of Teaching Reading Skills

The teacher's first concern, whether he is working with first graders, sixth graders, or twelfth graders, is with the development and measurement of reading skills. Broadly, these may be divided into the two areas of oral and silent reading.

ORAL READING

In the primary grades much class time is spent in oral reading so that the teacher may observe, usually informally, pupil progress in sight vocabulary and the use of phonetic analysis. In the middle and upper grades the emphasis shifts to consideration of how fluently the reader presents the author's main ideas to his audience. Among high school and college students, as well as other adults, the effectiveness of oral reading is judged by how well the reader is able to act as a *communicator* for the author. This demands that the reader understand the author himself; observe punctuation that has been used; retain the phrasing of words and emphasis on ideas suggested by the writer; and avoid misinterpretation of the material read, by slurring or speeding through the presentation of some ideas and lingering over others.

Standardized oral reading tests are often given at regular intervals in a school system, but perhaps not at the most useful times. Some tests do not have enough forms for the teacher to be able to use them frequently for evaluation. Occasionally a teacher might like to use a method of evaluating oral reading that is more objective than informal observation and not as exhaustive in diagnosing difficulties, or as precise in locating grade level, as a standardized test.

The teacher can quickly devise such an instrument for evaluating oral reading by using materials he has at hand. First, he lists the types of errors which he wishes to check. Among the most common are mispronunciation, omissions, substitutions, insertions, repetitions, and disregard of punctuation. For each of these errors the examiner must decide a code for marking. A study of those used for standardized tests will be helpful. Second, the teacher selects the material to be read. For Grade II it might be part of a page of a supplementary reader; for Grade V it might be two or three paragraphs from a book in the content areas. For Grade XI it might be a portion of a literary selection. For Grade XIV it might be a short poem or part of a long poem. Third, the teacher carefully constructs a number of questions for the pupil to answer after his oral reading.

Now the teacher is ready to test pupils individually. Two copies of the reading selection are needed, one for the reader, one for the teacher. Prior to testing, the teacher prepares his own book. Over the selection to be read the teacher clips a sheet of clear tracing paper on which pencil marks do not smudge easily; on this the tester writes the pupil's name, the date, the name of the book, its page number, and incloses in brackets the sentences, paragraphs, or verses to be read aloud. As the pupil reads, the teacher records on the tracing paper the errors made, using the key for errors he devised earlier. He may also write comments on the sheet.

If the school owns a tape recorder, the teacher can have the pupil record his oral reading. Older students may even make their recordings independently, running the machine themselves. The use of the tape recorder has several advantages: it is possible for the teacher to check the tape at a later and perhaps more convenient time; it is possible for the pupil to hear and evaluate his own oral reading; it is possible to compare students' oral reading records made at different times; it provides high motivation for improving oral reading, especially for boys; it is possible for groups of pupils to hear and evaluate samples of oral reading.

Such plans for evaluating oral reading have several advantages: (1) the teacher can test pupils on the particular kind of material they have been learning to read; (2) the teacher has a permanent record on the tracing paper which can be put into the child's cumulative folder; (3) retesting using the same or a similar passage can be done later if this seems desirable; (4) the teacher can get some measure of the child's ability to read orally several different types of material by using a number of different selections; and (5) the teacher can use the findings to determine individual differences in order to plan the next steps in teaching or reteaching.

Silent reading in the classroom. The classroom teacher evaluates the effectiveness of teaching silent reading every day that he meets with his pupils. Early in Grade I, children are encouraged to read silently, and at once they are engaged in answering questions which attempt to measure how well they comprehend what they have read. From that day on, through high school, college, and even graduate school, how effectively one reads is measured by the level of comprehension he attains.

In the elementary school, the teacher evaluates the directed reading in the basic reader, at least in an informal way, following the reading of every story, whether the pupils are in Grade II or Grade VIII. Generally, the teacher is interested in the progress of the class in comprehension, vocabulary, and reading rate, so that evaluative devices tend to be designed to measure these aspects of reading.

Several criteria may be used to judge the effectiveness of one's teaching of reading. The teacher may be asked:

1. Do you make careful evaluation a part of every reading lesson or unit involving reading? This means more than selecting at random one or two questions from the teacher's guidebook or asking one that can be answered quickly without any concentration on the part of group members. Evaluation must always be related to the teacher's immediate and particular objectives.

2. Do you use evaluative techniques that are appropriate for the grade level? You would not expect a second grader to write a detailed outline of reference material from an encyclopedia. On the other hand, with older pupils we often retain the easy-answer questions because they are quickly scored without arguments about the correct answers. This kind of evaluation is, in reality, a disservice to the student, because he is led to believe that all reading should be this simple.

3. Do you use a variety of techniques other than the most common one of requiring the reader to answer questions orally or in writing? These may be expedient, but they are not always the most appropriate.

4. Do you use questions at distinct levels of difficulty so that readers are challenged by, and receive practice in answering, the more penetrating types of queries?

5. Do you use many "open-ended" questions (as contrasted with true-false and multiple-choice items) which demand that the reader function independently without suggested responses? We know that

many youngsters, particularly the bright ones, often use a process of elimination on multiple-choice-item tests and make higher scores than they would if the questions were stated and required one- or two-sentence responses. In informal, day-to-day evaluation, the teacher is in a favorable position to give the reader opportunities to gain skill in answering "open-ended" questions.

6. Do you have occasional, brief checkups that can be kept for a period of time as a part of the pupil's individual record of reading progress? Brief checkups which show one's progress in developing a particular skill often serve as motivation to continue work on that skill or to move on to attack a more complex one. The main advantage of keeping such papers over a period of several weeks, or even months, is that the child is able to see, after a while, that he really is improving in reading skills, though he is seldom aware of this from day to day.

7. Do you discuss with the pupil his responses to questions, helping him judge his strengths and weaknesses in reading skills? I believe there would be fewer reading failures in our schools if teachers and pupils held more frequent "post mortems" following the daily checkups and unit tests. The teacher owes it to his pupils, especially beyond the second grade, to discuss with them the kinds of errors they are making in reading, to try to find out why such errors are being made, and to suggest ways in which each pupil may help himself.

Challenging Questions to Measure Comprehension

Comprehension questions may easily be classified at a number of different levels of difficulty. In this discussion let us consider how the teacher may use questions at five levels.

A Level I question requires a factual response which is clearly stated in the selection read. Such questions may be identified in the evaluation of reading materials as early as Grade I. Even within this level there are questions which vary in difficulty. For example:

Where did the Winslow family spend Thanksgiving?
In what year did the Pilgrims arrive in America?
Give three kinds of experience which prepared the aviator for his flight across the Atlantic.
How many lines are there in a sonnet?
Who was the goddess born from the head of Jupiter?
In explaining the meaning of "supercilious," what synonym does the writer use?

A Level II question requires an answer in which the reader must make some reorganization of the author's material. This may involve choosing a title for the selection, stating the main idea, summarizing, or outlining. Again, Level II questions may be used with beginning readers. Questions at this level, when used with high school and college students, make more and more intellectual demands on the readers. Examples of the more difficult Level II questions include:

What is the chief objective of Thurber's essay?
In line 13 the poet says, "Sculptured like some young god's." In what other words does the poet reinforce this idea?

A Level III question requires an answer in which the reader must make inferences within a framework relevant to ideas which are not directly stated. This usually involves anticipating possible outcomes, drawing relevant conclusions, and making relevant judgments. Questions at this level would include:

What will Fred do after he finishes playing baseball?
Did the author feel optimistic or pessimistic at the time he wrote this selection?
Why did the poet begin with a description of the father's hands?
What do you think the author's attitude is toward the youth in the story?
Give at least two reasons why you believe the author is writing about an incident which happened one year before he wrote this account.

A Level IV question requires an answer in which the reader shows a knowledge of figurative, idiomatic, or picturesque language, and the connotations or denotations of words, if he is to interpret the selection accurately. Even young readers can answer Level IV questions. Some examples of this level of questioning are:

What does Sandburg mean when he says, "The fog comes on little cat feet"?
"He left the U.N. assembly, followed by a little group of his satellites." How is this use of the word "satellite" different from its most common use today? What are the meanings of this word?
What does line 6 mean, "Hands vocative in spirited dispute"?
What does the author mean by the phrase "ever seeking Lotos-lands"?

A Level V question requires an answer in which the reader must evaluate ideas in the selection, weighing them against those of another author or authors, or comparing them with those of the reader himself. This level demands that the reader draw upon his own resources and experiences. Examples of Level V questions include:

In the story Bill chose a puppy at the pet shop. What would you have done if you had been in Bill's place? Why would you have made your selection?

In what ways were the early years of Andrew Jackson like those of Abraham Lincoln? What other similarities do you notice between the two men?

Bacon and Emerson both write about friendship. Emerson's element of Truth is most like which of Bacon's fruits of friendship?

Analyze and compare the three philosophical positions which have been presented. Which of the three most nearly approximates your own philosophy?

It is through experience with and practice in answering comprehension questions at different levels of difficulty that mature and careful readers develop. Only when the classroom teacher is aware of his role in this situation can the school be expected to fulfill this important function for its pupils.

The Effectiveness of Developing Reading Interests and Attitudes

Since the classroom teacher does not work single-handed in the development of reading interests and attitudes, he should not try to work alone in appraising these aspects of the reading program. Where he can secure the aid of others, he certainly should do so. Often both parents and librarians are in better positions than the classroom teacher to observe the genuine reading interests and attitudes of children and young people. Those pupils who seek the approval of their teachers may answer reading-interest questionnaires or fill out individual reading records in a way which appears to reflect the teacher's objectives. This presents a problem that has long plagued teachers, particularly at high school and college levels, in evaluating the quality and amount of the free reading of pupils; that is, how to determine whether books listed or reported on, orally or in writing, have actually been read. Conversely, when the reader doubts that a book is on the "approved" list, he may omit reporting that he has read it at all.

Another factor teachers should consider when evaluating the reading interests and attitudes of pupils is that the books reported read may represent a selection from quite limited available materials rather than a series of genuine, first-choice interests. The child who must rely on the offerings of a bookmobile, excellent though such services are, may read quite different books from those he would select if he lived across the street from a large-city branch library. The reported reading interests of the child who attends a school with a library of five hundred volumes can hardly be compared with those of the pupil in a school with a library of three thousand books.

How can the parent help the teacher to evaluate the reading interests and attitudes of his child? First, there must be a warm and friendly relationship between the home and school, and recognition that it is the child who is the first concern of both. Second, the parent must understand not only the broad objectives of the school but also the particular goals in reading at the child's present level. Notice that I suggested the *reading achievement* level and not the grade level of the pupil. These may or may not be the same. Third, communication between the home and school must be easy and relatively frequent.

In informal conversations the teacher probably can secure the best help from parents about the reading interests and attitudes of their children. Questionnaires may be sent home, but here, too, parents, anxious as their children are anxious, may report information which they expect to meet with teacher approval. Often this is done more wishfully than deliberately.

What questions about reading can the classroom teacher use as a guide in conversation with parents? Every teacher can devise a set that will be most appropriate for his situation. However, a few are suggested here as an initial core.

1. What book titles or magazines does your child ask for or buy independently? This list is not the same as one which contains the names of books which the parent, fond uncle, or family friend adds to the child's collection.

2. What does your child do in his leisure time when no adults plan his activities? Does he read?

3. What does your child read in private, that is, when he isolates himself from the rest of the family, in his own room if he has one, or on the porch, or somewhere away from other people? What books or magazines do you find under his pillow or his bed or stacked away in his closet? In what kind of book- or magazine-trading does he engage?

4. How do you feel about your child's reading of comic books? Do you think this is interfering or has interfered with his development of more mature reading interests?

5. Do you know what your child is reading right now—this week—today? Do you ever discuss with him the things he reads for recreation? Does he consider the sharing of ideas and incidents he comes upon in his reading a natural adjunct to reading?

6. Does your child know, if he is in the middle grades or above, what you, his mother and father, are reading currently? Does he ever hear you discuss your recreational reading with anyone? As a teen-ager, does

he ever read biography, fiction, or non-fiction because you recommend it?

7. Does your child recognize and enjoy references to well-known literature with which he is familiar? A recent magazine cover by Charles Addams showed a present-day space man lying on a strange planet, red-orange in color. His rocket ship was in the distance, and far off in the sky was the earth, with its North and South American continents dimly discernible. But the space man was not relaxing; he was staked to the ground by hundreds of ropes or strings being applied by myriads of twentieth-century Lilliputians. A teen-ager who showed this to me remarked, "What do you know, a modern Gulliver in distress!" Without the knowledge of the literary reference, the drawing would have been merely amusing, and the artist's efforts to say a great deal in a little space would have been wasted.

From answers to such questions, added to his own keen observations, the classroom teacher can appraise his pupils' present reading interests and attitudes toward reading.

Summary and Conclusions

Evaluation is useful only when it is related to carefully defined objectives. The two major aspects of reading that have been discussed are the evaluation of the effectiveness of teaching the skills of both oral and silent reading and the appraisal or reading interests and attitudes. For measuring oral reading, informal testing has been suggested. Criteria for judging the effectiveness of the evaluation of silent reading in the classroom have been presented. A plea has been made for the classroom teacher to work conscientiously and thoughtfully to improve the breadth and depth of the questions he uses to evaluate reading comprehension. Five levels of questioning have been proposed, ranging from the simplest level of factual response which is clearly stated in the selection to a level which requires the reader to recall, evaluate, and compare what he has read with everything he knows about the subject. In addition to what the classroom teacher observes about the reading interests and attitudes of pupils, information should be secured from parents whenever possible.

The chief purpose of evaluating the effectiveness of reading should be to make clear to the teacher the next steps needed to aid the child in making continuous intellectual growth.

60. Determining Reading Achievement

WILLIAM G. CARR (1935)

Kinds of tests used by teachers whose work is outstanding. Insofar as the present study is representative, reading tests constructed by teachers for use only in their own classrooms are used by nearly all teachers in all grades. Nearly two-thirds of the first- and second-grade teachers and more than three-fourths of the teachers and more than three-fourths of the teachers in Grades III to VI also use standardized reading tests. In about one-fourth of the cases, citywide tests are administered, that is, tests constructed by supervisory officers, with or without the assistance of teachers, for use in all the schools in the system. In about 10 percent of the cases, tests are constructed by the principal, or a committee of teachers, for use in all comparable classrooms in the same building. These facts, shown in Table 1, suggest the important place that testing occupies in the total reading program. Apparently most of the teachers selected to take part in this investigation use not only the tests which they prepare but also at least one other type of standardized or semi-standardized test.

Number of tests given per year. Table 2 shows the average number of standardized and informal reading tests, respectively, which teachers use in the various grades. In general, standardized tests are given two or three times per year; informal tests thirty to forty times a year, or roughly once a week.

The administration of reading tests. Standardized tests are used in the great majority of cases in a uniform testing program involving the whole school system. Approximately two-thirds of the replies indicated that they were used only in that way. In about one-fourth of the cases, standardized tests are used in uniform testing programs; and, in addition, teachers use them more or less extensively in their teaching. Only about 10 percent of the teachers use them solely to measure achieve-

SOURCE: *Better Reading Instruction*, NEA Research Bulletin, XIII, 5 (November, 1935), 315–318. Reprinted by permission of the publisher.

TABLE 1. Extent to Which Reading Tests of Various Types Are Used by 1527 Successful Teachers

KIND OF TEST	PERCENT OF TEACHERS USING TESTS; GRADE					
	I	II	III	IV	V	VI
1	*2*	*3*	*4*	*5*	*6*	*7*
Tests prepared by teachers for use in their own classrooms	90	94	92	99	95	97
Standardized reading tests	64	67	80	79	76	80
Tests prepared for citywide use	26	29	25	27	24	20
Tests prepared for use thruout a given school building	9	11	13	8	11	10
Number of teachers' reports on which the percents are based	288	260	270	225	229	255

ment in their own classrooms, without reference to the work of other teachers in the same school system.

When uniform testing programs are being carried out, 50 to 60 percent of the teachers reporting say that they themselves are responsible for administering the standardized tests. In 15 to 20 percent of the cases, the tests are administered by the principal or the superintendent, and in about 10 percent, by supervisors. Occasionally they are administered by a special examiner, the psychologist, or some other teacher.

Types of test exercises which teachers find most helpful. Except in the first grade, completion and multiple-choice tests are rated as the most valuable types of informal classroom tests, with true-false and matching exercises ranking third and fourth, respectively. In the first grade, matching exercises are rated as the most helpful type; then true-false, multiple-choice, and completion in the order named. The essay test is rated far below all these types by the teachers of every grade.

TABLE 2. Average Number of Standardized Reading Tests and Informal Tests Given in Each Grade by 1527 Successful Teachers

KIND OF TEST	AVERAGE NUMBER GIVEN PER YEAR; GRADE					
	I	II	III	IV	V	VI
1	*2*	*3*	*4*	*5*	*6*	*7*
Standardized reading tests	2.0	2.3	2.5	2.3	2.5	2.4
Informal reading tests	32.7	42.0	36.0	35.1	37.2	32.8

Uses made of test scores. An average of 55 to 65 percent of the teachers in the various grades enter the scores from certain reading tests as part of the pupils' permanent records. The extent to which test scores are presented graphically to pupils to motivate their work is indicated in Figure 1. Graphs showing individual achievement are the ones most teachers select for frequent use. The percent of teachers making frequent use of graphs of both types increases considerably between Grades I and VI.

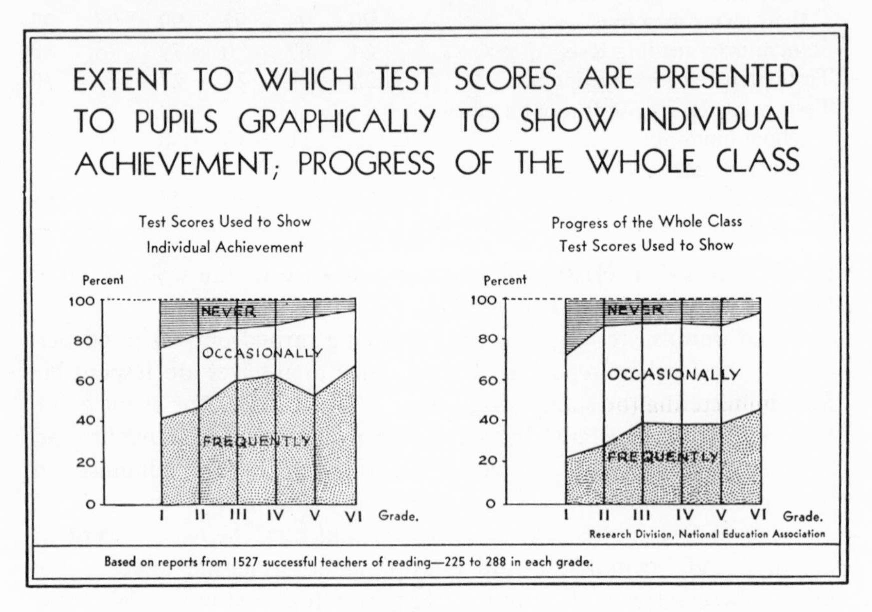

Figure 1.

How test results are most helpful. The teachers who participated in this study agree almost unanimously as to the ways in which reading tests contribute to classroom instruction. The use of tests in diagnosing reading difficulties is given the highest average rank by the teachers in all six grades. Other ways in which reading tests are helpful, listed in the order of importance assigned to them by the teachers in every grade, are: classifying pupils according to reading achievement, determining the initial ability of pupils in order to plan classroom work to the best advantage, establishing goals of achievement, motivating the work of a class, and, least important of all, determining pupil progress. Since we are so often inclined to think of tests almost wholly in terms of the last named function, every teacher may well reexamine this phase of the work, raising the question: Am I using reading tests as effectively as possible, not merely as a checkup, but as a means of understanding my pupils and planning my work?

Troublesome testing problems. There is also close agreement in the opinions of teachers at the various grade levels with respect to the testing problems that are most troublesome. Listed according to difficulty on the basis of teacher opinion these problems are: (1) obtaining test materials; (2) the clerical work involved; (3) constructing informal reading tests; (4) interpreting test results; (5) selecting appropriate published tests; (6) administering tests; (7) finding adequate time for tests without interfering with other necessary activities.

Standards of achievement which teachers employ. From 168 of the school systems included in this study, approximately three-fourths of the supervisors report that norms on standardized tests are set up as criteria, or standards of achievement, for pupils in the various grades. In about two-thirds of the cases, the course of study in use sets forth certain definite abilities and skills that pupils in each grade are expected to develop. In about 45 percent of the schools represented, local norms on standardized tests are used instead of, or in addition to, published norms. Thirty-six percent of the reports indicate that the amount of material covered is used as one important standard of achievement. From these percents it is obvious that definite standards of two or more types are often used as goals of achievement. On the other hand, even among these schools, where outstanding results in reading are being achieved, 15 percent report that *no definite or objective standards* have been adopted.

Amount of reading expected in the various grades. The number of books which teachers expect the average pupil to read varies not only from one grade level to another but also from classroom to classroom in any given grade. Certain teachers in every grade from the first to the sixth report that their average pupils read not more than 5 books during the year. Others report a standard of 30, 40, and sometimes 50 books per year. Figure 2 shows the average number for each grade, increasing from 8.6 in Grade I to 17.8 in Grade VI. These standards indicate clearly that the teachers who cooperated in this study look upon extensive reading as an essential element in correct reading instruction. This is in harmony with the findings of several research studies, showing the superiority of extensive reading to intensive study and drill, except in the case of very slow learners.[1] Washburne points

[1] See especially: Field, Helen A. *Extensive Individual Reading vs. Class Reading.* Contributions to Education, No. 394. New York: Teachers College; Columbia University, 1930. 52 p. Hilliard, George H. "Extensive Library Reading vs. Specific Drill as an Aid in Improving Certain Reading Abilities." *Educational News Bulletin* (Western State Teachers College, Kalamazoo) 2: 6–12; June, 1932. Hunt, C. W.

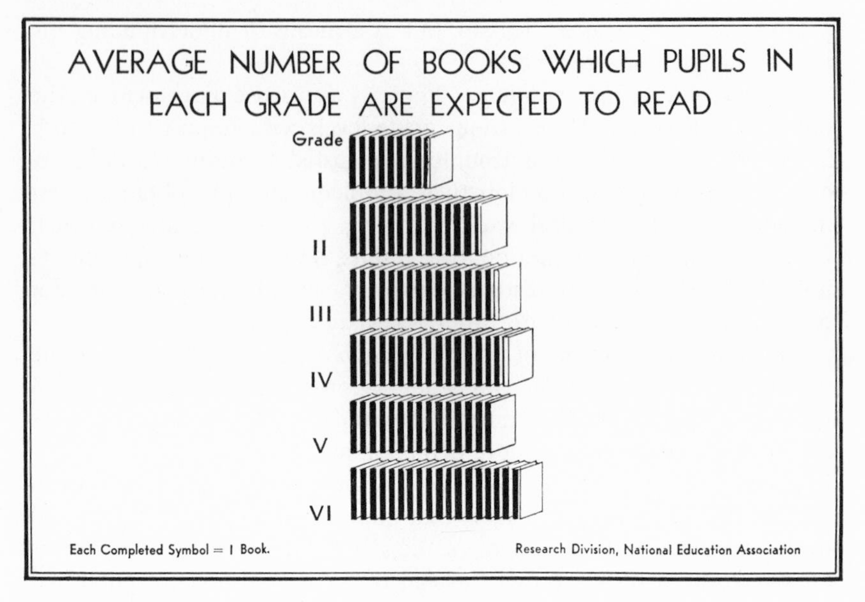

Figure 2.

out that "on the average, when a pupil has completed about 15 books on his grade level he will have raised his reading level to the next higher grade."[2]

Zirbes has proposed a standard for pupils' reading at various grade levels, based not on the number of books read—which is at best a variable criterion—but on the number of thousand-word units.[3] On the basis of her observations of practice, she classifies schools according to the amount of reading pupils do in each grade, in the manner indicated in Table 3. It may be helpful in interpreting these standards to recall that an ordinary third reader contains about thirty thousand-word units; earlier readers a smaller number; advanced readers, 60, 70, and sometimes more than 100 units.

"Extensive Reading: A Factor in Developing Reading Ability." *School and Society* 11: 260–61; February 28, 1920. O'Brien, Ida. "A Comparison of the Use of Intensive Training and of Wide Reading in the Improvement of Reading." *Educational Method* 10: 346–49; March, 1931. Scruggs, Sherman D. "Improving Reading Ability in Grades V and VI by Extensive Reading." *University of Kansas Bulletin of Education* 3: 3–10; April, 1931. Zirbes, Laura; Keelor, Katharine; and Miner, Pauline. *Practice Exercises and Checks on Silent Reading in the Primary Grades.* New York: Lincoln School, Teachers College, Columbia University, 1925. 66 p.

[2] Washburne, Carleton W. "How to Fit Reading to Each Individual Child." *Individual Instruction* 1: 2–7; December, 1928.

[3] Zirbes, Laura. *Comparative Studies of Current Practice in Reading.* Contributions to Education, No. 316. New York: Teachers College, Columbia University, 1928. p. 80–93.

TABLE 3. Number of Thousand-Word Units Read by Pupils in Classrooms Where Instruction Varies in Efficiency

TYPE OF INSTRUCTION	NUMBER OF THOUSAND-WORD UNITS PUPILS READ; GRADE					
	I	II	III	IV	V	VI
1	2	3	4	5	6	7
Traditional	10–15	20–35	30–55	50–100	100–200	150–250
Unprogressive	25–30	40–65	60–130	150–275	300–550	350–600
Superior	35+	70+	150+	300+	700+	800+

SOURCE: Zirbes, Laura. *Comparative Studies of Current Practice in Reading.* Contributions to Education, No. 316. New York: Teachers College, Columbia University, 1928. p. 92.

Proposed standards for rate of silent reading. Rate standards are usually expressed in one of three ways: (1) number of words per minute; (2) number of words per second, or per 100 seconds; or (3) a point score on a reading test without specific reference to number of words or time units. Since all standardized rate tests have norms showing the rate of performance expected of pupils at various age or grade levels, these need not be reviewed here. It may be helpful, however, to bring together some of the rate standards, expressed in words-per-minute, which have been proposed at one time or another by various research workers. This is done in Table 4. There is considerable discrepancy

TABLE 4. Rate Standards for Various Grades Proposed by Different Students of Reading Problems

STANDARDS PROPOSED BY:	WORDS PER MINUTE; GRADE				
	II	III	IV	V	VI
1	2	3	4	5	6
O'Brien[a]	...	...	236	278	293
Brown[a]	...	...	213	269	272
Gray[b]	90	138	180	204	216
Courtis[a]	...	...	160	180	220
Oberholtzer[c]	...	138	156	186	234
Starch[a]	108	126	144	168	192

[a] Quoted in *Silent Reading.* Twentieth Yearbook, Part II. National Society for the Study of Education. Bloomington, Ill.: Public School Publishing Co., 1921. "The Development of Speed in Silent Reading," Ch. 4, p. 73.
[b] Quoted by Clarence R. Stone in *Silent and Oral Reading.* Boston: Houghton Mifflin Co., 1926. p. 21.
[c] Oberholtzer, E. E. "Testing the Efficiency of Reading in the Grades." *Elementary School Journal* 15: 313–22; February, 1915.

among the recommendations, and none are based on recent investigations. The standards proposed for the sixth grade by Gray, Courtis, Oberholtzer, and Starch are lower than O'Brien's standard for fourth-grade pupils. O'Brien's standards, however, may be somewhat higher than most classes can be expected to achieve, for he was one of the most successful early champions of rapid silent reading. Gray's proposed standards are probably representative of satisfactory achievement without undue emphasis on rate of reading.

Other standards of achievement. Norms on the various standardized comprehension and vocabulary tests undoubtedly constitute the best available standards for pupil achievement in these phases of reading. Other standards, somewhat less objective perhaps, but important none the less, are sometimes defined in terms of new abilities acquired, correct habits established, and wholesome attitudes developed. The desirable levels of achievement at the end of each of the growth stages in reading which characterize the elementary-school period are set forth in the Twenty-fourth Yearbook of the National Society for the Study of Education.[4] These deserve the careful attention of all teachers of reading.

Selected References

1. Briggs, Thomas H. "A Dictionary Test." *Teachers College Record* 24: 355–65; September, 1923.
2. Burgess, May A. "*The Measurement of Silent Reading.*" New York: Russell Sage Foundation, 1921. 164 p.
3. Dewey, Joseph C. "Consistency of Pupil Response on Tests of Reading Comprehension." *Elementary School Journal* 34: 533–36; March, 1934.
4. Gates, Arthur I. "A Series of Tests for the Measurement and Diagnosis of Reading Ability in Grades 3 to 8." *Teachers College Record* 28: 1–23; September, 1926.
5. Gates, Arthur I. "A Test of Ability in the Pronunciation of Words." *Teachers College Record* 26: 205–19; November, 1924.
6. Jorgensen, Albert N. "Use of Diagnostic Tests in Teaching Silent Reading." *Elementary English Review* 9: 86–98; April, 1932.
7. McAnulty, Ellen A., and Clark, Willis W. "A Study of Primary Reading Tests." *Los Angeles Educational Research Bulletin* 10: 6–16, 2–10; January–February, 1931.
8. Madsen, Iver N. *Educational Measurement in the Elementary Grades.* Yonkers-on-Hudson, New York: World Book Co., 1930. 294 p.
9. Monroe, Marion. *Children Who Cannot Read: The Analysis of Reading Disabilities and the Use of Diagnostic Tests in the Instruction of Retarded Readers.* Chicago: University of Chicago Press, 1932. 206 p.

[4] National Society for the Study of Education. *Report of the National Committee on Reading.* Twenty-fourth Yearbook, Part I. Bloomington, Ill.: Public School Publishing Co., 1925. p. 44, 54, and 62–64.

10. Odell, Charles W. *Educational Tests for Use in Elementary Schools.* University of Illinois Bulletin, Vol. 24, No. 49. Urbana: the University, 1927. 44 p.
11. Raguse, Florence W. "Qualitative and Quantitative Achievements in First Grade Reading." *Teachers College Record* 32: 424–36; February, 1931.
12. Rock, R. T., Jr., *Reading Tests for the Primary Grades.* Catholic University of America, Educational Research Bulletin, Vol. 2, No. 4. Washington, D.C.: Catholic Education Press, 1927. 36 p.
13. Sangren, Paul V. *Improvement of Reading Through the Use of Tests.* Kalamazoo: Extension Department, Western State Teachers College, 1932. 207 p.
14. Shank, Spencer. "Student Responses in the Measurement of Reading Comprehension." *Journal of Educational Research* 22: 119–29; September, 1930.
15. Simpson, Mabel E. "Qualitative and Quantitative Standards of Attainment in Reading, Grades 1–6, abstract." Reviewed in *Elementary School Journal* 29: 728–30; June, 1929.
16. Smith, Henry L., and Wright, Wendell W. *Tests and Measurements.* New York: Silver, Burdett and Co., p. 196–234.
17. Wilson, Guy M., and Hoke, Kremer J. *How to Measure.* New York: Macmillan Co., 1928. p. 121–67.

61. What Constitutes an Adequate Testing Program

THEODORE L. TORGERSON (1938)

While standardized tests had their origin near the beginning of the present century, the measurement movement really did not make its influence felt among the schools of this country until the close of the World War. Since 1920 the construction and use of objective tests of achievement, intelligence, aptitude, interests, and more recently, personality and adjustment, have developed at a rapid rate. The functions served by these tests have, however, undergone a marked change. At

---

SOURCE: *Education*, May, 1938, 553–556.

first teachers gave the tests to satisfy their curiosity about the tests and how they worked. Later, teachers gave the tests to satisfy their curiosity about how well their classes did in comparison with others or with the norm for the test. In the majority of cases the pupils received no direct benefit in the nature of remediation.

At present, objective measurement is rapidly becoming an integral part of the teaching procedure. There is a growing recognition of the fact that education in terms of individual needs must be based upon a knowledge of the whole child. Many factors have operated to bring about this changed point of view. The increased size and heterogeneity of the school population, due to more stringent attendance laws, better schools, increased interest in education, and a scarcity of jobs, are some of the factors which have made the problem of providing for indivdual differences more acute and increased the complexity of instructional problems. More complete information about each pupil, made possible through the use of objective tests, has become indispensable. Furthermore, the emphasis upon providing education in terms of individual needs, the acceptance of the importance of developing outcomes other than information, and the growing tendency for the school to accept responsiblity for the development of the whole child, has resulted in demands upon test technicians to develop new tests that will enable teachers to study the several aspects of child development and to determine a child's needs more completely in terms of the ultimate goals of education.

Measurement is not an end, but a means to an end. The objective of the measurement program is to know the child and his needs. Teachers should use standardized tests because they provide an efficient and reliable method of securing data about their pupils which will enable them to promote an educational program in terms of individual needs. Instruction in terms of individual needs requires a knowledge of individual pupil capacities, aptitudes, interests, and adjustments as well as a measure of present levels of attainment. Standardized tests are instruments of measurement which should enable the teacher to diagnose the difficulties underlying scholarship and adjustment as well as to determine educational and mental maturity. Such a program necessitates the use of valid and reliable tests which measure the emotional, social, educational, and mental development of every pupil. The nature and difficulty of the materials of instruction as factors which condition learning must be studied in order that the proper adjustments may be made to the individual needs of the pupils. Curricular differentiation to meet the needs of bright and dull pupils also demands differentiation in instruction in accordance with the psychological characteristics of slow and rapid learners. Problems related to the efficiency of the teacher may involve a study of teacher traits, attitudes, and abilities. A more complex constellation of factors that may be termed teacher-pupil relationships, which involve teacher traits, attitudes, and practices and their effect upon the pupils, present a new and unexplored field.

The second step in a testing program is that of selecting tests that are valid[1] and reliable.[2] The tests must not only meet these criteria, but they must also be selected because the results obtained from their use will provide the data needed for the solution of the specific problems to be studied. The nature of the problems studied will determine the nature of the tests to be used. Problems involving educational status ordinarily require the use of intelligence tests and survey tests of achievement. Problems concerning the nature or specific character of educational disabilities require the use of diagnostic tests of achievement and tests of intelligence and aptitudes. Problems concerning scholarship difficulties or the adjustment of pupils generally necessitate the use of tests and rating scales of pupil adjustment, intelligence tests, achievement tests, aptitude tests, and as comprehensive a measure as possible of all the factors that condition learning and adjustment. Diagnostic tests of achievement which measure several abilities must provide a reliable measure of each ability measured.

It is obvious that many of the tests published a decade or more ago have become outmoded. Some of the newer tests are more diagnostic, others measure the more complex work habits, and the general trend is in the direction of the measurement of objectives other than information. Tests measuring scientific attitudes, social attitudes, inferences, work type skills, and personal adjustment enable the teacher to secure important information about the effectiveness of instruction and to discover basic causes which prevent the development of certain valuable outcomes. Tests of personality and adjustment provide objective information about the nature and degree of pupil maladjustments and form the basis for a more complete understanding of the pupil and his problems. Some of these newer type tests are listed at the end of the article.

[1] In using achievement tests it is of the utmost importance to select tests that have a high curricular validity. The tests must provide an adequate sampling of the subject matter actually taught. Furthermore, the specific objective measured, such as information, skill, understanding, attitude, or appreciation, must be clearly recognized.

[2] A reliability coefficient of at least .90 based upon the range of talent of single grade is the minimum acceptable reliability for a test used to analyze individual performance.

It is obvious that a testing program is of little value unless the results are utilized for a careful follow-up program which will eliminate causes and correct the deficiencies that have been discovered. The proper utilization of the results will in a large measure depend upon the clarity of the objectives or problems to be solved and the adequacy of the tests employed. Methods of handling test scores, analysis and interpretation of the results which calls for a certain degree of expertness, are likewise important aspects of any testing program. The nature of the remedial work should be apparent if the problems initiating the testing program are well defined, the tests chosen in the light of the problems to be solved, and a careful interpretation made of the several factors in relationship to the problems studied. However, the average teacher has neither the time nor the skill necessary to prepare adequate remedial material. The usual review and reteaching is generally unscientific and ineffective. While test technicians are aware of the necessity for preparing better tests, they have not accepted the responsibility for preparing remedial material based upon the difficulties measured in the areas of learning tested.

The following summary lists the important steps involved in a successful testing program:

1. A testing program should be an outgrowth of important educational problems in which the teachers are vitally interested.
2. The problems should be concerned with the factors that condition the growth and development of the pupils in harmony with the objectives of education.
3. The tests employed must have statistical and curricular validity, high reliability, and be chosen for the express purpose of providing the data needed for the solution of the specific problem.
4. The tests must be administered by trained examiners.
5. The analysis and interpretation of results must be thorough and made in accordance with the problems to be solved.
6. The remediation must be based upon individual needs as revealed by the tests and consist of a thorough program based upon the underlying causes of the disabilities studied.

62. Values and Limitations of Standardized Reading Tests

ARTHUR E. TRAXLER (1958)

In discussing my topic, I am going to reverse the key words in the title and consider the limitations first and the values second. This reversal does not mean that I believe the limitations are more important than the values, but there are certain limitations which are inherent in the reading process and which logically ought to be considered first of all.

Limitations

The *first kind of limitation* is to be found in the nature of the reading act, and this limitation can never be entirely resolved. If reading were wholly, or even mainly, a mechanical process, as is implied in some theoretical discussions and some methods for the teaching of reading, then measurement would be comparatively simple. An observable manifestation of the mechanics of reading is found in eye movements, which are measurable and, in fact, have been measured precisely for many years.

But learning to read is much more than learning the mechanical aspects, as every teacher knows from experience and as Gates,[1] Gray,[2] and other reading specialists have frequently emphasized. Reading is a complex, unified, continuous activity which does not naturally fall into subdivsions or measurable units. In this respect, reading differs from other basic skills, such as arithmetic and spelling. You can take a problem in multiplication or a set of such problems, or you can take a list

[1] Arthur I. Gates, "Character and Purposes of the Yearbook," *Reading in the Elementary School,* p. 3. Forty-eighth Yearbook of the National Society for the Study of Education, Part II. Chicago: University of Chicago Press, 1949.
[2] William S. Gray, "Essential Objectives of Instruction in Reading," *Report of the National Committee on Reading,* p. 16. Twenty-fourth Yearbook of the National Society for the Study of Education, Part I. Bloomington, Ill.: Public School Publishing Co., 1925.

SOURCE: *Proceedings of the Annual Conference on Reading,* XX (December, 1958), 111–117. Reprinted by permission of the University of Chicago Press.

of spelling words representing, let us say, the *i-e e-i* rule, and study pupils' achivement on these in isolation. But reading is a process which flows past as you try to appraise it. You can arrest the flow to examine some aspect, but then it ceases to be reading.

Moreover, reading which is at all mature is an associative thinking process deep within the recesses of the mind. There is no way for an observer to be sure at a given moment whether a subject reading silently is gleaning facts or gathering main ideas or evaluating the writer or gaining aesthetic satisfaction or, in fact, whether he is really putting his mind to the printed page at all. Much can be inferred about the person's ability by having him read aloud. An oral reading test is undoubtedly one of the best ways of appraising the reading ability of a pupil but, since it must be administered individually, this kind of measure requires too much time for extensive use with large numbers of pupils.

Since, except for a superficial estimate of speed, no aspect of silent reading can be measured without interrupting the process, we customarily resort to a kind of addendum to the reading process itself. We ask a series of questions when the reading is finished and hope that the answers to these will indicate the quality of the comprehension which took place while the reading was being done. This isn't as good as we would like it to be, but it is about the best we can do, and, as will be indicated later, this rather clumsy procedure does yield valuable information about reading comprehension.

Since we cannot measure reading "all of a piece" while the act is taking place, we usually have recourse to some artificial and presumably logical analyses of the process and then build our tests upon the elements into which reading was analyzed. These analyses are likely to be somewhat different, depending upon the predilections of the persons doing the analysis. As I reported in an earlier one of this series of conferences, a survey of twenty-eight published reading tests showed that attempts were being made to measure forty-nine different aspects of reading ability, although some of these differed little except in the names assigned to them by the test authors.[3]

Factors analysis is of some help in identifying the fundamental areas of reading which ought to be measured. For instance, Davis[4] carried on a factor analysis of the Cooperative Reading Comprehension Test some

[3] Arthur E. Traxler, "Critical Survey of Tests for Identifying Difficulties in Interpreting What Is Read," *Promoting Growth toward Maturity in Interpreting What Is Read*, p. 196. Ed. William S. Gray. Supplementary Educational Monographs No. 74. Chicago: University of Chicago Press, 1951.

[4] Frederick B. Davis, "Fundamental Factors of Comprehension in Reading," *Psychometrika*, IX (September, 1944), 185–97.

years ago and reported that most of the variance was accounted for by two factors—word knowledge and reasoning in reading. However, the components of reading logically identified by reading specialists may differ considerably from those based on statistical analysis.

There is considerable agreement among those who have constructed reading tests based upon logical analysis of the reading process that three broad aspects of reading on which information is needed are speed, vocabulary, and comprehension. But if these are accepted as the main components toward which measurement should be directed, a *second kind of limitation* arises because of the complex nature of the subdivisions.

For instance, the measurement of rate of reading is not the simple procedure it may at first seem to be. There is not just one rate of reading for an individual; there are innumerable rates depending upon the nature of the material and the purposes of the reader. The speed at which a good reader covers an exciting novel may be several times as fast as his rate of reading a research article in a professional journal. The more mature the reader, the more his speed will vary. If a rate score of three hundred words a minute is obtained for a pupil on a reading test, one cannot say that this is his normal reading rate; one can say only that this was his rate on the material used in the test and under the kind of motivation which the test provided.

Most individuals, however, maintain somewhat similar *relative* reading speeds in different reading situations. So a pupil's standard score or percentile rating is likely to be fairly stable from one reading test to another, provided the test is long enough to yield reliable results. In some reading tests an attempt is made to obtain a speed score in just one minute of reading time. This is much too short an interval. Three minutes of reading time is the minimum for a reliable rate score, and at least five minutes of reading time would be preferable.[5]

Similarly, the measurement of reading vocabulary is complicated by a number of variables. There is not only a general reading vocabulary; there are also vocabularies of special fields. An individivual's standing within a norm group will be affected to some extent by the relative weight given in the vocabulary test to the different special fields. If a major proportion of the test words happen to come from the fields of mathematics and science, pupils with special reading facility in the humanities and social studies will be handicapped, and vice versa. Nevertheless, a reading vocabulary test which is carefully and scientif-

[5] Arthur E. Traxler, "The Relationship between the Length and the Reliability of a Test of Rate of Reading," *Journal of Educational Research,* XXXII (September, 1938), 1–2.

ically prepared is one of the most reliable and valid of all tests for use in placing an individual in a norm group.

The anomalous nature of part scores on reading tests is nowhere more evident than it is in the case of reading comprehension tests. The kinds of questions used and the manner of responding to the questions differ widely. In some comprehension tests the subject may refer back to the reading material while answering the questions, whereas in others he must recall what he has read. Some comprehension tests consist largely of factual questions, others stress main ideas, and still others attempt to measure critical thinking, inferences, or appreciation stimulated by the reading passage.

When the comprehension score is broken down into part scores, the variety of the scores may be inferred from the names of some of the parts. These include, among others, paragraph comprehension, main ideas, fact material, directed reading, level of comprehension, general significance of a passage, use of references, relevant and irrelevant statements, true and false deductions, and ability to perceive relationships.

Yet research indicates that attempts by testmakers to differentiate among various aspects of comprehension have not usually been very successful. The intercorrelations of the subscores, when corrected for attenuation, tend to be so high that they suggest that almost the same thing is measured by the different subtests.[6] This seems to be something closely akin to what Davis called reasoning in reading, or something very similar to that broad area of general intelligence which is measured by paper-and-pencil group tests of mental ability.

This brings us to a *third limitation of reading tests*—the lack of clear differentiation between measurement of reading comprehension and measurement of intelligence. In a sense, the better and more searching the reading test is, the greater this limitation becomes. It was pointed out earlier in this paper that reading, particularly high-level reading, is actually a form of thinking. But thinking is the process through which intelligence is manifested. So, when we give a reading test that really probes ability to think about the reading material, are we measuring reading or intelligence? The answer is that scores on this kind of test represent a composite of both intelligence and ability to read. Hence, it is very difficult to predict how much the scores of individuals who are low on such a test may be improved by teaching. For some individuals

[6] Arthur E. Traxler, "A Study of the Van Wagenen-Dvorak Diagnostic Examination of Silent Reading Abilities," *1940 Fall Testing Program in Independent Schools and Supplementary Studies*, pp. 33–41. Educational Records Bulletin No. 31. New York: Educational Records Bureau, 1941.

the possibilities of improvement are considerable; for others the main determiner of low reading comprehension scores is low verbal intelligence, and the prognosis for significant improvement is not favorable. Teachers need to recognize this failure of even the best reading tests to differentiate between reading comprehension and intelligence and to be prepared to accept the fact that not every pupil with a low reading score is capable of much improvement. But it is almost impossible to predict in advance which pupils with low reading scores are capable of improvement and which ones are not, unless scores are also available on such measures as an individual intelligence test and a listening comprehension test.

A *fourth limitation of reading tests* is the time-consuming nature of the measurement of reading, particularly reading comprehension. Vocabulary test items can be done quickly, but reading comprehension tests are not efficient because of the necessity of covering both reading passages and questions based on them. It is not unusual for a reading test to require the reading of a paragraph of two hundred words or so in order for the pupil to be able to answer four or five questions. Since many schools demand tests which can be administered within forty minutes, the number of comprehension questions used is likely to be too small for high reliability. If attempts are made to subdivide the comprehension test into parts measuring different aspects of comprehension, as is true of some reading tests, and if the comprehension test, along with a vocabulary test and a speed test, is squeezed into a forty-minute period, one may expect the subtest scores to be almost valueless for the study of individuals, although of some use in the study of groups.

This limitation of reading tests can readily be removed if schools will agree to devote a period of two or three hours to the measurement of reading instead of forty minutes or less.

Values

Notwithstanding the limitations of standardized reading tests, it would be next to impossible to plan and carry on a modern reading program without them. They have a number of positive values for instruction in reading in all schools. Some of these were referred to in connection with the discussion of limitations.

Perhaps the *most important value* of a reading test, or any other standardized test, is that it lends a certain amount of definiteness to our thinking about the achievement of a pupil or a group. Without reading tests it is possible to say in a vague or general way "Here is a pupil who appears to be a good reader; here is another who doesn't read well; and here is another who doesn't seem able to read at all." But we cannot be very confident about our classification when it is done simply on a subjective basis.

Reading tests enable us to speak about reading ability in quantitative terms with considerable confidence, provided we keep in mind that every test score contains an error of measurement and that we recognize the unimportance of small differences in score.

A reading test may be given to a seventh-grade class, and then it is possible to say, "That pupil reads about as well as the average ninth grader; this pupil is approximately at the fifth-grade level in reading ability; and here is a very retarded pupil whose reading is still on the level of Grade II." Moreover, if the test yields part scores, we can make such further quantitative statements as "In comparison with the norms for his grade, John has a rate of reading percentile of 96; a vocabulary percentile of 52, but a comprehension percentile of only 15."

These kinds of information lend definiteness and direction to the planning of reading instruction for both groups and indivduals. They provide a reasonably firm basis for developmental, corrective, and remedial programs, even though teachers need to remind themselves occasionally that the basis is not quite so solid and dependable as the bald, bold figures suggest, because of the limitations of reading tests already mentioned.

A *second value* of reading tests is for the appraisal of growth of individuals and groups in a developmental reading program. Is the total reading program of the school well designed to bring about normal or better growth of pupils at all grade levels and levels of ability? If not, where do the weaknesses exist? Such questions as these cannot be answered simply through the use of observation and teacher judgment. But if different forms of tests yielding comparable scores are used annually, and if the results are carefully studied, a constant check can be kept on the reading program as a whole and on the rate of reading growth of individual pupils.

A *third value* of reading tests lies in diagnosis of the strengths and weaknesses of groups and individuals as a starting point for corrective or remedial work. However, it should be kept in mind that reading tests are not in themselves diagnostic. They yield worthwhile information for diagnosis only when someone attempts to relate the results to other kinds of information about the pupil.

Still another value of reading tests lies in the early identification of gifted pupils. Nearly all gifted pupils read well, particularly in the field of their greatest ability and interest. Not infrequently, one of the first indications of unusually high mental ability is the tendency of a young child to begin reading on his own a year or two before he reaches the age of school entrance. When he enters school, his reading ability may be beyond the usual reading test designed for the lower primary grades, and a more difficult test may be needed in order to measure his actual achievement. It is desirable to supplement the school's regular testing program with reading tests appropriate to the ability level of very superior children so that suitable activities may be planned for them. Too often attempts to identify the gifted are delayed until the junior or senior high school level. This is frequently too late, for by that time many potentially outstanding children will have fallen into habits of an easy mediocrity in reading, as well as in other school activities.

Values and Limitations of Different Kinds of Reading Tests

Now I should like to comment briefly on the values and limitations of several types of reading tests.

One kind is that which yields only one total score. Forty or fifty years ago, when the first objective tests appeared, a number of reading tests were one-score tests, but tests of this kind almost disappeared from the scene until 1957, when the Sequential Tests of Educational Progress (Educational Testing Service, 1957), or STEP, were published. At each level, the reading test of this series is a seventy-minute test yielding only one over-all score. The STEP Reading Test is a most carefully constructed test, but it is difficult to see how it will be of much value in a reading program if used alone.

However, there is also in the STEP series a Listening Comprehension Test. It is believed that a listening test is one of the best measures of potential reading ability, although more research evidence is needed on this point. In any event, the STEP Listening Test and the STEP Reading Test, when used together, should furnish some information having broad diagnostic value.

At the other extreme, there is the kind of reading test in which an attempt is made to obtain within a class period a large number of part scores for purposes of diagnosis. This type of test is well illustrated by the Iowa Silent Reading Tests (World) and the California Reading Tests (California Test Bureau). Such tests, in which the time limits for the parts are very brief, either will have a large speed component in all scores, or the number of questions in each part will be so small that the scores will be low in reliability, or both. The total scores on these tests are often highly reliable, but it is more appropriate to use the part scores on tests of this kind for the study of groups than for individual diagnosis.

A third kind of reading test is aimed at the measurement of three aspects of reading believed to be especially important, such as rate, vocabulary, and power of comprehension. Fairly reliable measures of these aspects may be obtained within a class period, although the reliability of the comprehension score tends to be somewhat low.

In the primary grades the measurement of three or more aspects of reading ability within the same class period presents difficulties because of the short attention span of young children. Gates met this problem by having his Primary Reading Tests (Bureau of Publications, Teachers College) printed separately—one each for word recognition, sentence reading, and paragraph reading. The Gates tests continue to be among the most satisfactory reading tests at this level.

The most logical way of meeting the needs for a quickly administered survey test and dependable diagnostic scores would seem to be through a co-ordinated battery in which the survey test would be given first, to be followed by diagnostic tests appropriate to the weaknesses indicated on an individual or small-group basis. Thus far, the only tests of this kind are the Diagnostic Reading Tests (Committee on Diagnostic Reading Tests, Inc.). The committee has also undertaken to provide teaching materials for use in overcoming the weaknesses revealed by the diagnosis.

As already suggested, reading tests furnish only a portion of the information needed in carrying on a school reading evaluation program. So far as is possible, these tests should be used in conjunction with individual tests of mental ability, listening ability, achievement tests in the content areas, measures of interests, and inventories of personal qualities. Standardized reading tests have a limitation, in addition to those mentioned earlier, in that they furnish no direct information about interests or personality. As all teachers know, the sources of reading difficulty are not always to be found in the learning area; they often originate in the pupil's home, in his social group, in health and physical handicaps, or in his general adjustment to the environment of the school.

Reading test scores reach their greatest meaning and usefulness when they fall into place in a comprehensive individual cumulative record.

X. Research in Reading

From what sources can a teacher get new ideas? How can he avoid the pitfall of perpetuating pet theories and attitudes? What can awaken a teacher's curiosity and revitalize his instructional procedures? The answers to these questions lie in educational research.

According to Cleland, research in reading instruction occupies more space in magazines, journals, books, etc. than any other instructional area. Unfortunately, the significance of a great number of these studies is questionable. Cleland (63), Strang (64), and Raygor (65) find many weaknesses in them and offer suggestions for improvement. In many instances, problems have not been carefully defined; materials, methods, and the scope of the investigations have not been controlled; groups have not been properly equated; evaluative instruments have not been reliable or valid; and as stated by Cook (66), consideration has not been given to the Hawthorne effect. Because of weaknesses such as these, studies are repetitious and the results of one study may contradict the results of another. Often an experimenter will end his statement of results with an apology indicating the need to improve and repeat the study.

When studies of significant worth are conducted and when findings are conclusively established, then what? Teacher apathy to reported research findings is too often reflected in outmoded classroom practices. It's reported that a lag of forty years will usually elapse before research findings are applied to classroom practice. Clymer (67) discusses the problem and informs us of some of the reasons for this delay. Apropos, too, are Clymer's suggestions as to how teachers can apply research findings to their instructional program.

In the closing article of this chapter, Gates (68) reviews the contributions made by early researchers in reading. This is followed by a discussion of phonics, individualized reading, and programmed learning. He then described a significant research pattern for the future. Do you not agree with Gates when he says that "large-scale, time-consuming investigations must be carried out in education as they are already being conducted in medicine and public health, and in many phases of science and engineering"?

63. Needed Improvement in Research Design in Reading

DONALD L. CLELAND (1964)

It would not be difficult to justify a conclusion that research on reading instruction comprises more space in magazines, journals, books, encyclopedias, etc., than in any other area of education. The late Dr. William S. Gray has estimated that approximately 4,000 scientific studies of the sociology, psychology, and teaching of reading are available. While it is true that most of these studies dealt with reading at the elementary level, according to Summers[1] approximately 1,000 research studies have been completed which dealt with reading at the secondary level. It would be a safe guess to say that the total number of studies, if all could be located, would nearly double the 4,000 mentioned. According to Gray,[2] the number of research studies increased each decade and reached a peak in the period 1931–1940 with a total of 1,071 studies. During the

[1] Edward G. Summers, *An Annotated Bibliography of Selected Research Related to Teaching Reading in the Secondary School: 1900–1960* (Pittsburgh: School of Education, University of Pittsburgh, 1963), pp. 183.

[2] William S. Gray, "Summary of Reading Investigations," *Encyclopedia of Educational Research*, ed. Chester W. Harris (New York: The Macmillan Company, 1960), p. 1087.

SOURCE: *Improvement of Reading Through Classroom Practice*, IX (1964), 244–249. Reprinted with the permission of Donald L. Cleland and the International Reading Association.

next decade, and possibly because of the second World War, the number of studies reported amounted to 915. Apparently, a resurgence occurred *post bellum* as over 700 studies were reported for the period 1951–1957. As testimony to the fact that the number of research studies in the area of reading is increasing year by year, Robinson[3] cites 185 studies completed during the period of July 1, 1962 to June 30, 1963. A little simple arithmetic, therefore, would indicate that approximately 2,000 studies might be completed during the decade 1961–1970.

Several reasons or forces may account for this upswing.

1. The increased emphasis upon reading and particularly at the secondary level. It would be safe to say that slowly, but definitely, teachers and administrators are realizing the tremendous role the skill of reading plays in all study activities.

2. The encouragement of research in reading by the United States Office of Education. Money to support research in reading has been made available by congressional action. Increasingly, year by year, more money has been made available. This fact alone has resulted in an increased number of proposals submitted for funds to support cooperative research projects. Mention should be made also of other funding agencies such as the Carnegie Foundation.

3. The efforts of the National Council on Research in English. Specialists in the field of reading are applauding the dynamic leadership of those responsible for the latest effort of NCRE to get support from the U.S. Office of Education for cooperative research. To me this is the most exciting adventure in research that it has been my pleasure to witness. As a member of a cooperative team, I have witnessed the combined efforts of the leaders in reading, psychology, and experimental design not only directed toward improvement in research design, but also directing the weight and force of their prestige in a manner that will ensure research proposals strong in both *internal* and *external* validity. The fruit of this effort should be more palatable and more generalizable than much of the race-horse type of research that has been so prominent in the past.

At this point in our discussion, let us turn our attention to research on research. Several such studies have been completed at the University of Pittsburgh—studies which critically examined research in spelling,[4] pho-

[3] Helen M. Robinson, "Summary of Investigations Relating to Reading, July 1, 1962–June 30, 1963," *The Reading Teacher*, Vol. 17 (February 1964), pp. 326–391.

[4] Stephen Pavlak, A *Critical Analysis of Scientific Research in Spelling*, Unpublished Doctoral Dissertation (Pittsburgh: University of Pittsburgh, School of Education, 1956).

nics,[5] and reading comprehension.[6] The conclusions drawn as a result of the critical appraisal of the research studies listed are revealing and further attest to the need for improvement in research design or a better control of certain variables.

In 1954, Pavlak[7] examined 234 references to spelling. After carefully examining them, he decided to study critically 121 of these studies to ascertain if they met research criteria which were formulated by Monroe and Engelhart,[8] namely: (1) definition and restriction of the experimental factor; (2) control of pupil factor; (3) control of important non-experiment factors; (4) accuracy and validity of measures of differences in achievement; (5) justification of generalization. After applying the criteria of scientific accuracy, forty-nine studies, or 40.5 percent, were rejected.

Of the 72 studies accepted, eighteen of the nineteen doctoral studies, thirty-six of the sixty-two masters' theses, and eighteen of the forty journal and monograph articles, were accepted. After critically studying these seventy-two studies, Pavlak[9] arrived at the following conclusion:

> After carefully studying and comparing the findings of the various scientifically accurate research studies; it was found that the studies did not agree as to the best general method of teaching spelling. According to the accepted investigations, neither the test-study method nor the study-test method was superior in the teaching of spelling. An analysis of the scientific studies showed that there was a trend toward conducting research on the value of the individual method of teaching spelling.

A similar evaluation of research studies in phonics was conducted by Morrone[10] in 1958. Of the 198 references secured and examined, 101 were selected for critical study, using again Monroe's and Englehart's criteria. Of the 101 studies examined critically, thirty-three were accepted as having satisfied the aforementioned criteria. Of the thirty-three studies accepted, thirteen of the eighteen doctoral dissertations, eight of the twenty-four masters' theses, and twelve of the journals and monographs were accepted.

[5] Victor E. Morrone. A *Critical Analysis of Scientific Research in Phonics,* Unpublished Doctoral Dissertation (Pittsburgh: School of Education, University of Pittsburgh, 1958).
[6] Arthur W. Schoeller, A *Critical Survey of the Scientific Studies of Reading Comprehension,* Unpublished Doctoral Dissertation (Pittsburgh: School of Education, University of Pittsburgh, 1950).
[7] Pavlak, *op. cit.*
[8] Walter S. Monroe and Max Engelhart, "A Critical Summary of Research Relating to the Teaching of Arithmetic," *Bulletin* No. 58 (Urbana, Illinois: University of Illinois Press, 1931).
[9] *Ibid.*, p. 212.
[10] Morrone, *op. cit.*

One of the conclusions drawn from a critical examination of the studies is very disconcerting. The following substantiates this point of view:

> After a careful analysis of the scientific research on phonics in reading, it was found that disagreement existed as to the approach and amount of phonic instruction teachers should utilize. Some of the investigations disclosed that phonics become meaningful and functional when they are used as an integral part of the reading instruction. Other studies revealed that phonics should be taught systematically each day in a specific period distinctly apart from the basic reading lessons. . . . The trend indicated that the process of teaching phonics should be one of analysis rather than one of synthesis. Phonics should be taught as a process involving whole words rather than isolated word elements.

It is interesting to note that the same conclusion was drawn in 1921 by Theisen:[11]

> The question of phonics or no phonics is perhaps of less importance than (the question) of just what, how much, and from whom. Present practice is exceedingly wasteful. . . . The phonic content taught should have a direct bearing upon the reading in hand.

A careful study and evaluation of scientific studies in reading comprehension further attests to the need for improvement in research design in reading. Schoeller[12] critically analyzed 211 studies in comprehension, which encompassed the period from 1884 to 1948. Of these studies, fifty-three were rejected as not meeting the criteria set forth by Monroe and Englehart.[13]

Of the 211 studies critically examined, four of the forty-four doctoral dissertations, thirty-six of the seventy-eight masters' theses and eighteen of the eighty-nine journals and monographs were rejected. One of Schoeller's conclusions is worthy of note:

> Research in this field is still sporadic and the types of problems attacked are not chosen in a systematic way. Many of the problems that have been investigated have been concerned with only a few grade levels, such as which skills begin to develop at certain age levels. Also, some of the problems, such as factors in comprehension, have been only partly investigated.

At this point, it would be revealing to recapitulate the findings as a result of the critical evaluation of studies in spelling, phonics, and read-

[11] W. W. Theisen, "Factors Affecting Results in Primary Reading," *Twentieth Yearbook, Part II*, National Society for the Study of Education (Chicago: University of Chicago Press, 1921), pp. 1–24.
[12] Schoeller, *op. cit.*
[13] Monroe and Engelhart, *op. cit.*

ing comprehension. Of the 433 scientific studies, 170 were rejected and 263 were accepted. *The bare unvarnished fact is that approximately 60 percent were accepted as having met the criteria selected.* Seventy-one of the eighty-one doctoral dissertations, eighty-six of the 164 masters' theses and 140 of the 188 studies reported in journals, etc., were accepted. It is interesting to note that the above falls into the following rank order: (1) doctoral dissertations; (2) journals and monographs; (3) masters' theses. It is shocking to note that 47.5 percent of the masters' theses examined and accepted for study were rejected.

It is true that these three studies were completed during the 1950's. I am confident, also, that during the last decade more sophistication has been brought to research studies in reading. Notwithstanding, however, few would have the audacity to suggest that we have reached the point beyond which no improvement could be made.

At this point in our discussion, let us turn our attention to a writer who enjoys stature in the area of reading.

In a recent article which appeared in the *Phi Delta Kappan,* McDonald[14] gives his reactions to an evaluation of research studies he reviewed during the last ten years.

The author lists sources of error in research studies. The list is quite thought provoking and supports the theme of this paper. An abbreviated form of these are as follows:

1. Failure to correct for regression to the mean.
2. Treating reading grade scores as empirically obtained indications of month-by-month progress. In reality, reading grade scores are extrapolated from one grade level to another.
3. Interpretation of test scores on the assumption that the tests used provide reliable and valid measures of the most important aspects of reading.
4. Spurious scores obtained from the use of a single test over wide educational (or performance) levels.
5. Use, for checking reading comprehension, of test questions which can be answered by most children from their background knowledge (i.e., without even reading the selection).
6. Errors in interpretation because of use of inappropriate norms, failure to allow for interform differences in equivalence, etc.
7. Failure to select a really comparable control group.

Previously in this article I mentioned that what was needed in research in reading was not necessarily improvement in research design, per se, but an elimination or better control through randomization of certain

[14] Arthur S. McDonald, "Some Pitfalls in Evaluating Progress in Reading Instruction," *Phi Delta Kappan,* XLV (April 1964), pp. 336–338.

variables so that the *information estimate* obtained can be contributed to the independent variable. Otherwise, the dependent or consequent variable may be explained by rival or alternate hypothesis. Except in the isolated science laboratory, it is extremely doubtful if research in the child's environment or in a simulated atmosphere can be cleanly controlled.

The task which we face, therefore, if we cannot control certain non-experimental factors, is to randomize them so that any confounding effect they might have on the information estimate is evident in both control and experimental groups.

Cognizance on the part of the experimenter of these confounding variables which may give rise to rival or alternate hypothesis will enable him to design experiments which will be strong in both *internal* and *external* validity, thus obtaining an information estimate that will be highly generalizable. Let us therefore look at variables that, if not controlled or randomized, may confound experimental results. As I explore these, you will instantly recognize that I have drawn heavily upon the literature, especially the *Handbook of Research on Teaching*[15] and a paper presented by Dr. Guba[16] to the faculty of New York University.

Certain conditions must exist if we are to secure an unbiased *information estimate*, not necessarily to prove a given hypothesis, but to build confidence in a conclusion each time new evidence has been uncovered. In fact Guba says,[17] "experimentation thus is a systematic procedure for exposing some hypothesis to disconfirmation." He goes on to say that the assertion that all swans are white can be disconfirmed at once if we can point to a black swan. Yet we build confidence in the truth of the assertion every time we inspect a swan and find it white. By the same token we build confidence in the superiority of Method A over Method B every time we see research which gives evidence that A is superior to B.

I have asserted that we need an unbiased *information estimate* if it can be generalizable. At this point, we might ask, what experimental and non-experimental conditions might give us a biased *information estimate?* A review of the literature would reveal many, among which might be the following:

1. History—the effects of events, situations, or experiences that occur simultaneously with the experiment. For instance, parents may attempt

[15] T. T. Campbell and J. C. Stanley, "Experimental and Quasi-Experimental Designs for Research on Teaching," Chapter V in Gage, N. L. (ed.), *Handbook of Research on Teaching* (Chicago: Rand McNally, 1963).

[16] Egon G. Guba, "Common Sense About Experimental Design in Educational Research" (Paper read at a Faculty Symposium, School of Education, New York University, February 25, 1963).

[17] *Ibid.*, pp. 2–3.

to aid their children in reading, using an approach that would be foreign to the antecedent variable.

2. Maturation—that is, effects of processes that may be associated with normal growth or maturation.

3. Testing—the effect of one testing upon another subsequent testing because of practice or memory effects, etc. For instance, this effect may be seen in certain speed reading courses in which pretesting is followed by reading exercises, the format of which is very much similar to both the pretest and the postest. In effect, the students are "trained" by the pretest and reading exercises to do better on the postest, thus giving rise to a rival hypothesis.

4. Instrumentation—the effect wrought by changes in instrumentation. This factor was referred to as *instrument decay* by Campbell and Stanley, a descriptive phrase which seems to explain this concept very neatly. Changes in the calibration of a measuring instrument or changes in observers or scorers used may bring changes to the obtained measurements.

5. Statistical regression—this extraneous variable is operative especially when groups have been selected on the basis of extreme scores. Students in a remedial reading group whose pretest scores are low almost inevitably will show gain since it is a statistical truism that any extreme group on retest will manifest a regression toward the population mean. By the same token, similar experiments on gifted children will also show a regression to the mean, which in this instance may be lower than the pretest mean. This regression toward the mean is a ubiquitous phenomenon. Any principal who observes that his highest IQ students do not necessarily have the highest achievement scores, and that his lowest IQ students may not have the lowest achievement scores, may be guilty of this *regression fallacy* if he concludes that the brighter students are underachieving and his dullest students are over-achieving, and consequently announces to the faculty that they are overstimulating the slowest and understimulating the brightest.

6. Differential selection—the effect of using groups that have not been selected randomly; thus, the groups may not be comparable according to some criterion or criteria. If two methods of teaching reading are being compared and one of the groups, either the experimental or control, has a significantly higher IQ than the other, any differences obtained cannot be as ascribed, *a priori*, to the independent variable. Or likewise, if one group were selected from a high income level where probably more intellectual stimulation is provided by the parents and the other group were selected from a low income group where, probably, little intellectual stimulation is provided, the end results may be attributed to a rival hypothesis.

7. Subject mortality—the effect of differential loss from experimental groups resulting in non-comparable groups. Mortality—families of children moving to another school district, cases on which only partial data are available, and dropouts from the experimental group because of lack of willingness to continue—is very troublesome to handle and is commonly, as one writer put it, swept under the rug.

These seven sources of rival or alternative hypotheses constitute major threats to the internal validity of an experiment. Thus, the *information estimate* gleaned from the research may be adulterated, and if so, does not permit generalization. How can researchers then rid experiments of these confounding variables? This can be done in two ways—by control and by randomization. If it were possible to control completely all confounding variables, the *information estimate* would be certain. This halcyon state is, however, impossible to achieve in practice. The other choice, therefore, is to randomize. In such a situation, the effect of these variables is not removed but is forced into a pattern which is predictable from statistical theory. The estimate of the size of the effect produced by these randomized variables is called an *error estimate*.[18]

It would not be amiss at this time to mention, very briefly, three true experimental designs which so neatly control the biasing effects of the seven rival hypotheses previously described. Campbell and Stanley[19] have described them as:

1. The Pretest-Postest Control Group Design. In this research design equivalency of groups is achieved through randomization. Both groups, the experimental and control, are given both pretests and postests, but only the experimental group receives treatment.

2. The Postest Only Control Group Design. In this design we have equivalency of groups achieved through randomization. Both experimental and control groups are tested *posteriori* but in which only the experimental group receives treatment.

3. The Solomon Four-Group Design. This design is really a combination of the Postest Only Control Group Design and the Pretest-Postest Control Group Design. This design calls for four groups—one experimental and three control. All four groups must be selected randomly. The experimental group receives a pretest treatment and postest; control group II receives no pretest, but treatment and postest; and control group III receives postest only.

I hope the theme of this presentation is readily apparent. In spite of the thousands of research studies in reading completed since 1884, many questions remain unanswered. Divination will not give us the answer. Research is committed to the settling of disputes regarding educational

[18] *Ibid.*, p. 13.
[19] Campbell and Stanley, *op. cit.*, pp. 183–197.

practices, as the way of verifying present practice, and as a way of establishing cumulative tradition as pertains to new practices. We must be mindful, however, that while settling disputes, verifying present practices, and establishing cumulative tradition, experimentation can also beget other controversies or disputes.

The three studies cited earlier in this paper point to the need for improvement of research design, or we might say, the need to rid research of confounding variables which give rise to rival or alternate hypotheses. Casting aside approximately 40 percent of studies as not having met selected criteria is a sad commentary on research. Another potent argument supporting the theme is the support the U.S. Office of Education has given to research. And still another, and perhaps more potent, is the prestige given by the National Conference on Research in English in behalf of research in reading. And finally, the classic effort of the American Educational Research Association offers mute evidence of this need. Only the most naïve would question the continuous need for improvement in research design in reading.

64. Reactions to Research on Reading

RUTH STRANG (1962)

I

Apart from clinical studies, there has been little research that has contributed to our understanding of the dynamics of the reading process. Coefficients of correlation do not indicate causation nor identify the forces that are actually influencing an individual. Factor analysis groups characteristics into clusters and highlights the ones that are dominant. However, it discovers no new factors; it only rearranges the factors that were originally put into the hopper. Surveys too often pool widespread

SOURCE: *The Educational Forum,* January 1962, pp. 187–192. Reprinted by permission of Kappa Delta Pi, An Honor Society in Education, owners of the copyright.

ignorance; they may reiterate unverified and possibly erroneous opinions, and lend authority to unevaluated procedures.

Many of the early experimenters used the comparable group research design to ascertain which of two methods was the more effective. These investigators were content to match groups with respect to age, grade, sex, intelligence test scores, and initial reading test scores. But what about the subjects' learning rates? Is this factor adequately indicated by intelligence test scores? And what about many of the other factors that have been found to be components of reading ability, such as linguistic abilities and listening comprehension? What about pervasive "mobilizers" such as the individual's self-concept, value system, purpose, and attitude toward reading? The teacher's personality, teaching skill, and relation to the pupils are also recognized as important influences on learning. Yet all of the comparable group experiments have ignored these factors. Even when the same teacher is employed in both groups, he usually shows greater enthusiasm and skill in teaching by one of the methods than in teaching by the other. Moreover, the effective teacher can hardly help modifying his method in response to the needs of his pupils. Thus the experimental method itself is contaminated.

Comparable group research is made still more complicated by differences in the classroom situation. Obviously some situations are more conducive to learning than others. In some groups the interaction among the pupils facilitates learning; in other groups it inhibits it. Innumerable factors within the situation may affect the results that are obtained by any method.

"Comparable" groups are never really comparable. There are always uncontrolled variables that may influence the results. Thus, at the end of the experiment, the investigator cannot choose but be apologetic; he cannot say with certainty that a given result was obtained by virtue of the particular teaching method which he wanted to study. The apparent differences in the two sets of results might be attributed to differences in the personality or enthusiasm of the teacher, the learning rate of the children, or any of the other factors that we have already mentioned. In short, the teaching-learning process is too complex to be studied by the predominantly statistical research designs that are now available.

How, then, can we prove that one method of teaching reading is in general better than another? I don't think we can—or need to. There is some truth in the Chinese proverb that "a good method used by a bad person brings bad results and a bad method used by a good person brings good results."

Instead of continuing to conduct inadequately controlled group experiments, it would be more useful to adopt the single group comparison type of experiment that is employed in the physical sciences. Here all the factors in a given situation are carefully described. Then one factor is modified and the resultant total effect is recorded. In this way we would gain some insight into the ways in which learning is affected by various complex conditions, including the pupils' prior experiences.

Another approach is the "simple research design" suggested by Dr. William Brownell. This involves:

1. Accurate, detailed study of the pupils in given classes—their abilities, backgrounds, learning rates, etc.
2. Carefully documented observation of the teaching-learning process as it is actually carried out in the classroom—including the dyadic relation between what the teacher says and does and the way the pupils respond.
3. An imaginative interpretation, coherent and logical, of each phenomenon observed, in the light of theory that gives meaning and direction to the inquiry.

Premature attempts to be scientific have produced misleading conclusions, which have had detrimental effects on the teaching of reading.

By attempting to make comparisons in a field under conditions where variability is inevitable, the experimenter reinforces the erroneous either-or attitude. The newer conception stresses flexibility and encourages combining the best features of several methods. To conclude that one method, used with selected teachers and a limited number of pupils who have had certain previous learning experiences, is poorer than another is to imply that the "poorer" method should be discarded. However, further analysis of the data might show that this method is very effective when used with certain pupils, or when used in combination with some other method.

II

One type of research seems to be basic to the improvement of reading instruction. It underlies programmed reading instruction with or without the use of machines; it is prerequisite to the construction of effective reading tests; it is essential for efficient instruction in reading at every age level. This research deals with the dynamic process by which individuals of different ages, mental abilities, interests, and backgrounds actually comprehend and interpret what they read.

Lacking this basic knowledge of the reading process, we have built up a superstructure of teaching methods which may be highly inappropriate and inefficient for many pupils. For example, bright children who have learned to read before entering school sometimes score low on reading readiness tests. Apparently they have developed a method of sensing the meaning that does not require the kind of auditory and visual discrimination that these tests involve. Similarly, older pupils may be hampered and frustrated by having to go step by step through a set of predetermined motions to reach a conclusion which they could arrive at more quickly by intuition.

How these pupils arrive at such effective comprehension is the complex problem of this proposed research. How do their minds work as they read? What forces are influencing them at the time? What developmental factors may have affected their reading progress?

Information of this kind can be obtained most directly from introspective and retrospective accounts. Adolescents have given me keen insights in freely written compositions, panel discussions, and interviews. For example, the following comments were made in a panel discussion in response to the question, "Why do some bright students fail in one or more subjects?"

> A bright student is able to read very fast and skips over many things, but when you read fast, you don't always get what you should and you say, "Oh, I'll remember this, I don't have to take notes." . . . I think even if you are bright you should take notes.

Another student described the effect of television on reading:

> I think that the intelligent person must judge, and I guess it is up to the parents of children of younger ages to judge where television should begin and reading should end.
>
> Television, like the comics, gives you a picture at the same time as you read. It leaves no room for your interpretation. . . . With reading you can seek out different interpretations. With television . . . you don't judge; you watch it and absorb it.
>
> In some ways television is a menace to the intelligence because it is so easy. You can sit there and don't have to do a thing. You can be lulled by it, and I think the more you watch television, the more your critical sense becomes dulled.
>
> I know that at the beginning of an evening when I have nothing to do or a few things to do that I don't want to do, I might start and watch one bad program and then another and another, and pretty soon I begin to enjoy them no matter how bad they are. I think it's really harmful if a bad television program keeps you away from a good book.

Could any psychologist have stated more lucidly or simply the subtle conditioning effect of television?

Following are two quotations that illustrate the kind of insights into the reading process that can be obtained from adolescents' compositions:

When I am up against some text material or something else that is concentrated and difficult to get immediately, I sometimes will go on reading without really coordinating my mind with the task; I will keep on reading the words without thinking about them at all. When I come to the end of a page, I wouldn't be able to say what was on it. I have read it, but it seems as though my eyes were working separately from my brain.

When I first started to read, I read very widely. I was kind of a bookworm in my younger days and I accepted what I read completely as fact. But once I started to go into a subject, I read many books about it. For example, after I had read about five or six books about Queen Elizabeth I, I began to run up against contradictions. . . . Then I began to think for myself a little more, and I think that is what makes a mature reader.

One can also obtain specific insights from some students in groups, immediately after they have read a passage and answered comprehension questions on it, by asking them questions such as these, which invite retrospection: How did you read the article; that is what method or process did you use? What did you do to get the main idea? What did you do to get important details? What did you do when you met words you did not know? One tenth-grade student reported that she "read parts carefully and skimmed through others; repeated details to herself; and tried to imagine what the unfamiliar word would be to make sense."

The worker who is successful in gaining the interest and co-operation of the pupil in an interview may gain insight into the reading process—even if the youngster has a low ability to verbalize.

From sixth-grade pupils who had been taught certain words which they did not know initially, and were then tested on them, William Elfert[1] obtained many explanations of both failure and success in learning the meaning of words. Auditory similarity accounts for some errors: one child defined *optimist* as "stubborn," obviously confusing it with *obstinate.* One boy confused *vertical* with *vehicle:* "A bicycle is a vertical; you ride on it." Visual similarity accounts for other errors: one youngster defined *immortal* as "bad," obviously confusing it with *immoral.* As E. L. Thorndike pointed out many years ago, one part of a word may have overpotency: one pupil defined *earnest* as "to earn something." Other errors occur because a word's meaning has become associated with the phrase in which it is commonly used. For example, *brawny* was defined as *smart* because of the association of "brains and brawn."

[1] William Elfert. "An Exploration of Sixth-grade Pupils' Acquisition of Word Meanings Through Classroom Instruction." Doctor of Education project report, Teachers College, Columbia University, New York, 1960. 121 pp. Typewritten.

Even more fascinating are the associations that give pupils the correct meanings of words:

Associations with their experience: *Unanimous:* "We voted for a new class president last month. Everyone was in agreement on one person, and the teacher said, 'It's unanimous. He's elected.' "

Associations with persons: *Dawdle:* "There's a boy in my class who is always wasting time. When we had the word *dawdle,* my teacher said, 'That's the boy who dawdles.' " *Brawny:* "I think of the wrestlers on TV."

Personal reference: *Confiscate:* "If the teacher sees somebody with a yo-yo or ball in class, she says, 'If you don't put that away, I'll confiscate it.' "

Dramatizing the word: *Encounter:* "We had an act on that. A boy was walking along reading the paper and another boy bumped into him."

Teachers' explanations and other activities also helped these pupils to remember the meanings of words. The dictionary was mentioned in only 7 out of the 786 responses having furnished the correct meaning of a word, although it was frequently used in every class.

III

The research procedure here proposed would be to present pupils of different ages and abilities with various kinds of reading tasks, obtain an adequate measure of their comprehension and interpretation, ask them to describe their reading processes, and then seek further clarification of what they have said, with the aid of specific questions as in the Rorschach method of "testing the limits." The pupil might also be asked to read a shorter passage and verbalize his process as he reads.

Some important aspects of this kind of study are illustrated by research now being carried on at the University of Chicago under the direction of Dr. Helen Robinson in projects with elementary, high school, and college students. One research worker used a narrative selection on the sixth-grade level to investigate the differences and similarities of good interpretation and poor interpretation. Another studied pupils' responses to poetry; another analyzed the respective contributions of language structure and language content to senior high school students' comprehension of literature; another examined the reading processes of twelfth-grade students when they were reading for details and when they were reading for general impressions; and still another assessed the influence of an unstructured reading situation as contrasted with a classroom reading assignment. In all of these researches student introspection and retrospection were major sources of significant data.

Piaget made extensive use of introspection as a major technique for collecting data on children's thought processes. Of late he has been criticized for collecting masses of data without first setting up hypotheses. But is there not a place for exploratory studies that are based on repeated observations and unhampered by preconceptions? Is not this the essence of the inductive method as it was developed by Francis Bacon and later used by Darwin? Have not some of the most important discoveries been made by persons who sought only to understand—who felt no obligation to adapt their findings to preconceived classifications or theories? At times it is well to drop preconceived notions and make a fresh start.

Piaget has also been criticized for neglecting to submit his data to statistical treatment. He replies that his unstructured interview data, based on questions which follow the leads of the subjects, do not lend themselves to statistical treatment—i.e., statistical treatment is not appropriate to this kind of data. Instead he uses clinical reasoning, or what Barbara Buks called "insightful analysis"—a kind of critical, creative thinking that adapts itself to the data that have been obtained.

If we agree that each individual is unique, why do we insist that doctoral students in education must always arrive at generalizations? Would it not be wiser, as Francis Bacon suggested, to refrain for awhile from trying to arrive at general conclusions, and from inferring more than is warranted from a single piece of research?

It is a characteristic of the behavioral sciences that they never yield perfect correlations; when we are working with an individual, we have no way of knowing whether he conforms to the central tendencies or is one of the extreme deviates. In fact, a mind that is predetermined to see everything in terms of the central tendency may be incapable of recognizing true individuality.

Would it not be more helpful to teachers and clinicians if researchers were to report individuality as well as commonality, and to describe and explain the processes which have produced certain responses?

Research oriented toward goals such as I have briefly outlined might supply unique insights into the dynamics of the reading process. This kind of information might either confirm or revolutionize our methods of teaching and testing reading.

65. Some Thoughts on the Current State of Research in Reading

ALTON L. RAYGOR (1964)

In spite of the fact that the act of reading has been the object of more research studies than any other single piece of human behavior, we still must face the fact that the development of a science of reading has been a very slow process, and that we do not know much more about it than we did fifty years ago. One reason is that we spend much more time trying to demonstrate that what we are doing has some effect than we do trying to find out what does, in fact, produce that effect. A recent look at about a thousand research studies in reading turned up about three hundred studies in which someone had given a reading test, taught a course, then given another reading test. In a few cases someone had even tested and retested a group *not* given a course. Two or three of the latter kind of study would have been useful to establish that one could influence test scores by teaching reading courses. The other two hundred and ninety-seven studies contributed very little to our knowledge of reading and represent a loss of experimenter time running into some twenty to thirty thousand hours. This is only one example of the fact that our research has been very repetitious and relatively uninformative.

How much more useful it would have been if some of the studies referred to above had been designed to evaluate the application of some specific method or material! Even more useful in the long run would have been an attempt to use this much research time and effort to study the basic process of reading.

Recent developments in learning theory have demonstrated the value of some research procedures in which traditional statistical research has given way to more complete experimental controls, making it possible to do significant studies using a relatively small number of subjects and more careful control of the experimental variables. The focus of attention is on the behavior of a single organism at a time, in an attempt to find out just what the organism is doing at any given time and what can

SOURCE: *Journal of Developmental Reading,* VII (Winter, 1964), 75–76. Reprinted by permission of the author and publisher.

be done to alter its responses. Such research procedures have produced our knowledge of the power of operant conditioning techniques, for example, and their resultant application in programmed instruction. It is time we began to study, with similar methods, the nature of the complex set of responses we call reading and the specific techniques for producing those responses.

A really scientific study of reading will involve, among other things, a closer look at the results of work in other related sciences. The art of teaching reading has probably developed about as much as it will without more attention to its scientific foundations. Just as the art of healing builds on scientific efforts in pathology, anatomy, chemistry, and other sciences, the art of teaching reading needs to be nourished by the body of scientific information provided by experimental psychology, linguistics, sociology, and other behavioral sciences.

Significant changes in the history of any field are always marked by points at which we increase our understanding of the basic processes involved and extend our control over them. So it will be in reading. Our "basic" research needs to be aimed at understanding the reading process, and our "applied" research should be directed toward the application of specific techniques and the observation of their effects.

66. The Hawthorne Effect and Reading Research

DESMOND L. COOK (1964)

The purpose of this paper is to examine a methodological problem encountered frequently in reading research investigations and which is popularly referred to as the *Hawthorne effect* phenomenon. I shall (a) provide a definition of the phenomenon, (b) discuss the significance of this phenomenon in general research methodology, and (c) present some illustrations of its direct relation to reading research.

SOURCE: *Improvement of Reading through Classroom Practice,* IX (1964), 249–253. Reprinted with the permission of Desmond L. Cook and the International Reading Association.

An operational definition of the Hawthorne effect has been presented by the author in an earlier paper.[1] It was defined then as ". . . an awareness on the part of the subject of special treatment created by artificial experimental conditions." Subject awareness becomes confounded with the independent variable under study, resulting in a facilitative effect on the dependent variable and causing ambiguous results. Under this approach, the phenomenon is truly an *effect* because it is created by certain causative situations. The definition also emphasizes that the phenomenon occurs in the *subject* participating in the experiment as opposed to assigning it to the experimenter or his surrogate as is often done. In the latter case, the investigator's enthusiasm for the experimental variable is said to result in the experimental results coming out as they do. The tendency for experiments to come out in terms of the experimenter's enthusiasm should best be placed under *experimenter bias* rather than the Hawthorne effect. In any given experimental situation, the degree of subject awareness is probably widespread between subjects.

Importance of the Hawthorne Effect Phenomenon

Concern over the role of the phenomenon described above as a contaminating variable in social and behavioral science research has developed primarily within the past two or three decades although early experimenters in education (e.g., McCall in 1923) suggested that some such phenomenon might occur and experimenters should be aware of it. The importance of the phenomenon has been brought into focus more and more because of a continuing failure to secure similar results when educational experiments are repeated outside of the setting of their original investigation. Correlated with this failure to observe similar experimental results in new situations is the fact that behavioral scientists began to develop a concern about certain social-psychological interactions between experimenter and subject which heretofore had not been carefully scrutinized. Some of the more current problems of this type being investigated are those of *experimenter bias* by Rosenthal[2] and the work on *demand characteristics* (implicit and explicit cues in experimental situations signaling the subject as to the purpose of the experiment) being done by Orne.[3]

[1] Desmond L. Cook. "The Hawthorne Effect in Educational Research," *Phi Delta Kappan,* XLIV: 116–122, p. 118.
[2] Robert Rosenthal. "On the Social Psychology of the Psychological Experiment: The Experimenter's Hypothesis as Unintended Determinant of Experimental Results," *American Scientist,* June 1963, Vol. 51, No. 2, pp. 268–283.
[3] Martin T. Orne. "On the Social Psychology of the Psychological Experiment: With Particular Reference to Demand Characteristics and Their Implications," *American Psychologist,* 17: 776–785, 1962.

The above remarks project an image of the Hawthorne effect phenomenon's being a negative feature of experimentation, and to the extent that it does exist in an experimental situation I believe this condition to be true. There are those, however, who do not look upon the Hawthorne effect as having negative valence but look upon it instead as possessing positive valence. Such a position is represented by recent writings of Uttal,[4] Caplan,[5] and Suchman.[6]

All of these writers feel that the Hawthorne effect has been or can be capitalized upon to motivate students to achieve. Suchman, in his studies on inquiry training at the University of Illinois, feels that his experimental treatments actually utilize the Hawthorne effect to secure greater motivation and thus increase achievement on the part of participating subjects.

The Hawthorne Effect in Research Designs

Accepting the operational definition of the Hawthorne effect as presented above, let us now turn our attention to its possible role in the design and conduct of research. Some time ago, I hypothesized relationships between possible components of the Hawthorne effect and the stages of experimental investigation.[7] The components of the Hawthorne effect were established by using four frequently encountered definitions or explanations of the phenomenon: namely—"novelty," "attention," "knowledge of results," and "teacher-pupil interaction." The research stages were defined as those activities carried out by an investigator *prior* to conducting the research, and those activities carried on *during* the research, and those activities employed as *post* research procedures.

Within this framework, it is possible to relate certain research activities to possible subject awareness. For example, the introduction of new, different, and/or novel materials as part of the research procedure might create feelings of novelty and thereby induce awareness. The use of selected pre-tests as part of the research preliminaries might also cause the subject to realize he is the center of attention and thus induce awareness. It would be possible also during the post experimental interviewing of

[4] W. R. Uttal. "On Conversational Interaction," in J. E. Coulson, *Programmed Learning and Computer Based Instruction*. Proceedings of the Conference on Application Digital Computer to Automated Instruction, New York: John Wiley, 1961, p. 196.

[5] Bernard A. Caplan. "Issues in Educating the Culturally Disadvantaged," *Phi Delta Kappan*, 45: 72–76, November 1963, p. 74.

[6] Personal Correspondence with Dr. Suchman.

[7] Desmond L. Cook. "The Relation of Possible Hawthorne Effect Components to Stages of Experimental Investigation." A paper prepared for a joint session of the American Educational Research Association and National Council on Measurements in Education, Chicago, Illinois, February 16, 1963.

subjects to signal them in such a way as to cause them to become more aware of experimental participation and hence then respond differently than would be normally expected. These interactions of research conditions and possible components could operate not only in an experimental group but also in a control group, thus accounting for the common finding of *no* differences. Such interactions would, however, be particularly heightened in situations where the experimental group alone received them. Observed differences between experimental and control groups could possibly be accounted for on this basis alone. In situations where both experimental and control groups received identical interactions, the absence of a difference between but resultant greater achievement in both groups might be attributable to an induced awareness on the part of *all* subjects.

This concept of interaction between experimental arrangements and subjects' feelings has been presented to some degree in the current *Handbook of Research on Teaching* in the chapter on experimental design by Campbell and Stanley[8] under the concept of *reactive arrangements.*

From the above possible interaction between components and procedures, some simple and early generalizations about controlling for the phenomenon appear. For example, activities such as pre-testing of subjects should be placed in the context of normal school activities insofar as possible. If testing is done normally in September, any groups participating in the research should be tested during that period and not during the middle of the year when the introduction of special tests create high subject awareness. Also, all experimental and control subjects should receive as nearly as possible identical experimental activities except for the variable under study. For example, unless increased teacher-pupil interaction is a concomitant of an experimental variable then both experimental and control groups should be treated the same with regard to this interaction during the application of treatment stage.

I would like to offer the suggestion that a necessary step of any experimentation be a *post-research inquiry.* The purpose of this inquiry would be to determine what research activities, if any, may have created awareness within the subjects. Such inquiry may be rather difficult to conduct at the elementary grade levels, but it might be helpful in explaining some research results. We have found in some preliminary work that students at the fourth grade level can and do recognize significant departures from normal routine, and as a consequence they realize their role as participants in a study. One of our research assistants reports

[8] D. T. Campbell and J. C. Stanley, "Experimental Designs for Research on Teaching," *Handbook of Research on Teaching,* N. L. Gage, editor. Rand McNally, 1963, pp. 171–246.

that one student could serve as a guide, describing the project going on in the school, he was so well acquainted with the nature of it. While the evidence for this step comes largely from studies using college students as subjects, the use of post-experimental inquiry has turned up many cues other than the experimental variable to which the students were responding. Hence, the technique has proved to be of value in constructing other experimental situations so as to reduce the effectiveness of such cues.

Relationship to Research on Reading

What specific implications of the Hawthorne effect phenomenon are there for research in reading? I would like to set forth some possible implications by citing some instances that have been called to our attention during our work on the Hawthorne effect wherein there has or has not been some concern with the possible presence of the Hawthorne effect in reading research.

If I were to state that a large percentage of reading research was contaminated by the possible presence of the Hawthorne effect, you would probably react to such a statement by feeling that this was an attack upon your area of interest by a relatively uninformed person. Fortunately, I do not have to make such a statement, because McDonald[9] and Chall[10] have highlighted the role of this phenomenon in recent writings.

Let me first cite instances to show the possible operation of the Hawthorne effect on an incidental basis in reading research. In an earlier article,[11] I made note about some work done in a small community in Wisconsin which created national interest[12] because of the controversy which centered around using the McGuffey readers. In reporting on the success of the study, the results were pretty much attributed to using the readers. I questioned at that time, and still do, the extent to which the publicity surrounding the reading program might not have in some way contributed to a greater motivation on the part of teachers, students, and parents and thereby reflecting a type of Hawthorne effect phenomenon. I would also like to call your attention to a recent study[13] in which

[9] Arthur S. McDonald. "Some Pitfalls in Evaluating Progress in Reading Instruction," *Phi Delta Kappan*, XLV: 336–338, April 1964, p. 338.
[10] Jeanne Chall. *Interim Report on a Study of Methods of Teaching Beginning Reading, The Carnegie Corporation*. October 10, 1962, p. 16.
[11] Cook, *op. cit.*, p. 120.
[12] "Kids with McGuffeys Way Ahead," *Columbus Dispatch*, Columbus, Ohio, June 13, 1962, p. 9A.
[13] David L., Clark. "The Hawthorne Effect and Educational Experimentation," An address delivered to the Research Commission of the American Vocational Association, Kansas City, December 1961.

some effort was made to study the relationship between color blindness, reading readiness, and reading achievement. One of two control groups (color-blind boys) did better in reading achievement than an experimental group of color-blind boys and a control group of non-color-blind boys. On this basis, it might be said that color blindness relates positively to reading achievement. Upon investigating the procedures, it was found that the teacher of this group was given information about the color-blind status of the students. Apparently, the teacher subsequently used this information to facilitate reading achievement for her group and thus surpass the other groups. It would seem to indicate that giving the teachers information regarding the pupils' condition in this case resulted in increased attention to the group of students and thereby created within them a possible Hawthorne effect.

There have been reported also instances of specific concern with the possible presence of the Hawthorne effect phenomenon in completed reading research. One instance was called recently to my attention.[14] The investigators were questioned, when reporting at a national meeting, about the possible reason for the experimental groups' continually coming out on top. Operating under an assumption that any novelty effect associated with the new method should wear off over time, the project was continued past its original termination date. Follow-up data were obtained from the original experimental-control pupils plus each new third grade group until all third grade pupils in the system had started to read using the experimental method. The results revealed that even over time, and with an increase in the number of subjects, the experimental group maintained their superiority over control subjects and the presence of any Hawthorne effect was discounted.

That the phenomenon is often overlooked in completed reading research can be partially documented by reference to a recent publication from the U.S. Office of Education entitled *Research in Reading for the Middle Grades.*[15] In summarizing the research done during 1955–1960 with regard to practices in the teaching of reading the bulletin points out that in one group of studies concerned with the role of grouping the experimental method always seems to come out on top. It seemed to matter little whether the research sought to evaluate homogeneous grouping, variations of the Joplin plan, reading block programs, pupils

[14] Margaret H. Greenman. "A Six-Year Experimental Study of Two Methods of Teaching Reading in the Elementary School," a paper presented at a joint meeting of the International Reading Association and American Educational Research Association, February 17, 1959.

[15] Warren G. Cutts. *Research in Reading for the Middle Grades:* An Annotated Bibliography, Office of Education Bulletin No. 31, U. S. Department of Health, Education, and Welfare, Washington, D. C.

pairs, or differentiated instruction. Although in one study the teachers recognized the influence of a Hawthorne effect, none of the investigators took steps to eliminate it or reduce it.[16]

One cannot approach only the Hawthorne effect from the point of view of checking completed research but one can try also to prevent it in projected research. I would call your attention to such an instance in a study[17] on teaching of reading in kindergarten being currently conducted by the Denver public schools. In correspondence with Dr. Oberholtzer,[18] superintendent of schools, he writes as follows:

> We are conscious of the implications of the Hawthorne effect on our study. Because of this we have attempted to provide similar treatment for teachers of pilot and control groups such as in-service meetings, assistance by teachers and special assignments, and curriculum bulletins. Also as can be seen from the research design, certain control groups become experimental and vice versa.

While I do not say that this will remove the Hawthorne effect completely from the research, the consciousness on the part of the investigators that it might operate prior to starting the experiment will lead them to adopt certain control procedures that might otherwise escape them and create problems when it comes to interpreting the research.

Another case of where prior attention has been given to the possible creation of a Hawthorne effect is a project[19] on critical reading recently funded by the U.S. Office of Education and being conducted by The Ohio State University. In this project, both experimental and control groups will receive special treatment. That is, while the experimental teachers are being trained in development of critical reading the control group teachers will have similar training periods but on children's literature materials. An attempt will be made to give equal attention to both experimental and control teachers during the course of the experiment. A further effort at minimizing the uniqueness of experimentation will be handled by informing all the teachers that an experiment is in progress. They in turn will be asked to tell the students.

[16] I. E. Aaron, Francis Goodwin, and Ada Kent, "Fourth Grade Teachers Experiment with Cross Class Grouping for Reading Instruction," *Elementary English*, 36: 305–307, May 1959.

[17] "The Effectiveness of Teaching Reading in Kindergarten," Cooperative Research Branch Project No. 1134. Office of Education. U. S. Department of Health, Education, and Welfare.

[18] Personal correspondence with Kenneth E. Oberholtzer, Superintendent, Denver Public Schools, April 23, 1963.

[19] "Critical Reading Ability of Elementary School Children," Cooperative Research Branch Project No. 2612, Office of Education, U. S. Department of Health, Education, and Welfare.

The validity of such techniques as described above in reducing the role of the Hawthorne effect is conjectural. The techniques do represent, however, typical approaches to controlling for the Hawthorne effect. More importantly, the experimenters are conscious of the phenomenon before they conduct the research.

Conclusion

Regardless of what one's particular beliefs are with regard to methods of reading instruction, one needs to be aware of his role as a researcher seeking the truth with regard to the best procedure for teaching reading. In this situation, the researcher becomes an impertinent questioner of his own procedures when conducting research and assumes the same role for the research of others. The researcher, therefore, tends to help resolve the conflict presented by Dr. Chall[20] in her summary remarks about a survey on reading methods she conducted.

> The conflict between enthusiasm and involvement (needed by the practitioner) and the cool, dispassionate observation and analysis (needed by the educational experimenter) may probably not be solved if the experimentation is left to those who are concerned primarily with "helping" rather than with knowing. The sincerity and commitment of the teachers and administrators, of whatever view in the controversy, may be functional for their role as educational practitioners, but dysfunctional for their roles as experimenters and understanders of methods.

Just as I am sure that you are sincere about what makes for effective reading instruction, I would ask you also to be equally as sincere in trying to understand the role that a phenomenon like the Hawthorne effect may play in your research. To the extent that such phenomena are better understood and controlled in research then more fruitful will be our efforts in trying to answer the many questions currently being raised about the best method of teaching reading in the schools of today and tomorrow.

67. The Real Frontier in Reading Research

THEODORE CLYMER (1958)

A major task, the real frontier in reading research, and one that needs constant attention, is *putting research to work in the classroom.* All the research findings in the field of reading instruction have little or no value until they are applied in the day-to-day job of teaching children to read. The task of applying what we know about reading to what we do in teaching reading is the focus of this article.

How Well Do We Apply Research Findings?

Surveys by competent authorities sometimes give discouraging reports of the degree to which school practices conform to research findings. Traxler (6) suggests, however, that the need to improve reading instruction is no greater now than it was formerly. Supporting Traxler's views are the reports of achievement of today's children when compared to the achievement of children of five, ten, or twenty years ago. See, for example, the article by Betts (1). These studies suggest equal or improved achievement for the children in today's schools. In view of this somewhat conflicting evidence, we must conclude that we may be doing an adequate job in applying research findings to the teaching of reading, but that much remains to be done to improve the situation. The job that we are doing is satisfactory—but it could easily be done much better.

What Prevents Application of Research Findings?

A wide range of causes is probably responsible when practice trails behind what research suggests is good reading instruction. The situation in any one school is likely to be somewhat unique, and to determine the cause or causes in a particular school would undoubtedly require careful study. The following list includes, in the writer's judgment, the major reasons for inadequate application of research findings to classroom in-

SOURCE: *The Reading Teacher,* XII (December, 1958), 92–97. Reprinted with the permission of Theodore Clymer and the International Reading Association.

struction: (1) lack of knowledge of research findings, (2) lack of knowledge of how to put these findings into practice, (3) lack of administrative and/or community support for changes in the reading program, and (4) lack of proper teaching conditions (such as reasonable work load, sufficient supplies and materials, appropriate class size, suitable school plant, etc.), which enable the teacher to do his best work.

If these lacks are the major causes of difficulty, let us examine the first two—knowledge of research and knowledge of how to put findings into practice—and suggest methods whereby these problems may be overcome. In the space available here, it is obvious that only a few suggestions in these two areas can be made. The problems of administrative and community support and proper teaching conditions can be mentioned only indirectly because of space limitations.

How Can We Gain Knowledge of Research Findings?

Robinson (5) clearly understands the problem of the teacher who goes to the research journals for an answer to his questions about classroom practices. He may find there is nothing available about his particular program, or he may discover so many reports based upon different designs and populations, and with differing conclusions, that he is hopelessly confused. What is the teacher to do? One answer must be, as Robinson points out, a collection and interpretation of research by qualified persons.

Reading research has been collected and interpreted in a variety of ways in the materials that are described below, and each deserves special consideration. These materials are ordered from the most general to the most specific in terms of their utility to the classroom teacher.

Basic readers and their accompanying workbooks and manuals. The authorship of modern basic readers assures the teacher that these teaching tools are constructed with a sound research foundation. The names of Gray, Gates, Betts, Russell, Bond, and many others appear on countless research articles, as well as on material intended for instructonal use. The teacher can be certain that the basic materials authored by such persons apply research findings in a careful, thoughtful manner. Thus, the teacher who is seeking help on an effective research-oriented way of teaching vowel principles, basic study skills, critical reading, or any other reading ability will find general help in any of the modern basic programs.

In certain localities, principals and supervisors are suggesting that teachers abandon all use of basic materials. Until teachers are as skillful in applying research findings as persons who devote their lives to the job, and until they are provided generous allotments of time to write materials, the basic programs are tools that should be available in all classrooms.

Professional books. Today the college instructor faces an embarrassment of riches as he guides his reading methods classes to professional books which are based upon research findings. Every few months, it seems, another valuable book appears. The classroom teacher may turn to these books to find answers to questions on classroom practice which are based on research findings. To be sure, not all these books will agree on all matters; but the agreement is greater than is sometimes supposed. The disagreements are helpful, for they provide the new frontiers in reading on which progress can be made. Today's professional books provide an excellent means of learning about research findings and how they can be applied in the classroom, for the current books illustrate research principles by descriptions of classroom practices. See, for example, Harris (3), and McKim (4). A study schedule of as little as one hour a week in these professional books will reward any teacher with enriched and more effective teaching.

Useful summaries of research. The Department of Classroom Teachers and the American Educational Research Association of the NEA have cooperated in bringing together the results of research in a form which is readily useful to teachers. A series of pamphlets which cover a wide range of subjects—from spelling instruction to homework assignments—is available for twenty-five cents per pamphlet from the NEA, 1201 Sixteenth Street, N.W., Washington, D.C. 20006. Professor Gates of Columbia has prepared the readable and practical pamphlet entitled *What Research Says to the Teacher: Teaching Reading.* The contents of this pamphlet are succinct and unequivocal in their application to the teaching of reading. A copy of this pamphlet should be on every teacher's desk.

The Encyclopedia of Eductional Research. This volume, organized and written through the auspices of the American Educational Research Association and published by The Macmillan Company, provides an expert evaluation of the research in countless areas of education. The current edition (1950) carries a thorough and concise summary of reading research by W. S. Gray. This material warrants the thoughtful attention of anyone who seriously wants to understand the research background of reading instruction. A revised edition of the *Encyclopedia* will be available in 1960.

Traxler's summaries of research. Arthur Traxler's three summaries (7, 8, 9) provide an overview of reading research beginning in 1930 and covering nearly twenty-five years. These carefully prepared bulletins, published by the Educational Records Bureau, provide annotated bibliographies grouped according to topic. These bulletins merit careful attention by all students of reading instruction.

AERA's Review of Educational Research. Every three years the American Educational Research Association devotes an issue of the *Review of Educational Research* to language arts and fine arts. These reviews—necessarily selective because of the broad areas covered—give a good overview of some of the major studies published during the period covered by that issue.

Gray's yearly summaries. In 1925 W. S. Gray published his *Summary of Investigations Relating to Reading,* which compiled and reviewed the research in reading up to that date. Since then, each spring Gray has published a yearly summary of reading research. These summaries, which now appear in *The Journal of Educational Research,* should be consulted for recent developments in reading research or for trends in reading over the past thirty years.

Professional journals. Sometimes the reading of research articles in professional journals is a frustrating experience because of the complex statistical vocabulary and symbols used. With a careful examination, however, the adequacy of the design and the major findings can be evaluated and perhaps applied to a particular classroom problem. Dolch's article (2) will be a major help to the classroom teacher in evaluating research studies.

Three journals frequently reporting reading research are *The Elementary School Journal, The Journal of Educational Research,* and *Elementary English.* Reports in these journals are generally not statistically complex and usually carry a clear interpretation of what the results mean for the classroom.

From the various sources discussed above the teacher may obtain information about research findings as they apply to the teaching of reading. Having obtained this information, the teacher faces a second and infinitely more difficult task—putting the findings to work in the classroom.

Careful Planning

The teacher's first job in applying research in the classroom is to consider carefully the application of research to his particular teaching area or age group. There can be no substitute for a careful, thoughtful interpretation of how the research will find applications in the teacher's particular situation. Generally, after studying the research, writing an outlined statement of how the research is to be applied will be a helpful exercise in clarifying thinking and in formulating plans for carrying out the change in instruction in the classroom.

Perhaps this careful consideration may include talking over your plans with a friend who is a teacher and who may be able to add additional insight. A friendly "give-and-take" discussion over coffee will usually provide ideas available in no other way. Usually the principal or the supervisor should be consulted, for they can provide wise counsel, offer suggestions of procedures and materials, or possibly point out areas in which problems are likely to arise. Some changes in instruction require a schoolwide planning program, and in these cases it is, of course, particularly important that the principal and the supervisor be consulted. In many situations where the changes are relatively major, the parents should be consulted so they have an understanding of the program, for in most communities parental opposition comes from a lack of understanding of the "whys" of a modern reading program. If procedures such as these are carried out, the teacher will have a much clearer idea of how the research findings may be applied in his particular situation.

Setting Up Classroom Procedure

The second step to be carried out in applying research findings in the classroom is to work out very carefully the classroom procedures which will be necessary to implement the research findings. This point cannot be overstressed. The need for a carefully planned and detailed program of what will happen step-by-step is essential to a successful program. This is not to suggest that the teacher would not welcome changes, or that unexpected events would not be utilized in the classroom to promote a vitalized learning program. But it is equally true that disappointment and chaos will come from a program in which the class procedures are worked out in an accidental and happenstance manner. The detailed plan of operation is particularly important when only part of the class will be involved in any one activity. This means that a careful program must be worked out for those children who are not immediately under the teacher's direction. At the beginning stages, it may be necessary to work out every step in an extremely detailed manner. Later, as the teacher's skill increases and as the students gain more maturity, it may be possible for the teacher to turn more of the planning over to the pupils to allow them greater freedom in the selection of the way and the manner in which they carry out the assignment.

Need for Modest Beginning

The third point to be kept in mind in applying the research findings to the classroom is that generally a modest beginning is best. The major mistake of most teachers in attempting to change their teaching to conform to research findings is to make too sweeping changes. A modest beginning will be helpful to the teacher because he is feeling his way in carrying out instruction in a new or somewhat different manner. A modest beginning will allow him to test out his ideas, to more or less feel his way along as he gains in understanding of the procedures and as he gauges the children's abilty to respond to the kind of instruction he hopes to give. A modest beginning is also helpful for the children because they, too, will be learning as this new program is put into effect. Making a slow, cautious approach in this manner may require more time to reach the goal of changing instruction, but the goal is more likely to be reached than in a case where the teacher immediately makes major changes, and then both the teacher and the children struggle to find their way in the new routine. The need for a modest beginning is perhaps illustrated most often in those cases where teachers are attempting to use multiple, flexible groups for the first time. Beginning teachers, for example, often start their grouping in an ambitious way for even an experienced teacher. Too sweeping a program results in chaos with neither the children nor the teacher prepared to handle it.

Need for Careful Evaluation

After the program is being carried out successfully in the classroom as the teacher would like it, one major step remains. This step is the careful evaluation of the results of the new teaching. Unfortunately, in a few school systems sweeping changes are made in the instructional program without the provision for checking the results of such changes. This means that no definite conclusions can be made about the changes in the children as a result of this instruction. The author recently visited an area where sweeping changes are being made in the manner in which children are being grouped for reading instruction. (Incidentally, the technique of grouping being used is not one supported by the research—at least as the writer would interpret it.) No systematic provision is being made for an evaluation of the results of the new technique of grouping. At the conclusion of their instructional period, using the new techniques of adjusting for indivdual differences, there will be no way to determine in these schools whether the new technique results in greater learning or whether the old technique provided the better means for promoting reading growth.

The suggestion is not being made that the teachers be called upon to carry out their own experimentation and design of research experiments. What is suggested is that when changes are made, an attempt should be made to evaluate, either formally or informally, the results of the new procedures. In the case of a schoolwide change, the principal, supervisors—or, in the larger systems, research directors—should aid in the designing of studies that will permit an adequate evaluation of the effectiveness of the new procedures.

When a teacher is carrying out procedures on his own, an informal evaluation may be made using standardized test scores, counts of books read, subjective measures of attitude changes, or any other measures which seem appropriate to the objectives of the experimental program.

This article has pointed out some of the major sources of research information which are valuable and useful to the classroom teacher, as well as some suggestions for putting into practice the changes indicated by research. Much of our reading research has yet to be interpreted and applied to the task of classroom instruction. For the classroom remains as the true frontier in reading research.

References

1. Betts, E. A. "Reading: Now and Then," *Education* 78 (October, 1957), 85–86.
2. Dolch, E. W. "School Research in Reading," *Elementary English*, 33 (February, 1956), 76–80.
3. Harris, A. J. *How to Increase Reading Ability*. 3rd Ed. New York: Longmans, Green, 1956.
4. McKim, M. G. *Guiding Growth in Reading*. New York: The Macmillan Company, 1955.
5. Robinson, H. M. "Educational Research for Teachers," *Elementary School Journal*, 54 (May, 1954), 487–89.
6. Traxler, A. E. "What Does Research Suggest About Ways to Improve Reading Instruction?," *Improving Reading in the Junior High School*, pp. 5–15. U.S. Office of Education, Bulletin No. 10, 1957.
7. Traxler, A. E., and others. *Ten Years of Research in Reading: Summary and Bibliography*. Bulletin No. 32. New York: Educational Records Bureau, 1941.
8. Traxler, A. E., and Townsend, Agatha. *Another Five Years in Reading: Summary and Bibliography*. Bulletin No. 46. New York: Educational Records Bureau, 1946.
9. Traxler, A. E., and Townsend, Agatha. *Eight More Years of Research in Reading: Summary and Bibliography*. Bulletin No. 64. New York: Educational Records Bureau, 1955.

68. The Future of Research in Reading[1]

ARTHUR I. GATES (1962)

The most important characteristic of teaching reading today is a general pattern. This pattern, which embodies a number of components of materials and procedures, is the result of nearly a century of evolution. It was suggested by a group of persons, including G. Stanley Hall, E. B. Huey, John Dewey, Edward L. Thorndike, Charles Judd, and others, who were active shortly before and after the turn of the century. Most of them were very critical of the program based upon difficult, literary basal readers, supplemented by a stiff system of phonics, then in use.

Huey, who became a spokesman for this group, stated in 1908 that this program "benumbed" children by its monotony and artificiality. The extensive drill on phonics is necessary, he stated, only when the material to be read is too difficult and "unnatural for children." "But the remedy is simple, for such matter should not be read, its very difficulty being the child's natural protection against what he is as yet unfitted for" (4, p. 348).

Dewey declared that if reading must be taught by this kind of program it should not be started until the child is eight years or older. Huey pointed to the superiority of an informal beginning with reading of miscellaneous materials at home. He wrote, "One can pick out the children who learned to read at home. They read naturally. . . . The child does not want to learn reading as a mechanical tool" (4, pp. 305–306). Once the child has learned to read "naturally" at home, he will later be helped rather than hindered by work in phonics and other skills, but that task should be "left to the school" (4, p. 334).

[1] This article is, in substance, a talk made at the annual meeting of the National Conference on Research in English, in Atlantic City, New Jersey, February 19, 1962.

SOURCE: *Education,* LXXXII (May, 1962), 545–554.

Contributions of the Twenties

These were recommendations of a pattern quite similar to the one which prevails today. Workers active during the twenties stressed the need of a more systematic and thorough program of instruction in the basic reading skills. They suggested readers carefully graded in difficulty, containing all kinds of reading material, and designed primarily to help teach reading, not literature or history or manners and morals.

The twenties introduced one largely new feature, the organized workbook or study program. This innovation grew out of the conviction that the 1900 emphasis on "natural" reading left too much to the "whole word" or "look-and-say" method which is essentially unguided, or trial-and-error learning. These workers believed that a carefully organized program of study materials and procedures was essential. The twenties, in short, witnessed the beginning of what today in many circles is called "programmed learning."

The leaders during the twenties did not suggest a less important role for individual guidance by the teacher. On the contrary, they recognized the crucial value of the teacher's art more clearly than did the 1900 group. They suggested that the use of workbooks and other teaching materials would provide the teacher with more time for engaging in this indispensable kind of personal instruction.

It was during the twenties that the most comprehensive and complex diagnostic and remedial programs were developed on the assumption that teachers could learn to function on a more advanced professional level. The basic purpose of the extensive work on diagnostic and remedial methods was to help teachers become more expert and more skilled in teaching individual children, including those handicapped in various ways.

As I wrote in my first book on remedial reading, published in 1927, and have repeated, in substance, at least a thousand times since then, "Remedial instruction, then, is first and primarily individual prescription for individual needs. . . . remedial teaching should follow the same general principles of learning that are, or should be, observed in any other type of instruction—with certain occasional departures to meet particular types of need. These variations represent not contradictions of the main principles but special applications of them which require unusual skill and understanding" (2, pp. 18–19).

Studies of diagnostic and "remedial" methods were carried out primarily to find ways of improving normal, everyday teaching of the puzzling variety of children which every teacher will encounter.

This in brief is the general pattern of teaching which has developed since 1900. Let us consider next the relationship of recent suggestions and controversies to this pattern.

Phonics

I feel that none of the recent suggestions for improving teaching is necessarily in conflict with this general pattern except possibly one, the teaching of phonics for weeks or months before the child has begun to read. As noted above, this procedure was strenuously objected to by the 1900 group, and before. To start the child off with phonic drill or any other such study instead of actual reading would seem to be more thwarting to the child's urge today, when he faces insistent electric signs, store placards, television inscriptions, and a flood of printed materials at every turn, than was the case a half-century ago.

In any event, it is, I think, now high time for a change in our activities in this area. For some years, we have been forced to spend time and energy in debating an almost nonexistent issue, the relative merits of the phonic and a nonphonic "whole word" or "word configuration" or "look-and-say" or the "whole word" plus "frequency of repetition method." No one advocates any one of the latter type of method; no one doubts the value of certain phonic skills.

All reading programs with which I am familiar provide for teaching phonics. There are disputes concerning the time to introduce phonics, the amount and kind to teach, the length of time to carry it forward, and the ways to relate it to other forms of instruction and other points. It is now time to get on with study and investigation of the real issues.

Recently I made a list of more than twenty-five phonic programs, of which about half are sufficiently different from each other to justify experimental comparison. For example, consider the differences between the following: the Carden method with its extensive made-in-advance drills extending from kindergarten through grade eight; the Bloomfield-Barnhart program of 250 or more "lessons" based on quite different phonetic principles; the inductive method represented in the practice materials of Donald Durrell and his colleagues; the schemes favored by Hunter Diack; and the program recently recommended by Dolores Durkin, which provides a comprehensive phonic system with rules and conventions as "resource" information which the teacher is to employ in individualized instruction.

I repeat that it is time to quit attacking the "look-and-say" straw man and start to work studying theoretically and experimentally the many rival programs now before us.

Individualized Reading

The advocates of "individualized reading" propose not a new pattern of teaching, but a new emphasis of its components. They call for more expertness and time for individual guidance by the teacher. In general, they propose that relatively more of the teaching be done by direct, oral instruction by the teacher and that relatively less be left to readers, workbooks, practice procedures, and mechanical aids. They object strongly to such practices as having a whole group work on the same basal reader at the same time, but some of them approve of using individually and to some extent various kinds of graded and workbook type material.

The questions raised about the more extreme "individualized" reading procedures concern the practice rather than the theory. The advocates of individualized reading, for example, maintain that every teacher should be sufficiently well informed and skillful to be able to teach any child, even a moderately handicapped one, to read by devising, as she goes along, a program nicely adjusted to his needs.

This is a statement that I should applaud wholeheartedly. Endorsing this basic principle of individualized reading, however, need not involve an acceptance of the assertion that children never have identical or very similar likes and dislikes for reading selections or needs for similar or identical lessons in basic techniques.

Neither does an acceptance of the ideal of individual instruction deny the value of every type of use of systematically organized study such as that embodied in a typical basal-reader and workbook program. For example, a basal-reader program can and should be introduced at the time, and used at the rate, in the manner, to the extent, and with the amount and kind of additional instruction that best suits each child.

It is here, of course, that we encounter the practical question. Can the typical teacher, with a class of thirty pupils before her, reasonably be expected to become sufficiently expert and to find sufficient time to conduct an extreme program of this type along with everything else she is called upon to do?

A number of persons believe that with the wealth of reading materials and information about teaching which are or could be made available today teachers should be able to do so. Others are doubtful. A quite emphatic "no" is given by many. In this connection let us consider the views recently presented by the advocates of instruction by "programmed learning."

Programmed Materials

B. F. Skinner and other psychologists contend that a major fault of current teaching is the fact that it proceeds by steps that are so large and imprecise that a learner can come a cropper at almost any point. Even the shrewdest teacher would rarely be able to detect these little slips.

The history of remedial reading bears out this idea as do studies of certain earlier forms of practice materials. Indeed, these major features of modern programming were introduced between 1915 and 1925. Nila B. Smith and Stuart Courtis, Carleton Washburn of Winnetka fame, and many others were developing practice materials which embody the basic idea.

My colleagues and I made up outfits varying from 400 to 1,000 pages of mimeographed teaching materials for use in experiments on teaching reading in the first grade in 1922. Some of it was tried out on normal children of various ages, including very young ones and on others suffering various handicaps, such as congenital deafness. These were "programmed" materials. Although judged by modern standards, they were crude, poorly controlled, and inadequate in many ways, they worked very well.

A number of similar programs were developed before and after that time, but it was soon apparent that schools were then not ready for them either theoretically or financially. The first preparatory book published as a companion to basal readers was a programmed outfit, but it included only a fraction of the several hundred pages of mimeographed material used for experimental purposes.

Programming, using psychological principles now available, could produce more detailed and otherwise better workbook types of material. It need not be thought of as opposed to the importance of shrewd individualized instruction. It could be the means of helping the teacher to acquire greater expertness and to save more time to devote to children individually. Indeed, this is Skinner's contention. I shall return to this critical issue later.

Many other possibilities of improving reading instruction now lie at hand. For example, possibilities of using sound-motion pictures, especially slow-motion pictures or television to portray various ways of tackling unfamiliar words, or later the methods of reading rapidly by "thought-units" instead of single words, and many other procedures have scarcely been explored.

The controversies now raging about us, the vigorous defense of and violent attacks on one or another of these policies give a misleading idea that they are incompatible with each other and hostile to the prevailing general pattern of teaching. To my mind, for example, "individualized teaching" and "programming" are really buddies. Each can help the other move along toward a good objective. We need more and better kinds of both.

Skinner and others have demonstrated the enormous potency of well-programmed procedures. It is, I think, now clear that good programming can be made so productive that it may often be the most vital factor in a teaching procedure. It may be unrecognized as the factor which determines the result of a comparison of two or more programs. A poor system of teaching word recognition techniques, for example, may surpass a good one by a wide margin if the poor one is programmed better than the good one.

Deficient Control Procedures

As powerful a variable as pencil and paper or mechanical programming is, another kind, the type of programming which a teacher provides in oral instruction, may be extremely potent. Indeed, skill in programming may be a major characteristic of the art of the master teacher.

In my own experimentation I have often come up against unmistakable evidence that the teacher's skill (programming if you like) was the decisive factor. The crucial influence, however, seemed often to be other characteristics of the teacher, such as the degree of her enthusiasm or her determination to make the program succeed.

As many critical reviews of research have suggested, complex programs usually leave uncontrolled so many variables that one often cannot tell which ones produced the results shown in a comparison of two or more of them. The experimental group nearly always wins, often as a result of no merit of its own.

The tendency of the new "experimental" procedure to win out suggests that in research as well as in daily practice we must be concerned with boredom and backsliding and, as in medicine, with the development of immunity.

I grew up in a small town in which religious activities were very prominent. Religious enthusiasm, even after it had been raised to a climax, seemed gradually to wane. Members of the congregation appeared to become less devout and less active, and not a few became "backsliders." This signified the need of a Revival Meeting. If some other local denomination or an itinerant group got into action first, every one was stirred up, quarrels broke out in each church, and quite a few members might join the new sect. The only remedy was to have revival meetings in one's own church first.

This may be the situation in reading today. The materials and methods have changed so little in the last couple of decades that teachers find them unexciting, if not boring. A little weary of teaching with them, the teachers have been inclined to rest on their oars. They may be disposed to look for something new—anything.

Any new program taught with reawakened alertness and drive will probably show up better in a control group test than an old one, taught lackadaisically, even if the latter is intrinsically better. But the "new" one of 1962 will become the dull old program of 1982, ready for easy defeat by another "new" one at that time.

A Research Pattern for the Future

All the foregoing considerations suggest the necessity of comparing programs over a period of several years, not merely to mitigate, if not eliminate, the effects of initial novelty and enthusiasm and of later complacency in the teacher, but also to evaluate the later as well as the immediate effect of a form of training.

The literature is full of instances in which, for example, first-grade procedure A excels B during the first year or two, but shows no superiority or even inferiority in later years, or cases in which teaching process A in grade three is helpful, whereas it is futile or detrimental if taught earlier or later.

When all these difficulties are considered, it appears that several requirements are encountered. One is that control group studies must be conducted on a wide scale, including a large number of carefully selected communities. Secondly, all the variables likely to be influential must be measured or appraised thoroughly at frequent intervals and kept under careful observation at all times during a course of several years. Third, a succession of similar groups should be launched at intervals of a year or two, each to be followed from a beginning to a fairly mature stage.

A new method needs to be appraised after it has settled down free of the honeymoon fervor. We simply must face up to the fact that large-scale, time-consuming investigations must be carried out in education as they are already being conducted in medicine and public health, and in many phases of science and engineering.

Statistical Methods

Many persons seem to feel that statistical procedures have been advanced in the last century to a point where they are about equal to any demand that could be made upon them by workers in our field. This is regrettably untrue. Despite the formidable array of correlational methods, factor analysis, analysis of variants and so on, procedures for deriving significant facts from certain types of extensive data about various characteristics of the members of one group, as for example one which has used a special reading program for many years, or two groups as in a control group study, are not available.

Many statistical procedures work well only when the data fall into certain straitjackets. Often when it is said that the data are not good enough to make a valid statistical analysis, a more significant statement would be that statistical methods now available are unequal to the task of revealing the facts that are probably there. It is for this reason, in part, that many able investigators resort to the use of "clinical" and other methods of generalization when trying to detect complex relationships.

In making these comments, I do not mean to imply that statisticians have not worked long, hard, and expertly, nor that they have not made splendid advances in their field. They have. I am merely saying that the problems they face are so numerous and so difficult that they have not yet solved them all.

Fortunately there are emerging some new possibilities. For example, some of the new, almost incredible electronic procedures, such as those used in "systems analysis," may be developed to reveal facts now hidden from us in the complexity of reading programs (5).

Hasty Changes

Leaders in the study of reading instruction must be prepared to defend progress against several threats, and the atmosphere of panic about everything which seems to surround us now and which tends to make us want to "do" something in a hurry.

Persons quite unqualified are proposing decisive action. Poorly informed school superintendents and principals occasionally force hasty changes. Professors of college English and others tell us exactly what to do. Men and women trained in psychology or other fields but innocent of knowledge of or experience in teaching reading undertake to develop teaching machine programs.

To prepare a first-rate, Skinner-type detailed program requires more, not less, knowledge of the field of reading than preparing a typical little workbook of the types now in use. "Programming reading" is no job for the amateur. I anticipate the marketing of a flock of new programs of all sorts, some of them incredibly bad.

One of the problems faced by enthusiasts for programming in reading became apparent a quarter of a century ago. This is the problem of motivation. When work with programmed materials such as workbooks, practice exercises, phonic and other types of drill booklets was carried too far, in comparison with reading of senseful material, most children got bored and restless (3). This was one of the reasons for Huey's statement, given above, that too much phonics before or during the beginning lesson in reading "benumbed" children.

The major principle growing out of nearly a century of investigation of teaching reading is that wide reading is the heart of the program. This idea is a fundamental feature of the pattern described in the first section of this paper. Persons developing programmed reading should take this fact into account. Programming, of course, can be only a means to this end.

Experimental and Analytical Studies

In this paper, I cannot deal with all the important needs for research in the future. Indeed, I have decided to give no more than a nod of recognition to two of the most important of all.

One is the whole field of laboratory, experimental, and analytical research. I shall merely say that the advances in teaching of reading have been based more fully than on anything else on such studies as those of James McKeen Cattell on perception of words between 1875 and 1900, those of Walter Dearborn, Charles Judd, and others on eye movements between 1905 and 1920, and those of Edward L. Thorndike on reading as a thinking or problem-solving process between 1910 and 1920. Research of these and similar types will be as indispensable in the future as it was in the past.

Teaching Advanced Techniques

Thorndike's suggestion that reading embodies all forms of higher mental processes suggests a second conviction which I shall be unable to discuss fully. It is that in our future research you should not be misguided, however great the pressure may be, into devoting your energies to minor needs to the neglect of major issues.

For example, I do not believe that study of phonics in the future compares in importance with the investigation of the diversity of complex and subtle forms of reading which we should be cultivating at the upper grades and at the junior and senior high school levels. In my recent survey of phonic and other methods, I noted ten or a dozen word study programs which, with some modifications and additions to give them a broader, more diversified coverage, would produce quite satisfactory results when taught by a reasonably expert teacher.

A much more conspicuous and important need, in my opinion, is to develop comprehension programs for teaching the wide variety of skills needed at higher levels—the abilities required to deal with all the complexities and subtleties encountered in the whole range of materials, from light fiction to heavy technical texts. It is here that current programs are most conspicuously inadequate and incomplete.

I can do no more today than to indicate what I mean by saying that we should soon have reliable data as guides in setting up a program such as that proposed by a group of New York City junior high school teachers for reading in grades 7, 8, and 9 (6). The fact that we do not have much evidence on the theoretical soundness or the practical effectiveness of such a program and additional procedures for teaching the reading skills unique in all the special subjects such as mathematics and physics is an indication of a major need of future research.

Role of the Teacher

A most important issue is the role of teacher in the program of reading instruction. The typical basal reader and workbook program which has gradually developed since 1900, as suggested in the first section of this paper, includes both programmed materials, chiefly in the workbook, and individualized teaching, in which the teacher follows her own ideas or suggestions given in the teachers' manual or both.

The ready-made workbook "program" is incomplete, leaving a great deal of instruction to the teacher. The strength of this plan is that it provides generously for tailoring the teaching to the individual, but this feature is also its most conspicuous weakness. If the teacher is able to carry out her responsibility expertly and fully, the results are splendid. If she is not, the returns may be poor.

For example, consider the teaching of phonic and other word study and word recognition skills. The small workbooks do not include a full program of instruction. The teachers' manual typically suggests additional guidance which should be adjusted to individual needs. (Individual differences in the amount and kind of instruction needed in this area are especially great.)

A good teacher would have at her command many teaching procedures, in addition to those contained in the basal series manuals, such as those outlined in comprehensive texts on teaching reading, and others derived from her own experience. She is free to teach as much or as little phonic and other word study skills, beyond those contained in the workbooks (which are often not provided at all in poorer communities) as she chooses. As a consequence, the amount and character of phonics taught varies greatly.

Such a plan has the strengths and weaknesses of other democratic processes. The teacher's freedom to teach in the way and to the extent which she thinks is best is accompanied by her freedom to do as little as she may choose.

This feature of the typical American program explains why certain control group and practical comparisons of the phonics taught in system A and B's basal reader and workbook program are not very meaningful unless the amount and kinds of teaching phonics are described fully. Results will vary from good to bad depending on the quality of the teaching. This fact suggests again how crucial is the question of deciding what the role of the teacher of the future should be.

How Much for the Teacher?

This is the question of what and how much instruction should be programmed in advance and what and how much should be left for the teacher. In the course of my early work in this field, I developed the conviction that teachers could and would gradually emerge from rule-of-thumb, routine teaching and slowly but surely ascend to a level of professional knowledge and skill equivalent to that of a first-rate physician.

Perhaps this was an unrealistic vision. Strong forces are now at work to return to one or another type of single, simple, fixed-in-advance type of routine teaching in which the teacher operates like the laboratory technician or nurse rather than the physician. The danger is that many different, almost automatic procedures will develop so independently of each other as to give us a hodgepodge of competitive devices.

Whether one conceives the teacher of the future as a slave to fixed routine or a master of the artistry of teaching, an important responsibility falls upon you, the leaders, to see to it that an over-all program of teaching is evolved in which each procedure is effectively coordinated with others.

Although I have had in recent years moments of doubt about the soundness of my conviction of long ago that teachers could become as well informed, as skillful and shrewd in diagnosis and guidance in their field as physicians or engineers are in theirs, I should hope that you leaders would engage in battle to achieve this type of teacher in the future.

In saying this, I do not mean to imply that the development of "programmed" materials, teaching machines, motion-picture demonstrations, and other mechanical devices is a threat to the cultivation of a higher level of performance by the teacher. These devices cannot fully supply all the features of a good reading program.

The lively world of tomorrow will confront every child with innumerable problems the solutions of which cannot be "programmed" for the reason that no one knows what the solution is. No person or machine could have programmed Darwin's principle of evolution before Darwin conceived it.

A teacher may say, "Come now, the children in my class are not Darwins." Oh yes, they are. They are, in the sense that their lives are full of little problems as perplexing for them as Darwin's big problems were for him. They must learn to solve them, *de novo*, in the same general way, by mental maneuvers which cannot possibly be foreseen by the maker of programmed materials. It is here that a highly trained and skillful teacher is most desperately needed.

Programmed Learning a Help

It is precisely here that we are likely to make the mistaken assumption that programmed learning and other such teaching aids are hostile to insightful and creative teaching. Properly employed, they should not hinder but help the teacher become more effective by giving her an understanding of learning in its most detailed and intricate form, and by releasing the precious time she must otherwise spend on routine teaching to do what only she can do.

Effectively used, programmed materials and other aids will not replace or degrade a teacher. A physician or surgeon is not made less important or less helpful by providing him with more and better tools with which to work. On the contrary, better equipment should increase his insight and effectiveness. In the same way, good use of the new products of our mechanical civilization should help the teachers of reading to become, to borrow the title of a recent report, the Torch Lighters of the teachers' profession of tomorrow (1).

If teachers of reading are to move up to the level of professional expertness instead of down to the level of vocational routine, they will need skillful and courageous leadership, and you, members of this group, are the ones to provide it. At no period in my professional lifetime, now nearing fifty years, has the danger of retrogression been so great or the opportunity for progress been so promising.

References

1. Austin, Mary C., and others, *The Torch Lighters* (Cambridge, Massachusetts: Harvard University Press, 1961).

2. Gates, Arthur I., *The Improvement of Reading* (1st edition, New York: The Macmillan Company, 1908).
3. Gates, Arthur I., and Russell, David H., "Types of Materials, Vocabulary Burden, Word Analysis, and Other Factors in Beginning Reading. I." *Elementary School Journal,* Volume 39 (September, 1938), pp. 27–35.
4. Huey, Edmund B., *The Psychology and Pedagogy of Reading* (New York: The Macmillan Company, 1908).
5. Mauch, James, "A Systems Analysis Approach to Education," *Phi Delta Kappan,* Volume XLIII (January, 1962), pp. 158–162.
6. *Reading Grades 7, 8, 9, A Teacher's Guide to Curriculum Planning,* Curriculum Bulletin, 1957–1958 Series, Number 11 (New York: Board of Education of the City of New York).

XI. Issues and Trends in Reading

There is one thing you can count on, we are told. And that is change. But is change synonymous with progress? In the reading field change may be initiated through experimental programs, new methods, and research. Some reading specialists and teachers become enthusiastic about method A while others prefer method B. The issues and controversies are many. The only aspect of the reading program on which all agree is that youngsters in today's schools must be helped to refine their reading skills in order to meet tomorrow's demands.

A selection by Austin (69) opens this chapter and provides us with faculty opinion on significant issues. The faculty represents teachers of courses in the fundamentals of reading instruction. Since institutions from various parts of the United States were represented, it is very interesting to learn what those who guide the thinking of tomorrow's teachers feel about significant issues. Do their opinions coincide with yours?

Austin (70) treats one of the many controversial issues that is of current concern. She poses the question "When Should Reading Instruction Begin?" The reader doubtless has seen popular articles devoted to the subject of "teaching your baby to read." Many parents have purchased materials that were advertised to do the job. After considering the advantages and disadvantages of teaching the very young to read as presented by Austin, what are your conclusions?

Few approaches to remedial reading have caused more furor than Delacato's "neuro-psychological" approach. According to Delacato (71) the only significant trait that poor readers have in common is their lack of neurological organization. In order to overcome this inadequacy, he suggests a remedial program that is radically different from those advocated by reading authorities.

To cope with the nonphonetic nature of the English language without changing traditional spelling, Gattengno evolved an approach which uses colors to differentiate sounds. The history of "Words in Color," this new and controversial method for the teaching of reading, is treated comprehensively by Sister M. Raphael (72).

The Augmented Roman Alphabet, now called the Initial Teaching Alphabet, is a 44-letter alphabet evolved in England by Sir James Pitman which is designed to simplify learning to read. It employs all letters in our alphabet except "x" and "q" plus 20 new symbols, some of which are combinations or augmentations of conventional letters. Each of the 44 letters in the alphabet stands for only one sound. What are the long-term effects of ITA on children with whom it is used? Opinions differ. "The Value of ITA" highlights the controversial nature of this approach to the teaching of reading. Two authors, Downing (73) and Cutts (74) present opposing views.

The phonics arena is one of perennial controversy. When did it all start? What is the status of instruction in phonics today? Durkin (75) furnishes us with information along these lines in her historical treatment of the phonics issue.[1]

Individualized reading, one of the most dramatic trends in reading instruction within recent years, is based on Olson's concepts of seeking, self-selection, and pacing. The program sets aside time for individual children to find their own reading materials and then to read them at their own rate. The teacher provides guidance during conferencing periods with individual children. Group activities and group instruction are not omitted. The values and limitations of this kind of program are discussed by Sartain (76) who comes to the conclusion that the basic reading program should not be jettisoned but should be combined with individualized reading.

Linguistics, another relatively new approach to reading instruction, is still developing and evolving. Bloomfield,[2] as early as 1942, outlined the implications of his concept of linguistics to the teaching of reading. Since that time, a number of linguists have written about the subject. Strickland (77) helps to clarify

[1] See Part IV for additional articles on phonics.

[2] Leonard Bloomfield, "Linguistics and Reading," *Elementary English Review*, 19 (April, May 1942), pp. 125–130, 183–186.

linguistics for us by setting forth the basic concepts commonly held by linguists. After discussing some of the similarities of their beliefs, she shows how Barnhart, Fries, and Smith—three linguists of note—differ in their approach, organization, and methodology. How does this new science of language make a contribution to the teaching of reading?

Ten thousand words a minute? Fifteen? Twenty? Are such rates possible? Are such rates desirable? Have we made a fetish of speed? The pros and cons to these questions can be found in a joint article from the NEA Journal titled "Speed Reading." Two authors, Wood (78) and Ehrlich (79), present opposing views on the subject.

A basic research study of significance was carried out by Walton (80) in 1957. By using the ophthalmograph to determine the reaction time of ten subjects in a reading situation in which comprehension was completely ignored, he arrived at a maximum reading speed that is anatomically and physiologically possible. If Walton's findings are valid, how does one explain reported reading speeds of 2,000 to 25,000 words per minute?

What lies ahead in the field of reading? What are some of the changes we can expect? More important, what can we do to bring about increased efficiency?

The college and university faculty members whose opinions on controversial issues were presented in the opening selection of this chapter were questioned about future changes. Austin (81) reports first on their dissatisfaction with the current state of affairs in education. She goes on to say, however, that the vast majority anticipate many changes. Unfortunately, the anticipated changes do not always coincide with what was felt to be desired changes.

Gates (82) closes our anthology with a challenge. "What Should We Be Doing Soon?" Gates places emphasis on the need for better basal research and suggests that the International Reading Association assume the responsibility of recruiting able young persons to do reading research. He also admonishes the IRA for not being more active in evaluating certain practices and setting up standards. Then in a series of inspiring paragraphs Gates invites educators "to enter into a new life—a life new in promise and prestige, a life which can be full of the gaiety of achievement."

69. Faculty Opinion on Significant Issues

MARY C. AUSTIN (1961)

Since reading instruction, like other areas of public education, has long been a popular target of lay criticism (1), professional opinion was sought on selected contemporary issues to ascertain whether college faculty members as a whole stand divided or united on these questions. At the outset, the general agreement on course content and methods of college instruction, reported earlier, was found to carry over in large measure to current issues in the field of reading instruction in the elementary school (2). Indeed, on the issues which follow, there was no real controversy in the sense that respondents clearly polarized in groups on disputed questions. Nor, except in one or two cases, was there a strong dissentient minority. The differences of opinion which appeared arose only on matters of emphasis or degree.

In the discussion which follows an effort has been made to summarize the general responses made to the questions concerning certain aspects of the elementary reading program. Comments supplied by the respondents have been used extensively to amplify their checked responses. Some respondents used the space afforded for such comments to support or justify their responses; others to illustrate their interpretation of their choice; others to offer an idea not appearing in the printed list of alternatives. The comments quoted were taken to suggest the range and tone of faculty thinking about reading problems and are not intended, therefore, to represent precisely the various percentages reported in the tables.

The Beginning Reading Program

READINESS FACTORS

In the early stages of development, what is chiefly responsible for the child's progress in reading or lack of it? Are there any measurable

---

SOURCE: Mary Austin, *The Torch Lighters* (Cambridge, Mass.: Harvard University Press, 1961), pp. 65–73. Reprinted by permission of the author, the publisher, and the President and Fellows of Harvard College.

traits or factors believed to determine reading achievement? In answering these questions, the college instructors in reading were asked to indicate what factors in their judgment were crucial to successful accomplishment of skills basic to beginning reading. The majority reaction was that such success depends not on one factor, but upon a combination of determinants. The commentaries stressed the need, as one instructor expressed it, "to delay the beginning reading program until the pupil has reached an adequate level of maturation on all levels." Similarly, another remarked that "the beginning reading process is a complex undertaking requiring a well-directed program of instruction including a variety of materials, techniques, and procedures, together with a favorable home environment, to ensure that each child will begin to learn how to read with security and genuine understanding."

Recognition of the role of the elementary teacher herself in the reading process was underscored by one respondent who stated, "I believe a child's success depends chiefly on how well the teacher succeeds in making him interested in and desirous of reading at the stage where he can handle the process successfully." Further support for the importance of the influence of the teacher came from another respondent who claimed, "the teacher's enthusiasm and the need to accept the child's individuality, pacing learning so that success is assured each step of the way is essential." Not forgotten was the need for "an understanding teacher with a pleasing personality and a love for children."

As stated above the major professional commitment, as far as achievement in the beginning reading program is concerned, appears to be a combination of determinants, including such qualitative factors as the home environment and teacher personality.

The Names and Forms of Letters: An issue of some controversy appears in the question: Should beginning readers be taught the names and forms of letters apart from simple words? If so, when? Before the words, or simultaneously with the words (sight vocabulary)?

In the present survey, only a few persons endorsed the method of teaching names and forms of letters before the sight vocabulary. The majority of the respondents, or 61 percent, held that it should be a simultaneous process. A large minority of 171, or 27 percent, on the other hand, maintained that the beginner should have no formal training in the names and forms of letters.

One instructor of the majority group stated that letters should be taught simultaneously with a sight vocabulary, provided that the child also learned "other word recognition and attack skills (phonetic and structural analysis) along with meaningful story content." Still another said that "because of the importance of phonetic analysis for the attainment of independence in reading, it is advisable to teach the child not only the letters of the alphabet, but also their sounds and simple combinations as needed." However, one member of the majority cautioned that "the emphasis put on learning names and forms of letters should be subordinate to that of teaching the sight words, but some recognition of the letter sounds and forms should be encouraged."

The minority opinion typically claimed that the child would learn many letters incidentally and that formal or definite instruction should be given later in the reading program, if needed. Other respondents stressed the possibility of teaching names and forms of letters "when the need arises in writing, spelling, and as they desire to know letters." For most respondents, however, it was a matter for simultaneous teaching, with sight words having a slight priority in the early grades. One description of the process follows:

> The children use their stock of sight words (*b*aby, *b*ig, *b*all, *b*ump, for example) for the purpose of comparison, i.e., those sight words all *sound* alike at the beginning and they all *look* alike at the beginning. They all start with the letter "b." So *after* some sight words are learned the letter name is given.

More briefly, the child should first learn "sight words, then develop an awareness of differences and likenesses in words (whole to part, and back to whole)."

Vocabulary: Is it better to teach young children new words in some systematic manner of grouping, classification, or ordering? Or is it better to let interests and motives run their course—to teach words on a demand basis or as the need arises? If vocabulary control (3) enters in, to what degree should control be exercised? And what provisions should be made for individual differences?

A large majority of respondents advocated some method of vocabulary control. One of those who preferred close vocabulary control claimed, "Books for developmental reading should have a closely controlled vocabulary. Provisions for individual differences," she continued, "may be cared for by supplementary work." Another respondent, while advocating close control, qualified her choice by saying that the question depended upon the pupil's abilities—"The superior child will be able to handle more than a moderately controlled vocabulary and should not be held to the basic requirements of a basic vocabulary." Along the same line, another added that the vocabulary should be "uncontrolled for the bright and gifted child."

One respondent felt that control should be a function of purpose; vocabulary should be controlled "closely during instruction, not so closely in recreational reading."

From the standpoint of increasing the child's understanding of words, one instructor sought a balance: "I think we need controls, but we also need to stimulate him to reach out independently as fast as possible."

Thus vocabulary control in the early program appears to be endorsed, although some question exists as to the degree. Control seems to depend upon many things. Among them are ability and maturity of the child, the purpose of the reading lessons (for comprehension or recreation), and pupil motivation. Thus, no single type of control was favored by a majority of respondents, but rather a combination of devices to insure proper vocabulary control. The consensus was expressed by one respondent as follows:

> Opportunity to handle and browse through many books of many types and areas of interest, secured from the school library, public library, or brought into the classroom through other means, should be provided. Vocabulary of parallel type and extending beyond this type should be introduced from the very beginning.

Phonetic Analysis: Phonetic analysis is a method of word attack which involves the association of speech sounds with letter symbols and combinations of the latter. Among the faculty in the present survey, opinion was sought on this method as a technique used in isolation and as one used in conjunction with other methods of word recognition.

There was considerable agreement that when used in isolation, phonetic analysis, like any other single method so employed, is of doubtful effectiveness. Over half of the faculty respondents indicated that under these conditions it was of little importance, and another 12 percent believed it to be of no importance at all. This technique in isolation, said one instructor, "is of little importance since its effectiveness depends upon its use with other techniques." When used alone, according to other respondents, the technique "may hinder reading programs . . . that is, it may hinder interest, comprehension, and speed." Rejecting the method altogether, one instructor believed that "it tends to confuse pupils except perhaps for the very bright who really do not need it."

The faculty viewed phonetic analysis more favorably when the technique was used together with other means of word attack. Over 80 percent believed that, in these circumstances, the method assumed considerable and even major importance in the reading program. "Phonetic analysis," said one instructor, "is important. If introduced gradually with other techniques and in meaningful ways, and if introduced sequentially at appropriate reading levels, it can materially aid reading . . ." The strength of phonetic analysis appears to lie in the aid it gives in the identification of unfamiliar words. The technique must apparently be used in balance with other approaches. As one instructor put it, "It should not be deleted from the program, nor should it be overstressed. Phonetic analysis should be considered as one of several ways of identifying a strange word." The need to view phonetic analysis as one of several techniques was further advanced by another respondent:

> When used in this way, phonetic analysis is most valuable. Children provided with significant ear training and association of visual and auditory techniques, when this training is done functionally, find considerable satisfaction in identifying unknown words.

Moderation in phonetic analysis as a technique for teaching children to read, its balance with other methods, and its judicious handling characterize a good program in the eyes of the majority of respondents.

Developing Reading Skills

The Role of the Basal Reading System: Preference for the use of basal readers for all elementary grades was expressed by one-half of the faculty surveyed. Another fourth would limit their use to the primary grades only; and 16 percent would not choose the reader as a chief tool of reading instruction.

The use of basal reading series is another of the few issues on which opinions differed significantly. But again, it is not a question of the exclusive dependence upon a reading series contrasted with no use at all. In fact, except for a minority of 16 percent, the respondents did not mutually exclude them. The opinions given suggested instead a search for the right point in the development of each child at which the basal reader might be left for more independent work, or for the right combination of teacher-devised materials and the published product.

It may be worth noting that a total of 75 percent of all respondents preferred the use of basal readers in the primary grades (50 percent would go beyond the primary grades), and recalling an earlier item (4), 85 percent indicated that a child's vocabulary should be closely or moderately controlled in the beginning reading program. The consistency here, in turn, suggests that the basal reading series finds favor as a vocabulary-controlled teaching tool.

On the use of basal readers for all grades, one respondent stated, "The practice provides for continuity in development of skills, assures no omissions. The skills will be applied in the content subjects." A number of respondents, however, also referred to what seems to them the restrictive nature of the basal reading series. Typical of their thinking is the following statement: "Basal reading texts cannot meet the reading needs of all the pupils. This is especially true for children who are excellent readers." Supporters of individualized reading programs declared that "in any grade the pupil learns best reading individually selected materials." A much stronger expression of the same opinion was: "The idiocy of thinking that a given book is so good that everybody must read it at the same time prevents individual growth."

The development approach to reading, favored by most teachers, is said to be most effectively supported by the use of basal readers. One respondent maintained that "an adherence to a basal text at all grade levels would safeguard the child's chances of being introduced to all essential skills in reading." It is not, of course, a question of exclusive use of the series, but rather one of relative reliance. One instructor thought that "equal emphasis should be given to library reading and to reading in the content fields. I would also," she continued, "use readers perhaps more in the primary grades than in upper grades." Another respondent stated, "Above the primary grades, the pupils should have sufficient skill in independent word identification so that many materials can be used . . ."

Judging from the respondents' comments another key issue of the basal reader question is the extent to which such a reader supplements or supplants the judgment of the teacher. On this issue the consensus was that it should be considered *one* tool of instruction (with strengths and limitations) to be used in teaching. As one instructor said:

Perhaps the most important question involved here is the ability of the teacher. A well-trained competent teacher need not be limited to a basal reading text provided she knows what skills can supplement any needed skills not covered in the text in use. Personally, I favor a basal text because of the sequence and continuity of the skills and because an inexperienced teacher needs the continued guidance of the teacher's manual. It must be recognized, however, that some teachers do not use a text properly or to the limit of its resources.

The caution implied is clear: do not allow the promise of order and continuity in the basal reading approach to prevent freedom and spontaneity.

Oral and Silent Reading: Is it better to stress oral reading over silent reading, silent reading over oral, or should there be equal amounts of each in the beginner's program? The question of oral versus silent reading drew forth a distinct division of opinion suggesting that this was one of the few genuine controversies. About as many respondents preferred a stress on oral reading as preferred equal emphasis on oral and silent reading. A small group, or 9 percent of the total, maintained that silent reading should receive more emphasis.

Of those who proposed that oral reading should prevail in the beginning, one instructor claimed that "oral reading is important in the program because of its personal, social, and diagnostic values. It gives the teacher a quick and valid way to evaluate progress in important reading skills, particularly those of word recognition and phrasing, and to discover specific instructional needs." Another pointed out that "it is as natural for a beginner to vocalize as it is to breathe. It is this vocalization that proves to him that he is reading. Silent reading first, of course, followed by oral."

The other group which held that there should be equal amounts of silent and oral reading in the early grades advocated this to prevent the child from "becoming just a word caller," and to avoid "lip readers which come from too much oral reading." The representative opinion of this group is exemplified in this statement:

> I believe that some oral reading daily is important for each child in the beginning reading program, not only because children at that age enjoy reading aloud, but also because the child and the teacher can check on his progress. Nevertheless, because real independence in reading can be attained only when the child is able to read silently, it seems to me that the teacher should also emphasize silent reading.

This issue demands empirical evidence for resolution.

The matter takes a different turn as a child advances in grade. In grades 2 to 6, a majority, or 73 percent, of the respondents felt that silent reading should be stressed; only 17 percent believed there should be equal amounts of oral and silent reading, and less than 1 percent advocated more oral reading than silent, at this level.

One instructor supplied the rationale for the majority view: "By this time in school the amount of reading material for the pupil to handle has greatly increased. He needs speed as well as accuracy. This can best be attained by a great deal of silent reading, particularly in the upper grades." The purpose of reading aloud changes, too, according to one respondent: "The portions of time used for oral reading drop drastically in the third grade. By the sixth grade oral reading should be used (1) for diagnostic purposes, (2) after previous study, and (3) in audience situations." That the case for oral reading is not wholly lost, however, is shown by one instructor who said:

But I do not interpret this (more silent reading) as many in the profession do, to mean practically no oral reading! Meaningful oral reading is desperately needed in middle and upper grades to protect our embattled mother tongue. Diction, grammar, enunciation, pronunciation, increased vocabulary, and "sharing" require continual oral reading. Our teen-agers' slurpy, sloppy speech, and meager vocabularies, etc., are partial results of mass neglect of oral reading in elementary school past second grade.

Thus a change of emphasis in oral versus silent reading appears to take place with advances in grade. In the first grades oral reading seems to be stressed and in the upper grades, silent reading. A balanced view was expressed by one respondent: "Both are important. It is not the amount of oral reading, but rather the quality and purposefulness of the oral reading which counts. Children need much silent reading in order to gain speed and in order to carry on the reading in other subjects."

Grouping: The grouping of children according to various plans for the accomplishment of various purposes is a technique of considerable importance for effective teaching in general and no less so for the teaching of reading. Therefore an attempt was made to secure opinions from the faculty in the present survey, opinions on practical as well as desirable grouping methods.

Grouping children according to their ability to read, but making some provision for individual instruction, would appear the approach most preferred, thus resolving the dilemma between what is desirable and what is expedient in educational practice.

A proponent of this approach advocated "group instruction according to reading ability and level, but provisions for other groups, e.g., interest groups in activities in which provision is made for reading at varied levels of difficulty; small skill groups, some individualized reading when the child is ready for it, and individual help as needed." Although, in the opinion of another, "individual instruction would be ideal, ability grouping is most feasible when enrollment continues to be high."

The importance of flexibility in grouping was stressed by one respondent who believed that "the best results are obtained by allowing the child to move as fast as possible—sometimes individually, sometimes with a partner or two, sometimes in a larger group, but always a part of the unit which meets his needs and ability."

The need for controlled research carried out under scientific conditions was urged by one faculty member in order to ascertain "the efficiency of all types of organizational procedures, including totally individualized instruction as well as intra-grade and cross-grade grouping plans."

The position on the organization of the reading program within the classroom appears to be sharply outlined with the great majority holding to group instruction according to level of reading ability as the criterion for pupil placement.

Assessing Achievement

READING AND PROMOTION POLICY

Among other subjects and interests, reading has a central role in the debate of promotion policy. Since many, if not all, subjects of study presume reading ability on the part of the student, reading achievement would seem an important element in a school's policy of promotion. In other words, if reading is the chief tool of formal and informal learning, to what extent is the child's promotion a function of this ability, particularly in the early grades?

In the Early Grades: Faculty opinion, polled in this survey, varied. About a third believed that in the early grades (one through three) success in meeting the established reading goals was of considerable importance; a fourth stated that such success was of major importance; and another fourth indicated only moderate importance. Less than 10 percent maintained it to be of little or no importance.

"Reading," said one instructor, "is only one part of the school's curriculum and the child should be promoted on the basis of total growth and development and his ability to achieve as in a case of slow learners." Some respondents simply did not believe in "retaining children on the basis of academic progress for which reading is certainly essential." The inevitability of advancement was proclaimed by one instructor who felt resigned to the fact that "overaged pupils will have to be promoted regardless of reading achievement." But, another felt that, "if a child fails to develop proficiency in reading in the primary grades, he cannot succeed in any of his school work in the upper grades," and therefore had better be retained.

Some respondents considered questions of promotion policy to be outside the powers of the college instructor and decisions of this type to belong squarely in the hands of the elementary school administration: "The teacher must abide by school policy and 90 percent of the schools seem to regard this (success in reading) as the primary criterion. "Children," this instructor added, "often merely lose another year by retention since they cannot adjust emotionally . . ."

The question of advancing from one grade to the next was less of a concern for some respondents than that of establishing the causes of the reading failure which prevented promotion. "If grouping were adequate," said one respondent, "and provided for individual needs, the question of promotion would depend on the competence of the teacher at each grade level to meet the child's needs." Although in the usual sense success means that the child has attained the goals set for him, the setting of goals may vary, and,

> Since these goals differ with various circumstances, and since many schools maintain a policy of no retention for lack of success in any single academic skill, many other factors would enter into this decision of promotion. A child reading below level for one or two years, may often be able to achieve his so-called "proper" grade level the third year.

Thus, for the early grades, faculty opinion was not crystallized on the point of using reading ability in promotion policy.

In the Intermediate Grades: Faculty opinion on promotion in the intermediate grades as indicated in the checked replies did not appear far different from those for the primary grades. Slightly fewer held reading success to be of major importance at this level—correspondingly, slightly more regarded it as of considerable or moderate importance.

The written comments of the faculty on this matter suggest greater differences than did the checked responses. "Here (on the intermediate level)" said one instructor, "he must read to learn." For some, the intermediate grades represented a getting down to the business of learning, and retention became a serious matter. One respondent wrote, "By this time failure in meeting established (reading) goals needs careful attention and diagnosis for aid, because of the personal frustration to the child in using the printed page in all content fields, as well as in the area of reading for pleasure and enrichment."

Reading success is equally important at this level because from this point on the work becomes increasingly complex: "The content in terms of meaning and vocabulary development increases greatly in grades four through seven; therefore, it is very important to have established reading goals, and to meet them." On the other hand, grade placement should not be thought of too rigidly. According to another instructor, "promotion should be an individual matter. For example, a student's needs might be met better in a fifth grade, despite the fact that he may read at a fourth grade level of efficiency."

While no hard and fast rule seems advisable on the relation of promotion to reading success, the implications of the problem are far-reaching.

> Established reading goals should be interpreted as those established for various mental abilities. Every effort should be made to use the full power of each child during any one year, but all factors in the child's growth should be considered for promotion. Children are individuals with distinct patterns of growth. When a child is in one of these grades and the teacher thinks of

him only in reference to established goals for the grade reader level, the child becomes a remedial problem, a personality problem, and a discipline problem.

Promotion policy based upon reading ability is, therefore, a matter complicated by many considerations. On the whole, faculty opinion in the present survey assigned from considerable to major importance the role of reading success in grade advancement, its overall importance being slightly greater in the intermediate grades.

Thus the foregoing analysis of faculty opinion on current issues in reading instruction shows that there is marked agreement among the college faculty. Where there are differences of opinion, they are concerned more with the amount of stress to be given a particular approach than with the values of the approach itself.

References

1. Cf. C. Winfield Scott, Clyde M. Hill, and Robert W. Burns, ed., *The Great Debate.* Prentice-Hall, Inc., (Englewood Cliffs, New Jersey, 1959) passim.
2. The data in this section were taken from responses to the Questionnaire, Part II, Items 13 through 24. See Appendix C.
3. Control, in the sense used here, refers to the vocabulary in the books children read. Teacher control, then, is exercised in selection of books and reading materials.
4. See Table 3, Appendix E.

70. Reading in the Kindergarten

MARY C. AUSTIN (1965)

One of the most controversial issues of the sixties continues to be that of teaching young children to read. On the one hand are those who advocate the beginning of formal reading instruction at the nursery school or kindergarten level. On the other is an equally vociferous group which denounces the introduction of reading instruction to three-, four-, and five-year-olds.

SOURCE: *The Instructor,* LXXIV (March, 1965), 20–22. Reprinted by permission of the publisher.

Regardless of its position in this debate, every school system would do well to reexamine and restate its educational goals and the classroom procedures related to them. For the many years of its existence, the kindergarten program has changed very little. It has been considered as the chief means of orienting children to school life, as well as the major way of helping them adjust to the children and adults whom they will encounter as they participate in the varied activities of a school setting. Traditionally, there has been little or no attempt to initiate formal instruction in the academic subjects.

Within the past few years, however, doubts have been expressed as to the soundness of this approach for *all* children. Some teachers have felt that children are being deprived of the opportunity to explore books beyond the listening, viewing, and touching stage. This feeling has been prompted by the knowledge that a large number of kindergarteners have spent a year or more in nursery schools and have enjoyed similar advantages.

Certainly a greater degree of preparedness for learning on the part of some boys and girls appears to be present. Some of them can read when they enter kindergarten. There has been more learning of the alphabet, more writing, more reading of signs and labels, and generally, more contact with the printed word. Many five-year-olds have traveled extensively in their short lives. They have many books and recordings in their homes. They speak of many matters with assurance and poise.

But we need not rely upon observations alone for evidence that young children have increased in language proficiency during the past three decades. Quantities of data on such indices as amount of talking, average sentence length, and percentages of complex and compound sentences were gathered during the 1930's. Studies in more recent years have reflected the advances in children's language development.

In a follow-up study in the same community in 1957, Templin (1), using the same methods and sampling techniques as Davis (2) and McCarthy (3), found children talking in significantly longer sentences and using larger vocabularies. Studies by Strickland (4) and Loban (5) confirm these findings and also lend support to the observation that children's speaking, listening, and reading abilities are directly related. Loban, for example, found that pupils who had the largest vocabularies and highest achievement in oral language in kindergarten continued to exceed other children in reading ability as they advanced from grades one through six.

Studies of Preschool Reading

Understandably, some teachers are plagued by feelings of guilt because they are not taking the factors mentioned above into account as they plan the year's work. Others do not consider them sufficiently important to warrant changes in the curriculum. Longitudinal studies of preschool reading may help teachers and administrators resolve these dilemmas. Several such studies are in progress, two of which will be discussed briefly.

Durkin's fifth-year report of the achievement of 49 Oakland, California, public school boys and girls who learned to read at home prior to first-grade entrance continues to favor an early start in reading (6). She indicates that "a majority of 'bright' preschool readers achieve higher in reading after only five years of school instruction than non-early readers of the same intellectual level who have had six years of school instruction." Durkin pointed out that these findings do not necessarily provide support for earlier school instruction in reading. Almost without exception, the early "home readers" were children who wanted to learn to read and had many opportunities to do so. Differences in attitudes toward reading, as well as reading achievement, might be great if the schools were to include formal reading activities for all children at the kindergarten level.

In a carefully designed and controlled experimental study involving approximately 4,000 pupils, the Denver Public Schools have provided instruction in beginning reading in kindergarten pilot groups since 1960. At the end of first grade these pilot groups of children scored significantly better on reading tests than did the control groups of children who had had the regular kindergarten program (7). The results revealed further that optimum reading achievement was obtained when adjustments were made in the first grade to take advantage of gains made in kindergarten.

The Denver study also considered the possibility that the early teaching of reading may cause an increased occurrence of problems related to vision, hearing, or social and academic adjustment. When each of these areas was checked in the first-grade pilot and control groups, it appeared that teaching beginning reading in kindergarten neither created nor prevented problems, since the differences found between groups were not statistically significant.

The Denver Public Schools have initiated a parallel study to determine how effectively parents can provide reading readiness activities for their preschool children. A guidebook entitled *Preparing Your Child for Reading* presented the instructional plan, and sixteen television programs demonstrated specific approaches which parents might use at home. Again, carefully structured research groups were established to test the preschool program.

Final evaluation of the Denver reading project will be forthcoming at the conclusion of the five-year study. In the meantime, annual progress

21. poor vision
22. poor attitude toward school
23. nail biting
24. poor present health
25. lack of interest
26. lack of motivation
27. lack of reading materials at home
28. a specific teaching method

These original studies indicated that groups of poor readers exhibited a lack of neurological organization as their most significant common trait. Our present studies indicate that approximately 70 percent of children seen by our reading clinics have some need for and do profit from neurological organization.

These children are not easily identified by the typical neurological and psychological tests unless they have gross disorganization or have a traumatic etiology. We have concluded that these children have suffered some slight developmental loss either in properly organizing subcortical neural levels or in establishing a complete dominance configuration. When these factors are changed through proper neurological organization we find that the technique used to teach them becomes secondary in importance to proper neural organization.

Let us analyze man who is a speaking and reading being to see how poor readers differ from the developmental norm of good readers. Man differs from lower forms of animals and has been able to conquer his planet because of the following neuro-psychological functions which are uniquely his. He can supinate and pronate his hand, he has finger-thumb opposition, he can stand fully upright, he has functional stereoscopic vision, and he has cortical hemispheric dominance. All of these have great causal implications for man's most significant neuro-psychological achievement—that of symbolic language and its concomitant, ideation.

If we analyze man's neurological development phylogenetically we find that the development of the nervous system from simple to complex takes a vertical course from the low spinal cord area, going vertically hrough the higher spinal area, medulla, mid-brain, corpus collosum, nd cortex. This phylogenetic development is recapitulated ontogenetilly in man. Man has added a lateral progression at the level of corx wherein the right or left hemisphere becomes the final point of minance. This orderly progression is an *interdependent continuum.* high level is unfunctioning or incomplete, the next lower level takes mand. A lack of organization at lower levels influences the func- of higher levels. It is the final lateral progression which enables

reports appear to show that parents are successful in helping their young children prepare for reading instruction and that early reading instruction has a "measurable, positive, continuing effect" (8).

Actually, the important issue for administrators, teachers, and parents to decide is not whether schools should teach reading to *all* kindergarteners, but whether each child who enters school has every opportunity to advance at a pace appropriate for his ability. Future research must consider the problems involved in discovering the optimum age for beginning reading for each child. Studies should also be directed toward an evaluation of various techniques to be used in determining readiness for reading so that schools can delay formal reading instruction for some individuals and accelerate it for others.

Early Reading Programs

Of what value are research findings pertaining to children's language development and early reading instruction to the teacher? Perhaps most obvious is the fact that improved classroom programs can be based upon this knowledge. Realizing that children today possess larger vocabularies and use more complex sentence structures than those of several years ago, the teacher can capitalize upon this situation by providing a wide variety of enriched learning experiences. She can take advantage of teachable moments by being sensitive to individual and group needs or interests. She can modify plans and keep a flexible schedule.

Recognizing that listening and speaking abilities are so important in determining success in reading, the teacher can place greater emphasis upon these skills from the very beginning of the year. She needs to be highly perceptive in knowing when to listen herself, when to question and clarify, and when to introduce related concepts. She will make certain that boys and girls have many experiences with stories and poems, including the retelling of story episodes in sequence. Perhaps some children will learn to operate a filmstrip projector so that *Hercules,** *Mike Mulligan and His Steam-shovel,** or another favorite can be shown as a child narrates the story. Sets of filmstrips with accompanying long-playing records are available also. What a boon to a busy teacher who occasionally can introduce a new story to one group of children by means of the sound filmstrip while she works with another group!

Knowing that some children have learned to read prior to school entrance, the teacher can provide the kind of instruction that is appropriate for the needs and accomplishments of these early readers. More often than not, she will take full advantage of materials and experiences which are already a part of the kindergarten. Visits to the local super-

* Produced by Weston Woods, Weston, Conn.

market or post office, for example, enlarge the children's horizons, result in the addition of new words to their vocabularies, form the basis of creative play and artwork, provide individual and group story content, and serve as springboards to many valuable reading skills. If a tape recorder is available, the teacher can use it for oral compositions and speech improvement activities. In these ways and others, she can help young readers develop into even better ones.

In today's world children are surrounded by many preschool experiences. Undoubtedly some American children are ready to read somewhat earlier than those in the past. In the present changing climate of opinion about the best time for beginning reading instruction, each school system will do well to examine current findings in child development, its own philosophy of education for young children, and the types of classroom approaches which will be compatible with its beliefs.

References

1. Templin, Mildred, *Certain Language Skills in Children, Their Development and Relationship*. University of Minnesota, Institute of Child Welfare Monograph Series, No. 26, 1957.
2. Davis, Edith A., *The Development of Linguistic Skills in Twins, Singletons with Siblings, and Only Children from Age Five to Ten Years.* University of Minnesota, Institute of Child Welfare Monograph Series, No. 14, 1937.
3. McCarthy, Dorothea, *The Language Development of the Pre-School Child,* University of Minnesota, Institute of Child Welfare Monograph Series, No. 4, 1930.
4. Strickland, Ruth G., *The Language of Elementary School Children: Its Relationship to the Language of Reading Textbooks and the Quality of Reading of Selected Children.* Bulletin of the School of Education, Vol. 38, No. 4. Bloomington, Ind.: Indiana University, 1962.
5. Loban, Walter D., *The Language of Elementary School Children.* Research Report No. 1. Champaign, Ill.: National Council of Teachers of English, 1963.
6. Durkin, Dolores, "A Fifth-Year Report on the Achievement of Early Readers," *Elementary School Journal*, Vol. 65 (Nov., 1964), pp. 76–80.
7. Brzeinski, Joseph E., "Beginning Reading in Denver," *The Reading Teacher*, Vol. 18 (Oct., 1964), pp. 16–21.
8. *Ibid*., p. 21.

71. Neuro-Psychological Factors as Causes of Reading Disabilities

CARL H. DELACATO (1960)

The *neuro-psychological* concept for the diagnosis of reading problems and *neurological organization* as the primary treatment modality is based on the premise that language is the distillate of man's phylogenetic neural development and that normal language function and reading are the distillates of a total ontogenetic neural development.

Our original studies aimed at finding the common characteristics among poor readers indicated *no significant correlation* between the fol lowing and poor readers as a group:

1. low intelligence
2. common socio-economic status
3. race
4. religion
5. divorce in family
6. very progressive schooling
7. very conservative schooling
8. emotional maladjustment
9. too much phonetic instruction
10. faulty school placement
11. changing teachers
12. social immaturity
13. rigid parents
14. lax parents
15. poor in arithmetic
16. restricted speaking vocabulary (bi-lingualism)
17. severe emotional conflicts at home
18. hostility on the part of the child
19. exhibitionism
20. poor hearing

SOURCE: *New Frontiers in Reading,* V (1960), 60–62
sion of Carl H. Delacato and the International Rea

man to accomplish those unique neuro-psychological functions mentioned above.

The neurological differences between man and slightly lower forms of animals are not cellularly important. The basic difference between man and the animal world is that man has achieved hemispheric dominance at a cortical level. Man has evolved to the point where the two hemispheres of the brain, although mirroring each other physically, have differentiated functions. Completely right sided humans are one sided: i.e., they are right eyed, right handed, right footed, with the left cortical hemisphere controlling the skill aspect of the organism. The opposite is true for completely left sided humans.

We have found that children who do not fit into this developmental pattern have language and/or reading problems.

Diagnostically we proceed from cortical function down. Where we find deviations from the normal progressions, treatment procedures have been established to facilitate neurological organization. When a child is neurologically organized he can profit from reading instruction. Without proper neurological organization most of our reading techniques prove relatively ineffective.

We begin at the level of cortex and hemispheric dominance.

1. Ascertain handedness using the usual techniques and adding supination-pronation and opposition bilaterally to better evaluate the handedness.
2. Ascertain footedness utilizing the usual techniques.
3. Ascertain the controlling eye in binocular vision. This is done via the Berner rationale utilizing tests 4, 5, and 6 of the Telebinocular. An evaluation of the sighting eye, although considerably less reliable than ascertaining the controlling eye, is also helpful.

Through the observation of the combination of the above, we can ascertain the natural laterality tendency and if any of the factors above do not fall on the side of natural laterality the appropriate treatment procedures are used.

1. Make the dominant hand the most skilled and most used hand by re-enforcement or re-education.
2. Establish the eye on the side of dominance as the controlling eye in binocular vision. This can be done through occlusion and re-training. This should begin at far point and then be followed at near-point.
3. Re-educate the child so that the proper foot is dominant.

The next level of diagnosis and treatment is the ascertainment of sub-dominant cortical functions. Since dominance implies the highest level of control, and since it is essential and what we are striving for, the irradiation of the sub-dominant hemisphere should be discontinued so far as possible. The primary sub-dominant function which interferes with the complete establishment of dominance is *tonality*. Music and singing should be deleted from the child's environment as much as possible at this time, as should be tonalized oral reading.

The next significant diagnostic area is at the mid-brain level. It is characterized by cross-pattern function. It can be evaluated by having the child creep or walk, and ascertaining the serialization of these acts. In proper cross-pattern creeping, the side toward which the head is turned has the arm flexed and the leg extended. As the head turns, the arm on the other side of the body is flexed and the leg on that side is extended. This should also hold true with normal walking, and both creeping and walking should be smooth and serialized. One can see this pattern beautifully exaggerated if he examines a still photograph of a sprinter running.

If this pattern is not followed, the child should be taught to creep and walk in a proper cross-pattern in order to facilitate greater neurological organization at this level.

The organization of the brain stem is ascertained during sleep. When asleep the properly organized child usually sleeps prone in the tonic-neck reflex position with the flexed arm and leg on the subdominant side and the extended arm and leg on the dominant side. An apparent disorganized sleep position, or mirrored pattern does not necessarily indicate neurological disorganization if turning the head elicits a tonic neck reflex, or the subject awakens.

A lack of organization at this stage indicates the need for re-education at a homolateral level. The patient can be organized at this level through crawling exercises in a homolateral pattern.

Having ascertained the areas of neurological organization which are lacking, a pre-remedial program aimed at establishing neurological organization is initiated. Reading activities are discontinued during this pre-remedial period. This usually lasts about 6 to 18 weeks, during which time periodic re-evaluations are made. When neurological organization is achieved the child is returned to his remedial and/or educational situation.

We find that those children who are properly neurologically organized become able to profit from remedial instruction whereas they had not been able to do so prior to the pre-remedial program.

The *neuro-psychological* approach to the diagnosis of reading problems and *neurological organization* as the remedial procedure is the result of the work of The Rehabilitation Center at Philadelphia, the Chestnut Hill Reading Clinic of Philadelphia, and Centro De Reabilitacao Nossa Senhora Da Gloria, Rio de Janeiro, Brazil. For a complete description of the basic research and rationale please see: (1) *The*

Neurological Organization of Development Stages of Mobility in the Severely Brain-Injured Child by Robert Doman, M.D., Eugene Spitz, M.D., Elizabeth Zucman, M.D., Carl H. Delacato, Ed.D., and Glenn Doman. This article has been accepted for 1960 publication in the Journal of the American Medical Association. (2) *The Treatment and Prevention of Reading Problems* by Carl H. Delacato, Ed.D., Charles Thomas Co., Springfield, Ill., 1959.

72. Color: A New Dimension in Teaching Reading

SISTER M. RAPHAEL (1966)

Color has added a new dimension to the teaching of reading. Throughout the country, primary children, children with reading difficulties, and illiterate adults are learning to read through this new approach to reading and writing called "color reading" or "visual dictation."

Dr. Caleb Gattegno, a British educator, developed the color reading system called "Words in Color" (WIC). He first saw children in Switzerland learning music through the use of color and was greatly impressed with the results. Under this inspiration, he introduced a system of learning arithmetic in which color was of special importance. In 1957, while working in Ethiopia on a UNESCO project, he discovered the value of mathematics and color in the teaching of Amharic, the official language of Ethiopia. He was able to reduce the learning time for reading and writing its 251 signs from a minimum of 4 or 5 months to 10 hours. After experimentation with the phonetic languages of Spanish and Hindi, he tackled the nonphonetic English language. After five years of work, he first demonstrated the teaching process in Washington, D.C., in 1964.

The irregularity of the English spelling has long been recognized as the biggest stumbling block for beginning readers. This is a major argument of those who oppose the phonics method of teaching reading.

SOURCE: *Catholic School Journal*, LXVI (October, 1966), 56–57. Reprinted by permission of the author and publisher.

Many children never overcome the confusion they encounter when letters are pronounced one way in one word and another way in other words. English, which is not phonetic, is full of such pitfalls.

For example, the same "oo" sound is represented by the ten different letter combinations in the following words: *to, too, two, crew, through, flu, true, fruit, shoe,* and *you.* Quite naturally, a child meeting these words for the first time and trying to decipher them with an ordinary phonics background will at least be confused, if not hopelessly lost. In "Words In Color" all the letters and combinations of letters which are pronounced "oo" are colored green. The color provides the key for reading the words.

Although Dr. Gattegno has identified more than 270 different sounds in the English language, which uses only a 26-letter alphabet, he simplifies these to 47 main sounds. The colors represent sounds, one each for the 20 different vowel and diphthong sounds in English and one each for the 27 consonant sounds. Teachers who use this system must have 47 colors of chalk at hand to represent the main sounds. The color for a sound is the same no matter how the word is spelled. For example, the *n* in *no,* the *ne* in *phone,* the *kn* in *know,* the *pn* in *pneumonia,* the *gn* in *gnat* are all lavender, the *n* sound in color.

An advantage of WIC is that the learner is allowed initially to view our nonphonetic language as a phonetic language without changing the traditional spelling. Reading books accompanying the program are in black and white, and all writing done at the blackboard is done with white chalk. The colored chalk is exclusively for the teacher's use.

Materials Needed

Three kinds of materials are required for color reading method: those for the teacher, those for the entire class, and those for the individual learner. The teacher has a teacher's guide which gives detailed suggestions for the content and sequence of the lessons. The entire class uses 21 charts in color with more than 600 words, eight phonic code charts in color, and word cards for more than 1200 words, printed in black on colored cardboard. Each student receives a word-building book, three reading books containing a 1200-word vocabulary, a story book, and worksheets.

The 21 charts progressively introduce the sounds of English, beginning with the most regular spellings and progressing through virtually all the regular and irregular signs of English. The set of eight phonic code charts is a systematic organization of the signs (spellings) occuring in English; four charts present the vowel signs with their various spellings and four charts present the consonants with their varied spellings. The word cards introduce words representing different parts of speech. Each part of speech is printed on a card of a special color. By putting the words together in sentences, learners discover the structural elements of complete sentences. If a word can be used as more than one part of speech, it is printed on more than one color card. Thus the student learns inductively that every complete sentence *always* has some structural element and only sometimes includes others.

All of the materials for the individual learner are printed in black on white. As soon as the teacher has introduced the first sounds, the learner can recognize these words in his word-building book, can learn words made up of these sounds in the first of his three reading books, and can use words on his first worksheet. Since the learner works almost simultaneously with words printed in color and words printed in black, at no point in the program does progress depend on remembering colors.

The use of all the materials is flexible. Their use depends upon the needs and level of readiness of the students. This flexibility easily allows for taking care of individual differences.

Teachers working with WIC have not found that the number of colors is confusing to the learners. One color with its sound is introduced at a time. A new color with its associated sound is not introduced until complete mastery of previous colors and the associated sounds have been mastered. At times, the closeness of colors has been deliberate. For example, the colors for *b* and *d* are purposely close so that beginners learn immediately that they must recognize the letters by shape differences.

Color-Blindness Is No Problem

Since the system is based upon distinguishing between so many colors, the question of what effect color-blindness might have naturally arises. Authorities agree that this is not a serious problem, since present research reveals that less than eight percent of the boys and about 0.5 percent of the girls in the average first-grade classroom will have some degree of color-blindness. Furthermore, many color-blind children see most colors naturally, and those colors which are distorted will still be distinguishable from the others.

Proponents of the color reading program say that continuing experiments may enable an average kindergarten child to read up to 2000 words after six months. WIC is being tested throughout the country. In the spring of 1965 the program was being used in some 600 classrooms by approximately 15,000 students. The program has been met with approval where it has been used. In the Santa Fe public schools, the program is considered a success and has been added to the approved textbook list of the state department of education.

For Adult Illiterates

The WIC reading program has been used successfully to teach adult illiterates and nonreaders of all ages. The program is now being tested under the antipoverty program in work camps for adults and teen-agers. Various cities have also initiated the WIC system. Program for Action by Citizens in Education (PACE) in Cleveland, Ohio, has joined the Cleveland public schools, the Cleveland Public Library, and other community organizations in a "Right-to-Read Project." Their object of teaching adult illiterates and poorly schooled adults is being realized partly through the use of WIC.

73. The Value of ITA: "We're Enthusiastic"

JOHN DOWNING and IVAN ROSE (1964)

Before speaking out on behalf of ITA, let us explain briefly what it is, for the benefit of those who may be unfamiliar with it.

ITA, which stands for Initial Teaching Alphabet, is the new beginning reading alphabet pioneered in British schools.

It was invented by Sir James Pitman, whose idea was to prevent children from experiencing difficulty and failure in the beginning stages of learning to read by giving them a simpler and more reliable alphabet and spelling.

Children use ITA until they have become confident and fluent in reading it. Then they transfer their skills and attitudes over to reading the traditional orthography (TO) of English. The characters of ITA and its spelling rules have been very carefully designed to make this transfer easy once ITA has given the children a flying start into reading.

In Britain, ITA's effects are being carefully studied by the Reading

---

SOURCE: *NEA Journal*, September, 1964, pp. 20–22. Reprinted by permission of the authors and publisher.

Research Unit at the University of London Institute of Education. Already the objective evidence collected during the first two years seems to show quite clearly (a) that beginning reading is much easier with ITA and (b) that children can readily transfer their superior reading skill from ITA to standard print.

In this research we are comparing the attainments of children using ITA with the achievements of pupils learning with TO. Everything except the one factor of the alphabet and spelling is being held constant in the two groups of classes.

The progress of the two groups has been very different. After only five months, the four- and five-year-old beginners who were using ITA materials were significantly in the lead, and their superiority increased as the months went by. For example, 25 percent of the ITA group (413 children altogether) had gone beyond the basal reader series by the end of the first year, compared with only 4 percent of the group using TO (687 children). At the end of two years, the comparative positions were 76 percent for ITA and 36 percent for TO.

All the objective data collected so far in this research have pointed in the same direction. On tests of comprehension, word recognition, and speed of reading, the children learning to read with ITA demonstrate astonishing superiority.

This testing indicates that for the following reasons ITA greatly lightens the load of learning at the beginning:

Pupils need to learn only one character for each letter of the alphabet (e.g. only *e* not *E* as well). Whenever capitals are needed, ITA uses a larger version of the same lower case shape.

Fewer whole-word representations need be learned in ITA. For instance, the ITA pupil has to learn only the one visual pattern for *dog* instead of the five or more patterns of TO. (i.e., Dog, DOG, etc.)

Fewer phonic print-signals have to be learned in ITA. For example, in TO the sound common to such words as *zoo, shoe, grew, through, do, blue,* etc. has thirty or more alternative phonic symbols. When ITA is used, there is only one single symbol to be learned for this one sound.

ITA has a simpler, consistent, spelling system. In ITA letters can generally be relied upon to keep the same sound value. For example, the letter *o* in ITA is not used to represent several different sounds as it is in the TO spellings *do, go, women, gone, one.* ITA is, therefore, much more consistent as a code for spoken English. Each of the different sounds in such words is signalled by a different printed symbol.

Consistency of *direction* of reading is the rule in ITA. In English we read words from left to right, but within many words in TO, the letters are not to be read from left to right in the early primitive decoding stage of learning.

For example in the words *cape, bite, dote, cute* the second sound is signalled by letters two and four, and so the child must *reverse* from right to left to read the final sound signalled by letter number three. In ITA the left-to-right rule of reading is never broken in this way.

Phonic symbols are less complex in ITA. Traditional orthography does not have enough letters to provide one letter for each of the forty odd sound units of English; instead, letters have to be used over again in a variety of combinations. For example, in TO, *c* is used for *cat, cup, cot; h* is used for *hat, hut, hop;* but in *chat, chop, chin, c* and *h* are used for a different single sound.

In ITA these sounds have been given their own special characters. The child learning to read in ITA can consistently apply reason and logic to the process; in TO this would not be true, for each rule has far too many exceptions. Thus, with ITA a child can approach a new word, a new book eagerly and confidently, knowing that his knowledge and skill will not let him down.

Tests made of the ITA pupil's ability to read *conventional print* show that transfer is quite easy. Only eighteen months after beginning to learn to read with ITA, children obtain very superior scores on tests printed in the *traditional alphabet and spelling.* The children who begin with ITA and later transfer to the standard print can read the latter with much greater accuracy and comprehension than the children who have been learning the traditional alphabet and spelling from the beginning.

74. The Value of ITA: "It's Too Soon to Know Definitely"

WARREN G. CUTTS (1964)

I would like to make clear at the start that I am NOT against ITA. On the contrary, I have continually encouraged further research with it. My reply to the article by Messrs. Downing and Rose is based upon

SOURCE: *NEA Journal*, September, 1964, pp. 20–22. Reprinted by permission of the author and publisher.

my sincere belief that we are not yet ready either to accept without reservation or to reject this new instructional medium. I regard myself as a "friendly gadfly."

My purpose is neither to discredit ITA nor to disparage the efforts of those who seek to demonstrate its usefulness. The founder of this system and the men associated with him, both in England and elsewhere, are individuals of highest integrity and ability. They should be applauded for their willingness to press forward with their educational experiments in the face of adverse criticism and, frequently, a lack of understanding on the part of teachers and administrators.

As pointed out by Sir Edward Boyle (then British Minister of Education) in the Parliamentary debates last March [1963]:

> A final evaluation of the ITA experiment will not be possible until some while after the children concerned have transferred to traditional orthography. But the promise of the results obtained so far is fulfilled, have no doubt that the use of this Alphabet will lead further, and that its significance will become more widely understood.

In other words, we should suspend judgment until more research has been completed and the data examined from a variety of viewpoints. Premature judgments can lead to rash statements which cloud the real issues and which compel teachers to take sides. This has happened many times in educational history, resulting in controversies that have generated more heat than light.

The ITA experiments in England are scheduled to continue until 1974. Educators should carefully consider interim reports from both British and American studies but should not at this time draw conclusions about the full significance of ITA.

Since many children in England and a significant number in the United States have already made the transition from ITA to TO (traditional orthography), why are we still reluctant to accept this new medium for beginning reading instruction?

Several factors make early appraisals of doubtful validity:

1. We do not know as yet the long-range effect of ITA on reading and spelling performance, and may not clearly see what effect (if any) it will have until pupils who have taken part in the experiment reach the fourth or fifth grade. It is entirely possible, although present evidence seems to indicate otherwise, that certain residual effects may later act as deterrents to fluent reading and accurate spelling. These possible effects need to be carefully weighed against the advantages claimed for early reading achievement.

2. We do not know as yet the extent to which the enthusiasm of teachers and the glamour of an experimental situation lift pupils to

higher reading achievement. We need to find out how well ITA expedites learning after the initial enthusiasm and glamour have worn off.

The "Hawthorne effect" can never be completely eliminated in educational experiments, since teacher enthusiasm is an uncontrollable variable. Of course, the fact that most of the experimental teachers have become enthusiastic about ITA may itself be considered a credit to the new system.

3. Although many children have made a successful transition to TO without any apparent difficulty, there may be some children whose mental abilities or psychological sets make it difficult for them to discard one medium and master another. Therefore, even if ITA is approved and recommended as an instructional medium for general use in beginning reading, we will ultimately need more refined experiments to determine the types of learners for whom it works best. We also will need to know the sort of program in which it functions best.

4. Too early acceptance is likely to bring about a sharp cleavage between the proponents and opponents of ITA. If educators will only suspend judgment until more evidence is available, it will be much easier to maintain a scientific atmosphere in which objective data can be weighed and sifted in the light of broader educational objectives.

It is important that reading researchers continue their efforts to simplify the learning task for beginning readers. (For example, simplification might come through linguistic programing of reading materials.) Whatever the avenue explored, we need the individual and cooperative efforts of others who, like Sir James Pitman, are willing to display imagination, resourcefulness, and determination. An inclination to accept ITA as a panacea might discourage such efforts.

5. Another reason for suspending judgment on ITA is the fact that several significant research studies have demonstrated that late starters tend to catch up with and even surpass in reading ability those children who have received direct, intensive reading instruction early in the first grade or in kindergarten. This is especially true when delayed instruction has been preceded by enriched readiness activities.

These studies, while not unassailable, at least suggest that some of our current concern for getting children off to an early start in reading may be misdirected.

75. The Controversial History of Phonics

DOLORES DURKIN (1962)

The teaching of reading has its own history. And at most times during that history some attention has been given to phonics. At most times too, however, the question "Should phonics be taught?" has been asked and conflicting answers have been heard.

Early History of Phonics

In colonial days, best depicted for purposes of this discussion through the *New England Primer*, a child learned to read by first learning the alphabet. As he was warned:

> He who will ne'er learn his ABC
> Forever will a blockhead be.

Once the child mastered the alphabet, he was then required to learn the pronunciation of various lists of syllables by spelling out the letters. On the assumption that the difficulty of learning the pronunciation of letter combinations is directly related to the number of letters combined, shorter syllables came first. Ultimately, words were introduced and, again, the sequence in which they appeared depended upon length and number of syllables.

While the sounds of letters received some attention during this colonial period, the spelling out of letters was the principal means used to help children learn to read syllables and, later on, words.

Following the American Revolution the matter of sounds took on new and special importance in reading instruction—in this instance, though, as a way of standardizing American speech. In his well-known *American Spelling Books,* which "taught millions to read and not one to sin," Noah Webster tried to rid the new nation of its dialects by emphasizing, through phonics, a common pronunciation of common words. In reading, the letters of the alphabet were still introduced ini-

---

SOURCE: Dolores Durkin, *Phonetics and the Teaching of Reading* (New York: Teachers College Press, 1962), pp. 8–14.

tially, but now their sounds received special attention. Syllables came next, and they too were organized according to sounds. Once learned, they were followed by lists of phonetically related words.

By 1840 Horace Mann had become a prominent educational leader; and about that time too he was reminding teachers and school administrators it was words that were familiar to young children, and it was letters and letter sounds that were unfamiliar. His reminder, coupled with other reactions against the ABC and sounding methods of teaching reading, led some schools to emphasize a whole-word method. In these instances a child learned to read by first learning whole words.

Later, the researcher Cattell demonstrated through tachistoscopic techniques that a reader reacts to words and groups of words, not to the individual letters within a word. As then interpreted his finding gave further impetus to the whole-word method, and even to sentence and story methods. During these same years, however, texts like the McGuffey and the Beacon Readers were used extensively in the schools, and both emphasized phonics. In some of their stories, for example, vowels in words were diacritically marked, silent letters were crossed out, and identical letter combinations were underlined. Consequently, even while Horace Mann lectured and Cattell worked in his laboratory, much repetition of *nip, nap, nup,* and *sit, bit, rit* was still going on in elementary school classrooms.

Later Developments

About the time of World War I the influence of Gestalt psychology reached educational circles. Its emphasis on the importance of "wholeness" in the learning process tended to discredit still further the phonetic method of teaching reading. So, too, did the exaggerated emphasis given to silent reading during the 1920's. These developments, together with growing interest in less formal and less structured teaching–learning situations, combined to put phonics somewhere in the background as a method of teaching reading. A few writers have said that by 1930 it was dispensed with, but this conclusion seems to be based more on a look at some of the textbooks of the time than on actual classroom observation.

In any case, by 1940 there was an open resurgence of phonics as one aspect of reading instruction. In 1955, however, came Rudolf Flesch's *Why Johnny Can't Read,* which—while indicting the schools for their failure to teach phonics and, consequently, reading—went on to become a best seller. Following *Why Johnny Can't Read* came much countercriticism, more controversy, and even some "new" phonetic systems. Consequently, it is relevant to ask at this point, Where do we now stand in regard to phonics?

The Current Scene

"To be or not to be" is no longer the focus of the phonics debate. Today, the value of phonics for a reading program is generally recognized, if and when it is given an appropriate role to play. What is its "appropriate role," therefore, comes forth as the current question to debate. And, while less dramatic than other questions, it too has been effective in stirring up controversy, and even hot tempers.

Like most debates, this current one has basically two sides. One side sees phonics as *the* method of teaching reading. The other side sees phonics as providing one possible kind of help in identifying new and unknown words. Both positions have certain consequences for classroom practice and both, according to the debaters, have important advantages and disadvantages.

Phonics as *the* Method of Teaching Reading

When phonics becomes *the* method of teaching reading, certain classroom practices logically follow. For example, phonics will necessarily be introduced at the time reading instruction begins. In this instance, initial instruction takes the form of telling the children the sounds of various letters. Later, these sounds are blended into syllables and then into words.

One well-known phonetic system, that of Julie Hay and Charles Wingo (4)—and this, incidentally, was enthusiastically recommended in Flesch's *Why Johnny Can't Read*—begins as follows. Pictures of an apple, elephant, Indian, ostrich, and umbrella introduce the short sounds of the vowels. Ten more pictures, these showing a squirrel, monkey, fox, rabbit, goat, nest, bear, tiger, pig, and dog, illustrate common sounds of the consonants *s, m, f, r, g, n, b, t, p,* and *d*. Once the short vowel sounds and the sounds of these ten consonants are learned they are blended together, first into syllables (su, so, si, se, sa), then into words (sun, sob, sit, set, sat). Following some of these initial blending exercises is a very brief "story" in which, at least for a time, some words are read by the children and some are supplied by the teacher. The very first of these stories is as follows:

Sam sat in the sun.
The sun is good for Sam.

While differences are to be found in the various systems that assume phonics to be *the* method of teaching reading, the pattern of Hay and Wingo is fairly typical of the group as a whole. Like the others, it proceeds deductively. That is, it begins with generalizations about the sounds of letters which are then applied to the pronunciation of specific syllables and words. Like the other systems, too, that of Hay and Wingo is a synthetic process in that it initially concentrates on parts of words which are later combined into whole words.

Phonics as One Kind of Help in Word Identification

When phonics is seen as providing only one possible kind of help in word identification, the sounds of letters do not have to be introduced at the time reading instruction begins. Instead, instruction can begin by teaching some words as whole words. In this instance, each word to be learned is presented as a unique and single symbol and the child is expected, in time and with practice, to remember it as such. When enough words have been learned in this way to provide examples of letter–sound relationships, then this is the time when phonics is introduced. Now, recurring parts of known words are used to arrive at generalizations regarding their sounds. For example, when a child knows *my*, *mother*, *must*, and *me*, or *big*, *baby*, and *bunny* he is ready to make generalizations regarding the sounds of the consonants *m* and *b*. And as more words are learned, more generalizations can be made about the sounds of other letters and letter combinations.

This particular way of progressing in phonics is often described as an *inductive* and *analytic* procedure. It is inductive because specific words are used to arrive at generalizations regarding the sounds of letters. It is analytic because whole words are analyzed to identify recurring letters and correlated recurring sounds.

How do the proponents of these two different approaches to phonics substantiate their respective positions? All, it would seem, speak loudest when pointing out disadvantages of the approach that is not theirs. They speak much more briefly, and meekly, when pointing out advantages of their own proposals.

For example, those who see phonics as *the* method of teaching reading usually claim it is only within this framework that phonics is systematically taught; that without a good foundation in phonics, reading problems follow. They also maintain that an approach to phonics which is unlike their own encourages guessing rather than reading, and dependence on the part of the reader rather than the hoped-for independence. They further claim that when children lack independence in working out the pronunciation of unfamiliar words, they are then forced to read dull and senseless texts in which the same words are repeated almost endlessly. The less timid in this group add, still further, that in learning to read whole words "the child grows tired and bored," but that the learning of sounds is "full of fun and adventure (7)."

Like this first group, those in the second—that is, those who look to phonics as providing only one kind of help in word identification—

also tend to substantiate their position mainly by pointing out flaws in the approach that is different from their own. They claim, for example, that immediate stress on phonics kills enthusiasm for learning to read and emphasizes pronunciation sometimes to the exclusion of meaning. They would also say that immediate stress on phonics allows for only a deductive approach; and this, in turn, encourages memorization to the exclusion of genuine understanding and insight. Other indictments point to inefficient eye movements, unnecessary lip movements, and slow, laborious reading as unfortunate results of too much phonics too soon.

What About the Teacher?

In the midst of these counterclaims and countercriticisms, which approach to phonics should the classroom teacher follow? Ideally, findings of carefully thought-out and worked-out research would change the substance of the various arguments from opinion to fact, and thereby would provide direction and justification for classroom practice. Unfortunately, however, existing research in phonics is characterized more by quantity than by quality. And because of the lack of quality, "data" can be found to support almost any claim or any point of view.

Basically, the cause of inferior research in phonics is neither single nor simple. In one sense, however, it can be said to be rooted in inadequate controls. For example, if a researcher examines the value of one method of teaching phonics as opposed to another, both methods ought to be carried out under identical, or at least very closely comparable conditions. Otherwise the researcher would not be justified in attributing differences in outcome or achievement to differences in method. Yet much of the published research in phonics shows little or no attempt to control for teacher-quality or for teacher-motivation. Too often, in fact, the teacher using the "newer method" is a volunteer who, most likely, has considerable enthusiasm for the method he is using, and is therefore much more likely to succeed than the less well motivated teacher—almost regardless of method.

Another related shortcoming in research arises when the researcher assumes controls which do not exist. Many of the earliest studies in phonics, for example, were designed to compare the reading achievement of two matched groups of children, one of which was given instruction in phonics while the other, supposedly, received none. Never taken into account in any of this research was the possibility that children in the so-called "No Phonics Group" actually received instruction in phonics at home or, what is equally possible, had developed their own phonics system. Consequently, what might really have been compared in this research is the reading achievement of children who receive formal classroom instruction in phonics, and the achievement of those who get help in phonics at home or who develop their own system of phonetic analysis.

A third kind of weakness in existing research lies in its tendency to examine, as the basis for making comparisons and drawing conclusions, only a limited segment of "reading achievement." Easily testable outcomes such as speed in reading, or ability to call off lists of words have most often been used as the basis for judging the value of some particular approach to phonics. The matter of a child's interest in reading or, perhaps, his ability to read critically or to draw inferences is usually sidestepped. Here, one serious barrier to better research has been the inability to identify specifically all of the skills and reactions that constitute good reading, coupled with the inability to measure adequately some already identified.

One further kind of flaw in the various studies could be attributed to the researcher's tendency to report in only a vague way what he does and what results he obtains. Often, for example, a particular "method" is given a label instead of a carefully detailed description. In addition, research findings are sometimes reported "in general" rather than in systematic, quantitative terms. And yet without exactness in research reporting it is impossible to compare meaningfully one study with another, or to cumulate the findings of several similar studies. What results, then, is a long list of small, isolated studies many of which are devoid of useful findings and of valid generalizations.

What has also resulted, therefore, is a long list of unanswered questions about the teaching of phonics. Still without definite answers are such basic questions as: How much is too much phonics—too much in the sense that it kills interest in reading, impedes its speed, and even obscures the meaning aspect of reading? Is there one sequence for teaching the various phonetic elements that is better than others? Is there a level of intelligence, or perhaps a special kind of intelligence, required for success in phonics? Is this being measured in currently available intelligence tests? What, specifically, can be done to help the child who knows the individual sounds of *b*, *a*, and *t*, but who seems unable to blend them into the familiar word *bat?*

Again—What About the Teacher?

At this point the teacher might well be asking, But what about me? I am still expected to make decisions about phonics. What do I do? Where do I begin? What do I do next?

Concerned as he is with immediate problems and responsibilities, the classroom teacher must have at least tentative answers to his questions. Consequently, until good research yields definitive, well-substantiated findings regarding many different aspects of phonics instruction, answers must continue to evolve from personal teaching experience and the teaching experience of others; from extensive classroom observation; from research findings in other areas of learning; and from objective, logical analysis.

References

1. Brown, Roger, *Words and Things*. Glencoe, Illinois: The Free Press,
2. Flesch, Rudolf, *Why Johnny Can't Read*. New York: Harper and Brothers, 1955.
3. Gray, Lillian and Reese, Dora, *Teaching Children to Read*. New York: Ronald Press Company, 1957.
4. Hay, J., and Wingo, C. E., *Reading With Phonics*. New York: J. B. Lippincott Company, 1948.
5. Kenyon, John S., *American Pronunciation; A Text of Phonetics for Students of English*. Ann Arbor, Michigan: George Wahr, 1937.
6. Smith, Nila B., *American Reading Instruction*. New York: Silver, Burdett and Company, 1934.
7. Terman, Sibyl and Walcutt, Charles Child, *Reading: Chaos and Cure*. New York: McGraw-Hill Book Company, Inc., 1958.
8. Thomas, Charles K., *An Introduction to the Phonetics of American English*. New York: Ronald Press Company, 1947.

76. Individual Reading—An Evaluation

HARRY W. SARTAIN (1963)

We all have doubts about the perfection of reading methods, but there is not the slightest doubt about the need for differentiating reading instruction to fit a wide range of pupil abilities.

Need for Differentiated Teaching

We know that when children enter the first grade they range in chronological age from about 5½ years old to about 6½ years old.

SOURCE: *A Report of the Nineteenth Annual Conference and Course in Reading* (Pittsburgh: University of Pittsburgh Press, 1963), pp. 55–60. Reprinted by permission of the publisher.

There usually is a spread of 12 months from the youngest to the oldest. However, the Stanford-Binet intelligence test norms show us that the spread in mental age is four times as great as the spread in chronological age. In any first grade class in a normal population there are children who are mentally only four years old along with others who are mentally five, six, seven, and eight. Because the most able children grow in mental ability at a faster rate than the average children, while the slower ones grow at a slower rate, this spread in inherited mental ability increases as the children move through school. By the time they reach the sixth grade the mental age range is something like seven or eight years instead of the four years that we had in first grade. This means that some sixth grade children have the mental ages of average third-graders while others have the mental ages of fourth, fifth, sixth, seventh, eighth, ninth, and tenth grade children.

Some school systems feel that they can reduce the range in academic aptitude appreciably by assigning so-called homogeneous groups to a classroom. However, these schools fail to take into account the fact that when you group children on the basis of any one average test score, you overlook the great range in ability in many specific traits that are combined in the average score.

Closer observation of testing will show that within the so-called homogeneous group there are individuals who are as weak on word analysis as any in the fastest group. In each "homogeneous" class there are individuals who are as weak in adopting speed to purpose and materials as the lowest in the slowest group and others who are as strong in this trait as the best in the fastest group. The more individual traits we look at, the more we see that there is no such thing as a truly homogeneous group. One of the more recent studies that illustrates this fact was published by Balow in the *Elementary School Journal* in October 1962 (1).

Time and time again studies have shown that when we attempt to adjust instruction to the capabilities of individuals, progress is significantly greater than when we teach all of the children in a class the same thing at the same rate. One of the frequently quoted studies on this topic was reported by Jones in 1948 in the *Journal of Educational Psychology* (2). Innumerable other studies support this finding. It is evident that reading instruction must be adopted to fit varied pupil needs and capabilities.

Misuses of Basal Programs

Individualized reading has received increasing attention as a reaction to the misuse of basic programs. These misuses have resulted in poorly differentiated teaching and in the development of unfavorable attitudes toward reading (3). Some of these malpractices in using basic programs are:

1. *Assigning all children in the class to read the same stories at the same rate.* When we are aware of the extent of individual differences we know how ridiculous this is. Unfortunately this practice is most common at the upper grade levels where the range of individual abilities is greatest.

2. *Limiting the reading program to one series of textbooks.* This occurs in spite of the fact that the teacher's manual of every good basal series tells us that the children learn development skills through the basic materials but that they must practice these skills in many, many other books.

3. *Requiring whole groups to follow in their books while individuals read aloud.* Oral reading should be related to listening, not to following visually in books. The practice of having children follow in books makes them bored with reading and develops unfavorable attitudes.

4. *Failing to utilize the skills program of the teacher's manual in a flexible manner to meet differing needs of pupils.* Every child does not need the same number of skills lessons.

5. *Employing practices which cause children to feel a stigma resulting from placement in inflexible reading groups.*

All of these procedures have been condemned by most reading authorities, but they are continued in situations where the teacher is uninformed or is not willing to put forth the amount of energy necessary to get to know the needs of individual children and undertake programs of instruction that provide for these needs.

Values in Individualized Reading

Proponents of completely individualized reading have made extensive claims about the values of this approach to instruction. Among these purported values are the following:

1. Children read more books.
2. Each child's interests are given consideration.
3. The teacher learns each child's needs and provides skills programs exactly fitted to meet those needs.
4. The plan works equally well with large or small classes.
5. The plan works equally well with the slow or able student.
6. Children and parents like this arrangement.

Dozens of experimental findings are quoted in support of these claims. Unfortunately, only a few of the experiments with individualized reading have been scientifically designed, and these are seldom quoted by the people who are enthusiastic about individualized reading.

Dangers in Individualized Reading

Some teachers who have experimented with individualized reading, and have been reluctant to adopt it as the sole method, have listed certain dangers that they observe in this approach (4).

1. There is no opportunity to teach new vocabulary and concepts that are needed before reading. Those people who say that there is no need for vocabulary control in reading instruction must never have worked with children who are average and slow learners. Also they must never have studied a foreign language, for they would find how quickly one becomes swamped if he cannot keep up with the new vocabulary load.
2. In the few minutes per week that one has to work with each individual pupil, it is practically impossible to provide a really systematic and complete program of skills. When one looks at the lists of skills that are taught in some individualized programs, one is shocked by how limited and inadequate they are. In many cases an individual teacher seems to emphasize word analysis skills to the near exclusion of comprehension and work study skills (5, 6).
3. It is exceedingly difficult to identify the individual difficulties that children have during the infrequent short conferences.
4. There is some doubt about the permanence of skills that are taught so briefly and are not systematically reviewed.
5. There is less opportunity for group interaction to develop critical thinking and literary appreciation than there is when instruction is provided in groups.
6. The slow learning pupils and others who do not work well independently become restless and waste a great deal of time. It seems that those youngsters who especially need a great deal of instruction suffer from lack of the teacher's frequent attention.
7. The method is inefficient because of the time required to teach skills to individuals instead of teaching several groups of children who are progressing at similar rates. It is the same as having thirty reading groups, when it might be possible to provide basic instruction in four to six groups with additional corrective teaching in flexible groups on various days.
8. The conscientious teacher becomes very frustrated in attempting to provide individual conferences for all of the pupils who need them each day, while the careless teacher is left without adequate direction (7).

Research Findings

More than three-fourths of the experimentation and research done with individualized reading is so poorly designed that it is of no help in making decisions about values and weaknesses of individualized programs (8). Some of the common errors in these studies are the following:

1. *Providing no comparison group as a control.* The fact that a person achieves some degree of success with one method does not prove that he would *not* do equally well with another method if he used the same materials, the same group of children, and the same amount of teaching effort.

2. *Failure to make the control situation exactly equivalent to the experimental situation when controls are used.* If the children in the control group do not have ready access to the same number of books, for example, as the children in the experimental group, it is not going to be possible for them to read as extensively or progress as rapidly. Other discrepancies are such things as providing more time for instruction with the individualized program than with the control program or providing additional assistance from student teachers with one program and not the other.

3. *The use of interested volunteers to teach one program while run-of-the-faculty-lounge teachers work with the other program.* All studies in education show that some teachers get better results than others. In a study where half-interested, average teachers employ one method and the other method is demonstrated by eager, enthusiastic teachers who are interested in individual children, there will be no doubt about the outcomes. The fact that one group demonstrates superior performance will be due largely to differences in teacher capability and performance rather than to differences in method.

4. *Comparing the experimental program with the weakest variety of standard practice rather than with the best model in standard use.* An example is the failure to provide any differentiation in the instruction of the control group. This is a way of stacking the deck in experimentation. When every child in the control group is given the same book, the experimenter can be certain in advance that the group will perform more poorly than a group where children are given books at their own differing levels of reading ability. When the experimenter claims that he compared an individualized approach with the "traditional" approach, the reader assumes that the traditional approach included both the use of basic materials and some effort to differentiate instruction through grouping within the classroom as competent teachers do. The results, when there is no attempt to differentiate teaching through grouping in the classroom, merely show a difference between differentiation and lack of differentiation in instruction, rather than between individualized reading and a correct use of a basal program. (As an example see Reference 9.) When we claim that we are comparing basal instruction with

individualized instruction it is professionally dishonest to provide an extremely poor-quality program for the control group instead of providing the quality of basal instruction that is recommended by the people who prepare the basal materials.

Objective Research Findings

A couple of years ago the more objective experiments with individualized reading were analyzed for their implications (10). Reports of studies since have not changed the conclusions that were offered then. In evaluating individualized reading one can be reasonably sure that the following statements are true:

1. The individualized reading approach can be somewhat successful under certain conditions.
2. The successful teaching of individualized reading requires especially competent teachers.
3. The less capable pupils are likely to be less successful in individualized reading programs than in programs that are more directed. (Of course, this will not be true if the comparison program makes no provision whatever for mental differences and attempts to require the same work of the slow child as the average.
4. Children read more books under the plan of self-selection with individualized instruction than they do in basal programs.
5. The personal conference between the pupil and the teacher is of special value.
6. Individualized reading does not allow adequate time for the setting of thought-provoking purposes for reading and for the introduction of new vocabulary.
7. The lack of a planned sequential skills program makes teachers uneasy about a wholly individualized organization.
8. Teachers using the wholly individualized approach are constantly pressed for time to provide conferences that pupils need.

In view of these findings, it seems wise to hesitate before we jettison every worthwhile feature of basic reading (11). At the same time, we need to recognize that basal reading programs are going to be entirely inadequate to meet the needs of individual pupils in our classes unless many adaptations are made.

A sensible approach is to combine strengths of excellent basic programs with strengths of individualized reading (12). This means that in our classrooms we should have many, many books at many, many levels in addition to the basic readers. Our children should be grouped for some standard basic instruction, but they should be stimulated to read innumerable other books independently in every spare moment. They should share their independent reading experiences individually with the teacher and with other children in personal conferences. Although the basal reading grouping might remain fairly constant during the year, there should be times every week when the children who have special interests or difficulties are brought together in temporary groups to receive the attention necessary for their continued stimulation. In this way the teacher will provide for the divergent needs of individual children without having to face the impossible task of tutoring each child separately.

References

1. Balow, Irving H., "Does Homogeneous Grouping Give Homogeneous Groups?" *Elementary School Journal,* Vol. 63 (1962) pp. 28–32.
2. Jones, Daisy M., "An Experiment in Adaptation to Individual Differences," *Journal of Educational Psychology,* Vol. 39 (1948) pp. 257–272.
3. Sartain, Harry W., "The Place of Individualized Reading in a Well-Planned Program," Ginn and Company Contributions in Reading No. 28.
4. Sartain, Harry W., "The Roseville Experiment with Individualized Reading," *Reading Teacher,* Vol. 13 (1960) pp. 277–281.
5. Hunt, Lyman C., Jr., "Individualized Reading: Teaching Skills," *Education,* Vol. 81 (1961) pp. 541–546.
6. Miel, Alice (Editor), *Individualizing Reading Practices,* (N.Y.: Bureau of Publication, Teachers College, Columbia University, 1958), Chapters 2, 3, and 4.
7. Sartain, Harry W. *op. cit.*
8. Sartain, Harry W., "Research on Individualized Reading," *Education,* Vol. 81 (1961) pp. 512–520.
9. Walker, Frederic R., "Evaluation of Three Methods of Teaching Reading," *Journal of Educational Research,* Vol. 54 (1961) pp. 356–358.
10. Sartain, Harry W. *op. cit.*
11. Lofthouse, Yvonne M., "Individualized Reading," *Reading Teacher,* Vol. 16 (1962) pp. 35–37.
12. Sartain, Harry W. *op. cit.*
13. Aronow, Miriam S., "A Study to the Effect of Individualized Reading on Children's Reading Test Scores," *Reading Teacher,* Vol. 15 (1961) pp. 86–91.
14. Groff, Patrick, "Comparison of Individualized and Ability-Grouping Approaches to Reading Achievement," *Elementary English,* Vol. 40 (1963) pp. 258–276.

77. Linguistics and the Teaching of Reading

RUTH G. STRICKLAND (1964)

A number of linguists have become interested in the teaching of reading. They are convinced that their knowledge of language in general, and the sound system of English in particular, can be put to use in the schools to help children learn to "crack the code" of English and to do it more rapidly.

The linguist's concept of reading is not the concept commonly held by the classroom teacher and the reading specialist—that reading is getting meaning from the print on a page. The linguist conceives the reading act as that of turning the stimulus of the graphic shapes on a surface back into speech. The shapes represent speech; meaning is not found in the marks but in the speech which the marks represent. In the linguist's concept a child can read when he can recognize symbol-sound correspondence to the point that he can respond to the marks with appropriate speech.

The linguist recognizes that the school cannot stop here. The rest of what the school calls teaching reading is actually teaching *thinking,* with and in response to what is found on the page.

An alphabet is a set of graphic shapes that represent speech sounds in a nearly one-to-one relationship. The sounds of English are represented in writing by the 26 letters of the Roman alphabet, though the language utilizes more than 26 sounds. A *grapheme* is a significant unit of graphic shape and *phoneme* is a significant unit of speech sound. Mastery of the correspondence between the phonemes (sound symbols) of the language and the graphemes (graphic symbols) used to represent them is essential to carrying on the reading process.

The task of learning to read, therefore, is the task of developing recognition responses to sets of patterns of graphic shapes.

SOURCE: *The Education Digest,* XXIX (April 1964), 47–50. This article appeared originally in the *Bulletin of the School of Education,* XL (January, 1964), 9–14, published by Indiana University. Reprinted by permission of *The Education Digest* and Indiana University.

Large numbers of English words are spelled in a regular manner, that is, the grapheme-phoneme correspondence is reliable. Some English words have changed in pronunciation so that the spelling is no longer a one-to-one symbol-sound correspondence. The word "knight" is an example, with many other examples in words borrowed from other languages.

If children are to learn symbol-sound or grapheme-phoneme correspondences efficiently, their first experiences with written words should be with words which are regular in spelling. There should be one sound for one letter until that is learned. Irregularly spelled words should be added later, and those in which correspondence is completely unpredictable and irregular should be encountered last.

Such a logical system is not presently utilized in the preprimers of reading textbook series now in popular use. A check will show preprimers including words in which "a" has three different forms.

Linguists hold that learning correspondences is made unnecessarily difficult by introducing confusion rather than systematic progression. There is logic in this contention. To the linguist, the eclectic method of the basal readers fails to take account of stages in the process of learning to read, and this makes little sense to him.

Three Proposals

Two recent books on the teaching of reading present schemes based on this hypothesis. The first to appear was *Let's Read,* in which Clarence L. Barnhart presents the plan of the late Leonard Bloomfield. The other is Charles Fries' *Linguistics and Reading.* Both books are based on the concepts just delineated, though there are differences in approach, organization, and methodology. A third linguist, Henry Lee Smith, Jr., is working on materials built on a linguistic plan. His point of view is set forth in a series of films entitled *Language and Linguistics,* which should be helpful to the teacher of reading.

These three linguists who have entered the field, and some critics who have not, appear in agreement that in present basal reader plans, grapheme-phoneme correspondences are treated as only one of a number of seemingly equally important clues for unlocking the identity of words. To them, this ignores the importance of the basic concept that needs to be taught, namely, that the writing is alphabetic and that the sets of graphic shapes represent speech sounds and patterns.

Barnhart, in *Let's Read,* presents in 245 lessons a program of reading that begins with mastery of the alphabet, so that the child can name both capital and lower-case letters accurately and confidently before beginning work with words. The first 36 lessons present the five vowels in two-letter and three-letter words, using only the "short" sound of each vowel. Consonant blends, pairs of vowels, and common irregular spellings are fed into the scheme after children have mastered the earlier lessons. It is a systematic scheme of teaching symbol-sound correspondences with constant use of oral reading. There is no emphasis on reading for meaning and little or no story content until the child has had many lessons on correspondences. The process is solely that of turning the stimulus of the graphic shapes into speech. When the child can do this, he can read.

Fries' Method

Both Fries' book and Smith's series of films offer differences in approach, organization, and methodology, though all are based on early learning of symbol-sound correspondences. Fries has tried to exclude everything not essential to the task so that full attention can be concentrated on learning symbol-sound correspondences. Concurrent learning of new words, grammatical structures, or meanings is ruled out, as is any attention to writing. The goal is high-speed recognition with complete accuracy, using only capital letters written as simply as possible, and moving from single letters to groups of two or three, which calls attention to contrasting shapes with no attention to words or meanings.

A second set of responses, which must be made automatic, are responses to the major spelling patterns of English. The spelling patterns begin with the simple vowel-consonant, consonant-vowel-consonant patterns. Attention is called through grouping and contrasts to the consonant sounds in words in which the sound for a letter is always the same sound. This is the stage of learning to respond to "bundles" of graphic shapes with practice until response is automatic. Certainly this involves the skill of "look-say," but with attention centered on grapheme-phoneme correspondences.

The last stage of developing ability to read comes, Fries says, when the reading process has become so automatic that it can be put to use for vicarious experience, the assimilation of ideas, appreciation, and all other purposes usually stated for the teaching of reading.

Harry Lee Smith, Jr., in contrast to Fries, would start children with sight words learned in meaningful contexts, then turn to reading material which is planned to teach recognition of correspondences and spelling patterns through simple stories of animals and the type of repetition found in the usual preprimer. The major difference lies in the fact that, with Smith's material, a letter has only one sound until the child has learned to recognize it in a variety of words of similar spellings. A few irregularly spelled words are added as needed for story action.

These three proposals for a linguistically based method of teaching reading are a start in what might prove a highly significant direction. At present, teachers recoil against the dullness and meaninglessness of it in spite of its logic. They want children to love reading and to approach each step of it with eager interest. The suggestions now available from the linguists scarcely fit this psychological need.

But others are turning their attention to the beginner. There is a spate of new books designed to interest him in reading. While the author of the Dr. Seuss *Beginner Books* is a better authority on child humor and fantasy than on linguistics, he has so far caught the idea behind the program of the linguists that his collaboration with them might conceivably produce scientifically sound material which also meets the psychological needs of the beginner in reading.

Linguists other than Bloomfield, Fries, and Smith have given little attention in their writing to the problem of teaching children to read. Several others are now beginning to give thought and time to it, as a result of present concern for teaching reading more rapidly and effectively. Those who have done so recognize their own need to know more about how reading is taught and the kinds of problems teachers encounter. It is difficult for anyone not familiar with the work of the first grade to recognize the differences that lie within six-year-old children—differences in mental maturity, background, sensory powers, neurological structure, and all the manifestations. The closer any scholar comes to the teaching arena, the less dogmatic he tends to become with regard to how to teach reading.

The Present Need

This does not stand in the way of educators who are willing to draw on the linguists' knowledge of languages for what to teach and the sequence in which it might be taught. Here is where the scholar who knows the structure of the language and how it operates can be most helpful. The need at the present time is for the linguists to provide clear statements of the sound and spelling patterns to be taught and the sequence for teaching based on regularity of pattern, frequency of occurrence, and general utility in reading.

All of the preceding is pointed toward the beginning stages of learning to read. To comprehend what he reads, the reader turns the visual stimulus of written language back into speech—overtly if he is inexperienced and immature, subliminally if he is a rapid, experienced reader. Because this is true, the more clearly the reader understands the patterning of his language the better will be his oral reading interpretation and his silent reading comprehension.

Understanding the function and operation of pitch, stress, and juncture helps children to turn what they read into the flowing, meaningful patterns of normal speech and, through the process, to gain the full component of meaning. Understanding subject and predicate patterns and patterns of elaboration and subordination is also necessary to recognize and respond to the signals on the page. Help with reading by patterns, and quantities of reading for practice, should help many children with comprehension in their silent reading and with interpretation in oral reading.

78. Speed Reading

EVELYN N. WOOD (1963)

Human tendency is to reject as impossible advanced ideas which do not fit common concepts and accepted standards. Pioneers, regardless of their fields, have usually been greeted by skepticism, doubt, and ridicule. Arthur Compton, atomic physicist and Nobel Prize winner, commented: "New discovery nearly always disturbs man's way of life. Its first products are often fear, suspicion, and malice. Unfortunately change does not come easily. I wish man could accept with eagerness the conditions of change."

The pioneering efforts represented by Reading Dynamics have met their share of skepticism and doubt. Some of you have accumulated bits of information about this new approach to reading from newspapers, magazines, a television show, a demonstration, or just hearsay. I want to tell you briefly what it is, what claims we make for it, how we teach it, and what test results show.

The Reading Dynamics method is a process of reading down the page rather than across each line, using the hand as a pacer. The aim is "visual reading" with virtual elimination of subvocal speech. Readers who have to "hear" as well as to see words never read very fast because they slow down to listen.

SOURCE: *NEA Journal*, April, 1963, pp. 44–46. Reprinted by permission of the author and publisher.

observed was no more than a hurry-up version of what we all do in reading. There was no mystic pattern of looking only at one spot on a page for a few moments before moving on, or moving the eyes straight down a page without regard for lines of print. Furthermore, test results showed that the subjects averaged only 50 percent in comprehension when they attempted high-speed coverage.

Is there nothing then to speed reading? Is it a complete hoax? By no means.

Practically every student I have met in my classes has been able to speed his reading without sacrificing comprehension. What is involved?

Most of us ordinarily read at speeds we find comfortable, and those speeds are below what we can do when we are pressed for time. If students practice reading faster than is comfortable, in a few weeks they can become habituated to higher speeds.

Most slow readers spend too much time going back over what they are reading. Students who practice reading without regressing eliminate much of this kind of wasteful activity in a few weeks and can read faster with good comprehension.

Practically every reader benefits from reading-comprehension exercises. As comprehension increases, speed generally increases along with it.

Improvement in reading vocabulary contributes to increased reading speed.

Learning the patterns in writing contributes to greater reading speed.

Using the aids a book provides, such as table of contents and preface, saves reading time.

Correction of any visual difficulties makes reading faster and more comfortable.

No tricks, no secret formulas, no magic, no need for fantastic claims. Next time you hear tales of the great reading speed achieved by graduates of this special course or that, ask what material was read and what was learned and what was remembered.

The important thing about reading is how much you get from it, not how fast you do it.

The first problem, then, is learning how to let words and ideas come into the mind faster, and the second is learning how to get meaning from words and ideas without relying on "inner speech."

The single word is no more important to the total understanding of what is read than the single film frame passing through the projector is to the understanding of the motion picture. As hundreds of single frames pass through a projector much faster than each single frame could be individually projected, they give the viewer the feeling, atmosphere, and detail of an entire film. Similarly, dynamic reading enables the reader to see a story much as the author thought it through.

Before judging the dynamic reading process, a person should try to determine directly from those in charge exactly what claims they make for it. I am not responsible for the gross distortions of figures on reading rates quoted by people who have not checked with me to determine the accuracy of the figures they quote. Our Reading Dynamics brochures state only that students who are willing to practice an hour a day, following the directions we give, can learn to read at three to ten times their beginning speed with no loss in comprehension.

Reading rates vary, depending on the material to be read. Simple reading requires one rate; study reading, another; and material calling for critical evaluation, still another. No one needs to read everything at the slow pace of oral reading.

A specially trained teacher is required to teach the Reading Dynamics method. Those who enroll in the course should be reasonably able readers who are willing to follow instructions. Students begin by reading very simple material, moving the eyes down the page in a zigzag fashion, catching as much of the content as possible. This is not reading, but practicing. As the student practices, he experiments by having his eyes follow his hand down the page at varying rates of speed until he discovers the rate of speed and the downward motion of hand and eyes that suits him best and that maintains adequate comprehension. Much practice and repetition and experience with many kinds of reading materials help him make this determination.

Students are amazed to find how much they can comprehend as their eyes sweep down the page. Comprehension is difficult to measure, however, because the degree of comprehension is affected by many things including motivation, the length of the material that is read, and familiarity with the subject.

If subjective evidence is any criterion, doctors, lawyers, students, clergymen, and United States Senators are among those who have expressed satisfaction with the results obtained from taking the course.

Checking the recall of what the students have read is an objective way to measure comprehension. Such checks have been made informally after demonstrations of the dynamic reading technique at meetings sponsored by the Association for Higher Education, an NEA department. Members of the Association selected the books to be used for the demonstration, timed the reading, asked questions on the material read, and the audience expressed general satisfaction with the performances of the selected students. Several members have expressed the hope that extensive research might be conducted.

At the University of Delaware, a careful study of the Evelyn Wood Dynamic Reading technique was made by William Liddle, a Ph.D. candidate, using a control and an experimental group. In reading nonfiction, he found no significant differences in comprehension between the two groups, despite the fact that the experimental group read at 1300 wpm—better than three times the speed of the control group.

I did not invent rapid reading, but I have found methods of teaching rapid reading more effectively to more people. There is no trickery or chicanery involved. We have been able to show that many people can read with satisfactory comprehension at faster speeds than they had thought possible. I am convinced that this is just the beginning of exciting new possibilities.

79. Speed Reading

EUGENE EHRLICH (1963)

The ease with which so many unqualified persons assume the title of "reading expert" was dramatized for me twice in the past few months. First, *The New York Times* carried an advertisement on October 14, 1962, offering a position as reading teacher. Pay—$80 to $100 a week. Travel—seven weeks in a city and then move on. Qualifications? *College graduate preferred.* Second, a twenty-two year old, who came to me for help in reading, turned out to read at no better than fourth-grade level. His occupation? Clerk in a well-known New York City speed reading school. As part of his duties he administers and scores reading tests.

SOURCE: *NEA Journal*, April, 1963, pp. 44–46. Reprinted by permission of the author and publisher.

Surely it is time to look critically at one of America's fastest growing industries, speed reading. How big this business is nobody knows for certain, but I can say without hesitation that it has reached the multimillion dollar class.

We hear a great deal about various new ways of reading. Advertising appears in our daily newspapers promising that we can learn to read "four to ten times faster" than we now do. The undergraduate newspaper published at Columbia University has carried advertisements this semester for two different reading institutes with quarters off campus. They tell students that they can learn to read 150 to 200 pages an hour in their textbooks, that they can learn to study at speeds of up to 20,000 and 30,000 words a minute.

At the very least, the claims of the speed reading merchants are just not consistent with what our best reading research tells us. The fastest adult readers I know of approach speeds of 700 to 800 words a minute. The exceptions to this upper limit I have encountered can be counted on the index finger of my left hand.

Some years ago, one of my students reached the phenomenal speed of approximately 1,000 words a minute in a magazine comparable in difficulty to *Harper's* or *Atlantic Monthly*. He had taught himself to read at high speeds through consistent practice over a period of decades. In my testing of thousands of adults and university students, I have found no others who can do as well as this.

Of course, many skillful readers can go through a novel at speeds greater than 1,000 words a minute, but such speeds are achieved by skipping more words than are actually read, by sacrificing the most important values of a novel to pursuit of plot alone. This can scarcely be called reading in the ordinary sense.

I tested a few graduates of the Reading Dynamics Institute in New York City on a page of typewritten material and found that they "read" at speeds close to 6,000 words a minute. Mighty impressive! Then to make certain they understood it, they all reread the page twice. This brought their average effective speed down to something over 1,70(words a minute. Still impressive—except for one thing. What they ha read had no meaning at all! It was a garbled amalgam I had put togeth from two different magazine articles. I had taken two lines from o article and two lines from the other alternately until the page was f A mean trick, but I heard no more from these men about how fast t read.

An analysis of eye-movement photographs made by Stanford E. lor, Educational Developmental Laboratories, of the "reading" of graduates of this same course appeared in the *Eleventh Yearbook* *National Reading Conference*. The photographs show that the r

80. Vision and Rapid Reading

HOWARD N. WALTON (1957)

Introduction

Within the past few years numerous reports have appeared describing the phenomenally high speeds achieved by students of speed reading training programs. Reading rates ranging from 2,000 to 8,000 words per minute are often reported. One newspaper article told of an individual reading at 30,000 words per minute. Information of this nature is being disseminated by various journals, magazines, brochures and circulars, with radio and television joining the chorus.

We often hear people speak of other reading feats, these being performed by mental giants, who are capable of reading a page at a glance and those, with a more "limited span," grasp complete paragraphs with a single fixation.

Since these reports are being circulated, it would seem desirable to conduct scientific inquiry concerning their validity.

Historical

In 1878, Javal (1), made a most significant discovery by simply watching the eye of a school child who was reading. His very eminent predecessors had assumed the truth of the common belief of "sweeping the eyes along a line of print." He found, not a steady sweep, but a series of little jumps (saccadic movements) with intervening fixation pauses.

It then became important to know whether we see during saccadic eye movements. Subsequent investigation revealed that only blurs and streaks are observed during version movements. Under various environmental seeing conditions and in reading these blurs and streaks are extremely brief due to the speed of the saccadic movement (from 1/25 to 1/50 of a second in reading) and very faint due to minimal brightness contrasts which normally prevail. Consequently, being of no practical value or interest, they are habitually disregarded and ignored (2).

SOURCE: *American Journal of Optometry*, February, 1957, pp. 73–82. Reprinted by permission of the author and publisher.

Peripheral Visual Acuity and Masking

In a study of peripheral visual acuity, Feinberg (3) [Table I] found the following values:

TABLE I. Peripheral Visual Acuity

Distance from Fovea	*Visual Acuity*
1°	20/30
2°	20/35
3°	20/50
4°	20/60
5°	20/70

In an earlier experiment Wertheim (4) determined a peripheral visual acuity curve which closely corresponds to the above figures. Acuity measurements made by Weymouth (5) and co-workers from 1.5 degrees to fixation also approximates the data obtained by Feinberg.

The letters in most printed material subtend an angle equivalent to a 20/60 letter (1.76 mm. at 16 inches). Thus on the basis of the above peripheral acuity figures, an individual would be able to identify two 20/60 letters separated by 2.2 inches with a single fixation provided he was fixating midway between standard block letters as follows:

E • H

2.2 inches

Peripheral visual acuity provides adequate vision 1.1 inch on either side of the fixation point, located 16 inches from the eyes.

Ruediger (6) presented tachistoscopically to his observers a white card on which was printed an "N" or a "U" at varying distances from a central fixation point. The card was 30 centimeters from the reader's eye. It was found that indirect vision was still satisfactory for perception of 11-point type when the letter was 2½ centimeters on either side of the central point.

Theoretically it would seem possible to span an entire line of 2.2 inches of standard block letters with a single fixation if fixating centrally. Yet, an eye movement is necessary before grasping the span. This is due to mutual interference or masking of the letters in indirect vision, as explained below.

Korte (7) [Graph 1] studied letters, words and nonsense syllables in indirect vision, recording the eccentricity measured as a tangent. The words, composed of German lower-case letters, ranged from 2 to 8 letters and were read at a distance of 30 cm. He found that a group of letters, in comparison with a single letter, must be brought closer to the fixation point in order to be read. As would be anticipated on the basis of peripheral visual acuity, he found that capitals were read further out than the lower case letters. Korte also determined that isolated letters were read further out than words, and the longer a word, the closer it must be brought to the fixation point.

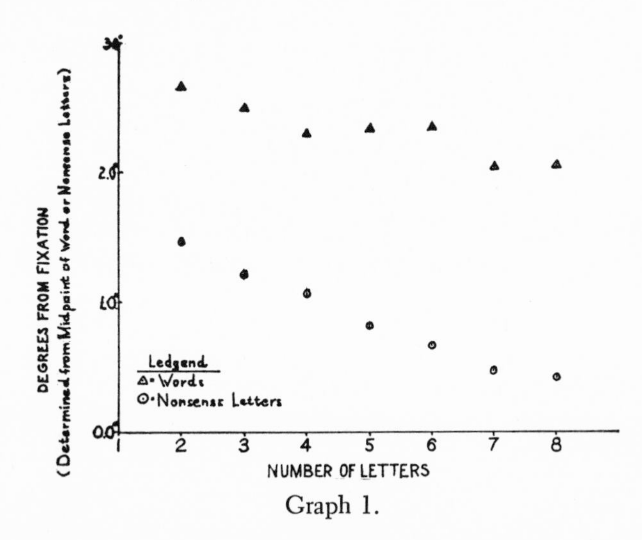

Graph 1.

The anatomical arrangement of the retina provides the basis for the explanation. The fovea centralis, according to Polyak (8), subtends an angle 1°40′ at the nodal point of the eye. At the fovea each cone is thinner and connected to only one ganglion cell. Its impulse is therefore much purer, and the image received by the brain much sharper than elsewhere in the retina, being as it were insulated from the impulses of neighboring cells. In the retina generally each visual cell is in relation with many, up to 100, ganglion cells (9).

Printers rarely use standard block form but usually some modification such as condensed, extra condensed, etc. Thus a 20/60 letter, 1.76 mm. vertically is usually 20/40, 1.17 mm., horizontally. This reduces the visual angle subtended to 2½° on each side of the fixation point or a total span of 1.4 inch. This span is further reduced by masking.

Hamilton (10) by use of the tachistoscope exposed a line of print at a speed allowing a single fixation with instructions for the observer to read from the left as far as possible. Typically, the observer read the first word or two correctly and beyond that made a guess which had some resemblance to the next word. The observer using such cues as general word shape, context and easily recognized prefixes and suffixes was able to supply an additional word. However, since the first word of the line was fixated, only half of the peripheral retina was utilized.

By extensive use of the tachistoscope in visual and reading improvement programs and by teaching students to fixate so as to take full advantage of the retinal cone mosaic nasally and temporally, Walton (11) has found that with a 1/100 of a second exposure, approximately 29 letter spaces, or 5 words or 5 letters each, may be read. About 17 letter spaces, or 3 words of five letters, are seen relatively clearly and by utilizing general word shape, context, and familar letter groups a word at either end of the central fixation point may be deduced. These observable results correspond closely to those that may be calculated on the basis of peripheral visual acuity, evaluating the vertical and horizontal components of the letters and the effects produced by masking of the letters in indirect vision.

Saccadic Eye Movements and Reaction Time

The function of the saccadic eye movement in a reading situation is to carry the eyes from fixation to fixation with the extent of the movement being determined by the number of words perceived at each fixation. A movement over a space of five letters of ordinary print, at a reading distance of a foot, takes 15 to 20 ms., or about 1/60 of a second. Table II from Dodge & Cline (12) gives the duration of longer movements, their extent being measured by the angle through which the eye swings. The table gives the averages derived from 3 subjects.

Although it might be assumed that the reaction time of the saccadic movement is very short, it is actually about the same as that of a hand response to a visual stimulus. The saccadic response to a stimulus ap-

TABLE II. Duration of Saccadic Eye Movement

Extent of Movement	*Duration of Movement*
5°	29 ms.
10°	39 ms.
15°	48 ms.
20°	55 ms.
30°	80 ms.
40°	100 ms.

For movements of twenty degrees or less, along a page held a foot from the eyes, each degree means approximately 1/5 of an inch, so that 5° = 1 inch, 10° = 2 inches, 15° = 3 inches, and 20° = 4 inches (more precisely, 4.23 inches).

pearing in indirect vision was found to be on the average 195 ms. with a range of individual averages from 125 to 235 milliseconds (13). More recently Westheimer (14), by use of two neon bulbs which could be moved to any position on a horizontal arc of 150 cm. radius, determined a reaction time which varied between 120 and 180 ms.

In a reading situation, at each fixation a period of time, the reaction time, elapses before the next saccadic movement is initiated. Obviously, the duration of the saccadic movements and the reaction time are limiting factors that must be considered in determining the ultimate speed that may be achieved in reading.

Apparatus

The apparatus in Figure 1, the ophthalmograph produced by the American Optical Company (15), consists of three main parts—the stand, headrest, and camera.

The headrest provides sufficient pressure to help the subject hold his head steady.

Light from a direct source (E) is reflected from the two corneas and focused on the film (L) by means of lenses mounted in telescoping tubes (D). These tubes may be moved in any direction to locate the beams of light from the corneas and thus make allowance for different pupillary distances.

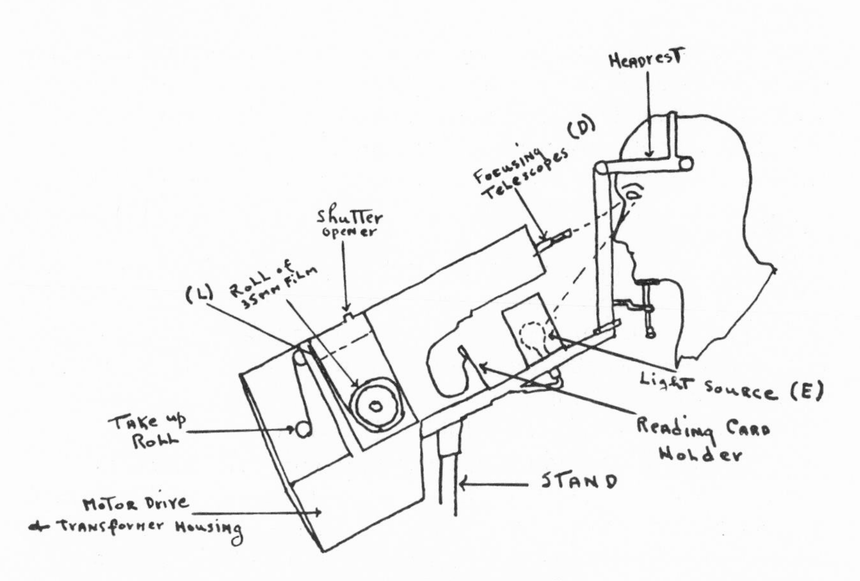

Figure 1. Ophthalmograph.

The film in the camera is traveling upward at a constant speed of ½ in. per second with the emulsion side toward the subject.

Subjects

Ten subjects were used in conducting this investigation. Of this number, one was an assistant professor at the Los Angeles College of Optometry and the remainder students of the senior class. Thus the participants were trained observers. All subjects were males ranging in age from 24 to 35 years.

Procedure

The procedure was designed to duplicate eye movements and fixations as utilized in a reading task while eliminating the factor of comprehension, thus providing a means of determining the reaction time per fixation. To gain this information the following card (Figure 2) was designed for use in the reading card holder of the ophthalmograph.

hat	map	may	key	mac
mad	hat	sad	sat	let
mal	tee	man	tan	fee
can	top	lap	cop	set
rot	tik	see	mop	hot

Figure 2. Arrangement of card used in determining reaction time.

Prior to being tested, each subject was thoroughly familiarized with the methodology, being given a duplicate of the card used in the experimental procedure. Five minutes of practice in quickly fixating each word was required, with instructions that during the test maximum effort should be utilized so as to achieve the greatest speed in performance.

Results

The reaction time was determined by projecting the ophthalmographic film strip upon a screen and measuring the length of each fixation. These calculations were converted to a time factor (milliseconds) based upon the fact that the film strip moves through the ophthalmograph at a speed of 0.5 inch per second.

The results are tabulated in Tables III and IV.

Buswell (16) has found that the average duration per fixation in silent reading for college students is 252 ms., which is only 33 ms. longer than determined in this study, where comprehension was not a factor.

In 70% of the cases regressions occurred at the beginning of four of the five lines. While the longest reaction time was determined on the

TABLE III. Reaction Time (Milliseconds)

Identification	*Mean Reaction Time*	*Shortest Reaction Time*	*Longest Reaction Time*	*Difference Longest—Shortest Reaction Time*
S.S.	292	170	450	280
R.M.	183	120	300	180
T.B.	172	125	260	135
E.H.	248	165	400	235
J.H.	170	115	275	160
O.K.	169	125	300	175
R.V.	194	120	350	230
C.S.	309	200	400	200
J.S.	254	150	315	165
B.L.	200	115	250	135

basis of a single fixation, the time required to consummate fixation of the first word would also include the duration of the regression. The greatest lapse of time in 80% of the cases occurred at the beginning of the line due to the appearance of the longest fixation or the combination of the first fixation and regression.

Woodworth (17) reports that the greatest amount of time is spent fixating the first quarter of a line of print, explaining that what lies further to the right is receiving some preliminary examination during this period of time. In view of peripheral visual acuity and masking, this explanation seems unlikely. However, the present investigation clearly indicates that the greater amount of time required at the beginning of a line is due to visual factors.

It is interesting to note the rather large range existing between the shortest and longest reaction time, indicating that factors other than comprehension enter into the determination of the duration of fixation.

Discussion

Ophthalmographic studies of adults who have not had the advantage of reading training indicate that they generally read by fixating each word. Buswell (18) has reported approximately ¼ sec. as the average

TABLE IV. Analysis of Reaction Time (Milliseconds)

Number of Subjects	*Mean Reaction Time*	*S.D.*	*SE Mean*
10	219	49.8	15.7

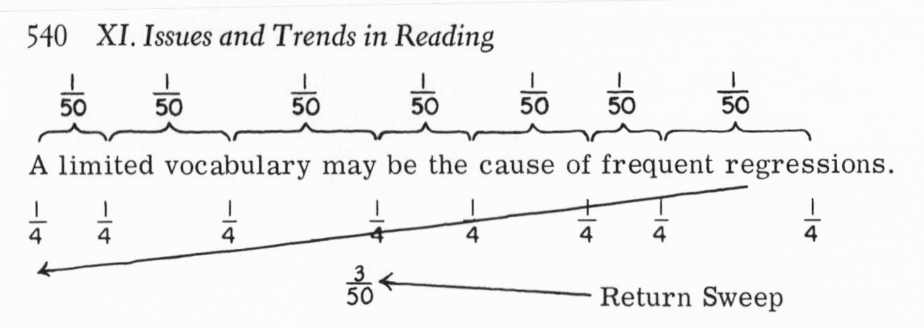

Figure 3. Typical adult reading pattern. Reading rate of 220 words per minute. $\frac{1}{50}$ and $\frac{3}{50}$ second, saccadic movements. $\frac{1}{4}$ second being the duration of fixation.

duration of fixation. Considering the time intervals for interfixations as shown in Table II, average reading rates may be calculated. This is shown diagrammatically in Figure 3.

The above reading speed falls within the range given by Harris (19) of rates for various college and educated adult groups, the variation being from 207 to 290 words per minute. Harris says that 250 W.P.M. may be taken as a rough estimate of the normal reading rate for high school and college students, and adults.

Ophthalmographic investigations of college students reading non-technical material shows that the average span of recognition is 1.25 words per fixation (20). Using the same values as in the previous example with the exception of 8 fixations per line, the reading rate is 272 W.P.M. as shown in Figure 4. Again this is within the range as shown above.

It is important to know the potential reading speeds that may be achieved when completely reading the printed page. Considering the anatomical and physiological limiting factors of peripheral visual acuity, masking, saccadic eye movements, and reaction time, calculations may be made that will approximate this potential. Various relationships among these factors are shown in Table V.

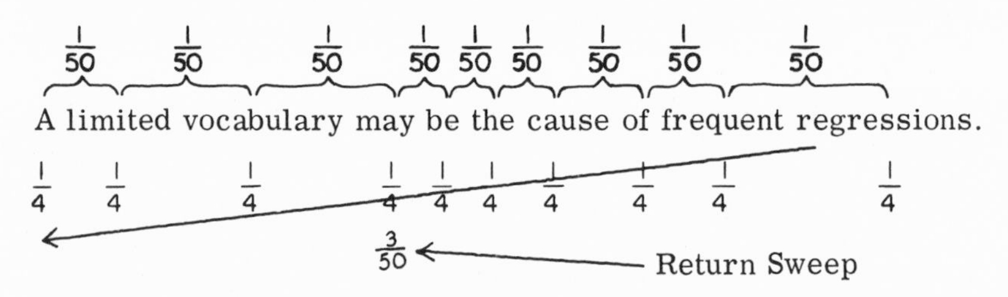

Figure 4. Typical college student reading pattern. Reading rate of 272 words per minute. $\frac{1}{50}$ and $\frac{3}{50}$ second, saccadic movements. $\frac{1}{4}$ second being the duration of fixation.

TABLE V. Reading Rates (Calculated on basis of 10 word line)

Reaction Time	*Number of Fixations*	*Interfixations* No.	*Interfixations* Time (Sec.)	*Return Sweep* No.	*Return Sweep* Time (Sec.)	*Reading Rate* W.P.M.
1/5	3	2	1/33	1	1/20	853
1/5	2	1	1/25	1	1/25	1250
1/6	3	2	1/33	1	1/20	982
1/6	2	1	1/25	1	1/25	1451

The average reaction time as determined by this study was 219 ms., slightly slower than 1/5 sec. Deducting one standard deviation (49.8 ms.), thereby including approximately 80% of the population, gives a reaction time of 169.2 ms., which is about 1/6 sec. Therefore the calculations in Table V were made on the basis of 1/5 and 1/6 of a second.

In view of the peripheral visual acuity curve and the effects of masking in indirect vision, three words may be seen relatively clearly, and by utilizing general word shape, context, and familiar letter groups, a word at either end of the central fixation point may be deduced. Thus calculations were made on the basis of 3 and 2 fixations per line.

How close an individual may come to reaching the limiting anatomical and physiological factors will depend upon such other considerations as educational background, experience, I.Q., and vocabulary.

The data indicate that if an individual is reading faster than 1,451 W.P.M., he is skimming; this reading skill is primarily concerned with locating and grasping main ideas. The data further indicate that it is not possible to grasp a page or a paragraph with a single fixation.

Summary and Conclusions

Within the past few years numerous reports have appeared in various periodicals describing phenomenally high speeds achieved by students of rapid reading training programs.

These reports must be considered in relation to present knowledge regarding vision and evaluated in view of Javal's significant discovery that the eyes move along a line of print by saccadic movements with intervening fixation pauses.

On the basis of peripheral visual acuity and masking, three words of 5 letters each may be seen relatively clearly, and by utilizing general word shape, context and familiar letter groups, a word at either end of the central fixation point may be deduced.

The ophthalmograph was used to determine the reaction time of ten subjects in a reading situation in which comprehension was completely ignored.

The results showed the following:

1. The mean reaction time was 219 ms., which is only 33 ms. shorter than the average duration per fixation for college students in silent reading.
2. The greatest lapse of time occurred at the beginning of the line due to the appearance of the longest fixation or the combination of the first fixation and a regression.
3. The investigation indicates that the greater amount of time required at the beginning of a line is due to visual factors.
4. The large range existing between the shortest and longest reaction time indicates that factors other than comprehension enter into the determination of the duration of fixation.

Considering the limiting anatomical and physiological factors of peripheral visual acuity, masking, saccadic eye movements, and reaction time, potential reading speeds may be calculated.

Reading rates of over 1,451 W.P.M. indicate that the individual is skimming.

The data indicate that it is not possible to grasp a page or paragraph with a single fixation.

References

1. Woodworth, Robert S., Experimental Psychology, p. 557, Henry Holt & Co., New York, 1950.
2. Ibid., pp. 591–4.
3. Feinberg, Richard, "A Study of Some Aspects of Peripheral Visual Acuity," Amer. J. Optom. & Arch. Amer. Acad. Optom., Feb. and March, 1949, Vol. 26, Nos. 2 and 3.
4. Duke-Elder, Stewart Sir, Text-Book of Ophthalmology, p. 936, C. V. Mosby Co., St. Louis, Mo., 1942.
5. Adler, Francis H., Physiology of the Eye, pp. 634–5, C. V. Mosby Co., St. Louis, Mo., 1950.
6. Ruediger, W. C., "The Field of Distinct Vision," Arch. Psychol., 1907, Vol. 1, No. 5.
7. Korte, Wilhelm, "Zeitschrift für Psychologie," Vol. 93, pp. 17–82, 1923.
8. Zoethout, W. D., Physiological Optics, p. 134, The Professional Press, Inc., Chicago, Illinois, 1947.
9. Wolff, Eugene, Anatomy of the Eye and Orbit, p. 117. The Blakiston Co., New York, 1954.
10. Woodworth, Robert S., op. cit., p. 721.
11. Walton, Howard N., "Visual and Reading Improvements in Industry," Amer. J. Optom. & Arch. Amer. Acad. Optom., Nov., 1955, Vol. 32, No. 11.

12. Woodworth, Robert S., op. cit., p. 584.
13. Woodworth, Robert S., op. cit., p. 585.
14. Westheimer, Gerald, "Mechanism of Saccadic Eye Movements," Arch. of Ophth., Nov., 1954, Vol. 52, No. 5.
15. Amer. Optical Co., Bureau of Visual Science, "The Analysis of the Reading Graph," Amer. Optical Co., 1950.
16. Buswell, Guy Thomas, "Fundamental Reading Habits: A Study of Their Development." Supplementary Educational Monographs, No. 21, University of Chicago Press, 1922.
17. Woodworth, Robert S., op. cit., p. 727.
18. Buswell, Guy Thomas, op. cit.
19. Harris, Albert J., "How to Increase Reading Ability," p. 450, Longmans, Green & Co., New York, 1950.
20. American Optical Co., op. cit., p. 6.

81. Reading Problems, Research and Changes

MARY C. AUSTIN (1961)

Neither the colleges nor the schools are entirely satisfied with the status of education today. . . .

The changes most frequently mentioned were concerned with programs of instruction at the elementary school level. The emphasis generally was on more individual instruction. However, only four people stated their belief that individualized reading programs would gain wider acceptance among educators, both in the public schools and in the teacher training departments of the colleges. In conjunction with this, it is anticipated that some organizational changes will involve a move away from the self-contained classroom teachers towards specialists in various elementary fields. Cross-grade and cross-class organization is also expected, as well as a wider adoption of the ungraded primary. All of this is based on the assumption that far greater importance will be at-

SOURCE: Mary Austin, *et al.*, *The Torch Lighters* (Cambridge, Mass.: Harvard University Press, 1961), pp. 122–136. Reprinted by permission of the author, the publisher, and the President and Fellows of Harvard College.

tached to provision for individual differences, with special emphasis on programs for gifted children. This will also involve more widespread use of small-group instruction.

Another change frequently cited dealt with materials to be used in the classroom, especially basal readers. While a small group of respondents saw a future where basal readers would cease to be major tools of instruction in the first grade (although not abandoned completely), others felt that their use would increase but with the materials themselves undergoing modification. Further changes in basal readers would include an over-all upgrading of content so that the material would more nearly coincide with a child's speaking and listening vocabulary at the various stages of his development. In addition, it was pointed out that basal readers in the future should include more material designed to capitalize on boys' interests in the primary grades. A general hope was expressed that readers for all grade levels would contain increasing amounts of high-interest materials, as well as formal instruction in reading skills for appropriate grade levels, at least through the elementary school and possibly through junior and senior high school as well.

With the recent increased development of audio-visual materials, it is perhaps only natural that the respondents should have had some definite ideas about their future use. It was anticipated that greater numbers of schools would adopt audio-visual materials as necessary tools of instruction, and that among other devices, recording machines would come into more prominent use. Indeed, the use of television at the college level is also being initiated. One midwestern institution reported that closed circuit television is now being used for instructional purposes with great success, and two other colleges, one in New England and the other in the South, were said to include such systems in their projected plans. Presumably other colleges will follow suit as their budgets permit.

Also at the college level and in connection with such changes in the curriculum as involve greater use of audio-visual materials, it should be noted that several respondents anticipated other alterations in the total teacher training program. These specifically concern the ratio between liberal arts and professional courses, with opinion about equally divided regarding the placement of major emphasis. State legislatures as well as presidents and deans in the seventy-four colleges have been advocating an increase in the amount of time devoted to liberal arts courses, and now that such an increase has been effected in many of these institutions, the authorities are waiting to see how these changes will affect the training of their students. Exceptions are to be found most frequently in those colleges that have not recently examined their programs or in those colleges which are beginning to realize that a fifth year may prove necessary for preparing elementary teachers.

The above anticipated changes were cited by a majority of the respondents. In addition, there were replies that differentiated sharply between changes they expected and those they desired to see take place but for which they have little present hope. Among the latter were the introduction of reading at an earlier age; a more integrated approach to the teaching of reading, involving a closer relationship with all other aspects of the elementary curriculum; greater emphasis on recreational reading; and a revision of the basal readers in an attempt to keep their content abreast of the times. This last feature, to be sure, was among those actually expected by some of the respondents, as already mentioned. Finally, several people expressed their belief that reading instruction in the future will have to be more firmly based on research findings, and that research in psychology will continue to be very influential in determining the most effective ways to teach children to read. This latter subject will be discussed in the following section.

Research

A number of respondents were convinced that research will play an increasingly important role in both the theory and practice of reading instruction in the future. Over the past thirty years there has been an enormous amount of it done in elementary education, particularly in the field of reading. Efforts have been made to approach the subject scientifically while keeping in mind that in teaching reading one is dealing with human beings who cannot be reduced to a test-tube level. There are few who would question that much of this research has accounted directly or indirectly for the improvement in the teaching of reading and in the training of elementary school teachers.

While almost all respondents had suggestions regarding future research in reading, nevertheless many were highly critical of past research and the way it is being utilized currently. One respondent stated categorically that, "nothing new has been done in the field of reading in the last twenty years." Others were less dogmatic, but their comments ranged from "We are not using the research findings we have" to the proposal that "nothing more should be done for four or five years" in order to let teachers assimilate the research of the past. Furthermore, those who approved of past research and believed that it had been responsible for much of the improvement in the teaching of reading also felt that it had lacked precision, had not been conducted under controlled conditions, and frequently had been utilized before any testing and verification of the results. On the other hand, it was frequently pointed out that the difficulty lay not in the research itself but in the way its results had been used. Few, if any, classroom teachers have had courses in research design and most are ill-equipped to deal with research findings, if in fact they bother to read them at all. One respondent suggested that a magazine, popular in tone, such as *The Instructor*, or *The Grade Teacher*, could do much to ensure that research findings would reach the people for whom they are intended. But an additional comment was made that most teachers would continue to ignore research findings even if they were made more readily available and more easily digestible. This particular respondent's view was that most classroom teachers had "closed minds" about research and, regardless of the validity of its results, would continue to teach as they had been teaching, without reference to new methods and ideas.

Although there were some respondents who felt that past and current research had been badly designed and poorly utilized, a substantial majority of those interviewed believed that future improvement in reading would result largely from increased research in the field. The area in which most of them saw a need for further investigation was that of adjusting instruction to the individual child, with special emphasis on the particularly able readers and on those readers who may, from a variety of causes, be termed "disabled." This would include research into enriching the reading program for the better reader and exploring his interests in an effort to motivate him more successfully. It would also include research to ascertain methods by which the poor or non-reader can better learn the techniques necessary to assure ease in handling written material. In the latter instance, research to determine what kind and degree of reading disabilities can be handled properly and successfully within the normal classroom was particularly emphasized.

Concern with the individual reader is seen in the interest evinced in the individualized reading programs which have been introduced in several school systems, notably in New York and California, and which have aroused the curiosity of professional educators across the country. This, more than any other aspect of adjusting instruction to the individual, is the one which respondents feel needs to undergo precise, empirical investigation involving measurement of results and evaluation. In connection with the individualized reading program, one respondent was convinced that too many beginning teachers were using this approach without proper training in its specific techniques and without any scientific evidence to substantiate its effectiveness.

During the discussion of the individualized reading program, many of those interviewed expressed their belief that the whole area of grouping merits further examination. Several cited their conviction that research was needed to clarify the problem of effective grouping within the classroom and to aid teachers in organizing their time and their materials more effectively, with a view toward giving children meaningful independent work. In addition, they were eager for research which would help them establish procedures designed to benefit those with particular handicaps in the field of reading.

The mechanics of reading is another area in which the respondents saw definite need for further research. Among the specific skills and techniques which would profit from further investigation were: phonics, techniques of increasing vocabulary, and a re-appraisal of readiness programs. Critical reading skills, as an area in need of further study, was mentioned more frequently than any other specific skill. Emphasis was also placed on developing better techniques of teaching dictionary and reference skills.

Other aspects of reading that were cited as needing research include: concept and interest levels, study skills, determination of frustration levels, investigation of the relative merits of oral and silent reading, and the frequently noted problem of effective evaluation techniques. Respondents indicated some need for research into the diagnostic tests now being used in the hope of improving them and embracing within them objectives not now covered.

As might be expected, there were many among those interviewed who felt that further research into the psychology of learning was necessary, with particular reference to the nature of the reading process and to principles of child growth and development. Included in this would be problems mentioned in other connections, such as precise identification of frustration levels and the optimum age for beginning reading instruction.

Other areas of needed research mentioned by at least one respondent include an appraisal of the use of machines to teach reading, a status study on the teaching of reading in junior and senior high schools, and the role of school administrators in upgrading instruction in the elementary schools.

This, then, is the picture given by respondents from the seventy-four institutions. Without question, most, if not all, were of the opinion that many specific areas of research in reading are needed. But almost as large a number are equally convinced that the job cannot be done merely by engaging in additional research, even though it be more precise, accurate, and scientific than in the past. Some way must be found to ensure that the findings of research are actively utilized in the classroom and thus affect those for whom they are intended—the children who are learning to read.

Summary

According to the personnel interviewed in seventy-four colleges and universities, the following issues are relevant to the total program for training prospective elementary school teachers: causes of reading disability, college-sponsored programs designed to upgrade instruction in the local schools, anticipated changes in reading instruction, and research in the field of reading. The faculty cited four areas of responsibility for the large number of reading disabilities: poor classroom teaching, lack of leadership at the administrative and supervisory level, poor organization and use of materials within the schools, and difficulties particular to the children themselves.

In view of the large number of children with reading disabilities in the schools today, respondents were asked what, if anything, their institutions were doing to help upgrade instruction in the local schools. Their replies indicated that a variety of programs are carried on by institutions, but that few are of a formal nature. Most are informal and dependent in large measure on the individual in charge of the particular program, with the college itself taking little or no responsibility for initiating such help. The lack of formal, specific programs was attributed to the difficulty in achieving close relations between the college and the school personnel, with each putting the blame on the other.

Many of the respondents, obviously dissatisfied with the state of education today, offered several suggestions regarding anticipated changes in the future. These concerned changes in programs of instruction, changes involving the materials used, organizational changes, and, among others, those in the curriculum prescribed for training prospective teachers. In addition, several instructors indicated areas where they would like to see alterations which they did not necessarily expect. These included the basal readers, more emphasis on the integration of reading with other areas of the elementary curriculum, and reading instruction more firmly grounded in research.

Finally, almost all respondents were convinced that research findings would play an increasingly important role in determining the philosophy and methods of reading instruction in the future. Areas in which they hoped that research would be undertaken include the following: adjustment of instruction to the individual child; the organization of reading programs based on self-selection; grouping; teaching the mechanics of reading; and the psychology of learning. Several respondents were critical of the way in which past research had been conducted and utilized, but almost all agreed that research was necessary and, with certain suggested improvements in its methods and application, would be even more important in the future in assuring that children were given every opportunity to learn to read successfully.

82. What We Should Be Doing Soon

ARTHUR I. GATES (1965)

As the title of my paper implies, I wish to suggest a few things we members of IRA should be doing soon. First in importance is the need to revive and redirect reading research. The extensive studies of Barton and Wilder (2) under the auspices of the Carnegie Corporation leave no doubt that scientific work in our field is at a low ebb. It is low in quantity—too few persons of high competence are devoting their time fully or even mainly to basal research. It is too limited to the more obvious, the more practical problems. It is restricted too much in range; it does not show sufficient activity in many promising lines now developing within sociology, anthropology, experimental psychology, biochemistry, statistics, and other new types of scientific approach such as systems analysis.

Change and Challenge in American Education (8), a 115-page book written by James E. Russell, Secretary of the Educational Policies Commission, presents the main idea so well that I shall quote from it.

> We may hope that specialists in educational research can find ways to alter their efforts in a rather profound way. The present thrust of most research consists in trying out someone's favorite ideas for reform and improvement. I have no resistance to most people's pet ideas. I also like to see the kind of research that tests whether phonics is better than sight-reading and what effect class size has on learning. I think too that educational television, team teaching, and programmed learning can be useful. . . . But the notion that all these peripheral actions can add up to profound improvement or change strikes me as fanciful.
>
> When our theoretical base is as incomplete as it is, . . . suggested solutions proliferate on the fringes. What we need is to know more of the mind, its structure and operation, and the forces and factors that influence it. I do not expect to find these insights . . . in programmed instruction, or in any fortuitous combination of advances on the periphery. We must plunge into the central question.

SOURCE: IRA Invitational Address, 1965. Reprinted with the permission of Arthur I. Gates and the International Reading Association.

One could wish that educators were highly mobilized on this front, but they are not. Although some years ago educational researchers of national reputation were involved, more recently there has been little educational research at this level. . . . This advance must come and come soon.

I should like to convince you that now, for the first time during my life, we can afford to undertake the kind of research we need to do. During my earliest professional years, I and my research associates prepared close to a thousand pages of experimental material for teaching reading during the first year, but no one would publish them. During the past forty years, reading readiness tests have been nearly squeezed to death by economic pressure. They must be cheap group tests; "we can't afford the time for individual testing." They must be very simple to understand and use; our teachers colleges cannot afford to train teachers to learn to use complicated or subtle techniques. And so the cheap, the quick, the simple, and consequently the necessarily superficial and inadequate appraisal of the beginning pupil prevails, and sooner or later is criticized quite justifiably for being what it is.

Research in the past has been penny-wise and pound-foolish. Let us be done with that policy. Let us assume that those days are over. Our best economic experts express no doubt about it. A recent Kiplinger letter, the big business man's favorite confidential adviser, stated, "Education is the big 'growth business,' now the most valuable of all. Capital will be poured into education but, mind you, we'll have it to pour." Most of our political leaders, including President Johnson, agree. The implications of this conviction are tremendous—we must plan our future on the assumption that we can afford to do almost anything which holds a reasonable promise of improving education.

Next I wish to convince you that truths (facts and principles) most significant for reading shine out of basal, scientific research, even that done in an apparently remote region, for example, on the antics of animals, and by an investigator who wasn't thinking about reading at the time. Indeed, I shall start out by declaring that a study of animals was responsible for the greatest revolution in the teaching of reading ever made.

The animals demonstrated the major principles involved in learning to read in 1898 (11). Their demonstrations got to us only because Edward L. Thorndike introduced for the first time a revolutionary method of study—the scientific method. His famous puzzle boxes enabled him to see the main features of learning and problem solving because the activities of cat, rat, and monkey were slower, more visible, and less subtle than those of children learning to read. Later, when Thorndike studied reading, he realized that when a child or adult tries to read a passage he is faced by the same confusion of possibilities; and he tackles the problem as does a cat or rat, with all the knowledge, skill, insight, and reasoning ability at his command. This idea made explicit in an article entitled "Reading as Reasoning" published in 1917 (12) was so fundamental, so far-reaching, that it resulted in a great number of improvements in teaching reading. The idea that reading is as complex, varied, and subtle as thinking itself has been the basis of our thinking about reading and learning to read for a half century, and it has confronted us with a myriad of practical problems which puzzle us even today.

Let me tell you now about another tremendous contribution to the teaching of reading made by a study of animals, especially Pavlov the pig. Pavlov the pig went to school with Pavlov the Professor more than a half-century ago in Russia (6). He was the most popular pig in school. He learned quickly. Every day he led the singing. He was always healthy and hungry, but even when he reached the dinner table first he didn't make a hog of himself.

Then one day Professor Pavlov introduced reading. He taught the pig that by pushing a lever when a circle appeared above it he would get some food, and if he pushed the lever when a square was shown, he would get an electric shock. Then the Professor began to introduce figures (that is, words) which resembled both the circle and the square in various degrees, such as the outline of a rounded bar of soap or the heel of a man's shoe. As the choices became harder, Pavlov the pig made more and more mistakes. He began to get jumpy and snappy. His singing began to go off key, and eventually he had a real nervous breakdown. Pavlov the pig really was the first reading disability ever studied in a genuinely scientific clinic. Apparently, when a pig suffers a reading disability, it hits him hard. It took over a year of hospital care to restore Pavlov to normalcy. Of course you must realize the pig suffered severe penalties for missing words. A mistake deprived him of food and subjected him to annoying electric shocks.

The majority of psychologists would probably say that the cause of Pavlov's breakdown was frustration resulting from efforts to learn something that is too difficult. And most of us might have continued to believe that mere difficulty did the damage, were it not for another study made on animals. Liddell (5) found that an animal did not become disorganized even when failures were frequent if—and I quote—"some freedom for evasion and procrastination is possible." What heresy is this? Possibly the pig's trouble was that it didn't know how to swear. It just had no way of saying, "The devil take this miserable business. I've had enough of it."

Not one of Liddell's animals broke down when an adequate avenue for escape—a way to save face—was provided. Here is an important principle for teachers of reading that might not have been discovered outside of the pigpen, so to speak. Indeed, studies of animals beginning with those by Pavlov and Thorndike have contributed greatly to our present information about motivation in reading and other human activities.

Studies of animals as well as of human beings have shown also that the significance of learning experiences varies, along with other things, with the character of the times—with the social and physical environment. Anthropologists and sociologists have also contributed greatly to our understanding of the influence of our environment on reading. We now know that to improve the teaching of reading the teacher should study all phases of each child's life and have a background of valid information to use in interpreting these data. For example, consider television. Although Paul Witty and others have labored long and hard to gauge television's influence, they would be the first to admit that it poses formidable problems as yet unsolved. For example, a positive correlation has sometimes been found between the amount of time spent by a child in viewing television and his reading ability. I suspect the relationship is spurious. For example, if every child stole as much time from his school work as he dared, the brighter child would spend more and the duller one less, a fact which would produce the positive correlation.

In a recent sociological type of investigation (9) it was found that in England youngsters who viewed TV extensively tended to advance beyond the typical low-grade, cowboy, and other violent programs to superior dramatic and informative shows as they grew older. The explanation seemed to be that the BBC did not supply enough programs of the poorer type to fill the youngsters' entire viewing time with the result that they tried other, better offerings and gradually learned to like them. American stations on the other hand pour out such a flood of this low-grade stuff that the youngsters never exhaust the supply and therefore do not learn to view anything better. Indeed, I understand that "Bonanza," full of fights and foolishness, is the most popular TV show in America.

It is possible that American children are smothered likewise by an avalanche of low-grade reading material? Would we do better with a smaller, more carefully selected diet? The child who is gorged all day with ice cream and soda pop is likely to lose his appetite for what my generation of mothers called "a decent meal." Recently at the big Barnum and Bailey Circus, where dozens of thrilling events were going on all over the place, I observed a youngster who apparently was bored and confused by it all and spent most of his time playing with a few simple trinkets he had brought along in his pocket. There is here an unsolved paradox.

One of the biggest conflicts in our world today is the battle between pictures and print. Pictures—pictures in newspapers, tabloids, books, magazines, advertising matter, in movies and overwhelmingly on TV—have been gaining on the printed words at a constantly increasing rate. If this recent deluge of pictures does not completely swamp the printed word, it at least poses the overriding educational and social problem of our time. In the face of this phenomenon, our investigations are pathetically inadequate.

In many other respects, life is different today from yesterday. We must recognize that people as well as physical objects change. When I was a child it was apparent that my elders had grown up during the Sweet Alice, Ben Bolt age. When I reached high school, I, as was the custom, got myself "a best girl." Her name was Alice and she was a very sweet girl, but I doubt that she ever wept with delight when I gave her a smile. Indeed if I offered several of my most bewitching grins, instead of weeping, I suspect she would have said, "What's on your mind now?" I am sure she never trembled with fear at any of my frowns.

Teachers' attitudes and techniques have changed greatly during my lifetime. I came into education with a background of premedical training and experimental psychology, and I soon developed the conviction that the teacher of the future would be thoroughly trained to diagnose and deal with children's educational and intellectual life as a physician was prepared to diagnose and prescribe for their physical life. I started in at once to try to develop useful tests, examinations, and diagnostic instruments corresponding to the visual charts, the stethoscope, blood sugar tests, etc., of the physician. But alas! this idea got better support in the decade beginning in 1920 than it did thirty years later. Mary Austin (1) and her committee's recent report suggests in fact that teacher training institutions have retreated before the stubborn enemies of professional preparation of this sort. The greatest of these enemies has been the old conviction that we can't afford it. I believe it is more needed now than ever and it is financially feasible.

I think that every teacher, at least every elementary school teacher, should be given an internship training during which she learns to make comprehensive case studies of individual children using all of the best technical equipment available. As many of our leaders have been demonstrating for years, we have sufficient information and techniques to enable any good teacher to teach all or nearly all children to read well, provided an adequate internship type of training is provided. To fail to equip teachers with those insights and techniques now is absolutely inexcusable. The IRA should assume the major responsibility for putting this idea into effect.

One of the areas which is in need of extensive study is suggested by the disagreements between the believers in systematic learning (practice) and progressive or "creative teaching." The quarrel here is older than I am and equally confusing. The advocate of one of these views can blacken the eye of anyone who insists on using his opponent's plan exclusively. So, since I learn from TV that a black eye is a noble characteristic of anyone who refuses to shift from his fixed taste, I must assume that stubbornness is a virtue.

This general issue is involved in various suggestions for teaching phonics and for using many kinds of detailed, ready-made "programmed materials" or machine teaching. (I must note in passing that the person who has been most active during the past twenty-five years in pushing the possibilities of programming is B. F. Skinner, a leader in animal psychology.) I am sure that E. L. Thorndike a half-century ago took a favorable view of programming in general when he said in effect (10), "Never let a teacher spend her precious time in doing what can be done as well by a few pieces of paper, but save her time to enable her to do better the things that only she can do." I have been doubtful that programmed materials could do all the "precious things" that a good teacher can do, but a recent cartoon in *Punch* made me pause. This cartoon shows a man reading a message just handed to him by a huge electronic computer. The computer's message said, "I would like to contribute a pint to the blood bank."

I suspect that these new programs and devices can do many useful things. Although I have not as yet seen a program for teaching reading that I thought was very good, the fault was in the materials programmed, not in the principles of programming. Research has already suggested that programs are not, as many persons assume, valuable only for routine drill work; on the contrary they seem to be better adapted to encouraging reasoning and problem solving of certain sorts. They can be made to detect errors very well. They can be adjusted nicely to different rates and to many, but not all routes of learning. Many practical issues are not solved as yet, but when Mr. Russell and I (and many others) insist that we must get back into much more extensive basic research, we do not mean to say that practical research is without value. All the basic research done since 1900 has not clarified all the general priniples of learning, much less the value of the hundreds of specific materials, methods, and devices now used by teachers of reading. Basal research, however, often reveals practical principles and throws doubt on practical policies which many of us might otherwise assume to be sound.

For example, a belief long held by many is that the greater the number of sensory channels employed to feed information to a learner the better he will learn. Thus, instead of having him merely see the word, you have him also sound it, write it, type it; you show a pictorial illustration of it, use it in a story, and so on. Let one sense be facilitated by another. Indeed many persons now warmly recommend a "combined method," one which uses many resources. Thus the classroom is filled with every available kind of book, workbook, phonic system, sound motion picture, teaching machine, TV lessons, and so on. Sometimes it seems that everything a teacher can get hold of is tossed into the hopper and ground into mincemeat, which she then seasons with additional suggestions as it is passed out.

A series of recent studies done not by us reading researchers but mainly in the psychological laboratory cast doubt on these policies. Robert Travers in his recent address as President of the Educational Psychology Division of the American Psychological Association summed up his review of many studies by saying, ". . . flooding the learner with information and stressing realism are likely to provide poor learning. Some schools do this, as if in the hope that the more information is available the more the learner will absorb. But the fact is that the learner has a limited ability for utilizing information, can generally utilize information from only one source at a time, and has a limited storage capacity . . . what is needed are principles which will indicate how information can be most effectively compressed and simplified . . ." not expanded and elaborated (13).

When new investigations like these threaten old convictions we must not be discouraged. Upsets like these are the inevitable and desirable fruits of scientific progress. The time to worry is not when we encounter changes and uncertainties but self-satisfied agreement among our experts. A state of agreement usually means merely that progress has come to a halt. Despite many such uncertainties we can and should soon be making real improvements in most of our materials and procedures. An enormous number of excellent investigations, both theoretical and practical, both "central" and "peripheral" (to use Russell's apt phrases) have been done in the past. Indeed, many investigations in the field of reading compare favorably with the work done in any of the behavioral sciences. Don't ever let anyone deceive you into thinking that the scientific as well as the practical contributions of E. L. Thorndike, Charles Judd, Walter Dearborn, Grace Fernald, Leta Hollingworth, William S. Gray, and David Russell (to mention only those who are regrettably no longer with us) are not outstanding.

The effects of the scholarly work of these fine men and women are sufficient to enable us to make many practical improvements now. For example, the basal reader outfits are still so fragmentary, incomplete, and difficult to use as to require a great deal of really shrewd additional work by a teacher to handle many children individually with them. These books are poor not because we do not know enough to make better ones but because everyone has assumed that we cannot afford better ones. Well, we can. And we should now be making materials that are more detailed, more comprehensive, and built deliberately for individual instruction as well as group activities. They may comprise many more packets, and in general bear little physical resemblance to the present reader-workbook outfits. I could give you many other illustrations but I must move on.

I want to tell you about another problem of greatest significance in reading research which some animals recently called to our attention. Psychologist Robert Rosenthal (7) divided a large group of rats into two groups equivalent in ability to run certain mazes. To one-half of his graduate student assistants he turned over one group of rats, which were said to be "rat geniuses." The other assistants got the equivalent group but they were described as "stupid rats." The assistants went to work teaching equivalent rats by prescribed, identical methods to run an identical maze. What happened? The "genius" rats learned noticeably better than the "stupid" ones.

This little study radiates with a host of implications of great importance. I am sure I do not as yet see them all but one seems clear. The differences seem to be due to something these teachers did differently while trying to teach in exactly the same way. Things they did differently are very subtle but they cry out that the role of the teachers is an overwhelmingly important factor in the learning situation even when the pupils are rats utterly blind to most of the things, such as the meaning of spoken words, which the teacher habitually uses.

This study demonstrates the unreliability, known for some time on the basis of other evidence, of the typical control group method widely used in education. Most of the control group studies of reading methods, especially those made during these recent years of turmoil and tempest, have yielded data which are mainly useless, indeed often misleading. So-called experiments of "demonstrations" of methods or materials which have been given great publicity are the worst offenders. They are loaded dice.

Only very extensive studies carried out for many years in many neutral schools by neutral teachers supervised by genuinely competent and neutral investigators in comparison with many other procedures will reveal reliably the relative merits of the various programs. We can afford them. We have simply got to have them. Few of us, I am sorry to say, have been trained to the level of expertness in the new science. A fine start in this direction has been made by the Federal Department of Health, Education, and Welfare in launching under supervison of Donald Durrell, Guy Bond, Theodore Clymer, and others some large-scale studies of first-grade reading. Dr. Bond, who is serving as the chief critic of evaluation in these studies, plays a difficult and extremely important role. I regret to say that too few "reading researchers" are equipped to do expert work of this sort. We need many more men and women capable of doing it well.

It is time perhaps for this association also to undertake the serious business of promoting and appraising the result of studies of principles and practices in reading. Scientific and professional discoveries in our field could now grow by leaps and bounds like the two youngsters who live in the apartment above me. I think that these two lively children, scientific and professional research activities will need much parental care and discipline. And I think the IRA should consider the advisability of becoming the foster parents. I am pretty sure that, if IRA doesn't do so, other organizations will. Some of the responsibilities the IRA might assume soon are new and strange to it. Its officials may feel like the Maine guide who declared to his obviously disgruntled clients, "I still say that I am the best guide in the state of Maine, but I think we're in Canada now." But Canada is not too far afield, and there are other guides like the American Psychological Association and especially the American Medical Association to lend us a helping hand.

I shall offer only a few suggestions on the many things that should be done. The IRA should launch a large-scale program of recruiting able young persons, especially those trained in other areas, to do research on problems in reading. A science progresses rapidly only when it is led by genius.

The IRA might assign a group to investigating chicanery and unsound practices, to gauge new proposals and ideas, to evaluate progress and needs, and in general to inform the public and the profession expertly and promptly about teaching reading.

Is it not significant that a committee not of IRA, but of the Social Science Research Council (a committee of very able persons) found it advisable to look into a recent development in our field? I quote their report on one (3).

A similar emphasis on fundamentals pervaded the committee's conference on reading, held in the fall of 1963. There is a bandwagon movement to reform primary reading with new alphabets, such as the Pitman alphabet imported from England. Meeting with proponents of those methods, we were able to clarify the problems of evaluating the claims put forward. But the linguists and experimental psychologists in the conference plunged much deeper. These new alphabets are haphazard artistic creations that have neither been adequately designed in the light of present knowledge of language and perception nor refined by proper empirical trial. Hence the conference identified questions far more basic than those being raised by reading educators.

The IRA should at least set up standards for professional training and launch a vigorous program to induce teacher training institutions to provide these standards and school systems to honor them. Certification standards should be suggested for classroom teachers, teacher assistants, reading specialists, reading supervisor, reading research workers, and others.

Every such venture can get out of hand and do more harm than good. There is danger of evolving an "Establishment" which defends the status quo, and curbs rather than encourages progress. Our main purpose should be not to perpetuate old views but to initiate and sustain new ventures. I must now say quite frankly that I am not sure that the IRA is the best organization to assume some of these functions. Perhaps the American Educational Research Association, for example, with its wider range of experts, would be better. At least the IRA should give the choice consideration. It should be done carefully and soon.

Despite a century of scientific study of reading, there are many other interesting and vital issues yet to be solved. For example, most persons who have come into the profession since 1940 have been urged to develop a kind of research attitude, learn some research techniques, and engage in some form of research work, such as "action research." Before accepting this as unquestionably good advice, consider this comment made by William James in his *Talks to Teachers*—a book which I regard as the most enlightening, the most warmhearted, the most enchanting ever written for teachers. In one of his *Talks* made in Boston in 1892, James (4) said:

> Least of all need you, merely *as teachers*, deem it part of your duty to become contributors to psychological science or to make psychological observations in a methodical . . . manner. . . . The teacher's attitude toward the child, being concrete and ethical, is positively opposed to the psychological observer's, which is abstract and analytic. Although some of us may conjoin the attitudes successfully, in most of us they must conflict.
>
> The worst thing that can happen to a good teacher is to get a bad conscience about her profession because she feels herself hopeless as a psychologist. . . . The best teacher may be the poorest contributor of child-study material, and the best contributor may be the poorest teacher. No fact is more palpable than this.

I must now gather up the scattered threads of my discussion. Before I do I must make sure that my earlier suggestion that the IRA consider taking on some very serious business does not mislead you into assuming that I should wish to curtail the association's service in providing at the annual convention a few days of relief from professional strain, a few days of good will and gaiety. The IRA has become a lively social club, admirably full of fun, food, and friendly frolic. The rapidly swelling membership is evidence that these features fill a need.

My long professional life has convinced me that, except for sheer intelligence, the greatest professional asset is a gay heart. The leaders in educational science I have known were extremely gay men and women. They were dedicated to their work, because they found it full of thrilling challenges. I now regard the deadly ever-serious scientist with some suspicion. He is almost sure to be a bore. When one of these persons has me cornered, my mind is likely to wing off to a sweet vision. It is the vision of my dog. When I get home I shall give him the signal that means, "Let's go for a walk in the woods." He will appear to go mad with joy. All over the place he will explode into geysers of gaiety. Is it not one of the wonders of the world that this beautiful, incredibly lively animal will seem to be filled with ecstasy at the prospect of taking a walk with me—with me, poor dull clod that I am, stumbling along at a snail's pace, insensitive to the thrills of forest smells and sounds that make him tingle with heavenly delight. Is this dog's rapture the outcome of a magic fountain of acquired gaiety or the culmination of inheritances of ages of sensitivity to the thrills of venturing into the realm of mystery? Both contribute, I think; each enlivens the other. And so I express the hope that all of you will discover the excitement of adventures in the hunting grounds which the profession and science of education provide.

We must wake up to the realities of today. We must do away with the picture of a teacher as a sad creature. Education is now America's biggest business; we are the largest professional group in the world. By any fair test education's promise for improving mankind is excelled by no profession. Education should and can command the best of scientific and scholarly works and facilities. What better tribute could you ask for than the action of one of the world's most distinguished men, a brilliant chemist and scientific theorist, a former President of Harvard University, James B. Conant, in joining our ranks?

Doesn't President Johnson's pride in and commitment to education give you a lift? These and many other world leaders invite educators to enter into a new life—a life new in promise and prestige, a life which can be full of the gaiety of achievement. Let us throw off the ancient shackles of timidity and face the world with self-confidence and pride.

To be sure, in all these ventures, luck and circumstances play a role, and many a hunting ground turns out to be barren of big game. But, lest you worry about such possibilities unduly, let me tell you about my neighbor's elk hound, who although living only thirty miles from New York City has gone forth every day of his long life and will venture again tomorrow, gaily confident that at the foot of the next knoll, or in the thicket surrounding the next bend in the little brook, he will at long, long last come upon an elk. You have perhaps heard someone say that the scientist and the teacher lead a dog's life. I can't imagine a more thrilling life than that of a well-trained, well-treated dog. This hope for a startling discovery on the next voyage into uncertainty makes a richly rewarding life for a dog or scientist or teacher. The great naturalist, Louis Agassiz, understood this kindred spirit of the lively animal hunter and the scientific and professional explorer when he said in substance to his crew standing ready to begin one of his scientific expeditions:

> We may not catch no whale
> But we will have a lovely sail.

Education is filled with more mysteries than any of the silent seas. I hope all of you will sail forth into some phase of it with the best scientific or professional tools in your hands and the spirit of gay adventure in your heart. May you have a thrilling sail; may you catch many a whale.

Bon voyage!

References

1. Austin, Mary C. et al. *The Torch Lighters: Tomorrow's Teachers of Reading*. Cambridge: Harvard University Press, 1961. 191 pages.
2. Barton, Allen H., and Wilder, David E. "Research and Practice in the Teaching of Reading: A Progress Report," in Miles, Matthew B. *Innovation in Education*. New York: Teachers College, Columbia University, 1965, pp. 361–398.
3. Cronbach, Lee J. "The Committee on Learning and the Educational Process," *Items,* Volume 18, No. 4, December 1964, pp. 54–55.
4. James, William. *Talks to Teachers*. New York: Henry Holt and Company, 1923. 301 pages.
5. Liddell, Howard S. et al. "The Comparative Physiology of the Conditioned Motor Reflex," *Comparative Psychology Monographs,* Volume 11, No. 1, December 1934, pp. 1–89.
6. Murphy, Gardner. "Behaviourism," Chapter XVI, *An Historical Introduction to Modern Psychology*. New York: Harcourt, Brace and Company, 1929, pp. 263–278. Pavlov's earlier studies did not cover all of the

details, some of which were selected from later writings of other authors in order to give a fuller picture of the findings.

7. Rosenthal, Robert et al. "The Effect of Experimenter Bias on the Performance of the Albino Rat," *Behavioral Science*, Volume 8, No. 3, July 1963, pp. 183–189.
8. Russell, James E. *Change and Challenge in American Education*. Boston: Houghton Mifflin Company, 1965. 115 pages.
9. Schramm, Wilbur (Ed.) The Effects of Television on Children and Adults. Number 1. Unesco.
10. This is the substance of a statement contained in Thorndike, Edward L. and Gates, Arthur I. *Elementary Principles of Education*. New York: Macmillan Company, 1929. 335 pages.
11. Thorndike, Edward L. *Animal Intelligence*. New York: Psychological Review Monograph Supplement, 1898. Volume 2, No. 4. 109 pages.
12. Thorndike, Edward L. "Reading as Reasoning: A Study of Mistakes in Paragraph Reading," *Journal of Educational Psychology*, No. 4, June 1917, pp. 323–332.
13. Travers, Robert M. W. "Transmission of Information to Human Receivers," *Newsletter of Division 15, Educational Psychologist*, December 1964, Volume 2, No. 1, pp. 1–5.